The Changing Leadership Landscape

THE SIOP PROFESSIONAL PRACTICE SERIES

Series Editor
Douglas Reynolds

TITLES IN THE SERIES

Performance Management Transformation: Lessons Learned and Next Steps
Edited by Elaine D. Pulakos and Mariangela Battista

Employee Surveys and Sensing: Challenges and Opportunities
Edited by William H. Macey and Alexis A. Fink

Mastering Industrial-Organizational Psychology: Training Issues for Master's Level I-O Psychologists
Edited by Elizabeth L. Shoenfelt

Mastering the Job Market: Career Issues for Master's Level Industrial-Organizational Psychologists
Edited by Elizabeth L. Shoenfelt

The Age of Agility: Building Learning Agile Leaders and Organizations
Edited by Veronica Schmidt Harvey and Kenneth P. De Meuse

Overcoming Bad Leadership in Organizations
Edited by Derek Lusk and Theodore L. Hayes

Talent Assessment: Embracing Innovation and Mitigating Risk in the Digital Age
Edited by Tracy M. Kantrowitz, Douglas H. Reynolds, and John C. Scott

Strategic Workforce Planning: Best Practices and Emerging Directions
Edited by Marc B. Sokol and Beverly A. Tarulli

Becoming a Talent Magnet: Lessons from the Field on Attracting and Recruiting Great People
Edited by Mark A. Morris

The Social Capital Imperative: Revealing, Developing, and Leveraging Organizational Networks
Edited by Kristin L. Cullen-Lester and Greg Pryor

Evolving the Employee Experience: An Integrative Perspective
Edited by Rose Mueller-Hanson, Evan Sinar, and Elaine D. Pulakos

The Changing Leadership Landscape: New Challenges, New Expectations, New Actions
Edited by Sheri L. Feinzig & Mariangela Battista

The Changing Leadership Landscape

New Challenges, New Expectations, New Actions

Edited by

SHERI L. FEINZIG
MARIANGELA BATTISTA

OXFORD
UNIVERSITY PRESS

OXFORD
UNIVERSITY PRESS

Oxford University Press is a department of the University of Oxford.
It furthers the University's objective of excellence in research, scholarship,
and education by publishing worldwide. Oxford is a registered trade mark of
Oxford University Press in the UK and in certain other countries.

Published in the United States of America by Oxford University Press
198 Madison Avenue, New York, NY 10016, United States of America.

CIP data is on file at the Library of Congress.

ISBN 9780197820049

DOI: 10.1093/9780197820070.001.0001

Printed by Marquis Book Printing, Canada

The manufacturer's authorized representative in the EU for product safety is
Oxford University Press España S.A. of El Parque Empresarial San Fernando de Henares,
Avenida de Castilla, 2 – 28830 Madrid (www.oup.es/en or product.safety@oup.com).
OUP España S.A. also acts as importer into Spain of products made by the manufacturer.

FSC
www.fsc.org
MIX
Paper | Supporting responsible forestry
FSC® C103567

For my three generations of the greatest support network imaginable: my mother Marilyn who overcame numerous societal obstacles on her path to leadership (and in memory of my father Stanley who supported her every step of the way); my spouse Steven always cheering me on while building his own leadership prowess; and my children Ileana and Zach, emerging leaders with incredibly bright futures ahead.

-Sheri L. Feinzig

For Concetta and Genesio, mom and dad, my first examples of great leadership.

-Mariangela Battista

Contents

SECTION III. DATA AND ANALYTICS THROUGH A LEADERSHIP LENS

SECTION IV. GLOBAL CHALLENGES

SECTION V. LEADERSHIP AND DIVERSITY

SECTION VI. CARING AND EMPATHY

SECTION IX. SUMMARY AND CONCLUDING THOUGHTS

List of Figures and Tables

Figures

Tables

List of Contributors

Robert E. Anderson Jr., MPA, is CEO of Anderson Global LLC, Dover, DE, USA.

Edward Barrows Jr., DBA, is Professor of the Practice of Leadership at Brown University, Providence, RI, USA.

Mariangela Battista, PhD, is Principal at Sirena Consulting LLC, New York, NY, USA.

Phaedra Boinodiris is Co-Founder of Future World Alliance, NC, USA.

Karen Boroff, PhD, is Professor Emeritus at Seton Hall University.

Anton I. Botha, PhD, is Adjunct Professor at the University of Cape Town, Cape Town, South Africa.

Christine E. Boyce is a practitioner-researcher in industrial and organizational psychology based in Holland, Pennsylvania. She is ABD from the Industrial-Organizational Psychology Ph.D. program at the University at Albany, SUNY.

Chelsi Campbell, PhD, is I/O Psychology Researcher at the American Institutes for Research, Washington, DC, USA.

Anthony W. Caputo, MA, is Chief Operating Officer, Chief People Officer, at Remesh Inc., New York, NY, USA.

Lynn G. Collins, PhD, is Global Co-Head Talent Insights and Assessments at BTS, New York, NY, USA.

Elisabetta Comini is Partner at Coreconsulting Spa, Milan, Italy.

Gena Cox, PhD, is CEO & Head of Advisory & Executive Coaching at Feels Human, LLC, FL, USA.

Andrea Derler, PhD, is Principal of Research and Value at Visier Inc., Vancouver, Canada.

Sheri L. Feinzig, PhD, is Adjunct Professor at New York University, New York, NY, USA.

Alexis Fink, PhD, is Principal at Propeller Insight, LLC, Battle Ground, WA, USA.

Cassandra Frangos, EdD, is Board Member and Partner at Spencer Stuart, Boston, MA, USA.

Amy D. Grubb, PhD, is Executive Advisor at the Federal Bureau of Investigation, in Wilmington, DE, USA.

Sandra B. Hartog, PhD, is Partner Emeritus, BTS Global Assessment Practice, at BTS, New York, NY, USA

Sarah Birrell Ivory, PhD, is Associate Professor at the University of Edinburgh Business School, Edinburgh, UK.

Angela Jackson, EdLD, is Director of Future Forward Institute, Boston, MA, USA; and Lecturer at the Graduate School of Education, Harvard University, Cambridge, MA, USA.

Archie Jones Jr., MBA, is Senior Lecturer of Entrepreneurial Management Unit at Harvard Business School, Harvard University, Boston, MA, USA.

Ruchin Kansal, MBA, is Professor of Practice at Seton Hall University, South Orange, NJ, USA.

Elizabeth Kolmstetter, PhD, is Chief People Officer (retired) at the Cybersecurity and Infrastructure Security Agency, Arlington, VA, USA.

Alex Liebscher is Senior Research Scientist at BetterUp Labs, Austin, TX, USA.

Brad MacKay, PhD, FRSA, FAcSS, is Professor at the University of St Andrews, St Andrews, UK.

Meisha-ann Martin, PhD, is VP People Research, Workhuman, Austin, TX, USA.

Gaurav Mukherjee is Director of Employee Success, Salesforce, CA, USA.

Haig R. Nalbantian, MPhil, is Co-President/Co-Founder the Workforce Sciences Institute, Jupiter, FL, USA.

Xolani Nghona, PhD, is Founder of Intrapreneurship Factory, Cape Town, South Africa; and Lecturer at Rotterdam School of Management, Erasmus University, Rotterdam, Netherlands.

Khoa Le Nguyen, PhD, is Senior Research Scientist at BetterUp Labs, Austin, TX, USA.

Kate Niederhoffer, PhD, is Chief Scientist at BetterUp Labs, Austin, TX, USA.

Mathian Osicki, PhD, is Integrated Talent Leader at GE Aerospace, Evendale, OH, USA.

Patricia Pedigo, PhD, is Executive Consultant (retired) at M&A Integration, HR Business Development, IBM, Seattle, WA, USA.

Ludmila N. Praslova, PhD, SHRM-SCP, is Professor of Graduate Organizational Psychology in the School of Business of Vanguard University of Southern California, Costa Mesa, CA, USA.

Kristina Rapuano, PhD, is Senior Research Scientist at BetterUp Labs, Austin, TX, USA.

George S. Reiswig, MA, is Principal User Experience Director at Propeller Insight, Battle Ground, WA, USA.

Alexandra Lycan Ronske, MA, is Instructor at West Point, NY.

Sandra L. Shullman, PhD, is Managing Partner of the Columbus Office at Executive Development Group, Columbus, OH, USA.

David G. Smith, PhD, is Professor of Practice at the Johns Hopkins Carey Business School, Baltimore, MD, USA.

Lorraine Stomski, PhD, is Chief Talent Officer at Walmart, Bentonville, AR, USA.

H. Colleen Stuart, PhD, is Associate Professor of Management and Organization at the Johns Hopkins Carey Business School, Baltimore, MD, USA.

Anna A. Tavis, PhD, is Professor in the Human Capital Management Department at New York University, New York, NY, USA.

Barbara Toffolo, PhD, is Partner and Coach and Head of CoreSchool at Coreconsulting Spa, Milan, Italy.

Anna Marie Valerio, PhD, is Adjunct Professor in the Psychology Department at New York University, New York, NY, USA; and President of Executive Leadership Strategies, LLC, Ridgefield, CT, USA.

Randall P. White, PhD, is Affiliate Professor of Leadership at HEC, Paris, Jouy-en-Josas, France; and Partner at Executive Development Group, Greensboro, NC, USA.

Kathlyn Wilson, PhD, is Associate Professor in the Department of Human Resource Management at the University of Hertfordshire, Hatfield, UK.

Woody Woodward, PhD, is Chief Coaching Officer, BetterUp, Washington, DC, USA.

Jane Wu, PhD, is Executive Consultant at IBM, Arlington, VA, USA.

SECTION I
INTRODUCTION

SECTION I
INTRODUCTION

1
Leadership Today
An Overview

Mariangela Battista and Sheri L. Feinzig

Introduction

Events of the early 2020s have indelibly changed how employees experience their work environment, and leadership practices must adapt in response. From COVID-19–related work and life decisions to social unrest, wars, and technological advances, the world is substantially different from just a few years ago. And all indications suggest the exponential change will continue. Some of these events accelerated workplace changes that were already emerging, while others resulted in entirely new workplace practices and mindsets. We have begun to see a shift to a more holistic and person-centered focus on employee experience, manifesting in new talent practices and leadership expectations.

What does the world of work look like today? Briefly, we see work becoming more fluid and dynamic thanks to new market demands, changing stakeholder expectations, rapid advances in technology, and the evolution of artificial intelligence (AI) (Deloitte, 2025). What does it mean to be a leader today? Is it enough to set vision and direction, create alignment, achieve results through others, gather resources, assist the team in overcoming barriers? These have been consistent expectations for leaders. Today we see organizational leaders also needing to navigate complex challenges like cost pressures, dwindling team morale, and the relentless need for organizational growth in volatile environments (Accenture, 2025). And yet this still does not fully describe what leaders face on a daily basis. Engaging with the rapid pace of technological changes, addressing our basic humanity and well-being in a world of daily stress, expanding upon inclusionary practices, rising above

Mariangela Battista and Sheri L. Feinzig, *Leadership Today*. In: *The Changing Leadership Landscape*.
Edited by: Sheri L. Feinzig and Mariangela Battista, Oxford University Press.
DOI: 10.1093/9780197820070.003.0001

constant chaos and turmoil, and simply addressing the unpredictability of any given day—together illustrate what the role of a leader entails.

Technology, Including Artificial Intelligence

Technology is dominating and impacting every facet of society, not just organizational life. Ever-changing technology and the evolution of AI are here, and not going away. Successful leaders will know how to best leverage this new technology for employee and organizational good. This means the ability for a leader to engage and understand the use and value of AI in all its forms. Change management is necessary to help teams engage with this new technology and ensure the correct usage so that it complements and enhances, rather than replaces, human capability. This also means determining when *not* to use this technology, and enabling teams with the ability to make crucial decisions in every scenario of whether AI is appropriate and beneficial or counterproductive and/or harmful. How does one lead change and mitigate risks for their organizations and their teams in this new age of AI?

In addition, technology now generates never-ending streams of data. What new sources of data and ways of using data have emerged, and how ready are leaders to be "data-driven?" Leaders need to be stewards of the data in order to make impactful decisions, and they need to safeguard their organizations from data mishandling, misuse, and exposure to breaches. Leaders of the future must be equipped to understand when and how to leverage data and technology, in combination with human capabilities, to enhance performance while nurturing human growth. Given this new dominance of technology and data, the nature of leadership will inevitably need to change and adapt (Chamorro-Premuzic et al., 2024).

Our Humanity

While technology and AI may dominate the current zeitgeist, that does not mean leaders can now ignore our basic humanity. Quite the contrary. Compassion and empathy have become even more important. According to the World Economic Forum's (2025a) Global Risks Report, we see declining optimism in the world due to the expansion and escalation of global conflicts, widespread political and societal polarization, a seemingly non-stop assault of extreme weather events amplified by climate change, and the continued spread of misinformation via social media.

The world of work has been strongly impacted by these numerous dramatic shifts and seemingly constant fury. While organizations expect employees to bring their best selves to work and perform optimally, that expectation may be unrealistic when events impacting their lives outside of work provoke deep anxiety. The topic of mental health, once rarely discussed openly, is now widely acknowledged as a relevant workplace concern (Grabarek & Sawyer, 2025). We have also seen changes in the balance of power between workers and leadership. The balance favored workers and organized labor during the accelerated hiring phase of the pandemic, but subsequent workforce reductions diminished worker leverage. We have seen increasing attempts among workers to unionize (Holt & Schmid, 2024) countered by some leaders' efforts to thwart unionization efforts (Semuels, 2022). Return to office mandates have created confusion and have not necessarily led to improved productivity or enhanced employee experience (Bloom et al., 2024). Accenture's Future of Work study found that only 29% of employees trust their leaders to have employees' best interests at heart (Accenture, 2025).

Global Diversity

Our world is quite diverse, and any pocket of a population will demonstrate its own diversity beyond the traditional constructs of gender and ethnicity. With every generation more diverse than the previous, have we made any progress in regard to our ability to lead more inclusively? While there have been changes—for example, diversity is now recognized as encompassing more than gender and ethnicity to include neurodiversity and physical ability—what we have seen is very slow progress.

In less than two decades, 99 out of 100 global economies have improved their overall gender parity scores—gaining an average six percentage points from their initial baseline score. However, the global gender gap score in 2025 for all 148 economies stands at only 68.8% of the gap closed. When considering the constant set of 100 economies covered continuously since 2006, the gap has narrowed by 0.4 of a percentage point, from 68.6% in 2024 to 69.0% in 2025. According to the World Economic Forum, "Based on the collective speed of progress of those 100 economies, it will take 123 years to reach full parity globally" (2025b, p. 5). Social scientists have basically found that the movement toward gender equity has stalled (Cooper & Fielding-Singh, 2024).

Increasingly, women are outperforming men at attaining education beyond high school or its equivalent. Despite this, women are still underrepresented in the workforce and in leadership roles—only 29.5% of college educated senior managers are women. Between 2015 and 2024, the share of women in top management rose from 25.7% to 28.1%, but progress has slowed post-2022. And as one female global leader has stated, there is still a double standard—expectations female leaders face that male leaders never do (Ardern, 2025).

Through all of this slow progress, we have also begun to see swings back to an earlier era when employment rules and regulations did not exist. An era when working conditions were far less favorable, work itself was far more dangerous, and large swaths of the working population were grossly underutilized and underrepresented. At the time of this writing, executive orders by the Trump administration in the United States are attempting to undo 60 years of employment law and progress. This feeling of constant chaos, and the subsequent need to create calm for employees, is generating additional challenges for organizational leaders.

The Era of "Polycrises"

All these societal and workplace shifts have demanded that leaders look for new ways to lead effectively in this changing world of work. Leaders face continued complexities among the myriad fast-paced changes and sociopolitical crises ("polycrises"), which makes the so-called VUCA (volatile, uncertain, complex, ambiguous) world of a few years ago seem tame and simple in comparison.

The world's challenges are not linear and well-defined. What we see are multiple fronts of increased complexity and unpredictability layering on current experiences. This era of polycrises began in 2008 (Chetty & Patel, 2023), and has intensified for almost 20 years. This is, and will continue to be, the state of the world. Specifics may change, but leaders will continue to be challenged to lead in an increasingly complex world.

All of these changes and complexities indicate new and constant challenges for leaders today. Deloitte (2025), in their Global Human Capital Trends report, outlines some of these fundamental tensions. They identify tensions between augmentation and automation, personalization and standardization, agility and stability, empowerment and control. All these tensions drive different leadership behaviors and expectations. And according to Deloitte, leaders find themselves stuck in a wait-and-see cycle, unsure of how to navigate the tensions and make the complex decisions necessary to move their organizations forward.

The Zeitgeist

It is not an understatement to say that the current and evolving zeitgeist requires much from leaders. Traits alone are not enough to successfully navigate this increasing complexity. Context plays a critical role in determining the most appropriate leader behaviors. Successful organizations will require leaders who understand and respond effectively to these changing expectations, and who continually sense and adjust as various possible futures emerge.

The world will continue to change in unpredictable ways. Leadership today is not for the faint of heart (Walker, 2024). Leadership is beyond the tactics of management and about creating the environment where individuals can be their best selves. So what is a leader to do? Are we expecting too much? How do we best prepare future leaders? How leaders navigate and lead through these unprecedented times and the unforeseen future challenges that will undoubtedly emerge— is the core focus of this volume.

About This Leadership Volume

This leadership volume is focused on answering these questions. It is organized around emerging macro themes—including technology and data, sociopolitical challenges, diversity and inclusion, compassion and empathy, and emerging attributes and trends relevant for developing leaders of today and tomorrow. All of these themes reflect current workplace change.

The chapters are meant to help leaders navigate the new world of work as well as build their adaptability and readiness for future challenges that will inevitably unfold. Each theme is addressed in multiple chapters discussing specific topics and recent research trends aligned with the theme.

The last section (Section VIII) of the volume provides practical and illustrative case studies depicting real-world examples of new leadership approaches in practice. It is never just one attribute or practice. Successful leadership is a combination of multiple attributes and behaviors. And context matters. The case studies provide holistic examples of organizations where leadership is thriving. These case studies individually and collectively reflect the full breadth of topics covered in the prior sections. They methodically illustrate how this guidance is put into action. These case studies reflect the private sector, public sector, and non-government arena demonstrating that good leadership can be replicated anywhere.

This volume brings together a wide range of perspectives and experiences from four dozen experts from across the globe. The authors represent a mix of academics, consultants, and internal practitioners with a diversity of backgrounds and lived experiences to inform and challenge the reader. Collectively, these experts provide thought-provoking insights grounded in research-based, real-world tested ideas and approaches.

The Rapidly Evolving World of Technology

We begin the journey in Section II, which is focused on how new and evolving technologies require new leadership knowledge, skills, actions, and accountabilities. Recent work by Chamorro-Premuzic (2023) and others view AI and other advancing technologies as ways for employees to "copilot" rather than "auto pilot." But these new ways of working will also demand new leadership skills. What is the impact of generative AI and applications such as ChatGPT? How should leaders lead when they are responsible for overseeing the work of a bot versus a human? What are the implications for teamwork and productivity? How will employees develop and grow when technology does the thinking for them? What are the risks and mitigation strategies as poorly understood technologies permeate the workplace at unprecedented levels? How will organizations manage knowledge to support training in a context of rapid change?

Boyce (Chapter 2) provides an enlightening overview of redefining leadership in this age of AI. She focuses on the rate of change and the need to upskill and reskill individuals and teams so they can work appropriately with AI. Boyce also examines the importance of emotional intelligence and empathy, how the human qualities of leadership will increase in importance in this age of AI, and how to lead oneself while also leading others through such a significant change.

Tavis and Derler (Chapter 3) go the next step with tangible examples of what we see today with the intersection of management and AI. They explore how AI-powered tools— including agentic AI, AI coaches, and digital twins—are already transforming the managerial function. They argue that data literacy and real-time analytics are increasingly important in tasks related to both defining and measuring managerial effectiveness. They provide case study examples demonstrating the effective integration of analytics and AI. Finally, they advocate for hybrid models where human insights with AI capabilities become essential for organizational success.

Niederhoffer and colleagues (Chapter 4) share research from the consultancy BetterUp emphasizing the increasing importance of human-centric leadership skills with the integration of AI in the workplace. Through a year-long study involving 12,000 US-based full-time employees, the authors identified two predominant AI mindsets: Pilots and Passengers. Pilots were found to embrace AI with optimism and agency. Pilots leveraged AI tools to enhance productivity, goal attainment, innovation, and job satisfaction. Passengers were found to exhibit apprehension and concern about AI's impact on job autonomy and quality. Their findings highlight shifting roles for leaders in this new era of generative AI. In order to cultivate the Pilot mindset, leaders must enable employees to adapt confidently to AI-driven changes, and they must manage with deeply human skills including listening, motivating, recognizing, and coaching. This chapter provides specific, data-driven strategies for leaders to facilitate the transition to AI-operated environments.

Woodward (Chapter 5) explores the intersection of coaching and AI in leadership development. He provides examples of tools and use cases, and details how AI can streamline administrative tasks, enable scalable support, and personalize feedback. Woodward introduces the concept of "braiding" AI into coaching processes, emphasizing integration rather than replacement.

While all these chapters mention potential concerns about this new and ever-growing technology, Boinodiris's concluding chapter of the section (Chapter 6) eloquently details substantial risks, which are often overlooked or underestimated in the zeal to adopt AI. This chapter outlines what leaders should know about AI and what actions they need to take when introducing these technologies, integrating them into their organizations, and maintaining them over time. Boinodiris identifies a specific leadership role—AI governance leader—that is needed in organizations to engender trust and ensure accountability for surfacing and mitigating risks through robust, ongoing processes, realizing benefits while protecting their businesses, employees, customers, and society from undue harm.

These chapters provide the reader with ample food for thought on the expanding capacity and use of technology in society and in organizations, and on the role of a leader in this technology-driven environment.

Data and Analytics through a Leadership Lens

Section III is focused on the emerging required competency of leveraging data and analytics to be a successful leader. The proliferation of data today creates an imperative for leadership expertise in navigating and optimizing data for organizational decision-making. How can leaders best make sense of data to arrive at fact-based decisions? What data are necessary? How can data accuracy be ensured?

Fink and Reiswig (Chapter 7) explore a range of sample metrics and data available to leaders and identify the challenges of extracting meaningful insights from what can at times be an overabundance of data, while still avoiding the consequences of bad data or inappropriate interpretation. They emphasize the importance of accurate, relevant, and ethically managed data to inform business decisions.

Nalbantian (Chapter 8) discusses how data, analytics, and context matter in the assessment and development of leaders, emphasizing that leader development is not a one-size-fits-all model. Based on his extensive client research, Nalbantian explores how advanced analytics and AI permit a new data-driven, analytics-based approach to assessing and developing leaders. The result is leadership development programs that are more objective, more context-sensitive, and more tailored to the organization and its business objectives.

These chapters open the reader to the importance of data and the criticality of understanding and interpreting data for effective decision-making.

Global Challenges Impacting Organizations

Section IV highlights some of the global challenges impacting organizations today, when leaders need to steer organizations through continual and unpredictable social, environmental, and economic turbulence.

Boston Consulting Group (Caye et al., 2022) has defined generative leaders as those who strive to leave the world a better place than they found it. Generative leaders want to do better not just for their shareholders, but for their customers, for their teams, for society, and for the planet as well. The 2025 Edelman Trust Barometer Global Report indicates that employees expect Chief Executive Officers (CEOs) to take a public stand on key issues and to address them. Therefore, leaders need to be proactive in thinking about societal challenges.

Birrell Ivory and Mackay (Chapter 9) outline the role that sustainability initiatives must play in thriving businesses. They posit that business exists to support a thriving society by producing goods and services, and in doing so makes a profit. Societal good and profitability are not mutually exclusive, and long-term profitability requires a thriving society to consume the goods and services produced. The authors further explore the origins of sustainability, its relationship to business, and how leaders might best approach this relationship in the future. Finally, they share tools useful for leaders who recognize the role of sustainability in ensuring the strategic success of their business.

The environment and context in which organizations operate present formidable leadership challenges. Since we live in the era of continued polycrises, crisis management skills are needed now more than ever (Nohria, 2024; Reed, 2025). Grubb and Anderson (Chapter 10) define crisis leadership and compare it to leadership in more settled, predictable, and lower-stakes situations. They describe crisis situations where the impact is immediate and the stakes, pressure, and spotlight are abnormally high. Poor leadership in such situations can lead to catastrophic results such as interrupted operations, reputational damage, significant financial loss, or even death and destruction. They outline key steps leaders can take before, during, and after a crisis to improve their ability to lead themselves, their teams, and entire organizations through crises and significant disruptions.

These two chapters provide a glimpse of the increasing global complexity that leaders face beyond the immediacy of what their teams demand.

Leadership and Diversity

Section V focuses on leadership and diversity, and the imperative of leading the entirety of the workforce in an increasingly diverse world. At the time of this writing, the notion of leading inclusively is under attack in the United States given Trump administration executive orders and the resulting cultural and societal fallout. Research and practice, evidenced by the chapters in this section, show that leading inclusively is more important than ever for organizational success and societal well-being.

Cox and Wilson (Chapter 11) focus on the shifting dynamics of diversity, equity, and inclusion (DEI) in organizations, including changed societal expectations and heightened scrutiny of DEI efforts. The authors directly acknowledge that not all employees understand or support DEI work. While recognizing the limits of the science and practice of DEI, the chapter offers practical guidance that includes widening the DEI lens to include all ethnicities (including the multitude of variations of "White" identity), centering respect to enhance employee engagement and innovation, reevaluating performance appraisal systems, and reconsidering how implicit bias training is used. The chapter assists leaders in navigating real-world DEI challenges, thereby driving systemic change to benefit employees and their organizations.

Valerio and Ronske (Chapter 12) provide a call to action in support of women's leadership. Although women have made substantial gains in education and workforce participation, they continue to be underrepresented in senior leadership positions. Despite increased awareness and efforts by many organizations, progress toward gender equity has been slow, particularly for women of color. The authors describe systemic issues embedded in organizational structures which result in the "Broken Rung," the "Glass Cliff," microaggressions, and biased promotion systems, arguing that real progress requires shifting focus from "fixing" individuals to transforming systems. They present a call to action encouraging leaders and HR professionals to implement practical, evidence-based strategies such as increasing board diversity, supporting mentorship, expanding flexible work options, and investing in leadership development.

Smith and Stuart (Chapter 13) argue that allyship is a crucial complement to inclusive leadership, equipping leaders with the skills needed to foster belonging and equity in workplaces where social identities matter. They provide readers with a practical roadmap for integrating allyship into organizational leadership, offering actionable insights for fostering more inclusive and effective leadership practices.

Praslova (Chapter 14) introduces us to neurodiversity and explains how the goal of "neuroinclusion" challenges traditional leadership models. She outlines a neuroinclusive approach to leadership based on the concept of holistic belonging—a framework that recognizes and values the unique ways humans think, feel, work, and interact (Praslova, 2024). Finally, she describes an alternative, neuroinclusive approach to creating leadership pipelines and neurodiverse leadership teams.

These chapters collectively illustrate key approaches to leading inclusively in today's increasingly diverse world, enabling organizations to more fully utilize the immense talent pool represented by this diversity.

Caring and Empathy

Section VI is focused on authentically leading with humanity in order to optimize worker, organization, and societal outcomes. Morgan (2023) defines a vulnerable leader as a leader who intentionally opens themselves up to the potential of emotional harm while taking action to create a positive outcome. We see powerful examples of vulnerability, and the benefits to be reaped, in the chapters of this section. The authors describe different ways to lead with empathy, compassion, humanity, and vulnerability, in order for leaders to engage all of their employees and lead successfully.

Comini (Chapter 15) specifically focuses on the role of psychological safety (Edmundson, 1999) and accountability. The COVID-19 pandemic amplified existing trends such as rising stress, burnout, and disengagement. While we have seen significant investment in employee well-being programs, the return on investment (ROI) of these programs has fallen short of expectations. Too often organizations have focused only on these initiatives without taking into consideration the role of management practices and how work is managed. This chapter introduces a practical framework that enables managers to support employee well-being, drive performance, and foster more supportive work environments. Grounded in recent research and real-world consulting experience, the framework balances speaking up with accountability, defined as a sense of ownership and personal agency. The chapter concludes with concrete, actionable advice for managers on how to initiate and sustain meaningful everyday conversations that build a culture of speaking up and accountability—one that benefits both individuals and the organization as a whole.

Martin (Chapter 16) introduces the idea of a "generous check-in," which "prioritizes the employee as a person above the work the employee does for the organization" (Martin, 2025, p. 386). A generous check-in, according to Martin, should foster psychological safety and encourage two-way dialogue, which in turn improves employee engagement and creates a supportive environment to engage in coaching, feedback, and praise. Generous check-ins should create space for the employee to say how they are doing, contain agenda items that are important to the employee, and, ideally, occur on a weekly basis. It is important for managers to be fully present for the check-in meeting and show up prepared to have a productive discussion. Too often managers are multi-tasking or distracted when in one-on-one conversations. When check-ins are done well, employees are more likely to feel psychologically safe and to contribute positively to the organization.

Frangos (Chapter 17) explores the changing nature of CEO and C-suite leadership, including capabilities that have become more important over time and that link to the performance of the business. The chapter focuses not only on the behaviors that will make executives successful but also on the behaviors and habits that top leaders will need to eliminate. Frangos provides a special focus on learning agility, describing why it is important and how leaders can build their learning agility muscle. She continues by exploring the role of vulnerability in learning, shares advice for leaders to unlearn outdated habits that can become problematic, and explains how to build trust and followership.

These chapters highlight the different ways leaders can lead with empathy and compassion, creating environments characterized by psychological safety, accountability, learning agility, and vulnerability—putting people first in the leadership equation.

Developing Leaders for the New World of Work

Section VII is focused on developing and enabling new and existing leaders to operate successfully in this new world of work. As leaders must adapt to the new reality of unpredictability and near-constant change, so must leadership development practices. What is required of leaders today and in the future to be successful? This section takes us through what has been identified as the most critical aspects of leadership by noted scholars.

Kansal, Boroff, and Caputo (Chapter 18) share their research findings based on their longitudinal "Future of Leadership Survey." The authors highlight the importance of trust as the foundational element of leadership effectiveness in today's world. They believe that the ability for leaders to instill trust should be elevated in leadership development. They propose a new conceptual model for assessing leadership effectiveness across defined time arcs: Potential (past), Performance (present), and Permanence (future). The authors conclude with practical guidance for leaders to enhance trust within their organizations in today's rapidly changing organizational landscapes.

Wu and Pedigo (Chapter 19), based on their cumulative decades of experience, describe the leadership skills and behaviors needed to lead through change in the world of mergers and acquisitions (M&A). M&A activity has grown significantly since 2016, with companies using this strategy to fuel organizational growth. Leaders from both the acquiring and acquired organizations assume a key role in guiding their employees through disruptive change while also working to ensure the success of the combined organization. Communications, culture, governance, and personal motivations are only a few crucial elements that every leader must intentionally address.

Jones, Nghona, and Jackson (Chapter 20) present the challenges and opportunities associated with cultivating an intrapreneurial mindset in the context of modern leadership development. They make a compelling argument for the benefits of bringing entrepreneurial skills and behaviors inside organizations to accelerate innovation and growth, and provide actionable insights for organizations to nurture intrapreneurial leaders from within to drive sustainable success.

Toffolo (Chapter 21) explores an often-overlooked dimension of leadership: relational presence and attunement. She posits that leading in today's complexity requires a new kind of focused presence between leaders and followers. Toffolo and her coaching colleagues share analyses based on years of coaching engagements where they examine the managerial tension between "doing" and "being." She describes how leaders can learn to meet their teams with greater emotional clarity, presence, and humanity beyond transactional encounters.

Finally, Barrows, White, and Shullman (Chapter 22) explore the evolution of executive education in today's business schools, consultancies, and corporations. How are these storied institutions defining and developing future executives and CEOs? Their survey of executive development scholars and practitioners, combined with their own decades of experience, reveals trends and criteria consistent with those discussed throughout this volume.

The chapters in this section identify specific leadership competencies and behaviors needed today and in the future—including trust, change leadership, intrapreneurship, and attunement, to mention a few.

Bringing Leadership Practices to Life: Case Studies

In Section VIII we see how all these ideas come to life with case studies and playbooks for leadership success. As evidenced by these examples, there is no one right way to lead. Some attributes or criteria are more important in some contexts than others. A great deal is expected and required of leaders today. These case studies provide concrete examples of how organizations have defined and developed their leaders for success. Case studies span public companies, the government, and non-government organizations (NGOs).

Botha, Osicki, and Campbell (Chapter 23) share the landmark leadership work conducted by the United Nations (UN). Since its founding in 1945, the UN has had to continually adapt its leadership and organizational approaches to meet the demands of a dynamic global environment. The authors detail how the UN incorporates innovative leadership training and core values like humanity and humility, along with data analytics and digital innovation to bolster adaptability and visionary leadership. They discuss how these transformations enhance the UN's capacity to contribute to global stability and set future leadership trends.

Stomski (Chapter 24) explores Walmart's strategic initiative to build compassionate leadership capabilities at scale through its Manager Academy program. In the wake of significant global events—including the COVID-19 pandemic, social unrest, and the rise of generative AI—the emphasis on empathy, compassion, and deep listening has become a core business imperative for the world's largest retailer. Stomski describes Walmart's people-centered culture and discusses how foundational values, dating back to founder Sam Walton, inform current leadership development efforts. She reviews the neuroscience and psychology behind empathy, and highlights the design of Walmart's Manager Academy. This design combines in-person learning, storytelling, leadership modeling, and immersive scenarios and technology aligned with Walmart's core values. The chapter reviews Walmart's approach as a scalable model for embedding empathy into leadership development while reinforcing corporate culture and driving business performance.

Mukherjee, Collins, and Hartog (Chapter 25) describe leadership development at Salesforce. They explore Salesforce's strategic investment in leadership development through its large-scale programs—Accelerate and Elevate—designed to build the capabilities of both aspiring and current frontline people leaders. The programs were designed to align with the company's business goals, foster a culture of accountability and trust, and equip leaders to thrive in an era of human-AI agent collaboration. The authors review the design, delivery, and measurable outcomes of each program, including high levels of engagement, increased leadership confidence, and improved business performance. The chapter outlines Salesforce's use of modular, virtual-first learning formats, gamification, peer coaching pods, and simulation-based learning to allow for scalability. Results from internal surveys and participant feedback illustrate the tangible benefits of leadership development at scale.

Kolmstetter (Chapter 26) describes a detailed blueprint for the role of a leader in establishing a new organization and culture. The chapter provides a valuable case study that underscores the vital role that leaders have in prioritizing people and culture in order to achieve key talent management outcomes—such as effective hiring, enhanced engagement, improved retention, leadership excellence, and a skilled workforce—that are essential for the US Cybersecurity and Infrastructure Security Agency (CISA) to achieve its national security mission. The chapter describes how the Chief People Officer, a pioneering role, adopted a human-centric approach to drive a healthy culture that CISA aims to integrate into the daily experiences of every employee. Organized around 12 Core Culture Principles—such as moral courage, empathy, imagination, inclusion, agility, lifelong learning, and resilience—this discussion illustrates how leaders and practitioners can effectively operationalize culture efforts, supported by relevant and practical examples. This chapter serves as an essential resource for those committed to fostering a thriving workplace culture.

Conclusion

Section IX is our summary and conclusion of main themes, reflections, and looking to the future (Chapter 27).

While the basics of leadership—strategy, vision, and alignment—remain important, their level of criticality has now increased, and the current geopolitical zeitgeist requires leaders to address complex external forces—including shifting technologies, attitudes, and expectations—like never before.

Leaders who understand the expectations and the zeitgeist also see the value of generating positive change and creating positive work environments where employees can be their best selves and perform at their optimal. Decades of research shows that these types of leaders will always be successful.

As we see increased expectations regarding the use of technology as part of managerial work, the use of technology needs to be approached with care. Dignity and respect for individuals' contributions must be kept in mind. Employees must feel valued, and that they are worth more than an AI-generated performance review, for example. Managers who leverage technology to make themselves better leaders are distinctly different from managers who use the tools to do their job. An employee deserves a focused conversation from their manager who truly understands their accomplishments as opposed to receiving AI-generated feedback. This can be perceived by the employee as a manager abdicating their role and responsibility. Technology has the potential to both enhance effective managers and exacerbate bad managerial practices. Fundamentally, leadership behaviors must instill trust in you as a leader. Humanity must still be in focus as the world continues to evolve. These are the leadership lessons and principles you will find throughout this volume.

We hope that this book will provoke thought, discussion, and action. Leaders do not (and should not be expected to) have all the answers, but they need to create the space for others to explore, build, and grow. Much is required of a leader today. Expectations are higher because the world is evolving at an ever-accelerating pace. The chapters collected in this volume are meant to provide thoughtful guidance and examples grounded in evidence-based work. Let the leadership journey in the new world of work begin.

References

Accenture. (2025). *Life trends 2025* https://www.accenture.com/content/dam/accenture/final/accenture-com/document-3/Accenture-LifeTrends2025-Report.pdf#zoom=40

Arden, J. (2025). *A different kind of power*. Crown Publishing Group.

Bloom, N., Han, R., & Liang, J. (2024). Hybrid working from home improves retention without damaging performance. *Nature, 630*, 920–925. https://www.nature.com/articles/s41586-024-07500-2

Caye, J., Hemerling, J., Lovich, D., Humblot-Ferrero, M., Potier, F., Werner, R. (2022). Why the world needs generative leaders. *BCG*. https://www.bcg.com/publications/2022/all-about-generative-leadership-and-its-benefits

Chamorro-Premuzic, T. (2023). *I, human*. Harvard Business Publishing.

Chamorro-Premuzic, T., Wade, M., & Jordon, J. (2024, January 22). As AI makes more decisions, the nature of leadership will change. *Harvard Business Review*. https://hbr.org/2018/01/as-ai-makes-more-decisions-the-nature-of-leadership-will-change

Chetty, S., & Patel, V. (2023). Everything all at once. *Dialogue*, Q4, pp. 24–27.

Cooper, M., & Fielding-Singh, P. (2024, November 1). Younger women's experiences show gender equity at work isn't inevitable. *Harvard Business Review*. https://hbr.org/2024/11/younger-womens-experiences-show-gender-equity-at-work-isnt-inevitable?ab=HP-hero-featured-text-1

Deloitte. (2025). *2025 global human capital trends*. https://www2.deloitte.com/us/en/insights/focus/human-capital-trends.html#balancing-tensions-in-the-work

Edelman. (2025). *Edelman trust barometer: Global report*. https://www.edelman.com/sites/g/files/aatuss191/files/2025-01/2025%20Edelman%20Trust%20Barometer%20Global%20Report_01.23.25.pdf

Edmondson, A. (1999). Psychological safety and learning behavior in work teams. *Administrative Science Quarterly, 44*(2), 350–383. https://doi.org/10.2307/2666999

Grabarek, P., & Sawyer, K. (2025). *Leading for wellness*. Wiley.

Holt, J., & Schmid, B. (2024). Unionization activity continues to surge in the U.S. *Employment Law Watch*. https://www.reedsmith.com/our-insights/blogs/employment-law-watch/102k1hz/unionization-activity-continues-to-surge-in-the-u-s/

Martin, Meisha-ann. (2025). The generous check-in. In Feinzig, S.L. and Battista, M. (Editors). *The Changing Leadership Landscape: New Challenges, New Expectations, New Actions*. New York: Oxford University Press.

Morgan, J. (2023). The reality of vulnerable leadership. *Dialogue, Q4*, pp. 38–41.

Nohria, N. (2024). As the world shifts, so should leaders. *Harvard Business Review*. https://hbr.org/2022/07/as-the-world-shifts-so-should-leaders

Praslova, L. (2024). *The canary code.* Berrett-Koehler Publishers.

Reed, W. (2025, April 28). 10 strategies for leading in uncertain times. *MIT Sloan Management Review.* https://sloanreview.mit.edu/article/10-strategies-for-leading-in-uncertain-times/#article-authors

Semuels, A. (2022, October 13). Some companies will do just about anything to stop workers from unionizing. *Time.* https://time.com/6221176/worker-strikes-employers-unions

Walker, D. (2024, October 20). There is no leadership without risk. *The New York Times.* https://www.nytimes.com/2024/10/20/opinion/leadership-crisis.html

World Economic Forum. (2025a). *The global risks report 2025, 20th edition.* https://reports.weforum.org/docs/WEF_Global_Risks_Report_2025.pdf

World Economic Forum. (2025b). *Global gender gap report 2025.* https://www.weforum.org/publications/global-gender-gap-report-2025

SECTION II

THE RAPIDLY EVOLVING WORLD OF TECHNOLOGY

2

We Didn't See That Coming

Redefining Leadership in the Age of Generative AI

Christine E. Boyce

Introduction

Depending on your definition, the earliest forms of artificial intelligence (AI, e.g., least squares regression) have existed for over 200 years. Coincidentally, they came into being in the same era as did the earliest theories of leadership (e.g., Thomas Carlyle's "Great Man Theory," which appeared in the 1840s). Much has changed since then, including both the development of what is now known as generative AI, and the realization that you do not have to be a man to be great. In modern times, these two ever-present forces—AI and organizational leadership—are interacting to create new ways of working, new challenges, new concerns, and new opportunities, and they are doing so at an incredible rate. This interaction and the speed at which it is disrupting work have significant implications for jobs, individuals, and organizations.

The desire to understand these implications is not new. It has been a focus of businesses, academics, and practitioners for many years. While we have been asking many of the right questions and seeing the answers evolve over time (e.g., "What makes a great leader?" and "How can technology create a competitive advantage?"), the speed at which we need clarity has completely changed. For example, in just two years' time, ChatGPT, one of today's most well-known generative AI tools, grew to more than 300 million weekly active users (Altman, 2025). To keep up, we must become better and faster at integrating divergent areas of research (e.g., technology and people leadership), ensuring that enduring human needs (e.g., autonomy, psychological safety) do not go unaddressed, and making decisions quickly and accurately (e.g., "How does a leader build the ideal AI-augmented team?"). Fortunately,

Christine E. Boyce, *We Didn't See That Coming*. In: *The Changing Leadership Landscape*. Edited by: Sheri L. Feinzig and Mariangela Battista, Oxford University Press. © Oxford University Press (2026).
DOI: 10.1093/9780197820070.003.0002

as we will see in this chapter, if we are open to it, AI can serve as an important partner in helping us cope.

In today's world, the proliferation of AI is approaching ubiquity, so much so that some have stated, "we eventually won't even know it's there" (Deloitte, 2024, p. 2). Even if we limit our view to the world of work, work is increasingly being augmented by AI, a powerful trend that is both creating and displacing jobs (World Economic Forum, 2025). While there are many reasons for this, including its ease of use and the fact that, in many cases, humans do not require any training to obtain benefits from using AI (Dell'Acqua et al., 2023), much is still unknown regarding the ways in which humans interact with their digital collaborators (cf. Ide & Talamàs, 2024 and Otis et al., 2023). This creates a unique challenge for those tasked with leading workers in today's fluid environment. To help address these challenges, the purpose of this chapter is threefold:

- To explore the work—i.e., the tasks and activities—of leaders and how it may be affected by generative AI
- To elaborate on the leader as a person and the human qualities of leadership that will increase in importance in generative AI–augmented workplaces
- To highlight areas that would benefit from additional research and scientific curiosity

As we explore these topics, it will become clear that generative AI is more than a tool leaders must manage. It is a force that is reshaping what it means to lead. To adapt, leaders must rise to the occasion, challenge the way things have been done in the past, and—above all else—focus on human connections.

Setting the Stage

Perhaps it is already cliché to say (which is in and of itself telling), but the field of AI is transforming rapidly. By the time this chapter is published, there will likely have been new advances and breakthroughs that did not exist at the time of this writing. For these reasons, it is important to begin by clarifying a few terms as they are used here.

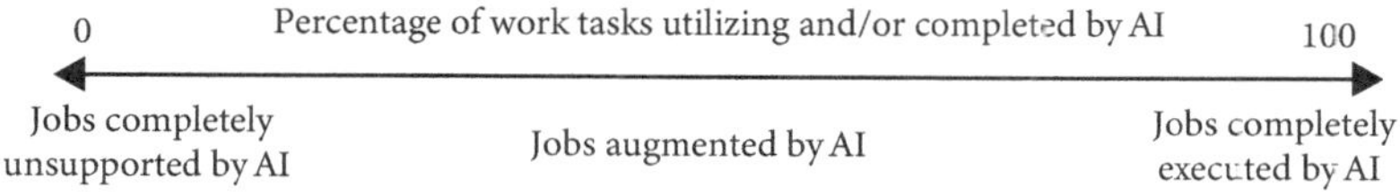

Figure 2.1 Continuum of AI Use in Jobs

For the purposes of this chapter, *AI* is defined as "a broad term referring to computer-based procedures that mimic the decisions, processes, or outcomes of humans so closely as to appear intelligent" (Tippins et al., 2021, p. 5). This includes a specialized form of AI known as *generative AI*, or AI that creates something new (e.g., text, audio, video, images). It also includes *AI agents*, which are systems or programs that can perform tasks on behalf of users or other systems (Gutowska, 2024). AI agents are goal-directed tools that can operate autonomously and seem poised to dramatically change how we work (Warren, 2025).

As we explore the use of AI, specifically the impact of generative AI on people at work and on the humans who lead them, it is important to keep in mind that the use of AI in the workplace is not an all-or-nothing approach. It can be easy to get caught up in thinking of individual jobs as being entirely replaced by AI, but as we will see, it is more likely that jobs will be reshaped or even transformed by such technologies. As a result, it is helpful to conceptualize the use of AI in any role as falling along a continuum from not at all used to AI fully executing the job, as shown in Figure 2.1. Readers thinking about specific jobs are encouraged to consider where along this continuum the role falls today, relative to where it might fall in the future.

Leaders at Work

Definitions of leadership continue to be numerous and varied (Yukl & Gardner, 2020), despite it having been researched for many years. To facilitate a review of the implications of generative AI for today's leaders, this chapter instead utilizes the employee lifecycle as a framework for the analysis of leader tasks. Specifically, the implications of generative AI are explored beginning with leadership tasks and activities related to the talent acquisition process, then discussing concerns around talent development and retention, next covering activities related to offboarding employees, and then

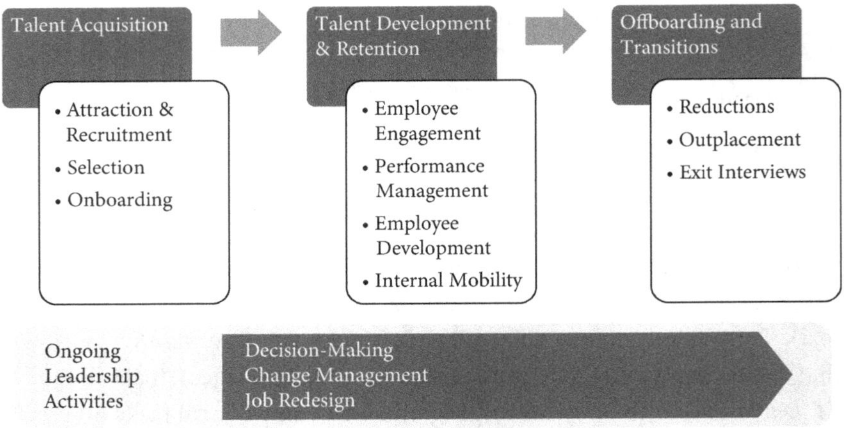

Figure 2.2 The Employee Lifecycle and Related Leadership Activities

looking at responsibilities of leaders that endure across these stages. This section concludes with mention of a "new" leadership task that is likely to increase in importance. The structure of this framework is depicted in Figure 2.2. Subsequently, this chapter discusses those personal leadership qualities that are likely to increase in importance because of generative AI and then explores a way of thinking about future research.

As evidenced by the chapters in this volume and elsewhere, the demands on leaders in organizations are ever-changing. However, some of these changes are so revolutionary that they have the potential to cause dramatic transformations across large classes of jobs, or even all jobs. Consider, for example, the use of electricity in manufacturing facilities, the invention of the computer, and the invention of the internet. Each of these transformed work—and for that matter, life—as we know it. Generative AI has the power to be just as transformative, as it is impacting every aspect of the employee lifecycle that leaders need to manage, as well as those enduring activities like decision-making and change management that are continuously required.

Talent Acquisition

Bringing on good talent is one of the most fundamental aspects of leadership. While an individual leader may not be involved in every step, the talent acquisition process includes attracting and recruiting individuals, choosing whom to hire, and onboarding employees so they can add value to the organization as quickly and easily as possible. In a generative AI–enabled world, the mechanisms by which organizations and potential employees proceed through each of these steps are rapidly changing. For example, AI-enabled chatbots can recruit, screen, and interview thousands of applicants at once, enabling leaders and organizations to consider a much larger and potentially more diverse pool of talent than ever before (see Boyce & Boyce, 2020 for an example). On the other hand, applicants can use AI to generate resumes, cover letters, and even cheat on video-based interviews (Alex, 2024). While the risk of making a bad hire has always been a concern, the chances of doing so are increasing. Lesser-skilled individuals can now more easily represent themselves as ideal candidates—and by using generative AI and AI agents, they can do so at scale in a more tailored and effective way. Today's leaders and their talent acquisition partners must sort through exponentially increasing numbers of what appear to be quality job applications, they must combat more sophisticated ways of cheating, and they must be on the lookout for AI-based talent acquisition processes that unintentionally impart bias into the process. At the same time, they have a much larger set of tools at their fingertips to reach greater numbers of potential applicants, to customize recruitment messages to specific audiences, and to utilize objective assessments throughout the screening process. Taken together, it is easy to see how this litany of new concerns increases the complexity of a single hire. Once that individual begins work, the onboarding process can then be facilitated using AI to create highly individualized plans and objectives which are connected to the overall business strategy. In utilizing these automated approaches, leaders will need to place additional emphasis on ensuring that employees do not lose sight of one of the most crucial elements of a successful onboarding experience—getting to know your (human) coworkers.

Talent Development and Retention

The global employee development market was around $340 billion in 2023 (Bersin, 2024), and the employee engagement software market size that same year was valued at $911 million (Fortune Business Insights, 2025). Clearly, organizations—and consequently, leaders—are investing time and money in these areas. Generative AI is remaking these critical activities in highly customized ways, creating learning content that is bespoke to an individual user, analyzing employee sentiment at scale in real time, and creating personalized surveys to proactively check in on employees. Generative AI–enabled performance management tools are automating evaluations, providing employees with real-time feedback and coaching, helping them create personalized development plans, and even identifying potential attrition risks. These advances can provide leaders with more data than ever regarding the status of their employees, which begs the question of how to interpret it for insights that a leader can use to take meaningful action. In addition, like other forms of electronic performance monitoring (see McNall & Roch, 2007 for some examples), the relationship between generative AI–related performance monitoring and employee perceptions of trust still needs to be explored. Once again, we see the inputs leaders must attend to increasing in both complexity and scope, highlighting the need for increased vigilance and sophistication when it comes to strategic thinking and decision-making.

Another implication of generative AI on employee development concerns the more basic issue of how people learn. In many organizations, junior employees learn by manually completing rote tasks over time—e.g., a junior marketer prepares competitor analyses by researching other companies and drafting a report. This individual might spend many hours on each report, toiling over document revisions before ultimately creating the final version. Using generative AI, that same person could spend a few minutes drafting a simple prompt and then almost immediately review a report draft that requires minimal editing before considering it complete. As a result, leaders developing their teams must now ask themselves how to help them develop the knowledge and skills necessary to be effective in the future, if the routine tasks from which they would normally learn can now be completed instead by generative AI. This may require figuring out how to let people try more complex activities having had less practice, which is another way of saying leaders may need to get comfortable letting people fail more often.

Today's leaders are also faced with the daunting challenge of determining what their teams should be learning in the first place. The World Economic Forum predicts that "on average, workers can expect that two-fifths (39%) of their existing skill sets will be transformed or become outdated over the 2025–2030 period" (2025, p. 6). When combined with the fact that "macrotrends-driven creation of new jobs is estimated to amount to 170 million jobs," (p. 18) or 14% of today's total employment, it becomes evident that leaders will be faced with a critical skills gap—i.e., current employee skillsets will be outdated, and we should somehow be preparing employees now for roles that do not exist yet.

Offboarding and Transitions

When talent is being offboarded, there is a resulting decrease in leadership activity. However, many of the same trends we have seen in prior employee lifecycle stages still apply. Leaders might be involved in deciding which jobs will be eliminated during a reduction, especially as workers' skills become less relevant over time. In these cases, generative AI–enabled tools can help the leader conduct analyses of different scenarios, taking into account vast amounts of data as they do. Leaders might be responsible for evaluating the performance of an outplacement provider, and/or analyzing data from employee exit interviews. In these cases, too, generative AI can be used to understand and help interpret the available data. From the perspective of the leader, the use of generative AI again enables greater ability to quickly combine and digest large amounts of data, while also requiring a corresponding increase in the mental capacity to use it. This includes a need for leaders to develop fact-checking skills to ensure that any outputs the AI produces are accurate, as it has been well documented that AI can make up incorrect responses to a question, a phenomenon often referred to as "hallucinating" (Maleki et al., 2024).

Ongoing Leadership Activities

Occurring throughout the employee lifecycle, two other leadership activities are particularly important to consider in a generative AI–enabled workplace: decision-making and change management.

Decision-Making. Considering each of the employee lifecycle activities, one trend becomes quite clear: AI helps leaders integrate huge amounts of data without requiring expert statistical or mathematical capabilities, while at the same time requiring leaders to derive insights from and act on a much more expansive and complex set of inputs. In theory, incorporating more data into a decision-making process should lead to better decisions. However, this is only true if high-quality, relevant, and unbiased data are used, and if leaders can interpret and apply these data effectively as part of the decision-making process. Thus, the leader's role as decision maker—even in entry-level leadership roles—requires a more expert-level approach to considering inputs and making critical choices for the business. Perhaps this is why the World Economic Forum found that "analytical thinking remains the most sought-after core skill among employers" (2025, p. 6). If used well, generative AI can also summarize and help interpret these inputs, taking multiple complex data points into account. But even then, the best leaders will be those who use their data-driven insights effectively and those who can determine when decisions are best made by AI and when they should be overridden by a credible expert.

As might be expected, an emerging research trend is that individuals with greater domain expertise are less trusting when using AI, and therefore less likely to blindly follow its recommendations (Otis et al., 2023; Zhang et al., 2020). While this skeptical approach can contribute to increased overall performance, it also requires humans to contribute sufficient unique knowledge to the decision-making process. There is still much to be learned about how to optimize AI-supplemented human decision-making, as both human (e.g., level of knowledge) and technological (e.g., the level of autonomy with which AI operates) factors can influence output quality. For example, Ide and Talamàs (2024) found that autonomous AI tended to benefit the most knowledgeable individuals, while non-autonomous AI benefited those who were the least knowledgeable. To mitigate the risks associated with high-stakes, AI-supported decision-making, humans are encouraged to always check their work and that of the AI, or risk arriving at a fate similar to those of automobile drivers in the early days of global positioning systems (GPS) who blamed the GPS for mishaps like driving directly into bodies of water.

Change Management. As new advances are made and new technologies are implemented, the words written by Kenneth Pearlman and Matthew Barney in the year 2000 (coincidentally in SIOP's tenth ever Professional Practice Series volume) seem just as accurate today. They stated, "Sweeping economic, demographic, and technological changes have seemingly overnight, reshaped the ... workplace in such fundamental ways ... In just the last ten years organizations have almost literally turned upside down" (p. 3). Connecting this to the role of leaders specifically, John Kotter noted a year later that "what leaders really do is prepare organizations for change and help them cope as they struggle through it" (2001, p. 1). Given the current world of work, it seems a safe prediction that change management will continue to be a necessary leadership skill over the long term. However, not all change is created equal, and the changes brought on by generative AI are unique in the rate at which they are happening, the expansiveness of their impact, and the simple fact that we are unable to accurately predict what new technologies will come to be or the resulting consequences. While it is often the case that leaders must simultaneously navigate both themselves and others through change, the scope here is larger, the speed is faster, and the novelty is greater than with other types of change, which makes the fear people naturally feel when exposed to changing environments even stronger and potentially more detrimental. For these reasons, the role leaders play in building human connections and psychological safety is essential for leadership success, as will be explained in the subsequent section, "The People Side of Leadership."

Increased Emphasis on the Redesign of Jobs

Yukl and Gardner (2020) argued that one reason technology "changes often fail to yield the desired benefits [is] because without consistent changes in work roles, attitudes, and skills, the new technology will not be accepted and used in an effective way" (p. 107). Similar to the reasons electricity took 40 years to show its effect on productivity in manufacturing—i.e., factories and the way they operated, including how talent was recruited, trained, and paid, needed to be completely redesigned (Harford, 2017)—jobs today must be similarly reinvented if we are to realize the potential benefits of AI.

While these changes mean that some jobs may eventually be completely replaced by AI, researchers seem to be coming to consensus that wholesale job elimination is less likely than shifts in focus for those performing the roles. Take, for example, the job of school bus driver, as described by Agrawal et al. (2018). In the example they provide, self-driving vehicles may one day eliminate the need for a human to drive a school bus. However, one of the major responsibilities of school bus drivers is also to monitor the children to maintain discipline and protect them from one another—i.e., a fundamentally human task. As a result, advanced technologies that allow school buses to drive themselves would not eliminate the role of school bus driver. Rather, they might shift the focus of school bus drivers from driving to childcare.

Some of these resulting shifts in focus will be less desirable than others. Consider, for example, a study conducted by researchers at the University of Cambridge that explored how the addition of drug dispensing robots impacted three different jobs within a hospital pharmacy

(Barrett et al., 2012). After the robots were implemented, pharmacists could delegate mundane tasks, freeing up time to elevate their roles and focus more on strategic and valuable activities like advising patients. Pharmacy technicians, on the other hand, experienced mixed results, expanding their roles to include technical expertise in maintaining the robots, causing the technicians to be seen as more essential, while also having to navigate an increased workload and increased dependency on the robots. Pharmacy assistants fared worst of all, being relegated to behind-the-scenes activities of loading the robots with drugs, facing increased supervision and a loss of autonomy, and feeling less valued overall.

The impact of generative AI on jobs and workers is not always intuitive. Leaders must consider the impact of AI on a case-by-case basis and look both at the individual tasks that are part of the job and at the psychological and emotional reactions of job incumbents. For example, in a thoughtful paper that explores, among other things, how generative AI may lead to productivity loss and the implications for human factors research in the AI space, the authors argue that generative AI has not only fundamentally restructured and shifted workflows, but it has also made "easy tasks easier and hard tasks harder" (Simkute et al., 2024, p. 1). To help their teams successfully navigate the use of AI in jobs today, leaders must go beyond standard evaluative metrics like cost savings and work output; in addition they should consider less tangible but equally important factors like the human experience of work. They must think about the relationships between people and jobs and consider what elements of specific roles may need to be adjusted to allow humans to achieve maximum benefits from the use of generative AI. The resulting changes are likely to also change the knowledge, skills, abilities, and other characteristics required for success in a role, thereby impacting things like recruitment, training, and compensation strategies. Once again, we see the role of leaders in organizations increasing in scale, complexity, and importance because of AI.

The People Side of Leadership

In addition to the tasks leaders must complete throughout the employee lifecycle, successful leaders of *human* employees in generative AI–enabled workplaces must also facilitate human connections and prioritize the employee experience. Contrast this with leaders of *digital* employees—i.e., leaders who only manage a series of AI bots or agents, as described by Warren (2025)—who can comfortably skip this section.

Humans want to be led by other humans. In fact, research has shown that people are more likely to intend to quit when they imagine their boss is AI (de Almeida et al., 2023). When employees in an organization experience a leader, they are experiencing those uniquely human leadership skills (or lack thereof) that are often referred to as "soft"—or, in more recent times, "power"—skills. The best leaders demonstrate "strong interpersonal skills, and leadership behaviors traditionally viewed as feminine (e.g., supporting, developing, empowering). These skills and behaviors ... are more important than in earlier times because of changing conditions in work organizations" (Yukl & Gardner, 2020, p. 363). Several of these stand out as particularly important for leaders and are discussed in Section VI of this volume (e.g., empathy, autonomy, psychological safety). They are also particularly important in a generative AI context and are highlighted here as well, among others. The list that follows represents a combination of qualities important for managing people and necessary for successful use of AI. A visual representation of a model for leadership in an AI-enabled organization can be found in Figure 2.3.

Empathy. Demonstrating empathy—i.e., the ability to share in the emotions of others—is one of the most universal aspects of humanity. Some have

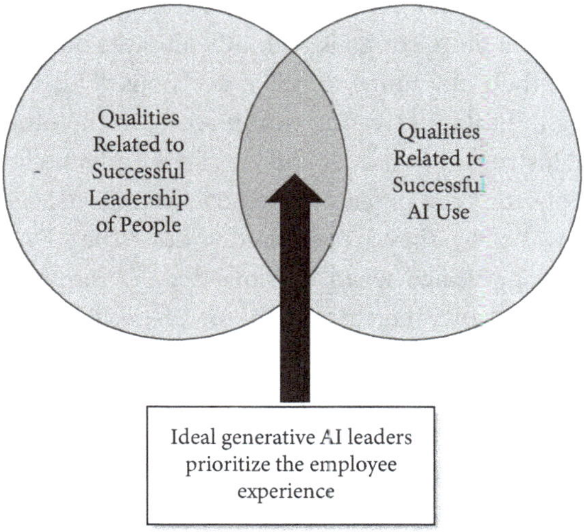

Figure 2.3 A Proposed Model for Successful Leadership in a Generative AI–Enabled Workforce

even predicted it will "play a supersized role in the economy of the future" (Tavis & Lupushor, 2022, p. 83). As employees navigate the complex changes described in this volume, being able to rely on their leaders to understand what they are going through is essential. Furthermore, as increasing amounts of work are being done by AI, those motivated by connecting (whether in person or virtually) with other humans in the workplace may find this need less fully met, making it even more important for human leaders to step in. While Tavis and Lupushor (2022, p. 83) have also argued that "emotionally intelligent machines" will one day "be teaching empathy back to humans," we are not there yet. In a similar fashion to what we see with what is known as the "uncanny valley"—i.e., that unsettling feeling one gets when seeing a robot or image that is "almost" human (Mori, 1970)—when generative AI attempts to imitate empathy, it is perceived as inauthentic, which mitigates any positive benefit of demonstrating empathy and creates what has been called a "backfiring effect" (Seitz, 2024). Those leaders who can demonstrate real empathy in real time will be the ones who are best able to care for their teams during these times of rapid change.

Autonomy. Feeling a sense of autonomy in one's work has long been understood to be a factor that increases an individual's motivation to perform (e.g., Deci & Ryan, 2000; Hackman & Oldham, 1976). This is one of the many reasons that micromanagement can be so demotivating. In a generative AI–enabled workplace, the effects of AI on autonomy can be both positive and negative. On the one hand, junior employees using generative AI are now enabled to complete more complex and difficult tasks on their own, potentially increasing their autonomy to make decisions. This can be a help to leaders looking to build motivating workplaces. On the other hand, when employees are instructed to use AI and/or when leaders rely heavily on AI to make decisions, this can potentially remove feelings of agency from individuals who now believe they are required to do as the AI suggests. Things get even more complicated when we consider the recent finding that as the quality of AI outputs increases, humans essentially "fall asleep at the wheel," getting lazy and failing to check their work, to the detriment of the quality of their outputs (Dell'Acqua, 2021). As a result, leaders must once again consider the implications of AI use on both specific jobs and specific individuals—including their existing experience, competency level, and motivations—to ensure that personal autonomy is not sacrificed in the name of implementing the latest technology. Much research remains to be done on the ideal structures for human–AI interactions in the workplace.

Psychological Safety. It is well established that psychological safety leads to a wide range of positive outcomes—from job performance to creativity, inclusion, and engagement (Edmondson & Bransby, 2023). As defined by Edmondson (1999), psychological safety is "a shared belief held by members of a team that the team is safe for interpersonal risk taking" (p. 350). She goes on to say that "it describes a team climate characterized by interpersonal trust and mutual respect in which people are comfortable being themselves" (p. 354). Given the numerous ways AI can be implemented in the workplace (e.g., as a monitoring system, as a performance enhancer, as a director of work activities), it is likely that the impact of AI on psychological safety differs depending on its use. For example, implementing an AI-based performance monitoring system might reduce someone's psychological safety, whereas using AI to equip junior members of the team with research and information they need to be successful might enhance it. In either case, to achieve the benefits and value associated with a psychologically safe workplace, it is ultimately up to human leaders to ensure those reporting to them feel safe to express concerns without fear of retribution. To help, leaders can involve employees in AI decision-making processes and emphasize transparency in AI usage.

Asking Better Questions. Exhibiting curiosity as a leader can be an important way to evaluate options, understand challenges, and get to know one's team. Research has shown that intellectual curiosity leads to a range of important outcomes from academic performance (von Stumm et al., 2011) to general well-being (Kashdan & Steger, 2007), in part because individuals who are more curious ask more open questions (Harrison & Dossinger, 2017). To the extent that leaders can be more curious about the impact of generative AI on their teams and their teams' jobs, they will be better equipped to understand the potential benefits and challenges brought on by AI and to help their teams navigate them effectively. On a more practical level, those who use generative AI directly may find themselves in a position of needing to write prompts—i.e., the input AI models use to generate an output. Prompts often take the form of questions, and the ability to ask better questions of generative AI models has a direct relationship with the relevance of the output the AI produces. This is likely a skill that all of us—not just leaders—will want to develop.

Inspiring Others. The ability to persuade and inspire and to rally people around a common goal is one of the hallmarks of people leadership. Whether or not a workplace incorporates the use of generative AI, leaders still need to achieve objectives and get work done. As noted throughout this chapter, the rate of change in workplaces today stemming from AI shows no signs of slowing down. As a result, today's leaders are called upon to continually engage their teams around new ways of working, and to inspire them to do so even though many may be fearful that the very technology they are using will one day take their jobs. This places increased importance on the ability of leaders to engage and inspire their teams around a compelling vision for the future.

Flexibility/Adaptability. The ability to incorporate generative AI in the workplace requires the ability to adapt to changes in the way that work gets done. As jobs continue to evolve, and as new jobs are created and others displaced (World Economic Forum, 2025), the truism that "the only thing that is constant is change" becomes ever more real. Leaders operating in this environment are simultaneously faced with generative AI–led changes to their own jobs, to their business strategies, to the work done by their teams, and to the expectations of their markets and customers—and they must find a way to cope. As Tomas Chamorro-Premuzic explains, "since leaders cannot outperform machines in managing data, information, or well-defined problems, they will predominantly compete in terms of their ability to manage people" (2019, p. 108–109). For some leaders, this will require the reallocation of time and energy to people over technology and process, and this cannot happen without being flexible. Adaptability also goes hand in hand with the change management aspects of leadership. Leading by example and demonstrating ways of adapting to change will help employees do the same.

Integrity. Demonstrating personal integrity and behaving in a way that is consistent with one's own values is crucial to effective leadership. It builds trust (see Covey, 2006 for an extensive review) and lays the foundation for effective team functioning. While it can at times be easy to spot a leader without integrity, in the context of generative AI, the situation is more complex. Leaders who wish to ensure that work processes are ethical and aligned with their values must now be responsible for ensuring that the AI tools they utilize also operate in accordance with the standards they have set. This is not always easy, especially when it can be difficult or even impossible to fully understand how AI works to deliver a result. That said, one of the benefits of AI is the fact that it can be utilized to help uncover human biases that already exist, allowing us to call them out into the open so that they can be addressed (Chamorro-Premuzic, 2023).

A Promising Area for Future Research

Throughout this chapter, we have seen that the responsibilities of leaders are changing. This includes both what leaders do and how they do it. The implementation of generative AI in the workplace requires leaders to adapt to new ways of doing things, despite not having a clear understanding of the effects of AI on their teams. Many of the resulting questions around how to realize the benefits of AI, how to promote autonomy and psychological safety in the workplace, and others raised here have yet to be appropriately studied. To address these, it is recommended that researchers continue to explore the characteristics of the ideal human–AI partnership. Ultimately, this will be about two things: calibration and balance. How do we calibrate the right level of AI involvement to achieve maximal performance? How much AI involvement is too much, and how much is not enough? Another way to ask this is: How can the synergy between AI and humans lead to the outcomes we would like to achieve? And perhaps even more importantly: How do we balance this relationship such that we also achieve the ideal human experience both at work and in life? We are early in the process of our understanding, and while it will be some time before we can say what best practice looks like, things are moving quickly.

With Great Power Comes Great Responsibility

As noted by both Voltaire and Spider Man, leaders have always had a great responsibility, and that is likely to continue. This is only enhanced by powerful tools like generative AI; we should think of AI as amplifying the role leaders play. Their job is becoming more intense in terms of data, decisions, and pace. At the same time, the ability to create human connections is increasingly important. In short, the role leaders play in today's world is ever more critical, and it still requires a combination of intelligence and interpersonal skills. However, the implementation of generative AI in the workplace is raising the bar in terms of the expectations we put on leaders in organizations. Under these circumstances, fast, accurate, executive-level decision-making and deeply caring for other humans and their experiences will be the primary methods by which leaders stay relevant over time. If used effectively, AI can help with these activities, but it will ultimately be the choices made by humans that determine success.

References

Agrawal, A., Gans, J., & Goldfarb, A. (2018). *Prediction machines.* Harvard Business Review Press.

Altman, S. (2025). Reflections. *Sam Altman.* https://blog.samaltman.com/reflections

Alex (2024). 8 tactics candidates are using to cheat in interviews. *Insights.* https://www.alex.com/blog/8-tactics-candidates-are-using-to-cheat-in-interviews

Barrett, M., Oborn, E., Orlikowski, W. J., & Yates, J. (2012). Reconfiguring boundary relations: Robotic innovations in pharmacy work. *Organization Science, 23*(5), 1448–1466.

Bersin, J. (2024, April 6). The $340 billion corporate learning industry is poised for disruption. *Josh Bersin.* https://joshbersin.com/2024/03/the-340-billion-corporate-learning-industry-is-poised-for-disruption/#:~:text=by%20joshbersin%20%C2%B7%20Published%20March%2023,Let%20me%20explain

Boyce, A. S., & Boyce, C. E. (2020). Talent identification in the digital age: Moving from selection to e-selection. In T. Bondarouk & S. Fisher (Eds.), *Encyclopedia of electronic HRM* (pp. 176–181). De Gruyter.

Chamorro-Premuzic, T. (2019). *Why do so many incompetent men become leaders? (and how to fix it).* Harvard Business Review Press.

Chamorro-Premuzic, T. (2023). *I, human.* Harvard Business Review Press.

Covey, S. M. R. (2006). *The speed of trust: The one thing that changes everything.* Free Press.

de Almeida, F., Kireeva, T., Orghian, D., Moreira, P., & Santos, S. (2023). My boss, the algorithm: AI leadership increases turnover through reduced psychological safety [unpublished manuscript]. https://www.researchgate.net/publication/379282580_My_Boss_the_Algorithm_-_AI_Leadership_Increases_Turnover_through_Reduced_Psychological_Safety

Deci, E. L., & Ryan, R. M. (2000). The "what" and "why" of goal pursuits: Human needs and the self-determination of behavior. *Psychological Inquiry, 11*(4), 227–268.

Dell'Acqua, F., McFowland, E., III, Mollick, E., Lifshitz-Assaf, H., Kellogg, K. C., Rajendran, S., Krayer, L., Candelon, F., & Lakhani, K. R. (2023). Navigating the jagged technological frontier: Field experimental evidence of the effects of AI on knowledge worker productivity and quality. [Working Paper 24-013]. Harvard Business School.

Dell'Acqua, F. (2021). Falling asleep at the wheel: Human/AI collaboration in a field experiment on HR recruiters [Working Paper]. Columbia Business School.

Deloitte. (2024). *Tech trends 2025.* Deloitte. https://www.deloitte.com/us/en/insights/topics/technology-management/tech-trends/2025/tech-trends-introduction-ai-is-everywhere.html

Edmondson, A. C. (1999). Psychological safety and learning behavior in work teams. *Administrative Science Quarterly, 44*(2), 350–383.

Edmondson, A. C., & Bransby, D. P. (2023). Psychological safety comes of age: Observed themes in an established literature. *Annual Review of Organizational Psychology and Organizational Behavior, 10,* 55–78. https://www.annualreviews.org/deliver/fulltext/orgpsych/10/1/annurev-orgpsych-120920-055217.pdf?itemId=/content/journals/10.1146/annurev-orgpsych-120920-055217&mimeType=application/pdf

Fortune Business Insights. (2025, January 13). Employee engagement software market size share & industry analysis. *Fortune Business Insights.* https://www.fortunebusinessinsights.com/employee-engagement-software-market-107130

Gutowska, A. (2024, July 3). What are AI agents? *IBM.* https://www.ibm.com/think/topics/ai-agents#:~:text=An%20artificial%20intelligence%20(AI)%20agent,to%20call%20on%20external%20tools.

Hackman, J. R., & Oldham, G. R. (1976). Motivation through the design of work: Test of a theory. *Organizational Behavior and Human Performance, 16,* 250–279.

Harford, T. (2017, August 20). Why didn't electricity immediately change manufacturing? *BBC*. https://www.bbc.com/news/business-40673694

Harrison, S. H., & Dossinger, K. (2017). Pliable guidance: A multilevel model of curiosity, feedback seeking, and feedback giving in creative work. *Academy of Management Journal, 60*(6), 2051–2072. https://doi.org/10.5465/amj.2015.0247

Ide, E., & Talamàs, E. (2024). Artificial intelligence in the knowledge economy. *arXiv*. https://arxiv.org/abs/2312.05481

Kashdan, T. B., & Steger, M. F. (2007). Curiosity and pathways to well-being and meaning in life: Traits, states, and everyday behaviors. *Motivation and Emotion, 31*, 159–173.

Kotter, J. P. (2001, December). What leaders really do. *Harvard Business Review*. https://hbr.org/2001/12/what-leaders-really-do?autocomplete=true

Malecki, N., Padmanabhan, B., & Dutta, K. (2024, June 25–27). *AI hallucinations: A misnomer worth clarifying* [Conference presentation]. 2024 IEEE Conference on Artificial Intelligence, Singapore. https://doi.org/10.1109/CAI59869.2024.00033

McNall, L. A., & Roch, S. G. (2007). Effects of electronic monitoring types on perceptions of procedural justice, interpersonal justice, and privacy. *Journal of Applied Social Psychology, 37*(3), 658–682.

Mori, M. (1970). The uncanny valley. *Energy, 7*(4), 33–35.

Otis, N. G., Clarke, R., Delecourt, S., Holtz, D., & Koning, R. (2023, December 21). *The uneven impact of generative AI on entrepreneurial performance*. OSF Preprints. https://doi.org/10.31219/osf.io/hdjpk

Pearlman, K., & Barney, M. F. (2000). Selection for a changing workplace. In J. F. Kehoe (Ed.), *Managing selection in changing organizations* (p. 3). Jossey-Bass.

Seitz, L. (2024). Artificial empathy in healthcare chatbots: Does it feel authentic? *Computers in Human Behavior: Artificial Humans, 2*(1), 100067. https://doi.org/10.1016/j.chbah.2024.100067

Simkute, A., Tankelevitch, L., Kewenig, V., Scott, A. E., Sellen, A., & Rintel, S. (2024). Ironies of generative AI: Understanding and mitigating productivity loss in human–AI interactions. *arXiv*. https://doi.org/10.48550/arXiv.2402.11364

Tavis, A., & Lupushor, S. (2022). *Humans at work: The art and practice of creating the hybrid workplace*. Kogan Page.

Tippins, N. T., Oswald, F. L., & McPhail, S. M. (2021). *Scientific, legal, and ethical concerns about AI-based personnel selection tools: A call to action*. Center for Open Science. https://www.academia.edu/98917015/Scientific_Legal_and_Ethical_Concerns_about_AI_Based_Personnel_Selection_Tools_A_Call_to_Action

von Stumm, S., Hell, B., & Chamorro-Premuzic, T. (2011). The hungry mind: Intellectual curiosity is the third pillar of academic performance. *Perspectives on Psychological Science*, 6, 574–588. https://doi.org/10.1177/1745691611421204

Warren, N. (2025). Five contrarian ideas about genAI in the workplace. *Exponential View*. https://www.exponentialview.co/p/five-contrarian-ideas-about-genai-at-work

World Economic Forum. (2025). *Future of jobs report*. World Economic Forum. https://www.weforum.org/publications/the-future-of-jobs-report-2025/

Yukl, G., & Gardner, W. L., III. (2020). *Leadership in organizations* (9th ed.). Pearson.

Zhang, Y., Liao, Q. V., & Bellamy, R. K. E. (2020, January). Effect of confidence and explanation on accuracy and trust calibration in AI-assisted decision making. In *Proceedings of the 2020 Conference on Fairness, Accountability, and Transparency* (pp. 295–305). https://doi.org/10.1145/3351095.3372852

3

From Algorithms to Leadership

Management in the Age of AI

Anna A. Tavis and Andrea Derler

Introduction

While the impact of artificial intelligence (AI) on the broader workforce has received significant attention, the equally critical yet less examined evolution of leadership and management in this era demands further investigation—not only for its profound implications for management practices but also for its direct business relevance (Paradis, 2024). For over a century, the debate over the distinction between management and leadership has persisted, often creating a false dichotomy between these two essential roles within organizations (Kotter, 1990). The act of leadership, defined as "influencing others through one's own socially accepted behavior in such a way that this directly or indirectly causes the person influenced to behave in the desired way," has long been elevated as the visionary and strategic force (Weibler, 2023, p. 24). Management, in comparison, often has been described as an operational and transactional oversight (Drucker, 1999). In fact, many voices have proclaimed the imminent demise of middle management, arguing that the advent of AI, automation, and data-driven tools would render these roles obsolete (Elliott, 2021). But this binary framing misses the mark and proves to be even less helpful in the age of AI, where the introduction of multimodal data, predictive analytics, agentic AI, AI coaches, and digital twins into the workflows of organizations requires a wider understanding of the complex intricacies of the ways in which leaders and managers affect people and business outcomes (IBM, 2021; Purdy, 2024; Terblanche et al., 2022).

In this chapter, we propose that, far from disappearing, the role of middle management is poised to expand in both impact and influence. With unprecedented access to data and business insights, talent trends, and work

Anna A. Tavis and Andrea Derler, *From Algorithms to Leadership*. In: *The Changing Leadership Landscape*. Edited by: Sheri L. Feinzig and Mariangela Battista, Oxford University Press. © Oxford University Press (2026). DOI: 10.1093/9780197820070.003.0003 outcomes, middle managers already do less of the mundane, repetitive managerial tasks they often struggled with in the past, but have been pivotal in driving strategic decisions, fostering innovation, and enhancing employee engagement. As AI is reshaping the very nature of work and organizational structures, the traditional distinction between leaders and managers is gradually blurring; it creates a more unified role that seamlessly integrates strategic vision with operational execution. Over time—and we already see the beginnings of it—middle managers, supported by AI, data, and analytics technologies, will become even more indispensable to organizational success in a whole new way.

The future of leadership and management cannot be effectively addressed without a deep awareness of how these roles are evolving in the era of AI, and how current developments in technology, AI, and data analytics impact managers' role in the organization. All professionals deeply involved in leadership strategy and development must reconsider how management and leadership will continue to adapt to emerging technologies. They must also understand the evolving leadership models that will shape the workplace of tomorrow (Simić, 2020). Their role is crucial in transforming management from an administrative function to a strategic one, focused on innovation, coaching, engagement, and human-centered decision-making.

These changes, already happening in organizations, demand more than a simple distinction between the roles; they require a deeper integration of leadership and management underpinned by data, real-time insights, and pathbreaking technologies. Building on this idea, we examine the significant paradigm shift that reshapes the role of managers in today's rapidly evolving workplace (Tabesh, 2022). We describe how the role of a manager is already changing vastly due to the integration of AI-based tools in work processes, requiring people managers to better understand their value and demonstrate it to the business and its workforce. Furthermore, we explain how the new ways of measuring managerial decisions and actions help redefine the purpose of management focusing on an impact-driven approach, and how new tools in data analytics and coaching position AI-powered technologies not as managers' foes but as collaboration partners. In conclusion, we question the relevance of traditional leadership development programs and preview a new AI-powered management paradigm, because, as the title of the article in *Financial Times* suggests, "AI is already changing management—companies must decide how" (Mollick, 2024).

Toward the Evolutionary Model of AI-Driven Management

For decades, effective leadership has been defined and thought of in the form of a trait theory, in that the personal attributes and qualities of leaders were the center of attention. Traditional trait theories of leadership, which emerged in the early twentieth century, suggest that leadership is primarily determined by inherent traits rather than learned skills or behaviors (Kirkpatick & Locke, 1991). A recent US industry study about the development of leadership models showed that many organizations continue to emphasize the identification and cataloging of specific behaviors and traits that embody effective leadership (NeuroLeadership Institute, 2019). The study's findings revealed a stubborn tendency to prioritize the leader as an individual; despite advancements in leadership research, many models still reflect a trait-centric approach, overlooking the relational and contextual aspects of leadership (Hollander, 1992).

For the most advanced organizations, however, this mindset is already changing—away from a focus on leaders' traits, to a focus on leaders' impact. With the proliferation of advanced technologies, organizations now have new opportunities to understand, measure, and shape the effect of leadership and management decisions, actions, and behaviors with greater precision and evidence than ever before. AI-based analytics tools that allow a real-time view into a much wider set of business functions have significantly enhanced the ability to integrate data from diverse sources, providing not only insights into the business and financial performance of managers' units or teams but also more rigorously validated perspectives on relational and contextual aspects of leadership (Visier Inc., 2024b). Human resources (HR) and business leaders are now able to connect metrics such as team engagement scores, turnover rates, and various inclusion data to tangible business outcomes, such as sales performance and customer service numbers.

Cartier, the French luxury goods company, has expanded the use of people analytics among its managerial ranks, reflecting the organization's view that data-driven insights are essential for creating business value and informing strategic decision-making. By expanding the value of people analytics beyond HR to other business functions, Cartier's example illustrates how enabling data access at the managerial level can support measurable organizational outcomes (Legret, n.d.). Such practices contribute not only to evaluating leadership effectiveness but also to reshaping organizational

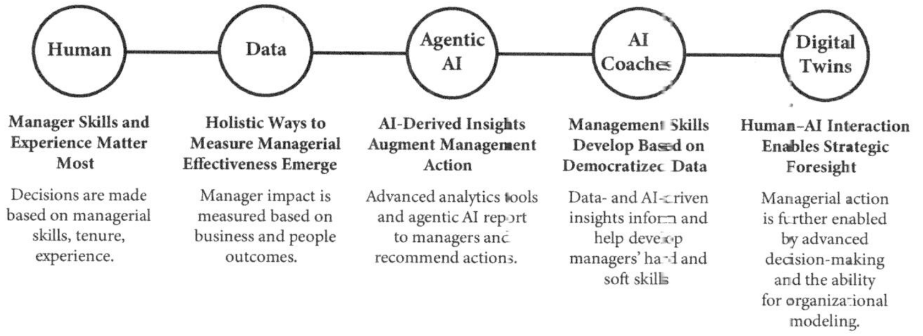

Figure 3.1 Evolution of Management in the Era of AI

conceptions of effective management. In addition to achieving financial performance, managers are increasingly expected to consider the processes by which outcomes are attained—promoting a more balanced and sustainable leadership model. This broader perspective expands a leader's objectives to include facilitating a positive work environment, supporting team members, and cultivating healthy team dynamics. By enlarging the lens from "who a leader is" to "what a leader makes possible," today's most advanced organizations pave the way for a more ethically grounded and organizationally aligned definition of leadership—one that is every bit as relational and contextual as it is individual.

In summary, we capture the overall trajectory of management evolution in Figure 3.1, starting from the human traits, through democratized data, to agentic AI, AI coaching, and ultimately to the still nascent digital twins.

Currently, we see the evolution of management in organizations that are embracing AI capabilities to enhance decision-making in five distinct stages. For many decades, managers' decisions hinged primarily on their personal skills, experience, and personality—a stage we call the "human" stage that predates access to data that would enable a more personality-oriented manager style. The next stage, which we call the "data" stage, reflects current times, and marks a significant shift toward evidence-based management. Managers have access to data about business and people to make their decisions, and at the same time see their own effectiveness measured through access to business and people outcomes on the organization's side. Progressing further, we currently envision the immediate future stage we call "agentic AI," whereby managers are equipped with AI-powered agents, comprehensive analytics, and recommendations to further support and enhance their data-informed managerial decision-making. Based on the insights that are emerging about managerial effectiveness in real time, the stage we call "AI coaches" reflects the democratization of AI-driven insights for managers, which simultaneously enables in-the-moment management coaching to improve manager effectiveness and fosters both technical and interpersonal skill building across management levels. Finally, the "digital twins" stage offers digital models of the organization to conduct advanced scenario planning to make proactive strategic decisions through a collaborative human–AI approach.

The growing availability of data and AI tools has refocused managerial priorities, driving up the demand for leaders who excel in soft skills like interpersonal effectiveness, communication, and coaching (Field et al., 2023).

Measuring Manager Effectiveness in Real Time

Measuring the impact of management and leadership on teams, individual, and unit performance is critical to both talent and business strategy. Yet, recent academic research underscores that many organizations still lack rigorous systems to evaluate managerial effectiveness. A study by Nguyen et al. (2024) highlights the need to reassess how organizations invest in and measure the performance of employees in managerial roles. The study found that managers with leadership responsibilities receive significant financial and career advantages over individual contributors—earning, on average, 33% more at the same organizational level and being 32% more likely to receive promotions. Given such significant financial investments in managerial roles, it is critical for organizations to implement comprehensive performance measurement systems to ensure they are receiving adequate returns. Such systems include but are not limited to the assessment of financial and talent-related metrics, and help quantify the value of managers compared to high-performing individual contributors.

A case in point is Standard Bank Group, a financial services institution with headquarters in Johannesburg, South Africa. The bank's goals include "guiding leaders to create ideal conditions for ... people to thrive," according to Werner Merbold, the head of Workforce Insights (Visier Inc., n.d., par. 7). People leaders are asked to align their approach to driving performance in the form of financial results to other value drivers such as client focus, operational excellence, and employee engagement. In the case of senior leaders, the achievement against these metrics is forming part of their performance evaluation and remuneration because "the business understands that the non-financial metrics are drivers of financial success" (Derler, 2024, p.10). The bank's approach to generate business results while carefully aligning business, management, leadership, and employee value drivers reflects a new era for the definition and measurement of leadership in business settings. Increasingly, effectiveness is defined according to the influence and impact a leader has on others, rather than solely their personal characteristics and skills.

As this example shows, managers are no longer judged solely by financial outcomes but also by how those results correlate with talent retention, as employers increasingly account for both direct and indirect managerial costs.

How Data and AI Transform Managerial Advancement

The evolution of managerial roles is reshaping the nomination and promotion process, as AI-based analytics tools now allow leaders to compare team-level metrics such as productivity, engagement, and retention across managers. Traditionally, managers were promoted from individual contributor roles based on their skills and their tenure at the organization. However, a recent study challenged conventional wisdom about the linear link between managerial experience and business outcomes (Visier Inc., 2024c). Researchers analyzed 3.4 million employee records across 85 enterprise-sized companies in North America and Europe during 2023 and found that only 30% of companies showed a continuous positive relationship between tenure and team performance. This research not only questions the weight that should be placed on a manager's tenure at the organization as a proxy for the value of experience and institutional knowledge, but also foreshadows the future of managerial effectiveness. Managers now are expected to have a strong understanding of how to leverage AI systems to optimize team performance and processes, making technical acumen and a growth mindset more important factors in promotions (Govindarajan et al., 2021). In other words, managers are increasingly expected to develop skills such as data literacy to better understand the interplay between people and work, respond to rapidly evolving contexts, and coach their teams with greater insight. At the same time, organizational leadership can monitor trends and performance through continuous, real-time analysis of business and talent outcomes, enabling more evidence-based decisions about top talent across the organization.

Insights-Enabled Manager Impact

Managers are generally open to a more data-driven way to manage work. A recent survey of 1,000 business leaders showed that 87% are even excited about using generative AI to help them in their role, and many would leverage AI tools for gaining insights into employee and team performance, correlate rewards with productivity, identify retention risks, improve diversity and inclusion efforts, and refine talent acquisition strategies (Visier Inc., 2024a). Lowes, the home improvement company, conducted a detailed analysis of its store performance by examining the relationship between employee engagement and financial outcomes. The company discovered a link between employee engagement and store performance, with highly engaged employees driving tangible business results (Bersin et al., 2024).

Only a few years ago, the retrieval of such insights would have been extremely time- and resource-intensive and elusive to most store managers. Business leaders interested in understanding how their leadership style impacts sales results, store customer satisfaction scores, turnover, or absenteeism rates, would have needed to ask for this information from HR, and wait for days if not weeks—if it was available to their organization at all. Nowadays, with sophisticated analytics practices and AI-powered analytics platforms they can not only access this type of information themselves via their organization's analytics platform, but do it by using simple targeted natural language prompts, and get an accurate, securely delivered answer promptly. Looking ahead, agentic AI will offer a deeper understanding of complex business contexts, allowing it to not just answer questions but also to provide nuanced interpretations, generate strategic recommendations, and even learn and adapt its approach over time (PwC, 2024).

The delivery of real-time performance and people insights to leaders and managers enables what is widely known as the "democratization of data." The integration of data makes an impact-oriented approach to measuring managerial outcomes possible, and will primarily serve managers. Those who understand how employee engagement in their retail store or call center correlates with management behaviors, customer satisfaction scores, and sales performance will be more successful than those who do not. Managers who are able to uncover the root causes of success or failure in their respective contexts can mitigate turnover or low performance earlier and quicker than others, leading to a differentiation of talent like never before.

Standard Bank Group has successfully democratized people insights to over 9,000 managers across multiple African countries by transitioning from a service-based to a platform-based approach. This shift allowed managers to access data independently, fostering a self-service culture for information retrieval. The bank's strategy involved defining clear metrics, building a team of champions, and consistently measuring progress. Their approach goes beyond simply measuring individual performance; it focuses on creating an environment where employees can thrive and contribute to organizational success. By linking success factors back to managers and incentivizing leadership effectiveness, Standard Bank has created a data-driven culture that empowers leaders and drives significant performance improvements across the organization (Gonzales, n.d.).

Emerging AI-driven agents present the next, even more promising outlook to enhance decision-making capabilities across various aspects of workforce management by analyzing and presenting workforce data to managers in real time. These tools can proactively identify trends, alert managers to shifts in team dynamics or business conditions, and provide tailored recommendations for action. By leveraging these insights, they will be able to address issues preemptively, cultivate stronger relationships within their teams, and optimize overall performance. Again, this expanded, data-informed approach validates and enhances our understanding of management and leadership, moving beyond static trait-centric models to embrace the dynamic relationship between managers, their teams, and the broader organizational context.

Augmented Management: Merging Human Insight with AI Capabilities

The transformative role of AI in organizational leadership and management extends far beyond data access and new skill acquisition. It requires a fundamental redesign of the institution of management—understood here as the structures, processes, and practices that govern how organizations are led and operated. As we proposed at the beginning of this chapter, this redesign introduces a new ecosystem where managers and leaders are complemented by AI-enabled expert systems, agents, coaches, and assistants, collectively redefining how organizations function. In the short term, AI is not set to replace human managers but it is driving a significant shift as the knowledge and skills leaders and managers have spent decades cultivating are being reorganized and reprioritized (Di Prima et al., 2024). The time for adaptation is running out fast.

Studies of the ongoing shifts in managerial roles due to the introduction of these new AI technologies have primarily focused on the categorization of skills. In the 2016 Harvard Business Review landmark article—"How Artificial Intelligence Will Redefine Management," published before the launch of ChatGPT—the authors explored how AI had been already reshaping managerial roles and leadership skills since the early twenty-first century. This article initiated numerous studies and discussions centered on five essential "skills," positioning them as the AI-era evolution of the classic trait theory (Kolbjørnsrud et al., 2016):

- Enhanced Decision-Making: AI's advanced data analysis capabilities enable managers to make more informed and objective decisions, reducing reliance on intuition and experience.
- Automated Routine Tasks: By automating administrative and repetitive tasks, AI allows managers to focus on strategic planning and creative problem-solving.
- Shift in Required Skills: The integration of AI necessitates that managers develop skills in data interpretation, technological literacy, and emotional intelligence to effectively collaborate with AI systems and lead human teams.
- Redefined Managerial Roles: As AI takes over routine tasks, managerial roles are evolving to emphasize coaching, mentoring, and fostering innovation within teams.
- Increased Collaboration: AI facilitates better communication and collaboration across departments by providing real-time insights and breaking down information silos.

What is captured in this article's framework is the convergence of two management paradigms: the static and the dynamic one. The authors observed, even in the early days of AI adoption, that the roles of managers and leaders had become increasingly context-dependent and shaped by the broader organizational dynamics. We argue that the role of managers and leaders is now undergoing an even more fundamental shift. AI is transforming leadership and management from individual job responsibilities and personality-based skills into collaborative processes, with numerous tasks enabled through an ecosystem of AI-powered assistants, copilots, coaches, and ultimately digital twins. These new management assistants provide unprecedented access to data, generate actionable insights, and simulate scenarios, enabling leaders and managers to operate at the "top of their 'human' license." This means focusing their energy and expertise on the most complex, high-impact decision-making tasks, while leveraging AI to handle information synthesis and contextual analysis.

Supporting Managers in the Age of "Non-Human" Collaborators

The true challenge for leaders and managers now lies in navigating the complexity of these AI-enabled inputs and translating them into human-directed actions. Their roles will continue to be defined by their ability to orchestrate and synthesize the contributions of a "blended team" of human and AI collaborators. This shift requires new behaviors: an openness to engaging with non-human agents, a capacity to interpret AI-generated insights critically, and adapting them to make decisions that align with both the evidence and the broader organizational vision.

How are managers supported by "non-human" management collaborators—AI assistants, agents, coaches, and digital twins—and experiencing the reshaping of the very essence of management and leadership in today's organizations? The following next generation of tools is being used to augment managerial roles:

1. Copilots for task integration.
2. Virtual agents and assistants for operational execution.
3. AI coaches for enhancing soft skills.
4. Digital twins for advanced decision-making and organizational modeling.

Redefining Management from the Outside in with Copilots

In March 2023, Microsoft introduced its Microsoft 365 Copilot, an AI-powered assistant designed to enhance productivity across its entire suite of applications. Integrated into tools like Word, Excel, PowerPoint, and Outlook, "a Copilot on every desk, every device and across every role is core to Microsoft's mission to empower every person and every organization on the planet to achieve more," according to Microsoft's Judson Althoff, Executive Vice President and Chief Commercial Officer (Althoff, 2024, para.1).

By embedding AI capabilities directly into globally used productivity tools, Microsoft has taken a significant step toward redefining every job and reshaping every managerial role, enabling leaders to focus more on strategic decision-making and less on administrative tasks.

Here are specific case studies of copilots implemented in a broad variety of industries to support managerial responsibilities:

- Financial Services: Morgan Stanley is actively integrating AI to enhance its operations, particularly within its wealth management division. The firm has initiated approximately 30 AI projects aimed at streamlining processes and improving client services, freeing up financial advisers to focus on building relationships with their clients (Chan et al., 2024).
- Software Engineering: Unlike traditional preprogrammed AI tools, copilots are built to deliver intuitive support by learning from their users and actively engaging with them, offering real-time suggestions and insights (e.g., GitHub Copilot). This new capability enables managers to better understand their team's needs, provide timely feedback, and make more informed decisions, strengthening relationships and enhancing people management effectiveness (Bharadwaj, 2024).
- Healthcare: Radfield Home Care is a UK-based company that employs ChatGPT copilots to improve business operations, particularly in marketing, HR, and software development, freeing up their staff to be more efficient, find cost-effective solutions, and provide better care for its patients (Ackerman, 2024).

An example of using a copilot for managerial responsibilities with teams can be seen in the team performance management case. A project manager overseeing a cross-functional team uses Microsoft Teams Copilot to enhance collaboration and productivity. The manager relies on this copilot to streamline communication, track progress, and address challenges in real time. Here are some examples from 10 best Microsoft Copilot Use Cases (Insight, n.d.):

- The manager asks Microsoft Copilot to "summarize the key points from this week's team discussions," and it provides a concise overview of updates, decisions, and unresolved issues (par. 4).
- During a team meeting, the manager uses Microsoft Copilot to "draft action items based on the conversation." Copilot creates a clear list of tasks assigned to each team member and shares it automatically (par. 3).
- To support team well-being, the manager requests Microsoft Copilot to "analyze recent sentiment in team chats," identifying potential signs of stress or disengagement and suggesting proactive interventions.(Microsoft, 2025)

As AI-driven tools become increasingly integrated into managerial practice, it is essential to emphasize the need for rigorous, ongoing evaluation and verification of AI-generated outputs. Despite their impressive capabilities, large language models (LLMs) remain prone to generating inaccurate or fabricated information, which is commonly referred to as "hallucinations." These errors are not rare anomalies but a fundamental limitation of current generative AI systems, particularly when they extrapolate beyond their training data or operate without grounding in verified sources (OpenAI, 2023; Singla & Sukharevsky, 2023). For managers, the challenge is not only to embrace these emerging technologies, but also to develop the skills and discernment required to collaborate with AI responsibly—ensuring their contributions are both accurate and aligned with organizational goals in this new era of augmented management.

The Rise of AI Agents: From Interactive to Proactive

2025 has been a pivotal year for the emergence of digital agents, marking a significant step forward in their adoption and signaling the coming of the "Agentic Economy." The term "Agentic Economy" has been used in various contexts for a long time, particularly within economic theory, where the concept of an "agent" refers to decision-makers such as individuals, firms, or governments that interact within the economy (Mitnick, 2006).

AI agents are a new class of AI systems that are transforming how work is being done. Unlike copilots and assistants, which are designed to follow human instructions and support specific tasks, agents operate with autonomy. These AI agents independently navigate complex environments and can take actions to achieve specific goals. Examples of full integration of such agents into management teams are still few but illustrative.

Fujitsu's Kozuchi AI Agent

Japanese multinational Fujitsu, a pioneer of information and communications technology since 1935, launched its Kozuchi AI Agent in October 2024. Kozuchi AI Agent is a groundbreaking AI service designed to act as a proactive team member in high-level business tasks without undermining human decision-making. It acts as a regular team member would—joining meetings, making proactive suggestions, and generating new, creative ideas. This agent currently supports functions like production management and legal affairs; Fujitsu plans to expand its application to areas like marketing, logistics, and HR (Fujitsu, 2024).

AI Agents in Contact Centers

In the evolving customer contact center[1] industry, AI agents are becoming crucial tools for improving human agent performance, particularly in the coaching process. One such example is AI Coach Assist, a transformer-based AI system[2] that leverages natural language processing (NLP) techniques to identify coaching opportunities in real-time. This AI agent analyzes call transcripts and evaluates the relevance of each call for coaching purposes, based on quality assurance (QA) questions posed by supervisors or managers.

AI Coach Assist works by combining the query from the supervisor with the call transcript to classify whether a given call is coachable or not. It uses pre-trained language models to make this determination, significantly speeding up the coaching process. By recommending the calls that are most likely to contain valuable coaching moments, it helps managers focus their attention where it is most needed, improving the effectiveness of their coaching efforts, some of which can be done by the AI coach. This results in better customer service and higher overall customer satisfaction (Laskar et al., 2023).

Collaboration on the Human–AI Agent Teams

This is still in its early stages, but researchers are exploring conditions under which human–machine collaboration is optimized and whether humans accept machines as teammates. The new role of a manager as a facilitator of such hybrid teams still remains largely unexplored. Early findings show that the integration of AI agents into human teams offers significant potential benefits but also introduces challenges. On the positive side, AI agents like the AI Coach Assist or reinforcement-learning-based managers in human–machine teams enhance decision-making by analyzing large data sets, identifying patterns, and proposing optimal solutions. For instance, AI agents can effectively delegate tasks to the most suitable team member, as demonstrated in hybrid driving scenarios where managers reduced errors and improved team performance by up to 187% (Fuchs et al., 2024).

However, this integration is not without drawbacks. Dependence on AI agents may reduce human team members' ability to maintain situational awareness or intervene effectively when the AI fails. Furthermore, the need to ensure AI's adherence to ethical guidelines and mitigate biases in its decision-making adds complexity. Balancing AI autonomy with human oversight is critical to avoid overreliance or unintended consequences in team dynamics. These pros and cons highlight the importance of thoughtful implementation and the role of a human manager on such teams (Srivastava et al., 2022).

Continuous evaluation of collaborative hybrid environments, particularly with an eye on the evolving role of the human manager, will not only be necessary but urgent. The success of such hybrid teams will depend on maintaining a balance between AI autonomy and human judgment and oversight and creating a collaborative ecosystem where both can successfully drive unprecedented innovation (Ackerman, 2024).

The Emergence of a Digital Twin as an Organizational Design Coach

A digital twin is a digital replica of a real-world entity or process, designed to simulate, predict, and optimize its real-world counterpart's performance (McKinsey & Company, 2024). It was originally developed in the first decade of the twenty-first century for industrial applications, such as in aerospace and manufacturing (Grieves, 2015). Digital twins enabled virtual models of physical systems to optimize design, performance, and maintenance, as well as predict future scenarios and outcomes, offering a forward-looking perspective that sets them apart from traditional data, which is rooted in historical analysis. Over time, advancements in Internet of Things (IoT), AI, and data analytics have expanded their applications to diverse fields, from healthcare and urban planning to organizational management, transforming the way systems are monitored and improved (Gubbi et al., 2013).

An example of how all-encompassing planning and decision-making is at the city/state level is the creation of the digital twin of the City of Singapore (GW Prime, 2022). In 2015, the Singapore government embarked on developing a comprehensive digital twin of the city, integrating real-time data from sensors across the city to simulate and analyze various scenarios from the impact of different urban policies, such as zoning laws or energy efficiency measures, and to make data-informed decisions about public housing, green spaces, and waste management. This initiative positioned Singapore as a global leader in smart city innovations, setting a benchmark for digital urban planning worldwide.

Just as Singapore optimized urban mobility, businesses can streamline workforce deployment, optimize remote work models, and improve employee productivity. Digital twins can provide real-time insights into employee well-being, engagement, and collaboration efficiency.

Although organizations are currently focused on implementing digital twins in operational and product-focused areas, early examples of their expansion into scenario-based planning, leadership, and management predictive decision-making are already emerging. When used as a coach, a digital twin acts as a personalized, AI-driven adviser that supports an individual's growth, decision-making, and strategic thinking (Edrisi et al., 2024). What such a digital tool allows us to do is to simulate and stress-test multiple scenarios of an organizational outcome. However, this application remains the furthest on the horizon of organizational implementation, lagging behind other forms of AI-driven coaching in adoption and integration (Ukko et al., 2022).

Virtual Coaches: The Future of Managerial Success

As AI handles routine tasks and agents assist with operations, managers are transitioning to roles requiring adaptability and skills for navigating not only higher-level human needs but also human–machine dynamics on their teams. AI coaching is emerging as a 24/7 solution, equipping managers with personalized guidance, insights, and strategies to navigate workplace shifts and transitions.

The first AI coaching services began to scale across organizations as a response to remote working during COVID-19. Alexi Robichaux, the co-founder of BetterUp, a pioneering technology-based coaching company, stated that "BetterUp was founded on the belief that coaching should be accessible to people everywhere, and it should be built on evidence-based practices that lead to real, positive impact" (Robichaux, 2022, para. 1).

However, as technology has become more sophisticated, AI-enabled coaches are becoming a go-to solution for coaches and leaders at all organizational levels. As employees receive coaching from the onboarding process through performance management and learning and development, managers and leaders are reaching out for more strategic levels of support.

Ray Dalio, the founder of Bridgewater Associates and author of Principles, Life and Work (Dalio, 2017) is developing an AI-powered digital version of himself to provide access to his mentorship and coaching for leaders who are looking for guidance. By leveraging generative AI, Dalio's platform will offer tailored advice on topics such as goal achievement, problem-solving, entrepreneurship, and personal development, drawing from Dalio's extensive experience and documented principles. This development is one of many others that represents a significant advancement in making expert coaching accessible to a broader audience, empowering managers to enhance their decision-making, leadership skills, and adaptability in complex environments with an experienced coach at their side (Jafar, 2024).

Conclusion: Toward an AI-Centered Model of Management and Leadership

The integration of data-driven and AI-powered technologies into management and leadership practices marks a pivotal shift in how organizations operate and succeed. AI's dual impact—transforming measurement and management—provides expanded opportunities to refine leadership practices, aligning them with the demands of today's hybrid workplaces. By synthesizing multi-modal and diverse data streams, AI enables organizations to measure leaders better; it helps leaders to make more data-driven decisions, adapt strategies in real time, and correlate behavioral patterns with measurable outcomes. This evolution moves leadership development from static, trait-based models to adaptive, evidence-based frameworks, ensuring that practices stay relevant in ever-changing environments.

For that very reason, we see traditional leadership training, often costly and inefficient, as no longer sufficient and probably redundant in today's fast-paced world (Beer et al., 2016). Organizations are already willing to spend less on it every year, according to Josh Bersin, global industry analyst. The majority of companies spend $500 or less per person per year (Bersin, 2023). Instead, it is possible that AI-powered coaching and real-time analytics will soon replace traditional learning and training developments for managers and leaders, and instead deliver tailored, continuous support, allowing organizations to identify impactful behaviors and offer personalized development. This approach ensures managers are equipped to lead effectively, fostering stronger human connections as AI handles routine tasks and data preparation.

For organizations, this means investing not just in advanced AI tools but also in cultivating leaders' ability to interpret and act on AI-driven insights ethically and strategically. As AI continues to evolve, it offers a transformative opportunity to redefine leadership—enhancing decision-making, improving team interactions, and driving sustainable success. The future of management lies in embracing this new paradigm where human potential is amplified by intelligent technology, demanding a strategic and efficient retraining of managers—an undertaking that AI will facilitate by providing targeted, individualized learning experiences that address specific developmental needs.

Notes

1. "Contact center" generally refers to a broader operation that handles communications across multiple channels (phone, email, chat, and social media). A call center, in contrast, traditionally focuses on inbound and outbound phone calls only.
2. The transformer is a deep learning architecture that employs self-attention mechanisms to process and analyze sequential data, such as text. Unlike earlier models, transformers can process entire sequences simultaneously rather than sequentially, enhancing efficiency for natural language processing (NLP) tasks. This design allows AI systems to better understand the context and relationships between words or phrases, enabling effective evaluation of call transcripts for coaching purposes.

References

Ackerman, N. (2024). Using ChatGPT in our care business gives us more time for people. *The Times*. https://www.thetimes.com/business-money/entrepreneurs/article/care-home-boss-on-using-ai-were-dealing-with-peoples-lives-enterprise-network-7pbmc9358?utm_source=chatgpt.com&egion=global

Althoff, J. (2024, April 24). Leading in the era of AI: How Microsoft's platform differentiation and Copilot empowerment are driving AI Transformation. *Official Microsoft Blog*. https://blogs.microsoft.com/blog/2024/04/24/leading-in-the-era-of-ai-how-microsofts-platform-differentiation-and-copilot-empowerment-are-driving-ai-transformation

Beer, M., Finnstrom, M., & Schrader, D. (2016). The great training robbery (working paper 16-121). *Harvard Business School*. https://www.hbs.edu/ris/Publication%20Files/16-121_bc0f03ce-27de-4479-a90e-9d78b8da7b67.pdf

Bersin, J. (2023). Companies have been neglecting their leadership, and it shows. *The Josh Bersin Company*. https://joshbersin.com/2023/11/companies-have-been-neglecting-their-leadership-and-it-shows

Bersin, J., Ioannidou, S., & Enderes, K. (2024). The definitive guide to people analytics: The journey to systemic business analytics. *Visier*. https://www.visier.com/lp/definitive-guide-people-analytics-josh-bersin

Bharadwaj, C. (2024). How AI copilots are spearheading workflow transformation—benefits, types and use cases. *Appinventiv*. https://appinventiv.com/blog/ai-copilot-use-cases

Chan, B., Cuccinello, H., Reed, A., & Brownstein, E. (2024). Here's everything we know about how Wall Street banks are embracing AI. *Business Insider*. https://www.proquest.com/docview/3149706230

Del Val Núñez, M. T., Aránega, A. Y., & Ribeiro-Soriano, D. (Eds.), *Artificial intelligence and business transformation: Impact in HR management, innovation and technology challenges* (pp. 163–176). Springer Nature Switzerland. https://doi.org/10.1007/9783031587047_10

Derler, A. (2024). Measuring manager effectiveness. *Visier*. https://www.visier.com/lp/measuring-manager-effectiveness-with-people-analytics

Di Prima, C., Bevilacqua, S., Bresciani, S., & Ferraris, A. (2024). The impact of artificial intelligence on organizations and managers: The skills needed for an effective leadership. In M. T. Del Val Núñez, A. Y. Aránega, & D. Ribeiro-Soriano (Eds.), *Artificial intelligence and business transformation: Impact in HR management, innovation and technology challenges* (pp. 163–176). Springer Nature Switzerland. https://doi.org/10.1007/978-3-031-58704-7_10

Drucker, P. F. (1999). *Management challenges for the 21st century*. Harper Business.

Edrisi, F., Perez-Palacin, D., Caporuscio, M., & Giussani, S. (2024). Developing and evolving a digital twin of the organization. *IEEE Access*, *12*, 45475–45494. https://doi.org/10.1109/ACCESS.2024.3381778

Elliott, B. (2021). It's time to free the middle manager. *Harvard Business Review*. https://hbr.org/2021/05/its-time-to-free-the-middle-manager

Field, E., Hancock, B., Imose, R., & Yee, L. (2023). Middle managers hold the key to unlock generative AI. *McKinsey & Company*. https://www.mckinsey.com/capabilities/people-and-organizational-performance/our-insights/the-organization-blog/middle-managers-hold-the-key-to-unlock-generative-ai

Fuchs, A., Passarella, A., & Conti, M. (2024). Optimizing delegation in collaborative human–AI hybrid teams. *ACM Transactions on Autonomous and Adaptive Systems*, *19*(4), 1–33. https://doi.org/10.1145/3687130

Fujitsu. (2024, October 23). Fujitsu to offer AI agents that can both collaborate and engage in high-level tasks autonomously. *PR Newswire Europe Including UK Disclose*. https://www.proquest.com/docview/3119372866

Gonzales, S. (n.d.). 6 insider tips for unlocking manager effectiveness from the experts. *Visier*. https://www.visier.com/blog/insider-tips-for-unlocking-manager-effectiveness-from-the-experts

Govindarajan, V., Sikka, N., & Srivastava, A. (2021). The uncertainty of middle management jobs—and how to stay relevant. *California Management Review*. https://cmr.berkeley.edu/2021/01/middle-management-jobs

Grieves, M. (2015). *Digital twin: Manufacturing excellence through virtual factory replication*. https://www.3ds.com/fileadmin/PRODUCTS-SERVICES/DELMIA/PDF/Whitepaper/DELMIA-APRISO-Digital-Twin-Whitepaper.pdf

Gubbi, J., Buyya, R., Marusic, S., & Palaniswami, M. (2013). Internet of Things (IoT): A vision, architectural elements, and future directions. *Future Generation Computer Systems, 29*(7), 1645–1660. https://doi.org/10.1016/j.future.2013.01.010

GW Prime. (2022). Virtual Singapore—building a 3D-empowered smart nation. *Geospatial World.* https://geospatialworld.net/prime/case-study/national-mapping/virtual-singapore-building-a-3d-empowered-smart-nation

Hollander, E. P. (1992). Leadership, followership, self, and others. *The Leadership Quarterly, 3*(1), 43–54. https://doi.org/10.1016/1048-9843(92)90005-z

IBM. (2021). What is a digital twin? *IBM.* https://www.ibm.com/think/topics/what-is-a-digital-twin

Insight, C. (n.d.). 10 best Microsoft Copilot business use cases. *C5 Insight.* https://c5insight.com/10-microsoft-copilot-business-use-cases

Jafar, B. (2024). Ray Dalio plans AI version of landmark Principles coaching. *Dow Jones Institutional News.* https://www.proquest.com/docview/3097751502

Kirkpatick, S. A., & Locke, E. A. (1991). Leadership: Do traits matter? *Academy of Management Perspectives, 5*(2), 48–60. https://doi.org/10.5465/ame.1991.4274679

Kolbjørnsrud, V., Amico, R., & Thomas, R. J. (2016). How artificial intelligence will redefine management. *Harvard Business Review.* https://hbr.org/2016/11/how-artificial-intelligence-will-redefine-management

Kotter, J. P. (1990). *A force for change: How leadership differs from management.* Free Press.

Laskar, M. T. R., Chen, C., Fu, X.-Y., Azizi, M., Bhushan, S., & Corston-Oliver, S. (2023). AI Coach Assist: An automated approach for call recommendation in contact centers for agent coaching. In S. Sitaram, B. Beigman Klebanov, & J. D. Williams (Eds.), *Proceedings of the 61st Annual Meeting of the Association for Computational Linguistics (Volume 5: Industry Track)* (pp. 599–607). Association for Computational Linguistics. https://doi.org/10.18653/v1/2023.acl-industry.57

Legret, J. (n.d.). 3 tips from Cartier on scaling people analytics to drive business impact. *Visier.* https://www.visier.com/blog/how-to-scale-people-analytics-drive-business-impact

McKinsey & Company. (2024). What is digital-twin technology? *McKinsey.* https://www.mckinsey.com/featured-insights/mckinsey-explainers/what-is-digital-twin-technology

Mitnick, B. M. (2006). Origin of the theory of agency: An account by one of the theory's originators. *University of Pittsburgh.* https://sites.pitt.edu/~mitnick/agencytheory/agencytheoryoriginrev11806r.htm

Mollick, E. (2024). AI is already changing management—companies must decide how. *Financial Times.* https://www.ft.com/content/389e505c-a1cc-4176-a592-dd1d0fa171b8

NeuroLeadership Institute. (2019). *Building brain-friendly leadership models.* https://cdn2.hubspot.net/hubfs/1927708/Idea%20Report_LeadershipModels_US_All_DIGITAL.pdf

Nguyen, K.-T., Friedrich, B., Cao, L., Bianchi, N., Smessaert, A., Derler, A., & Haig, D. (2024). The individual contributor penalty. *Visier.* https://www.visier.com/lp/visier-research-report-individual-contributor-penalty

OpenAI. (2023). GPT-4 technical report. *arXiv.* https://arxiv.org/abs/2303.08774

Paradis, T. (2024). AI will reshape the global labor force. Employers will need to help their workers keep up. *Business Insider.* https://www.businessinsider.com/ai-will-change-most-jobs-employers-help-workers-keep-up-2024-8

PwC Middle East. (2024). Agentic AI: The new frontier in GenAI. *PwC.* https://www.pwc.com/m1/en/publications/documents/2024/agentic-ai-the-new-frontier-in-genai-an-executive-playbook.pdf

Purdy, M. (2024). What is agentic AI, and how will it change work? *Harvard Business Review.* https://hbr.org/2024/12/what-is-agentic-ai-and-how-will-it-change-work

Robichaux, A. (2022). Our commitment to human transformation through coach quality. *BetterUp.* https://www.betterup.com/blog/human-transformation-coach-quality

Simić, I. (2020). Da li su menadžeri i lideri jedno te isto? *Ekonomika*, *66*(3), 1–12. https://doi.org/10.5937/ekonomika2003001s

Singla, A., & Sukharevsky, A. (2023, August 1). *The state of AI in 2023: Generative AI's breakout year*. McKinsey.

Srivastava, D. K., Lilly, J. M., & Feigh, K. M. (2022). Improving human situation awareness in AI-advised decision making. *2022 IEEE 3rd International Conference on Human-Machine Systems (ICHMS)* (pp. 1–6). IEEE. https://doi.org/10.1109/ICHMS56717.2022.9980783

Tabesh, P. (2022). Leadership vs. management: A false dichotomy. *California Institute of Advanced Management*. https://mlari.ciam.edu/leadership-vs-management-a-false-dichotomy

Terblanche, N., Molyn, J., de Haan, E., & Nilsson, V. O. (2022). Comparing artificial intelligence and human coaching goal attainment efficacy. *PLoS ONE*, *17*(6). https://doi.org/10.1371/journal.pone.0270255

Ukko, J., Saunila, M., Nasiri, M., Rantala, T., & Holopainen, M. (2022). Digital twins' impact on organizational control: Perspectives on formal vs social control. *Information Technology & People*, *35*(8), 253–272. https://doi.org/10.1108/itp-09-2020-0608

Visier Inc. (2024a). Managers know AI tools make them more effective, can HR deliver? *Visier*. https://www.visier.com/lp/ai-tools-manager-effectiveness-thanks

Visier Inc. (2024b). Visier announces world's first analytic AI agent platform to augment and extend every employees' performance and productivity. *Visier*. https://www.visier.com/company/news/visier-announces-worlds-first-analytic-ai-agent-platform

Visier Inc. (2024c). Visier Insights™ Report: How tenure affects manager performance. *Visier*. https://www.visier.com/lp/manager-performance-and-tenure-thanks

Visier Inc. (n.d.). Standard Bank Group leads the way in measuring manager effectiveness. *Visier*. https://explore.visier.com/standard-bank-group

Weibler, J. (2023). *Personalführung* (4 ed.). Vahlen.

4

Cultivating the Pilot Mindset in the Age of AI

The Importance of Agency and Optimism in the Evolving Management Landscape

Kate Niederhoffer, Alex Liebscher, Kristina Rapuano, and Khoa Le Nguyen

Historical Context: From Manual to Knowledge Work to AI-Enhanced Work

Historically, major technological revolutions have been heralded as the driving force behind large-scale economic restructuring and the redefinition of organizational frameworks. The Industrial Revolution replaced manual labor with mechanized processes, enabling and prioritizing efficiency and productivity (Mokyr, 1990). Employees could use machines and factory systems to produce goods more efficiently, thereby freeing time and resources for additional tasks and roles (Abis & Veldkamp, 2020). Each wave of technological change introduces increasingly sophisticated workplace tools that radically impact efficiency, productivity, and innovation. Technological tools are often portrayed as the principal catalysts for shifting models of leadership and talent development.

Widespread access to and adoption of generative artificial intelligence (AI) has catalyzed another paradigm shift in management expectations and practices, reminiscent of past transitions from manual labor to knowledge work, only accelerated (Abis & Veldkamp, 2020). In this chapter, we examine how AI is redefining not only how we work but also how we relate to one another in the workplace, reshaping leadership expectations and influencing the ways leaders develop. Drawing on socio-technical systems

Kate Niederhoffer et al., *Cultivating the Pilot Mindset in the Age of AI*. In: *The Changing Leadership Landscape*. Edited by: Sheri L. Feinzig and Mariangela Battista, Oxford University Press.
DOI: 10.1093/9780197820070.003.0004

theory (Trist & Bamforth, 1951), technology acceptance models (Davis, 1989), and mindset theory (Dweck, 2006; Lee & Hancock, 2024), we underscore the central role of individual perceptions of utility, agency, and trust in shaping technology adoption. We argue that in the era of generative AI, effective organizational change requires the joint optimization of both the technical and social components. In particular, mindsets, behaviors, and interpersonal workplace dynamics ultimately determine the trajectory of AI adoption, leadership development, and broader organizational transformation.

As AI becomes embedded in daily operations, managers must skillfully navigate both technical and relational complexities (Brynjolfsson et al., 2023; Cascio & Montealegre, 2016). In addition to overseeing workflows, setting performance goals, and guiding strategic directions, managers must also address resistance to change (Oreg et al., 2011) and support a culture conducive to AI adoption (see the section "The Evolving Role of Management"). In an AI-enhanced context, leadership styles emphasizing empowerment, autonomy, and constructive feedback can help employees align with organizational objectives and maintain their sense of control (Chiaburu et al., 2014).

Objectives and Significance

Drawing from social psychology, industrial/organizational psychology, organizational behavior, communications, and management science, this chapter aims to provide empirical support for the importance of cultivating a particular mindset of high agency and optimism for empowering employees to adopt new technology that may improve their efficiency and innovation while maintaining critical thinking skills. The chapter offers insights on what organizations can do to foster more adaptive perspectives and practical insights for managers to help employees not only accept AI as part of their work but also capitalize on its potential to enhance productivity, creativity, and job satisfaction.

To investigate these goals, we present findings from a year-long study of nearly 12,000 US-based full-time employees, focusing on their experiences with and attitudes toward AI in the workplace, and the mindsets about AI that shape usage and outcomes.

Research Methodology

Beginning in May 2023, we launched a monthly survey online via the participant recruitment platform, Prolific (Palan & Schitter, 2018). In addition to a short battery of items that remained consistent across months, we rotated in validated scales, hypothesis-driven experiments, and topical questions. The last continuous survey was administered in April 2024, with one additional in August 2024; all the surveys were written in English. Respondents were paid for their time.

The sample included 11,938 US-based full-time employees, ages 18+, with full demographics shown in Table 4.1. Respondents who met each of the following criteria were included in the final sample: (1) currently employed at 40+ hours a week; (2) had not participated in a previous survey from this study; (3) correctly answered attention and comprehension check questions; and (4) met a minimum participant quality rating. The final sample was not matched or weighted to reflect nationally representative demographic distributions.

Empirical Results

Decades of psychological research demonstrate that people have mindsets, which are strong core assumptions that function as implicit theories about

Table 4.1 Demographics of Attitudes toward AI in the Workplace

	Demographic Category	Percentage (%)
Age	18–24	9.8
	25–34	38.0
	35–44	26.4
	45–54	16.5
	55–64	7.8
	65+	1.6
Ethnicity	Asian or Asian American	8.7
	Black or African American	14.3
	Hispanic or Latino	7.2
	White	66.4
Gender	Female	52.2
	Male	46.0
	Nonbinary Self-described	1.8

Table 4.2 Items on the AI Mindset Scale

Mindset Dimension	Item
AI Optimism	Using AI is fun and enjoyable for me. Using AI facilitates my learning and growth. Using AI is harmful to me.*
AI Agency	I'm good at using AI to do things that are important to me. Using AI to do things makes me feel dependent on it.* I feel like using AI makes me less capable.*

*Indicates reverse scoring

their relationship to powerful forces in their lives (Dweck, 2006; Crum et al., 2017; Yeager et al., 2019). They are "frames of mind" that orient people toward particular sets of associations and expectations about things or processes in their lives, like whether the nature of their intelligence is fixed or changeable (i.e., a growth mindset) or if stress is enhancing or harmful (i.e., a stress mindset). These mindsets can have powerful downstream effects on perception, cognition, and behavior. People also have mindsets about powerful digital forces in their lives, such as social media and, more recently, AI (Lee & Hancock, 2024). Technology mindsets are the beliefs, associations, and expectations that people draw on automatically to make sense of new or unfamiliar technology, shaping how they perceive and engage with novel innovations.

To determine the AI Mindsets, we performed an exploratory factor analysis on a set of five optimism items and six agency items in our first month's survey. These items were adapted from the Social Media Mindsets Scale (Lee & Hancock, 2024) to an AI context. Two clear factors emerged, representing perceived optimism about AI and agency over AI. The three most predictive items of each factor were retained for subsequent monthly surveys and are included in Table 4.2. Women were less optimistic about AI than men. Older individuals reported slightly higher agency than younger individuals. Education, ethnicity, and being in a managerial position did not relate to an individual's agency nor optimism.

To examine the relationships between AI Mindsets and related workplace attitudes, we analyzed correlations between our AI Mindset factors (agency and optimism) and items from several validated scales, including the General Attitudes toward AI Scale (GAAIS, Schepman & Rodway, 2020) and Eudaimonic Workplace Well-Being Scale (EWWS, Bartels et al., 2019). The strongest positive correlations were observed with items from the GAAIS representing job-relevant confidence, curiosity, and optimism toward AI; and negatively with concerns about job displacement and worry about reduction of work value due to AI. These relationships support the construct validity of our scale and indicate that individuals with higher agency and optimism tend to view AI as a tool for personal and professional enhancement. Moderate correlations were also found with EWWS indicators of purpose, emotional vitality, and growth at work, suggesting that AI Mindsets are associated not only with attitudes toward technology adoption but also with broader indicators of employee thriving and engagement.

The Pilot Mindset

We define a Pilot mindset as one in which the individual is high in both optimism and agency about AI. Conversely, a Passenger mindset is one in which the individual is low in both optimism and agency toward AI. Individuals who did not meet the threshold for either category are considered to be forming their views, and are classified as Undecided. Individuals with the Pilot mindset report that using AI facilitates their learning and growth, and describe themselves as empowered through AI to do things that are important to them and their work. By contrast, those with the Passenger mindset are more likely to believe that AI is taking away their power, and making them feel less capable and more dependent on the technology.

For simplicity, we communicate that an individual is a Pilot (Passenger) if they have a self-reported Pilot (Passenger) mindset. However, as with other leadership competencies, mindsets are malleable. In total, 38% of participants were categorized as Pilots and 5% as Passengers. Sixty-two percent of respondents reported high agency (feeling in control over AI), while 72% were optimistic about the future of AI. Conversely, 26% felt low agency (powerlessness), and 17% expressed pessimism about the future of AI. While only a relatively small percentage of our population reported as high agency and high optimism, Undecided individuals likely encompass several subtypes, well beyond their classification as low agency, high optimism (19%), or low optimism, high agency (8%). Future work may refine this typology using cluster analysis. Recognizing these nuances can help leaders tailor interventions more effectively, rather than relying on one-size-fits-all messaging or training.

Impact and Influence of AI Mindsets

1. Employees' mindsets toward AI are strong predictors of their use of AI at home and at work, and their curiosity and confidence toward the technology. When people use AI at work, the Pilot mindset has a strong relationship with important organizational metrics, including employee engagement, productivity, and intent to leave. For example, compared to Passengers, Pilots are 13.7 times more likely to use AI once a week or more (both at work and outside it),
2. and 6.5 times more likely to use AI at work once a week or more.

In other words, Pilots are more likely to adopt AI both in their personal lives and workplaces. Their curiosity toward AI and optimism about its value, consistent with relationships reported earlier (see the section "The Pilot Mindset"), likely drive the intrinsic motivation necessary to learn and integrate the technology into their workflows. These findings suggest that the Pilot mindset may serve as a psychological mediator between AI exposure and key outcomes such as productivity, engagement, and intent to stay, helping to explain why some individuals thrive with AI while others resist or disengage. This mediating role aligns with technology adoption models (e.g., Davis, 1989) and mindset theory (Dweck, 2006), which posit that internal beliefs and perceived control influence behavioral uptake of new tools.

The Pilot mindset is associated with frequent and productive AI use at work. In contrast, Passengers often experience decreased productivity and higher intent to leave their jobs when required to adopt AI tools. This suggests that productivity at work may be impacted by AI use—however, in opposite directions depending on the individual's AI Mindset. Additionally, Passengers are more fearful of AI-driven job replacement and are more likely to be actively looking to leave their role as their use of AI at work increases, unlike Pilots. This suggests that underprepared employees (Passengers) may seek out less threatening work environments, whereas Pilots may seek greater opportunities for achievement within an organization that leverages new technologies. Otis et al. (2024) similarly found that the benefits of using an AI mentor were distributed unequally across entrepreneurial demographics. Those with high levels of performance prior to the introduction of AI reaped more rewards, while lower performers experienced stagnation or performance declines. This mirrors our finding that without the proper mindset (i.e., the Pilot mindset), generative AI use can reduce productivity.

Introducing AI into the daily workflow of Passengers could be frustrating or unproductive. Cultivating the Pilot mindset may be a prerequisite for successful AI adoption.

The Evolving Role of Management

These findings underscore the central thesis of this chapter: the need for leaders to attend not only to technical onboarding but also to shaping the psychological conditions that support effective AI use. As AI tools become more widely integrated into daily work, managers face new demands that require not only technical knowledge but also strong relational skills (Brynjolfsson et al., 2023; Cascio & Montealegre, 2016). In line with socio-technical systems theory (Trist & Bamforth, 1951), organizations must jointly optimize technological capabilities and human well-being and belonging. In the context of rapidly evolving AI innovations, managers bear primary responsibility for ensuring this balance. The success or failure of AI adoption hinges partly on how well leadership practices align with employee needs for clarity, empowerment, and psychological safety (Edmondson, 1999; Van Quaquebeke & Gerpott, 2024).

Unlike many prior technologies, generative AI is associated with unique risks such as unpredictability, hallucinated outputs, opaque reasoning processes, and variable reliability (Brynjolfsson et al., 2023). As such, leaders must balance encouragement of experimentation with clear standards for oversight. This includes validating AI-generated content, training teams to identify limitations, and establishing clear decision boundaries for AI use. Additionally, establishing norms that explicitly support non-use of AI, or allow human judgment to override algorithmic output, as it is to disclose when AI has been used.

The integration of generative AI into the workplace is increasingly marked by volatility, uncertainty, complexity, and ambiguity, driven in part by unclear workplace policies around AI usage, ethics, and ownership (van Quaquebeke & Gerpott, 2024). In such environments, employees often face heightened ambiguity about expectations and accountability. To maintain trust and motivation under these conditions, relational and participative leadership styles, such as shared leadership (Carson et al., 2007), are especially important for sustaining trust and motivation (Chiaburu et al., 2014; Gerpott et al., 2019). In a series of five experiments, Santoro and Monin

(2023) demonstrate that exposure to AI elevates the perceived importance of attributes like empathy, moral judgment, and trust. The authors term this phenomenon the "AI Effect." This suggests that in times of technological volatility, skills rooted in human connection are not diminished but rather amplified in salience. As AI becomes increasingly capable across a wide range of tasks, research suggests a paradox: people come to value distinctively human traits even more.

As AI assumes responsibility for some routine and data-driven tasks (whether this is appropriate or not is outside the scope of this chapter), managers' interpersonal sensitivities become a primary channel for fostering team cohesion and performance outcomes (Cascio & Montealegre, 2016). This trend aligns with our research findings indicating that individuals prefer human managers to retain ownership of tasks requiring socioemotional competencies—precisely the capabilities most predictive of performance in the era of generative AI. When asked to differentiate tasks best performed by humans versus AI, individuals consistently, over the course of the year from August 2023 to August 2024, reported that motivating team members, actively listening to feedback and concerns, recognizing contributions, and providing constructive feedback were functions that should remain within the domain of human managers. In contrast, tasks such as tracking performance metrics and managing deadlines are perceived as more appropriately delegated to AI. These findings, shown in Figure 4.1, underscore the evolving role of managers, highlighting the irreplaceable nature of human-led interpersonal interactions in team performance. Empathy fosters psychological safety, which is essential for risk-taking and experimentation (Edmondson, 1999). Managers must demonstrate an understanding of employees' fears and aspirations, tailoring support and guidance in ways that bolster agency, especially over AI (Trist & Bamforth, 1951; Davis, 1989).

Collectively, these findings highlight deeply human attributes that organizations can foster to optimize outcomes. For example, organizations with high levels of belonging and psychological safety offer a foundation for fostering the Pilot mindset. Individuals who perceive strong support from their organization are 88% more likely to experience an increase in both agency and optimism through coaching over a four-month period of at least three one-on-one coaching sessions, as compared to those who endorse average or low levels of organizational support. Managerial influence is equally important. Leaders who themselves adopt the Pilot mindset are two to three times more likely to have direct reports that exhibit similar optimism and

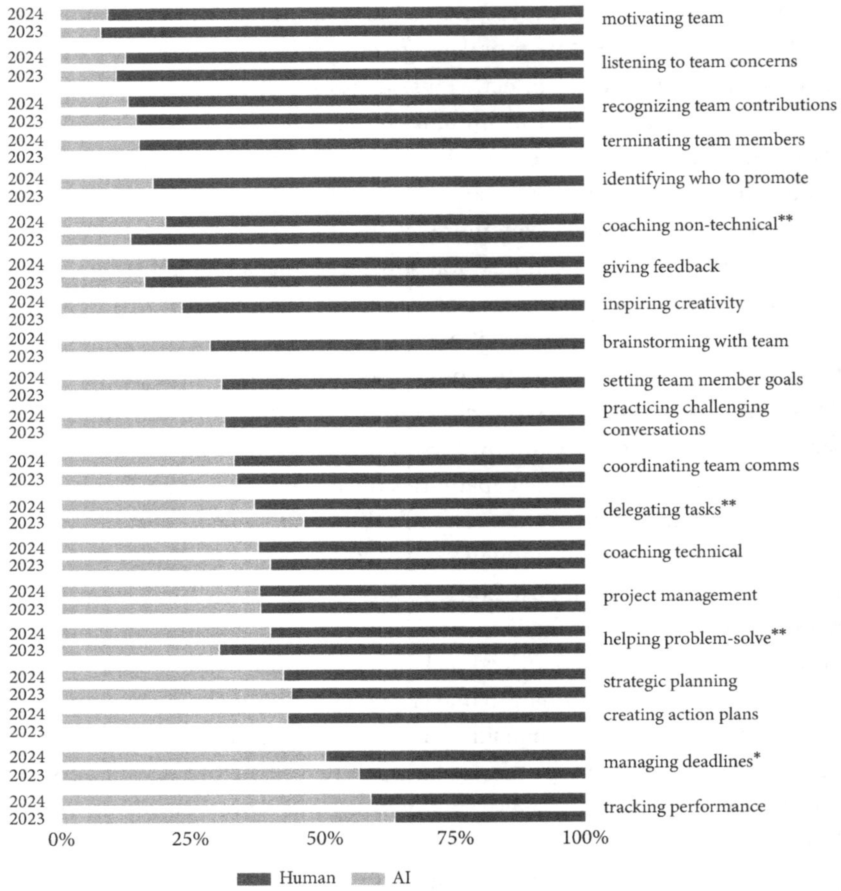

Figure 4.1 Preferences for Human and AI Management Tasks

Note: Estimates represent predicted probabilities *denotes statistical significance, *$p < .01$, **$p < .001$, $n_{(2023)} = 928$, $n_{(2024)} = 994$.

agency. Finally, perceived warmth in managerial style is also associated with AI adoption. Employees who view their managers as approachable and encouraging are 1.5 times more likely to use AI at work.

Recent fieldwork demonstrates that AI "teammates" reshape traditional team dynamics, often redistributing perceived expertise away from less experienced humans to algorithmic agents (Dell'Acqua et al., 2025). This can be beneficial in distributing the workload and automating otherwise manual workflows, but only if teams are trained to engage critically with AI contributions and maintain human collaboration as a central process.

Coaching Specific Mindsets and Behaviors

Consistent with growth mindset theory (Dweck, 2006) and research on stress mindsets (Crum et al., 2013), self-awareness and a belief in one's capacity to adapt are central to high-agency orientations toward AI. Managers can encourage employees to frame their challenges with AI not as threats but as opportunities for learning—a perspective that, as research on psychological empowerment shows, increases agency, or self-efficacy and initiative (Seibert et al., 2011; Bandura, 1986). Activities such as self-reflection, frequent feedback exchanges, and skill-building workshops may help employees move from the tentative Passenger mindset to the more proactive Pilot mindset.

Framing and Communication

Leadership communication about AI plays a defining role in shaping employees' attitudes and usage patterns (Van Quaquebeke & Gerpott, 2024). Drawing on the technology acceptance model (Davis, 1989), our experimental research (not reviewed in this chapter; see Lee et al., 2024) confirms that employees who hear about AI's "machine-like strengths" are significantly more likely to trust and effectively leverage AI tools, boosting optimism and perceived control. Conversely, framing AI as human-like can induce confusion and mismatch between expectations and actual AI capabilities.

Transparent, purposeful communication that highlights AI's potential but also acknowledges employees' concerns can reduce resistance and foster psychological safety (Kotter, 1996; Oreg et al., 2011). Clarity about AI's nonjudgmental nature, for instance, mitigates employees' anxiety around potential mistakes and encourages exploratory learning (Edmondson, 1999). Logg, Minson, and Moore's recent work (2019) demonstrates that individuals often exhibit "algorithm appreciation," showing a preference for algorithmic over human judgment even when the algorithm's performance is flawed. Furthermore, promoting digital literacy is essential. Hancock and Lee (2024) discuss the effectiveness of digital media literacy interventions in building resilience against misinformation, suggesting that similar approaches could enhance employees' engagement with AI outputs. This underscores the necessity for leaders to communicate the limitations of

AI, ensuring that employees remain vigilant and have agency in using AI. By communicating AI's capabilities and limitations, fostering psychological safety, and enhancing digital literacy, leaders can ensure that employees maintain agency and oversight in an AI-integrated workplace.

Clear Leadership Communication

As detailed in the section "Framing and Communication," leader communication quality is one of the strongest predictors of mindset adoption. This aligns with findings from change management literature emphasizing transparent, purposeful communication (Kotter, 1996). Participants who felt that their supervisors or organizations encourage AI use show higher levels of engagement and curiosity. This cultural endorsement can normalize AI experimentation, alleviating fears of job displacement or failure.

Pilot Mindset Psychoeducation Intervention

Based on theories of implicit beliefs (Dweck, 2006; Yeager et al., 2019) and empirical work on technology mindsets (Lee & Hancock, 2024), we have begun preliminary experimentation with a brief "Pilot mindset" psychoeducation-based intervention exploring optimism and agency as learned orientations to AI. In a standard Alternate Uses Task to measure creativity, participants provided with a concise explanation that emphasizes AI as a powerful tool, rather than a threat, demonstrate preliminary evidence that they adopt more creative approaches to AI-based tasks. By contrast, employees without the intervention show higher rates of "copy-and-paste" behavior, essentially offloading problem-solving to AI and diminishing their own learning. Those guided to adopt the Pilot mindset found unique, innovative ways to integrate AI's capabilities with their own expertise, enhancing ownership of both the process and results. This aligns with research on identity-based motivation (Oyserman, 2009) and highlights that short, targeted interventions can catalyze lasting changes in how people approach novel technology. Such an approach is also consistent with broader "growth mindset" interventions in education and the workplace, where even brief exposures can yield significant improvements in performance and resilience (Yeager et al., 2019).

Implementation Strategies

Building on these insights, the emergent leadership paradigm in AI-augmented contexts hinges on cultivating "deeply human" skills and the Pilot mindset. Recent scholarship points to four core domains:

- Active listening and emotional intelligence: Leaders who are attentive to verbal and nonverbal signals can preempt concerns around job security or skill obsolescence (Glikson & Woolley, 2020).
- Motivation and recognition techniques: Grounded in self-determination theory (Deci & Ryan, 2000), effective leaders satisfy employees' needs for competence and autonomy by celebrating small wins and encouraging innovative use of AI.
- Frameworks for AI integration: Through clear communication and explicit norms about usage and disclosure of AI usage, managers can scaffold employees' transitions toward more confident and effective AI usage and trust (Ford et al., 2018; Schilke & Reimann, 2025). Leaders should align AI rollout strategies with broader ethical commitments, framing AI as a tool in service of human values, not a replacement for them.
- Building trust in AI-enhanced environments: Fostering trust depends not just on technical reliability but on inclusive, transparent practices where purpose is clearly communicated (Awad et al., 2018; Tambe et al., 2019). Leaders will need to model responsible use: socializing prompting strategies, triangulating and validating outputs from generative AI, and encouraging discernment in usage alongside critical thinking.

These competencies prepare organizations to maintain a supportive atmosphere where AI becomes an enabler rather than a point of conflict, and where employees feel equipped to navigate ongoing technological changes (Cascio & Montealegre, 2016).

Foster an Environment Open to Tool Experimentation

Organizations high in belonging, psychological safety, and manager support offer a foundation for growth in agency and optimism. As described earlier (see the section, "The Evolving Role of Management"), high belonging and psychological safety enable mindset shifts. Coaching can amplify these effects. Our research also found that communication by an organization's leaders matters. Participants with supervisors or organizations that encourage the use of AI tools are more likely to be Pilots.

Invest in Managers as Change-Makers

As noted in the section "The Evolving Role of Management," managerial mindset has cascading effects on team orientation and behavior. Thus, interventions targeting manager beliefs may yield multiplicative benefits. Additionally, employees who perceive their managers as warm are more likely to adopt AI at work. Specifically, team members who see their managers as approachable and supportive are 1.5 times more likely to use AI. Overall, investing in managers' mindsets, skills, and behaviors may have multiplicative effects on an organization's successful adoption of generative AI.

Coach for Individuals' Mindsets

Coaching specific mindsets and behaviors fosters growth in agency and optimism. In particular, increases in self-awareness and a growth mindset act as powerful levers of growth in agency. Becoming a Pilot is also associated with behavioral improvements in goal setting and identifying multiple paths to achieve goals.

Educate Employees on the Pilot Mindset in Their Workflow

As explained in the section "Pilot Mindset Psychoeducation Intervention," a brief psychoeducational intervention explaining the Pilot mindset had a profound effect on people's approach to using AI. Illustrating to people the importance of agency and optimism helped them be more creative with AI and reduced their dependency on AI. Those who did not receive the psychoeducation intervention were more likely to simply copy-and-paste the AI's output. In other words, a small dose of education on what the Pilot mindset is can increase perceptions of ownership, ensuring AI is seen as a tool in an employee toolbox to augment, not displace, one's own creativity.

Establish Training and Development Programs

Part of fostering a safe environment for employees to experiment with generative AI is creating spaces where they can learn from experts how to use the tools available to them within their organization to accomplish goals that are important to them. Elements of a training and development program to consider include explaining how to access generative AI tools, enabling trial-and-error learning with minimal risk, psychoeducation of the Pilot mindset, and demonstrating effective expert usage. In addition to this, group learning through sharing information, storing collective knowledge, and facilitating knowledge retrieval can be an effective training framework (Wilson et al., 2007).

Conclusion

As generative AI becomes further integrated into the workplace, organizations and leaders can anticipate needing to continue developing managers' and workers' skillsets and designing new roles and responsibilities. In addition to improvements in our understanding of individuals' relationships to AI, this chapter shared a series of practical strategies that organizations can implement that are built on the foundation of a mindset of agency and optimism.

Acknowledgments

The authors gratefully acknowledge Jeffrey Hancock and Angela Lee for their central contributions to the development of the Pilot mindset research program. Their collaboration has informed the conceptual framing, survey design, data collection, analysis, and interpretation across multiple studies. In particular, the adaptation of the AI Mindset Scale is derived from their original Social Media Mindset Scale (Lee & Hancock, 2024), which provided a critical foundation for our empirical work. Their partnership was instrumental in shaping the theoretical and methodological integrity of this chapter.

References

Abis, S., & Veldkamp, L. (2020). The changing economics of knowledge production. *The Review of Financial Studies, 37*(1), 89–118. https://doi.org/10.1093/rfs/hhad059

Awad, E., Dsouza, S., Kim, R., Schulz, J., Henrich, J., Shariff, A, Bonnefon, J. F., & Rahwan, I. (2018). The Moral Machine experiment. *Nature, 563*(7729), 59–64. https://doi.org/10.1038/s41586-018-0637-6

Bandura, A. (1986). *Social foundations of thought and action: A social cognitive theory.* Prentice-Hall.

Bartels, A., Peterson, S., & Reina, C. (2019). Understanding well-being at work: Development and validation of the eudaimonic workplace well-being scale. *PLOS ONE 14*(4).

Brynjolfsson, E., Li, D., & Raymond, L. (2023). *Generative AI at work* (No. 31161). National Bureau of Economic Research, Inc.

Carson, J. B., Tesluk, P. E., & Marone, J. A. (2007) Shared leadership in teams: An investigation of antecedent conditions and performance. *Academy of Management Journal, 50*(5). https://doi.org/10.5465/amj.2007.20159921

Cascio, W. F., & Montealegre, R. (2016). How technology is changing work and organizations. *Annual Review of Organizational Psychology and Organizational Behavior, 3*(1), 349–375. https://doi.org/10.1146/annurev-orgpsych-041015-062352

Chiaburu, D. S., Smith, T. A., Wang, J., & Zimmerman, R. D. (2014). Relative importance of leader influences for subordinates' proactive behaviors, prosocial behaviors, and task performance: A meta-analysis. *Journal of Personnel Psychology, 13*(2), 70–86. https://doi.org/10.1027/1866-5888/a000108

Crum, A. J., Salovey, P., & Achor, S. (2013). Rethinking stress: The role of mindsets in determining the stress response. *Journal of Personality and Social Psychology, 104*(4), 716–733. https://doi.org/10.1037/a0031201

Crum, A. J., Akinola, M., Martin, A., & Fath, S. (2017). The role of stress mindset in shaping cognitive, emotional, and physiological responses to challenging and threatening stress. *Anxiety, Stress, & Coping, 30*(4), 379–395. https://doi.org/10.1080/10615806.2016.1275585

Davis, F. D. (1989). Perceived usefulness, perceived ease of use, and user acceptance of information technology. *MIS Quarterly, 13*(3), 319–340. https://doi.org/10.2307/249008

Deci, E. L., & Ryan, R. M. (2000). The "what" and "why" of goal pursuits: Human needs and the self-determination of behavior. *Psychological Inquiry, 11*(4), 227–268. https://doi.org/10.1207/S15327965PLI1104_01

Dell'Acqua, F., Ayoubi, C., Lifshitz, H., Sadun, R., Mollick, E., Mollick, L., Han, Y., Goldman, J., Nair, H., Taub, S. & Lakhani, K. (2025). *The cybernetic teammate: A field experiment on generative AI reshaping teamwork and expertise* (No. 33641). National Bureau of Economic Research. https://doi.org/10.3386/w33641

Dweck, C. S. (2006). *Mindset: The new psychology of success.* Random House.

Edmondson, A. C. (1999). Psychological safety and learning behavior in work teams. *Administrative Science Quarterly, 44*(2), 350–383. https://doi.org/10.2307/2666999

Ford, J. K., Baldwin, T. T., & Prasad, J. (2018). Transfer of training: The known and the need to be known. *Annual Review of Organizational Psychology and Organizational Behavior, 5*, 201–225. https://doi.org/10.1146/annurev-orgpsych-032117-104443

Gerpott, F. H., van Quaquebeke, N., & Schlamp, S. (2019). An identity perspective on ethical leadership to explain organizational citizenship behavior: The interplay of follower moral identity and leader group prototypicality. *Journal of Business Ethics, 156*(4), 1063–1078. https://doi.org/10.1007/s10551-017-3625-0

Glikson, E., & Woolley, A. W. (2020). Human trust in artificial intelligence: Review of empirical research. *Academy of Management Annals, 14*(2), 627–660. https://doi.org/10.5465/annals.2018.0057

Kotter, J. P. (1996). *Leading change.* Harvard Business School Press.

Lee, A., & Hancock, J. T. (2024). Social media mindsets: A new approach to understanding social media use and psychological well-being. *Journal of Computer-Mediated Communication, 29*(1). https://doi.org/10.1093/jcmc/zmad048

Lee, A. Y., Rapuano, K., Liebscher, A., Sudhof, M., Niederhoffer, K., & Hancock, J. T. (2024). Who wants to talk to a chatbot? Psychological determinants of preferences for self-disclosure to AI. Manuscript in preparation for publication.

Logg, J. M., Minson, J. A., & Moore, D. A. (2019). Algorithm appreciation: People prefer algorithmic to human judgment. *Organizational Behavior and Human Decision Processes, 151,* 90–103. https://doi.org/10.1016/j.obhdp.2018.12.005

Mokyr, J. (1990). *The lever of riches: Technological creativity and economic progress.* Oxford University Press.

Oreg, S., Vakola, M., & Armenakis, A. (2011). Change recipients' reactions to organizational change: A 60-year review of quantitative studies. *The Journal of Applied Behavioral Science, 47*(4), 461–524. https://doi.org/10.1177/0021886310396550

Otis, N., Clarke, R., Delecourt, S., Holtz, D., & Koning, R. (2024). The Uneven Impact of Generative AI on Entrepreneurial Performance. *Available at SSRN 4671369. https://dx.doi.org/10.2139/ssrn.4671369*

Oyserman, D. (2009). Identity-based motivation: Implications for action-readiness, procedural-readiness, and consumer behavior. *Journal of Consumer Psychology, 19*(3), 250–260. https://doi.org/10.1016/j.jcps.2009.05.008

Palan, S., & Schitter, C., (2018). Prolific.ac—A subject pool for online experiments. *Journal of Behavioral and Experimental Finance, 17*(2), 22–27.

Santoro, E., & Monin, B. (2023). The AI Effect: People rate distinctively human attributes as more essential to being human after learning about artificial intelligence advances. *Journal of Experimental Social Psychology, 107,* 104464. https://doi.org/10.1016/j.jesp.2023.104464

Schepman, A., & Rodway, P. (2020). Initial validation of the general attitudes towards Artificial Intelligence Scale. *Computers in Human Behavior Reports, 1,* 100014.

Schilke, O., & Reimann, M. (2025). The transparency dilemma: How AI disclosure erodes trust. *Organizational Behavior and Human Decision Processes, 188,* 104405. https://doi.org/10.1016/j.obhdp.2025.104405

Seibert, S. E., Wang, G., & Courtright, S. H. (2011). Antecedents and consequences of psychological and team empowerment in organizations: A meta-analytic review. *Journal of Applied Psychology, 96*(5), 981–1003. https://doi.org/10.1037/a0022676

Tambe, P., Cappelli, P., & Yakubovich, V. (2019). Artificial intelligence in human resources management: Challenges and a path forward. *California Management Review, 61*(4), 15–42. https://doi.org/10.1177/0008125619867910

Trist, E. L., & Bamforth, K. W. (1951). Some social and psychological consequences of the longwall method of coal-getting. *Human Relations, 4*(1), 3–38. https://doi.org/10.1177/001872675100400101

Van Quaquebeke, N., & Gerpott, F. H. (2024). Artificial intelligence (AI) and workplace communication: Promises, perils, and recommended policy. *Journal of Leadership & Organizational Studies, 31*(4), 375–381. https://doi.org/10.1177/15480518241289644

Wilson, J. M., Goodman, P. S., & Cronin, M. A. (2007). Group learning. *Academy of Management Review, 32*(4), 1041–1059. https://doi.org/10.5465/amr.2007.26585724

Yeager, D. S., Hanselman, P., Walton, G.M., Murray, J. S., Crosnoe, R., Muller, C., Tipton, E., Schneider, B., Hulleman, C. S., Hinojosa, C. P. and Paunesku, D. (2019). A national experiment reveals where a growth mindset improves achievement. *Nature, 573*(7774), 364–369. https://doi.org/10.1038/s41586-019-1466-y

5

The Transformative Power of Coach-Led AI-Driven Leader Development

Woody Woodward

Introduction

Traditional leadership development programs have a long history of struggling to demonstrate meaningful and sustained impact. At the same time, the promise of coaching has been a mixed bag. Far too often, coaching initiatives feel disconnected from the flow of work and difficult to measure. Enter the digital coaching revolution. The rise of digital coaching platforms and the proliferation of artificial intelligence (AI) in human transformation is changing the leadership development landscape in dramatic fashion. This chapter explores the role of coaching in leader development and how the latest digital and AI technologies are being developed and deployed to create highly customized coach-led leader development experiences that are integrated into an organization's learning strategy.

The Role of the Coach in Leader Development

At the most basic level, leadership is about influencing action. In other words, leaders must work through others by inspiring and motivating them to behave in ways that create movement toward goals. The role of a coach is to assist the leader in this endeavor. Vendaveer and Frisch (2022) explain that when working with organizational leaders, the role of a coach is to "(a) elevate their performance and effectiveness as leaders, (b) develop required skills for advancing into leadership roles in organizations, and/or (c) prepare for transitions into different leader roles (e.g., higher level or international assignment) using evidence-based methods grounded in scientific research" (p. 3).

Woody Woodward, *The Transformative Power of Coach-Led AI-Driven Leader Development*.
In: *The Changing Leadership Landscape*. Edited by: Sheri L. Feinzig and Mariangela Battista,
Oxford University Press. © Oxford University Press (2026). DOI: 10.1093/9780197320070.003.0005

Executive-level coaching engagements often center around high-level leadership themes such as setting and communicating a vision, making strategic decisions, navigating role transitions, or managing organizational change. Coaches act as confidential sounding boards, challenging assumptions and supporting the exploration of alternative perspectives. As the relationship deepens, executive coaches focus more specifically on developing interpersonal and social skills, such as self-management, emotional regulation, and communication impact.

Over time, executive coaching has increasingly become embedded within broader leader development programs that include classroom training, experiential learning, and cohort-based initiatives. These hybrid models balance curriculum-based group learning with individualized coaching tailored to the leader's strengths, personality, and organizational context. The trend of integrating coaching into development strategies has accelerated in recent years, thanks to digital and AI technologies.

The Evolving Role of AI in Coaching

Digital coaching platforms have broadened access to coaching and created opportunities to manage, scale, and measure coaching programs. Providers are now weaving AI into coaching processes in several ways. Generally, AI applications in coaching fall into three categories: AI for supporting coaching, AI for delivering coaching, and AI braided into coaching. AI-enabled coaching tools and their uses are described in this section and summarized in Table 5.1.

AI for Supporting Coaching

At its most basic, AI supports administrative and manual tasks, helping coaches streamline workflows. Tools like Otter.ai and RaeNotes transcribe sessions, while platforms like Optify assist in managing engagements and generating reports. More advanced tools—sometimes called "copilots"—go further by analyzing sessions, recommending resources, and tracking commitments. For example, Ovida provides coaches with session analytics and personalized feedback.

Table 5.1 Summary of AI-Enabled Coaching Tools and Their Uses

Tool/Platform	Category	Primary Use	Example Use Case
Otter.ai and RaeNotes	AI for Supporting Coaching	Session transcription and automated notetaking	Captures key points from a coaching session automatically
Coaching.com, Optify	AI for Supporting Coaching—Software-as-a-Service (SaaS) tools	Coach workflow and engagement management	Tracks client commitments and schedules follow-ups
Ovida	AI for Supporting Coaching—AI Copilot	Real-time support and feedback on conversations with session analysis	Provides users with feedback and analytics after each session/conversation
Coach Vici, Evoach, Nadia, and Sherlock	AI for Delivering Coaching—Autonomous Generative AI Chatbots	Early AI chatbots for structured goal setting	Guides users through coaching style sessions (e.g., GROW) for finding resources and achieving short-term goals
BetterUp AI, ChatGPT, Claude, Sesame	AI for Delivering Coaching—Generative AI Chatbots	Human-like interaction, scalable support	Uses natural conversation to challenge thinking outside of sessions
Loupe	AI Braided into Coaching—for Feedback Collection	Real-time, flow-of-work peer feedback	Sends short surveys to colleagues for just-in-time reputation data
BetterUp Grow AI Role-Play, Ovida, Yoodli	AI Braided into Coaching—Role-Play & Skills Practice	On-demand simulated conversations	Leaders practice delivering tough feedback to a virtual employee
Google Gemini and Microsoft Copilot	AI Braided into Coaching—AI Workflow Assistant	Summary of meetings, tracking tasks and commitments	Generates action steps from coaching session recordings
Humu by Perceptyx	AI Braided into coaching—AI for Nudging and Microlearning	Drive behavior change through tailored nudges	Sends weekly behavioral prompts based on team goals and leadership best practices
Grain	AI Braided into Coaching—Session Recap and Sharing Across Communication Platforms like Slack & Hubspot	Turn sessions into highlight reels or insight clips	Coach shares one-minute video insight with client as reinforcement

AI for Delivering Coaching

Autonomous AI coaching tools, or coachbots, are AI-powered chatbots trained on coaching models such as GROW (Goal, Reality, Options, Way Forward). Early examples—Coach Vici, Evoach, Pocket Confidant, Rocky AI, and Sherlock—were often text-based, rule-bound tools designed to assist users with goal setting and reflection. Though limited in conversational nuance, they pioneered the notion of scalable coaching support.

The release of ChatGPT by OpenAI in late 2022 marked a turning point in the development of conversational AI. With its ability to produce context-aware, human-like interactions, generative AI opened new possibilities for AI coaching agents. These chatbots powered by large language models (LLMs) simulate natural dialogue, respond dynamically, and offer generalizable coaching support across a variety of topics.

A key distinction, however, is that these systems remain reactive—they must be prompted by a human user. Unlike human coaches who may proactively challenge or redirect a conversation, current AI coaches are limited to response-based interaction.

Researchers such as Passmore and Tee (2021) define AI coaching as "the application of artificial intelligence methodologies to the coaching environment" (p. 3), delivered either synchronously or asynchronously via computer-based coach agents. Similarly, Terblanche et al. (2022) describe coachbots as expert systems designed for a narrow domain, often trained to replicate coaching logic within a specific topic. Essentially, these specialized bots are designed to mimic a coach. Similar to human coaches, the way they interact depends on the philosophy of the developer and the particular models being used to train the AI. In addition to traditional coaching approaches, these AI coachbots may also take on the roles of mentoring, advising, and/or training.

As AI in delivering coaching is very new, there is little academic research on the subject. Most papers tend to focus on exploring the concept, defining terms, and discussing ethical use. However, there is emerging research around AI for supporting goal attainment, detecting emotions, and acceptance by users.

AI Coaching in Goal Attainment: There is an extensive body of well-established research on goal setting and goal attainment (Locke & Latham, 2002). This research has had a tremendous influence on the coaching profession spawning a multitude of models and approaches. The longest standing and most applied model of goal attainment or performance coaching is the

GROW model, which was first introduced by Sir Jonathan Whitmore in his 1992 book *Coaching for Performance* now in its sixth edition (Whitmore & Gaskell, 2024). Given the popularity and evidence-based grounding of models like GROW, it stands to reason that many AI coaching agents have been trained on goal theory and goal attainment approaches.

One particular study did explore the potential for a text-based AI coachbot in delivering basic goal attainment. The researchers conducted two longitudinal randomized control trials to compare goal attainment of those subjects working with a trained professional coach vs. those working with an AI trained on goal theory (Terblanche et al., 2022). The coachbot used in the study was created by the lead researcher and was a pre–generative AI coachbot. In other words, it was a more command-control style AI very specifically designed to take the user through the GROW process.

Although the study did demonstrate the efficacy of the coachbot in basic goal attainment, there are limitations. It is also worth noting that most executive coaching engagements are far more complex than simple goal attainment exercises. Executives face a lot of complexity where the stakes are high and they must navigate internal politics, market forces, changing regulations, and geopolitical influences. Thus, executive coaching requires the coach to understand context and adjust and adapt to the evolving needs of the client, not just set and pursue goals.

AI Coaching and Emotional Detection: One can argue that the foundation of the professional executive coaching relationship is the ability of the coach to connect with their client and allow them to feel heard and safe (Bachkirova & Kemp, 2024). This sets a tone and allows for the client to be open and vulnerable during the session and across the arc of an engagement. Bachkirova and Kemp (2024) sought to compare an "AI coach" to their definition of a professional coach by examining how an AI may differ across six characteristics of an ideal coach. The authors point out the criticality of connecting and being present with the client through attention, deep listening, and empathy. We typically think of this level of connection as uniquely human. However, there is early research that has called these beliefs into question.

To explore this notion of feeling heard, researchers at the University of Southern California (USC) examined the ability of ChatGPT to create responses to written narratives authored by human subjects. The idea was to test whether an AI could generate responses that made humans feel heard. In their study Yin et al. (2024) found that "AI-generated messages made recipients feel more heard than human-generated messages and that AI was better at detecting emotions" (p. 1). There was also an interesting twist.

The USC team found that "recipients had more positive reactions when they believed that the response came from another human (vs. AI). In other words, they devalued the response when it was labeled as AI rather than human generated" (Yin et al., 2024, p. 2).

AI and User Acceptance: In the specific case of the USC study, an AI was better able to perform one of the core functions of human engagement than actual humans. However, their findings underscore the ongoing debate about the acceptance of AI-generated content in response to human prompting. In other words, the AI may perform better, but will we accept it? That said, it is important to note that this is only one study and the subjects in the comparison group tasked with writing the human responses (to compare against the ChatGPT responses) were not trained coaches. Nonetheless, the findings do call into question our understanding of what it means to feel heard.

The nonjudgmental nature of interacting with a coachbot is what appears to be attracting younger users (Yin et al., 2024). Part of creating a safe space within the container of the coaching session is ensuring there will be freedom from judgment. Coachbots trained to take a pure coaching approach where they ask questions, reflect responses, and challenge assumptions (as well as ensure confidentiality) may be able to engender a higher level of trust with some populations. It is worth noting that many of those from these younger populations will make their way into leadership roles. Thus, their expectations of coaching may differ from those held by today's leaders.

While empirical studies remain limited, early findings are encouraging. As referenced in the section AI for Delivering Coaching, the controlled study by Terblanche et al. (2022) did show that the AI coach could demonstrate efficacy in guiding participants through structured goal processes. Still, the researchers noted that real-world executive coaching is far more complex than goal setting alone, often requiring nuanced engagement, contextual awareness, and adaptive emotional intelligence.

AI Braided into Coaching

AI in coaching and development has rapidly progressed to become more than just add-on tools like personality assessments or scheduling apps. While coachbots will continue to improve and work more autonomously, they will likely be deployed as either copilots for coaches or autonomous bots designed to service individual contributor and early-stage supervisor/manager levels where human coaching is cost-prohibitive. AI-powered coachbots have already been shown to be capable of novice-level coaching (Terblanche et al., 2022). However, the challenges facing developing leaders who must operate in an increasingly complex, ambiguous, and disruptive world are fundamentally different.

In discussing the science of developing deep expertise pioneered by Anders Ericsson, Wharton professor Ethan Mollik notes that developing complex skills is much more than time and repetition. Mollick (2024) states, “Instead, deliberate practice requires serious engagement and a continual ratcheting up of difficulty. It also requires a coach, teacher, or mentor who can provide feedback and careful instruction, and push the learner outside their comfort zone” (p. 183). In other words, humans will most certainly remain critical to the development of other humans, particularly when it comes to coaching humans around the complex skill of leading other humans. However, optimizing human capability has always required technology, and AI in coaching is no different. For executive coaches to be successful, they will have to embrace and master AI.

The future of AI in coaching lies not in replacement but in *integration*. This concept—referred to by the coaching provider BetterUp as “braiding”—describes the seamless incorporation of the human expert (coach), behavioral science (the evidentiary foundation), and AI into every stage of a coaching engagement. Rather than functioning as stand-alone tools, AI systems can be braided into the human experience of coaching to enhance the entire arc of development.

Braiding AI into the executive coaching process certainly has the most promise for enhancing the human transformation process at the more senior levels. There are three core challenges that coaches face where braiding digital and AI technologies into the process can enhance the impact of leadership coaching: collecting credible and meaningful feedback, converting learning into action, and expanding access to resources.

Collecting Credible and Meaningful Feedback: Feedback is critical to leader development, and feedback is constantly coming at us from all around (Frisch et al., 2012; Riordan, 2020). Feedback from a leader’s colleagues and reports can give coaches a sense of the context the leader is operating in and facilitate more acute conversations around self-insight. The challenge is that getting high-quality feedback that is relevant to the development of a leader is no easy task. Coaches must rely heavily on the leader for information about how their quest for positive behavioral change is actually going. As a result, coaches get an incomplete picture of the true nature of how others experience their client in the work environment. Personality theorist Robert Hogan refers to this as the leader's identity. Hogan has theorized that there are two critical aspects to understanding an individual's behavior: identity and reputation. "Identify" refers to our own observations of our behavior, whereas "reputation" concerns the observations made by others. In other words, our identity comes from the stories we tell ourselves, and our reputation comes from the stories others tell about us (Hogan, 2007). Historically, coaches have had to rely heavily on the identity of their clients or the stories they have crafted about themselves. This can be a challenge for coaches when it comes to getting a sense of how their work is going, particularly if their focus is on interpersonal interactions and communication. Knowledge of a leader's reputation and the way in which others experience that leader in the flow of their work is critical to their development. When the coach has to rely on the subjective recounting of experiences by their coaching client, they risk being misled, either intentionally or unintentionally. The challenge is how to best get this feedback as quickly and accurately as possible.

According to Riordan (2020) feedback consists of four basic elements: "The feedback provider ('source'), the actual message, the context in which it is provided, and the perceptions and attitudes of the recipient" (p. 13). The challenge is that getting information from feedback providers about reputation has been limited. Feedback in coaching has traditionally been conducted through the deployment of quantitative tools such as the classic 360-degree questionnaire and qualitative approaches like semi-structured/structured interviews with select colleagues. These approaches essentially provide a snapshot of the leader at a specific point in time, a snapshot that is static and may or may not be relevant to work being done with the coach. In addition, these traditional 360-style feedback approaches tend to be top-down processes that often originate from the human resources (HR) function and are not always well suited for coaching.

Fortunately, advances in digital technology and AI are enabling coaches and leaders to access high-quality feedback in ways we never thought possible. We know from decades of research that feedback is more likely to be well-received and acted upon if perceived as credible and timely. Credible feedback must come from someone well-intentioned and who has a direct line of sight to our behaviors. In other words, feedback must come from those who experience the leader in the flow of their work. Feedback must also come in a timely fashion. Out-of-date feedback from someone you no longer work with can be a distraction. The idea is to get a sense of how someone currently experiences you throughout the workday.

Advances have been made in AI technologies that now allow coaches to collect real-time feedback in the flow of work. Pioneering technologies like Loupe give coaches the capability to deploy simple targeted surveys to employees/colleagues who had direct experience with the leaders they were working with. There are also technologies that allow coaching service providers to integrate with HR information systems (HRIS) to gather real-time progress data on both self-report and objective metrics. These technologies enable us to expand our ability to collect credible and meaningful data that can be used to provide feedback. In addition, wearable technologies like the Oura ring can give us real-time feedback on how you are physically functioning and showing up in the workplace. Just imagine being able to get feedback on how you are performing on a task or how well you presented in the meeting you just wrapped up. That day is here. Startups like the aforementioned Loupe, along with others, have been deploying these technologies in enterprises for a few years, and they continue to get better.

We live in an on-demand world where we expect answers instantly. Getting feedback is no different. Younger workers (our future leaders) will not be interested in waiting for a 360 or annual performance evaluation to get backward-looking feedback. The world is moving too fast for static 100-question 360-degree feedback assessments to be applicable.

Converting Learning into Action: Coaching is a safe space where a leader can be open, honest, and vulnerable. This allows them to think outside of the normal confines of their leader persona and explore alternatives. One of the challenges is helping the client take the insights and desired behaviors gleaned from the container of the coaching engagement back to the work environment. The fact is that old habits are tough to change and new ones can be even tougher to establish. In addition, the prompts and cues of the work environment can be incredibly powerful. As Stanford researcher B.J. Fogg (2020) notes, "Life is filled with an overwhelming number of prompts that we don't want, but there are plenty that we do want" (p. 97). Part of a coach's role is to help leaders identify the environmental factors that can both help and hinder their ability to apply new learning. The challenge is that most work environments are not well suited for behavioral experimentation. However, digital and AI technologies are changing the landscape. We are more connected than ever before, and our ability to monitor our own movements and behaviors is improving.

For years coaches have been adapting AI transcriber tools like Otter.ai and RaeNotes to capture basic session notes. Now Microsoft Copilot and Zoom AI provide advanced versions of these transcriber tools that allow the coach to capture notes, highlights, and commitments instantly. These can then be quickly converted into targets and action steps. Now there are AI tools that are always on and engaged, particularly from the digital coaching providers, that can assist coaches and leaders with keeping track of commitments to goals, ensuring progress is being monitored, and teammates are being communicated with for feedback and support. As these tools continue to be seamlessly integrated into our standard suite of office communication tools, there is no doubt they will become standard accepted practice.

Walking back into the treadmill of work is tough. In this fast-paced environment it can be difficult to take the time to try those experiments and there is always a risk. This is why tracking, nudging, and interactive technologies are critical to ensuring leaders go back and apply what they committed to trying. For example, technologies like Humu (acquired by Preceptyx) deliver science-backed nudges throughout the workday that are designed to drive small behavioral actions. The selected behavioral actions are based on survey responses from employees that can be reviewed and co-created with a coach. Managers and HR administrators (and sometimes coaches) have access to dashboards to keep them apprised of real-time progress on behavior change across the organization.

Expanding the Repertoire of Resources for Coaches: Let's face it, we are all limited by our experiences as well as our ability to recall those experiences. AI has access to vast databases of information that can be specifically curated for the needs of the end user. They can be deployed as on-demand conversational training tools for coaches as well as curated learning resources for leaders.

Developmental feedback for coaches is a real challenge for the profession. For the most part, coaches do not get much objective data on how they are performing as a coach. Coaches have traditionally relied on some combination of satisfaction surveys and verbal feedback from the client. Coaches rarely get the opportunity to hear and see themselves in action.

This is beginning to change. Conversational video platforms like Ovida can now combine objective data collected by an AI with observations from a trained expert to provide a more robust developmental experience. This idea is certainly not new. Consider the fact that most professional sports have a long history of relying on video and data in developing players. Quite simply, the coach shows a player video of their performance along with statistical analysis and benchmark data. Based on this information, the sports coach provides specific guidance on how to improve their performance. Ideally, executive coaches will begin making use of AI-powered video and audio capture tools to integrate continuous learning into their own development as coaches. In addition to providing the coach with objective competency-based data, these data-capture tools can also be used to assess and provide feedback on leader conversations. As video platforms like Zoom and MS Teams become more standardized and integrated into daily business practice, conversational analysis tools will begin to gain more acceptance.

There are also autonomous AI tools where users can interact directly with a trained AI. Publicly available conversational tools like Ovida and Yoodli as well as tools like Grow AI deployed by coaching provider BetterUp allow coachees to actually role-play with a trained coachbot on a very specific type of conversation. These tools can assist an executive with conversations ranging from a hostile journalist to a frustrated employee. One can even practice a difficult conversation with a direct report where the leader must provide tough feedback. AI role-play tools like these allow the executive to confidentially practice conversations on their own time where they can experiment without any judgment. This allows for on-demand access to these AI chatbot developmental aids between sessions with trained professional coaches.

Just as every human, every coach has their limits, particularly when it comes to knowledge and resources. We can only access and recall so much information. The LLMs allow the AI to search vast databases and convert findings into easily digestible and customized formats in mere seconds. As stated by Ethan Mollick, "AI is good at finding facts, summarizing papers, writing, and coding tasks. And, trained on massive amounts of data and with access to the internet, LLMs seem to have accumulated and mastered a lot of collective human knowledge" (2024, p. 180). However, it is worth noting that most AI tools still make mistakes and the successful use of any AI tools requires the user to have enough domain expertise to catch any errors or falsehoods. That said, with the guidance of experts, organizations and coaching providers are now able to develop proprietary models of leadership based on the specific values, philosophies, and competencies of the organization that can be ingested by an LLM. AI coachbots are then trained on these models to more precisely guide their interactions with leaders. This allows leaders to access curated resources that specifically support their development within the context and culture of their organization.

As AI in coaching has evolved, there have been attempts at crafting standards. In 2024, the International Coaching Federation (ICF) released the AI Coaching Framework and Standards (ICF, 2024). The nearly 100-page document outlines considerations developers should contemplate when creating AI tools for coaching. Nicky Terblanche, a coaching researcher from Stellenbosch University, published the Designing AI Coach (DAIC) framework as a guide for integrating established coaching science and ethics into AI coachbot development. According to the DAIC model, effective coaches must demonstrate trust, empathy, transparency, predictability, reliability, ability, benevolence, and integrity in order for chatbots to be ethically used in coaching. Bottom line, developing standards for AI in professional coaching is a work in progress.

The idea of an autonomous AI coaching a human is certainly not without controversy. There are many who see AI agents as dangerous and even view AI as an existential threat to their livelihoods. It will really depend on how the AI coach is trained, deployed, and supervised. Many early generative AI coach bots emphasized mentoring and advising approaches over the more traditional Socratic-based coaching approaches embraced by many coaching professionals. For the moment, the use of AI in delivering coaching is focused on more junior-level employees, as access to human coaches is both cost- and time-prohibitive at this level. Essentially, this is scaling or democratizing coaching (or human development) within and across organizations. Although the conversational capabilities are impressive, the ability to delve into complex leadership challenges is still far away. Thus, the use of AI agents autonomously coaching executive-level leaders without supervision is unlikely anytime soon.

At this point it is difficult to keep track of all the AI coaches currently available on the market. Similar to the early challenges faced by the personality assessment industry, nearly anyone can produce an AI coach and get it out on the market without any real scientific validation or scrutiny. The debate is certainly much more complex than can be covered here, but the reality is that these tools are out there and will continue to proliferate at a break-neck pace.

While the potential benefits of AI in coaching are numerous, risks must be acknowledged. Here are some key concerns along with ideas for mitigation:

- *Loss of human connection*: AI cannot fully replicate the empathy, intuition, and rapport of a human coach. *Mitigation*: Use AI as a supplement, not a replacement, especially for executive-level coaching.
- *Data privacy and confidentiality*: Coaching involves sensitive information, and AI tools often involve third-party platforms. *Mitigation*: Vet vendors carefully, ensure data encryption, and establish clear agreements on data use, storage, access, and management.
- *Bias and misinformation*: AI models may reflect biases present in their training data. *Mitigation*: Choose tools trained on coaching-relevant data and audited for fairness and accuracy.
- *Overreliance on AI*: Clients may become too dependent on AI tools for support. *Mitigation*: Encourage reflective practice and blend human coaching with AI for balanced development.

Conclusion: What Now?

One of the unique features of being human is our ability to create technology. From tools for making fire to engines that convert fire into energy, we have always sought to enhance ourselves through technology. Throughout our evolution, every major technological advancement has upended the way we think, work, and live. We have moved from walking to riding horses to driving cars to flying planes. In more recent times, just think back to when we asked ourselves questions like: How can we conduct meetings over a phone? How can we coach over a video call? How can we possibly build a team remotely?

The integration of AI into coaching is inevitable—and transformative. Leaders and practitioners must understand that AI is not here to replace human development but to enhance it. For organizations, this means reimagining leader development programs with AI as a strategic enabler. For coaches and leaders being coached, it means embracing AI as a partner in practice. Stay informed about AI developments relevant to leadership and coaching. Ultimately, the future of leadership development will belong to those who can skillfully braid human insight with technological innovation.

References

Bachkirova, T., & Kemp, R. (2024). 'AI coaching': Democratising coaching service or offering an ersatz? *Coaching: An International Journal of Theory, Research and Practice, 18*(1), 27–45. https://doi.org/10.1080/17521882.2024.2368598

Fogg, B. J. (2020). *Tiny Habits: The small changes that change everything.* Houghton Mifflin Harcourt.

Frisch, M. H., Lee, R. J., Metzger, K. L., Robinson, J., & Rosemarin, J. (2012). Becoming an Exceptional Executive Coach: Use your knowledge, experience, and intuition to help leaders excel. AMACOM.

Greif, S., Moller, H., Scholl, W., Passmore, J., & Muller, F. (2022) Defining coaching and coaching concepts. In *International handbook of evidence-based coaching* (pp. 1–12). Springer.

Hogan, R. (2007). *Personality and the fate of organizations.* Lawrence Erlbaum Associates, Mahwah, NJ.

International Coaching Federation. (2024). *The artificial intelligence (AI) coaching framework and standards.* International Coaching Federation.

Locke, E. A., & Latham, G. P. (2002). Building a practically useful theory of goal setting and task motivation. A 35-year odyssey. *American Psychologist, 57,* 705–717. http://dx.doi.org/10.1037/0003-066X.57.9.705

Mollick, E. (2024). *Co-intelligence: Living and working with AI.* Portfolio Penguin.

Passmore, J., & Tee, D. (2023). Can chatbots like ChatGPT replace human coaches? Issues and dilemmas for the coaching profession, coaching clients and for organizations. *The Coaching Psychologist, 19,* 47–54.

Riordan, B. G. (2020). *Feedback fundamentals and evidence-based practices.* Routledge.

Tavis, A., & Woodward, W. (2024). *The digital coaching revolution: How to support employee development with coaching tech.* Kogan Page.

Terblanche, N., Molyn, J., de Haan, E., & Nilsson, V. O. (2022). Comparing artificial intelligence and human coaching goal attainment efficacy. *PLoS ONE, 17*(6).

Vandaveer, V. V., & Frisch, M. H. (2022). *Coaching psychology: Catalyzing excellence in organizational leadership.* American Psychological Association.

Vandaveer, V. V., Lowman, R. L., Pearlman, K., & Brannick, J. P. (2016). A practice analysis of coaching psychology: Toward a foundational competency model. *Consulting Psychology Journal: Practice and Research, 68,* 118–142.

Whitmore, J. & Gaskell, T. (2024). *Coaching for Performance: The principles and practice of coaching and leadership.* John Murry Press, London, UK.

Yin, Y., Jia, N., & Wakslak, C. J. (2024). AI can help people feel heard, but an AI label diminishes this impact. *PNAS Proceedings of the National Academy of Sciences of the United States of America, 121*(14), Article e2319112121. https://doi.org/10.1073/pnas.2319112121

6

Leveraging AI Opportunities and Mitigating Risks

What Leaders Need to Know and Do

Phaedra Boinodiris

Introduction

The integration of any form of artificial intelligence (AI)—whether traditional predictive AI (which forecasts outcomes based on historical data), generative AI (which creates new content such as text, images, or code), or agentic AI (which can autonomously plan, make decisions, and take actions toward a goal)—represents a powerful opportunity for transformation, but also a profound challenge. Organizations that *strategically* invest in AI—ensuring alignment with their overall business objectives—often experience significant improvements in employee productivity, process efficiency, and business model innovation. But the costs of doing AI *wrong* can hurt your bottom line, hurt you personally, and/or harm others and society. If you choose the wrong AI strategy, the cost estimates for implementing generative AI can be off by 500%–1000% as projected by industry analysts (Gartner, 2025). In addition to financial impact, a long list of additional risks has been identified, including inaccurate output, information usage violations, increased vulnerability to data breaches, human exploitation, and more. See Table 6.1 for a partial list of AI risks; see IBM's AI Risk Atlas for a broader set of risks (IBM, 2024b).

To truly harness AI's potential, organizations must not only "do the right AI"—choosing the right AI model use cases to invest in that are aligned to the mission strategy—but also "do AI right." In order to "do AI right" organizations must move beyond a focus on infrastructure, models, and operations to address the sociotechnical challenge of earning trust.

Phaedra Boinodiris, *Leveraging AI Opportunities and Mitigating Risks*. In: *The Changing Leadership Landscape*. Edited by: Sheri L. Feinzig and Mariangela Battista, Oxford University Press. © Oxford University Press (2026). DOI: 10.1093/9780197820070.003.0006

Table 6.1 Partial List of AI Risks

AI Harms		
Attribute inference attack	Confidential data in prompt	Confidential information in data
Copyright infringement	Dangerous use	Data acquisition restrictions
Data bias	Data contamination	Data poisoning
Data privacy rights alignment	Data transfer restrictions	Data usage restrictions
Decision bias	Evasion attack	Exposing personal information
Extraction attack	Generated content ownership and IP	Hallucination
Harmful code generation	Harmful output	Human exploitation
IP information in prompt	Impact on affected communities	Impact on cultural diversity
Impact on education: bypassing learning	Impact on education: plagiarism	Impact on environment
Impact on human agency	Impact on jobs	Improper data curation
Improper retraining	Improper usage	Inaccessible training data
Incomplete advice	Incomplete usage definition	Incorrect risk testing
Jailbreaking	Lack of data transparency	Lack of model transparency
Lack of system transparency	Lack of testing diversity	Lack of training data
Legal accountability	Membership inference attack	Model usage rights restrictions
Non-consensual use	Non-disclosure	Output bias
Over- or under-reliance	Personal information in data	Personal information in prompt
Poor model accuracy	Prompt injection attack	Prompt leaking
Prompt priming	Reidentification	Revealing confidential information
Spreading disinformation	Spreading toxicity	Toxic output
Uncertain data provenance	Unexplainable output	Unreliable source attribution
Unrepresentative data	Unrepresentative risk testing	Untraceable attribution

Trust in AI systems cannot be achieved solely through technical solutions—it requires a holistic approach encompassing people, processes, and tools. Trust must be intentionally built through transparency, education, and inclusivity.

Who Is Accountable? The Answers Are Troubling

When I ask at AI summits, "Who in your organization is accountable for ensuring responsible AI outcomes?"—the responses I receive are troubling. The most common response is, "No one." This is not just alarming—it is an abdication of responsibility. AI is already influencing business decisions, customer interactions, hiring practices, healthcare diagnostics, and even legal proceedings. If no one is accountable, then who ensures that AI systems align with ethical, legal, and organizational values? Who makes sure that biased models do not lead to discriminatory outcomes? The absence of ownership in AI governance increases the likelihood of AI systems causing harm, whether through unintended bias, security vulnerabilities, or opaque decision-making.

The second most common response is, "We don't use AI." This answer is almost always inaccurate. The reality is that AI is already embedded in many of the tools and software applications organizations rely on daily—whether they explicitly develop AI or not. Employees are likely using AI-powered tools for tasks like document summarization, chat-based assistance, data analytics, or even hiring and performance evaluations. AI is also built into enterprise software from vendors like Microsoft, Salesforce, and SAP. If organizations believe they do not use AI, it is often because they are not tracking or governing AI usage. This lack of awareness can lead to shadow AI (unsanctioned AI use outside IT oversight, creating risks in data privacy, bias, and security)—where employees or departments adopt AI tools without oversight, creating unknown risks for compliance, security, and bias.

The third most frequent response is, "Everyone." At first glance, this might sound like a positive approach—AI accountability should be a shared responsibility, if you have any role to play in an AI lifecycle. But when "everyone" is responsible for governance, it often means that no one is truly accountable. Without a defined ownership structure, AI governance itself becomes fragmented, and critical decisions—such as evaluating ethical implications, monitoring biases, or ensuring regulatory compliance—can fall through the cracks. Just as cybersecurity, financial reporting, and risk management require dedicated leadership, responsible AI governance demands clear roles, accountability, and structured oversight.

Why AI Governance Requires More Than Good Intentions

Responsibly curating AI may be one of the hardest things humanity has ever undertaken—because it demands not just technical precision but also ethical clarity, cultural humility, and a willingness to confront our own blind spots. This is a rapidly evolving field that requires deep expertise, cross-domain dialogue, ongoing monitoring, and organizational alignment.

Organizations must ensure that their AI models reflect their values and their users' expectations, and they must be cognizant of the broader societal impact of their technology. This means the following:

- *Value Alignment*: AI designers, developers, and business leaders must collaborate to embed ethical considerations into AI systems from inception. AI should align not only with business goals but also with the ethical standards of the organization and the communities it impacts.
- *AI model inventory*: Having a robust inventory to keep track of all AI models procured and developed along with their critical metadata is essential.
- *AI model auditing*: Organizations should have processes in place to understand how these models are behaving and how to interpret audit results.
- *Regulatory Readiness*: The global AI regulatory landscape is shifting, with new laws emerging, such as the European Union AI Act and the evolving policies from the US Federal Trade Commission (FTC), the National Institute of Standards and Technology (NIST), and the International Organization for Standardization (ISO). To operate within this evolving environment, organizations must track AI model inventories, assess compliance risks, and prepare for regulatory shifts.
- *AI Ethics and Literacy*: Accountability starts with awareness. AI literacy programs should be mandatory—not just for technical teams but for leadership, human resources (HR), legal, and procurement teams who

engage with AI-powered tools. Employees should understand the risks of AI systems that may be "lawful but awful"—technically compliant but ethically problematic.

The Two Pillars of Scalable AI Governance

For AI governance to be effective, organizations must establish clear, sustainable frameworks that scale with the complexity of AI adoption. There are two fundamental components: organizational AI governance and automated AI model governance.

Organizational AI governance addresses the strategic and operational approach to AI governance within the organization. It includes the following:

- *Defining AI Policies and Principles*: What stance does the organization take on AI ethics, fairness, transparency, and security? How do these principles translate into specific functional and non-functional requirements for AI models? Functional requirements define what the system must do—for example, flagging biased outcomes or generating user-facing explanations. Non-functional requirements define how well the system must do it—for instance, how much detail is in the generated explanations, how accurate fairness checks must be, or what standards it must meet for security and auditability.
- *Establishing AI Literacy and Training Programs*: How are employees educated on responsible AI practices? Is there applied training for developers, business leaders, and procurement teams? Are there diverse and inclusive communities of practice where people can be learning and sharing how to do the work required?
- *Structuring AI Governance Teams*: Who is responsible for AI governance? Is there a cross-functional AI ethics board, compliance officers, and/or AI risk managers?
- *AI Model Inventory and Oversight*: Does the organization track what AI models are in use, who owns them, and how they are being evaluated? Are there formal intake and monitoring processes in place?

Here is a list of people who should be involved in organizational AI governance: business leaders, AI ethics boards, other domain experts, data and AI leaders, policy and regulatory experts, Chief Product Officers (CPOs), Chief Information Security Officers (CISOs), and legal teams.

Beyond policy and training, AI governance requires technical enforcement. *Automated AI model governance* focuses on the lifecycle of AI models—from development to deployment and monitoring. Key components include the following:

- *Model Lineage & Transparency*: Organizations must be able to trace the origins of AI models—where data come from, how models were trained, and what assumptions were made.
- *Risk and Bias Detection*: Automated tools can continuously assess AI models for bias, fairness, explainability, and security vulnerabilities.
- *Monitoring Model Performance and Drift*: AI models must be regularly monitored to ensure they perform as intended. For example, an AI-powered hiring tool may start with minimal bias but could drift over time as it processes new data, leading to discriminatory outcomes.
- *Compliance Audits and Reporting*: AI governance platforms, such as IBM's watsonx.governance™ (an enterprise-grade solution for monitoring and validating AI models), can provide real-time insights into AI risks, compliance gaps, and AI model performance.

Here is a list of people who should be involved in automated AI model governance: development teams, IT leaders, Chief Data and Analytics Officers (CDAOs), software and data science leaders, and Machine Learning Operations (MLOps) teams.

Challenging the Powerful: Listening to All Voices for Responsible AI

A cornerstone of earning trust in AI is listening to voices that are often overlooked. The importance of diversity in AI development cannot be overstated. The larger the variance in human beings, the better—AI quality improves and risks are reduced when people with differing lived world experiences are included. An example from the healthcare industry illustrates the real-world impact of failing to consider relevant perspectives in development of a predictive AI tool. This tool failed marginalized communities in a way that was both avoidable and deeply revealing. The model, designed to flag patients who would most benefit from extra medical care, used historical healthcare spending data as a proxy for illness. On paper, it seemed efficient. But in practice, the algorithm baked in decades of systemic inequities. Patients who had historically lacked access to quality care—primarily low-income individuals, people of color, and those from immigrant backgrounds—had spent less on healthcare not because they were healthier, but because they were underserved. Clinics in their neighborhoods were underfunded or non-existent. Their insurance coverage, if they had any, was often inadequate. Many had experienced medical racism and did not trust the system to begin with.

Because the model did not see them as "high-cost," it did not flag them for support. Their chronic illnesses went unmanaged, their risks ignored. Meanwhile, wealthier and often white patients who had long enjoyed better access to care were prioritized. The AI was technically "accurate" based on its design, but ethically disastrous (Obermeyer et al., 2019).

This kind of failure—where technical precision masks systemic injustice—can only be prevented by shifting who gets to design, evaluate, and hold AI systems accountable. One organization exploring a different path is the Distributed AI Research Institute (DAIR) Strickland, E. (2022, March 31), founded by Dr. Timnit Gebru. While I cannot personally vouch for all of their work or its measurable impact, their mission deeply resonates: to build AI grounded in the lived experiences of those historically excluded from its development. DAIR's focus on decentralization, worker rights, and community-led research offers a promising counterweight to dominant narratives in AI development that too often prioritize speed and scale over justice and care. Their model is a reminder that inclusive governance is not just a compliance measure—it is a design choice that must start from the beginning. (Gebru, T. (2021, December 2))

Organizations that champion diversity as a key factor in creating equitable and impactful AI emphasize that inclusive teams produce better-performing technologies that reflect the needs of all stakeholders. Leaders must embrace these principles, ensuring that AI systems are both equitable and effective by integrating diverse voices throughout their development—voices representing vastly differing lived world experiences, who can approach AI development by focusing on human outcomes and behaviors.

Governance processes are critical to sustaining trust in AI systems. Accountable parties within the organization must maintain inventories of AI models, track regulatory compliance, and establish clear guidelines for ethical use. But AI governance is not just a compliance exercise—it is about creating a culture where challenging others' decisions is encouraged, and systemic biases are identified and addressed. By embedding *psychological safety* and *a growth mindset* into these processes, organizations not only have a better chance of mitigating risks but also of discovering opportunities for innovation that might otherwise go unnoticed. In this context, leaders must view AI not as a tool for replacing human intelligence but as a complement that could amplify human creativity, judgment, and empathy.

A huge challenge with governance processes today is the very big (and erroneous) assumption that all people understand and can recognize disparate impact. Most organizations that build or buy a lot of AI rely on intake forms to help assess when an AI model should go through formal review. Here are some questions included in these forms:

- Have any risks or exposures been identified?
- Is Personal Information (PI) or Sensitive Personal Information (SPI) being collected or processed?
- Where AI is used, is there an opt-out of the AI approach defined or accommodation provided for the user?
- What information is provided to users to explain how the AI works and how the AI outputs are determined?
- Where is this disclosure information located?
- Has bias testing been conducted?
- Are there any security concerns relevant to the use case?
- Are there any safety concerns relevant or could this use case potentially be used to cause inadvertent harm?
- Does this use case comply with all applicable laws?
- Describe the source of the training data

In general, here is what we have found:

- People are not incentivized to be thoughtful when filling out these forms.
- People often do not realize that what they want to build or buy falls under the definition of AI.
- They assume because it is using a specific technology, or worse, because it is hosted on a particular cloud, that there are no risks.
- They assume the third party will take on all the risks.
- People oftentimes have zero understanding of disparate impact.

- People assume 'a Human will be in the Loop' is a governance strategy onto itself.

This is why a holistic education on the topic of AI is so very important.

One of the most effective ways to bridge this knowledge gap is through design thinking workshops, where diverse, multi-disciplinary teams collaborate to analyze and mitigate disparate impact in real-world AI use cases. Using human-centered design frameworks, we guide participants—ranging from AI developers to policy and business leaders—through exercises that help them identify hidden biases, simulate AI decision-making in different demographic scenarios, and prototype safeguards to mitigate risks before deployment. These sessions emphasize empathetic problem-solving, allowing participants to step into the shoes of those affected by AI decisions and recognize unintended consequences that traditional intake forms fail to surface. Moreover, design thinking provides teams with a structured way to translate broad AI principles (like fairness and transparency) into actionable functional and non-functional requirements that inform what AI systems should be built or purchased. This ensures that governance is not just a compliance exercise but a thoughtful, iterative process that embeds responsible AI practices into every stage of development and deployment. Those that are best suited to lead such workshops are individuals that can truly engage those who may feel like they do not belong in a conversation about AI. (I sometimes refer to these individuals as "scout leaders" or "camp counselors"- they naturally engage and draw people in.)

I am often asked about the number-one skill to double down on for an AI-enabled future. The answer is—know how to be a *lifelong learner*. Success in this rapidly evolving world of AI lies in having humility and a growth mindset. Know that you will continue to learn how to leverage technology to amplify human capabilities while nurturing accountability, inclusivity, and growth within the organization. The leaders of tomorrow will be those who navigate this complexity with courage, empathy, and clarity.

In the Absence of Regulation, There Is Always Litigation

In the absence of comprehensive AI regulations, litigation has become a pivotal mechanism for addressing the challenges and harms associated with AI technologies. Organizations like TechTonic Justice—though modest in size—have made notable strides in this arena by equipping legal aid programs with the necessary skills and tools to challenge unfair automated decisions. TechTonic Justice supports low-income communities nationally to litigate cases where AI-driven systems wrongly deny Medicaid, public benefits, employment, housing, and more—highlighting the profound and real-world impacts of these systems on marginalized populations (TechTonic Justice, n.d.). Similarly, the American Civil Liberties Union (ACLU) has utilized legal avenues to promote transparency and accountability in AI applications. By filing Freedom of Information Act (FOIA) requests, the ACLU seeks to uncover governmental use of AI, particularly in surveillance and national-security contexts. For example, in March 2024, the ACLU submitted a FOIA request to the National Security Agency (NSA) for internal studies, reports, and roadmaps on its AI programs (American Civil Liberties Union. (2024a, March 7))—and when the agency failed to comply, the ACLU filed a lawsuit in April 2024b (*ACLU v. NSA*) (American Civil Liberties Union. (2024b, April 25)) to compel disclosure of documents that could significantly impact civil liberties.

These legal actions underscore the critical role of litigation in scrutinizing AI practices, especially when formal regulations are lacking. Through lawsuits and FOIA requests, advocates aim to hold entities accountable, ensure ethical AI use, and protect individuals from potential abuses stemming from unregulated AI systems.

Getting It Right: Investing in an AI Governance Leader

How can organizations successfully navigate this complexity and realize AI's benefits while protecting their businesses, employees, customers, and society from undue harm? A specific leadership role—AI governance leader—is needed to implement, drive, and oversee robust, ongoing AI governance processes.

A great AI governance leader is not just a steward of technology but also a champion of ethics, inclusivity, and trust. At their core, these leaders must possess a deep understanding of the sociotechnical nature of AI systems—recognizing that technology, people, and processes are inextricably linked. This requires a rare combination of technical literacy, ethical foresight, and an unwavering commitment to accountability. Noteworthy attributes of model AI governance leaders include the following:

- *Bravery*: Many of the most effective AI governance leaders I have encountered are among the bravest—willing to risk reputation and challenge profit-first priorities to protect societal interests.
- *Visionary Storytellers*: Exceptional leaders in AI governance see beyond immediate functionality and profitability. They anticipate the broader societal impacts of AI systems, from the risks of bias and exclusion to the potential for transformative good. They consistently ask, "Is this not just lawful but also ethical?" and ensure their teams are empowered to do the same. They are consummate storytellers as they must impart wisdom in ways that resonate with the widest range of people using words that are easily understandable, so that they can get people to *care* about the mission and achieve value alignment.
- *Collaborative and Inclusive*: These leaders must achieve value alignment to get all parts of the organization to understand *why* de-risking AI is so critical to the success of their organization. They must value diverse perspectives and foster environments where voices from all backgrounds—technical and non-technical, senior and junior, local and global—are heard and integrated into decision-making. They actively dismantle silos, knowing that unless everyone is on board—*all* leadership—the ship will flounder.
- *Accountable and Transparent*: A great AI governance leader does not shy away from accountability. They define clear ownership for AI outcomes, ensuring someone is always responsible for monitoring, maintaining, and governing AI systems. Transparency is their cornerstone—they openly communicate the purpose, limitations, and risks of AI systems to both internal teams and external stakeholders.
- *Empathetic and Adaptable*: Governance is not just about enforcing rules; it is about understanding people—both those developing the systems and those impacted by them. Leaders in this space must exhibit empathy, connecting with teams and users to understand their concerns and aspirations. They also are dedicated to nurturing their communities of practice, vigilant protectors of psychological safety, and remain adaptable, responding to the rapid evolution of AI technologies

and regulations with agility and foresight. They know that there is a "pandemic of not belonging"- meaning, that most people feel because they do not have the requisite technical degrees, they have no business being in working groups to discuss AI ethics or governance. Part of their job is to ensure that they engage those who can contribute valuable insights into which principles should be reflected in AI and how these principles manifest into feature and function.

- *Committed to Continuous Learning*: The best AI governance leaders recognize that they, too, are on a journey of discovery. They invest in their own learning and the development of their teams, fostering AI literacy and staying abreast of emerging technologies and regulations. They ensure their organizations evolve alongside the technology, cultivating cultures of lifelong learning.

Ultimately, great AI governance leaders combine technological expertise with human-centered leadership. They are as much architects of trust and inclusion as they are guardians of compliance and performance. These leaders too must be empowered, and given a *funded mandate* to do the work. In this rapidly changing landscape, these qualities will define the leaders who successfully guide their organizations toward responsible and impactful AI innovation.

What Leaders Must Understand and Do about AI

Let me be direct: the power and peril of AI is now squarely a leadership issue. It is no longer sufficient for executives to defer to technical teams or innovation labs. If you are in a position of leadership, AI is already shaping your business, your people, and your public impact—whether you realize it or not. So, what does that mean for you?

You Must Deeply Understand the Risks and Know How to Mitigate Them

This is not about checking boxes. It is about understanding that AI systems—especially generative and agentic ones—have consequences that stretch beyond efficiency and into ethics, society, and law. They can replicate historical injustices, hallucinate disinformation, leak confidential data, or disempower your workforce if deployed carelessly. But these risks are not reasons to avoid AI—they are reasons to lead with intention. That means you must:

- Know the limitations and risks of the tools you are putting into the hands of your people.
- Ask hard questions like, "Who might this harm?"; "What aren't we seeing?"; and "Are we solving the *right* problem?"
- Invest in fluency, not just for yourself, but across your leadership bench—because distributed ignorance is a breeding ground for crisis.
- Become fluent in the language that describes the functional and non-functional requirements that you need to see from anything you buy or build.
- Understand what the 'humans in the loop' will really need to be able to be proficient in their work, including HOW they are measured.

If you want to lead in the age of AI, then risk literacy and ethical imagination are not optional. They are core competencies.

You Must Shape the Culture with Your Words and Your Actions

People inside your organization are watching you. How you talk about AI will become how others behave with it. If you frame AI as a silver bullet or a cost-cutter, you are telling your teams to prioritize speed over care. If you talk about AI as a tool to amplify *human dignity, creativity, and accountability*, you are shaping a culture that centers values over hype. Leaders must model:

- *Vulnerability*: Say "I don't know" when you don't. That invites learning.
- *Empathy*: Bring lived experience and marginalized voices into your AI development cycles.
- *Curiosity*: Normalize questions like, "How might this system unintentionally exclude or harm?"

Culture change does not happen in all-hands meetings and presentations. It happens when people see that integrity matters more than convenience. It happens when the message from the top is, "Doing AI right is everyone's job—but I'm going first."

You Must Build, and Fund, the Governance Structures That Make Accountability Real

Let's stop pretending that AI governance is someone else's job. If you are a senior leader, your *visible sponsorship* of governance work is nonnegotiable. Without it, nothing sticks. No one has time. No one has a budget. No one takes the ethical high road if shortcuts are rewarded more than scrutiny. So what does this leadership look like in practice?

- *You fund the work*: That means resources for model inventories, ethics reviews, regulatory preparation, and education programs.
- *You backstop governance boards*: That means standing behind cross-functional groups that are designed to ask uncomfortable questions and slow things down when needed.
- *You assign ownership*: Because when "everyone" is responsible, no one is.

You also must create a *culture of psychological safety*, where people are rewarded—not punished—for surfacing concerns. Governance without safety is performance art. Governance with safety is innovation that does not cause harm.

You Must Hold Your Vendors Contractually Accountable

Let's not sugarcoat this—most organizations are already using AI. But in many cases, it is *third-party* AI, buried inside vendor tools and platforms. That does not make the risk disappear. It makes it harder to see—and harder to manage.

Vendor relationships must be governed with the same scrutiny as internal AI development—and that scrutiny must be built into the contract. As a leader, you must ensure that your procurement and legal teams are not just checking for conformity with the General Data Protection Regulation (GDPR) and basic compliance. They need to be asking vendors:

- What data were used to train this system? Were they representative and obtained ethically?

- What are your model update and monitoring processes? How often are you assessing for bias or drift?
- Can you provide transparency into how decisions are made?
- Do we have rights to audit your system or access performance reports?
- What happens if harm occurs? Who is liable?
- How will you notify us if vulnerabilities or failures are discovered after deployment?

Put these requirements into your *procurement language*. Make model cards (short documents explaining intended use, how the models were evaluated, etc.; IIAP, 2023), factsheets (details about AI models including creation information, data used, and lifecycle management; IBM, 2024a), and independent audits part of the deliverables. And—this is important—make sure your contracts include enforceable shared *accountability clauses*, not just aspirational values.

Also, do not assume your vendors are keeping up with global regulation. You must evaluate their preparedness for compliance across jurisdictions (EU AI Act, FTC oversight, NIST, ISO standards, etc.) and ensure that your organization is not inheriting risk by default.

Remember, your reputation is downstream of your vendors' practices. Vendor shared accountability is not a nice-to-have—it is your line of defense against ethical, legal, and operational fallout. Great leaders do not just govern what they build. They also govern what they buy.

Concluding Thoughts

Let's be honest: this is hard. Leading in the AI era means getting comfortable with ambiguity. It means choosing to do what is *right*, not just what is easy or profitable in the short term. It requires developing a deeper understanding of AI technologies—how they work, what they can achieve, the risks they carry—and imparting that knowledge and understanding throughout the workforce. It requires investing in AI governance and a capable AI governance leader. But the leaders who step up now—who ask the brave questions, resource the right systems, and center human values—will not only avoid the pitfalls. They will earn the trust that becomes a lasting competitive advantage. This is your moment. Make it count.

References

American Civil Liberties Union. (2024a, March 7). *ACLU files FOIA request for NSA AI transparency* [Press release]. https://www.aclu.org/documents/nsa-ai-foia-complaint

American Civil Liberties Union. (2024b, April 25). *ACLU v. NSA—FOIA lawsuit seeking records about the NSA's use of artificial intelligence* [Press release]. https://www.aclu.org/cases/aclu-et-al-v-nsa-et-al-foia-lawsuit-seeking-records-about-the-nsas-use-of-artificial-intelligence

Gartner. (2025). *Gartner IT Symposium/Xpo: Future of AI strategy and governance.* https://www.gartner.com

Gebru, T. (2021, December 2). Timnit Gebru launches independent AI research institute to counter Big Tech. *Distributed AI Research Institute.* https://www.dair-institute.org/press-release

IBM. (2024a). *AI governance documentation: Get started with watsonx.governance.* https://dataplatform.cloud.ibm.com/docs/content/wsj/catalog/get-started-aigov.html

IBM. (2024b). *AI risk atlas.* https://www.ibm.com/docs/en/watsonx/saas?topic=ai-risk-atlas

International Association of Privacy Professionals. (2023). *5 things to know about AI model cards.* https://iapp.org/news/a/5-things-to-know-about-ai-model-cards

Obermeyer, Z., Powers, B., Vogeli, C., & Mullainathan, S. (2019). *Dissecting racial bias in an algorithm used to manage the health of populations. Science,* 366(6464), 447–453. https://doi.org/10.1126/science.aax2342

Strickland, E. (2022, March 31). Timnit Gebru is building a slow AI movement. *IEEE Spectrum.* https://spectrum.ieee.org/timnit-gebru-dair-ai-ethics

TechTonic Justice. (n.d.). *Inescapable AI: The ways AI decides how low-income people work, live, learn, and survive* [Report overview]. https://www.techtonicjustice.org/reports/inescapable-ai

SECTION III

DATA AND ANALYTICS THROUGH A LEADERSHIP LENS

7
Leading and Deciding with Data

Alexis A. Fink and George S. Reiswig

Introduction

Changes in the business and tech sectors have accelerated dramatically in the past decade or so. As a result, leaders' instincts that were honed over the many prior years, but in materially different circumstances, may be less relevant as guides for how to approach current challenges. Previously reliable practices may no longer yield the same outcomes under new conditions. Leaders' own personal experiences from earlier moments in their career may still be emotionally resonant, but not practically relevant—especially as many roles, teams, and organizations are fundamentally changed through the adoption of AI and other advanced tools. Taken together, these realities mean that, now more than ever, leaders must make effective use of data to guide their decision-making in organizations.

It is important to recognize that effectively using data is not as simple as many people believe. Data must be accurate and relevant. Data must be handled ethically, including appropriate storage, use, and sharing. While all data require care to ensure accuracy and appropriate use, data about people require particular care to protect the privacy of the individuals involved; consulting with human resources (HR) or an employment attorney is advised to ensure that people data are appropriately and legally handled. The topic of privacy concerns around Personally Identifiable Information really merits its own dedicated chapter, and will only be touched upon here. The implications of failures to appropriately consider the privacy requirements of people data and analytics are both broad and deep, having legal, organizational, and cultural ramifications.

While demands and business conditions have changed, so have the resources available to effectively manage teams and organizations. Increased availability and accessibility of data, and improved tools for analysis of those

Alexis A. Fink and George S. Reiswig, *Leading and Deciding with Data*. In: *The Changing Leadership Landscape*. Edited by: Sheri L. Feinzig and Mariangela Battista, Oxford University Press. © Oxford University Press (2026). DOI: 10.1093/9780197820070.003.0007 data, create tremendous opportunity for insight. Taking full advantage of these new capabilities is critical for navigating new challenges for leaders, such as new structures around management of people and organizations as well as evolutions in business opportunities and risks. The increasing availability and use of advanced tools such as AI also significantly increase risks associated with data use in organizations. Especially when significant decisions are being made, it is critical to take steps to ensure the accuracy of the output being provided by these systems.

To realize the greatest benefits of good data work, leaders and managers must be able to use data and analyses not only to identify key patterns (the "what"), but also to answer questions about why something matters (the "so what") and then translate that understanding into an action plan (the "now what") (e.g., Rolfe et al., 2001). In many cases, it is more effective to begin with a particular decision or action and work backward to the data questions, rather than starting with data questions and hoping to find a practical implication or application for the insight that is discovered along the way.

This chapter will provide an overview of key ways leaders can incorporate good people-data practices into their work as leaders and managers. We will walk through some of the foundational data considerations necessary for leaders to effectively execute their jobs and manage their organizations, and share sample people data and metrics for leaders to incorporate as they manage their teams and organizations.

Pulling a Thimble of Insight from an Ocean of Data

Modern organizations typically have enormous volumes of data that are at least theoretically available to them. Some examples include:

- *Digitized processes*: As more and more business is conducted electronically, systems generally have the ability to store data; so, anything tracked, produced, invoiced, paid, collected, processed, or distributed will generate "digital exhaust." This might include both internal processes like time measurements, and external data like customer conversions.
- *Finance systems*: These sophisticated systems capture business performance, and Enterprise Resource Management (ERM) systems may

capture things like productivity, downtime, budgets, quality, and shrinkage or other data about business processes.

- *HR Information Systems (HRIS)*: Modern HR systems store enormous quantities of data, from selection processes through performance and promotion and on to exit. Many will also include information about training, competency or skill information, team structures, management hierarchies, and information about things like geographic distribution of teams. In many cases, these systems include default reporting or querying capabilities that can provide basic reports, such as headcount, exit data, or span of control. It is also frequently possible to conduct analyses that include compensation data based on these systems; extreme care must be taken when accessing especially sensitive personal information such as compensation. Although leaders often see compensation data as part of their direct reports' performance management processes, additional considerations are required before broader reports can be pulled or analyses conducted. Any inquiry including compensation data should be managed in partnership with your legal partners.
- *Employee listening*: Many organizations today capture employee sentiment in an online format. These are frequently confidential; that is, identifying information is collected for analytical purposes, but individual responses are not shared. Rather, results are aggregated to some minimum threshold. This serves two key purposes. First, it protects the confidentiality of the respondent, which has the happy consequence of increasing the likelihood that they will be honest in their responses. Second, aggregating responses can give you confidence that the scores generated are reliable measures of the actual sentiment. Confidential surveys also make it possible, with appropriate constraints, to connect employee sentiment to other organizational information, like tenure, level, job profile, performance, business unit, geographic location, work setting (such as in-office, hybrid, or remote), or other variables that can, in aggregate, give a picture of the health and risks in an organization or team.
- *Security and timekeeping systems*: While these data can be very sensitive and must be handled with appropriate privacy and other considerations, these systems can in some cases capture data such as attendance and location information, allowing organizations to consider things like co-location of team members. Before accessing these sorts of data,

leaders should consult with their organization's data privacy teams or employment attorneys to ensure that appropriate privacy considerations are respected.

Given this ocean of data, a key challenge is in identifying those critical pieces of data that, when taken together, provide the insight required to support effective decision-making. Most of this tsunami of data will be capturing transactions that are processed by one of the core systems; simply harvesting the data that are available may not yield much in the way of insight. That is, these types of transactional data may help you answer "what" questions, but not "why" questions. Even the "what" can be obscured by the sheer volume of water in this ocean. For example, learning that the average tenure at exit is 52 months may help you plan for future recruiting needs, but it does little to help an organization reduce the cost of turnover and begs questions such as, "Is that good or bad?" Deeper analysis, likely including information about capabilities measured at hire, experiences on the job, performance, career mobility, sentiment, and similar factors are likely required to help an organization plan for and manage attrition risk, as well as related talent management considerations.

Advances in analytical techniques and AI will transform the way we work, as well as the way we work with data. In particular, the ability of algorithms to identify outliers and unexpected patterns will vastly accelerate and expand our ability to catch problems before they become crises, and, in an ideal case, to identify and capitalize on opportunities more quickly and effectively. However, like humans, algorithms' abilities to generate insight is constrained by the data available to them.

Increasingly, organizations are turning to advanced systems that can respond to queries in natural language. For example, a leader might ask "what was our attrition rate last quarter" rather than hunting for the dashboard that gives her or him the data in question. There are a lot of benefits to this approach, especially the speed and ease of use. However, given unevenness in data quality, the risks of generative AI hallucinations, and variations in definitions, leaders should consider these quick and easy answers to be directional rather than definitive in most cases.

In many organizations, data quality is poor, limiting the usefulness of the data. In many cases where data are of poor quality, it is better not to analyze them at all, rather than generating some result with false precision that may lead organizational leaders to make bad decisions. This can be especially risky when asking AI to analyze the available data, as these systems, by design, extrapolate from available patterns and typically provide a specific answer.

Ironically, one of the ways that we can best ensure our ability to find meaningful insight in the current tsunami of data may be to add to this tsunami. More specifically, organizations and leaders may find that more valuable insight can be uncovered when we add richer data to our information systems. For example, folding in qualitative data, or data gathered intentionally beyond the automatically produced data that comes from passive transactions, can shed light and insights on the digital exhaust. In many cases, the quantitative data can illuminate what is happening, but not why it is happening, the consequences of it happening, or how to make a different thing happen—essentially the "so what" and "now what" elements of inquiry. Often quantitative data can identify a risk, but, alone, it cannot tell you how to mitigate that risk. As leaders, our roles require that we do both—proactively identify risks and guide the organization in such a way to avoid or minimize those risks.

Thoughtful attention to what information will support evaluations and decisions is an important way to build a data ecosystem that can help support "so what" and "now what" questions, and help leaders and managers effectively use data to improve their organization and outcomes.

Smaller teams in particular may find advanced techniques and large-scale reporting to be of less value; for frontline managers and leaders of smaller teams, qualitative data can be particularly rich and valuable. Advanced analytical techniques generally require large amounts of training data that may not be available for smaller teams; generalizing with data from elsewhere may power the AI, but make the output less relevant and useful. Where they are reasonable to collect, qualitative data are often more informative than quantitative data or generically produced AI output. Additionally, the mere act of engaging with employees around key questions can be the start of a change process.

Many organizations will have a minimal size team or number of respondents or cases required to provide access to quantitative data. In cases involving employee or customer sentiment data, this may be to protect privacy. In other cases, such as attrition, it may be because quantitative data are not particularly valuable or diagnostic to small teams. For example, if an organization typically has about 10% attrition, a team of five who lost no people in one year, and one person in the second year would be exactly on average across the two years. But attrition is often tracked either year to date or 12 months at a time (rolling 12-month cycles), resulting in the same team going from one of the "best" on retention (0% in that year), to "unacceptable" (20%) the following year. For that team of five, tracking annual attrition numerically might not make very much sense; a practice like "stay interviews," where HR or a leader initiates a conversation about satisfaction at work, might be a more illuminating and useful approach. It can be useful to "zoom out" and examine larger sets of data to find patterns, but it is important to be thoughtful about the criteria for what is included or excluded. Simply rolling up to the next highest group may do more harm than good if the basic characteristics—for example, tenure, level, role, or location—are materially different. Combining outcomes for a group of entry-level individual contributors with another team of more tenured deep experts is more likely to obscure useful patterns than to illuminate them.

Broadly, leaders and managers need to think about and work with data in two ways. First, they need to use data to effectively manage their organizations. This will involve developing a clear system of measures, and using those to guide things like prioritization of resources and evaluation of performance. Where automated systems or AI tools are deployed, embedding core definitions so that they are consistently deployed is essential. Second, many managers and leaders will have opportunities to use data for insight. Here, leaders will be exploring hypotheses and opportunities. These two types of work complement one another. These might even be thought of as the work of managing and the work of leading. The insight work guides decisions about what an organization should do, and the management work helps organizations determine how well they are doing it, highlighting where they might need to adjust to meet their objectives.

Effectively Managing Your Organization with Data

Figuring out what information is important to share, who should have access to the data, and how they should be formatted and shared are all more complicated questions than they seem. Many take a "ready, fire, aim" approach to this type of work, resulting in organizations that are littered with reports that overlap in content and often conflict with one another, or receive only narrow or short-term use. This approach relies on the recipients' ability to parse what they are receiving correctly, and the resulting differences in subjective interpretation feed confirmation biases which facilitate poor decision-making.

Furthermore, when multiple versions of similar reports are shared across an organization, a lot of time can be spent trying to reconcile the numbers to ascertain which of the reports are correct, if any. This means organizations are wasting time both on creating duplicative assets, and wasting time quarreling about what is true and who is most expert at interpreting the conflicting results rather than turning insight into action. At minimum, this all-too-frequent phenomenon represents an inefficient use of analyst and leader time.

This problem is likely to get worse as many organizations democratize access to data. Absent very thoughtful data quality and data governance investments, it is highly likely that each individual querying the data system will receive a slightly different set of results. It is also not uncommon for individuals to keep varying their queries until they get an answer they like. This sort of fishing expedition can meet the emotional needs of the leader ("See! I was right!"), but is often counterproductive in terms of informing effective decision-making. Especially when multiple leaders within a single team begin defining their queries differently to confirm what they already believe to be true, it becomes very difficult to take coherent action or build coherent strategies at the level of a larger organization.

The ability to do near-real-time exploration is a great leap forward in many ways, and, while still imperfect, advanced tools have greatly increased capabilities in this area. While it can be tempting to simply make all data available to everyone, it is worthwhile to invest the time to identify, first, which data need to be thoughtfully managed to ensure accurate results and appropriate privacy considerations. Next, it is important to be strategic in determining what information will be useful, to whom, how often, and how it should be delivered. As a general rule, it is advised to provide data only to those people who are accountable for using those data; providing data to satisfy curiosity is often demanded, but can have unintended consequences. For example, individual performance data and personal demographic data such as gender, ethnicity, disability status, or veteran status, are generally only accessible to a very narrow set of individuals with a specific business need for that information, such as supporting legal requirements. Additionally, providing open access to high volumes of data increases the risk that critical data will be missed; too much data essentially buries the needle of important information in a haystack of noise.

Oceans of data can overwhelm, confuse, or unintentionally mislead users. Good data stewardship and interpretation requires a principled, consistent approach to questions around what data to share, with whom, how frequently it should be delivered, and how we can get it into the right people's hands. Organizations will face new challenges in determining what data are useful and how to efficiently and effectively use data to support organizational decision-making. Building and using an effective reporting ecosystem requires thoughtful consideration of features like the "what," "when," "how," and "who" of sharing data, as well as savvy choices about which data are critical to consider and which are simply more noise in the system.

Data and Strategy

Organizations frequently aspire to be data-driven. Indeed, as change continues to accelerate, the availability of timely, relevant data to support effective decision-making is becoming even more essential. Data play a key role in developing strategy through research processes. Data are also useful in refining and supporting strategy. The process of operationally defining strategies in such a way that they can actually be measured can in itself be important in clarifying what really matters to the organization and how to achieve strategic goals.

It is often helpful to begin the exercise identifying a very short set of items or goals that get at the core purpose of the group, organization, or key strategy. These are the items for which the top leaders are ultimately accountable. Those top strategic metrics are consistent over multiple years, and are generally aligned to critical outcomes. It can be tempting to use a qualitative metric here; doing so can erode trust in the overall system, as judgment calls are hard to verify and quantify in a way that captures improvement or degradation. Qualitative evidence is critical in many domains, but ideally the guiding purpose of an organization can be captured in a way that can be objective and defensible. If you are having difficulty building a metric for one of these key organizations or strategies, a shorthand approach is simply to ask, "Why does this matter" and "How will we know?"

Taking the time to build these operational definitions of key strategies is an illuminating strategic exercise in itself. Frequently, the translation from abstract aspiration to something countable reveals differences of opinion within a leadership team or helps home in on a specific audience or outcomes of importance. In these cases, arguments are not a failure; they are an essential part of the process of getting to clarity and meaningful alignment.

3M's "New Product Vitality Index"—the proportion of revenue coming from products less than five years old—is a good example of a durable metric, aligned to the core strategy of 3M as an innovation company. The 30% goal for this metric helps guide decisions around determining investment priorities and operational goals, and other decisions to ensure that their product portfolio is appropriately refreshing and the company does not risk irrelevance through resting on stale products.

"Internal mobility" is an example of a people goal that can be operationally defined in several different ways. One organization might choose a goal of 50% of roles being filled with internal candidates. Another might focus specifically on filling 75% manager roles from within the company. A third could focus on how long employees are staying in their roles, with a goal of no more than 20% of employees below a certain level going more than 36 months without a promotion or job move. Each of these reflects a nuance in a talent strategy that may emerge only when taking the time to build out a metric.

Organizational leaders are well served by taking the time to identify key strategic people metrics in order to effectively manage their organizations and drive strategic people decisions. Failure to identify, manage, and measure key people outcomes leaves ambiguity in the organization, which in turn dampens performance. Depending on the nature of the company, the culture, and the population, a number of metrics could be appropriate, but all organizations need a handful that are aligned to their particular needs and strategies.

Here are some examples of people-centered metrics for effectiveness against different strategic priorities:

1. An organization focused on *efficiency* might examine *actual headcount* as a *percentage of budgeted* headcount.
2. One with a core strategy about *talent attraction* might instead consider *offer acceptance rate.*
3. An organization for which *stability* is critical might instead choose to focus on the proportion of *leadership positions filled from succession plans* as they consider the success of their people strategies.
4. An organization prioritizing *developing and retaining* their staff may focus on a metric like *internal mobility* in the form of measuring the percentage of people who change roles through *transfer or promotion* in a given year.

5. An organization with an emphasis on *performance* may track involuntary attrition or *performance improvements* against critical quantitative outputs.
6. An organization navigating an *acquisition integration* may monitor *sentiment* for problem areas or risks.
7. An organization *changing strategies* (for example, adopting AI) might capture *skill demonstration* aligned with the new strategy as a measure of progress toward full performance.

The next step is to translate these strategic priorities into a set of more granular, nearer-term indicators, aligned to those key, durable top strategic measures. These are things organizations might adjust periodically to make sure the overall trend is supporting the key strategic goals. If those top metrics can be thought of as capturing strategy, this next set of measures are more aligned to individual component parts that contribute to the success of those strategies. Where leaders are accountable for the top strategic measures depending on the situation, it may be appropriate for program managers or others to be accountable for this larger set of indicators. Some samples can be seen in Table 7.1.

Table 7.1 Sample Strategic Measures and Related Granular Indicators

Top Strategic Measures	Granular Indicators
• Actual headcount as a percentage of budgeted headcount	• Average time to fill open roles • Attrition rate • Engagement survey—intent to stay
• Offer accept rate	• Offer declines for compensation • Offer declines for location • Offer declines for type or level of work
• Leadership roles filled from succession plans	• Succession plan completeness ("Ready now" successors) • Succession plan uniqueness • Attrition among successors • Engagement survey—confidence in leaders
• Internal mobility—% of staff who are transferred or promoted	• % of staff who are promoted • % of staff who transfer to a new team but keep the same job profile • % of staff who transfer into a new job profile • Engagement survey—confidence in career opportunity

Top Strategic Measures	Granular Indicators
• Performance improvement (quality, speed, capacity, cost, etc.)	• Cycle time improvement • Defect rate reduction • Uptime • Cost reductions • Engagement survey—have what I need to succeed
• Acquisition—top line sentiment	• Intent to stay (as measured by survey or stay interviews) of acquired employees • Attrition of acquired employees • Performance outcomes of acquired employees • Promotion rates of acquired employees (compared to acquiring)
• Strategy shift—new skills	• Training rates for new skills • 360-degree evaluation of new skills • Promotion rates and performance outcomes for those with new skills • Attrition rates for those with new skills

Operational Measures

Operational measures are generally owned by managers or by others who are more directly responsible for various strategies and programs within an organization. These indicators tell leaders and managers whether the organization is trending toward success and provide the organization early opportunities to change course as necessary.

Not all organizations and teams will have specific, intentional people strategies, and therefore may not find value in strategic measures like those we have already discussed. Even in those cases, organizations will benefit from detailed operational monitoring of their people data and metrics. While the list of metrics that could be captured approaches the infinite, a sample of typical metrics for organization leaders to consider tracking are shown in Table 7.2. Leaders can identify a selection of core metrics, aligned to their key priorities or areas of risk, to consider on a regular basis.

The list in Table 7.2 explicitly does not include diversity data and metrics. Personal demographic characteristics are typically considered sensitive information, and access to that information may be restricted. Where it is legal and appropriate, many of the measures listed in Table 7.2 can also be examined for inconsistencies among demographic groups. Any inconsistencies found could indicate a problem that HR should explore.

Table 7.2 Sample Operational Measures

Top Strategic Measures	Granular Indicators
• Headcount	• Hires • Current headcount • Actual vs. budgeted headcount • Cost per head • Attrition
• Recruiting	• Time to fill • Offer accept rate • Time to full performance • Quality of hire • First year attrition • Recruiting cost to fill • Pass through rate • Interview hours per hire
• Compliance	• % Mandatory training completion • % Policy violations • % Exits for policy violations
• Operational effectiveness and efficiency	• Revenue per employee • Profit per employee
• Organizational health	• % New employees (e.g., less than one year) • % New managers (e.g., less than one year as manager) • Average tenure
• Organization design	• Average span of control • Level mix • Ratio of staff to line roles • % Co-location (e.g., employees co-located with at least one teammate)
• Careers and engagement	• % Internal transfers • % Employees with development plans • % Engagement (employee survey) • % Intent to stay (employee survey)
• Attrition and absenteeism	• % Absenteeism • % Attrition for top performers • % Attrition for leaders • Exit rate for poor performers
• Performance and promotion	• % Promotions • % Top performers without promotions • % Below-standard performance/poor performers
• Leadership and succession	• % Leadership roles filled from succession plans • Ratio of unique successors to targeted roles

Evaluating Metrics

Identifying data or metrics to monitor is important but, ultimately, organizations must also determine how to evaluate those data, and how to evaluate changes in those data. That is, leaders must put a stake in the ground about what good looks like. One common approach is to explore using benchmarks to determine whether the organization is doing well in comparison to others. Benchmarks can offer an external comparison, frequently against leading organizations or leading practices, although comparing units within an organization, or comparing the same organization to a prior time period, can also be effective and often offer more apples-to-apples comparisons. Generative AI tools can provide tempting certainty about what "typical" practices or performance might be; be aware that these are usually inferences rather than specific, verifiable data points.

There are at least three cautions to bear in mind when considering external benchmarks. First, when benchmarks are collected across separate organizations, rather than separate units within an organization, definitions and terminology can differ, resulting in comparisons that are essentially apples and oranges. A few examples can illustrate this problem:

- *Level comparisons*: Where employees' levels may be described the same way— e.g., "Grade 5"—the responsibilities and scope can differ substantially from one company to the next, or even within the same company, particularly if that organization operates in multiple countries or has been built by acquisition.
- *Span of control calculations*: These might vary dramatically, with some organizations including open roles, various forms of temporary workers such as interns and contractors, and administrative staff in their span of control numbers—and others not.
- *Organizational design differences*: Differences in how jobs and even departments are constructed and described might mean that the way one organization describes its ratio of staff to line roles could be quite different.
- *Attrition calculations*: Attrition, often a hot topic, is notorious for the different definitions that can be applied: Do retirements count as attrition? Deaths? Exits of temporary workers or those on short-term contracts? Do exits during a probationary period count? Do we count exits of people who were on a performance improvement plan differently

from other exits? Do we track voluntary and involuntary exits differently? Are layoffs included in attrition calculations? Simply asking for an "attrition rate" might yield very different results depending on answers to questions like these, even for the same period of time in the same organization.
- *Sentiment measurement*: How exactly are the questions and response scales worded? Is a midpoint included in the scale? Does the reporting reflect a percent favorable, a mean score, or a metric like Net Promoter Score?

These discrepancies abound, both in implementation and interpretation of the benchmarks. Inconsistencies like these mean that it is important for organizations to interpret many external benchmarks with some degree of caution. To be fair, there are some benchmarks and benchmarking organizations that have put significant work into ensuring consistency across organizations; in particular, there are some benchmarks for compensation (e.g., Radford), and some sentiment consortia (e.g., Mayflower Group) fall into this category.

Second, benchmarks are typically not sensitive to the features that make organizations unique. These can include fairly essential things like assets and strategies. For example, revenue per employee might differ dramatically between firms that sell similar products, where one produces those products in house and the other outsources the manufacturing and distribution. In that case, revenue per employee would likely be dramatically different. Average pay, attrition rates, injury rates, time to hire, junior/senior mix, and many others would likely be materially different between them. Most generalizable benchmarks consider employees (those directly employed by the organization), rather than considering workers (all those individuals in the flow of work, independent of their direct employer). A simple benchmark in this case could be quite misleading. Differences such as these are real, and can make it such that a very general benchmark is not applicable to an organization with unique characteristics. Finding other organizations with similar traits to benchmark against is helpful.

Third, benchmarks operate outside of strategy. They are generally constructed to reflect a specific segment of the performance distribution across organizations. Sometimes this is represented as an average or typical approach or performance. In other cases, it is framed inspirationally, highlighting the practices or performance at the top of the class. The only way to know whether average is "good enough" is to have a clear idea of your strategic differentiators. Occasionally, a benchmarking study reveals that no one is doing a particular thing very well. In the absence of strategy, it can feel like a relief to learn that you are not behind. If your strategy hinges on being effective at something, then learning that others are behind can help you understand the size of your strategic advantage in being the first to master this something.

Some (e.g., Levenson, 2015) have argued that, at best, benchmarks can drive to a sort of average performance. Thus, benchmarks may be useful in ensuring efficient operations in the more commodity areas of your business or organization, but savvy organization leaders will leave benchmarks aside and align their structures and practices to the demands of their strategies in those areas that are most unique, or those areas where they are driving differentiation for competitive advantage. The flip side of this coin is that an organization which does not in some way incorporate benchmarking into its strategy, and instead leans heavily on sets of "ever better" goals, risks setting up a demoralizing culture: as the theoretical maximum is achieved, the capability is no longer there to get better, but the goal may still remain. This approach also creates conditions of diminishing returns; continued metric improvements may no longer produce meaningful overall performance improvements.

Advances in AI are also likely to dramatically distort benchmarks as some organizations adopt new AI capabilities more quickly or more broadly. While there are certainly significant efficiency gains from technology advances, in some cases the workload and cost will be moving from one team or organization into another; fully accounting for the larger system of work is important for apples-to-apples comparisons, especially where cost and efficiency are key considerations.

In some cases, such as span of control or attrition, a benchmark may function as a goal. However, there are additional and often better ways to set a performance target or mechanism for evaluating a specific metric. In some cases, a goal is rooted not in what others have shown to be achievable, but in the performance level required to support or deliver a higher-order organizational outcome. While this will more often be the case for business metrics rather than people metrics, it is possible to develop goals by working backward from a necessary outcome to the performance required in the component parts to achieve that outcome. Other goal-setting strategies can include incremental performance improvements—for example, a 10% improvement in some outcome or other. It is often wise to examine the full range of current performance and set a target or goal at the upper end of current performance rather than beyond what any team is producing today; we have long known that specific, challenging goals help support good performance, but unachievable goals will have the opposite effect (e.g., Locke & Latham, 1984).

In some cases, a goal is inappropriate; for example, it would be inappropriate to have a goal around Family Medical Leave utilization. Rather, in situations like these, tracking leave utilization is not about triggering action to increase or decrease leaves; it is about identifying thresholds where additional leave coverage strategies, such as engaging contractors or offering temporary transfers as stretch assignments, might be necessary. In this case, the leaves themselves are not where the goals are set—but rather the volume of temporarily unfilled roles.

It is important for organizations to have mechanisms for ensuring that they are not creating harmful unintended consequences in pursuing their strategies and goals. Building out guardrails to monitor alongside the goals is a useful strategy. These guardrails are in essence a type of goal that is about staying within a healthy, realistic, and effective zone for whatever is being measured. Guardrails are useful when it is important to maintain—rather than to change—something, and specifically to ensure that improvements in one domain do not come at the expense of a different domain. Guardrails are in essence a measurement system against unintended consequences.

Often these types of data and information work together. For example, an organization may wish to reduce its cost to hire, but wants to ensure that efficiency in hiring does not come at the expense of lowered quality of hire or increased attrition. In this case, the measurement system may include:

1. An external *benchmark* about cost to hire for a particular skill set in a specific industry or geography
2. A *goal* around reduction of a certain percent for cost to hire
3. *Guardrails* requiring no change in 90-day quality of hire or overall attrition

In this way, multiple approaches to considering data come together to frame an organizational strategy or tactic.

Effectively Generating Insight with Data

Addressing metrics and reporting typically forms the bulk of most data teams' data work, and will form the core of ongoing data that a leader should consider. However, some of the most important data work falls in a different category—insight work. Here, leaders and organizations look to data to inform their strategic choices.

It is natural for people to arrive at a hypothesis and then seek data to support what they already think. In fact, it is so common that there is a name for it—confirmation bias, the tendency to interpret information in a way that supports your existing ideas (e.g., Hart et al., 2009). While this approach to data can be very satisfying, it is ultimately risky, as it allows faulty assumptions to persist and robs leaders of opportunities to thoughtfully consider alternative, better approaches.

Fortunately, there are well-established alternative approaches that support effective use of data in decision-making. One common method is to set up an A/B test. In large organizations this can look like a pilot test, where a change is implemented in one store or shift or other unit as an opportunity to evaluate impacts and risks. Analytically, it is important to compare the change (or lack thereof) in the unit with the intervention compared to the change (or lack thereof) in a matched unit that did not receive the intervention. In A/B tests, finding valid comparison groups is important so that researchers can be reasonably confident that the intervention is the only difference, and therefore can reasonably be assumed to be the cause of changes in performance. Validity, in this case, refers to finding groups with sufficiently similar characteristics and sufficiently high numbers. Simply seeing a difference in the pilot unit at the end of the experiment does not necessarily mean that the intervention was the cause; identifying a valid comparison group in advance is an important way to gain confidence in the effect of the intervention apart from other factors that might be happening at the same time.

Other data-driven improvement approaches are common in business and can have good applicability to people practices in organizations. Approaches like Six Sigma (e.g., Tennant, 2001), which seeks to identify and eliminate sources of variability (quality defects) in a process, and approaches like Lean (e.g., Krafcik, 1988), which focus on removing waste from a system or process, can be effectively applied to identify sources of improvement opportunity.

Organizations frequently request models that can forecast people outcomes, and attrition is generally at the top of the list. Attrition is expensive and disruptive, and employees leaving the company are easily counted. While in some situations, attrition is good, the effort and expense of recruiting and training new employees is significant, as can be the disruption when a valued employee leaves, and her or his work must be covered by others. It can be very tempting to develop a crystal ball to identify, in advance, where and how significant attrition risks are in an organization. However, for most organizations, attrition is materially influenced by factors outside of the organization, such as the larger economy or labor market. So once again, the data from the larger context and system must be factored into the analysis in order to identify the useful and appropriate insights.

Additionally, attrition forecasting has some specific considerations that other forecasting models might not, such as important questions about whether individual employees are identified as attrition risks, to whom they are identified, and what actions may be taken based on that risk assessment. Given the risks associated with individual identification, it is generally recommended to report attrition forecasts at an aggregate level and use those forecasts to inform decisions like adjustments to hiring strategies and fine-tuning core operational functions like ensuring the optimal staffing level for a recruiting team rather than deploying individual level interventions with specific at-risk employees.

While it can be very tempting to consider individual employee-level strategies, it is not only unethical, but also risks creating self-fulfilling prophesies; if a manager believes that Employee A is at risk for exit, that manager is less likely to invest in that employee. In turn, the employee, seeing better assignments go to peers or similar hedges from the manager, sees fewer reasons to stay and is more open to external possibilities. In this case, the manager inadvertently created the very circumstance he or she wished to avoid.

Qualitative Data

Insight work in teams and organizations often benefits from a combination of quantitative (numerical) data and qualitative (more categorical) data. When considering attrition, for example, it is helpful to understand why people are choosing to leave—through exit surveys, exit interviews, or examination of outcomes, behavior, and sentiment in the period leading to their departure. An entire chapter could be devoted to how to obtain and use good qualitative data, but once again that is beyond our scope here. For now, suffice it to say that qualitative and quantitative data are complementary measurements, and the insights gained from their combined use can be more meaningful and accurate than either system used on its own. And, just as there are pitfalls in how quantitative data are used, similar pitfalls apply when obtaining and interpreting qualitative data. Finding the right people to do this work is worth the time.

While business leaders may be more comfortable with quantitative data, qualitative data can offer rich meaning as to why something is happening—and knowing why something is happening is important to changing it. For example, quantitative data may reveal that one unit experiences more quality defects than a comparable one, but qualitative data may be most helpful in uncovering the reasons behind the difference, and, therefore, the best opportunities to bring the lesser-performing unit up to the standards of the better-performing one.

Common sources of qualitative data include employee surveys (especially regular sentiment and exit surveys), live conversations in the form of interviews, focus groups, or increasingly, data gathered through automated and AI tools. While all of these approaches seem very straightforward, effectively building them to enable useful information requires not only forethought but also specific expertise. In particular, when seeking to improve organizational performance, the ability to prioritize problems or opportunities is an important part of qualitative work. Asking for ratings based on importance as well as satisfaction, for example, can help prioritize risks identified through the qualitative exercise. Categorical sorting or ranking can also help leaders focus on the most pressing of problems identified.

In practice, this may look like an open conversation or brainstorming exercise, followed by a prioritization exercise in the form of ratings, rankings, or categorizing to identify the most critical opportunities. In addition, where privacy policies allow, teams and organizations can use large language models to ingest and categorize the most frequently mentioned challenges employees are experiencing in their work from sources like employee surveys or internal communication tools such as Slack.

Doing effective, high quality qualitative work is more complicated than it seems; ensuring that the participants feel able to be honest and that the lines of inquiry generate results that are useful and accurate is a subspecialty of its own. Where qualitative work is required, organizations are generally well advised to seek the help of a neutral third party with specialized capabilities in qualitative research to ensure the best results.

Qualitative methods have the advantage of exploring not only what is currently creating barriers to effective performance, but also what could make things better. This can come in the form of direct questions in qualitative exercises as well as through exploring practices or features that differentiate better-performing groups or units from worse-performing ones, and applying those better-performing practices more broadly. Experts in qualitative research are able to help people articulate issues, opportunities, and ideas to reveal insights that can be relevant and helpful.

To the extent that insight work is generally undertaken with an eye toward improvement, it is important to ensure that analyses do not unintentionally obscure the interesting parts. Frequently, group averages or a total of some sort are collected and analyzed. When seeking to improve performance, however, the greatest opportunities are in the places with the highest variability. To that end, leaders and analysts supporting them should consider including tools and techniques that highlight the variability of the data obtained. These might include calculating standard deviations, displaying whisker plots, or using scatter plots to evaluate the full data set.

Presenting Data

Both management and insight data benefit from effective visualization. Data visualization is not simply a matter of beautification; good data visualization makes patterns apparent and simplifies comparisons. Data patterns are often more quickly and easily processed when presented visually rather than in a tabular format. Progress against a goal, comparisons to similar units, and performance compared to a prior year are all more easily grasped when presented visually.

There is a robust literature (e.g., Nussbaumer Knaflic, 2015) and practice community for good data visualization. Fully exploring this is beyond the scope of this chapter. Common methods for the sorts of people data we are describing in this chapter will include proportions, comparisons, distributions, and changes over time, or time series. In each of these, thoughtful choices about what to display can make discerning the underlying story easier.

A lot of organizational data are some form of a time series. It can also be helpful to consider different ways to present time series data. Most organizations will track headcount and headcount changes. Here are three different examples of how to express monthly total headcount for an organization over a three-year period. The approach will be similar for other sorts of time series data, such as changes in attrition over time.

Figure 7.1 is simply total headcount per month over the entire three-year period. Here, the volatility is apparent, as is the fact that starting and ending headcount are quite similar to one another. Figure 7.2 shows the same data, but lays the years over one another to make the seasonality more obvious. In Figure 7.3, the patterns are expressed as change in headcount throughout the year. Here, rather than counting absolute values as in the previous two charts, the chart shows change from headcount on January 1. Finally, Figure 7.4 displays the data for the theoretical Year 3 used in the prior examples, but in the form of a waterfall chart. A simplified single year headcount waterfall shows realized exits, forecasted future exits, realized hires, forecasted future hires, and a planned upcoming unit divestiture. This style of chart has the added benefit of showing both additions (hires) and subtractions (exits) rather than just net change, allowing better determination of risks and opportunities.

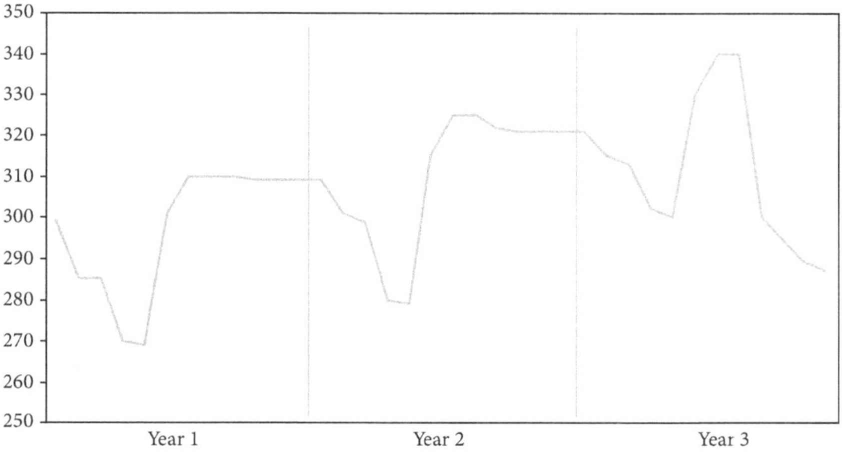

Figure 7.1 An Example of Showing a Simple Trend over Three Years, Emphasizing Volatility of the Data for the Entire Period

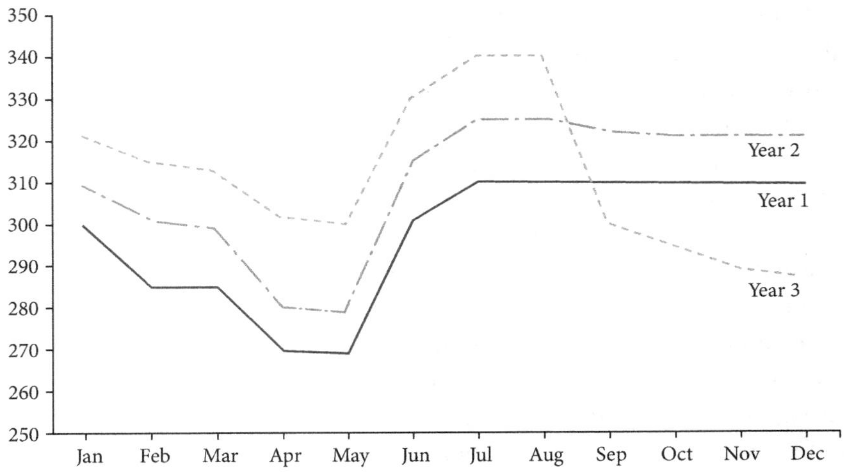

Figure 7.2 An Example of a Year-over-Year Chart, Showing the Relationships between the Three Years Including Possible Seasonality

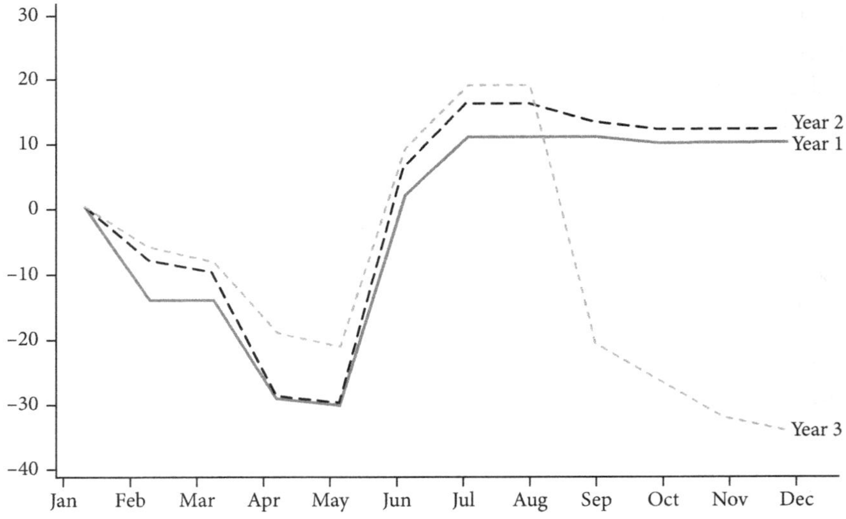

Figure 7.3 Ignoring the Absolute Values for Headcount, Instead Focusing on the Positive or Negative Delta in Headcount over the Course of Three Years

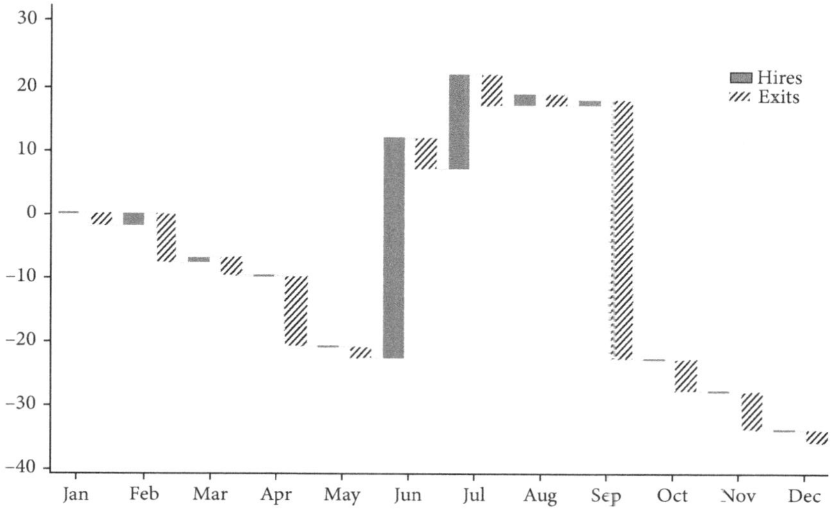

Figure 7.4 A Waterfall Chart Showing the Contributions of Hiring and Exits (Two Bars per Month) to the Headcount for a Single Year as They Relate to the Trend for Headcount

When and How to Share Data

Modern tools, including new generative AI tools, make always-on reporting easy and accessible. Many modern data-reporting platforms allow configuration of custom reports that can be repeated and set to a schedule to run and be delivered to a target user, supporting consistent definitions and calculations, and therefore removing sources of error and confusion that can come with one-off reports or generative AI queries.

A lot of business data are highly volatile, making it reasonable to examine results frequently or even continuously. In most cases, HR data change more slowly. Promotions and performance reviews often happen at fixed times of the year, meaning that any promotion or performance data would be analyzed and considered only then. While organizations increasingly gather sentiment data continuously, the small sample sizes often used mean that data must be aggregated over days or weeks to have a large enough pool of responses to be reliable. Many organizations have significant seasonality to their hiring, making recruiting data most valuable at specific times. On the other hand, span of control and office location are generally quite stable.

All of this means that it is generally advisable to review people metrics on a less frequent basis. Some data need only be reviewed annually, such as performance data, while others will be appropriate for quarterly or monthly consideration. Attrition is often considered more frequently; even so, monthly is generally adequate for most teams' or organizations' needs. Given the costs and consequences of headcount overall, many organizations will examine headcount on a monthly basis, and some will assess headcount even more frequently.

Most modern systems will allow both "pull" (the user actively navigates to the report or data) and "push" (the system generates and sends data or reports on a pre-set schedule) functionality. Many online systems suffer from low monthly active users; that is, people do not proactively review the data on a regular basis. Systems can be designed in such a way that people are notified if interesting or alarming thresholds are being approached in either direction, putting the burden of monitoring the metrics on the system, rather than individuals with other work to do. This is a space where advanced analytics can be extremely helpful; an automated tool can more easily search a large data set for outliers that might indicate a risk. Automated tools can search much more quickly and much more thoroughly than a human. At a minimum, overall people data should be considered as part of an annual strategic planning process.

Conclusion

Managing any organization at scale requires a thoughtful data strategy to ensure effective operations. Building out a coherent, strategically aligned approach to supporting and managing the human resources of an organization can help mitigate risk and accelerate performance. Intentionally designing an approach to obtaining and interpreting data, setting strategic goals, and revisiting all of that over time seems prima facie daunting and of questionable return on investment. However, organizations that have done so have reaped the benefits of this approach, and the results are reflected in their bottom lines.

References

Hart, W., Albarracin, D., Eagly, A. H., Brechan, I., Lindberg, M. J., & Merrill, L. (2009). Feeling validated versus being correct: A meta-analysis of selective exposure to information. *Psychological Bulletin*, *135*(4), 555–588. https://doi.org/10.1037/a0015701

Krafcik, J. F. (1988) Triumph of the Lean Production System. *Sloan Management Review, 30*, 41–52.

Levenson, A. (2015). *Strategic analytics: Advancing strategy execution and organizational effectiveness*. Berrett-Koehler Publishers.

Locke, E. A., & Latham, G. P. (1984). *Goal setting: A motivational technique that works!* Prentice Hall.

Nussbaumer Knaflic, C. (2015). *Storytelling with data: A data visualization guide for business professionals*. John Wiley & Sons.

Rolfe, G., Jasper, M., & Freshwater, D. (2001). *Critical reflection for nursing and the helping professions: A user's guide*. Palgrave Macmillan.

Tennant, G. (2001). *SIX SIGMA: SPC and TQM in manufacturing and services*. Gower Publishing, Ltd.

8

Leadership Development in the Age of Analytics and AI

Context Matters

Haig R. Nalbantian

Introduction

The executive committee of a major global consumer products company—"ConsumerCo"—was determined to significantly increase the diversity of its managerial workforce and executive leadership.[1] As the company's growth was largely driven by expansion in markets outside the United States and Europe and by a consumer base that was primarily female and increasingly non-white, the consensus view was that the future success of the business required changes in their leadership profile. Traditional corporate diversity, equity, and inclusion (DEI) efforts emphasizing hiring and career development had failed to significantly change the demographic makeup of their managerial population and executive leadership. The committee sought to better understand the reasons why and aggressively address the problem. They turned to their data and advanced analytics to uncover the root causes of their failures.

The analysis team examined the running record of the company's workforce data housed in their human resources information system (HRIS). Specifically, they statistically modeled the drivers of promotion, performance, retention, and pay, the key talent flows and rewards that ultimately create an organization's workforce. The analysis of these "internal labor market (ILM)" dynamics (Nalbantian et al., 2004) revealed a number of factors impeding the ability of ConsumerCo to sustainably increase representation of women and people of color in the middle and upper ranks.[2] One of the major impediments was the operation of their integrated talent

Haig R. Nalbantian, *Leadership Development in the Age of Analytics and AI*. In: *The Changing Leadership Landscape*. Edited by: Sheri L. Feinzig and Mariangela Battista, Oxford University Press. © Oxford University Press (2026). DOI: 10.1093/9780197820070.003.0008 evaluation and performance management system which was a lynchpin of their approach to leadership development (LD).

ConsumerCo had long embraced a "nine-box" approach to talent and performance management, eliciting reviews and ratings of salaried employees on both performance "results" and leadership capability and effectiveness, each on a three-point scale.[3] The analysis revealed that, all else being equal, women and people of color (with the exception of one racial group) were equally likely to be rated highly on "results" as their male and white counterparts respectively. On the other hand, people of color were significantly less likely to receive a high rating on the leadership dimension, with estimated disparities ranging from a low of roughly −17% to a high of over −36%, depending on the specific racial group considered. Given the strong weight of leadership ratings in predicting promotion and turnover probabilities, the career impact of these disparities in leadership ratings was devastating. Moreover, there was high year-to-year persistence in leadership ratings which made the promotion barrier more like a concrete wall.

The executive committee was shocked and genuinely perturbed by these findings. It was unfathomable to them that there could be such a wide and persistent demographic gap between "results" and "leadership" ratings. Aside from outright bias, an obvious explanation for the gap lay in the leadership model on which the company was relying. In effect, the company was operating a monolithic, one-size-fits-all model of leadership, one that identified a set of favored factors—attributes, work experiences, and behaviors—ostensibly associated with leadership effectiveness. The factors that defined effectiveness at ConsumerCo mirrored those of current members of the executive team which consisted almost completely of middle-aged, white males who had come up through the ranks. If leadership assessments hewed to a model that favored factors representative of the current leadership team—something exceedingly common in practice—it should be no surprise that the organization would continue to replicate the existing leadership profile and thwart efforts to advance diversity in the company's managerial and executive ranks.

The executives of ConsumerCo recognized that their current approach to LD was inconsistent with business needs. Wholesale transformation was required. They decided to abandon the nine-box and build a new, multidimensional model of leadership, one that embraced the notion that effective leadership can manifest itself in different ways and often carries a cultural dimension. For instance, not every "leader" may be publicly vocal, muscularly assertive, or exhibit a Western-style, "take-charge" mentality that often entails calling attention to one's own accomplishments. Some leaders may be more reticent, more modest and reflective, and still be effective in their roles. Their leadership may be exhibited by becoming the "go-to" members of their teams. They lead quietly by example. ConsumerCo's executives recognized that there were likely many future leaders being overlooked as a consequence of the imposition of a monolithic model.

Monolithic LD models also fail to recognize the contextual nature of effective leadership. What makes for good leadership in one setting or historically may not make for good leadership in another setting or as business and cultural realities change. Relying on a rigid, narrowly specified leadership profile can prevent adaptation to contextual factors and new realities. ConsumerCo's leaders were largely home-grown. The company was strongly oriented to build-from-within, emphasizing career value as the basis of rewards. Prior DEI efforts had prioritized hiring senior female and minority talent directly into executive levels because the company wanted to show quick progress. But no matter how capable these new hires were, no matter how accomplished their track record, it could be overwhelmingly challenging to quickly navigate an environment where institutional knowledge and know-how, and the strength and duration of internal networks, were pivotal to success. The cards were stacked against them. Not surprisingly, senior hires did not stick. A DEI strategy oriented to "buying" diverse talent was in direct conflict with a leadership and talent model anchored in a "build" strategy. These could not be reconciled without major revision in the organization's approach to LD and talent management.

The executive committee's decisive action to start fresh with their LD and talent models signaled the end of business as usual. The impact was swift and large. Within a couple of years, they succeeded in diversifying their management and senior leadership. They adjusted their DEI strategy to align hiring and career development with the build-talent strategy of the firm, bolstering the strength of their leadership pipeline. The fact that business results, including shareholder return, improved dramatically as well gave further credence to the value of the LD and talent management revolution they had launched.[4]

The ConsumerCo story highlights issues that lie at the heart of changes in how leaders can and should be developed in organizations. It speaks to the perils of monolithic LD models that rely on pre-set, generic characteristics, either from established research or from assessments of the attributes of the current leadership team. It reveals what can happen when an organization fails to recognize the contextual nature of effective leadership. It shows how LD interacts with other components of workforce strategy—in this case, the company's talent and DEI strategies—acting as part of a system of practices that influence the kind of leadership an organization secures. In these circumstances, achieving alignment with other system components may be more important to success than implementing any so-called LD "best practice." Finally, it shows how a rigorous, analytics-based approach, relying on advanced analytics applied to longitudinal data, can help objectively identify key drivers of leadership effectiveness and the factors that condition their influence. In the rest of this chapter, we dig deeper into the value of analytics-based LD and the specific methods that can bring this approach to fruition.

LD in Theory and Practice

Leadership effectiveness and development is one of the most researched areas in the domain of human capital management. Academic approaches to LD have typically involved identification of different models and "styles" of leadership, as well as detailing sets of attributes and behaviors required to execute these models successfully. Some models are most applicable to "steady-state" environments where change is incremental and top priorities for leaders are to maintain stable, efficient operations and anticipate and manage economic and operational risks. The Transactional Leadership Model (Burns, 1978; Bass, 1985; Judge & Piccolo, 2004) and Custodial Leadership Model (Davis, 1981) are prominent examples of this thinking. Broadly speaking, they emphasize task orientation, hands-on supervision, performance management and performance-based rewards. Other models are designed to recognize the unique requirements of leading organizations through major business transformation. The focus is on what is needed to navigate major business transitions, often technologically driven. They are also concerned with leading through economic turbulence and the special attributes required to do so successfully. For example, the Transformational Model emphasizes an appeal to "higher-order" motivations of employees and their developmental needs to support employee commitment to achieving a clearly articulated vision of organizational direction (Burns, 1978; Bass, 1985; Wang et. al. 2011). This approach is viewed as most relevant to innovation-dependent organizations in fast-changing sectors like the technology sector. The Servant Leadership Model, with its employee-centric perspective, focuses on worker well-being, growth, teamwork, collaboration, and employee empowerment, and also aligns with change environments by fostering organizational cohesion and what might be called reflexive adaptability to changing business conditions and requirements (Greenleaf, 1970, 1977; Van Dierendonck, 2011).[5]

Another category of LD models, competency-based models, are less focused on overall leadership styles than on the specific attributes, skills, and behaviors—"competencies"—associated with effective leaders (McClelland, 1961; Boyatzis, 1982; Spencer & Spencer, 1993).[6] They emphasize continuous assessments, often involving 360-degree feedback, to ensure learning and development programs are geared to promote essential competencies and address identified shortfalls in the competencies and experience of prospective leaders. These models became dominant in practice in the late 1990s and the first decade of the twenty-first century, with companies adapting them to the unique requirements of their business.

Some practitioners have applied stylized models of leadership, developed in academia, following the academic playbook. General Electric and IBM are famous for their extensive investments in LD, each creating home-grown competency models that integrated features of different academic models. Ford Motor company partnered with the leadership guru Noel Tichy to build their approach to LD around his constructs of "leaders at all levels," leaders as teachers, continuous learning through formal training, and on-the-job learning (Tichy & Cohen, 1997; Tichy, 2002). LD programs emphasized internal mobility.

Many practitioners have applied competency-based models in a more eclectic, ad hoc manner. Their approach has involved careful scrutiny of what makes for effective leadership within their own walls, eliciting input from successful (effective) leaders in their midst, especially top executives. As with ConsumerCo, they look to what made their own executives successful to inform the selection of potential leadership talent as well as training and development needs of up-and-coming leaders, and to support succession planning.

Measuring LD Effectiveness

The customized, competency-based approach to LD is only as sound as the markers of success that are used to define "effectiveness:" How accurate and predictive of future success are the performance measures used for evaluation purposes? The rapid proliferation of electronic data systems, increased accessibility of analytical tools, and now the advent of widely available AI tools and methods enables a more disciplined and expansive assessment of the factors making for effective leadership.

A key requirement of this approach is determining which markers of success will be used for modeling purposes. What outcomes are you, in fact, trying to predict? The most common approach is to rely on individual outcomes associated with success—for example, individual performance ratings, rate and degree of promotions, or the trajectory of pay increases. These are common proxies for actual performance and effectiveness. Rather than relying completely on subjective assessments of what predicts these outcomes, organizations can build predictive models that attempt to identify and quantify causal relationships between attributes, capabilities, experiences, and a higher likelihood of success.

A key part of the methodology is empirical estimation of a success profile. The composition and ranking of the elements of such a success profile are drawn from coefficients estimated from models of critical outcomes. Figure 8.1 shows results from a model estimating the drivers of promotion probability in another large, global products firm, "ConsumerRetailCo."

Interestingly, the modeling revealed that all else being equal, situational or "circumstantial" factors dominated individual attributes in predicting career advancement among salaried and managerial employees. These factors included roles as well as business unit and supervisory relationships assigned to employees. At the very top of the list was expatriate experience. In this organization, being in an expatriate role was pivotal to success. While the direction of the result aligned with executive team expectations, the size of the effect surprised them. All else being equal, those who took such positions were almost 130% more likely to be promoted and over 200% more likely to receive a top performance rating, dominating other individual and situational factors. They effectively surged relative to their peers in advancing into leadership positions. Being in certain functions also conferred a large advantage as did reporting to high-performing and high-level supervisors.

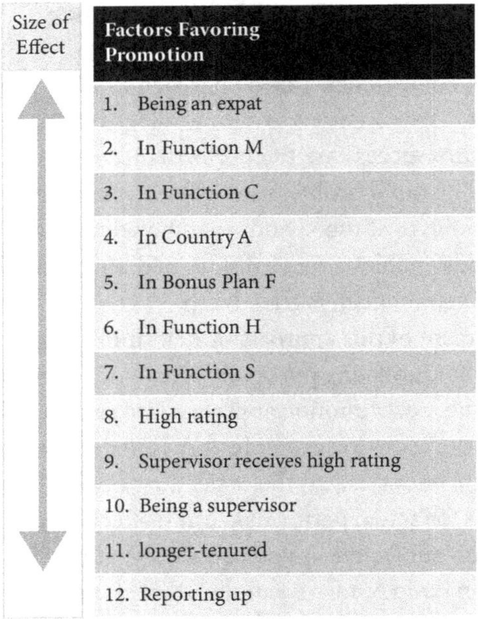

Based on results from estimation of multivariate statistical model of the drivers of promotion, incorporating individual, organizational and labor market factors.

Figure 8.1 ConsumerRetailCo's Empirically Determined Individual Success Profile

Length of service, an individual attribute, was predictive as well, though far less important than where the employee "sat" in the organization. This was critical to their developmental journey. For the leaders of ConsumerRetailCo, the key learning was that their LD model needed to be anchored in career development and proactively managed experience. Given that certain demographic groups were less likely to have the experience profile that predicted accession to leadership, the findings also helped them develop an action plan for increasing access of high-potential employees in under-represented groups to key roles, functions, and the more influential supervisors.

While Figure 8.1 only relates the ordinal ranking of the various factors covered, behind the rankings are quantitative estimates of the weights attached to these factors. This is an important benefit of the analytics-based approach described here. Quantification allows for prioritization of effects and suggested actions. LD experts often rely on directional relationships alone or on subjective determination of importance. But *economic* decisions require an understanding of dimension as well as direction because you are always comparing projected outcomes to known costs or estimated risks. The analytics-based approach permits LD experts to view leadership development through an economic lens as well as psychological or behavioral ones.

The outsized importance of situational factors at ConsumerRetailCo is something we see quite often when doing such modeling work. It raises important concerns about excessive reliance on individual outcomes as markers of true value and contribution. A good evaluation system needs to take into account the circumstances that affect the output of any work. This is an age-old challenge, but the advent of readily accessible data and analytics offers opportunities to address it effectively to support the design of effective LD programs.

Nowhere has this been more successful than in Major League Baseball, where the sabermetrics revolution has changed the very process by which talent is identified, developed, and managed. The decision makers in baseball have understood that individual performance always takes place in a group setting. It is affected by circumstances related to the caliber of the player's teammates, the decisions made by the team's manager, the quality of the player's coaches and resources supporting him, and the characteristics of the field the team plays on, among other things. To properly measure true value and contribution, it is necessary to account for these factors— i.e., "the hand you're dealt."

The analytics revolution allowed for the creation of a new set of "advanced" metrics in baseball that do just that. And it has had a huge effect on the evolution of the game and industry. To give an example, in 2010, the Seattle Mariners pitcher, Felix Hernandez, won the Cy Young Award as best pitcher in the American league despite having a won–lost record of 13–12—a paltry winning percentage of .52. He won against a field of other pitchers with 18, 19, and 21 wins and winning percentages over .70. Felix Hernandez had a winning percentage far below the norm ever considered worthy of notice. His "wins" were low, but the new measure—"Wins above Replacement" (W.A.R.)—was by far the highest of all the other pitchers considered. In effect, once you accounted for the fact that Hernandez played for a team that was weak offensively—they were lowest in runs scored, team batting average, and home runs—it was apparent that his performance was actually exceptional. He pitched far better than predicted given the hand he was dealt. Sabermetric analysis showed that the typical pitcher performing under the same conditions would have considerably fewer wins. Similar assessments were behind the Cy Young Awards earned by the pitcher, Jacob DeGrom, in 2018 and 2019. Despite his low winning percentages, his W.A.R. stood out, revealing capability and value otherwise obscured by traditional raw metrics. The latter reflected far more the adverse impact of his team's characteristics than his own remarkable contributions.[7]

The extensive use of advanced analytics in Major League Baseball allows the league to differentiate raw performance from true value or capability. Baseball today has arrived at a point where traditional raw measures are no longer emphasized—and new, more informative methods and measures of evaluation dominate. Can baseball's insights and approach translate to business organizations beyond the sports sector?

Analytics-Based LD in Practice: ClubCo goes to W.A.R.

A powerful example of how similar advanced analytics can be applied to develop more informative measures of value and capability, and how the resulting learnings can inform LD program development, is seen in the experience of a large national, not-for-profit organization that we will call "ClubCo" (Nalbantian, 2016). A few years back, the leadership of ClubCo set out to develop a new LD model to help advance the organization into a new era of growth and community impact. The mission of the organization was to provide educational and recreational services to communities throughout the United States, through active memberships of participants. The leaders of greatest interest to the executive team were those at the site and regional levels, the ones who forged and executed programs that drive membership and attendance and who were in charge of raising funds from state and local governments and from private foundations. ClubCo's senior leaders' objective was to create a new LD program customized to the organization's unique mission, operating model, and long-standing culture. Rather than rely on sector benchmarks or best practices from other leading not-for-profit service organizations, they decided to look for their own best practices within. They deployed a combination of quantitative and qualitative analytics to empirically identify the factors most associated with effective leadership at ClubCo.

Here are the key precepts behind ClubCo's approach to developing their LD model:

- The leadership model is about the *future*: it must deliver the capabilities, experience, and behaviors required to meet *future* organizational requirements.
- One size does not fit all: what makes for a good leader in one environment may not be the same in another environment.
- Decisions about the shape and content of the leadership model should be fact-based and keyed to learnings specific to the organization, not generic formulas or presumed universal "truths."
- Empirical identification of factors driving leader success at ClubCo should play the central role in shaping the LD model.

Critical to ClubCo's approach was recognition that inferences drawn from analysis of the factors influencing leader effectiveness were only as good as the performance measures on which the analysis is based. Like Major League Baseball, they appreciated that the raw performance measures on which they typically relied—i.e., unit or regional income, grants received, membership levels and growth, total customers served, attendance—may mask true leader effectiveness because they fail to account for environmental or situational factors that systematically affect these outcomes but have little to do with the local leader's actual contribution. So, for example, raising funds is easier in an affluent suburb than it is in a low-income, inner-city neighborhood. Achieving high attendance may be less challenging in an area with great facilities and easily accessible transportation than in one where facilities are old and run-down and transportation hard to come by. As such, to the extent performance measures could be adjusted to tease out the effects of such situational factors and capture performance relative to "expectation," the reliability of these measures in identifying true value would be enhanced.

The analysis team constructed a predictive model of performance using the "production function" construct from economics. As shown in Figure 8.2, the conceptual model mapped how individual club leader characteristics and behaviors translated into financial and operational outcomes, conditional on the influence of a set of situational factors—i.e., location and customer/member characteristics, unit facilities/infrastructure, unit human capital—and random noise that also affects those outcomes.

Multivariate regression modeling was applied to multiple years of unit and regional facility-level data to estimate the marginal impact of these various factors—bucketed as environmental ("E-Factor"), managerial ("M-Factor"), and human capital ("H-Factor"). The analysis covered

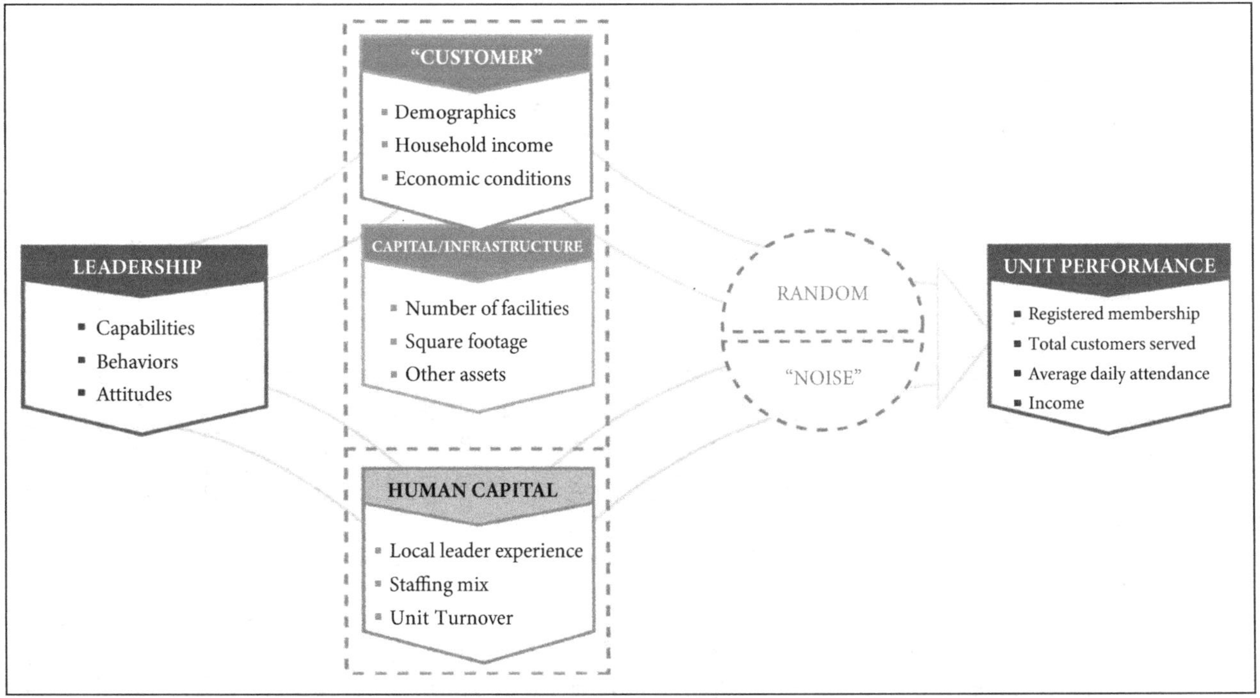

Figure 8.2 The Leader "Production Function:" Modeling the Impact of Leader Capabilities on Business Results
Source: Nalbantian (2016).

the characteristics and performance of hundreds of local units across the United States over multiple years. Estimated coefficients were used to create a hierarchy of influence as shown (impressionistically) in Figure 8.3.

The estimated coefficients were then used to create an "expected" performance level for each unit leader across the various dimensions of performance. The organization could then compare raw performance to expected performance of each unit leader to create a new composite measure of effectiveness, analogous to "W.A.R." in baseball. Leaders could then be ranked by effectiveness, based on the more refined assessment. In this way, leaders who were "lucky" to be working under advantageous conditions and looked good in terms of raw performance would not be ranked systematically higher than those working under more adverse conditions. Leaders facing serious challenges who outperformed expectations would be recognized for their effectiveness in face of adversity.

Once the most effective leaders were identified based on archival data, the analysis team undertook qualitative assessments using a population segmentation based on the performance category. The analytical team surveyed and interviewed the top 25% of high-performing leaders to better understand how they approached their work. The focus was on behaviors and attitudes exhibited in executing their roles. These responses were then compared to those offered by those in lower-performance categories. Combined with archival data about the backgrounds and experience of the various leaders, the analysis team could then specify a new LD model that detailed an optimal profile of effective leaders. The profile specified "who the best leaders are" in terms of identifiable attributes, and "what effective leaders do" in terms of how they think about their roles and go about their jobs. The former included factors such as educational background, prior work experience outside and inside the organization, and length of service, among others. The latter contained items such as prioritization of activities and tasks, time management, interactions with staff and members, and managerial functions. For instance, it was found that the top-performing leaders across both the financial and customer outcomes were more comfortable with specialization in their roles than were their lower-performing counterparts. The top-performing leaders were far more likely to prioritize their financial responsibilities, focusing on fundraising and delegating to staff more of their program development and member relations activities. They experienced less tension about the trade-off between spending time with funders versus time with members. Aligned with their focus, they also tended to achieve more stability in their local teams, as seen in lower staff turnover.

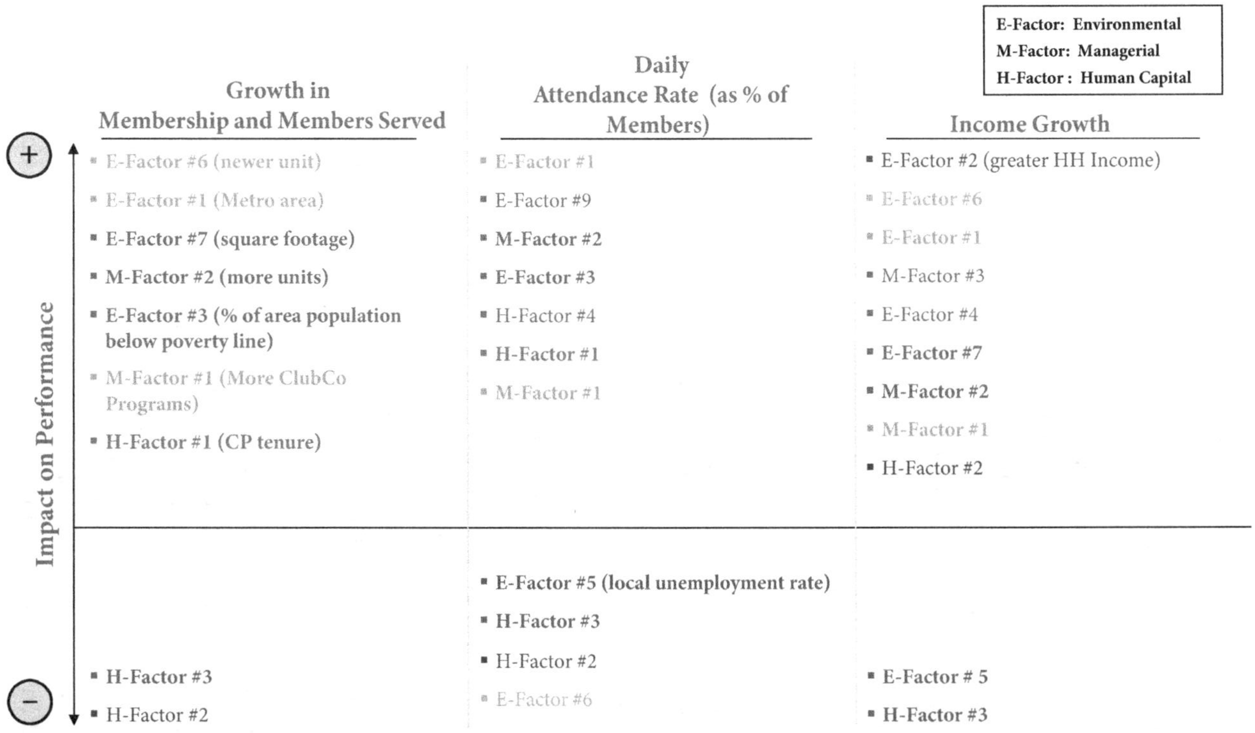

Figure 8.3 Identifying and Quantifying the Individual and Situational Factors Influencing Leader and Unit Performance

Source: Nalbantian (2016).

As the diagnostic process uncovered significant differences in what good leaders did at ClubCo, the resulting LD model could be very granular in its specifications. Moreover, the analysis results allowed for a tailoring of the LD model to local circumstances; they showed how specific explanatory factors were conditioned on purely situational factors affecting the units. Finally, because design decisions were informed by hard evidence on leader effectiveness in relation to the realities of ClubCo's unique mission, operations, and culture, the LD model was credible to those who would implement it and operate under it. This made the rollout and implementation of the new model easier than had it been a generic model developed and imposed from outside the organization.

Benefits of the Analytics-Based Approach

The benefits from pursuing an analytics-based approach to LD design are compelling. They include breaking down organizational myths and biases, enabling more accurate measures of actual leader contribution by accounting for the influence of situational factors, and identifying the full system-wide impact on LD effectiveness.

The Analytics-Based Approach Provides a Mirror of Reality

The analytics-based approach offers new opportunities to enhance the impact of LD in organizations and deliver new insights to advance LD research. One major benefit is that the approach helps break organizational myths and biases that form and influence executive decisions. The power of data to upend preconceptions was evidenced in the case of "MultiCo," a large, diversified media company that some years ago set about to revisit their entire talent and leadership development strategy.[8] Their CEO was convinced that changes in the business required a reset of their leadership profile and LD model.—Historically, the company had pursued a model that favored subject matter specialists with a proven track record across their businesses. Leaders came from the ranks of artisans who knew their craft and inspired others through their long-term commitment and success. The company de-emphasized pedigree in deference to longevity and proven "fire in the belly." The CEO felt that the demands of digitization and globalization, and the need for new products based on cross-business collaboration, required a type of talent different from their historical prototypes. He sponsored a program focused on acquiring top MBAs from a select few of the top business schools. He believed these would be the company's future leaders.

Internal labor market modeling similar to that undertaken by ConsumerCo and ConsumerRetailCo painted a sobering picture of the results of the CEO's program. All else being equal, those who came into the organization through the CEO's program were indistinguishable from their less pedigreed peers in terms of their trajectory of success: they were no more likely to receive high performance ratings, no more likely to advance or experience higher pay growth than those with the more conventional profile. On the other hand, they were significantly more costly due to their command of premium pay on entry and were also 25% more likely to turn over in any year. One interpretation was that this talent was not in fact of high value at MultiCo. Home-grown, specialized expertise was in fact what drove business performance. Alternatively, the results might mean there was a form of "organ rejection" taking place at MultiCo, reflecting a poor cultural fit. The kinds of people graduating from the top of the class at top business schools might feel stifled by the tightly managed environment and artisan-oriented culture of MultiCo. This culture might not be aligned with their needs and expectations. The company could do the hard work of culture change. Or, it could recognize what their data were showing and accommodate to their own realities.

The CEO was surprised by the findings—resisting at first, but ultimately reconciling to the reality the data revealed. The CEO program was scaled back significantly and emphasis restored on identifying the best of those within who matched their historical success profile.[9]

The Analytics-Based Approach Enables Creation of Innovative Measures That Are Informationally Powerful

We saw in the case of ClubCo how quantitative modeling helped demystify leader performance, allowing creation of adjusted measures of performance that were more revealing of actual contribution and could thus be used to ascertain leadership effectiveness. This contribution was hugely consequential for the organization.

The analytics-driven approach also provides the basis for measuring potential explanatory factors that have been elusive in practice. For instance, competency models commonly call out the importance of "agility" as a driver of leader effectiveness. But what exactly is agility and how does one measure it? Recruits and employees do not walk around with "agility" branded on their sleeves. Agility is a classic "unobservable" variable that can only be inferred imperfectly. Conventionally, input on agility would come from the feedback of supervisors and coworkers queried during the performance review cycle. Modeling permits creation of less subjective measures. For instance, since agility is fundamentally about the ability to adapt quickly and effectively to changing circumstances, a plausible signal of agility in an individual is a record of consistent success in the face of job or other situational changes. Professional and managerial employees who consistently perform well as their work and work environment change might well be regarded as demonstrating agility. With ample workforce data available to objectively measure the direct work environment of employees, modeling allows for identification of those who manage change well.

The Analytics-Based Approach Reveals the Operation of LD "in Context"

The analytics-based approach helps show how LD plays out within the system of workforce management practices that determine its effectiveness. We saw in the case of ConsumerCo how strongly LD was conditioned by the company's underlying build-from-within talent strategy and how it affected the outcomes of their DEI strategies. None of this would be obvious looking at the parameters of the LD program alone.

These kinds of interactions are common to LD across organizations. As an example, "ProductCo," a large global manufacturer, embraced an LD program predicated on frequent, planned job changes, both within and across functions as well as across geographies. See Nalbantian & Guzzo (2009). Drawing on insights from an academic guru's model of leadership, the company associated leadership with breadth of knowledge and experience, most easily developed through internal mobility.

In isolation, it appeared the LD program was working. Data analysis showed that internal moves were strongly predictive of advancement, providing incentives for up-and-coming leaders to pursue lateral moves.

The company itself experienced exceedingly high velocity of talent movement among up-and-coming leaders. The average time in the role was between 15 and 18 months. If one looked beyond the LD program, the high velocity of talent movement looked far more problematic. First, there was a fundamental misalignment of such high velocity with the firm's production structure. Product launches were of long duration—typically three to five years. That meant that by the time a product actually went to market, those responsible for core decisions at the onset of the launch team were two to three jobs removed from the team. A negative byproduct of these moves was a loss of accountability for product design and production decisions. The fact that the company pursued a build-from-within talent strategy compounded the problem. This meant that each time a launch team member was moved to another part of the organization, the team would have to look within for the replacement. They could not go to market to plug the gap. This led to a cascading of internal moves that destabilized launch teams throughout the organization. This is a classic "externalities" problem whereby the importing team gains all the benefits of the talent it recruits within while sharing none of the costs they impose on the team which has exported the talent. It was not surprising that mobility would turn excessive and the net result was a quality implosion evidenced by surging defect rates and slumping customer ratings. Failure to accommodate the LD design to the production and talent realities of the organization undermined what ProductCo thought was a state-of-the-art LD program. Once revealed, the issues were obvious. Amazingly, the reality had not been apparent to the executive team before the comprehensive data analysis was undertaken.

Challenges to Implementing the Analytics-Based Approach

For all its benefits, there are some challenges to implementing an analytics-based approach to LD design, which practitioners need to take into account.

Data Requirements Are Not Insignificant

A potential roadblock to the implementation of an analytics-based approach to LD program development is its data requirements. Whether modeling at the individual or unit levels, the methodology works best when the workforce, performance, and environmental factors captured by the data are comprehensive and of high quality. It also works best when the data are longitudinal with adequate history to be able to build robust models and test for structural changes. Longitudinal data are best not only because they are more likely to help identify causal relationships, but because many of the variables of greatest consequence to leadership effectiveness (and to human capital management generally) have no meaning unless measured over time. Learning is by nature a time-dependent variable. Leadership models keyed to continuous learning cannot be captured unless prospective leaders are tracked over time. The same is true when considering the effects of promotion, job change, and different forms of internal mobility. Insights derive from capturing what happens to the individual as she or he acquires different kinds of experience as they change jobs. Similarly, the influence of supervisors in nurturing leadership talent cannot be assessed unless viewed over time.

Fortunately, for larger organizations, modern HRIS and related electronic information systems typically house the vast majority of employee, organizational, and financial information required to create reliable models. Indeed, data are seldom an issue anymore. For smaller organizations, data requirements may be insurmountable. They may not have invested in the data systems required, so they need to construct the data sets by hand. And they may not have the population sizes of managers and professionals in feeder jobs required to reliably estimate statistical models. Generally speaking, population sizes of at least 500 employees should suffice to conduct such modeling at the individual level—that is, focused on individual outcomes such as promotion, performance, and pay. The more years of history available, the lower the population count can be. When it comes to modeling at the unit level, as in the case of ClubCo, constraints created by having too few units to track within the organization—say, fewer than 15 to 20—can be at least partially overcome by measuring performance outcomes at more frequent intervals. So, for instance, depending on the measure, one might use monthly or quarterly performance data rather than annual, as is customary. In the end, it all depends on the variability of shorter-term measures—e.g., because of seasonality—and the comprehensiveness of explanatory and control variables to be included in the model(s). The fewer the units available to cover in the modeling, the longer the time period and/or the more frequent the measurement of outcomes will be necessary.

History Is Not Always the Best Teacher

Analytics-based approaches inevitably rely on historical data. But LD ultimately is about the future. Over-reliance on historical data can lead to a distorted picture of what it takes to be an effective leader in changing circumstances. What made for effective leaders in the past may not be the same as what will make for effective leaders in the future. As there are no hard data on the future, this inevitably means that informed opinion must remain an important input into the development of LD models. Querying those inside and outside the organization who are best positioned to observe and understand how the business or mission is changing and how economic conditions will likely affect the performance of the organization seems an essential part of the evolving approach to LD design.

This does not mean data and analytics cannot inform LD changes responding to future transitions. With longitudinal data, statistical modeling of critical outcomes can help surface structural changes affecting LD programs. One can measure quite specifically how the influence of specific factors is changing over time, either by breaking the time series data set into overlapping periods which are then modeled separately, or by looking at interactions between explanatory factors and "dummy" variables used to account for time.

We must recognize, however, that sometimes examination of historical data alone is not a reliable basis to inform decisions about LD design. This is particularly true in cases of full-scale business transformation where heeding insights about historical success can actually impede adaptation to the requirements of the future.

A case in point, detailed in Guzzo (2019), is the experience of General Electric (GE) and the approach it took to understand the talent and leadership implications of its move toward digital manufacturing in its production facilities.[10] GE executives appreciated that the long-standing, highly structured, competency-based approach to LD that had been in place for many years may not work as effectively in supporting the radical transformation of production technology and operations they were undergoing. They also recognized that the strong, legendary culture they had developed over the years could get in the way of the speedy talent and leadership transformation required.

Rather than take a data-driven approach, GE chose to pursue a systematic qualitative analysis, tapping into the early experience of a number of its showcase digital operations in the United States, Europe, and Asia. A combination of interviews and surveys were conducted along with direct observation by their assessment team of the digital operations in these factories. The evaluation revealed and documented that while certain knowledge and experience areas such as cost management capabilities and shop floor experience would remain staples for effective leadership, a significant expansion and alteration of substantive knowledge and experience would be required to make the plant-level leaders effective in the future. The greatest need for change related less to subject matter than to modes of thinking and interactions with others—for example, critical thinking, strategic mindset, social skills, and change management. Most revealing of all, the experience at the plant level revealed that those best suited to lead the transformation effectively could well come from unconventional sources, including from jobs and occupations not traditionally targeted for recruitment. This was a giant leap for an organization that historically prized pedigree and internal longevity in developing their leaders. The kind of workforce transformation required to achieve the goals of digital transformation could butt up against historical pillars of GE's LD approach. Balancing the competing pressures of changing leader requirements and GE's strong organizational culture would be critical to delivering on the promise of technological change.

In cases like this, there is no substitute to qualitative, expert-driven diagnostics, even an appeal to external and internal benchmark experience or best practices. Quantitative diagnostics may still be useful, but in this instance the value may come more from identifying impediments to adaptation rather than future requirements. By uncovering patterns in the data which are misaligned with emerging LD requirements, it can help speed adaptation to emerging needs.

Executive Resistance Can Be a Showstopper

Another potential impediment to the effectiveness of an analytics-based approach to LD design is executive resistance. Those who work with data and analytics are prone to believe that data are gold and that tight, empirically backed arguments will win the day with business decision makers. Unfortunately, this is not always or even mostly the case. Like many areas of human capital management, executives often have firm, passionately held beliefs about what makes for effective leaders. After all, they have achieved their own success following certain precepts and channels and have first-hand experience with the developmental journey. They have seen many successful and unsuccessful leaders along the way and have developed clear ideas on what differentiates them. Sometimes this translates into rigid philosophies about LD to which they adhere.

It is foolhardy to discount the importance of philosophy or belief when it comes to LD. I once had the CEO of a major, global professional services firm say to me, "I don't know what I would do if results of your analysis were at odds with my own experience and what I believe." I appreciated her candor even as she declined to proceed with the proposed work. The incident reminded me that data and evidence only go so far. Understanding the attitudes of decision makers and the emotive aspects of their views in this area is essential if the value of an analytics-based approach is to be secured.

Summary and Conclusions

Leadership is a subject of huge—possibly, outsized—fascination in both academic and popular circles. The research literature on LD is voluminous and has spawned a plethora of LD models that have infiltrated businesses. Some of these models have been embraced wholesale; some have been modified and implemented in hybrid form, with varying success. Today, the practice of LD is at a cross-roads. Rapid economic, technological, and cultural changes are challenging LD orthodoxy, transforming what it takes to be an effective leader and how the next generation of leaders can be identified and developed.

This chapter has examined dimensions of the changing LD landscape in practice. It has shown how advanced analytics and AI now permit a new analytics-based approach to LD, upending the application and value of monolithic LD models, and changing the very business agendas that leaders are required to execute.

The data and methods required to deploy an analytics-based approach have been around a long while now. With AI bursting on the scene with accessible, easy to use tools and processes, the ability to pursue this approach in an efficient manner and in real time is only getting easier. This requires some adaptation on the part of organization leaders. For one thing, they have to check their egos at the door. They cannot assume that what made them successful leaders is the recipe for the successful development of future leaders. Second, getting comfortable with data and modeling is a prerequisite for understanding and acting on results. They cannot rest on platitudes, LD boilerplate, or simply articulating the tenets of LD "universals" of the past. Getting comfortable with analytics is emerging as a new competency for effective leadership.

The analytics-based approach to LD requires work, but for organizations the payoffs can be enormous. Better leaders, tailored to the unique demands of their business, operations, and culture, are likely to be produced when LD programs are informed by hard, contextually derived evidence on what works and does not. For academic researchers, the take-up and dissemination of this approach also provides important benefits. It can offer the basis for transformational research that opens new windows on what makes for great leaders and new opportunities for empirical study. Results from such extensive empiricism based on organizational data and naturally occurring experiments in organizations can also become the basis of entirely new theories of LD, leading to a reflowering of a field that might otherwise be spent.

Key Takeaways

- LD is at a cross-roads due to the rapid proliferation of archival data, accessible analytics, and AI.
- A new analytics-based approach enables organizations to pursue LD design anchored in empirical assessments of the drivers of leader success.
- Monolithic, one-size-fits-all approaches to LD are giving way to program designs tailored to the unique requirements of the business.
- LD programs are context-sensitive and must align with business strategies, operations, culture, and other human capital practices.
- A critical part of the analytics-based approach is to ensure that key performance measures used for assessment purposes are adjusted to deal with situational realities—i.e., "the hand you're dealt."
- As there are no data on the future, the analytics-based approach alone falls short for organizations undergoing major business transformation; qualitative assessments of future needs are still required.

Notes

1. This chapter draws on case examples from client projects I delivered during my long tenure as Senior Partner at Mercer and a founder/leader of its Workforce Strategies and Analytics Group. I wish to acknowledge the contributions of the remarkable colleagues who worked with me on these projects, including Rick Guzzo, Brian Levine, Karen Marciniak, Mathieu Sauterey, Lingzi Liang, Katie Noonan, Anna Marley, and Luis F. Parra, among others.
2. A comprehensive description of the specific methodology used—"internal labor market (ILM) analysis"—is presented in Nalbantian et al. (2004).
3. ConsumerCo's nine-box system was an adaptation of the original GE 9-Box Grid developed in the 1970s. ConsumerCo's version called out leadership capability and effectiveness rather than the more generic "potential." For a description of the original GE version of the nine-box, see Coyne (2008).
4. More technical detail on the ConsumerCo findings appears in Nalbantian (2017).
5. Useful characterizations of these models are also found in Bass and Stogdill (1990).
6. Another notable contribution to the development of Competency-Based Models is Mendenhall et al. (2013).
7. Baseball statistics cited in this section are drawn from Baseball Reference.com. 2010 American League Cy Young Award. https://www.baseball-reference.com/bullpen/2010_American_League_Cy_Young_Award; 2018 National League Cy Young Award. https://www.baseball-reference.com/bullpen/2018_National_League_Cy_Young_Award; 2019 National League Cy Young Award. https://www.baseball-reference.com/bullpen/2019_National_League_Cy_Young_Award
8. A comprehensive summary of the MultiCo case is presented in Guzzo et al. (2014).
9. Further discussion of how internal labor market modeling can be used to assess the impact of learning and specific types of experience on career development and advancement is offered in Guzzo & Nalbantian (2014)
10. A more detailed description of how GE adapted its approach to leadership development to accommodate technological transformation can be found in Guzzo (2019).

References

Bass, B. M. (1985). *Leadership and performance beyond expectations.* Free Press.
Bass, B. M., & Stogdill, R. M. (1990). *Bass & Stogdill's handbook of leadership: Theory, research, and managerial applications* (3rd ed.). Free Press.
Boyatzis, R. E. (1982). *The competent manager: A model for effective performance.* Wiley.
Burns, J. M. (1978). *Leadership.* Harper & Row.
Coyne, K. (2008). Enduring ideas: The GE–McKinsey nine-box matrix. *McKinsey Quarterly.* https://www.mckinsey.com/capabilities/strategy-and-corporate-finance/our-insights/enduring-ideas-the-ge-and-mckinsey-nine-box-matrix?wapp_id=eda2ed85-dbcc-4337-9a60-70f4a831caf2
Davis, K. (1981). *Human behavior at work: Organizational behavior* (6th ed.). McGraw Hill.
Greenleaf, R. K. (1970). *The servant as leader.* Robert K. Greenleaf Publishing Center.
Greenleaf, R. K. (1977). *Servant leadership: A journey into the nature of legitimate power and greatness.* Paulist Press.
Guzzo, R. A. (2019). Workforce readiness in times of change: Employer perspectives. In F. L. Oswald, T. S. Behrend, & L. L. Foster (Eds.), *Workforce readiness and the future of work* (pp. 73–91). Routledge.
Guzzo, R. A., & Nalbantian, H. R. (2014). Assessing learning's impact on careers. In C. D. McCauley, D. S. De Rue, P. R. Yost, & S. Taylor (Eds.), *Experience-driven leadership development* (pp. 523–528). Wiley.

Guzzo, R. A., Nalbantian, H. R., & Parra, L. F. (2014). A big data, say-do approach to climate and culture: A consulting perspective. In B. Schneider & K. Barbera (Eds.), *Oxford handbook of organizational climate and culture: Antecedents, consequences and practice.* (pp. 197–211). Oxford University Press.

Judge, T. A., & Piccolo, R. F. (2004). Transformational and transactional leadership: A meta-analytic test of their relative validity. *Journal of Applied Psychology, 89*(5), 755–768.

McClelland, D. C. (1961). *The achieving society.* Van Nostrand.

Mendenhall, M. E., Osland, J. S., Bird, A., Oddou, G. R., & Maznevski, M. L. (2013). *Global leadership: Research, practice, and development* (2nd ed.). Routledge.

Nalbantian, H. R. (2016). *From wins to W.A.R.: What HR can learn from baseball's sabermetrics revolution* [Keynote address]. *Talentball Conference*, hosted by Best Practice Institute and the Texas Rangers baseball club, Arlington, TX.

Nalbantian, H. R. (2017). The internal labor market paradigm: A model for using analytics to evaluate and interpret workforce and business performance data. In D. R. Berger & L. Berger (Eds.), *The talent management handbook* (pp. 542–555). McGraw Hill.

Nalbantian, H. R., & Guzzo, R. A. (2009). Making mobility matter: Moves that develop a leader. *Harvard Business Review, 87*(3), 76–84.

Nalbantian, H., Guzzo, R. A., Kieffer, D., & Doherty, J. (2004). *Play to your strengths: Managing your internal labor markets for lasting competitive advantage.* McGraw Hill.

Spencer, L. M., & Spencer, S. M. (1993). *Competence at work: Models for superior performance.* Wiley.

Sports Reference. (n.d.). Baseball-Reference. https://www.baseball-reference.com/

Tichy, N. M. (2002). *The cycle of leadership: How great leaders teach their companies to win.* HarperBusiness.

Tichy, N. M., & Cohen, E. B. (1997). *The leadership engine: How winning companies build leaders at every level.* HarperBusiness.

Van Dierendonck, D. (2011). Servant leadership: A review and synthesis. *Journal of Management, 37*(4), 1228–1261. https://doi.org/10.1177/0149206310380462

Wang, G., Oh, I.-S., Courtright, S. H., & Colbert, A. E. (2011). Transformational leadership and performance across criteria and levels: A meta-analytic review of 25 years of research. *Group & Organization Management, 36*(2), 223–270.

SECTION IV

GLOBAL CHALLENGES

9

Sustainability and Leadership

Sarah Birrell Ivory and Brad Mackay

Understanding Business

Why does business exist? This seemingly simple question posed at the start of sustainability training programs more often than not creates an immediate buzz amongst participants. In our experience, there are those who struggle to form a coherent answer, despite years of working in business, sometimes at very senior levels. Yet there are many others who confidently know the answer and indeed believe it is obvious and universally accepted. However, it soon becomes apparent that an answer that is obvious to one person does not reflect the response of their neighbor. The question is not, therefore, so simple after all.

In order to get to the crux of the debate, it can help to present two different statements and ask which one people agree with most:

1. Business exists to make a profit, and does so by producing goods and services.
2. Business exists to produce goods and services, and in doing so makes a profit.

We have found that the room tends to split on which answer resonates with individual views. This is not surprising. Historically, the response to this question has evolved over time from the writings of the Scottish enlightenment philosopher Adam Smith in his seminal *The Wealth of Nations* (Smith, 1776), who had a nuanced view of business and self-interest as a force for societal good (provided it was grounded in ethics), through to Marx (1867) who saw business and the surplus value, or private profits, that they generate as inherently exploitative, dehumanizing, and ultimately destabilizing, to the work of the economist Milton Friedman (1970) and his eulogizing

Sarah Birrell Ivory and Brad Mackay, *Sustainability and Leadership*. In: *The Changing Leadership Landscape*.
Edited by: Sheri L. Feinzig and Mariangela Battista, Oxford University Press. © Oxford University Press (2026).
DOI: 10.1093/9780197820070.003.0009

of shareholder value above all else. But the most interesting thing about the debate today is the number of people in each camp who do not recognize the other camp at all.

So, this fundamental question about why business exists is contested. This is not necessarily a problem—people can have different views on the purpose of business, and indeed different businesses can exist for different reasons. But it does become an issue when we consider the important role and function of business in society, as well as the significant environmental and social issues we are facing, in which business also plays an important part.

Global challenges, which range from climate change to income inequality, community breakdown, resource scarcity, and biodiversity loss are increasingly tipping over into crises, highlighting the increasing urgency and growing impact of such issues. They have also laid bare the role everyone, including—and especially—business, must play in driving change, innovation, and contributing to solutions for what are the defining issues of our age.

As such, it is often useful to pose a third option:

3. Business exists to support a thriving society, by producing goods and services, and in doing so makes a profit.

From this perspective, businesses have *purpose*. Law firms exist to uphold laws that maintain the stability of society through the idea of fairness, justice, and the rule-of-law. Agricultural companies exist to grow food to feed people. Pharmaceutical companies exist to provide medicines to treat health ailments. Energy companies exist to keep the lights on, so to speak. Transport companies exist to move people and things around. Communications companies exist to keep people connected. Waste collectors exist to maintain clean and hygienic cities and streets. And so on. That is, this option posits the idea that business exists for society's benefit—not solely or even primarily for the wealth accumulation of owners or shareholders, often called "shareholder primacy," even though that is an important secondary outcome of well-run businesses in a competitive market economy.

This dominant ideology of shareholder primacy is explored by Lynn Stout, a Cornell Law Professor, in *The Shareholder Value Myth* (Stout, 2012). She outlines the damage such an ideology is doing to society, to companies, and to shareholders themselves, debunking the myth of shareholder value through the lenses of history, law, and evidence. Arguably, the primacy of shareholder value over societal benefit has been a key determinant in the recent rise of angry, divisive populism across the world. This is not, however, an anti-profit argument. It is questioning the aim of *maximizing* profit, the *temporal* period over which profit maximization dominates attention, the *distributive* question of "profit for whom?" and the question of "profit at what costs?"—that is, the *externalities* of profits.

When did shareholder primacy come to dominate? There are a number of complex answers to this question. Lounsbury (2007) suggests that differences in approaches to investment management between Boston and New York provides a possible divergence. Until the 1950s, the investment industry in the United States was centered on Boston. It was dominated by a trusteeship approach, focused on investment in chosen companies over the longer term, capital preservation, and intergenerational transfer. From the 1950s, there was a geographic and ideological shift: from Boston to New York's Wall Street, and from trusteeship to a narrow focus on economic performance. The latter focused on short-term annualized returns linked to growth funds which were more speculative and led to more trading of shares, rather than long-term ownership of companies.

Many blame this short-term focus on the issues of social and environmental externalities from business-as-usual operations. Returning to the three options posed at the start of this chapter, this approach fits squarely within the first one, where the primary raison d'etre of business is to make profit. However, there is some evidence that we are seeing a shift as more businesses explicitly focus on how they support a thriving society while making profit. The growing number of social and hybrid enterprises are an example of this, including the burgeoning B Corps movement. This movement covers small, medium, and large organizations under the "Benefit Corps" umbrella who commit to balancing returns to owners with their contribution to both societal and environmental outcomes.

In 2009, Unilever's then CEO Paul Polman, for instance, announced that the company would no longer issue quarterly earnings guidance, urging shareholders who did not share his long-term orientation to invest elsewhere. This decision was emblematic of Polman's broader approach to corporate sustainability leadership, which sought to redefine value creation as "equitable, shared, and sustainable" rather than narrowly financial (Boynton, 2015, para. 2). By deprioritising short-term market expectations in favour of long-term societal and environmental impact, Polman positioned Unilever as a leading example of purpose-driven capitalism.

This orientation closely mirrors the principles underpinning the B Corps movement, which emphasises stakeholder governance, accountability beyond shareholders, and the integration of social purpose into core strategy. Polman's stance thus foreshadowed and legitimized a wider shift toward business models that reconcile profitability with responsibility.

The influential US-based Business Roundtable—which boasts 200 of America's most prominent Chief Executive Officers (CEOs)—had, until 2019, an enshrined philosophy that "the paramount duty of management and of boards of directors is to the corporation's stockholders" and that "the interests of other stakeholders are relevant as derivative of the duty to stockholders." (Business Roundtable, 2019, para. 2). Then, in 2019, they released a Statement on the Purpose of a Corporation which dramatically refocused their philosophy not on the stockholder, but on all of their stakeholders, stating that "we commit to deliver value to all of them, for the future success of our companies, our communities, and our country" (Business Roundtable, 2019, para. 13). According to Morgan Stanley Capital International (MSCI) data, nearly 75% of large public companies in developed markets outside of the United States, for example, now disclose their Scope 1 and Scope 2 carbon emissions, although in the United States the proportion is closer to 45% (Lee, 2024).

Recently, however, we have seen a rise in anti-ESG (environment, society, governance) sentiment with some major businesses pulling back on previous commitments. This has been partly driven by its politicization, where somewhat paradoxically, or perhaps more likely cynically, sustainability has become associated with liberalism (paradoxically because the term "conservative" derives from the Latin *conservare*, meaning "preserve"—an idea at the heart of sustainability; cynically because its weaponization for political reasons is contrary to the overwhelming consensus in science of the direction of travel of climate change and biodiversity loss, and gives cover to some of the more powerful players in the corporate world to renege on their responsibilities to future generations); and partly because much of the low-hanging fruit, particularly as it relates to environmental sustainability, such as emissions disclosures, has been picked. Further progress transitioning to a more sustainable world requires complicated and sometimes, although not always, costly investment, reigniting tension between short-term profit and longer-term societal benefit—and creative leadership.

In summary, the ongoing debate about why business exists, and its relationship to the externalities it causes, has not yet and is unlikely to ever reach consensus. However, we are seeing pockets of industry or types of organizations shift away from profit maximization at all costs. Even for those who maintain profit as a primary focus, many recognize that the two are mutually dependent *on* and reinforcing *of* each other in the longer term. This is reflected in the amount of private investment, for example, now flowing into renewables and the opportunities that new technologies will bring. To explore these ideas further, the next section will explore sustainability and how it links to current global trends and issues.

Understanding Sustainability

Many of the externalities of business, and wider social and environment trends, have been gathered together, for better or for worse, under the umbrella term "sustainability." Exploring the origins of the concept, and its relationship to business, can help to better understand why and how leaders have acted on these issues, and how they might approach them in the future.

In 1987, the UN's Brundtland Commission coined the famous definition of sustainable development as "development that meets the needs of the present without compromising the ability of future generations to meet their own needs" (Brundtland, 1987, p. 43). While this concept was targeted at a macroeconomic level of analysis, it soon trickled down in different ways to specific entities, like businesses.

In being translated to the level of business, a popular conceptualization of the "triple bottom line" came to prominence in the 1990s (Elkington, 1994). This idea was typically depicted as a Venn diagram where economy, society, and the environment overlapped in a central "sustainability sweet spot" (Savitz, 2006). Such a simplified depiction of complex interrelated components made a useful introductory tool to explain sustainability, but it had drawbacks. Elkington himself declared that "there are limitations inherent in the over-simplified delineation of economy, society, and environment" (Elkington et al., 2006, p. 14), and indeed tried to issue a "management concept recall" of the triple bottom line (Elkington, 2018). Objections to the concept include the failure to acknowledge the tensions and trade-offs which are ever-present in sustainability issues (Hahn & Figge, 2011); as well as the concept being hijacked to become an instrument of the "business case" for sustainability (Holliday et al., 2002), where social and environmental bottom lines are relevant only to the extent that they can materially and measurably contribute to the economic bottom line.

In part as a response to such criticisms, a more sophisticated visual depiction of sustainability sees the components as nested, rather than overlapping: the economic nested within the social, which in turn is nested within the environmental (Porritt, 2007). Such a depiction intends to reflect the fact that the global economy is a subsystem of human society, which is in itself a subsystem of the totality of life on earth. Economic health is ultimately dependent the stewardship of the finite resources of a healthy natural world. If the world, or even part of it, is dying, then sooner or later economies will follow.

This nesting approach has most recently been incorporated into Kate Raworth's "Doughnut Economics" (Raworth, 2018), which looks to define the safe and just space for humanity as existing within a regenerative and distributive economy. This relies on maintaining strong social foundations (including education, peace and justice, social equity, and health) without overshooting ecological ceilings (comprising issues like climate change, ocean acidification, freshwater withdrawals, biodiversity loss, and air pollution). Assessments suggest that many of these social foundations are suffering from a shortfall, and a number of the ecological ceilings from overshoot (Raworth, 2018). The implication is that, unless we address these issues, we will be unable to achieve a safe and just space for humanity. A number of these social foundations and ecological ceilings overlap with the UN's 17 Sustainable Development Goals (SDGs) adopted in 2015, which provide a "shared blueprint for peace and prosperity for people and the planet, now and into the future." (UN, n.d., para. 1). The original aim was to achieve these goals by 2030; however, a recent report has found that only 15% of SDGs are on track to be achieved, 49% show minimal or moderate progress, and 36% show signs of stagnation or regression (UN, 2024).

Such stark messages beg the question of where sustainability sits in the priorities and focus of business leaders. Sustainability is often introduced to leaders as an important topic they should consider for the protection of the environment and the betterment of society. While noble, such a framing has some drawbacks. First, it puts sustainability into the same bracket as all the many noble issues leaders could and perhaps should think about. But with incredibly busy schedules, and when being pulled in many different directions, it can end up being treated as another peripheral issue. And until something moves from peripheral to a core strategic priority, it is likely to be only paid lip service, if that.

Second, issues which fall under the umbrella of sustainability are often difficult for a business to address easily for a number of specific reasons. They are rarely the responsibility of just one organization, but rather have been referred to as "grand challenges" (Ferraro et al., 2015) and "super wicked" problems (Levin et al., 2012). Taking climate change as a representative example, as an issue it lacks immediacy and urgency due to a "mismatch between the timescales of business and that of the climate [making it] difficult to grasp what climate change means for organizations in the future" (Howard-Grenville et al., 2014, p. 615). This has allowed individuals and organizations to hold contested views on the importance of climate change and on the role of individual businesses in its resolution, especially given its "tragedy of the commons" traits (Gardiner, 2011).

A classic tragedy of the commons problem emerges whereby specific efforts are resourced and implemented by an individual business (e.g., sourcing lower emissions energy supply), but the benefits (e.g., reduction of emissions) are enjoyed by the collective, including businesses who have not invested in such efforts (Ostrom, 1990). This description could be used for other sustainability issues like community breakdown or resource usage. What makes climate change such an all-pervasive issue is that something that started as global temperature rises from increased greenhouse gas emissions in the atmosphere, largely from burning fossil fuels, is having wider and more devastating environmental and social impacts. This includes extreme weather, sea-level rise, drought, and flood. As a result of these widespread environmental issues, as well as the low carbon transition that has begun, we are seeing significant and disruptive societal transitions. Areas of the world will become unlivable, communities based around fossil fuel production may see their economy dry up, and the number of lives and livelihoods lost to extreme weather will grow. However, attributing this to the specific decisions of individual businesses is difficult.

Third, framing sustainability as a noble cause, or as an issue too great for one business alone, detracts from the notion of the sustainability concept as fundamental to the strategy and operations of business itself. This also runs the risk of leaving the concept open to politicized criticism, which we have seen in some countries. Such politicized criticisms of sustainability initiatives, or the related concept of ESG, are increasingly being imbued with associations to specific political ideologies. Given the broad range of issues that sit under the sustainability umbrella, such criticism has the potential to be widespread and affect initiatives that have no particular ideological aspects, and may well make good business and economic sense for shareholders and society alike.

For these reasons, we are seeing leaders increasingly disaggregate sustainability into specific issues such as supply chain resilience, energy security, customer segregation and targeting, talent attraction and retention, and stakeholder relationships. This allows businesses to be strategic and focus on key issues that either strategically affect them anyway or that they intentionally choose to take a stance on for brand, reputation, or leadership reasons.

Understanding Leadership and Sustainability

Irrespective of whether leaders choose to pay attention to sustainability issues, ignore them, or dismiss them outright, every business leader globally is being affected by a number of issues that sit under the sustainability umbrella. This is because we are seeing an increasingly disrupted world, linked to a number of environmental, political, and social issues. Such embedded and ongoing disruption saw Bennis and Nanus (1985) coin the acronym "VUCA" to describe the changing nature of the world. VUCA stands for "volatility, uncertainty, complexity, and ambiguity." This concept can be described as follows:

- *Volatility*: Change is a constant and happens quickly, but the nature, speed, volume, and magnitude of change are not predictable.
- *Uncertainty*: A lack of predictability of issues or events means past issues or events cannot be used as predictors for future outcomes, making forecasting difficult and the future uncertain.
- *Complexity*: Everything is related or interconnected, and actions we take can have unpredictable and unintended consequences for many other things.
- *Ambiguity*: Increased volatility, uncertainty, and complexity may mean that the best solutions or reactions are unclear, while the meaning of events may also be obscure or vague.

In response to this framing, leadership academic Bob Johansen (2012) argues that a VUCA world must be met by a VUCA leader. Specifically, he suggests the following:

- Volatility must be met with *vision*—a stable reference point for the organization that does not need to change even during turbulent times and goes to the heart of their purpose and measures of success.
- Uncertainty must be met with *understanding*—especially understanding key stakeholders like employees, through effective and consistent two-way communication about the uncertainties the organization is facing.
- Complexity must be met with *clarity*—being able to cut through the chaos to see clearly what matters most to the organization and what can be ignored.
- Ambiguity must be met with *agility*—being able to quickly and effectively implement solutions to challenges and adapt.

The notion of a VUCA world helps to explain *why* further progress on sustainability necessitates VUCA leadership skills capable of integrating sustainability issues into leader's thinking and increasingly into their strategy and understanding. It also contributes to understanding *what* position, particularly in highly charged political contexts, they need to achieve. But it lacks a prescription about *how* leaders might go about this. We suggest two concepts that can help leaders envision what they can do. The first focuses on an individual's progression through different stages of sustainability integration, and the second offers a tool that can be used to frame differing approaches to sustainability as an issue.

Our research of global companies found that individuals tasked with scaling sustainability within their organizations adopted three distinct approaches for integrating sustainability into their practice: an assimilation approach, a mobilization approach, and a transition approach (Ivory & Mackay, 2020). The *assimilation approach* focuses on conforming to the existing organizational success parameters—typically, profit. Leaders demonstrate how sustainability initiatives contribute to cost savings, efficiencies, or sales. While sustainability remains peripheral to the core of the organization, sustainability initiatives are nevertheless introduced incrementally and typically become successful because they are linked to business performance and represent quick wins.

Progressing one step further is the *mobilization approach*. This is the start of attempts to integrate sustainability more deeply into the organization by leveraging pockets: "warming-up" specific senior executives, exciting departments like R&D, reducing costs, improving efficiencies, expanding market segments, or initiating pilot projects. This approach can move forward incrementally and experimentally. Finally, the *transition approach* looks to achieve a wholesale adoption of sustainability as a mindset, mission, and purpose, specifically by shaping policies, processes, and attitudes toward sustainability principles. Key at this stage is integrating sustainability in education, training, and coaching.

Of course, the three approaches are not completely discrete in that individuals link their approaches—progressing from assimilation, to mobilization, and finally transition where sustainability becomes a strategic priority. As such, while assimilation may seem unambitious, it may be an important first step for a leader to gain "insider" status, or for sustainability to gain acceptability and credibility with internal and external stakeholders. The ability to enroll the support of increasingly senior leadership (and vice versa) within organizations by demonstrating at every stage the links between sustainability initiatives and wider senior management and board-level priorities such as financial performance is an important thread throughout each stage. Equally, messages from senior leadership that well-designed sustainability initiatives are an important strategic priority, and will improve economic performance, enable buy-in and scaling more widely within the organization.

The second concept which may help leaders envision what they can do, draws on a holistic view of the interplay between sustainability issues and business. This is necessary because while much of traditional strategy focuses on the competitive advantage of the firm and achieving individual company success, sustainability is a unique problem. As the saying goes, you cannot have a successful company in a failed world: "Successful corporations need a healthy society ... At the same time, a healthy society needs successful companies" (Porter & Kramer, 2006, p. 5). Therefore, to effectively integrate sustainability into an organization's strategy, one needs to look honestly not just at what the company gains, but what society gains.

We developed the Of/On Sustainability Framework to consider the impact *of* sustainability issues *on* business, and then *of* business *on* sustainability issues. Moreover, it considers these from both a negative and a positive perspective. This is related to the concept of "double materiality," accepting that

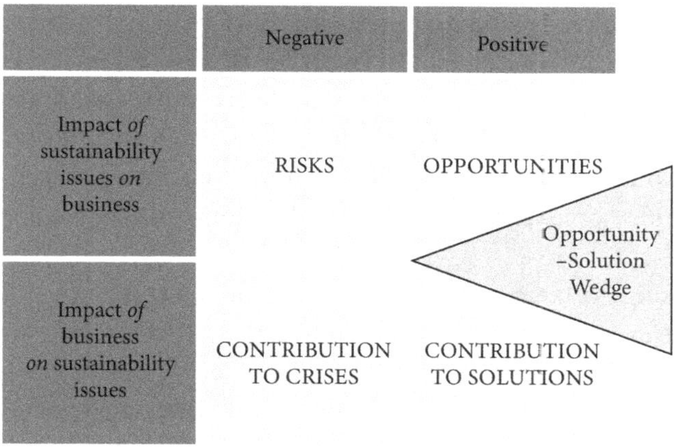

Figure 9.1 The Of/On Sustainability Framework

business needs to consider what is material for its success as well as what material impact it has on the success of sustainability issues and, therefore, society.

The impact *of* sustainability issues *on* business can be considered Risks (in the negative) and Opportunities (in the positive). The impact *of* business *on* sustainability issues can be considered Contribution to the Crises (in the negative) and Contribution to Solutions (in the positive) (see Figure 9.1).

The Of/On Sustainability Framework provides a number of benefits for leaders looking to both understand and act on sustainability issues. The first benefit is that it clarifies positions in discussions about this topic. Too often, people are speaking past each other without realizing it. One speaks with a focus on the business and the other with a focus on the sustainability issue. So long as participants are aware of this, a useful conversation can ensue. But too often, there is confusion instead of a dialogue.

The second benefit, which should not be underestimated, is that this framework helps individuals cope with the sense of being overwhelmed. Sustainability issues can create a sense of helplessness or even anxiety at the scale of the issues we are facing. The framework presented here can be used to focus attention on what can be achieved.

The final benefit is that it helps to prioritize action. A key aspect of the Of/On Sustainability Framework is the importance of balance across all four quadrants. It encourages the organization to consider their position and response in each quadrant. That said, while attention to all quadrants is important, there is a natural progression which may be comfortable for most businesses. We hesitate however to call this an "order." This is because the initiatives, projects, and solutions are likely to straddle different quadrants, or because action in one quadrant may—even with the greatest will and investment in the world—still take some time to reach fruition. However, we offer some thoughts on the relative importance and approach for each quadrant.

Addressing the business's *Contribution to the Crises* is an obvious place to start. If businesses do not effectively address this, or have a plan to address it, action in other quadrants becomes questionable. For some industries this is relatively easy, while others will find this difficult. Irrespective of how well the business addresses its Contribution to the Crises, it should then be moving on to further quadrants.

We suggest that the *Risks* quadrant is a plausible next step. This is especially important for risks with short-term implications. This ensures that the business continues to operate. As a society, we need many businesses driving toward solutions. Therefore, a form of protection or survival instinct should not only be allowed, but it should also be encouraged.

The next step is to look at the *Opportunities* that sustainability issues offer (for example, new product offerings or clients, diversifying supply chains or input materials, or leveraging government policy). These, however, should be immediately assessed with reference to the final quadrant, *Contribution to Solutions*. Where an opportunity for the business overlaps with a contribution to a solution for a sustainability issue, we can conceptualize this as the "Opportunity–Solution Wedge" (see Figure 9.1). Importantly, gaining support for initiatives within the wedge from stakeholders should be relatively easy, irrespective of their focus or interest. Those interested in strategic success for the business will be appeased, as will those interested in addressing sustainability issues.

Finally, it should be noted that there are initiatives that may sit within Opportunities or Contribution to Solutions but not within the Opportunity–Solution Wedge. These are to be encouraged but are likely to get more support from all stakeholders if there are other initiatives within the wedge which are being pursued at the same time.

In summary, the first step is that leaders understand they are operating in a VUCA world caused in part by sustainability challenges. Understanding how they can be a VUCA leader is essential, as is appreciating the progression from assimilation through to transition when looking to integrate sustainability. Considering the holistic interplay between sustainability and the business enables leaders to think about where to prioritize action: either with the focus on sustainability or with the focus on the business. The final section of this chapter provides guidance on how to approach education and training, and associated tools, to support leaders on this journey.

Integrating Sustainability through Education and Training

When looking to use education and training as a tool to introduce, increase, or integrate sustainability into a business, it is important to first think about the audience. Too often it is only people in formal leadership roles who receive attention and are offered places on programs. This tendency ignores the fact that leaders of the future are often those not currently in leadership roles, and "leadership" in relation to sustainability can come from people not in leadership roles at all: newer employees, those at the front line, or those more junior. The potential for these employees to lead on sustainability issues can be attributed to generational factors, interest, and also time: senior leaders already have a lot on their desks.

When it comes to designing interventions, it is important to have *dedicated* sessions. These are education, training, or coaching-focused sessions which explicitly explore sustainability issues. They are most effective when designed in a bespoke way with direct links made between the sustainability issues and the industry, business, and role of those attending. The sessions also need to provide specific courses of action, often co-developed by attendees and the session facilitator. Without attention to these elements, such sessions run the risk of being too abstract or losing the interest and attention of busy leaders (whether in formal roles or not) who have many competing priorities.

In addition to dedicated sessions, it is also important to have a *distributed* approach. That is, all other education, training, and coaching should touch on aspects of sustainability. This approach ensures that sustainability is not framed as an "add-on" to core business strategy.

Irrespective of whether the education, training, and coaching are offered across the leadership spectrum in both dedicated and distributed interventions, these are unlikely to pay off unless other aspects of the business are aligned to support the leader when they return to their role. As such, one of the greatest failures of such programs is the expectation that a small group of people can create change without the explicit and proactive support of the most senior leaders. Indeed, our research (Ivory & Mackay, 2020) found that buy-in from top leadership is essential throughout the entire process: developing and maintaining their support and commitment should be the primary and ongoing focus. It can also help to introduce drivers from the external environment—that is, leverage a competitor's behavior or client's expectations, embracing them opportunistically to gain support and urgency for sustainability interventions. Finally, internal policies and metrics are essential in integrating sustainability into the strategic heart of a business. For example, the human resources (HR) department should be altering key performance indicators (KPIs), recruitment expectations, and remuneration and bonus criteria, while the finance department should be willing to adjust internal rates of return for longer-term projects.

Conclusion

We started this chapter exploring why business exists. There will not be thriving businesses on a dying planet, and while nature's timelines do not operate on short-term financial reporting timelines, it is within the power of business leaders to help to contribute to a safe, secure, prosperous, and thriving world. Equally, there is sufficient evidence to suggest that sustainability is not mutually exclusive with sound financial performance, and indeed can enhance it and open up new business opportunities. However, the leadership approaches of the past, which have contributed to some of the global crises we face, should not be the leadership of the future. We hope this chapter has provided a sense of why leadership needs to integrate sustainability, and what leaders of the future might look like.

References

Bennis, W., & Nanus, B. (1985). *Leaders: The strategies for taking charge.* Harper.

Boynton, A. (2015, July 20). Unilever's Paul Polman: CEOs can't be "slaves" to shareholders. *Forbes.* https://www.forbes.com/sites/andyboynton/2015/07/20/unilevers-paul-polman-ceos-cant-be-slaves-to-shareholders

Brundtland, G. H. (1987). *Report of the World Commission on Environment and Development: Our common future.* United Nations General Assembly, document A/42/427.

Business Roundtable. (2019, April 19). *Business Roundtable redefines the purpose of a corporation to promote "an economy that services all Americans"* [Press release]. https://www.businessroundtable.org/business-roundtable-redefines-the-purpose-of-a-corporation-to-promote-an-economy-that-serves-all-americans

Elkington, J. (1994). Towards the suitable corporation: Win-win-win business strategies for sustainable development. *California Management Review*, *36*(2), 90–100.
Elkington, J. (2018, June 25). 25 years ago I coined the phrase "triple bottom line." Here's why it's time to rethink it. *Harvard Business Review*. https://hbr.org/2018/06/25-years-ago-i-coined-the-phrase-triple-bottom-line-heres-why-im-giving-up-on-it
Elkington, J., Emerson, J., & Beloe, S. (2006). The value palette: A tool for full spectrum strategy. *California Management Review*, *48*(2), 6–28.
Ferraro, F., Etzion, D., & Gehman, J. (2015). Tackling grand challenges pragmatically: Robust action revisited. *Organization Studies*, *36*(3), 363–390.
Friedman, M. (1970, September 13). The social responsibility of business is to increase its profits. *The New York Times*. https://www.nytimes.com/1970/09/13/archives/a-friedman-doctrine-the-social-responsibility-of-business-is-to.html
Gardiner, S. M. (2011). *A perfect moral storm: The ethical tragedy of climate change*. Oxford University Press.
Hahn, T., & Figge, F. (2011). Beyond the bounded instrumentality in current corporate sustainability research: Toward an inclusive notion of profitability. *Journal of Business Ethics*, *104*(3), 325–345.
Holliday, C. O., Schmidheiny, S., & Watts, P. (2002). *Walking the talk: The business case for sustainable development*. Greenleaf.
Howard-Grenville, J., Buckle, S. J., Hoskins, B. J., & George, G. (2014). Climate change and management: From the editors. *Academy of Management Journal*, *57*(3), 615–623.
Ivory, S. B., & MacKay, R. B. (2020). Scaling sustainability from the organizational periphery to the strategic core: Towards a practice-based framework of what practitioners "do." *Business Strategy and the Environment*, *29*(5), 2058–2077.
Johansen, R. (2012). *Ten new leadership skills for an uncertain world* (2nd ed). Berrett-Koehler Publishers.
Lee, L-E. (2024, February 29). US firms fall further behind global peers on climate disclosure. *MSCI Sustainability Institute*. https://www.msci-institute.com/insights/us-firms-fall-further-behind-global-peers-on-climate-disclosure
Levin, K., Cashore, B., Bernstein, S., & Auld, G. (2012). Overcoming the tragedy of super wicked problems: Constraining our future selves to ameliorate global climate change. *Policy Sciences*, *45*, 123–152.
Lounsbury, M. (2007). A tale of two cities: Competing logics and practice variation in the professionalizing of mutual funds. *Academy of Management Journal*, *50*(2), 289–307.
Marx, K. (1867). *Capital: A critique of political economy. Volume 1, Part 1: The process of capitalist production*. Cosimo.
Ostrom, E. (1990). *Governing the commons: The evolution of institutions for collective action*. Cambridge University Press.
Porritt, J. (2007). *Capitalism as if the world matters*. Earthscan.
Porter, M. E., & Kramer, M. R. (2006). Strategy and society: The link between competitive advantage and corporate social responsibility. *Harvard Business Review*, *84*(12), 78–92.
Raworth, K. (2018). *Doughnut economics: Seven ways to think like a 21st-century economist*. Random House Business Books.
Savitz, A. (2006). *The triple bottom line*. Jossey Bass.
Smith, A. (1776). *The wealth of nations: An inquiry into the nature and causes of the wealth of nations*. W. Strahan and T. Cadell.
Stout, L. (2012). *The shareholder value myth: How putting shareholders first harms investors, corporations, and the public*. Berrett-Koehler Publishers.
UN. (2024). *Progress towards the Sustainable Development Goals: Report of the Secretary-General*. General Assembly Economic and Social Council.
UN. (n.d.). *The 17 Goals*. Retrieved 05/01/2026, from sdgs.un.org/goals

10

Leading in a Crisis

Practical Considerations for Disruptive Situations

Amy D. Grubb and Robert E. Anderson Jr.

Introduction

Almost every leader will face a significant crisis in their career. It is not *whether* there will be a crisis to lead through, it is *how* leadership is demonstrated through that crisis that determines success as a leader and impact to the team and to the organization. This chapter highlights what a crisis is, the key differences in leadership through a crisis as compared to day-to-day operations, and what leaders should focus on before, during, and after a crisis to be best positioned for success.

A typical leader or employee in any given organization likely has little to no background in crisis management, and yet extremely disruptive events can happen in any industry at any time. These disruptions can overwhelm typical resources, processes, and coping mechanisms. Leadership in a crisis situation presents opportunities to rise to the occasion. Preparation for a crisis which may never happen is essential so that when that "never event" happens, a leader can be ready to lead through the chaos.

In this chapter, we will focus on practical approaches and techniques for leaders dealing with a crisis situation. The content primarily derives from our collective experience leading in crisis contexts and advising leaders in public- and private-sector organizations who are navigating a crisis. The goal is to focus on a core set of key practices that have shown to be effective for a range of crisis situations such that (a) leaders have a basic framework of how to start preparing for and navigating a crisis, and (b) researchers may have a framework under which to conduct additional research in this space.

Amy D. Grubb and Robert E. Anderson Jr., *Leading in a Crisis*. In: *The Changing Leadership Landscape*.
Edited by: Sheri L. Feinzig and Mariangela Battista, Oxford University Press. © Oxford University Press (2026).
DOI: 10.1093/9780197820070.003.0010

What Is a Crisis?

A crisis can be a personal or professional situation that is sudden, disruptive, impactful on financial or human capital, significantly complex, with a high degree of uncertainty both in terms of possible cause and possible outcome. While this chapter focuses on leadership in a crisis in the workplace setting, personal situations for employees can precipitate or be exacerbated when there is a significant threat to personal safety, health, financial stability, or the well-being of loved ones.

Experiencing personal crisis while in a leadership role can greatly impact that leader's ability to make decisions and respond to the needs of employees. In addition, leaders should have awareness of significant crises in the personal life of employees to support their well-being, reallocate workload, and find additional personnel to help meet organizational objectives while someone is experiencing a personal crisis.

We will focus the rest of this chapter on leading through a business crisis. This is not to downplay the role of personal crisis and its impact on work performance, but rather to focus on the novel situations that leaders can face when their team, business, or industry is experiencing a crisis and how to best demonstrate leadership during those situations.

The sudden, disruptive, complex event that impacts an organization to the degree that it can be considered a crisis can lead to decreased public trust, loss of property or data, impact to operations and fulfilling business purpose, significant and irrecoverable financial loss, or significant injuries or loss of life (employee or public). Examples of a business crisis include a catastrophic cyberattack or market event that causes considerable loss to the company, workplace accidents or violence, theft of organizational intellectual property, compromised product safety or contamination, or even poor public behavior on the part of employees or executive management that leads to backlash against the company. In government organizations, there can also be such world events as a mass casualty incident, bombing, or infrastructure attack.

The defining experiences of leaders and employees during *any* type of crisis are the feeling of being unprepared, facing immense pressure to make critical decisions under duress, and a perception of a profound sense of uncertainty and lack of control over the unfolding events. These situations often evoke strong emotional responses like fear, anxiety, and confusion, which further complicate the ability to think clearly and act effectively, especially for those without prior experience in navigating such turbulent circumstances. Consequently, during a crisis, leaders need to highlight aspects of their leadership in a different manner than that which would normally be executed in a day-to-day state of normalcy.

Similarities and Differences in Leading Day-to-Day versus Leading in a Crisis

Leading in a business environment requires a blend of consistent practices and adaptable strategies, but the approach shifts significantly when comparing day-to-day operations to crisis situations. In day-to-day leadership, the focus is often on maintaining stability, fostering growth, and executing established plans. This involves setting goals, delegating tasks, managing performance, and nurturing a positive organizational culture. Leaders typically work within predictable frameworks, relying on data analysis, strategic planning, and established communication channels to guide their teams. They aim to optimize efficiency, promote collaboration, and ensure long-term success through steady progress and continuous improvement. While day-to-day leadership emphasizes process and development, crisis leadership emphasizes immediate action, resilience, and adaptability. Both require strong leadership skills, but they are applied in distinct ways to address vastly different circumstances so that the team can continue to be effective and successful in a different mode of working and context.

Leading in a crisis demands a starkly different approach than leading in a steady state of work, primarily because the information coming to a leader during a crisis is overwhelming in volume and often highly inaccurate. Additionally, the employees executing on the crisis are operating in an extraordinarily complex, ever-changing, and ambiguous environment which leads to stress. As such, two crucial differentiators require a shift in leadership approach within the crisis situation: decision-making and communication.

Because of the urgency of a crisis situation, the amount of time to analyze the information at hand as fully as a leader may want to make decisions is appreciably less than that of the average organizational context. Additionally, the quality of the information is significantly diminished in a crisis situation: there are substantial gaps in data, the data are likely inaccurate, and the facts of the situation will change rapidly. Finally, the consequences of the decisions are more significant, with survival (human or corporate) possibly being at stake.

The role of stress within the crisis creates a sizable dimension to leadership in that the uncertainty and complexity of the situation results in physical and emotional reactions as well as a constant swirl in thinking. While there are complexities and ambiguities in the typical work environment, the impact of the subsequent decisions and actions are not as high-stakes, nor is there the time pressure and volume of input that a crisis creates. Typical situations allow employees and leaders alike to process information and act at a pace that works for them. The level of discomfort that comes with the urgency and ambiguity of a crisis situation can result in fragmented attention, leading to lower-quality decisions and actions and the need for leaders to communicate in ways that provide clarity and focus for others.

Both the challenges of decision-making and the stress component within the crisis, which demands changes in communication practices, are extremely uncomfortable for most leaders, even the most seasoned crisis-handlers. Preparation for crisis leadership allows for people to have some semblance of control and confidence in navigating whatever a future crisis might be. This allows the leader to demonstrate calm and steady leadership in the chaos surrounding the situation and have a sense of control and predictability.

Leading through Phases of Crisis

We propose that it is important for leaders to dissect how to approach a crisis in three distinct phases: before, during, and after the crisis. These phases have related but separate actions that any leader can take to calmly and successfully lead any team through whatever crisis will emerge (these actions are summarized in Table 10.1).

Phase 1: Before a Crisis

Crisis leadership really begins *before* a crisis occurs. When scoping what a leader can do to prepare, there are key areas where a leader can act and make improvements now to be more successful in leading through a crisis:

- Plan for various scenarios to develop crisis management and business continuity plans
- Build trust and resilience in the team

Table 10.1 Critical Leader Behaviors during Each Stage of a Crisis

Before	During	After

• Plan for possible scenarios to build crisis management plans and business continuity plans
• Build trust and resilience in team
  o Train and develop team on key skills and attributes
• Understand your own knowledge and skill limitations, gather experts to serve as advisers
• Hone communication skills and plans
• Secure financial and technological resources that might be necessary (or develop plans to acquire them)
	• Decide quickly on available (albeit inaccurate and incomplete) information
	  o Acknowledge that direction will change
	  o Communicate with clarity
	• Execute Plans
	• Check in on team members
	• Empower others to make decisions at their level
	• Inspire and demonstrate confidence
		• Shift oneself as the leader out of crisis mode and back to day-to-day mode
		• Conduct after-action reviews and revise processes and plans accordingly
		• Expand advisory experts as necessary
		• Give time and space for recovery for personnel and processes

- Know your experts
- Have communication plan
- Secure technology and financial resources that may be necessary

Plan for Possible Crisis Scenarios

While a defining element of a crisis is that it is sudden and unanticipated, leaders can still prepare themselves to face a crisis and develop the thought processes and action orientation to navigate any crisis successfully. The nature and types of crisis that an organization can face are endless, and preparing for each individual possible crisis is simply beyond scale and scope. However, with businesses and industries facing a new crisis on a daily basis, a key action to take right now is for leaders to ask, "What if that happens here?" as other organizations face a crisis of their own. While this might not prepare a leader for the exact crisis context that arises, it certainly pressure-tests critical levers needed to navigate a team through any crisis. It also addresses the wide range of possible disaster scenarios so that the leader can at least cursorily think through what resources and actions would be needed if that type of scenario happened in their own organization. Some significant events only become crises if leaders have not taken steps to prepare themselves and others for when such events occur.

Proactive crisis leadership centers on anticipating potential problems and taking preventive action *before* they escalate. This involves a continuous process of risk assessment, where leaders identify vulnerabilities within their organization or industry and evaluate the potential impact of various threats. This could range from natural disasters and economic downturns to technological failures, supply chain disruptions, or reputational damage. By rigorously analyzing these potential scenarios, leaders can develop strategies to mitigate their likelihood or minimize their impact. It is the role of the leader to be proactive and to understand the people who will look to the leader to calmly and effectively navigate the situation. Business leaders must also adopt a proactive stance in preparing the organization and its people for a crisis, embedding preparedness into the organization's DNA long before any disruptive event occurs. This entails scanning the talent and resources available to execute on a crisis, and arming the team with the awareness of plans, providing tools, and fostering resilience.

A leader needs a detailed crisis management plan (CMP) that outlines clear roles, responsibilities, communication protocols, and operational procedures for various crisis scenarios. This plan focuses on how the crisis itself will be run. Simultaneously, a business continuity plan (BCP) should be developed to ensure the continuation of critical business functions, including strategies for data recovery, alternative worksites, and supply chain resilience.

At the core of any crisis is the communication element; therefore, the cornerstone of proactive crisis management is the development of a comprehensive crisis communication plan. This plan outlines clear protocols for disseminating information to all stakeholders, including employees, customers, suppliers, and the public. It establishes communication channels, designates spokespersons, and prepares key messages for different crisis scenarios. Regular training and drills ensure that everyone understands their roles and responsibilities during a crisis, enabling a swift and coordinated response. This clear delineation and coordination of roles maximizes the limited resources and time that a crisis situation demands.

Build Trust and Resilience

The nature of a crisis requires that certain tasks be performed by a leader in the decision-making, logistics, resourcing, and communications space. However, leaders lead people, so building resilience within the organization's people is equally crucial. This involves fostering a culture of adaptability, flexibility, and trust where employees are empowered to think critically and respond effectively to unexpected challenges. Leaders can achieve this by investing in employee training and development, promoting cross-functional collaboration, and creating diverse teams with a wide range of skills and perspectives. This can build a culture where change is embraced, and where continuous improvement through learning and adapting to the situation is celebrated during the day-to-day times. Preparing the team and building the cultural environment where they can be successful during a steady state sets the stage for those behaviors and thought processes to become ingrained in the fabric of how business is done, so that they continue automatically during a crisis. Leaders can also build trust in how they react to bad news during typical business interactions. There is no shortage of bad news in a crisis and leaders need to build the psychological safety for employees to bring problems forward—and even more so when navigating a crisis. A resilient organization at all levels of leadership and employees that can share, absorb, and handle bad news in day-to-day business is better equipped to withstand shocks and emerge stronger from adversity. With strong frontline leadership to support this way of thinking, whatever the type of crisis, it will be handled much better in the long run.

Know Your Experts

Establishment of critical partnerships is essential in successfully guiding the organization through a crisis. Internal partnerships are indispensable, as no leader knows everything about every element of a crisis. Knowing the primary experts in the different functions within the organization (finance, human resources, communications, etc.)—especially those that the leader is less familiar with—can become a multiplier of resources in a crisis situation. A leader does not and should not have to know everything about every topic, they just have to know someone who does know. Taking inventory of their own and others' skill sets and supplementing with internal partners can save significant time and maximize probability of success. Proactive leaders also prioritize establishment of strong relationships with key external stakeholders. This includes building trust with customers, maintaining open communication with suppliers, and engaging with the community. These relationships can be invaluable during a crisis for providing support, resources, and goodwill.

Hone Communication Skills and Secure Resources

Effective communication strategies as a leader are paramount, necessitating the identification of key stakeholders, the establishment of diverse communication channels, and the training of spokespeople to deliver clear, consistent, and empathetic messages. This takes a lot of time to do well; leaders need to think about how to achieve this within the organizational practice, policies, and structure available, as well as spend dedicated time in honing their own communication skills and plans. When in the midst of a crisis, the time invested before the crisis in practicing how to be decisive, directive, and clear in communications (and with whom) will show value immediately. Communication does not only mean the messages that the leader puts forward, but also asking good questions and truly listening to the information that is being brought forward, not just the confirmatory or the negative information.

Furthermore, a core resource in times of crisis is the organizational culture. Leaders must cultivate a crisis-ready culture by promoting awareness, encouraging reporting, investing in regular training, and exemplifying a commitment to preparedness. Trust in the leadership overall, the boss, and the processes are paramount for success when the eventual crisis arises. By showing that preparedness is a cultural value, leaders foster trust in the team and build confidence in themselves. This builds resilience in team members to be successful in whatever they face together. Valuing preparedness also positions leaders to serve as a role model for individual dedication to planning for the unknown, to relying on people with skills different from one's own, and to continuously developing oneself.

In addition to building resilience and capability within the people working directly for the leader, securing other critical resources such as financial reserves, robust technology, and other key personnel with whom to partner is essential to overcome a crisis. By diligently addressing these areas before a crisis happens, business leaders can build resilient organizations capable of effectively navigating crises and minimizing potential damage.

In essence, proactive crisis leadership is not a one-time effort but an ongoing commitment to preparedness. It requires vigilance, foresight, and a willingness to invest in preventive measures. Furthermore, working to improve one's own leadership attributes that are essential to navigating a crisis (such as calmness, decisiveness, empathy, and adaptability) is much easier and more effective to do when in a steady organizational state and not in the midst of a crisis situation. By embracing a proactive and dedicated approach to crisis preparation, leaders can significantly reduce the likelihood and severity of crises, which in turn protects their organization and stakeholders, and increases the probability of long-term success. This requires significant investment of time and dedication to revising and reviewing for the eventual "what if" that will be sudden, unexpected, and complex. The more prepared a leader is, and the more they engage in critical self- and team-evaluation of readiness and skill, the more likely it is that the organization will emerge from crisis with minimal damage and the ability to bounce back and thrive more quickly. Ultimately, ethical and transparent leadership, coupled with a commitment to learning and continuous improvement, will guide the organization through the crisis and pave the way for recovery and future preparedness.

Phase 2: During the Crisis

To effectively lead during a crisis, business leaders must embody a combination of key traits, characteristics, and strategies. Being trustworthy, calm, decisive, and adaptable are paramount, enabling leaders to make swift, informed decisions while remaining flexible in the face of evolving circumstances. Clear and consistent communication is essential to maintain trust, as this ensures all stakeholders are informed of the situation, the response, and any changes. Empathy and compassion are crucial for understanding and addressing the concerns of those affected, which fosters a sense of unity and support.

Leaders should also demonstrate resilience, which inspires confidence and perseverance throughout the organization. Maintaining a calm and steady presence through actions and words, even when one feels neither calm nor steady, can give others the space and calm needed to make decisions and garner their own resources to address the crisis. A focus on strategic thinking helps prioritize actions, allocate resources effectively, and mitigate potential damage. Collaboration and empowerment of team members is vital in order for disparate team members, some of whom may not have worked closely together before, to leverage the diverse skills and expertise required to navigate the crisis.

Decide Quickly on Available (Often Inaccurate and Incomplete) Information

A crisis, whether it is a natural disaster, a financial meltdown, a public relations disaster, or a sudden operational failure, introduces a high degree of uncertainty, urgency, and pressure. In these situations, leaders must pivot rapidly, making critical decisions with incomplete information and under immense time constraints.

Initial information in a crisis can often be unreliable and overwhelming, and the degree of unreliability, uncertainty, and volume cannot be overstated. During a crisis, information is often gleaned incorrectly for several reasons, many of which are endemic to the nature of a crisis. The situation is usually chaotic and fast-moving, leading to confusion and misinterpretation of events. Stress and fear can affect people's perception and memory, making eyewitness accounts unreliable. Early reports often come from incomplete or fragmented sources, and there may be a lack of established communication channels to gather and verify information quickly. Additionally, there is often pressure to provide immediate updates, which can lead to the dissemination of unverified or inaccurate details.

As the crisis evolves and continues, the quality and accuracy of information improves. The challenge in this, however, is that a leader cannot wait for better information to make decisions in the early moments of a crisis. Crisis leadership prioritizes decisive action, clear and frequent communication, and the ability to stabilize the situation, mitigate damage, and restore confidence. A critical behavior in the early moments of a crisis is to keep making decisions. A leader should continue to take actions, direct the team and resources according to the information at hand in the moment, and not let the enormity of the situation lead to paralysis. A bias for action and decisions is required for survival.

On balance, leaders must exercise caution and avoid jumping to conclusions based on initial reports. Instead, they should prioritize verifying information from multiple reliable sources and establishing a clear process for information gathering and validation, and make smaller, action-based decisions in shorter time increments. It is crucial to communicate the uncertainty to stakeholders and to team members, acknowledging that the situation is still evolving and that the understanding of it may and will likely change. Leaders should also foster an environment of continuous learning and adaptation, where new information is integrated into the response strategy as it becomes available. This involves remaining flexible, being prepared to revise plans, and maintaining open communication channels to ensure that everyone is working with the most accurate and up-to-date information possible.

During a crisis, leaders must overtly acknowledge that information is often incomplete and rapidly evolving. This creates a state of constant change, where initial understandings and plans may shift significantly as new data become available. Leaders need to communicate this reality to their teams, emphasizing that the situation is dynamic and that adjustments will be necessary. It is essential to avoid presenting a facade of certainty when the situation is inherently uncertain, as this can erode trust when changes inevitably occur.

Effective crisis communication involves providing regular updates, even when those updates indicate that the situation is still unfolding. Leaders should explain what is known, what is unknown, and what processes are in place to gather further information. Leaders should also explicitly state that the direction of effort will likely change as the crisis situation evolves. Transparency and honesty are paramount. Team members need to understand that the evolving nature of the crisis may require changes to strategies, priorities, and timelines. Team members should also bring forward information early and often to continue to clarify the situation, trusting the leader to absorb the new information and to maintain an environment where bad news is as welcome as good news.

To manage the uncertainty, leaders should establish clear communication channels and protocols. This ensures that information is disseminated quickly and accurately, minimizing confusion and rumors. Regular meetings, updates, and feedback mechanisms can help team members stay informed and adapt to the changing circumstances. It is also important to manage expectations, letting the team know that the situation may take hours, days, or even weeks to fully resolve. Communication channels should also allow for information to flow upward, as those with "boots on the ground" often have nuanced knowledge that can lead to clarity and better decision-making.

Ultimately, leading through the chaotic and stressful change of a crisis requires a combination of clear communication, transparency, and adaptability. Leaders must keep their teams informed, manage expectations, and foster a culture of resilience and trust. By overtly acknowledging the dynamic nature of a crisis and providing ongoing support, leaders can help their teams navigate uncertainty and work effectively toward a solution. Furthermore, a leader continuing to evaluate the evolving information to make new decisions, even decisions that are contradictory to previous decisions, demonstrates a cadence of confidence when the leader has prepared themselves and the team to work as adaptively as possible when in the "non-crisis" times. Leaders and their teams will be uncomfortable during a crisis; as long as the leader continues to make decisions and add one incremental, small piece of certainty, however temporary it may be, the team can continue to move forward through the crisis.

As with the steady state of work, there are two key tracks of thought for a leader navigating a crisis: the operational side which is very task- and decision-oriented, and the people side, which has a focus on the empathy, trust, and communication necessary for success. This distinction between managing tasks and leading the people during a crisis is vital to surviving the crisis and thriving afterward; both elements are related, both need attention, but they require different approaches.

Execute Plans

The before-crisis phase emphasized the need for plans—crisis management plans and business continuity plans, both of which include a communication plan aspect. The purpose of developing these robust processes and documents is for executing in a time of crisis. When the uncertainty emerges, relying on the work that was done in the before-crisis phase can give stability and clarity to the leader, which in turn engenders trust in the team. Plans were made, and the crisis is the time to follow them, knowing that as the crisis emerges, there will be significant moments where all the planning did not take into account the novelty of this particular crisis. Plans are the starting point and a reference guide. That said, there are core functions in managing the tasks and activities on the operational side that are universal irrespective of the nature of the crisis. These primarily involve the logistic and operational aspects of crisis resolution. Essentially, the logistic and operational side is organizing and controlling the actual work that needs to be done to resolve the crisis. This is the part of crisis leadership that the team and those adjacent will actually *see* a leader do during the crisis. This part includes the following:

- *Assessing the situation*: Gathering information, evaluating the damage or impact, determining further possible threats.
- *Reporting*: Getting the accurate information to the right people.
- *Developing a plan*: Creating a step-by-step outline of actions to be taken, prioritizing tasks, and allocating resources.
- *Implementing the plan*: Directing the execution of the plan, assigning responsibilities, and coordinating activities.
- *Monitoring progress*: Tracking the implementation, measuring results, and adjusting.
- *Obtaining resources*: Ensuring that the team has the resources needed to complete the tasks in an effective and timely manner.

Check In on Team Members

In a crisis, both managing and leading are crucial. A leader needs to effectively manage the tasks to ensure that the practical steps are taken to address the situation. A leader also should focus on the people to ensure that they are motivated, supported, and working together effectively to achieve the desired outcome. The "leading the people" is the part of crisis leadership that the team and those adjacent will *feel* during the crisis, and it can be a large contributor to the dedication and commitment to the objective from others when the exhaustion of working a crisis sets in. It can also lead to clearer thinking, strategizing, and decision-making.

Leading the people focuses on the human side of the crisis and may be more important than any tactical plan or decision. In the instance of crisis leadership, leading the people focuses on the following aspects:

- *Providing direction*: Communicating a clear vision of how the crisis will be resolved and what the future will look like.
- *Motivating and inspiring*: Encouraging people to stay focused, committed, and productive, even in the face of adversity.
- *Supporting and empathizing*: Understanding the emotional impact of the crisis on individuals, addressing their concerns, and providing support.
- *Communicating*: Maintaining open, honest, and frequent communication with all stakeholders, including employees, customers, and the community.

- *Building trust*: Fostering a sense of confidence and assurance that the situation is being handled effectively and that everyone is working toward a common goal.
- *Empowering*: Giving team members the autonomy and resources to make decisions and act, fostering a sense of ownership, responsibility, and trust.

Empower Others to Make Decisions at Their Level

As the leader processes large volumes of information with varying degrees of quality and ensures the team is prepared, resourced, and executing as strongly as possible, bandwidth is critical. By attending to the human side of the crisis and empowering team members to make decisions within their lane, that "big-picture bandwidth" can grow and allow the leader to make the tactical and strategic decisions necessary to coordinate resources and resolve the crisis. Leaders in the before-crisis stage should have built some capability and trust in the team within an environment where people feel secure to speak up and act within their competence. This creates a situation where the leader does not have to feel the pressure of every decision and every action being required to emanate from them, which frees up an enormous amount of cognitive load.

This focus on empathy and the "people" element during a crisis seems counterintuitive. When one typically thinks of a leader navigating a crisis, the image is that of someone barking orders and driving tasks. While this is true to an extent, the manner in which it is done—calm, clear, hearing others, and making decisions quickly while attuned to the state of emotions and physical stamina of the personnel—can greatly impact the outcome. The care and concern for the people on the ground is a force multiplier for action and a core differentiator between those leaders who successfully navigate a crisis back to a steady state and those for whom the crisis never seems to end.

Inspire and Demonstrate Confidence

One of the most straightforward ways to demonstrate confidence and inspire others is to encourage them to act on the skills and talents that they bring to the table. This is true in steady-state work, and even more so in working through a crisis. A leader instills confidence in others by trusting their team members to do the right thing, provide the right information, and act within their boundaries in a chaotic situation. It is motivating for people to feel trusted and capable; a leader who role-models confidence by making decisions and allows others to do the same within their own space can bring about a perpetual motion machine that continues to drive forward and becomes self-motivating with each small success. Additionally, admitting what is unknown and relying on others to bring their knowledge to the table demonstrates the humanity and confidence of a leader and shows that it is acceptable to not know or be able to do everything, and that leveraging others brings about success.

Phase 3: After the Crisis

There is an end point to every crisis, although knowing exactly when to declare a crisis over is more of an art than a science. Some crises have clear end markers, such as a hostage negotiation resulting in the release of hostages and surrender of the captor. For most business and organizational crises, the end is less clear, but the need to declare a crisis over and redirect people and resources from crisis mode to steady-state mode is essential. A crisis can be considered resolved when the information flow becomes more consistent and accurate; the immediate threat to life, property, or business operations is addressed and the organization is in the process of working through a resolution of the disruption; the complexity of understanding the causes and outcomes of the event is becoming more straightforward and certain; and the operating tempo has shifted to a regular cadence that "feels" like regular work. There can be instances when resolution of one crisis leads to the onset of another. For example, an airplane crash has a crisis onboard prior to the crash itself, but the rescue and recovery operation is another crisis, and perhaps the initial investigation may have a crisis element to it as well. In most cases, however, there is a point at which the crisis is over, and because that point can be ambiguous, a key leadership behavior is to overtly declare the crisis over.

While this may seem trivial, the leadership act of declaring a crisis over and shifting oneself and others out of crisis mode and back to day-to-day steady state of work is important for the recovery and growth of the team and the leader. Although the crisis may be over and resolving to steady state, the work of the leader continues through the third phase, which also involves crucial actions to take, including conducting after-action reviews and giving the team members time and space to recover and get back into their own steady-state rhythms.

After-Action Reviews

While there are numerous methodologies for conducting an after-action review, the key components in every model include identifying what went well and what could be done better for the future. Timing of the review should occur soon after the crisis event itself, so that nuanced key lessons to share are captured and not forgotten. There can be a brief "beat" of time between crisis ending and after-action occurring so that there is some small distance from the event when reflection can occur. Once the crisis is declared over, an after-action review should happen.

It is not enough to do the after-action review, although the review itself can be helpful and even cathartic for team members and the leader. Once the after-action is done, the work to return back to the "before the crisis" phase of preparation begins again, and leaders must work and act to refine, revise, and restore the plans and the team. They need to ask the following questions:

- Do the crisis management plans and the business continuity plans need updates?
- What communication strategies and methods need to be highlighted or modified for the future?
- Do roles and responsibilities need to change?
- What additional experts and resources should be on hand?
- What training and growth opportunities do team members need to prepare for the next crisis (or steady state)?

These questions focus on the task management part of crisis leadership. The other, even more important focus, should turn to the team members themselves. Just as a person needs rest and recovery time after a strenuous workout, people need recovery time after a stressful crisis to be effective in the steady state and to be rested and prepared for the next potential crisis. Fundamental questions to consider about the team and the leader in the after-crisis phase include:

- How did team members shine in the crisis? (The leader should provide feedback accordingly.)
- What can the leader do to gradually bring people back to steady state mentally and physically?

- How can the leader balance workloads and assignments to give team members the time and space to recover and pace themselves?
- How can the leader role-model the "recovery" for themselves as well?
- How can the leader enhance their own leadership in a steady state to build/maintain trust and resilience?

Conclusion

Leading in a crisis highlights both the strengths and flaws of every leader. Leaders should relentlessly prepare for the inevitable crisis, whether it be learning from watching others navigate a crisis and game-planning those scenarios for the organization, or continually building trust and resilience in the team. Every meeting, decision, and interaction with the team can be a moment to ready oneself and others for a crisis. By capitalizing on what makes a great leader in the steady state, a leader can build culture and capability for the team to be able to navigate, survive, and possibly even thrive in a crisis. During a crisis, despite knowing that much of the information at hand is likely wrong, continuing to make decisions on the best information available, giving clear concise direction while acknowledging it will change, and looking out for the people on a personal level as they execute on the crisis plans is essential for successful navigation of the crisis in the moment. Declaring the crisis over at the appropriate time, and reviewing the events to revise plans and give the team time and space for recovery, will lead to a more adept handling of the next (inevitable) crisis.

SECTION V
LEADERSHIP AND DIVERSITY

11

Inclusive Leadership

Bridging Divides and Building Stronger Organizations

Gena Cox and Kathlyn Wilson

The Evolving Landscape of Diversity, Equity, and Inclusion in US and UK Organizations

As societies and workforces change, leaders must adapt (Lin et al., 2024; McKinsey & Company, 2024). The changing face of the available workforce compels leaders to ensure that their culture-building and leadership practices can optimize a workforce that is ever more diverse. This chapter explores this issue through a US and UK lens and offers strategic and tactical recommendations for leaders.

In both the United States and the United Kingdom, there have been long-standing efforts to understand and positively impact the experiences of minoritized people—for example, Indigenous people, descendants of the enslaved, and those from other groups that have been subordinated and underrepresented (Witherspoon et al., 2020). Since the 1960s and due to the Civil Rights Movement (Aiken et al., 2013), the experiences of minoritized people at work have become a more prominent part of this effort.

Diversity, equity, and inclusion (DEI) is a term that has been widely used to represent distinct, yet interconnected workplace approaches for enhancing the representation and integration of people from marginalized social identity groups, ensuring all employees feel valued and included (Fitzsimmons et al., 2023). We will use the term "DEI" throughout the chapter because of its recognizability. However, we prefer the term "equity, diversity, and inclusion" (EDI) which is also widely used. For example, EDI is the term of choice of the American Psychological Association (n.d.) because the organization prioritizes equity (removal of systemic inequalities/barriers), viewing equity as foundational to diversity and inclusion (Andoh, 2025). Some argue that the term "DEI" overemphasizes diversity

Gena Cox and Kathlyn Wilson, *Inclusive Leadership*. In: *The Changing Leadership Landscape*.
Edited by: Sheri L. Feinzig and Mariangela Battista, Oxford University Press. © Oxford University Press (2026).
DOI: 10.1093/9780197820070.003.0011

and underemphasizes equity and inclusion. Equality involves giving everyone the same thing or treating them the same, whether the treatment is beneficial to them or not (Cox et al., 2025, p. 102). Equity, on the other hand, is about each person getting what they need to succeed: "equity exists—not when people and groups are treated exactly alike—but when practices exist in an organization that enable fair and just access to experiences, opportunities, services, treatment, and equal outcomes" (Cox et al., 2025, p. 102). We acknowledge the ongoing debate surrounding using these terms (Green, 2024). In this chapter, we will use the term "equity" (Ruggs & Holmes, 2024).

In recent decades, immigration and population growth within immigrant communities have altered the US demographics (Jensen et al., 2021) such that the country is expected to become "minority White" by 2045 (Colby & Ortman, 2014). Vespa et al. (2020) predict that multiracial or multiethnic individuals will be the fastest-growing group over the next few decades. The UK population is also becoming more diverse as the proportion of White individuals is decreasing while other ethnic groups are growing. The fastest-growing UK demographic is people from mixed or multiple ethnic backgrounds, 60.5% of whom are under the age of 25—the highest percentage within this age range among the five aggregated ethnic groups (Gov.UK, 2023).

In addition to the long-standing focus on minoritized status based on race and ethnicity, various other social movements with hashtags like #MeToo, #stopAAPIHate, #blacklivesmatter, #neurodivergent, and #loveislove garner global attention to the experiences of people from subordinated groups. We recognize that other dimensions of difference are important and may be legally protected in the United States via the Civil Rights Act of 1964 and other laws (Equal Employment Opportunity Commission, n.d.) and in the United Kingdom via the Equality Act of 2010 (EHRC, 2018) and other regulations (e.g., the requirement for mandatory gender pay-gap reporting [GOV.UK, 2024a]). However, this chapter will focus only on the dimensions of race and ethnicity. By race we mean "the social construction and categorization of people based on perceived shared physical traits that result in the maintenance of a sociopolitical hierarchy" (APA, 2023a, para 1), and by ethnicity we mean, "characterization of people based on having a shared culture (e.g., language, food, music, dress, values, and beliefs) related to common ancestry and shared history" (APA, 2023b, para 1). Even though we will not discuss other dimensions of difference at length in this chapter, the analysis and recommendations we present offer a strategic approach to DEI that covers any of the dimensions on which a company might focus.

Although there is a perception that race and ethnicity have been extensively covered in the diversity and inclusion literature (e.g., Farndale et al., 2015), these dimensions have received less focus in management and organization studies with the emergence of the concept of diversity (Nkomo, 2021). A review of the DEI literature from 1928 to 2022 found that gender was the most cited diversity category and was mentioned twice as often as race (Fitzsimmons et al., 2023).

Our focus acknowledges the historical context and draws attention to systemic barriers experienced by racial and ethnic minorities in hiring, career progression, and pay, for which strategies are needed to achieve equity. Different underrepresented groups face unique experiences and challenges with their own implications for practice. The challenges are further exacerbated by the intersectional impact of gender and race stereotyping (Pogrebna et al., 2024). For example, Black men are often stigmatized, while Black women face marginalization (Livingston & Rosette, 2021). Asian women are regularly stereotyped as compliant and deferential (Mukkamala & Suyemoto, 2018). Black and Latina women often face biased appraisals of their competence (Rosette & Livingston, 2012; Niemann, 2004) and are criticized for being "too aggressive" (Holder et al., 2015). As a result, women from these racial and ethnic groups are underrepresented in the workplace, particularly in leadership roles (LeanIn.Org & McKinsey & Company, 2024).

This chapter aims to provide insights on how leaders can actively work to reduce racial bias and its potential impact within organizational settings and build inclusive organizations. We define diversity as "the degree to which a workforce reflects the demographic characteristics of the available labor force" (Cox, 2022, p. 30), including the varied work styles and perspectives that individuals from different identity groups bring (Thomas & Ely, 1996). We define inclusion as the extent to which individuals in positions of power and privilege in organizations involve the less powerful in participatory work systems and share information and power (Nembhard & Edmondson, 2006; Roberson, 2006), creating work environments where all employees feel respected (Cox et al., 2025).

The Current State of Inclusion in Organizations

Despite decades of attention to DEI issues, patterns of exclusion remain deeply embedded in organizational practices that shape access to opportunity, advancement and leadership. Examining empirical evidence on workforce composition and leadership representation can clarify exclusion and inclusion patterns as they currently manifest in organizations.

The Reality of Exclusion

Minoritized ethnic groups have historically been underrepresented in public- and private-sector organizations in the United Kingdom and the United States (Andrews & Ashworth, 2015; United States Department of Labor, 2024). People from minority ethnic backgrounds comprise 18.3% of the population in England and Wales (Office of National Statistics, 2022), with 66.5% of working age, compared to 62.1% of the White population (GOV.UK, 2024b). In the United Kingdom, ethnic minorities are underrepresented in senior roles, with significant variation across groups. In the private sector, minoritized ethnic groups hold 10.3% of senior roles, an increase of only 1.1 percentage points since 2014. Black employees hold just 1.5% of these roles, reflecting little progress over the past decade (Palmer, 2020). In the public sector, Black representation in leadership has stagnated at 1% over the same period (Business in the Community, 2020).

The pattern is similar in the United States, where representation of minority racial/ethnic groups is lower than would be predicted based on their representation in the overall workforce (United States Department of Labor, 2024). Black and Latino workers are underrepresented in professional occupations (Guynn & Fraser, 2023), and Black, Latino, and Asian workers are underrepresented in management and executive roles.

To better understand the challenge, we now provide context regarding how historically based systemic inequities exist in the workplace today.

The Role of Performance Appraisals in Underrepresentation Patterns

Selection and hiring practices play a role in racial disparities in the workforce, but performance appraisals are uniquely impactful because they form the basis of critical career decisions such as promotion and pay. Although there is much discussion about the future of performance appraisals

(Murphy & DeNisi, 2023), they are still widely used (Morley et al., 2021). Sixty-two percent of UK organizations (CIPD, 2024) and about 90% of US companies (SHRM, 2014) use individual performance evaluations to manage pay progression. However, the challenge from a DEI perspective is that ethnic minorities receive significantly lower ratings than their White counterparts (McKay & McDaniel, 2006; Stauffer & Buckley, 2005; Wilson & Jones, 2008, 2018). The focus of academic empirical research has been on determining the *magnitude* of difference in ratings across racial/ethnic groups (statistical effect sizes) rather than what *underlies* these differences (Wilson, 2010). In their review of appraisal research, DeNisi and Murphy (2017) argue that although some large-scale studies report significant effects of race, race is a weaker factor than other variables. Other studies (McKay & McDaniel, 2006; Sackett & DuBois, 1991) provide evidence that these differences are both statistically and practically significant. Stauffer and Buckley (2005) found that Black and White raters both rate Black staff lower but disagree on the magnitude of the difference. White raters gave significantly higher mean ratings to White staff when compared to Black raters. The practical implication is that for White ratees, the race of their supervisor does not matter, but for Black ratees it does (Stauffer & Buckley, 2005). The research is not definitive about whether these differences in ratings stem from racial bias, overestimated ratings for White staff, a positivity bias, or depressed ratings for Black staff (Greenwald & Pettigrew, 2014). Research suggests supervisors may emphasize distinct factors when summarizing performance across ethnic groups. Wilson (2010) found that supervisors emphasized interpersonal and social factors in summarizing the performance of Asian and Black bank staff, which were inconsistent with their performance ratings (also see Disability Rights UK, 2015). This aligns with previous correlational studies showing that supervisors emphasize interpersonal and social factors for ethnic minority staff (e.g., Cox & Nkomo, 1986).

Despite dissatisfaction with performance appraisal systems (Cappelli & Tavis, 2016; DeNisi & Murphy, 2017), these processes serve an essential function in organizations. Whether organizations abandon them and move, for example, to ongoing conversations (Adler et al., 2016), performance will always be evaluated in some manner. Examining the organization's appraisal process is critical to addressing disparities in progression and pay. Educating raters to optimize their accuracy is crucial.

Current Trends and Backlash against DEI Initiatives

Although US and UK businesses have tackled DEI for decades, progress has been slow (Newkirk, 2019). Historically, leaders from minority ethnic backgrounds have been assigned to handle corporate DEI issues (Paluch & Shum, 2024), and top-level leaders have not handled DEI like the key strategic imperative it should be (Cox, 2022). The murder of George Floyd by a police officer in the United States in May 2020 sparked a global DEI movement. Between 2020 and 2023, more corporate executives became directly involved in addressing DEI issues (Ceron, 2023; World at Work, 2021). In the United Kingdom, the government launched its "Inclusive Britain" strategy (GOV.UK, 2022; Race Disparity Unit, 2024). However, by summer 2023, the momentum had slowed (Ceron, 2023; Kalita, 2023; Rogers et al., 2024).

Legal Context

Legal challenges to DEI are not new but ramped up when in June 2023 the Supreme Court of the United States (2023) ruled that affirmative action in college admissions was unconstitutional. Affirmative action in this ruling refers to policies and practices in college admissions that consider race as one of the factors to promote diversity and correct past racial discrimination. This case is explicitly related to using numerical targets in college admissions, not corporate DEI. Nevertheless, leaders began to retreat from DEI as litigation challenges increased (Delikat & Kiselica, 2024; Murray, 2024), even though most DEI work remains legal.

Political Context

Political changes have also impacted DEI progress. In the United Kingdom, amid growing anti-immigration sentiment, the political environment has increased public scrutiny and made it more difficult for organizations to pursue inclusive policies. In 2024, the UK government announced a plan to publish new civil service guidelines to limit DEI work to only statutory obligations (Markson, 2024). A UK government commission tasked by Prime Minister Boris Johnson to investigate race and ethnic disparities concluded that geography, cultural traditions, and family structure within different ethnic groups, and their perceptions of their own individual and group agency, contribute to the problem. The report also concluded that biases are limited in explaining observed disparities (GOV.UK, 2021). In his first term (2017–2021), US President Donald Trump signed Executive Order 13950 banning DEI in the federal government (Trump, 2020, September 22). In November 2024, voters reelected Donald Trump to serve a second term (2025–2029). On the first day of his second term in office, Trump signed an executive order entitled "Ending Radical and Wasteful Government DEI Programs and Preferencing" (Trump, 2025, January 20), which revoked Executive Order 13985 (Advancing Racial Equity and Support for Underserved Communities through the Federal Government), which had been put in place by his predecessor, President Joe Biden. Trump's order also directed federal agencies to terminate their internal DEI positions and work. On January 21, 2025, the president issued an order "Ending Illegal Discrimination and Restoring Merit-Based Opportunity" (Trump, 2025, January 21), which revoked Executive Order 11246, thereby ending affirmative action in federal contracting. The Office of Federal Contract Compliance (OFCCP), which was responsible for promoting diversity in federal contracting, was ordered to immediately stop its work. Section 4 of the Executive Order 11246 encouraged the private sector to end "illegal DEI" and directed the Attorney General to create a strategic plan to target industry sectors and identify specific companies that practice "illegal DEI." DEI Executives are challenged to decide how to respond to these executive orders (Goldberg, 2025b) because they must now ensure that their efforts to avoid discriminatory actions do not violate the "illegal DEI" provisions (Goldberg, 2025b).

Because of these anti-DEI efforts, although most leaders still support DEI work (Butcher, 2024; Meyersohn, 2024), few organizations overtly express that support as they did between 2020 and 2023 (Herbert, 2024; Hudson, 2024). Several large corporations have explicitly said they will reduce their DEI efforts (Nassauer, 2024), and others are avoiding the term "DEI," using alternative language to describe their efforts (Telford & Mark, 2024).

Employee Context

Not all employees support DEI work. Research (Kanitz et al., 2024, p. 1644) indicates that employees tend to fall into one of four categories regarding their responses to DEI. The category names are intentionally self-descriptive. According to the authors, "The first term captures the characterizing affective experience, such as 'excited'. The second term denotes the broader stance toward the initiative, such as 'supporters.'" Excited Supporters, who respond most favorably to DEI initiatives, represented 70% of the research sample. Calm Compliers (who are not very enthusiastic about the work but are not resistant and will comply) were 21% of the respondents. Torn Shapers are conflicted. They feel a mix of positive and negative emotions about the work and were 6%. Discontent Opponents (who see little benefit to DEI initiatives) were 3%. In October 2024, about 52% of US employees said that companies doing DEI work was a good thing (Minkin, 2024)—a four-point decline from September 2023. In the United Kingdom, about 66% of workers thought in 2023 that DEI work was essential as they considered job opportunities (Bansal, 2023).

Although these broad contextual factors significantly influence DEI work today, the next section provides specifics about the narratives that fuel that resistance.

Arguments That Power the Resistance to DEI

We group the current resistance to DEI into four categories: (1) the conflation of DEI with "affirmative action," (2) the perception that DEI initiatives disadvantage the majority racial/ethnic group, (3) concerns that DEI drives a political agenda and is divisive, and (4) the criticism that DEI is ineffective.

Misperceptions about DEI and Affirmative Action

Leaders often discuss DEI and affirmative action if they are the same (Alqasser et al., 2024). DEI is an umbrella term for a wide range of actions that broadly promote fair workplace experiences, while affirmative action seeks *specific* proportional workforce representation. Affirmative action practices have been contentious for decades (Crosby et al., 2006) because opponents view them as an unfair form of preferential treatment, synonymous with quota systems. However, affirmative action only requires that an organization *study and understand* its workforce's characteristics and address any gaps they identify (Crosby et al., 2006); affirmative action does not demand quotas. However, very few organizations use affirmative action extensively in the way detractors describe it (Atkinson & Headley, 2024).

DEI Disadvantages the Majority Group

Another argument against DEI is that it disadvantages individuals from majority groups—typically White people and men—in favor of individuals from historically underrepresented groups, such as Black and Indigenous people. According to Pew Research (Minkin, 2024, para 5), "far more Americans say DEI hurts White men than say it helps them" (36% vs. 14%). This view often leads to the charge of "reverse discrimination" (Guynn, 2023), a term used to describe efforts to correct racial or gender imbalances that lead to discrimination against members of the majority group (Legal Information Institute, 2024). Critics contend that when organizations prioritize race, ethnicity, or other protected characteristics in hiring, promotions, and decision-making, they risk overlooking the qualifications and merit of majority group members, effectively replacing one form of perceived unfairness with another (Hernandez, 2024). However, research challenges the notion of a neutral meritocracy, illustrating that meritocracy reinforces inequality because it ignores systemic inequalities like unequal access to education and resources and assumes a level playing field that does not exist (Sandel, 2020). Recent research indicates that once people understand that merit is more complex and situation-dependent than they thought, they are less likely to say that meritocracy is fair and more likely to support diversity initiatives (Goya-Tocchetto, 2024).

DEI Drives a Political Agenda and Is Divisive

DEI is grounded in universal human rights concepts such as those enshrined in the US Declaration of Independence (1776) and the United Nations Sustainable Development Goals (UN, 2015). DEI is not inherently political but operates in a social and organizational context where politics, identity, and values intersect (Yoshino, Glasgow, 2024). For example, some in the United States view DEI as politically charged due to its origins in the Civil Rights Movement. As of this writing, many Americans' opinions about DEI are highly correlated with their political beliefs and party affiliation (Minkin, 2024). Even some DEI advocates say the work is "divisive" (Witherspoon, 2024).

DEI Is Ineffective

It is true that after decades of effort, corporate DEI work has not always delivered the desired results (Newkirk, 2019). Some DEI actions are more effective than others (Robb & Rana, 2024). However, it is also true that DEI work offers many benefits to organizations (Sitzmann et al., 2024; McCarter et al., 2023), including positive impacts on business outcomes like innovation, team collaboration, and sales professional performance (Zhang, 2020; Kim et al., 2021; Park et al., 2023; Shimul et al., 2024).

Against this backdrop, industrial-organizational psychologists continue working to help leaders understand the purpose and value of DEI and adopt evidence-based practices to help them achieve their DEI goals. However, since politicization and cultural backlash have dramatically altered the DEI landscape in the last two years, (Sitzmann et al., 2024), proponents of DEI need novel approaches if the work is to have the intended impact.

The Need for a New Approach to Inclusive Leadership

As organizations face the challenge of how to lead for inclusion (Tu, 2024), researchers have sought to identify leadership behaviors and attitudes that facilitate inclusion (e.g., Korkmaz et al., 2022; Roberson & Perry, 2022) and how inclusive leadership relates to other leadership styles. In exploring this question, it is essential to consider whether current leadership theories are inclusive. Research in this field has been produced primarily in the United States and Europe (Yukl, 2012) and the leaders studied primarily White men in male-dominated organizations (Ensari & Riggio, 2021). Indeed, behavioral science research has been criticized as being based on WEIRD (western-educated, industrialized, rich, and democratic) societies (Henrich et al., 2010), leading to a limited understanding of non-Western norms and values. Researchers have mainly tested Western leadership models in non-Western cultural contexts. There is much less examination of the value of non-Western leadership models in Western contexts. Although there has been some research on leadership in some other cultures—for example, Chinese leadership style (Tsui et al., 2004; Xing et al., 2023)—this narrow perspective fundamentally impacts our understanding and practice of leadership. The need is even more critical in inclusive leadership research (Klarsfeld et al., 2019). This skewed research perspective can distort practitioners' perceptions and conclusions when this research is applied to understanding leaders from different cultural groups (Ensari & Riggio, 2021).

Research examining inclusive leadership has been conducted from two different theoretical perspectives—diversity management and leadership. The diversity management perspective conceptualizes inclusive leadership as leader behaviors that are focused on facilitating group members' sense of belonging (*belongingness*) while maintaining their individuality (*uniqueness*), all while contributing to group processes and outcomes (Randel et al., 2018; Shore et al., 2011). On the other hand, the leadership perspective views inclusive leadership as a specific relational style (Roberson & Perry, 2022). Edmondson (1996) and Nembhard and Edmondson (2006, p. 297) found that inclusive leaders exhibit behaviors that "indicate an invitation and appreciation for others' contributions." The consequence of these two different perspectives is that the observations and practical applications from the two streams are fragmented, potentially reducing their impact (Roberson & Perry, 2022).

Inclusive leadership has been associated with work-related outcomes such as creativity and innovation (Carmeli et al., 2010; Choi et al., 2017; Choi et al., 2015; Javed et al., 2019), psychological safety (Nembhard & Edmondson, 2006), work engagement (Cenkci et al., 2021; Choi et al., 2015), employee well-being (Choi et al., 2017), and unit performance (Hirak et al., 2012). However, more research is needed to determine which components of inclusive leadership best predict workplace outcomes (Chrobot-Mason & Roberson, 2022). Roberson and Perry (2022) note some common elements between the diversity management and the leadership approach to inclusion: (a) inclusive leadership incorporates behaviors that foster a sense of shared identity, addressing needs for belongingness; (b) both streams include behaviors to reduce status differences—soliciting voices of those not typically valued; and (c) both emphasize participation and involvement in decision-making even when views might be divergent from others, valuing uniqueness.

A systematic review of inclusive leadership research (Korkmaz et al., 2022) identified four dimensions of inclusive leadership (at the individual, team, and organization levels): fostering employees' *uniqueness*, strengthening *belongingness* within a team, showing *appreciation*, and supporting *organizational efforts*. Research on the behavioral indicators of inclusive leadership (what inclusive leaders *do* to facilitate inclusion) and on the antecedents of inclusive leadership (the conditions or behaviors that lead to inclusive leadership) is limited (Korkmaz et al., 2022; Roberson & Perry, 2022). From a practice perspective, we know more about the *outcomes* of inclusive leadership than the behaviors needed to *facilitate* inclusion.

Practitioners should recognize these gaps and that leaders may struggle to distinguish between actions for diversity management and those for fostering inclusion (Roberson & Perry, 2022).

Inclusive Culture for All: Shifting the Narrative to Include All Ethnicities

Inclusion is the "glue" that holds diversity efforts together and ensures that individuals feel represented, engaged, and empowered. Without inclusion within DEI work itself, organizations risk exacerbating feelings of division and resentment. Ethnic majority group members may perceive that leaders overlook their needs, and employees from minoritized ethnic groups may disengage and voluntarily leave their organizations. We, therefore, recommend that leaders consider inclusion as much as they do diversity by designing organizational cultures that anticipate the challenges any employee (not just those from minority ethnic groups) encounter as they work within the business ecosystem (with one another, their managers, and leaders, clients, customers, patients, business partners, and suppliers). This approach could lay the groundwork for all other critical DEI work.

Since the primary problems that DEI work addresses still need to be solved (Nittrouer et al., 2024), business leaders must recognize them. Organizations need talent, and that talent will be more diverse in the future. Additionally, organizations must ensure that the products and services they bring to market will be attractive to a more diverse marketplace. Although leaders may experience some pressure from opponents of DEI (Meyersohn, 2024), they must continue building inclusive organizations—regardless of how they label their work (Emerson, 2024).

Ideally, future DEI policies and practices will promote inclusion and equity for all employees, focus on the systemic nature of inequity, and help all employees understand why this matters and how it benefits them. Pragmatic leaders should consider that when majority group members feel excluded or believe DEI policies are unfair, it can create division, resentment, and lower support for diversity efforts. A healthy DEI framework should balance the needs of all groups within society while seeking to address historic disparities.

Addressing the Concept of White Ethnicity

Ethnic groups, defined by shared religious, linguistic, or racial/color characteristics, possess a common cultural tradition and a collective sense of identity (Cox & Nkomo, 1990). Explorations of race/ethnicity in DEI work have focused on minoritized ethnic groups (Grimes, 2001; Welp & Schein, 2021), excluding White as an ethnicity from the conversation. However, "White" is also an ethnicity (Chrobot-Mason, 2004), and inclusion is equally about White men and women as any other ethnic group or gender (Welp & Schein, 2021). We need to expand the domain to acknowledge this broader perspective.

Broad classifications such as "Asian," which includes individuals from East and South Asia (Marks et al., 2024), and "Black or African American" (e.g., for African Americans, Nigerians, and Ethiopians) ignore cultural differences and focus too much on the superordinate category of race (or color). Similarly, it is misleading to consider White individuals as comprising a homogenous ethnic group because there is much cultural, historical, and geographical diversity within the White group (Frankenberg, 1993). The census in England and Wales includes multiple White ethnic groups: English, Welsh, Scottish, Northern Irish, or British; Irish; Gypsy or Irish Traveller; Roma; and Any Other White Background. The census in Scotland uses eight classifications for White: Scottish, Other White British, White Irish, White Polish, Gypsy or Traveller, Roma, Showman/Showwoman, and Other. Encouragingly, in March 2024, the US Office of Management and Budget (OMB) updated its standards, introducing a combined race/ethnicity question for self-reporting and enabling the "collection of detailed race/ethnicity data beyond the minimum categories" (p. 22185). The new question "What is your race and/or ethnicity?" will allow respondents to select one or more racial/ethnic groups. It also provides the option to report their national origin. For example, those selecting "White" can further select from English, Italian, German, Polish, Irish, and Scottish (or use a write-in box) and those selecting "Black" have the option of selecting from African American, Haitian, Jamaican, Nigerian, Somali, and Ethiopian. Crucially, individuals can select more than one option. These changes are to be implemented for the next US Census in 2030. This represents a step in the right direction.

The demographic and social changes we have described clarify that there is a need to develop more nuanced approaches to understanding the role of race and ethnicity in fostering inclusion in organizations. For example, even acknowledging that none of the race and ethnic groups are monolithic means that the leadership task would be made more complex. Increasing globalization will result in more one-, two-, and multi-way labor movements from migrants and international assignees. This will blur the distinction between the "local," familiar dimensions of racial/ethnic diversity and the new dimensions these movements will reveal. DEI practices must adapt to these inevitable realities (Wilson & Schwabenland, 2012). Leaders have two options for fostering inclusion in the face of this complexity. They can attempt to customize their leadership to match each variation. Or they can focus on treating all employees equitably, regardless of the variations. As discussed earlier in the chapter, equity is about each person getting what they need to succeed. This requires organizational practices that enable fair and just access to experiences, opportunities, services, treatment, and equal outcomes. Organizations can foster equity-first approaches by using data to establish criteria for what equity looks like and then identifying and addressing deviations from those criteria.

Practical Recommendations for Leaders

Now that we have specified the challenge of leading DEI in the current environment, the next section shifts to actionable strategies and tactics to empower leaders to lead the inclusion conversation in their organizations.

Strategic Recommendations

Recognize the Gaps in Our Knowledge and Self-Awareness

Be aware that our theories are underpinned by Western attitudes and values, embodying the cultural perspectives on which they are based. Reflecting on your own cultural identity, biases, and preferences is foundational to appreciating the power of diverse talent and embracing inclusion (Ferdman & Roberts, 2014).

Use Respect as the Primary Inclusive Leadership Outcome

We propose *respect* as the outcome against which DEI efforts can be measured. Studies have shown that respect is the foundational currency of interpersonal interactions (Baumeister & Leary, 1995), especially in situations, like workplaces, with power imbalances where trust matters (Dunning et al., 2016). Employees who feel respected are more productive, loyal, and likely to contribute innovative ideas (LaGree et al., 2023; Enwereuzor & Ugwu, 2021; DeCremer, 2002).

A comprehensive review of the respect research literature reveals two kinds of respect: *owed or generalized respect* (the kind accorded equally to all members of a workgroup or organization based on their humanity) and *earned or particularized respect* (the type that recognizes individuals based on achievements or socially valued attributes) (Rogers & Ashforth, 2017). Owed respect is the kind that matters to all employees and in DEI work.

Though the respect literature is comprehensive, the bottom line is that employees feel respected when they are *seen*, *heard*, and *valued*, and we encourage leaders to use that simple definition. All employees value respect, and the concept is unlikely to elicit defensive reactions from DEI detractors, yet it is undervalued and overlooked as a potential tool for addressing DEI challenges. Building cultures of inclusion based on respect could enable leaders to measure if and how much employees feel respected, whether respect is increasing, declining, or staying the same, and solicit employee feedback about optimizing their respect experience.

Organizations can integrate respect into organizational practices, such as their values and codes of conduct (Cox, 2022). Research indicates that fewer than 40% of US companies list respect as a corporate value (Sull et al., 2020), so there is room for greater adoption of this value. Nestlé and American Express are two companies that have long used respect as a cultural anchor. Nestlé says on their website (Nestlé, n.d.) that their values are "rooted in respect," and their CEO says that "[r]espect has a special and powerful meaning at Nestlé. It profoundly influences the way we work and run our business. Our values are visible in our behaviours, our actions and our decisions" (para 6.) The company details those values as Respect for Ourselves, Respect for Others, Respect for Diversity, and Respect for the Future. American Express (2024) says its nine Blue Box values are at the heart of the

Table 11.1 Sample Employee Survey Respect Questions

Respect Dimension	Sample Respect Question
Seen	I feel *seen*—noticed and acknowledged by my colleagues (or manager) for simply being a human on the team.
Heard	I feel *heard*—I have space to express my opinions and ideas. My colleagues (or manager) listen(s) to, use(s), and act(s) upon my opinions, ideas, and needs.
Valued	I feel *valued*—recognized by my colleagues (or manager) for my contributions at work.
Comment Question	What would need to change in your work environment in order for you to feel respected?

Source: Adapted with permission from Cox (2022).

company's culture. One of those nine values is, "We respect people: We trust and respect one another for who we are and what we contribute" (p. ii).

Organizations can help managers create respectful work environments by measuring respect in employee surveys, conducting cultural audits to assess how employees across targeted groups experience respect, and incorporating respect into performance evaluations. Some example language from the Cox (2022) respect model that could be incorporated into those tools is provided in Table 11.1.

Practice Inclusive Behaviors and Reward Them

Explicitly invite the views of employees and show a genuine appreciation for their contributions (Nembhard & Edmondson, 2006). Chrobot-Mason and Roberson (2022) have developed a useful checklist to help leaders reflect on inclusive behaviors in daily interactions and identify areas for development. Examples are shown in Table 11.2.

This can be supplemented with leadership development initiatives in which participants practice inclusive leadership behaviors (Roberson & Perry, 2022). It is essential to build accountability by offering managers rewards for demonstrating inclusive behaviors (Roberson et al., 2020).

Use "the Leadership Case" Instead of "the Business Case"

The business case for diversity seeks to demonstrate that diversity is good because organizations gain business benefits (usually financial outcomes) when it is present. However, although using the business case as the basis

Table 11.2 Inclusive Leader Behaviors (Examples)

Type of Interactions	Inclusive Leadership Behaviors
One-on-One	I make eye contact with the person. I treat each and every person with respect and dignity. I ask open-ended questions to learn more about the other person.
As Team Leader	I identify unique skill sets of team members. I ask everyone on the team what and how they want to contribute. I ask everyone on my team for input and through different means.

Source: Adapted with permission from Chrobot-Mason & Roberson (2022).

of leadership action on DEI may make executives feel they are maintaining their shareholder obligation, that framing has unintended negative consequences. When the business case is the primary rationale, decision makers are less likely to hire people from historically subordinated groups (Williams & Cox, 2022). This happens because with the business-case framing, decision makers think of DEI as a commodity and one that is only helpful when it benefits the organization. As a result, they focus less on addressing systemic inequalities. Another unintended consequence of the business-case framing is that people from the underrepresented groups feel like instruments and less like humans (Georgeac & Rattan, 2023). That is why we recommend the leadership case for DEI work. This human-centered approach emphasizes that each leader is responsible for effectively leading every employee in her remit. This approach calls for employees to feel that their immediate leader will be their advocate, even if no one else in the organization is (Cox, 2022). In this way, each employee will know the leader is in their corner.

Action Recommendations

Know and Use the Practices That Work and Avoid the Rest

According to Sitzmann et al. (2024), many standard DEI practices, such as diversity and harassment training and grievance procedures for reporting discrimination, negatively correlate with increasing diverse representation.

On the other hand, maintaining jobs that focus on desired DEI outcomes (for example, Chief Diversity Officers), maintaining diversity task forces, formal mentoring, and targeted recruiting are effective.

Calibrate Implicit Bias Training

Implicit bias—the automatic, spontaneous associations, thoughts, and evaluations we make about members of a particular group—is real (Kim & Roberson, 2022). And it makes sense that implicit bias training has become a tool in many organizations' DEI toolkits. However, organizations often implement implicit bias training in an ad hoc manner without a clear connection to any DEI strategy. Additionally, not all implicit bias training is grounded in psychological science (Hagiwara et al., 2020; Hagiwara et al., 2024). We recommend that organizations use implicit bias training only as one tactic in a comprehensive DEI strategy, only as part of an overall curriculum, and not as a stand-alone solution. Any DEI training, including implicit bias training, should be made available to all employees, not just to a targeted subset.

Examine Performance Evaluation Processes

Ensure staff are being evaluated against the organization's stated appraisal criteria rather than leaders' personal beliefs about what constitutes effective performance—their implicit theories of performance (Klimoski & Donahue, 2001). Pay attention to patterns in ratings that emerge when the rater and ratee are from the same ethnic group, versus those when the rater and the ratee are from different ethnic groups.

Clarify the Function of Employee Resource Groups

Employee Resource Groups (ERGs) are a typical component of DEI work (Catalino et al., 2022) and can be valuable. However, without clear strategic direction, ERGs can become isolated spaces that do not integrate well with the broader organizational culture. For ERGs to be effective, they must be aligned with the organization's DEI strategy, and their goals should be defined in business terms. People who join ERGs often expect to advocate for the identity group that formed the ERG. However, that is not usually the ERG's primary goal from the executive leadership perspective. One way to reduce this confusion is to link ERG activity to professional development. Help leaders and members of ERGs understand that the primary benefit they will get from participating in ERGs is access to opportunities for personal and professional growth. This will enhance the alignment between employee expectations and their actual experience in these groups (Welbourne, 2024).

By implementing these actions, leaders can create a collaborative, system-focused approach to DEI that fosters real change, empowers all employees, and delivers mutual benefits across the organization.

Conclusion

DEI is a critical leadership responsibility that can help all employees thrive and power business success. This chapter supports leaders by providing a multifaceted understanding of the challenges and offering actionable recommendations to drive meaningful, systemic change. The work must be done within a complex legal, political, and social landscape, but organizations must do it to compete in a fast-changing world. The psychological and practical context and recommendations in this chapter are meant to help leaders understand how they can navigate this complexity using thoughtful strategic approaches grounded in science and experience.

References

Adler, S., Campion, M., Colquitt, A., Grubb, A., Murphy, K., Ollander-Krane, R., & Pulakos, E. D. (2016). Getting rid of performance ratings: Genius or folly? A debate. *Industrial and Organizational Psychology*, *9*(2), 219–252. https://doi.org/10.1017/iop.2015.106

Aiken, J. R., Salmon, E. D., & Hanges, P. J. (2013). The origins and legacy of the Civil Rights Act of 1964. *Journal of Business Psychology*, *28*, 383–399. https://doi.org/10.1007/s10869-013-9291-z

Alqaseer, F., Davis, L., & James, R. (2024, February 26). DEI in an era of unrest: A few truths and a path forward. *Harvard Law School Forum on Corporate Governance*. https://corpgov.law.harvard.edu/2024/02/26/dei-in-an-era-of-unrest-a-few-truths-and-a-path-forward

American Express. (2024). *My company. My code*. https://www.americanexpress.com/content/dam/amex/en-us/newsroom/pdfs/AMEX-Code-of-Conduct-Policy_English.pdf

American Psychological Association. (n.d.). *Racial equity action plan: Psychology's role in dismantling systemic racism*. https://www.apa.org/about/apa/addressing-racism/racial-equity-action

American Psychological Association. (2023a). APA dictionary of psychology. https://dictionary.apa.org/race

American Psychological Association. (2023b). APA dictionary of psychology. https://dictionary.apa.org/ethnicity

Andoh, E. (2025, January 1). Sustaining EDI efforts in a challenging new normal. *APA Monitor on Psychology*, *56*(1). https://www.apa.org/monitor/2025/01/trends-equity-diversity-inclusion

Andrews, R., & Ashworth, R. (2015). Representation and inclusion in public organizations: Evidence from the U.K. Civil Service. *Public Administration Review*, *75*(2), 279–288. https://doi.org/10.1111/puar.12308

Atkinson, K., & Headley, T. (2024, December 6). Naval Academy's use of race in admissions upheld by judge. *Bloomberg Law*. https://news.bloomberglaw.com/daily-labor-report/trial-judge-upholds-naval-academys-use-of-race-in-admissions

Bansal, B. (2023, July 10). DEI in the workplace: Unveiling employees' attitudes in Great Britain. *YouGov.com*. https://business.yougov.com/content/46953-dei-in-the-workplace-unveiling-employees-attitudes-in-great-britain

Baumeister, R. F., & Leary, M. R. (1995). The need to belong: Desire for interpersonal attachments as a fundamental human motivation. *Psychological Bulletin*, *117*(3), 497–529. https://doi.org/10.1037/0033-2909.117.3.497

Business in the Community. (2020). *The race at work Black voices report*. https://www.bitc.org.uk/wp-content/uploads/2020/08/bitc-report-race-blackvoices-august20.pdf

Butcher, J. (2024, November 27). Restoring equality in employment: Sinking the DEI ship. *The Heritage Foundation*. https://www.heritage.org/progressivism/report/restoring-equality-employment-sinking-the-dei-ship

Cappelli, P., & Tavis, A. (2016). The performance management revolution. *Harvard Business Review*, *10*, 58–67. https://hbr.org/2016/10/the-performance-management-revolution

Carmeli, A., Reiter-Palmon, R., & Ziv, E. (2010). Inclusive leadership and employee involvement in creative tasks in the workplace: The mediating role of psychological safety. *Creativity Research Journal*, *22*(3), 250–260. https://doi.org/10.1080/10400419.2010.504654

Catalino, N., Gardner, N., Goldstein, D., & Wong, J. (2022, December). Effective employee resource groups are key to inclusion at work. Here's how to get them right. *McKinsey*. https://www.mckinsey.com/capabilities/people-and-organizational-performance/our-insights/effective-employee-resource-groups-are-key-to-inclusion-at-work-heres-how-to-get-them-right

Cenkci, A. T., Bircan, T., & Zimmerman, J. (2021). Inclusive leadership and work engagement: The mediating role of procedural justice. *Management Research Review*, *44*(1), 158–180. https://doi.org/10.1108/MRR-03-2020-0146

Ceron, E. (2023, May 25). Companies that made DEI promises after Floyd murder still have work to do. *Bloomberg*. https://www.bloomberg.com/news/newsletters/2023-05-25/companies-that-made-dei-promises-after-floyd-murder-still-have-work-to-do

Choi, S. B., Tran, T. B. H., & Kang, S.-W. (2017).Inclusive leadership and employee well-being: The mediating role of person–job fit. *Journal of Happiness Studies*, *18*(6), 1877–1901. https://doi.org/10.1007/s10902-016-9801-6

Choi, S. B., Tran, T. B. H., & Park, B. I. (2015). Inclusive leadership and work engagement: Mediating roles of affective organizational commitment and creativity. *Social Behavior and Personality*, *43*(6), 931–943. https://doi.org/10.2224/sbp.2015.43.6.931

Chrobot-Mason, D. (2004). Managing racial differences: The role of majority managers' ethnic identity development on minority employee perceptions of support. *Group & Organization Management*, *29*(1), 5–31. https://doi.org/10.1177/1059601103252102

Chrobot-Mason, D., & Roberson, Q. (2022). Inclusive leadership. In P. G. Northouse (Ed.), *Leadership: Theory and practice* (pp. 322–351). Sage Publications.

CIPD. (2024). Pay, performance and transparency 2024. *London: Chartered Institute for Personnel Development*. https://www.cipd.org/globalassets/media/knowledge/knowledge-hub/reports/2024-pdfs/8551-pay-performance-and-transparency-report-web2.pdf

Colby, S. L., & Ortman, J. M. (2014). Projections of the size and composition of the U.S. population: 2014 to 2060: Current Population Reports. U.S. Census Bureau.

Cox, G. (2022). *Leading inclusion: Drive change employees can see and feel.* Page Two Books.

Cox, G., Feinzig, S., & Ferdman, B. (2025). Reimagining "DEI": Centering strategic impact and employee experience. In E. Sinar Mueller-Hanson & E. Pulakos (Eds.), *Evolving the employee experience: An integrative perspective* (pp. 95–120). Oxford University Press.

Cox, T., Jr., & Nkomo, S. M. (1986). Differential performance appraisal criteria: A field study of Black and White managers. *Group and Organization Studies, 11*(1), 101–119.

Cox, T., Jr., & Nkomo, S. M. (1990). Invisible men and women: A status report on race as a variable in organizational research. *Journal of Organizational Behavior, 11*, 419–431. https://doi.org/10.1002/job.4030110604

Crosby, F. J., Iyer, A., & Sincharoen, S. (2006). Understanding affirmative action. *Annual Review of Psychology, 57*, 585–611. https://doi.org/10.1146/annurev.psych.57.102904.190029

De Cremer, D. (2002). Respect and cooperation in social dilemmas: The importance of feeling included. *Personality and Social Psychology Bulletin, 28*(10), 1335–1341. https://doi.org/10.1177/014616702236830

Delikat, M., & Kiselica, E. (2024, September 24). Litigation targeting large company DEI programs on the rise. *Harvard Law School Forum on Corporate Governance.* https://corpgov.law.harvard.edu/2024/09/18/litigation-targeting-large-company-dei-programs-on-the-rise/#more-168095

DeNisi, A. S., & Murphy, K. R. (2017). Performance appraisal and performance management: 100 years of progress? *Journal of Applied Psychology, 102*(3), 421–433. https://doi.org/10.1037/apl0000085

Disability Rights UK. (2015, March). *Tackling health and disability-related barriers to progression within the Civil Service.* Cabinet Office. https://www.gov.uk/government/publications/tackling-health-and-disability-related-barriers-to-progression-within-the-civil-service

Dunning, D., Fetchenhauer, D., & Schlösser, T. (2016). The psychology of respect: A case study of how behavioral norms regulate human action. In A. J. Elliot (Ed.), *Advances in motivation science* (pp. 1–34). Elsevier Academic Press.

Edmondson, A. C. (1996). Learning from mistakes is easier said than done: Group and organizational influences on the detection and correction of human error. *The Journal of Applied Behavioral Science, 32*(1), 5–28. https://doi.org/10.1177/0021886396321001

Emerson, J. (2024, December 13). Continuing the work of DEI, no matter what your company calls it. *Harvard Business Review.* https://hbr.org/2024/12/continuing-the-work-of-dei-no-matter-what-your-company-calls-it

Ensari, N., & Riggio, R. E. (2021). Exclusion of inclusion in leadership theories. In B. Ferdman, J. Prime, & R. Riggio (Eds.), *Inclusive leadership: Transforming diverse lives, workplaces and societies* (pp. 25–38). Routledge.

Enwereuzor, I. K., & Ugwu, L. E. (2021), Clarifying the interface between respectful leadership and intention to stay. *Journal of Health Organization and Management, 35*(4), 443–457. https://doi.org/10.1108/JHOM-06-2020-0258

Equal Employment Opportunity Commission. (n.d.). *Equal employment opportunity laws.* https://www.eeoc.gov/equal-employment-opportunity-laws

Equality and Human Rights Commission. (2018, 6 August). *Equality Act 2010.* https://www.equalityhumanrights.com/equality/equality-act-2010?return-url=https%3A%2F%2Fwww.equalityhumanrights.com%2Fsearch%3Fkeys%3Dequality%2Bact

Farndale, E., Biron, M., Briscoe, D. R., & Raghuram, S. (2015). A global perspective on diversity and inclusion in work organizations. *International Journal of Human Resource Management, 26*(6), 677–687. https://doi.org/10.1080/09585192.2014.991511

Ferdman, B. M., & Roberts, L. M. (2014). Creating inclusion for oneself: Knowing, accepting and expressing one's whole self at work. In B. M. Ferdman & B. R. Deane (Eds.), *Diversity at work: The practice of inclusion* (pp. 93–127). John Wiley & Sons. https://doi.org/10.1002/9781118764282.ch1

Fitzsimmons, S., Özbilgin, M. F., Thomas, D. C., & Nkomo, S. (2023). Equality, diversity, and inclusion in international business: A review and research agenda. *Journal of International Business Studies, 54*(8), 1402–1422. https://doi.org/10.1057/s41267-023-00642-x

Frankenberg, R. (1993). *White women, race matters: The social construction of whiteness.* University of Minnesota Press.

Georgeac, O. A. M., & Rattan, A. (2023). The business case for diversity backfires: Detrimental effects of organizations' instrumental diversity rhetoric for underrepresented group members' sense of belonging. *Journal of Personality and Social Psychology, 124*(1), 69–108. https://doi.org/10.1037/pspi0000394

Goldberg, E. (2025b, February 10). Alarmed, employers ask: What is "illegal D.E.I."? *The New York Times.* https://www.nytimes.com/2025/02/10/business/trump-dei-employers.html

GOV.UK. (2021). *Commission on race and ethnic disparities: The report.* https://www.gov.uk/government/publications/the-report-of-the-commission-on-race-and-ethnic-disparities

GOV.UK. (2022, March 17). *Inclusive Britain: Government response to the Commission on Race and Ethnic Disparities.* https://www.gov.uk/government/publications/inclusive-britain-action-plan-government-response-to-the-commission-on-race-and-ethnic-disparities/inclusive-britain-government-response-to-the-commission-on-race-and-ethnic-disparities

GOV.UK. (2023, March 31). *UK population by ethnicity: Age groups.* https://www.ethnicity-facts-figures.service.gov.uk/uk-population-by-ethnicity/demographics/age-groups/latest/#main-facts-and-figures

GOV.UK (2024a). *Gender pay gap reporting: Guidance for employers.* https://www.gov.uk/government/publications/gender-pay-gap-reporting-guidance-for-employers

GOV.UK. (2024b, May 21). *Working age population.* https://www.ethnicity-facts-figures.service.gov.uk/uk-population-by-ethnicity/demographics/working-age-population/latest/#working-age-population-by-ethnicity

Goya-Tocchetto, D., Kay, A. C., & Payne, B. K. (2024). Can selecting the most qualified candidate be unfair? Learning about socioeconomic advantages and disadvantages reduces the perceived fairness of meritocracy and increases support for socioeconomic diversity initiatives in organizations. *Journal of Experimental Psychology: General, 153*(12), 2962–2976. https://doi.org/10.1037/xge0001525

Green, J. (2024, October 28). Companies are dropping the D or E from DEI to avoid criticism. *Society for Human Resource Management.* https://www.shrm.org/topics-tools/news/inclusion-diversity/companies-are-dropping-the-d-or-e-from-dei-to-avoid-criticism

Greenwald, A. G., & Pettigrew, T. F. (2014). With malice toward none and charity for some. *American Psychologist, 69*(7), 669–684. https://doi.org/10.1037/a0036056

Grimes, D. (2001). Putting our own house in order: Whiteness, change and organization studies. *Journal of Organizational Change Management, 14*(2), 132–149. https://doi.org/10.1108/09534810110388054

Guynn, J. (2023, December 20). DEI under siege: Why more businesses are being accused of "reverse discrimination." *USA Today.* https://www.usatoday.com/story/money/careers/2023/12/20/dei-reverse-discrimination-lawsuits-increase-woke/71923487007

Guynn, J., & Fraser, J. (2023, March 16). Corporate diversity database: A USA Today investigative series inside the nation's most powerful companies. *USA Today.* https://www.usatoday.com/in-depth/news/investigations/2023/02/16/corporate-company-diversity-in-america-exclusive-searchable-database/7484640001

Hagiwara, N., Cuffy, C., Cyrus, J., Harika, N., Watson, G. S., & Green. T. L. (2024). The nature and validity of implicit bias training for health care providers and trainees: A systematic review. *AAAS Science Advances, 10*(33). https://doi.org/10.1126/sciadv.ado5957

Hagiwara N., Kron F. W., Scerbo M. W., & Watson G. S. (2020). A call for grounding implicit bias training in clinical and translational frameworks. *Lancet, 395*, 1457–1460. https://doi.org/10.1016/S0140-6736(20)30846-1

Henrich, J., Heine, S. J., & Norenzayan, A. (2010). The weirdest people in the world? *Behavioral and Brain Sciences, 33*(2–3), 61–83. https://doi.org/10.1017/S0140525X0999152X

Herbert, E. (2024, December). Cisco swims against the Big Tech tide to set standard in workplace equality. *Financial Times.* https://www.ft.com/content/58b6b437-69b6-4675-8104-89333b8a6b7e

Hernandez, T. K. (2024, June 17). Can CRT Save DEI? Workplace diversity, equity & inclusion in the shadow of anti-affirmative action. *UCLA Law Review.* https://www.uclalawreview.org/can-crt-save-dei/?

Hirak, R., Peng, A. C., Carmeli, A., & Schaubroeck, J. M. (2012). Linking leader inclusiveness to work unit performance: The importance of psychological safety and learning from failures. *The Leadership Quarterly, 23*(1), 107–117. https://doi.org/10.1016/j.leaqua.2011.11.009

Holder, A. M. B., Jackson, M. A., & Ponterotto, J. G. (2015). Racial microaggression experiences and coping strategies of Black women in corporate leadership. *Qualitative Psychology, 2*(2), 164–180. https://doi.org/10.1037/qup0000024

Hudson, C. (2024, September 13). Jamie Dimon among Fortune 500 CEOs defying diversity backlash. *Bloomberg Law.* https://news.bloomberglaw.com/esg/jamie-dimon-among-fortune-500-ceos-defying-diversity-backlash

Javed, B., Naqvi, S. M. M. R., Khan, A. K., Arjoon, S., & Tayyeb, H. H. (2019). Impact of inclusive leadership on innovative work behavior: The role of psychological safety. *Journal of Management & Organization, 25*(1), 117–136. https://doi.org/10.1017/jmo.2017.3

Jensen, E., Jones, N., Rabe, M., Pratt, B., Medina, L., Orozco, K., & Spell, L. (2021, August). *2020 U.S. population more racially and ethnically diverse than measured in 2010.* U.S. Census Bureau. https://www.census.gov/library/stories/2021/08/2020-united-states-population-more-racially-ethnically-diverse-than-2010.html

Kalita, S. M. (2023, June 27). Looking back on three years of performative diversity efforts. *Time.* https://time.com/charter/6290473/undoing-workplace-diversity-gains

Kanitz, R., Reinwald, M., Gonzalez, K., Burmeister, A., Song, Y., & Hoegl, M. (2024). Supportive, resistant, or both? A person-centric view on employee responses to diversity initiatives. *Journal of Applied Psychology, 109*(10), 1635–1658. https://doi.org/10.1037/apl0001190

Kim, J. Y., & Roberson, L. (2022). I'm biased and so are you. What should organizations do? A review of organizational implicit-bias training programs. *Consulting Psychology Journal, 74*(1), 19–39. https://doi.org/10.1037/cpb0000211

Kim, Y., Jeong, S. S., Yiu, D. W., & Moon, J. (2021). Frequent CEO turnover and firm performance: The resilience effect of workforce diversity. *Journal of Business Ethics, 173*, 185–203. https://doi.org/10.1007/s10551-020-04534-0

Klarsfeld, A., Knappert, L., Kornau, A., Ngunjiri, F. W., & Sieben, B. (2019). Diversity in under-researched countries: New empirical fields challenging old theories? *Equality, Diversity and Inclusion: An International Journal, 38*(7), 694–704. https://doi.org/10.1108/EDI-03-2019-0110

Klimoski, R. J., & Donahue, L. M. (2001). Person perception in organizations: An overview of the field. In M. London (Ed.), *How people evaluate others in organizations* (pp. 5–43). Lawrence Erlbaum Associates.

Korkmaz, A. V., van Engen, M. L., Knappert, L., & Schalk, R. (2022). About and beyond leading uniqueness and belongingness: A systematic review of inclusive leadership research. *Human Resource Management Review, 32*(4), 100894. https://doi.org/10.1016/j.hrmr.2022.100894

LaGree, D., Houston, B., Duffy, M., & Shin, H. (2023). The effect of respect: Respectful communication at work drives resiliency, engagement, and job satisfaction among early career employees. *International Journal of Business Communication, 60*(3), 844–864. https://doi.org/10.1177/23294884211016529

LeanIn.org & McKinsey & Company. (2024). *Women in the workplace 2024: 10th anniversary report*. https://leanin.org/women-in-the-workplace

Legal Information Institute. (2024). Reverse discrimination. https://www.law.cornell.edu/wex/reverse_discrimination

Lin, L., Menasce, J., & Fry, R. (2024, December 10). Key labor force trends. *Pew Research Center*. https://www.pewresearch.org/social-trends/2024/12/10/key-labor-force-trends

Livingston, R., & Rosette, A. S. (2021). The complexity of social disadvantage across gender and race. In B. Ferdman, J. Prime, & R. Riggio (Eds.), *Inclusive leadership: Transforming diverse lives, workplaces and societies* (pp. 39–59). Routledge.

Marks, R., Jones, N., & Battle, K. (2024, 4 December). *What updates to OMB's race/ethnicity standards mean for the Census Bureau*. https://www.census.gov/newsroom/blogs/random-samplings/2024/04/updates-race-ethnicity-standards.html

Markson, T. (2024). McVey announces "common sense" plan to streamline equality and diversity work. *Civil Service World*. https://www.civilserviceworld.com/professions/article/government-to-scrap-equality-and-diversity-roles-minister-says

McCarter, S. A., Wilson, M. L., & Anderson, D. (2023). Evidence-based strategies to improve the effectiveness of diversity, equity, and inclusion training. *Journal of Ethnic & Cultural Diversity in Social Work, 33*(6), 327–339. https://doi.org/10.1080/15313204.2023.2210850

McKay, P. F., & McDaniel, M. A. (2006). A re-examination of Black–White mean differences in work performance. *Journal of Applied Psychology, 91*(3), 538–554. https://doi.org/10.1037/0021-9010.91.3.538

McKinsey & Company. (2024, July 15). *Aiming higher: Embedding "systematic ambition" to drive UK corporate growth*. https://www.mckinsey.com/uk/our-insights/aiming-higher-embedding-systematic-ambition-to-drive-uk-corporate-growth?

Meyersohn, N. (2024, December 17). DEI isn't actually dead. *CNN*. https://www.cnn.com/2024/12/17/business/dei-isnt-actually-dead/index.html

Minkin, R. (2024, November 19). Views of DEI have become slightly more negative among U.S. workers. *Pew Research Center*. https://www.pewresearch.org/short-reads/2024/11/19/views-of-dei-have-become-slightly-more-negative-among-us-workers

Morley, M., Murphy, K. R., Cleveland, J. N., Heraty,N., & McCarthy, J. (2021). Distal context and performance appraisal: A 22-country study linking three facets of home and host country context to performance appraisal processes and purposes. *Human Resource Management, 60*, 715–736. https://doi.org/10.1002/hrm.22056

Mukkamala, S., & Suyemoto, K. L. (2018). Racialized sexism/sexualized racism: A multimethod study of intersectional experiences of discrimination for Asian American women. *Asian American Journal of Psychology, 9*(1), 32–46. https://doi.org/10.1037/aap0000104

Murphy, K., & DeNisi, A. (2023). New approaches to dealing with performance management: Getting rid of performance appraisals is not the answer. *IIM Ranchi Journal of Management Studies, 2*(2), 143–158. https://doi.org/10.1108/IRJMS-09-2023-0074

Murray, S. (2024, June 20). Rescuing diversity from the DEI backlash. *Financial Times*. https://www.ft.com/content/18a8e9c4-d515-4d9b-aac1-d88c02b46028?

Nassauer, S. (2024, November 25). Walmart rolls back DEI programs. *The Wall Street Journal*. https://www.wsj.com/business/retail/walmart-rolls-back-dei-programs-66a5201a?mod=Searchresults_pos1&page=1

Nembhard, I. M., & Edmondson, A. C. (2006). Making it safe: The effects of leader inclusiveness and professional status on psychological safety and improvement efforts in health care teams. *Journal of Organizational Behavior, 27*(7), 941–966. https://doi.org/10.1002/job.413

Nestlé. (n.d.). *Promoting ethical business at Nestle*. https://www.nestle-cwa.com/en/csv/what-is-csv/ethical-business-new?utm_source=chatgpt.com

Newkirk, P. (2019). *Diversity, Inc.: The failed promise of a billion-dollar business*. Bold Type Books.

Niemann, Y. F. (2004). Stereotypes of Chicanas and Chicanos: Impact on family functioning, individual expectations, goals, and behavior. In R. J. Velásquez, L. M. Arellano, & B. W. McNeill (Eds.), *The handbook of Chicana/o psychology and mental health* (pp. 61–82). Lawrence Erlbaum Associates Publishers.

Nittrouer, C. L., Arena, D., Silver, E. R., Avery, D. R., & Hebl, M. R. (2024). Despite the haters: The immense promise and progress of diversity, equity, and inclusion initiatives. *Journal of Organizational Behavior, 46*(1), 188–201. https://doi.org/10.1002/job.2835

Nkomo, S. M. (2021). Reflections on the continuing denial of the centrality of "race" in management and organization studies. *Equality, Diversity and Inclusion: An International Journal, 40*(2), 212–224. https://doi.org/10.1108/EDI-01-2021-0011

Office of National Statistics. (2022, November 29). *Ethnic group, England and Wales: Census 2021.* https://www.ons.gov.uk/peoplepopulationandcommunity/culturalidentity/ethnicity/bulletins/ethnicgroupenglandandwales/census2021

Palmer, S. (2020). Black employees hold just 1.5 per cent of senior roles, research reveals. *People Management, Chartered Institute for Personnel and Development.* https://www.peoplemanagement.co.uk/article/1744977/black-employees-hold-just-1-5-per-cent-of-senior-roles

Paluch, R. M., & Shum, V. (2024). The Non-White standard: Racial bias in perceptions of diversity, equity, and inclusion leaders. *Journal of Applied Psychology, 109*(7), 971–986. https://doi.org/10.1037/apl0001106

Park, Y. W., Voss, G. B., & Voss, Z. G. (2023). Advancing customer diversity, equity, and inclusion: Measurement, stakeholder influence, and the role of marketing. *Journal of the Academy of Marketing Science, 51*(1), 174–197. https://doi.org/10.1007/s11747-022-00883-6

Pogrebna, G., Angelopoulos, S., Motsi-Omoijiade, I., Kharlamov, A., & Tkachenko, N. (2024). The impact of intersectional racial and gender biases on minority female leadership over two centuries. *Scientific Reports, 14*(111). https://doi.org/10.1038/s41598-023-50392-x

Race Disparity Unit. (2024, 20 March). *Report on the Inclusion at Work Panel's recommendations for improving diversity and inclusion (D&I) practice in the workplace.* https://www.gov.uk/government/publications/inclusion-at-work-panel-report-on-improving-workplace-diversity-and-inclusion/c281303b-e075-483d-940f-456c92942bec?trk=public_post_comment-text#summary-of-recommendations

Randel, A. E., Galvin, B. M., Shore, L. M., Ehrhart, K. H., Chung, B. G., Dean, M. A., & Kedharnath, U. (2018). Inclusive leadership: Realizing positive outcomes through belongingness and being valued for uniqueness. *Human Resource Management Review, 28*(2), 190–203. https://doi.org/10.1016/j.hrmr.2017.07.002

Robb, D., & Rana, S. (2024). Cutting the cord: Good riddance to ineffective DEI programs. *Industrial and Organizational Psychology, 17*(4), 507–510. https://doi:10.1017/iop.2024.38

Roberson, Q. M. (2006). Disentangling the meanings of diversity and inclusion in organizations. *Group & Organization Management, 31*(2), 212–236. https://doi.org/10.1177/1059601104273064

Roberson, Q., King, E., & Hebl, M. (2020). Designing more effective practices for reducing workplace inequality. *Behavioral Science & Policy, 6*(1), 39–49. https://doi.org/10.1177/237946152000600104

Roberson, Q., & Perry, J. L. (2022). Inclusive leadership in thought and action: A thematic analysis. *Group & Organization Management, 47*(4), 755–778. https://doi.org/10.1177/10596011211013161

Rogers, K. M., & Ashforth, B. (2017). Respect in organizations: Feeling valued as "we" and "me." *Journal of Management, 43*(5), 1578–1608. https://doi.org/10.1177/0149206314557159

Rogers, T. N., Temple-West, P., & Bushey, C. (2024, December 5). "Crazy ideology": U.S. companies drop diversity efforts as conservative pressure mounts. *Financial Times*. https://www.ft.com/content/0c8974ee-60bf-4edb-839c-bc24b8ecbc81

Rosette, A. S., & Livingston, R. W. (2012). Failure is not an option for Black women: Effects of organizational performance on leaders with single versus dual-subordinate identities. *Journal of Experimental Social Psychology, 48*(5), 1162–1167. https://doi.org/10.1016/j.jesp.2012.05.002

Ruggs, E. N., & Holmes, O. (2024). Why dropping the E in DEI is a mistake. *Harvard Busines Review*. https://hbr.org/2024/08/why-dropping-the-e-in-dei-is-a-mistake

Sackett, P. R., & DuBois, C. L. (1991). Rater-ratee race effects on performance evaluation: Challenging meta-analytic conclusions. *Journal of Applied Psychology, 76*(6), 873–877. https://doi.org/10.1037/0021-9010.76.6.873

Sandel, M. J. (2020). *The tyranny of merit: What's become of the common good*. Farrar, Straus, and Giroux.

Shimul, A. S., Azim, S. M. F., & Cheah, I. (2024). Deciphering the impact of diversity, equity, and inclusion (DEI) on B2B salesperson's performance. *Journal of Global Marketing*, 1–21. https://doi.org/10.1080/08911762.2024.2424826

Shore, L. M., Randel, A. E., Chung, B. G., Dean, M. A., Holcombe Ehrhart, K., & Singh, G. (2011). Inclusion and diversity in work groups: A review and model for future research. *Journal of Management, 37*, 1262–1289. https://doi.org/10.1177/0149206310385943

Sitzmann, T., Bassani, G., & Stansifer, M. L. (2024). Don't get bogged down by the backlash. *Industrial and Organizational Psychology, 17*, 525–529. https://doi.org/10.1017/iop.2024.45

Sitzmann, T., Schwartz, S., & Stansifer, M. L. (2024, June 14). The most common DEI practices actually undermine diversity. *Harvard Business Review*. https://hbr.org/2024/06/research-the-most-common-dei-practices-actually-undermine-diversity

Society for Human Resource Management. (2014). *HR professionals' perceptions about human resource management effectiveness*. https://www.shrm.org/hr-today/trends-and-forecasting/research-and-surveys/Pages/2014-performance-management.aspx#sthash.DoYdBNJT.dpuf

Stauffer, J. M., & Buckley, M. R. (2005). The existence and nature of racial bias in supervisory ratings. *Journal of Applied Psychology, 90*(3), 586–591.

Sull, D., Turconi, S., & Sull, C. (2020, July 21). When it comes to culture, does your company walk the talk? *MIT Sloan Management Review*. https://sloanreview.mit.edu/article/when-it-comes-to-culture-does-your-company-walk-the-talk

Supreme Court of the United States. (2023, June 29). *Students for Fair Admissions, Inc. v. President and Fellows of Harvard College*. No. 20–1199. https://www.supremecourt.gov/opinions/22pdf/20-1199_l6gn.pdf

Telford, T., & Mark, J. (2024, May 2024). DEI is getting a new name. Can it dump the political baggage? *The Washington Post*. https://www.washingtonpost.com/business/2024/05/05/dei-affirmative-action-rebrand-evolution

Thomas, D. A., & Ely, R. J. (1996). Making differences matter: A new paradigm for managing diversity. *Harvard Business Review, 74*, 79–90. https://store.hbr.org/product/making-differences-matter-a-new-paradigm-for-managing-diversity/96510?srsltid=AfmBOooxOsVOEwxcOD00na2BlgLTeCoVtMtoMpDVcY_rEOBqZl7oGzup

Trump, D. J. (2020, September 22). Combating race and sex stereotyping (Executive Order No. 13950). *Federal Register*, 85, 60683–60689. https://www.federalregister.gov/d/2020-21534

Trump, D. J. (2025, January 20). Ending radical and wasteful government DEI programs and preferencing (Executive Order No. 14151). *Federal Register*, 90, 8339–8341. https://www.federalregister.gov/d/2025-01953

Trump, D. J. (2025, January 21). Ending illegal discrimination and restoring merit-based opportunity (Executive Order No. 14173). *Federal Register*, 90, 8633–8636. https://www.federalregister.gov/d/2025-02097

Tsui, A. S., Wang, H. U. I., Xin, K., Zhang, L., & Fu, P. P. (2004). "Let a thousand flowers bloom": Variation of leadership styles among Chinese CEOs. *Organizational Dynamics*, *33*(1), 5–20. https://doi.org/10.1016/j.orgdyn.2003.11.002

Tu, L. (2024, November/December). A new era of EDI work. *American Psychological Association Monitor on Psychology*, *8*(55), 24–29. https://www.apa.org/monitor/2024/11/edi-approach-political-backlash

United Nations Department of Economic and Social Affairs. (2015). *Sustainable development.* https://sdgs.un.org/goals

United States Department of Labor. (2024, January 26). *Current population survey. Labor force statistics from the current population survey.* https://www.bls.gov/cps/cpsaat11.htm

United States Office of Management and Budget. (2024, March 29). Revisions to OMB's Statistical Policy Directive No. 15: Standards for maintaining, collecting, and presenting federal data on race and ethnicity Federal Register. (89 Fed. Reg. 22182). https://www.govinfo.gov/content/pkg/FR-2024-03-29/pdf/2024-06469.pdf

Vespa, J., Medina, L., & Armstrong, D. M. (2020). *Demographic turning points for the United States: Populations projects for 2020 to 2060.* https://www.census.gov/content/dam/Census/library/publications/2020/demo/p25-1144.pdf

Welbourne, T. M. (2024). ERGs at the crossroads: The state of employee resource group report. *CEO Action for Diversity and Inclusion.* https://ceo.usc.edu/wp-content/uploads/2024/04/USC-CEO-ERGs-Crossroads_ResearchReport_Final_042324.pdf

Welp, M., & Schein, E. H. (2021). The role of White male culture in engaging White men to be inclusive leaders. In B. Ferdman, J. Prime, & R. Riggio (Eds.), *Inclusive leadership: Transforming diverse lives, workplaces and societies* (pp. 363–378). Routledge.

Williams, B. W., & Cox, J. (2022). The new principle–practice gap: The disconnect between diversity beliefs and actions in the workplace. *Sociology of Race and Ethnicity*, *8*(2), 301–314.

Wilson, K. Y. (2010). An analysis of bias in supervisor narrative comments in performance appraisal. *Human Relations*, *63*(12), 1903–1933. https://doi.org/10.1177/0018726710369396

Wilson, K. Y., & Jones, R. G. (2008). Reducing job-irrelevant bias in performance and appraisals: Compliance and beyond. *Journal of General Management*, *34*(2), 57–70. https://doi.org/10.1177/030630700803400204

Wilson, K. Y., & Jones, R. G. (2018). Performance appraisal. In T. Cornish & T. Calvard (Eds.), *The psychology of ethnicity in organisations* (pp. 58–82). Palgrave Macmillan.

Wilson, K. Y., & Schwabenland, C. (2012). International and intranational cultures in organizations: Overlapping or contested terrain? *Industrial and Organizational Psychology*, *5*(3), 357–361. https://doi.org/10.1111/j.1754-9434.2012.01460.x

Witherspoon, B. (2024, July 21). "DEI" has become too divisive—It's time for a rebrand. *The Hill.* https://thehill.com/opinion/civil-rights/4781691-diversity-equity-inclusion-language

Witherspoon, D. P., Bámaca-Colbert, M. Y., Stein, G. L., & Rivas-Drake, D. (2020). Hidden populations: Uncovering the developmental experiences of minoritized populations across contexts. *Developmental Psychology*, *56*(8), 1425–1430. https://doi.org/10.1037/dev0001055

World at Work. (2021, September 28). *More than 80% of organizations have taken action on DEI initiatives in 2021.* https://worldatwork.org/about/press-room/more-than-80-percent-of-organizations-have-taken-action-on-dei-initiatives-in-2021?

Xing, Y., Liu, Y., Froese, F. J., & Huang, M. (2023). Advancing Chinese leadership research: Review and future directions. *Asian Business and Management*, (22), 493–508. https://doi.org/10.1057/s41291-023-00224-7

Yoshino, K., & Glasgow, D. (2024, January 5). DEI is under attack. Here's how companies can mitigate the legal risks. Harvard Business Review. https://hbr.org/2024/01/dei-is-under-attack-heres-how-companies-can-mitigate-the-legal-risks

Yukl, G. (2012). Effective leadership behavior: What we know and what questions need more attention. *Academy of Management Perspectives, 26*(4), 66–85. https://doi.org/10.5465/amp.2012.0088

Zhang, L. (2020). An institutional approach to gender diversity and firm performance. *Organisation Science, 31*(2), 439–457. https://doi.org/10.1287/orsc.2019.1297

12

Women's Leadership

A Call to Action for Senior Leadership in Organizations

Anna Marie Valerio and Alexandra Lycan Ronske

The Case for Women Leaders

Although women in the United States earn the majority of bachelor's and master's degrees and represent nearly half of the entry-level workforce, they still hold only a small percentage of C-suite and board roles.[1] Despite decades of organizational change initiatives and growing awareness, women remain underrepresented in senior leadership roles across sectors (McKinsey, 2024; Valerio, 2022). This underrepresentation persists even as women continue to outpace men in educational attainment and enter the workforce in comparable numbers (National Center for Education Statistics, 2023). However, advancement into executive leadership has not mirrored these achievements. Research has consistently shown that organizations with greater gender diversity in leadership report higher financial performance, stronger governance, and improved employee engagement (Cohen et al., 2023; Laidlaw & Sandberg, 2023; Post & Byron, 2014). The gap between women's qualifications and their representation in leadership highlights both a systemic failure to leverage talent and a critical need for action (Valerio, 2018).

Furthermore, women—especially women of color (WOC)—face compounding barriers such as microaggressions, limited sponsorship opportunities, and exclusion from key developmental experiences (Holder et al., 2015; McKinsey, 2020a, 2024; Randel et al., 2021). These challenges are not merely individual hurdles but reflect broader organizational and societal systems that inhibit inclusion (Glass & Cook, 2018; Morgenroth et al., 2020; Ryan & Morgenroth, 2024). Progress has also been stalled by persistent stereotypes and hidden biases in hiring and promotion practices, despite

Anna Marie Valerio and Alexandra Lycan Ronske, *Women's Leadership*. In: *The Changing Leadership Landscape*. Edited by: Sheri L. Feinzig and Mariangela Battista, Oxford University Press. © Oxford University Press (2026). DOI: 10.1093/9780197820070.003.0012 growing evidence that inclusive leadership styles—particularly empathetic leadership—enhance organizational culture and performance (Eagly & Carli, 2007; Nowack & Zak, 2020; Van Bommel, 2023). Addressing these interconnected issues requires a fundamental shift from "fixing women" to reforming the systems that constrain them, in an effort to fully realize the economic contributions of women in the United States (Catalyst, 2022).

While these issues are often complex and interconnected, they are not insurmountable. Addressing them requires coordinated efforts across research, policy, and practice. Drawing on empirical evidence, the chapter offers actionable strategies for individuals, organizations, societies, and international systems to advance gender inclusion and fully realize women's leadership potential.

In light of current trends, the focus of this chapter will be on the following areas which were selected as having special relevance to the impact of women leaders in organizations for both the present and the future:

- Educational achievement trends
- Career progression and leadership outcomes
- Compounded barriers for women of color
- Early pipeline breakdowns
- Persistent bias in evaluation and opportunity
- Unequal career risk in leadership roles
- The need for systemic change

Demographic Data: When Achievement Does Not Lead to Parity

The data on women's educational attainment show increasing levels of achievement. According to recent National Center for Education surveys, women have continued to outpace men in the number of post-secondary degrees earned (National Center for Education Statistics, 2023). Figure 12.1 shows that in 2023, women earned 14% more bachelor's degrees, 20% more master's degrees, and 6% more doctoral degrees than men across all fields.

In some fields of study, specifically "hard sciences" such as science, technology, engineering, and mathematics (STEM), men still outpace women in post-secondary attainment. However, in 2022, women received almost 60% of legal and professional studies degrees and earned an equitable amount of business-related post-secondary degrees compared to men. As seen in

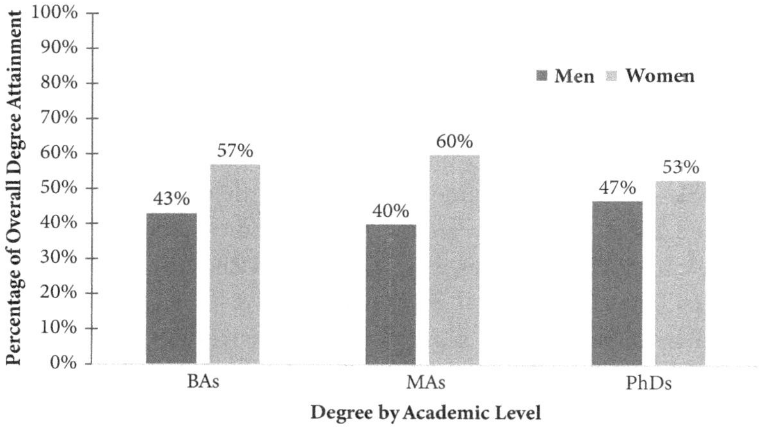

Figure 12.1 Educational Attainment for Men vs. Women in 2023
Source: National Center for Education Statistics (2023).

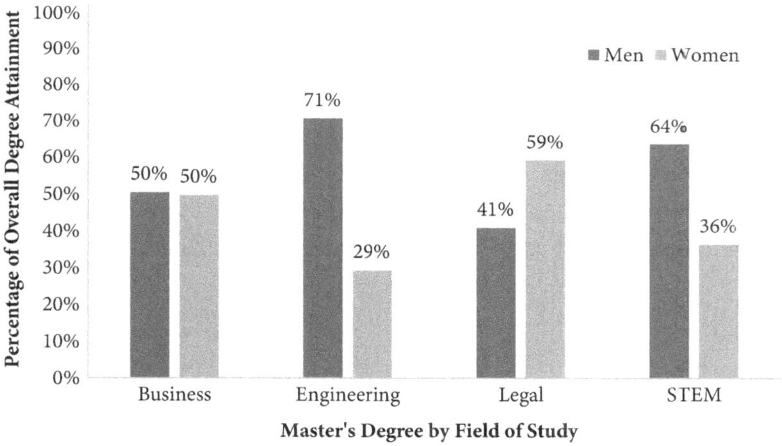

Figure 12.2 Master's Degree Attainment by Sex of Student and Field of Study for Men vs. Women in 2022
Source: National Center for Education Statistics (2022a, 2022b).

Figure 12.2, men and women earned the same number of Master of Business Administration degrees (MBAs) as of 2022. This current statistic indicates that women are just as qualified as men when entering the pipeline, so what is still preventing them from getting to the top?

Since the 1990s, many businesses have attributed the low level of women in C-Suite and Board of Director positions to a "lack of qualified candidates."

There is a misconception that women need to obtain higher levels of education before they can be taken seriously at work. In the business world, women have done just that! While women have made progress—it has been painstakingly slow. For example, as Figure 12.3 shows, in Fortune 500 companies in the United States women held 10% of Chief Executive Officer (CEO) roles in 2024, compared to 1995 when there were no women in CEO roles. It has taken 30 years for 10% of women to achieve CEO status in Fortune 500 companies, despite their elevated levels of educational attainment. One analysis, using data on Standard & Poor's (S&P) top executives over a five-year period, suggests that differences in the networks and credentials of men and women limit access to organizational leadership opportunities and therefore contributes to this trend (Ingersoll et al., 2024). Additionally, while women may advance to executive roles more quickly than men, women's advancement to the top in an organization slows once one woman is appointed to an executive role; these data suggest that organizations may appoint women to executive positions in order to improve public appearances and appease stakeholders (Bonet et al., 2020).

At the same time, the percentage of women on boards has moved from 10% to approximately 30%. In recent years, many organizations have established hiring quotas which require them to change hiring practices and likely contribute to the 20 percentage point increase (Ferreria et al., 2020; Smith, 2014). Studies suggest that organizations may find it more feasible to add women to boards than address deeper, structural challenges, such as biases

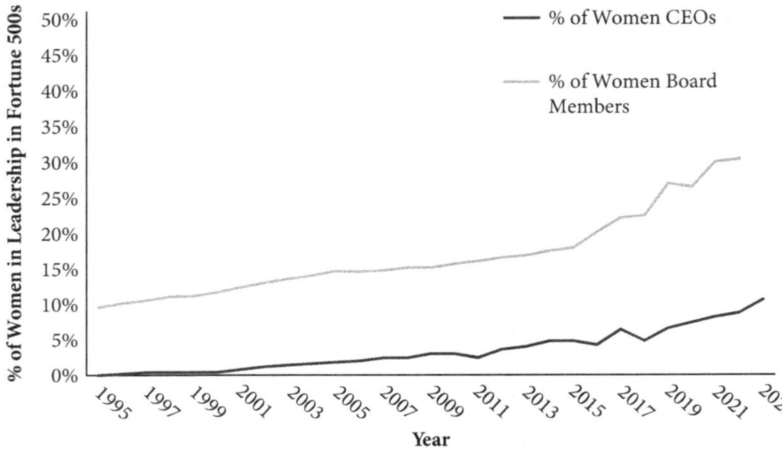

Figure 12.3 Women Leaders in Fortune 500 Companies

Source: Pew Research Center, Schaeffer (2023).

in promotion practices, that affect the selection of women for CEO positions (Adams & Ferreira, 2009; Post & Byron 2014). In essence, organizations might increase the representation of women on boards as a symbolic gesture rather than creating a substantive change. It is also important to note that using quotas to increase the number of female board members may hinder the advancement of women to executive roles (Gilbert & Fedorets, 2024).

Overall, the data show a significant imbalance between women's educational attainment and their achievement of leadership roles; although women are achieving higher and higher levels of education, their individual progress is not resulting in advancement to executive roles. In fact, at the current rate of advancement it may take at least another 50 years to achieve equity for all women in corporate America (McKinsey, 2024). This imbalance is of great concern, considering the implications from a potential loss of workforce talent.

Specific Challenges for Black Women and WOC

This slow progress and lack of parity is even more painstaking for WOC and minorities within the business sector. Although these women are achieving educational advancement and entering the pipeline, there is an even greater underrepresentation of minority women in senior leadership roles than white women; specifically, they struggle to make it to managerial and C-suite leadership positions. Black women and WOC face many more challenges that include a wider range of subtle verbal and nonverbal slights and insults (also known as microaggressions), being promoted more slowly, being least likely to be identified for growth opportunities, and limited interaction with senior-level managers. All these challenges contribute to decreased chances for upward mobility when compared to white women, but also when compared to men (McKinsey, 2020a, 2020b, 2024). Statistics shown in Figure 12.4 from the Bureau of Labor Statistics highlight this disparity for WOC.

Women in US Government Leadership Roles

The trend of slow advancement for women, and even slower advancement for minority groups, is also pervasive within US government roles. Regarding US political leadership since 1975, there continues to be an upward

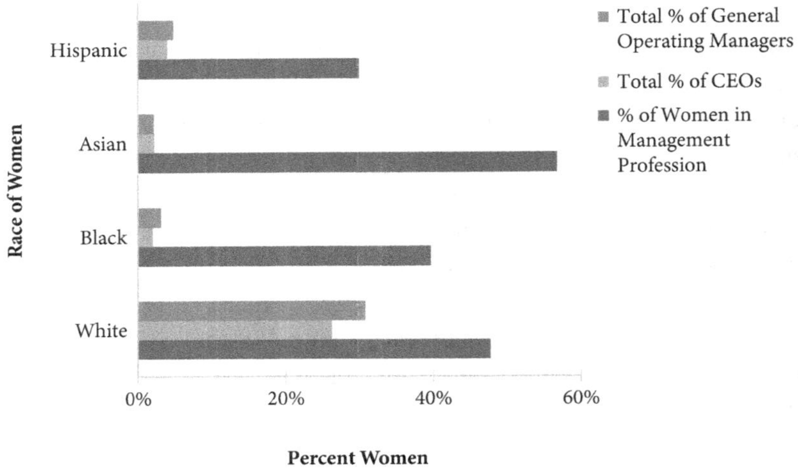

Figure 12.4 Women in Management Professions vs. % Women in Leadership by Race
Source: Bureau of Labor Statistics (2023).

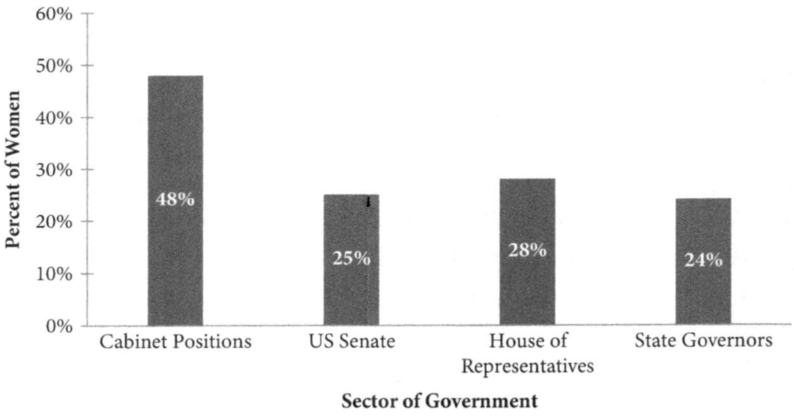

Figure 12.5 Women in Government Leadership Positions by Sector
Source: Pew Research Center, Schaeffer (2023).

trend for women in legislative roles in the US Senate, House of Representatives, and state legislators. Even though women make up more than 50% of the population in the United States, they hold between 25% and 28% (i.e., roughly one-quarter) of positions in the US Senate, House of Representatives, and State Governor seats, as illustrated in Figure 12.5.

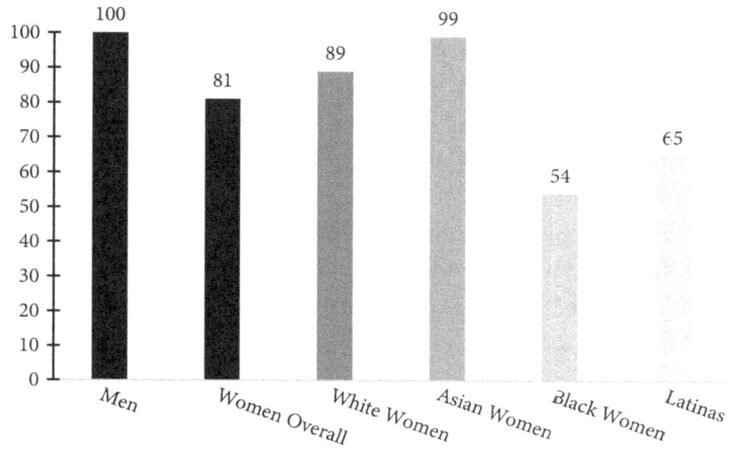

Figure 12.6 Promotion Rates of Women to Manager Compared to Men
Source: McKinsey (2024).

Within these political arenas, WOC are even less represented. In 2023, there were 24 female state governors, 23 of them were white women and only one was Native American. Figure 12.6 illustrates this lack of parity by race in sectors of government.

The "Broken Rung"

The slow advancement of women might be due to the "Broken Rung" phenomenon. In the first several steps up from entry levels to higher managerial levels, women frequently receive feedback that they need "one more assignment" to develop their leadership skills and move upward. Women represent 51% of the population and are earning comparable degrees to men in many fields, and 48% of entry-level employees are women (McKinsey, 2024). However, while women start out well-represented in the workforce at entry levels, they quickly fall behind when progressing to higher levels. As women lose ground to men in career advancement, the overall result is significantly slower progress for women early in their careers, especially in traditionally male-dominated fields. Consequently, because of the "Broken Rung," women fall behind, and often never catch up. Recent studies of women in the workplace showed that organizations promote fewer women in the first step up to manager and this has the effect of producing fewer women in senior leadership pipelines (McKinsey 2020b, 2024). Specifically, in 2024, for every 100 men who were promoted to manager only 89 women were promoted. As shown in Figure 12.6, these effects are even more detrimental for WOC (McKinsey, 2024). There is a common societal misconception that the "Broken Rung" is due primarily to circumstances—that women may be more committed to their families than their careers and choose to leave the workforce at critical junctions. However, according to survey data collected in 2023, women are just as committed to their careers as men (McKinsey, 2023).

Understanding Current Issues to Find Future Solutions

Understanding the current issues facing all women as they strive toward career success is timely at this juncture in our history. As the statistics show, women have been equipping themselves with educational experiences necessary to achieve success prior to entering the pipeline, but these achievements are not translating to gender parity in the workplace. According to one study conducted by McKinsey (2024), it will take 22 years to achieve parity for women in general and 48 years to achieve parity for WOC. The progress toward gender parity in organizations has been surprisingly slow despite impressive evidence that increasing the number of women in leadership roles will increase profits. Supporting this point, a 2019 study found the following: companies with female Chief Financial Officers (CFOs) generated excess profits of $1.8 trillion, companies with a female CEO or CFO generated greater stock price performance (when compared to market average), and companies with more female board members were more profitable overall than their peers with less board diversity (Laidlaw & Sandberg, 2023).

Another highly relevant issue for the inclusion of women in the workplace is empathy. As our world grows increasingly more complex in the post–COVID-19 era, empathy might be a necessary trait for organizational leaders to obtain success. Research shows that empathetic leaders create a plethora of positive outcomes within organizations. According to research by Catalyst, empathetic leaders boost productivity, increase innovation, foster inclusion, and decrease employee intent to leave (Van Bommel, 2023). All these outcomes could contribute to higher performance and organizational output. Additionally, WOC who have empathetic leaders experience less burnout (Van Bommel, 2023). Since women leaders typically exhibit more transformational and participative leadership styles compared to men (Kaiser, 2024; Nowack & Zak, 2020), they may be more empathetic leaders.

Statistics on performance and research on leadership traits of women point to a strong potential for success when women are appointed to leadership roles. As a result, current leaders of industry should be concerned about a systemic failure to harness the potential of women for the betterment of their organizations. Women continue to see their gender and race as barriers to advancement, and younger women and WOC receive less of the support needed from their managers to be successful (McKinsey, 2024). The first step to solving this problem is acquiring a better understanding of the challenges facing women because of racial, cultural, and other demographic characteristics that are critical to future progress.

The next sections of this chapter, Changes in Gender Stereotyping and Hidden Biases: the "Glass Cliff," Microaggressionson and Other Challenges provide an overview of more recent shifts in gender stereotyping, and the continued hidden biases in women's placement into leadership roles, suggested potential solutions for new ways of working in organizations. Overall, leaders should take a solution-focused perspective, adopting a "call to action" to address and overcome impediments in the progress in women's leadership attainment, rather than continuing to place the burden for success on women alone.

Changes in Gender Stereotyping

Gender stereotype research over the last 50 years provides helpful context for the progress of women in leadership. Gender stereotypes are generalizations about individuals' characteristics: communion (compassion, sensitivity, warmth, and connection with others) has been associated with women, while agency (ambition, independence, aggression, and acting assertively) has been associated with men (Bakan, 1966; Eagly & Carli, 2007; Heilman et al., 1995; Koenig et al., 2011; Schein, 1973). Stereotypes have continued to disadvantage women along the agentic–communal continuum. Women, viewed as either too "agentic" or too "communal," are caught in a "double bind," vulnerable to risks of derailment (Catalyst, 2007;

Eagly & Carli, 2007; Lyness & Heilman, 2006). Meta-analyses on patterns of leadership behavior show that women leaders adopt leadership styles that are participative (democratic) and collaborative. In contrast, male leaders showed more directive (autocratic) behaviors and tended toward delayed decision-making. Female leaders also tend to mentor and coach their subordinates more than male leaders (Eagly & Johnson, 1990; Eagly et al., 2003). However, the perceived effectiveness of certain leadership skills may vary by gender. This impact of pervasive gender stereotypes on leadership may be more prevalent in highly masculine or directive cultures, such as the military. For example, military superiors have a positive view of humble behaviors within junior leaders; however, men receive more benefit from acting humbly than their women counterparts (Swain & Korenman, 2018).

Notably, research shows that stereotypes are not fixed but have the capacity to change over time. A recent meta-analytic study included perceptions of competence in addition to communion and agency, as measured in US public opinion polls spanning seven decades with a large sample of over 30,000 respondents. Perceptions of women's competence appear to have shifted over time. Competence includes the ability to create or invent new things, as well as the traits of being innovative, intelligent, and logical (Eagly et al., 2020). As the authors illustrate, women have become increasingly competent through education and labor-force participation; as women increasingly occupy leadership roles, the perception and acceptance of both their leadership and agency are likely to increase. The upward trends in leadership may also be seen when women occupy roles as scientists and leaders, since the barriers in science and leadership may be weaker and challenges more manageable (Eagly, 2021). However, hidden biases still exist for women that need to be addressed and overcome.

Hidden Biases: The "Glass Cliff," Microaggressions, and Other Challenges

Although the increase in achievements and competence bodes well for women's leadership, there are two other problematic phenomena besides the "Broken Rung"—the "Glass Cliff" and microaggressions—that continue to contribute to the slowness in women's progress in organizations today. Organizations that can successfully combat and overcome these often hidden biases will strengthen the pipeline of talent and enable the success of all leaders. Hidden biases emerge from the interaction of organizational systems, leadership norms, and cultural expectations, influencing women's leadership opportunities in subtle but meaningful ways. These dynamics reflect systemic conditions rather than individual shortcomings and are reinforced through routine organizational practices related to selection, evaluation, and support (Ryan & Morgenroth, 2024; Valerio, 2018). Empirical research shows that such biases can shape both leadership placement and day-to-day experiences, increasing career vulnerability and interpersonal strain for women in leadership roles (Morgenroth et al., 2020; King et al., 2022). The "Glass Cliff" and microaggressions illustrate how these hidden dynamics operate across organizational contexts and leadership levels (Ryan & Haslam, 2007; Morgenroth et al., 2020; King et al., 2022).

The "Glass Cliff"

When organizations experiencing financial downturns appoint women to senior management positions, these women may be more likely than men to find themselves on a "Glass Cliff"— that is, their positions of leadership carry a greater risk of failure. It has not been uncommon for women to receive assignments to organizations in crisis. In fact, research shows that women are more likely to be appointed to leadership positions during times of crisis than men (Morgenroth et al., 2020). But if failure occurs, it is women, rather than men, who face the consequences including criticism and blame, and often job loss (Ryan & Haslam, 2007).

Women in leadership often bear the consequences of preexisting corporate struggles, reinforcing the precarious nature of "Glass Cliff" appointments. In the "Glass Cliff" scenario, women are promoted into roles in which they are not set up for success, and they either fail or are pushed out of the organization. As mentioned in the press in recent years, women in leadership roles in major companies (such as Boeing, Under Armor, Bed Bath & Beyond, Twitter (now X Corps), Citigroup, Walgreens, General Motors, Yahoo, and others) had to navigate many preexisting challenges (Cook & Glass, 2014; Holman, 2024; Khan, 2025). Examples of such corporate challenges have included operational inefficiencies, financial instability, declining stock prices, and investor dissatisfaction.

According to a recent meta-analysis, the "Glass Cliff" phenomenon is also present in other domains such as higher education and politics

(Morgenroth et al., 2020). Less research exists about women's appointment to precarious leadership positions in higher education as compared to the corporate sphere (D'Apice et al., 2024). However, women presidents at higher education institutions experience many of the same barriers to advancement based on gender as their corporate counterparts (Hagan & Olivier, 2022). The recent uptick in resignations may indicate underlying societal and organizational issues. From 2023 to 2024, there was an increase in female university presidents who resigned from the top 30 schools in the United States; the majority of these positions were subsequently filled by men (Nietzel, 2024). This statistic could potentially indicate the larger scrutiny that women face from stakeholders when their organizations experience challenges and the presence of the "Glass Cliff" phenomenon in academia (Kelderman, 2024). Regardless of the context in which they lead, women in leadership often bear the consequences of preexisting organizational challenges, reinforcing the precarious nature of "Glass Cliff" appointments (Glass & Cook, 2019; Morgenroth et al., 2020; Ryan & Haslam, 2007).

However, in a reexamination of the "Glass Cliff" phenomenon with a larger, more recent sample of women appointed as CEOs in precarious situations, greater education has a positive impact on CEO job security. Though selected and promoted during crises involving poor company performance, many companies are reluctant to fire women due to the negative publicity that would accompany the termination (Elsaid & Ursel, 2017). It may also be possible that "Glass Cliff" appointments result from an individual's long-term career strategy focused on balancing risky career moves, rather than isolated incidents of high-risk appointments (Glass & Cook, 2018). Furthermore, to overcome systemic biases, these leaders may deliberately pursue riskier career paths, such as pursuit of high-risk jobs, assignments, and leadership opportunities. Thus, female and minority leaders may pay a substantial risk tax for continued upward mobility within their organization.

It is clear that further exploration of the "Glass Cliff" phenomenon is warranted. Although there has been strong evidence for it in many organizations (e.g., Ryan & Haslam, 2007), many factors may influence it, such as country/cultural norms, differences across disciplines and industries (examples include blue-collar vs. white-collar, retail industry vs. STEM industries), and the geographical environments in which firms operate. Another avenue for exploring the myriad issues surrounding women's leadership may lie in seeking a better understanding of the conditions that enable talented women to thrive and grow their organizations (Li et al., 2025). In agreement with these authors, there are many opportunities for further studies by researchers and practitioners that would be important in advancing and enabling women's leadership across industries, organizations, and societies.

Microaggressions

Microaggressions may be defined as the subtle everyday verbal, nonverbal, and environmental slights, snubs, or insults, whether intentional or unintentional, that communicate hostile, derogatory, or negative messages to target persons based solely upon their marginalized group membership. Microaggressions may be evidenced in subtle behaviors toward others such as exclusion, invisibility, and assumptions about the universality of one's experiences. Unfortunately, as microaggressions may be subtle and difficult to identify, they nevertheless serve to undermine confidence and self-esteem, motivation, and job performance. Microaggressions serve to reinforce systems of disadvantage (King et al., 2022).

These subtle forms of discrimination also occur for women who are underrepresented in STEM fields, particularly in positions of leadership. For women in STEM fields, microaggressions can harm their work identities and trigger a cycle of rumination and self-doubt that may lead them to leave STEM (Fattoracci & King, 2023).

Other Challenges

Although many women face challenges in managing the phenomena of the "Broken Rung," "Glass Cliff," and microaggressions, such challenges are especially common for WOC. In comparison with their colleagues of other races and ethnicities, Black women experience many more challenges at work (McKinsey, 2020a, 2024). The more severe challenges for Black women include facing a wider range of microaggressions, being promoted more slowly, underrepresentation in senior leadership, and fewer interactions with senior leaders (McKinsey, 2024). Racial microaggressions impact the confidence, emotional and cognitive well-being, and inclusion of Black women, which may impact their ability to be successful in corporate leadership roles and lead to more frequent burnout (King et al., 2022). Solutions include providing opportunities to harness the power of allies for support to raise awareness and counter the negative effects of microaggressions (Kim & Meister, 2023). Coping strategies have included support networks, sponsorship and mentorship, and self-care (Holder et al., 2015).

What are the implications of this research for women's leadership? In addition to the underrepresentation of women in leadership roles, there is also a lack of representation in research—e.g., few empirical studies focus on the experiences of Black and Asian women (Otaye-Ebede & Shaffakat, 2024). Of the limited research regarding the unique challenges faced by WOC in career advancement, most focus on barriers to advancement such as effects of discrimination and racial microaggressions (Holder et al., 2015; McCluney & Rabelo, 2019). In fact, most management research is focused on the general experience of women (e.g., Powell & Butterfield, 2015) and does not include the unique challenges associated with intersectionality (Crenshaw, 1991). Increasing our understanding of how the intersectionality of race and gender create larger disadvantages for WOC is a critical step in moving toward overall equality and fairness. Because few studies focus on potential solutions to increase career advancement opportunities and success (Otaye-Ebede & Shaffakat, 2024; Smith et al., 2019), this is an "area of opportunity" for practitioners and researchers alike.

A Call to Action: Senior Leaders Must Act Now!

The focus on HR systems and processes can be beneficial within and across many organizations. However, a more comprehensive approach may be necessary to understand the challenges facing today's workforce by looking at what is needed at three levels of context: organizational, individual, and societal (Valerio, 2009). Although many positive societal and organizational changes have occurred in recent decades, the outcomes are painstakingly slow. Clearly it is time for a renewed "call to action" (Valerio, 2018) to accelerate the pace of change for workplace gender equality. Potential HR actions for addressing the issues of the "Glass Cliff," the "Broken Rung," and microaggressions include examining the extent to which these occur within a given organization. These may be evaluated along with the larger framework of how HR structures and processes are measured and used in the assessment and promotion of employees in organizations (Valerio, 2018). The call to action for C-suite and senior leaders in organizations starts by asking: To what extent are women given the work opportunities that lead to senior leadership roles?

Potential evaluation methods for these opportunities include the examination of organizational leadership models and frameworks for hidden, unconscious biases, thus ensuring that an organization's stated goals for values, strategy, and success include gender inclusion. It is also critical that commonly used HR metrics, such as performance evaluations and 360-degree feedback, remain bias-free—particularly when leaders use them to identify, select, and develop talented individuals. Equally important are utilizing clear and objective evaluation criteria for feedback, recognition, rewards, and hiring; as well as holding managers accountable for fairness in performance reviews and promotions. In addition, organizations may track and measure demographic data associated with the utilization and assignment of established learning and development opportunities such as mentoring programs, coaching, and key developmental experiences throughout the organization.

It is clear, therefore, that there are many HR functions that benefit from a reexamination of both the processes and their implementation to enable the advancement of talented women. As the demographics and statistical data included in the section "Demographic Data: /When Achievement does not lead to Parity" indicate, women have continued to attain the educational degrees necessary to pursue managerial and professional roles. Many organizational cultures continue to perpetuate these gender inequities by placing constraints and limitations on the ambitions, achievements, and skills of women. Underlying factors such as gender stereotyping and hidden biases are leading hordes of women to opt out of organizations when professional advancement is blocked or slowed, which is surprising given the amount of time and effort put forth to obtain educational degrees.

A more effective approach begins with a more comprehensive understanding of how organizational context, systems, and structures influence women's ambitions, interpretations of their skills, and motivation to succeed in organizations (Ryan & Morgenroth, 2024). Rather than place the focus on women's limitations, it is important to understand how organizational systems, structure, and culture can shape and constrain women's ability to obtain and succeed in leadership positions. Instead of simply encouraging and motivating women to aspire for high-level leadership positions, organizations should focus on sustaining an organizational culture and policies that promote women's success—i.e., "fixing the system" (Ryan & Morgenroth, 2024).

Organizations need a proactive approach to enable more talented women to move into leadership roles, with the result of generating even greater success and higher profits for organizations, rather than passively accepting the current systems. The following section provides practical ideas and solutions that HR professionals and their organizations can implement to improve the pace of change and enable women's advancement in organizations.

New Actions for Change in HR Organizational Practices, Policies, and Leadership

In examining trends within organizations, there are areas of practice that would enable leaders to infuse organizations with new ideas and talent, advance inclusion in their workforces, and increase innovation, profitability, and growth. The areas discussed in this section offer opportunities to leverage change in current HR practices and foster learning from "best practices" as well. Senior leaders and their organizations may well benefit by focusing on the following four areas of opportunity for organizational growth and increased profits: Women on Boards, Sponsorship and Mentorship, Flexible Work Policies, and Leadership Education and Executive Coaching.

Women on Boards

There is greater recognition that gender diversity on boards of directors is important for corporate governance, but progress toward increasing women's representation on boards has been slow. A meta-analysis involving 60,648 organizations across 36 countries showed that the national context for gender equality moderates the extent to which characteristics of organizational leadership relate to women's board representation (Halliday et al., 2020). That is, the larger cultural perspective of gender within a region or county, or the national context, impacts the relationship between certain characteristics of leadership within an organization (i.e., CEO's gender, chair's gender, CEO's age, board members' age, etc.) and women's representation on boards (Halliday et al., 2020). While the macro level impacts of national context on women's board representation matter, organizations should first understand both theoretical and practical implications for increasing the representation of women on boards.

In a study on women's impacts on firms' practices and policies, Glass & Cook (2018) focused on board composition and CEO's gender in areas of governance, product development, and equity at Fortune 500 companies. Results showed that gender-diverse boards foster innovation in business and equity practices, and that the presence of influential women in top leadership positions can result in numerous positive benefits. These benefits include, but are not limited to, enhanced financial performance, more inclusive workplace culture, and improved corporate social responsibility (Cohen et al., 2023; Glass & Cook, 2018; Post & Byron, 2014). The authors conclude that boards should be diversified and include more women leaders.

Results from recent large-scale, technology-assisted studies may hold promise in understanding how the use of gender stereotypes serve to perpetuate women's underrepresentation in leadership positions. For example, gender stereotypes are expressed in language of agency (assertiveness and decisiveness), which is often associated with male leadership. In contrast, women are often seen in less agentic terms than men. A study using natural language processing techniques to analyze more than 43,000 documents containing 1.23 billion words found that hiring female CEOs and board members was associated with changes in organizations' use of language—i.e., being a woman became more similar to the semantic meaning of agency (Lawson et al., 2022). The authors suggest that hiring women into leadership positions helps to associate women with characteristics of the positive aspects of agency that are critical for leadership success (e.g., independent and confident), but not at the cost of losing communality (e.g., kind and caring). This is significant since female leadership may result in a more inclusive culture—one in which members of the organization do not just perceive women dichotomously as either competent or likable but acknowledge complexities outside of the normal gender stereotypes. For example, female board representation has been positively related to human capital developmental policies that benefit all firm employees (Callahan et al., 2024). These results indicate that as women advance in positions of power in greater numbers in organizations, the current negative stereotypes associated with women are highly likely to change over time.

Sponsorship and Mentorship

Although the terms "Sponsorship and Mentorship" have often been used interchangeably, over time, greater clarity has evolved and their differences are now better understood. Mentorship involves the transfer of knowledge and the guidance provided by a more experienced person (the Mentor) through the sharing of their advice, knowledge, and experience with a less-experienced individual (the Mentee) (Ibarra et al., 2010). Sponsorship involves the actions associated with the support of superiors with a particular focus on their advocacy for promotion opportunities for a less-experienced person (Griffeth et al., 2021). At an earlier time, emerging from the research on sponsorship and mentorship was the idea that sponsorship is a more effective path toward leadership roles than mentorship (Catalyst, 2011; Ibarra et al., 2010). Some researchers have proposed that sponsorship may be a more important factor for career advancement than just mentorship alone (Singh & Vanka, 2020). In a similar vein, another view suggests that one of the reasons women are underrepresented in executive ranks is because they are mentored more than sponsored and lack the advocacy more easily provided between men (Griffeth et al., 2021). At this point in time, however, the literature is unclear as to whether sponsorship or mentorship programs matter more to women's upward trajectory in organizations. It is possible that both may be important in differing ways and are likely to merit further research efforts.

It also may be possible that the key to success lies in the way an organization formalizes and rewards the efforts of sponsors, mentors, and mentees and takes into consideration demographic variables. Sponsorship has great potential to increase career advancement for high-potential African American candidates. Given the challenges facing Black women and other WOC, sponsorship may be especially important to enable them to attain positions of leadership in their organizations (Randel et al., 2021). Leaders and their HR professionals may serve to advance the talent in their organizations by being proactive about identifying sponsorship opportunities (Chow, 2021) as well as tracking the outcome along a variety of appropriate dimensions. However, efforts to promote women into leadership often focus on only a few barriers within organizations, rather than considering the larger scope and the wide variety of barriers that exist across all organizational levels. In addition to focusing on strategies to enable the upward advancement of women in organizations, research shows that addressing barriers across all societal levels, albeit a daunting task, may be the best approach to help organizations create gender-equitable leadership environments (Diehl & Dzubinski, 2016). Sponsorship and mentorship programs provide opportunities for women to learn and navigate the challenges and the potential opportunities in their respective disciplines. Mentoring specifically can serve career functions (e.g., exposure-and-visibility, protection, and challenging assignments) and psychosocial functions (e.g., role modeling, acceptance and confirmation, and friendship) to help individuals develop workplace skills (Kram, 1983). Organizations that employ these types of programs will foster the growth of individuals through career and psychosocial functions, and enable the advancement of talented women.

Flexible Work Policies

The utilization of flexible work policies increased because of the COVID-19 pandemic, including hybrid and work-from-home (WFH) options which tended to promote a healthier integration of work and life for many people. As described by Wheatly et al. (2023), the WFH online delivery of women-only leadership programs enabled the participants to enhance their leadership skills, navigate unexpected challenges, and build collegial networks to advance their careers. All of these carry the potential to increase adaptation when future crises and industry disruptions occur suddenly. The rapid expansion of flexible work policies since 2020 has occurred faster than systematic research assessing their effects across difference employee populations. Therefore, especially important to this field of research is the impact of an organization's flexible work arrangement policies across varying demographics, such as gender, age, socioeconomic status and other variables.

An organization's flexible work policies and parental leave policies provide a large area of opportunity for research. For example, flexible workplace policies may have greater impacts on women depending upon the different stages of their careers—i.e., early to mid-career as well as later in career. Specifically, women in their early to mid-careers may have greater concerns about gender equality, sharing household duties, and be more open to using external childcare than their male counterparts (Offermann et al., 2021). In a similar vein, women who are at mid-career and beyond must often contend with many life-stage challenging experiences that include workplace age discrimination and threats to job security, and, within the same time frame, building sufficient wealth to fund their children's college tuitions and accumulating sufficient savings for a comfortable retirement. A recent study of the diversity and organizational practices that increase the proportion of women and people of color at the top showed that the more diversity management and family-friendly practices an organization implemented, the higher the proportion of women in management positions (Schoen & Rost, 2020). Unsurprisingly, these results provide valuable insight for organizations who seek to increase workforce diversity and opportunities for women's upward trajectory.

The recent creation of an online database provides further details regarding paid parental leave at large US public companies and serves as a valuable resource for employees and future research (Travis, 2024). Many developed countries have paid parental leave laws nationally; however, the United States is not among them. As of 2023, only 27% of private-sector workers had access to paid family leave (Bureau of Labor Statistics, 2023). The database shows the top 51 companies that publish the details of their paid parental leave policy publicly on their websites from 500 of the largest US public companies. In a review of research on gender differences in salary negotiations, the evidence suggests that "fix-the-institution" initiatives are more effective than "fix-the-women" initiatives in reducing gender differences in negotiation outcomes. The strongest evidence on effectiveness in narrowing gender disparities is found for policies that increase transparency—i.e., knowing what outcomes to expect from the negotiation process (Recalde & Vesterlund, 2020).

For researchers and practitioners interested in this topic, there is likely to be research data across organizations and countries that provide data and insight into how best to implement paid parental leave practices in the United States. For example, the results of a survey of 402 employed men and women supported the idea that work–life initiatives, regardless of gender, are positively related to leadership aspiration. The study showed that initiatives such as flexible work arrangements, leaves of absence, and on-site childcare assistance may encourage leadership aspiration for both genders (Fritz & van Knippenberg, 2018). Hence, the availability of work–life initiatives may remove barriers to advancement for all employees and increase available leadership talent pools.

In addition, it is important to note that Fritz and van Knippenberg (2018) have also provided examples of practical recommendations, based on the research results, that may be effective across organizations and cultures. These recommendations include a variety of initiatives, such as flexible work arrangements, on-site childcare, further education regarding work–life initiatives, or financial assistance programs that are associated with enhanced leadership aspiration and attainment. The authors suggest that it is important to create an environment for such work–life initiatives to be widely accepted to move an organizational culture toward a more family-friendly culture, and that these initiatives not be designed in a gender-exclusive manner. Such goals may be accomplished when top management and HR work together to develop alternative career paths to leadership roles that would consider how to incorporate telework, leaves of absence, and part-time work into the fabric of a career path. Using key performance indicators (KPIs) that measure the impact and acceptance of these initiatives to reduce their potential negative effects is a worthy endeavor that could help to find the best way to embed work–life initiatives in the organization. Both researchers and practitioners have a shared role in helping talented high-potential leaders integrate their leadership aspirations with their work and family life.

Leadership Education and Executive Coaching

In the past decade, both leadership education and executive coaching have become important staples of executive development efforts. Although at an earlier time both leadership education and executive coaching were provided mainly through in-person, off-site meetings, one of the outcomes of the pandemic and new technology was the recognition that these may be just as effective, as well as less costly, when delivered virtually. Leadership development initiatives offer unique opportunities to broaden access to peers and mentors, and empower women to enhance leadership skills and create collaborative relationships (Wheatly et al., 2023). In addition, it is important to recognize that there has been a greater appreciation for new leadership paradigms that prioritize traditionally "soft skills," such as humility, caring, and empathy, that are increasingly regarded as necessary for leadership success. Leaders who combine agentic and communal leadership styles are more likely to be successful in navigating the complex and rapidly changing world (Nowack & Zak, 2020; Valerio, 2022).

Fortunately, the cost-effectiveness of online delivery has enabled more people to avail themselves of these leadership development opportunities that provide many benefits. For young and emerging leaders, coaching leads to larger changes in leader identity, self-concept, humility, sense of purpose, satisfaction with life, and psychological well-being (Brown et al., 2021). The fact that these educational experiences may be provided on a large scale with positive outcomes, greater efficiency, and less cost suggests opportunities for organizations to reap many benefits from supporting leadership development and executive coaching initiatives.

Future Research

Building on the proposed organizational interventions, future research must prioritize evaluating the impact on advancing women's leadership. In a comprehensive overview of studies published in management, psychology, and diversity journals from 2000 to 2020, Lau et al. (2023) point out that less than 5% of studies on gender inequality in the workplace published in management, psychology, and diversity journals identify practical interventions for solving gender inequality in organizations. The authors emphasize the need to move beyond problem identification and toward the development and empirical testing of actionable solutions (Lau et al., 2023). Their review proposes that gender equality interventions exist in different ecological microsystems at the individual, interpersonal, and the broader societal levels. They propose future directions for research that would encourage women's greater awareness of incidences of gender discrimination, develop women to be proactive agents of change, and recognize the role of change agents such as leaders, male and female colleagues, spouse and/or family members. Suggestions for future research efforts include identifying factors for system-wide interventions and the impact of technology, such as the reinforcement of gender stereotypes, women's underrepresentation in STEM, and the biases inherent in artificial intelligence (AI) that impact gender equality.

While it remains important to understand current and ongoing issues, it is even more imperative to identify solutions, particularly given the favorable demographic trends for women's leadership cited in the section "Demographic Data."" The areas highlighted in this chapter indicate the value of shifting research focus from diagnosing barriers for women's leadership to testing interventions and driving systemic change. Organizations must act, thereby mobilizing and generating solutions through both research and practice (Valerio, 2018, 2022). As several studies suggest (Glass & Cook, 2019; Lawson et al., 2022, Ryan & Morganroth, 2024), future research on women's leadership may be especially well served by large-scale studies, longitudinal designs, and meta-analytic techniques increasingly made possible through technological advancements.

Conclusion: Reimaging Leadership through Organizational Change

There continues to be a concerning discrepancy between women's qualifications and their leadership representation in the United States (McKinsey, 2024; National Center for Education Statistics, 2023). Despite individual achievement and equal representation in entry-level jobs, women are systematically underrepresented in higher-level leadership roles across all sectors; in fact, if no action is taken, it will take 50 years for women to achieve parity (McKinsey, 2024). A renewed call to action is necessary to prevent continued stagnation and the underutilization of women in the workforce (Valerio 2018, 2022). Women face unique challenges such as the "Broken Rung," "Glass Cliff," and microaggressions, which inhibit and drastically slow progress. Full utilization of women in the workforce will increase not only the profits of individual organizations but also economic contributions at a societal level (Catalyst, 2022; Cohen et al., 2023; Laidlaw & Sandberg, 2023). Now is the time to act—not only because inaction will limit financial returns, but because the leadership landscape is shifting in the rapidly changing world. Research increasingly points to the value of empathetic leadership that fosters inclusive, high-performing cultures and is particularly well-suited to navigating today's complex organizational challenges (Kaiser, 2024; Nowack & Zak, 2020).

In conclusion, there is a shared responsibility and urgent need for intentional and systemic change. Women must continue to strive for excellence in education and qualifications, but organizations, researchers, and practitioners must implement and prioritize evidence-based solutions. Initiatives such as women on boards, sponsorship/mentorship, flexible workplace policies, leadership education, and executive coaching will act as organizational levers for more rapid change. Hopefully this call to action will spur the motivation for many to apply their respective skills as researchers and practitioners to apply solutions to overcome gender inequality for the generations to follow. With women's gains in educational and work achievements, it is imperative that organizations, individuals, and societies find ways to utilize their talents, resolve work–life issues, and become more adaptive in the twenty-first century. It is time to stop asking what holds women back, and focus on how we can collectively move them forward!

Note

1. The views expressed in this article reflect those of the authors and do not represent the official policy or position of the U.S. Military Academy, the Department of the Army, or the Department of War.

References

Adams, R., & Ferreira, D. (2009). Women in the boardroom and their impact on governance and performance. *Journal of Financial Economics, 94*, 291–309. https://doi.org/10.1016/j.jfineco.2008.10.007

Bakan, D. (1966). *The duality of human existence.* Addison Wesley.

Bonet, R., Cappelli, P., & Hamori, M. (2020). Gender differences in the speed of advancement: An empirical examination of top executives in Fortune 100 companies. *Strategic Management Journal,41*(4), 1–30. https://doi.org/10.1002.smj.3125

Brown, R. P., Varghese, L., Sullivan, S., & Parsons, S. (2021). The impact of professional coaching on emerging leaders. *International Journal of Evidence Based Coaching and Mentoring, 19*(2), 24–37.

Bureau of Labor Statistics. (2023). *House-hold data from current population: Table 11. Employed persons by detailed occupation, sex, race, and Hispanic or Latino ethnicity.* https://www.bls.gov/cps/cpsaat11.htm

Callahan, C., Mitra, A., & Sauerwald, S. (2024). Ethics of care and employees: The impact of female board representation and top management leadership on human capital development policies. *Journal of Business Ethics.* 195,615–629. https://doi.org/10.1007/s10551-024-05673-4

Catalyst. (2007). *The double-bind dilemma for women in leadership: Damned if you do, doomed if you don't.* https://www.catalyst.org/en-us/insights/2007/the-double-bind-dilemma-for-women-in-leadership

Catalyst. (2011). *Sponsoring women leaders to success.* https://www.catalyst.org/research/sponsoring-women-to-success

Catalyst. (2022). *Women in the workforce: United States (quick take).* https://www.catalyst.org/insights/2022/women-in-the-workforce-united-states

Chow, R. (2021). Don't just mentor women and people of color. Sponsor them. *Harvard Business Review.* https://hbr.org/2021/06/dont-just-mentor-women-and-people-of-color-sponsor-them?autocomplete=true

Cohen, S., Kadach, I., Ormazabal, G., & Reichelstein, S. (2023). Executive compensation tied to ESG performance: International evidence. *Journal of Accounting Research, 61*(3). https://doi.org/10.1111/1475-679X.12481

Cook, A., & Glass, C. (2014). Women and top leadership positions: Towards an institutional analysis. *Gender, Work and Organization, 21*(1), 91–103.https://doi.org/10.1111/gwao.12018

Crenshaw, K. W. (1991). Mapping the margins: Intersectionality, identity politics, and violence against women of color. *Stanford Law Review, 43*, 1241–1299.

D'Apice, H. K., Song, J., & Wotipka, C. M. (2024). A milestone in the pursuit of gender equality: Predicting first women presidents in U.S. higher education institutions, 1980–2018. *Sociology Compass, 18*(4), e13204. https://doi.org/10.1111/soc4.13204

Diehl, A. B., & Dzubinski, L. M. (2016). Making the invisible visible: A cross-sector analysis of gender-based leadership barriers. *Human Resource Development Quarterly, 27*(2), 181–206.

Eagly, A. H. (2021). Hidden in plain sight: The inconsistent gender gaps in STEM and leadership. *Psychological Inquiry, 32*(2), 89–95. https://doi.org/10.1080/1047840x.2021.1930764

Eagly, A. H., & Carli, L. L. (2007). *Through the labyrinth: The truth about how women become leaders.* Harvard Business School Press, Boston, MA.

Eagly, A. H., Johannesen-Schmidt, M. C., & van Engen, M. L. (2003). Transformational, transactional, and lais-sez-faire leadership styles: A meta-analysis comparing women and men. *Psychological Bulletin, 129*(4), 569–591. https://doi.org/10.1037/0033-2909.129.4.569

Eagly, A. H., & Johnson, B. T. (1990). Gender and leadership style: A meta-analysis. *Psychological Bulletin, 108*(2), 233–256. https://doi.org/10.1037/0033-2909.108.2.233

Eagly, A. H., Nater, C., Miller, D. I., Kaufmann, M., & Sczesny, S. (2020). Gender stereotypes have changed: A cross-temporal meta-analysis of U.S. public opinion polls from 1946 to 2018. *American Psychologist, 75*(3), 301–315. https://doi.org/10.1037/amp0000494

Elsaid, E., & Ursel, N. D. (2017). Re-examining the glass cliff hypothesis using survival analysis: The case of female CEO tenure. *British Journal of Management, 29*(1), 156–170. https://doi.org/10.1111/1467-8551.12241

Fattoracci, E. S., & King, D. D. (2023). The need for understanding and addressing microaggressions in the workplace. *Perspectives on Psychological Science, 18*(4), 738–742.

Ferreira, D., Ginglinger, E., Laguna, M., & Skalli, Y. (2020, November). *Closing the gap: Board gender quotas and hiring practices* (ECGI—Finance Working Paper No. 520/2017). https://doi.org/10.2139/ssrn.2992213

Fritz, C., & van Knippenberg, D. (2018). Gender and leadership aspiration: The impact of work–life initiatives. *Human Resource Management, 57*(4), 855–868 https://doi.org/10.1002/hrm.21875

Gilbert, A., & Fedorets, A. (2024). Lifting women up: Gender quotas and the advancement of women on corporate boards. *Corporate Governance: An International Review, 33*(3), 407–435. https://doi.org/10.1111/corg.12609

Glass, C., & Cook, A. (2019). Pathways to the glass cliff: A risk tax for women and minority leaders? *Social Problems, 67*(4), 637–653. https://doi.org/10.1093/socpro/spz045

Griffeth, L., Malik, R., Charas, S., & Randall, N. (2021). Sponsorship: An intervention to accelerate women's career velocity. *The IUP Journal of Soft Skills, 15*(3), 7–22.

Hagan, A. C., & Olivier, D. F. (2022). Women presidents of higher education institutions: A mixed-methods phenomenological study of the relationship between self-efficacy, transformational leadership, gender-based barriers, and support structures. *Research Issues in Contemporary Education, 7*(3), 1–28.

Halliday, C. S., Paustian-Underdahl, S. C., & Fainshmidt, S. (2020. Women on boards of directors: A meta-analytic examination of the roles of organizational leadership and national context for gender equality. *Journal of Business and Psychology, 36*(2), 173–191. https://doi.org/10.1007/s10869-019-09679-y

Heilman, M. E., Block, C. J., & Martell, R. F. (1995). Sex stereotypes: Do they influence perceptions of managers? *Journal of Social Behavior and Personality, 10*(6), 237–252.

Holder, A. M. B., Jackson, M. A., & Ponterotto, J. G. (2015). Racial microaggression experiences and coping strategies of Black women in corporate leadership. *Qualitative Psychology, 2*(2), 164–180. https://doi.org/10.1037/qup0000024

Holman, J. (2024). When that job promotion is really a "Glass Cliff." *The New York Times.* https://www.nytimes.com/2024/07/12/business/glass-cliff-effect.html#

Ibarra, H., Carter, N. M., & Silva, C. (2010). Why men still get more promotions than women. *Harvard Business Review, 88*(9), 80–126.

Ingersoll, A., Glass, C., & Cook, A. (2024). Gender, credentials, and success: An examination of educational attainment of top management teams. *Social Science Research, 124.* https://doi.org/10.1016/j.ssresearch.2024.103078

Kaiser, R. B. (2024). Has empathy really become more important to leadership since the COVID-19 pandemic? *Consulting Psychology Journal, 76*(2), 113–136. https://doi.org/10.1037/cpb0000273

Kelderman, E. (2024). A year ago women were the majority of ivy league presidents. Now most of them have quit. *The Chronicle of Higher Education.* https://www.chronicle.com/article/a-year-ago-women-were-the-majority-among-ivy-league-presidents-now-most-of-them-have-quit

Khan, R. (2025). Leadership at the edge: Navigating the glass cliff. *Society for Human Resource Management.* https://www.shrm.org/in/topics-tools/news/leadership-at-the-edge—navigating-the-glass-cliff

Kim, J. Y., & Meister, A. (2023). Microaggressions, interrupted: The experience and effects of gender microaggressions for women in STEM. *Journal of Business Ethics, 185*(3), 513–531.

King, D. D., Fattoracci, E. S. M., Hollingsworth, D. W., Stahr, E., & Nelson, M. (2022, April 28). When thriving requires effortful surviving: Delineating manifestations and resource expenditure outcomes of microaggressions for black employees. *Journal of Applied Psychology, 108*(2), 183–207. http://doi.org/10.1037/apl0001016

Koenig, A. M., Eagly, A. H., Mitchell, A. A., & Ristikari, T. (2011). Are leader stereotypes masculine? A meta-analysis of three research paradigms. *Psychological Bulletin, 137*(4), 616–642. https://doi.org/10.1037/a0023557

Kram, K. E. (1983). Phases of the mentor relationship. *Academy of Management Journal, 26*(4), https://doi.org/10.2307/255910

Laidlaw, J., & Sandberg, D. J. (2023, August). Breaking boundaries: Women poised for milestone achievement in parity amid otherwise bleak outlook. *S&P global Market intelligence.* https://www.spglobal.com/esg/documents/breaking-boundaries-women-poised-for-milestone-achievment-in-parity-amid-otherwise-bleak-outlook.pdf

Lau, V. W., Scott, V. L., Warren, M. A., & Bligh, M. C. (2023). Moving from problems to solutions: A review of gender equality interventions at work using an ecological systems approach. *Journal of Organizational Behavior, 44*(2), 399–419. https://doi.org/10.1002/job.2654

Lawson, M. A., Martin, A. E., Huda, I., & Matz, S. C. (2022). Hiring women into senior leadership positions is associated with a reduction in gender stereotypes in organizational language. *Proceedings of the National Academy of Sciences of the United States of America—PNAS, 119*(9), 1–11. https://doi.org/10.1073/pnas.2026443119

Li, X., Moyer, O., Pfeiffer, O., Velthuis, R., & Zaleski, P. (2025). Female CEO selection: Does the glass cliff exist? *The Leadership Quarterly, 36.* https://doi.org/10.1016/j.leaqua.2024.101853

Lyness, K. S., & Heilman, M. E. (2006). When fit is fundamental: Performance evaluations and promotions of upper-level female and male managers. *Journal of Applied Psychology, 91*(4), 777–785. https://doi.org/10.1037/0021-9010.91.4.777

McCluney, C. L., & Rabelo, V. C. (2019). Conditions of visibility: An intersectional examination of Black women's belongingness and distinctiveness at work. *Journal of Vocational Behavior, 113,* 143–152.

McKinsey. (2020a). *State of Black women in corporate America.* https://leanin.org/research/state-of-black-women-in-corporate-america

McKinsey. (2020b). *Women in the workplace.* https://womenintheworkplace.com

McKinsey. (2023). *Women in the workplace.* https://www.mckinsey.com/featured-insights/diversity-and-inclusion/women-in-the-workplace

McKinsey (2024). *Women in the workplace.* https://womenintheworkplace.com

Morgenroth, T., Kirby, T., Ryan, M., & Sudamper, A. (2020). The who, when, and why of the Glass Cliff phenomenon: A meta-analysis of appointment to precarious leadership positions. *Psychological Bulletin, 146*(9), 797–829. https://psycnet.apa.org/doi/10.1037/bul0000234

National Center for Education Statistics. (2022a). *Table 318.30. Bachelor's, master's, and doctor's degrees conferred by postsecondary institutions, by sex of student and field of study: Academic year 2021–22* (Digest of Education Statistics, 2023 ed.). U.S. Department of Education. https://nces.ed.gov/programs/digest/d23/tables/dt23_318.30.asp

National Center for Education Statistics. (2022b). *Table 318.45. Number and percentage distribution of STEM degrees and certificates conferred by postsecondary institutions, by race/ethnicity, level of degree/certificate, and sex of student: Academic years 2012–13 through 2021–22* (Digest of Education Statistics, 2023 ed.). U.S. Department of Education. https://nces.ed.gov/programs/digest/d23/tables/dt23_318.45.asp

National Center for Education Statistics. (2023, October). *Degrees conferred by postsecondary institutions, by level of degree and sex of student: Selected years, 1869–70 through2031–32* (Table 318.10). https://nces.ed.gov./programs/digest/d20/tables/dt20_318.10asp

Nietzel, M. (2024). The number of women who are presidents at top rated institutions has decreased. *Forbes.* https://www.forbes.com/sites/michaeltnietzel/2024/07/07/the-number-of-women-presidents-at-top-universities-has-decreased

Nowack, K., & Zak, P. (2020). Empathy enhancing antidotes for interpersonally toxic leaders. *Consulting Psychology Journal: Practice and Research, 72*(2), 119–133. https://doi.org/10.1037/cpb0000164

Offermann, L. R., Lanzo, L. A., Foley, K. O., & Harvey, T. J. (2021). College women leaders, 1985–2015: Achievement motivations across generations. *Journal of Managerial Psychology, 36*(1), 89–117. https://doi.org/10.1108/jmp-03-2019-0140

Otaye-Ebede, L., & Shaffakat, S. (2024). Breaking the concrete ceiling: Resources and strategies for career success amongst Black and Asian minority ethnic women leaders. *Journal of Occupational and Organizational Psychology. 97*(4), 1243–1281. https://doi.org/10.1111/joop.12520

Post, C., & Byron, K. (2014). Women on boards and firm financial performance: A meta-analysis. *Academy of Management Journal, 58*(5). https://doi.org/10.5465/amj.2013.0319

Powell, G. N., & Butterfield, D. A. (2015). The glass ceiling: What have we learned 20 years on? *Journal of Organizational Effectiveness: People and Performance, 2*(4), 306–326.

Randel, A. E., Galvin, B. M., Gibson, C. B., & Batts, S. I. (2021). Increasing career advancement opportunities through sponsorship: An identity-based model with illustrative application to cross-race mentorship of African Americans. *Group & Organization Management, 46*(1), 105–142.

Recalde, M. P., & Vesterlund, L. (2020). *Gender differences in negotiation and policy for improvement* (National Bureau of Economic Research (NBER Working Paper No. w28183). http://www.nber.org/papers/w28183

Ryan, M. K., & Haslam, S. A. (2007). The glass cliff: Exploring the dynamics surrounding the appointment of women to precarious leadership positions. *The Academy of Management Review, 32*(2), 549–572. https://doi.org/10.2307/20159315

Schaeffer, K. (2023, September 27). *The data on women leaders.* Pew Research Center. https://www.pewresearch.org/social-trends/fact-sheet/the-data-on-women-leaders/

Ryan, M. K., & Morgenroth, T. (2024). Why we should stop trying to fix women: How context shapes and constrains women's career trajectories. *Annual Review of Psychology, 75*(1), 555–572. https://doi.org/10.1146/annurev-psych-032620-030938

Schein, V. E. (1973). The relationship between sex role stereotypes and requisite management characteristics. *Journal of Applied Psychology, 57*(2), 95–100. https://doi.org/10.1037/h0037128

Schoen, C., & Rost, K. (2020). What really works?! Evaluating the effectiveness of practices to increase the managerial diversity of women and minorities. *European Management Journal, 39*(1), 95–108. https://doi.org/10.1016/j.emj.2020.06.005

Singh, S., & Vanka, S. (2020). Mentoring is essential but not sufficient: Sponsor women for leadership roles. *Development and Learning in Organizations: An International Journal*, *34*(6), 25–28.

Smith, N. (2014). Gender quotas on boards of directors. *IZA World of Labor*, *7*, 1–10. https://doi.org/10.15185/izawol https://wol.iza.org/uploads/articles/7/pdfs/gender-quotas-on-boards-of-directors.pdf

Smith, A. N., Watkins, M. B., Ladge, J. J., & Carlton, P. (2019). Making the invisible visible: Paradoxical effects of intersectional invisibility on the career experiences of executive Black women. *Academy of Management Journal*, *62*, 1705–1734.

Swain, J., & Korenman, L. (2018). In their humble opinion: How expressions of humility affect superiors' assessments of leadership potential in the US Army. *Military Psychology*, *30*(6), 507–527. https://doi.org/10.1080/08995605.2018.1503002

Travis, M. (2024, September 18). Which largest U.S. companies score highest on paid parental leave? *Forbes*. https://www.forbes.com/sites/michelletravis/2024/09/17/which-largest-us-companies-score-highest-on-paid-parental-leave

Valerio, A. M. (2009). *Developing women leaders: A guide for men and women in organizations*. Wiley/Blackwell. https://doi.org/10.1002/9781444315967

Valerio, A. M. (2022). Supporting women leaders: Research-based directions for gender inclusion in organizations. *Consulting Psychology Journal*, *74*(2), 178–193. https://doi.org/10.1037/cpb0000208

Valerio, A.M. (2018). Wherefore art thou all our women high potentials? *HR People & Strategy*, *41*(1), 32–36. http://www.executiveleadershipstrategies.com/docs/HRPS_41_1

Van Bommel, T. (2023). Power of empathy in times of crisis and beyond. *Catalyst*. https://www.catalyst.org/reports/empathy-work-strategy-crisis

Wheatly, M. G., Reed, L. N., Garland, M., & Jackson, C. C. (2023). Lessons learned from the pandemic: Syracuse University women embraced the online pivot in leadership education. *Journal of Leadership Studies*, *16*(4), 46–52. https://doi.org/10.1002/jls.21836

13
Why Allyship Matters for Leadership

David G. Smith and H. Colleen Stuart

Introduction

Organizations across industries face ongoing workforce challenges—including recruitment, talent development, skills alignment, engagement, retention, and advancement (Hastwell, 2023). In addition to technological advancements such as artificial intelligence (AI), jobs becoming less physically demanding, and the rise of remote work, many of these challenges are associated with—if not caused by—shifting workforce demographics. Compared to the past seven decades, today's workforce is more diverse in terms of gender and race, more educated, older, more likely to be unmarried, and more likely to have caregiving responsibilities (Cobbe et al., 2024; Maestas et al., 2023; Scheid, 2022). These shifts create both challenges and opportunities for leadership, particularly as businesses strive to remain competitive in a global marketplace that values diversity in markets, customers, talent, and ideas (Dillon & Bourke, 2016).

While research continues to assess the benefits of a diverse workforce (Gompers & Kovvali, 2018), it is increasingly clear that improving employment outcomes—such as engagement, retention, advancement, and performance—with a more diverse workforce requires leadership that fosters a culture of belonging (Carr et al., 2019). However, leadership teams remain disproportionately homogenous, often composed of individuals with majority identities—predominately white men. In such a context inclusive leadership is key, yet estimates suggest that only about 5% of leaders demonstrate inclusive leadership behaviors (Tapias et al., n.d.).

Over the past 40 years, leadership research has expanded beyond traditional transactional leadership models to more relational approaches. Leadership concepts such as authentic leadership, empowering leadership, ethical leadership, humble leadership, servant leadership,

David G. Smith and H. Colleen Stuart, *Why Allyship Matters for Leadership*. In: *The Changing Leadership Landscape*. Edited by: Sheri L. Feinzig and Mariangela Battista, Oxford University Press.
 DOI: 10.1093/9780197820070.003.0013

and transformational leadership have become popular for their focus on employees' needs and development (Amundsen & Martinsen, 2014; Brown et al., 2005; Liden et al., 2014; Walters & Diab, 2016; Walumbwa et al., 2008; Wang & Howell, 2010). Inclusive leadership has emerged over the last 20 years as a critical approach for managing a modern, diverse workforce (Carmeli et al., 2010). In this chapter, we provide an overview of this model and highlight a complementary concept—allyship.

Allyship, though relatively new in mainstream discourse, focuses on how members of dominant groups can actively advance equity by changing power structures that maintain the status quo. Given its potential to disrupt existing systems, allyship is sometimes perceived as anti-establishment, raising questions about its adoption within organizations. However, understanding how allyship develops and its impact on diverse workforces, leadership, and organizations offers valuable insights.

We examine how allyship is defined, conceptualized, analyzed, developed, and measured, using a typology that operationalizes allyship in leadership contexts. Like inclusive leadership, allyship presents implementation challenges, but together the two can complement one another in fostering workplace equity. We discuss ways in which these two concepts intersect and illustrate their application through a case study, demonstrating how allyship enhances leadership effectiveness in fostering inclusive and equitable workplaces.

A Typology of Inclusive Leadership

As its name implies, inclusive leadership is centered on fostering an environment where all employees feel valued, supported, and engaged. More than simply avoiding bias and discrimination, inclusive leaders actively promote inclusion through their interactions with employees (Randel et al., 2018). As summarized in Table 13.1, this leadership style operates at multiple levels—employee, team, and organization—through behaviors that embrace employees' uniqueness (e.g., promoting diversity), cultivate belonging within teams (e.g., building relationships), demonstrate appreciation (e.g., recognizing contributions), and support broader organizational inclusion efforts (e.g., advancing inclusion-related initiatives; see Korkmaz et al., 2022). Each of these dimensions of inclusive leadership unlocks important employee outcomes such as increasing organizational and team identification, empowerment, performance, and retention (Randel et al., 2018).

Table 13.1 Typology of Inclusive Leadership Behaviors

Dimension	Sample Behaviors
Fostering Employee Individuality	• Makes themselves available to employees • Recognizes individual differences • Collaborates with employees in decision-making processes • Supports employees' career growth and development
Developing Belongingness	• Ensures fair and equitable distribution of rewards • Fosters strong workplace relationships • Encourages transparency in decision-making
Showing Appreciation	• Acknowledges employees' contributions and efforts • Celebrates individual and team achievements
Supporting Organizational Inclusion Efforts	• Advocates for change • Communicates the alignment between organizational practices and inclusion initiatives

Source: Adapted from Korkmaz et al. (2022).

Dimensions of Inclusive Leadership

The behaviors that encompass inclusive leadership provide a framework for understanding, applying, and developing inclusive leadership. In the section "Developing Allyship Skills in Leaders," we compare them to allyship behaviors to explore how the two concepts can complement each other. In the inclusive leader typology, fostering an employee's uniqueness encompasses four unique dimensions (Korkmaz et al., 2022).

Fostering Employee Individuality

Supporting employees as unique individuals begins with leaders making themselves available, offering guidance, and paying attention. These actions signal that employees matter and that leadership genuinely cares about their well-being (Ellington, 2023), which in turn strengthens organizational identity and commitment.

Inclusive leaders also promote diversity by recognizing differences, valuing unique qualities, and actively encouraging employees to contribute. This set of behaviors relies on a high level of awareness and cultural intelligence. Depending on the type of diversity in the team, leaders may need to develop a deeper understanding of how to appreciate employees' distinct traits and help them apply those strengths to their work.

To empower employees, inclusive leaders foster autonomy, collaborate in decision-making, and look for opportunities for employees to offer insights on work processes. Empowerment is a key driver of engagement and performance, yet diverse employees often face biases that hinder their ability to assert themselves. Leaders who actively help employees navigate these biases—or better yet—create practices that eliminate biased behaviors for everyone—create more equitable workplaces. For instance, modeling a norm of amplifying new ideas and crediting the originator before moving forward with the discussion ensures that contributions are recognized.

Finally, supporting employees' learning and development involves developing their strengths, understanding their growth needs, and providing meaningful feedback. In this capacity, leaders take on the role of coaches and mentors, motivating employees and helping them navigate their unique career paths.

Developing Belongingness

The second dimension of inclusive leadership focuses on strengthening belongingness with a team (Korkmaz et al., 2022). A sense of belonging starts with equity, which is demonstrated through fair representation, unbiased decision-making, and a fair distribution of rewards (and consequences). Leaders who prioritize equity create an environment where all employees feel valued and treated fairly.

Beyond equity, belongingness is fundamentally rooted in positive and meaningful relationships with coworkers and supervisors. An employee's overall work experience—often measured through job satisfaction and employee engagement—hinges on a work environment where employees feel valued and cared for (Kennedy et al., 2021; Spehar et al., 2016).

Finally, employees experience true belonging when they are actively involved in decision-making. This involves collaboration, valuing diverse opinions, and taking the time to explain the reasoning behind decisions. Too often, leaders assume they can direct employees without their input or the need to explain themselves.

Showing Appreciation

The third dimension of inclusive leadership centers on displaying appreciation (Korkmaz et al., 2022). Recognition—whether it is through valuing employees' contributions, engaging in meaningful conversations about their work, or celebrating achievements—is arguably one of the easiest behaviors to practice, but is often missed by leaders. And it requires little in the way of resources other than time and attentiveness.

Supporting Organizational Inclusion Efforts

The final dimension of inclusive leadership involves supporting organizational inclusion efforts (Korkmaz et al., 2022). This requires leaders to embrace organizational change, by actively seeking opportunities for improvement to drive systemic inclusion. Addressing biased practices and policies that create inequities is a critical responsibility of inclusive leaders. By fostering systemic change, inclusive leadership makes the workplace more equitable for everyone and not just one person. Notably, changes initiated based on the experiences of a particular group of people often benefit many groups, or even everyone. Finally, inclusive leaders promote the organization's mission for inclusion by developing a diverse workforce and connecting everyday workplace practices to inclusion efforts.

Many leaders inherit existing workplace structures, and it is incumbent on inclusive leaders to understand them and apply their insights and resources to reform these systems. For those in startup environments, there is a unique opportunity to build inclusion and equity into organizational policies and practices from the outset.

These four sets of inclusive leadership behaviors are practical, developmental, and actionable, providing concrete examples that can be role-modeled, emulated, and put into practice. Moreover, these behaviors can be assessed and measured if desired. Regular assessment helps leaders receive feedback, stay motivated, and identify areas for growth and improvement. Inclusive leadership demands a growth mindset and a commitment to lifelong learning, as human behavior is complex and adaptive to change.

Conceptualizing Allyship as Leadership

The concept of "allyship" has existed for over 60 years, likely originating in the gay and transgender rights movement of the 1960s, where straight allies played a crucial role in advocating for civil rights and equality. Over time, allyship expanded to include racial allies but did not gain widespread

Table 13.2 Typology of Allyship Behaviors

	Individual Accountability	Interpersonal Accountability	Organizational Accountability
Reactive Behaviors	Addresses and regulates personal biases	Confronts and disrupts biased actions	Challenges and reforms biased systemic practices
Proactive Behaviors	Builds self-awareness and cultural intelligence	Advocates for people	Creates and implements new equitable practices

Source: De Souza & Schmader (2025); Smith & Johnson (2020).

recognition until the 2010s when it was applied to gender equality, specifically in the context of men as allies for women. In 2021, Dictionary.com recognized the growing significance of the term by naming "allyship" as its word of the year (Dictionary.com, 2021).

From a research perspective, allyship has emerged as a significant multidisciplinary field in the early twenty-first century. However, because of its popularity and application by several social identity groups before being studied by researchers, the latter have faced challenges in defining, modeling, conceptualizing, typifying, and measuring allyship behaviors.

For the purposes of this chapter, we define allyship as actively promoting fairness and equity in the workplace through supportive and collaborative personal relationships and public acts of sponsorship and advocacy intended to drive systemic improvements in workplace culture (Smith & Johnson, 2020). This definition aligns with the allyship typology outlined in Table 13.2, which categorizes reactive and proactive behaviors across individual, interpersonal, and institutional levels (De Souza & Schmader, 2025). Alternatively, these three levels of analysis can be evaluated based on levels of accountability—holding oneself accountable, others accountable, and the organization/institution accountable (Smith & Johnson, 2020). By integrating accountability into the framework, allyship becomes more than just an abstract concept—it becomes actionable, practical, and an expected leadership behavior.

Levels of Allyship

At the individual (intrapersonal) level, reactive allyship behaviors focus on recognizing and regulating one's own biases—acknowledging when we may be perpetuating bias and actively working to correct it (De Souza &

Schmader, 2025). Proactively, individuals can develop awareness and cultural intelligence to create positive interactions with others. In both reactive and proactive intrapersonal behaviors, accountability is at the personal level, focused on oneself.

At the interpersonal level, reactive allyship behaviors involve confronting and disrupting biased actions when they occur. When an ally witnesses discrimination or bias, they have a responsibility to confront the offender and hold them accountable. At the same time, they must hold themselves accountable for taking action rather than remaining passive. Proactively, interpersonal allyship includes advocating for people, increasing inclusion and belonging through everyday acts of support. This can take the form of recommending someone for an opportunity, celebrating achievements, and advocating for individuals—especially when they are not in the room to advocate for themselves. These actions may occur informally or through formal sponsorship programs within an organization.

At the institutional (organizational) level, reactive allyship means challenging biased practices and policies that contribute to systemic inequities, such as pay disparities or lack of representation. Proactive allyship at this level involves creating and implementing new equitable policies and practices that increase the institution's capacity for inclusion. This work often involves changing cultural norms but can also be driven by leaders role-modeling the desired behaviors.

Developing Allyship Skills in Leaders

Examining both inclusive leadership and allyship typologies, behaviors, and actions reveals significant alignment, a few key differences, and an opportunity to view them as complementary approaches to leading a diverse workforce. By focusing on their differences, we can highlight opportunities for integration and leadership developmental considerations that enhance both inclusive leadership and allyship capabilities.

Individual Leader Development

At the individual leader level, a key distinction of allyship is its emphasis on self-awareness, awareness of others, and cultural intelligence. Developing allyship skills requires leaders to recognize that others may experience the workplace differently than they do. This requires a healthy dose of humility and vulnerability, as well as continuous self-education, along with intentional social interactions with people from diverse backgrounds to understand different experiences and perspectives.

A crucial skill in this process is generous listening—a practice where the listener focuses on understanding the speaker's experiences rather than offering solutions (Smith & Johnson, 2020).

Another critical component of developing individual allyship is valuing and being receptive to feedback (Melaku et al., 2020). Well-intentioned actions may sometimes fall short or have unintended consequences; without feedback, leaders may be unaware of their impact. Again, demonstrating humility and vulnerability are valuable traits in demonstrating that a leader is open to feedback and wants to hear it (Smith et al., 2021). However, receiving feedback—especially when unexpected or direct—can trigger defensiveness. If a leader responds in a way that dismisses or discourages feedback, they risk creating an environment where others are reluctant to provide it in the future.

Organizational Leader Development

As organizations navigate today's complexities, inclusive leadership serves as a key driver of meaningful transformation. Embracing inclusive leadership and allyship is essential for fostering lasting organizational change. As we consider both frameworks, each has an emphasis on organizational change. While both frameworks emphasize organizational change, only allyship incorporates accountability, transparency, and clarity as critical factors in creating equitable workplaces (Bohnet, 2016).

Accountability motivates action and fosters a sense of ownership, often reinforced through performance evaluations and incentive structures. Establishing clear expectations that employment decisions—such as hiring, promotions, and pay raises—must be justified can encourage leaders to self-monitor their decisions to ensure fairness.

Transparency also plays a crucial role in reinforcing accountability. When key diversity, equity, and inclusion (DEI) metrics are visible across teams and business units, leaders can see how their team is performing compared to other teams. These comparisons can motivate action and, in some cases, collaboration. A truly inclusive work environment promotes knowledge sharing that helps everyone create a higher-performing and more equitable workplace.

Moreover, organizational transparency regarding equity and inclusion efforts builds trust (Smith et al., 2021). While many organizations hesitate to share imperfect results, openly communicating progress—especially when challenges arise—demonstrates a genuine commitment to improvement. Employees who see their organization acknowledge gaps and take action develop a stronger sense of belonging, leading to higher retention, engagement, and net promoter scores—a measure of how likely employees and customers are to recommend the company.

Taking transparency a step further, organizations that publicly disclose their inclusion and equity data gain a competitive advantage. Some investors are more likely to support companies with strong DEI commitments, and diverse candidates are more likely to apply (Markets Insider, 2019).

One critical area of focus for organizations today is transparency related to promotion and pay processes. Wage gaps and a lack of representation—often caused by unfair or hidden promotion processes—are forms of systemic inequity that can be mitigated through increased organizational transparency. In general, research shows that the more transparency an organization has, the more equitable it tends to be (Brandes & Darai, 2017).

Scaling Up Allyship for Inclusive Leaders

One of the most effective ways to proliferate inclusive leader behavior is through role-modeling. Witnessing inclusive leadership in real time—or hearing relatable stories and examples—motivates subordinates to adopt these behaviors as norms. An exception is when leaders are seen as inauthentic or performative in their allyship or inclusive leader behaviors (Birnbaum et al., 2024). When leaders fail to "walk the talk," their espoused behaviors lose credibility, and the attempted role-modeling is ineffective.

Recent research underscores that context matters when modeling authentic allyship behaviors. In male-dominated workplaces, even when subordinate men identify with a leader, they may not automatically emulate allyship behaviors (Lyubykh et al., 2024). However, when leaders use a narrative and storytelling to illustrate these behaviors, allyship is more likely to be adopted. The power of storytelling lies in its ability to bring values and norms to life through relatable examples (Passon, 2019).

When strategic messaging is incorporated into storytelling, it can be particularly effective in clarifying why allyship and inclusion are critical to an organization's success. The allyship narrative often includes a personal experience or story about someone the leader values, and how they were impacted by exclusionary or biased behaviors that activates a listener's emotional response to unfairness or injustice (Smith et al., 2021). The leader then ties the narrative back to the organization's mission or business outcomes, explaining why an equity initiative or change is needed for the success of the organization and why they need everyone's help and commitment to accomplish it. The power of storytelling cannot be overestimated in allyship and leadership.

One last difference between allyship and inclusive leadership is the lack of emphasis on work–life integration and whole-person perspective in the framework of inclusive leadership. Organizations create workplace policies and practices that impact employees outside of work, particularly in the areas of remote work, hybrid work, and flexible schedules. Additionally, caregiving responsibilities—such as parental leave or eldercare support—affect a growing segment of the workforce. Caregivers remain one of the least understood employee groups in terms of their needs, expectations, and self-identification (Lam et al., 2022). Due to gendered norms, women are impacted more severely, which causes systemic inequities in pay, retention, and promotion (Stefanova et al., 2023).

A Case Study: Postpartum Allyship in Leadership

To highlight the importance of allyship for leaders, we close with recent research examining postpartum allyship in the workplace. The reentry experiences of postpartum mothers play a pivotal role in shaping their identity as working parents well beyond the postpartum period. These experiences have far-reaching career implications, influencing factors such as turnover intentions, work-goal progress, and career advancement. They also impact family dynamics (e.g., work–family capital, work–family balance satisfaction, work–family conflict), and psychological well-being (e.g., postpartum depressive symptoms) (Chawla et al., 2024). Given the motherhood and caregiving biases that penalize women across their careers, employing an allyship framework to postpartum transitions presents a high-impact intervention for retaining mothers in the workplace and fostering equity.

This case study identified four types of allyship behaviors that led to positive outcomes for postpartum mothers. The first one was an interpersonal reactive set of actions that provided transparency in how to interpret and share knowledge about human resources policies while encouraging the mother to advocate for herself. The second type was an individual reactive set of actions and organizational proactive set of actions that used awareness of her unique needs to help with her transition back to work. They included supporting remote work options, allowing her to bring her baby into the workplace safely, providing access to a suitable lactation room, crafting her own return-to-work transition, providing schedule flexibility and structure breaks. The third allyship action was a proactive interpersonal action that validated her worker identity by celebrating her return to work. Finally, the last type of allyship behaviors was proactive interpersonal actions that validated her identity as a mother. This included giving gifts for the baby and parents, providing the mother with tangible comfort and support, asking about her well-being, asking to see pictures and videos of the baby, generously listening to her experiences and recognizing the tension and challenges of being at work as a new mother.

These allyship experiences played a crucial role in strengthening women's work–motherhood self-efficacy and alleviating feelings of guilt. In turn, this contributed to lower turnover intentions, enriched family lives (greater work–family capital), and enhanced well-being (reduced postpartum depressive symptoms) (Chawla et al., 2024).

Conclusion

In reviewing the typologies of allyship and inclusive leadership, we highlighted their commonalities and distinctions, reinforcing the idea that these frameworks complement each other in leading a diverse workforce. Both emphasize that effective leadership today requires humility, vulnerability, authenticity, a collaborative approach to decision-making and problem-solving, and a deep appreciation for uniqueness and diverse perspectives.

While not all leaders naturally exhibit these traits, they can be learned and developed through workplace socialization and formal leader development programs. However, one of the challenges organizations face in expanding allyship among leaders is a reluctance to engage with diversity. Research indicates that men, in particular, may hold implicit biases that holds them back from engaging with diverse colleagues. They may also experience anxiety about these interactions, concerns about social perceptions, or even fear of backlash (Johnson & Smith, 2016).

Using an inclusive leader framework that includes complementary allyship skills and techniques may be an effective intervention to men's reluctance to engage with diverse people. By legitimizing allyship as an expected leadership responsibility—including mentoring and advocating for underrepresented groups, such as women—organizations can help alleviate the anxiety and fear, while helping majority men feel included in a diverse modern workforce.

References

Amundsen, S., & Martinsen, Ø. L. (2014). Empowering leadership: Construct clarification, conceptualization, and validation of a new scale. *The Leadership Quarterly, 25*(3), 487–511. https://doi.org/10.1016/j.leaqua.2013.11.009

Birnbaum, H. J., Wilson, D., & Waytz, A. (2024). Advantaged groups misperceive how allyship will be received. *Organizational Behavior and Human Decision Processes, 181*. https://doi.org/10.1016/j.obhdp.2024.104309

Bohnet, I. (2016). *What works: Gender equality by design*. Belknap Press of Harvard University Press.

Brandes, L., & Darai, D. (2017). The value and motivating mechanism of transparency in organizations. *European Economic Review, 98*, 189–198. https://doi.org/10.1016/j.euroecorev.2017.06.014

Brown, M. E., Trevino, L. K., & Harrison, D. A. (2005). Ethical leadership: A social learning perspective for construct development and testing. *Organizational Behavior and Human Decision Processes, 97*(2), 117–134. https://doi.org/10.1016/j.obhdp.2005.03.002

Carmeli, A., Reiter-Palmon, R., & Ziv, E. (2010). Inclusive leadership and employee involvement in creative tasks in the workplace: The mediating role of psychological safety. *Creativity Research Journal, 22*(3), 250–260. https://doi.org/10.1080/10400419.2010.504654

Carr, E. W., Reece, A., Kellerman, G. R., & Robichaux, A. (2019, December 16). The value of belonging at work. *Harvard Business Review*. https://hbr.org/2019/12/the-value-of-belonging-at-work

Chawla, N., Gabriel, A. S., Prengler, M., Rogers, K., Rogers, B., Tedder-King, A., & Rosen, C. C. (2024). Allyship in the fifth trimester: A multi-method investigation of women's postpartum return to work. *Organizational Behavior and Human Decision Processes, 182*. https://doi.org/10.1016/j.obhdp.2024.104330

Cobbe, T., Mumford, D., Mantooth, J., Van Gaal, C., Balint, A., Wrobel, M., Raimondi, A., & Keenan, T. A. (2024, May). Working while caregiving: It's complicated. *S&P Global*. https://www.spglobal.com/content/dam/spglobal/global-assets/en/special-reports/Workingwhilecaregiving_Itscomplicated.pdf

De Souza, L., & Schmader, T. (2025). When people do allyship: A typology of allyship action. *Personality and Social Psychology Review, 29*(1), 3–31. https://doi.org/10.1177/10888683241232732

Dictionary.com (2021). Dictionary.com's word of the year is.... https://www.dictionary.com/articles/word-of-the-year-2021

Dillon, B., & Bourke, J. (2016). The six signature traits of inclusive leadership: Thriving in a diverse new world. *Deloitte University Press.* https://www2.deloitte.com/content/dam/insights/us/articles/six-signature-traits-of-inclusive-leadership/DUP-3046_Inclusive-leader_vFINAL.pdf

Ellington, L. M. (2023). Mattering: Shaping organizational leadership practices. *International Journal of Adult Education and Technology, 14*(1), 1–11. https://doi.org/10.4018/IJAET.329603

Gompers, P., & Kovvali, S. (2018, July–August). The other diversity dividend. *Harvard Business Review, 96*(4), 72–77.

Hastwell, C. (2023, April 21). Employee training and development: The benefits of upskilling or reskilling your team. *Great Place to Work.* https://www.greatplacetowork.com/resources/blog/employee-training-development-benefits-planning

Johnson, W. B., & Smith, D. (2016). *Athena rising: How and why men should mentor women.* Routledge.

Kennedy, J. T., & Jain-Link, P. (2021, June 21). What does it take to build a culture of belonging. *Harvard Business Review.* https://hbr.org/2021/06/what-does-it-take-to-build-a-culture-of-belonging

Korkmaz, A. V., Van Engen, M. L., Knappert, L., & Schalk, R. (2022) About and beyond leading uniqueness and belongingness: A systematic review of inclusive leadership research. *Human Resource Management Review, 32*(4). https://doi.org/10.4018/IJAET.329603

Lam, W. W. Y., Nielsen, K., Sprigg, C. A., & Kelly, C. M. (2022). The demands and resources of working informal caregivers of older people: A systematic review. *Work & Stress, 36*(1), 105–127. https://doi.org/10.1080/02678373.2022.2028317

Liden, R. C., Wayne, S. J., Liao, C., & Meuser, J. D. (2014). Servant leadership and serving culture: Influence on individual and unit performance. *Academy of Management Journal, 57*(5), 1434–1452. https://doi.org/10.5465/amj.2013.0034

Lyubykh, Z., Alonso, N. M., & Turner, N. (2024). Beyond allies and recipients: Exploring observers' allyship emulation in response to leader allyship. *Organizational Behavior and Human Decision Processes, 181.* https://doi.org/10.1016/j.obhdp.2023.104308

Maestas, N., Mullen, K. J., & Powell, D. (2023). The effect of population aging on economic growth, the labor force, and productivity. *American Economic Journal: Macroeconomics, 15*(2), 306–332. https://doi.org/10.1257/mac.20190196

Markets Insider. (2019, June 19). Investors representing $1.61 trillion in assets demand that companies disclose their workplace equity data. *Business Insider.* https://markets.businessinsider.com/news/stocks/investors-representing-1-61-trillion-in-assets-demand-that-companies-disclose-their-workplace-equity-data-1028291967

Melaku, T. M., Beeman, A., Smith, D. G., & Johnson, W. B. (2020, November–December). Be a better ally. *Harvard Business Review, 98*(6), 135–139. https://hbr.org/2020/11/be-a-better-ally

Passon, B. (2019). The power of storytelling for behavior change and business. *American Journal of Health Promotion, 33*(3), 475–476. https://doi.org/10.1177/0890117119825525d

Randel, A. E., Galvin, B. M., Shore, L. M., Ehrhart, K. H., Chung, B. G., Dean, M. A., & Kedharnath, U. (2018). Inclusive leadership: Realizing positive outcomes through belongingness and being valued for uniqueness. *Human Resource Management Review, 28*(2), 190–203. https://doi.org/10.1016/j.hrmr.2017.07.002

Scheid, B. (2022, March 10). More-educated US workforce will worsen historic labor shortage. *S&P Global.* https://www.spglobal.com/market-intelligence/en/news-insights/articles/2022/3/more-educated-us-workforce-will-worsen-historic-labor-shortage-69319768#:~:text=The%20American%20workforce%20is%20more,industries%20like%20retail%20and%20hospitality

Smith, D. G., & Johnson, W. B. (2020). *Good guys: How men can be better allies for women in the workplace.* Harvard Business Review Press.

Smith, D. G., Johnson, W. B., & Stromberg, L. (2021, May 12). How men can be more inclusive leaders. *Harvard Business Review*. https://hbr.org/2021/05/how-men-can-be-more-inclusive-leaders

Spehar, I., Forest, J., & Stenseng, F. (2016). Passion for work, job satisfaction, and the mediating role of belongingness. *Scandinavian Journal of Organizational Psychology*, *8*(1), 17–27.

Stefanova, V., Farrell, L., & Latu, I. (2023). Gender and the pandemic: Associations between caregiving, working from home, personal and career outcomes for women and men. *Current Psychology*, *42*(20), 17395–17411. https://doi.org/10.1007/s12144-021-02630-6

Tapias, A. T., Polonaskaia, A., Wang, Y., Hezlett, S., & Orr, E. (n.d.). Head and heart: Inclusive leaders for an equitable future. *Korn Ferry*. https://www.kornferry.com/content/dam/kornferry-v2/pdf/marketo-migration/Korn-Ferry-Head-and-Heart-Inclusive-Leaders.pdf

Walters, K. N., & Diab, D. L. (2016). Humble leadership: Implications for psychological safety and follower engagement. *Journal of Leadership Studies*, *10*(2), 7–18. https://doi.org/10.1002/jls.21434

Walumbwa, F. O., Avolio, B. J., Gardner, W. L., Wernsing, T. S., & Peterson, S. J. (2008). Authentic leadership: Development and validation of a theory-based measure. *Journal of Management*, *34*(1), 89–126. https://doi.org/10.1177/0149206307308913

Wang, X. H. F., & Howell, J. M. (2010). Exploring the dual-level effects of transformational leadership on followers. *Journal of Applied Psychology*, *95*(6), 1134–1144. https://doi.org/10.1037/a0020754

14

Neurodiversity and Leadership

One Size Fits None

Ludmila N. Praslova[*]

Introduction

Leadership as traditionally conceived is failing both organizations and individuals. On the one hand, increasing leadership job demands increase the risk of leader burnout (Shapiro, 2023). On the other hand, traditional career advancement models systematically exclude a significant portion of talented professionals from leadership roles and limit their ability to contribute (Chamorro-Premuzic, 2019; Doyle, 2025; Praslova, 2024, 2025). Both leadership selection and leadership training prioritize a narrow set of traits, such as confidence and extraversion (Chamorro-Premuzic, 2019; Gutmann, 2023; Praslova, 2023), potentially resulting in homogeneity in leadership teams and one-size-fits-all leadership strategies. These strategies often leave behind neurodivergent talent.

Research reveals stark gaps in opportunities for neurodivergent professionals. Unemployment rates for autistic adults with college degrees in the United States may exceed 80% (Lorenz et al., 2016; Patton, 2019). Even when employed, neurodivergent workers report higher rates of stress, exclusion, and burnout due to a lack of accommodations, unclear expectations, and the need to mask (perform neurotypical behavior) to survive (Raymaker et al., 2020).

Traditional leadership models operate under a fundamentally flawed assumption: that a single approach can effectively manage, motivate, and engage all employees. This one-size-fits-all paradigm is not merely

[*] *Positionality statement*: The author is a late-diagnosed autistic person with a Ph.D. in Industrial-Organizational Psychology who strongly identifies with the neurodiversity movement. This work is in part informed by the author's experience with systemic barriers in the workplace.

Ludmila N. Praslova, *Neurodiversity and Leadership*. In: *The Changing Leadership Landscape*.
Edited by: Sheri L. Feinzig and Mariangela Battista, Oxford University Press. © Oxford University Press (2026).
DOI: 10.1093/9780197820070.003.0014

ineffective; it is actively destructive, systematically excluding talented individuals different from the procrustean norms and dramatically limiting organizational potential. Leadership research indicates that the most effective leadership is flexible, context-specific, and individually tailored (Deng et al., 2022; Parr et al., 2013; Parr & Hunter, 2014). Neurodiversity represents one of the most important dimensions of human differences demanding an adaptive approach rather than one-size-fits-all models.

The Limitations of Traditional Leadership Models

Traditional leadership models are fundamentally rooted in *neuronormative* cultural expectations—a set of arbitrary social constructs that define what is considered "normal" or "ideal" in human behavior, cognition, emotional expression, and interaction (Walker, 2021). While neurobiological diversity is a natural human characteristic, societies consistently develop narrow perceptions of acceptable human functioning, categorizing individuals through limiting and reductive descriptors.

Neurological Diversity and the Arbitrary Nature of "Normal"

The concept of neuronormativity reveals a critical insight: definitions of "normal" are deeply contextual and historically contingent—in other words, relative. The "normality" expectations in ancient Greece, medieval Japan, and modern Australia would be dramatically different, underscoring the socially constructed nature of these standards.

To understand human dynamics based on nervous system differences, neurodivergent thought leaders developed terminology to describe human neurological variation without using pathologizing labels. The term "neurotypical" describes individuals whose neurobiology aligns with prevailing cultural standards and who can meet neuronormative expectations with minimal personal strain (Praslova, 2024; Walker, 2021).

In contrast, "neurodivergent" refers to a broad range of human neurological experiences that diverge from cultural norms and expectations. This comprehensive term includes variations in physical coordination, sensory processing, emotional intensity and expression, cognitive processing styles, and social interaction approaches (Praslova, 2024; Walker, 2021). Neurodivergence encompasses a wide variety of experiences, from dyslexia and attention deficit/hyperactivity disorder or difference (ADHD) to less recognized variations such as stuttering and neurological differences resulting from trauma or long-term health conditions. Some of these differences are generally viewed as neutral or positive, for instance, synesthesia (a difference in which stimulation of one sensory pathway leads to activation of another, such as "seeing" music or "tasting" words) and intellectual giftedness.

The term "neurominority" is more specific, identifying groups of neurodivergent people who face systemic discrimination due to an innate neurological variation. This terminology allows for a more nuanced understanding and recognition of specific neurological experiences (Walker, 2021).

The Cost of Neuronormative Leadership

Traditional leadership models perpetuate systemic bias through several critical mechanisms. Perhaps the most pervasive is the similarity bias, where leaders unconsciously favor employees who think, communicate, and interact most similarly to themselves. This unconscious preference creates homogeneous environments that exclude or burn out neurodivergent talent (Davies et al., 2023; Praslova, 2024; Raymaker et al., 2020; Whelpley & May, 2022).

Neuroexclusion occurs across the employment cycle. Interviews often rely on neuronormative cues, with dramatic negative impact on the rates of selection of neurodivergent candidates (Whelpley & May, 2022). Communication assumptions presume that direct eye contact indicates engagement, enthusiastic body language signals commitment, and preference for social interaction represents leadership potential. Each of these assumptions marginalizes people with different neurological profiles, regardless of their performance and goodwill (Bury et al., 2020; Crosbie, 2016; Davies et al., 2023; Whelpley & May, 2022). Furthermore, the cultural limitations embedded in neuronormative expectations also reflect specific cultural interpretations of "professional" behavior that may be entirely inappropriate or alienating for individuals from different neurological types (Austin & Pisano, 2017; Bury et al., 2020) or cultural backgrounds.

Performance evaluations also often measure success through a neuronormative lens that privileges rapid verbal communication, extroverted social engagement, and linear problem-solving, while neurodivergent productivity is often ignored and not rewarded. This productivity is also not supported or even impeded by one-size-fits-all productivity misconceptions. Standard work environments include uniform 9-to-5 schedules, open-plan collaborative spaces, standardized meeting and communication protocols, and one-size-fits-all motivation strategies. These approaches ignore the significant variations in how different people most effectively work, process information, and contribute to organizational goals (Austin & Pisano, 2017; Parr et al., 2013; Praslova, 2024).

The consequences of the dominance of neuronormative leadership approaches are profound. Organizations systematically exclude neurodivergent talent, reduce potential innovation, increase employee stress and burnout, lose access to unique perspectives, and diminish workplace psychological safety (Bury et al., 2020; Praslova, 2024; Whelpley & May, 2022). Neuroinclusive leadership calls for a different framework.

The Holistic Belonging Framework: A Comprehensive Approach to Inclusive Leadership

This part of the chapter outlines an approach to leadership based on the concept of "holistic belonging"—a framework that recognizes and values the unique ways humans think, feel, work, and interact (Praslova, 2024). The holistic belonging approach goes beyond traditional diversity and inclusion efforts, offering a comprehensive lens that addresses the complex, multidimensional nature of human experience in the workplace, fundamentally reimagining human-centered leadership. This approach is structured around four crucial and interconnected domains of difference associated with neurological diversity: *social*, *cognitive*, *emotional*, and *sensory/physiological*. Holistic belonging requires honoring all of these.

Leading for Social Inclusion

Social inclusion represents a critical dimension of neuroinclusive leadership. Traditional leadership approaches typically enforce standardized social expectations that disadvantage neurodivergent employees (Longmire et al., 2025). Leaders implementing a holistic belonging framework recognize that social differences represent natural human variation rather than deficiencies to be corrected, and develop approaches that support diverse social needs while maintaining organizational effectiveness.

While the vast majority of neurodivergent people want and need social connection and belonging, they often experience social interactions differently than neurotypical colleagues (Praslova, 2024). Some may find large group situations overwhelming due to the complex sensory and social processing demands; they may also need significant solitude time for recovery. Others might struggle with implicit social rules that neurotypical colleagues find easier to navigate.

Leaders practicing social inclusion recognize that these differences reflect neurobiological variations rather than a lack of social interest or skill. By acknowledging these differences without judgment, leaders can create environments where neurodivergent team members can socially engage in ways aligned with their needs rather than exhausting themselves through constant masking.

Leaders practicing social inclusion develop multiple pathways for workplace engagement that accommodate diversity in social and relational needs (Longmire et al., 2025; Praslova, 2024). Here are some examples of how neuroinformed leadership can make social life in the workplace more inclusive:

- Traditional leadership models often equate social success with specific behaviors that disadvantage the more reserved or task-focused neurotypes, such as visible networking, impromptu public speaking, or charismatic presentation styles. Leaders practicing social inclusion develop more nuanced definitions of social effectiveness that recognize multiple approaches to building relationships and influencing outcomes. This redefinition begins with separating *social style* from *social impact*. Neuroinclusive leaders evaluate relationship-building effectiveness based on outcomes, such as trust development, information sharing, and collaborative problem-solving, rather than specific behavioral approaches (Praslova, 2024). They recognize that an employee who builds deep, trust-based working relationships with a smaller number of colleagues may contribute at least as much outcome value as one who maintains broader but shallow connections.
- Leaders practicing social inclusion understand that workplace social events often create significant challenges for neurodivergent employees due to unpredictable social demands, sensory overwhelm, and implicit participation pressure. Neuroinclusive leaders communicate that participation in social events is truly optional. They schedule

events during regular work hours when possible, rather than requiring additional time commitments that may disproportionately burden neurodivergent employees who may need more recovery time from social interactions.

- Leaders informed by an understanding of neuroinclusion also develop alternatives to traditional celebration approaches. Public recognition events that place employees in the spotlight may create significant distress for some neurodivergent people, while others might strongly prefer written acknowledgment over verbal praise. By offering multiple recognition channels and respecting individual preferences, leaders ensure that accomplishments receive an appropriate celebration without creating unintended social pressure.
- Neuroinclusive leaders also establish norms around communication preferences. They encourage team members to share their optimal communication channels and styles, whether through direct conversation, team-building exercises, or formal documentation. They respect these preferences in daily interactions while helping team members understand and adapt to each other's needs. This mutual accommodation creates more effective communication while reducing unnecessary social friction.

Addressing and Preventing Conflict

Social misunderstandings occur in all workplaces, but they can have disproportionate impacts on neurodivergent talent. Leaders practicing holistic belonging also develop specific resolution processes for social misunderstandings. These might include facilitated conversations with clear speaking boundaries, written exchange options for those who process social information better in text, or other structured frameworks that ensure all perspectives receive fair consideration.

Prevention strategies represent another crucial element of addressing social misunderstandings. Neuroinclusive leaders proactively educate team members about communication differences, create explicit norms for specific interaction contexts, and develop shared understanding of how social processing varies across team members. This preventive approach reduces misunderstanding frequency; it also builds team capacity for navigating human differences with care and civility.

Leaders practicing holistic belonging also address casual ableism and neuroableism in workplace social contexts. They intervene when neurological differences become the subject of jokes or stereotypes, address problematic language or assumptions, and model respectful engagement with neurodiversity concepts. Such cultural intervention creates safer social environments for neurodivergent team members and elevates the overall quality of team interaction.

Leading for Cognitive Inclusion

Cognitively inclusive leadership requires a fundamental shift away from standardized practices toward recognition of diverse thinking and perceptual styles as valid and valuable human differences that can be organizational assets (Grandin, 2023; Praslova, 2023). Effective cognitive inclusion begins with leaders' understanding of cognitive differences associated with neurodivergence. This means moving beyond simplistic generalizations about dyslexia, ADHD, or autism to develop a nuanced awareness of the full range of cognitive strengths and challenges associated with neurodivergence (Praslova et al., 2023). This may require challenging common stereotypes; autistic or ADHD neurotypes may or may not demonstrate exceptional creative problem-solving during periods of hyperfocus, and dyslexic employees may or may not have leadership aspirations. It is important not to pigeonhole employees based on assumptions about specific neurotypes. Leaders do not need to become psychologists, but they do need to become experts on flexible work organization and communication.

Here are a few specific tips for advancing cognitive neuroinclusion:

- Cognitively inclusive leaders adapt communication approaches to ensure that information is accessible to diverse processing styles. This includes providing written documentation alongside verbal instructions, establishing clear agendas and objectives for meetings, and allocating preparation time before discussions requiring significant cognitive processing.
- Effective leaders also recognize that some people benefit from time to consider information before responding, while others process and articulate thoughts simultaneously. Creating space for both immediate and delayed responses ensures that all team members can contribute their best thinking rather than merely their fastest thinking. This might

include introducing structures such as "think time" during meetings or establishing channels for post-meeting contributions (Praslova, 2024).

- Traditional leadership often attempts to "develop" employees by focusing on perceived weaknesses rather than leveraging existing strengths. This deficit-oriented approach particularly disadvantages neurodivergent professionals whose cognitive profiles may include pronounced variations in capabilities across different domains—what Milton (2012) calls "spiky profiles." Cognitively inclusive leaders instead employ strengths-based assignment strategies, aligning tasks with individual cognitive profiles whenever possible.
- Effective cognitive inclusion also involves providing appropriate autonomy in task execution. Neurodivergent professionals often develop unique approaches to problem-solving that may not follow conventional methods but nevertheless produce excellent results. Leaders practicing holistic belonging resist the urge to standardize work processes, instead focusing on outcomes while allowing for cognitive diversity in approaches. This flexibility enables team members to leverage their distinctive strengths rather than struggling to conform to processes designed for different neurotypes.
- Physical work environments significantly impact cognitive function, particularly for neurodivergent professionals. Sensory sensitivities and energy regulation differences all influence an individual's ability to access their cognitive strengths (Markram et al., 2007; Meng et al., 2021; Raymaker et al., 2020). Cognitively inclusive leaders work to create environments that support diverse best-performance needs rather than forcing people to deal with standardized conditions (Doyle, 2025; Praslova, 2024). By providing options ranging from quiet spaces to collaborative areas to remote work and focusing on evaluation of outcomes, leaders enable team members to select environments that support their best work.
- Schedule flexibility is a crucial component of cognitive support. Traditional scheduling ignores significant variations in circadian rhythms, energy cycles, and optimal focus periods. Inclusive leaders support flexible scheduling that allows team members to work during their peak cognitive periods rather than arbitrary timeframes. This might include core hours for collaboration combined with flexible periods for independent work, asynchronous communication options, and adaptable deadlines that accommodate different work rhythms.

- Cognitively inclusive leaders redesign decision structures to incorporate diverse thinking. This includes providing background materials in advance, using structured formats that ensure all perspectives are heard, and incorporating multiple feedback channels. The timing of decisions also requires careful consideration. Organizations frequently impose artificial urgency (Denham Smith, 2023; Frei & Morriss, 2023). This may disadvantage the more deliberative thinkers. Inclusive leaders distinguish between genuinely time-sensitive decisions and those that would benefit from more thorough consideration. By creating appropriate timeframes for different decision types, they ensure that both quick insights and deeper analyses contribute to organizational success.

Cognitive inclusion also requires organizational professional development approaches and learning designed to support different cognitive profiles. This professional growth must include the entire career span (Praslova, 2024; Doyle, 2025); neuroinclusive leadership development is considered in the third part of this chapter (the section "Developing Neurodivergent Leadership: Beyond the Mythical 'Ideal Leader'").

Leading for Emotional Inclusion

Emotional inclusion is one of the most overlooked yet critical dimensions of neuroinclusive leadership (Praslova, 2024). Traditional workplace norms often enforce rigid expectations for emotional expression, disproportionately disadvantaging neurodivergent employees whose emotional processing may differ from neurotypical patterns. Leaders guided by the holistic belonging framework understand that emotional diversity constitutes a natural aspect of human variation rather than a deficiency to be corrected, or even a moral failing.

Neuroinclusive leaders develop an understanding of how emotional processing varies across neurotypes. Many neurodivergent people experience emotions with heightened intensity (Markram et al., 2007; Meng, 2021) while others experience delayed emotional processing, or struggle to identify emotions as they occur. Effective leadership begins with acknowledging these differences without pathologizing them. Rather than labeling people with more intense emotional responses as "unprofessional" or those with controlled emotional expression as "unengaged," neuroinclusive leaders recognize the full spectrum of emotional processing. They understand that it reflects neurobiological differences rather than character flaws or performance issues. This recognition creates psychological safety for neurodivergent employees to experience emotions authentically rather than expending limited emotional resources on masking (Praslova, 2024).

Here are some practical suggestions for creating emotionally safe environments:

- Begin by modeling emotional acceptance. Neuroinclusive leaders demonstrate appropriate vulnerability, acknowledge their own emotional responses, and normalize discussion of emotions in professional contexts. They might openly discuss feeling disappointed about a missed opportunity, excited about a new project, or frustrated by an unexpected challenge. This modeling sends powerful signals that emotional authenticity is welcome within the organization. Transparent emotional communication also directly supports neuroinclusion. When leaders clearly label their own emotional states—"I feel concerned about this deadline" or "I'm excited about your proposal"—they reduce interpretation demands for neurodivergent employees who might otherwise struggle to decode emotional tones. This practice creates shared understanding while modeling healthy emotional expression within professional contexts.
- Physical environments significantly impact emotional regulation, particularly for neurodivergent employees. Open-plan offices with constant visibility create additional emotional management burdens, as employees must constantly monitor their facial expressions and body language. Neuroinclusive leaders advocate for spaces that provide privacy for emotional processing. These might include quiet rooms where employees can privately self-regulate, flexible work arrangements, or remote work options that reduce the constant demand for emotional labor.
- Neuroinclusive leaders recognize that emotional labor requirements often reflect arbitrary cultural norms rather than legitimate job requirements. They question whether constant smiling, enthusiastic verbal tone, or animated facial expressions genuinely contribute to job performance or merely satisfy unexamined cultural preferences. Another example of neurotypical preferences creating extra demands for neurodivergent people is the expectation to always be on camera during

virtual meetings. This demand is likely to create nonverbal overload (Bailenson, 2021), which might be particularly exhausting for some neurodivergent people. By distinguishing between emotional performances that serve concrete business purposes and those that merely reinforce neuronormative expectations, leaders can eliminate unnecessary emotional labor demands.

- Performance evaluation is a critical context for addressing emotional labor disparities. Traditional evaluation approaches often implicitly assess emotional performance alongside substantive contributions, disadvantaging neurodivergent employees whose emotional expression may differ from neurotypical expectations (Praslova, 2024). Neuroinclusive leaders develop evaluation frameworks that focus on concrete contributions, skills, and outcomes rather than subjective assessments of "attitude," "enthusiasm," or "team spirit" that often serve as proxies for conformity to emotional demands.

Emotionally inclusive leadership may seem like a high demand on leaders. At times, it can be. However, by normalizing a range of human expression, leaders also help create social norms that allow them to be more authentic, reducing emotional demands for all (Duke, 2006; Raymaker et al., 2020). In addition, allowing for preventive emotional regulation and emotional hygiene rather than demanding emotional suppression until emotions boil over (Ruan et al., 2020) may create an environment with fewer conflicts and crises.

Leading for Physical and Sensory Inclusion

Physical and sensory inclusion is a foundational element of neuroinclusive workplaces. Traditional systems often create significant sensory and physical barriers for neurodivergent professionals, many of whom experience heightened sensory sensitivity (Markram et al., 2007), different movement needs, or unique responses to environmental factors. Leaders practicing holistic belonging understand that these physical and sensory considerations directly impact cognitive functioning, emotional well-being, physical health, and professional performance rather than representing mere preferences (Praslova, 2024).

Effective sensory inclusion begins with leader education about how sensory processing varies across neurotypes. Many neurodivergent people experience sensory information with heightened intensity—perceiving sounds, lights, textures, or other stimuli that may be barely noticeable to neurotypical colleagues as overwhelming or even painful (Markram et al., 2007; Meng, 2021; Praslova, 2021). Others may experience sensory seeking, requiring additional stimulation to maintain focus and engagement. Some neurodivergent people experience both sensitivity and seeking needs.

Neuroinclusive leaders recognize that sensory profiles vary dramatically even within specific neurotypes (Finnigan, 2024; Praslova, 2024). Two autistic employees might have completely different sensory needs, with one requiring minimal auditory stimulation while another needs constant movement for the best focus. This understanding prevents leaders from implementing one-size-fits-all systems or even well-intended but not effective accommodations (e.g., relying the generic advice such as "using headphones" may prevent desirable sound stimulation while doing nothing to alleviate bothersome smells or glare), and encourages personalized approaches based on individual sensory profiles.

Leaders practicing holistic belonging also understand how sensory experiences impact other dimensions of personal and professional functioning. An employee experiencing sensory overwhelm may appear emotionally dysregulated, cognitively disengaged, or socially withdrawn, when in fact they are simply responding to an overwhelming sensory environment. By recognizing these connections, leaders can address root causes rather than misattributing sensory-based responses to performance or attitude issues.

Leaders can do much to support sensory-inclusive physical environments, and it does not have to be expensive. Here are some examples:

- Lighting represents a critical consideration for sensory inclusion. Many neurodivergent people have significant sensitivity to fluorescent lighting, which may trigger migraines, visual processing difficulties, or general discomfort. Neuroinclusive leaders implement multiple lighting options, including natural light, adjustable task lighting, and reduced overhead lighting in certain areas. They advocate for lighting controls that allow individual adjustment.
- Acoustic considerations significantly impact neurodivergent people, many of whom struggle with auditory filtering. Background conversations, equipment noises, or environmental sounds that neurotypical employees might easily ignore can become profoundly distracting or distressing for neurodivergent colleagues. Leaders practicing sensory

inclusion create zones with different acoustic profiles in mind, from quiet areas with sound absorption to collaborative spaces where conversation is expected. They implement sound-masking technologies as needed and establish norms covering sound levels in different work areas (Praslova, 2024).

- Movement accommodation represents another crucial component of physical inclusion. Many neurodivergent individuals, particularly those with ADHD, regulate attention and emotional states through movement (Elahi et al., 2025). Traditional office expectations to remain still for extended periods create significant barriers for these employees. Neuroinclusive leaders implement movement-friendly policies, including walking meetings, standing desk options, fidget tools, and flexible break schedules that accommodate movement needs.
- Physical workplaces inevitably create sensory environments that will be suboptimal for some employees due to the diversity of human sensory profiles. Leaders informed by a holistic belonging framework recognize that remote or hybrid work arrangements often represent accessibility *needs* rather than convenience *preferences*. These arrangements allow neurodivergent talent to create individually optimized sensory environments that support peak performance.

Beyond accommodating individual needs, neuroinclusive leaders advocate for fundamental changes to workplace design standards (Praslova, 2024). Traditional office environments often reflect outdated assumptions about human functioning, prioritizing cost efficiency or aesthetic trends over human sensory needs. Neuroinclusive leaders emphasize that sensory-supportive environments benefit all employees, not just those who disclose as neurodivergent. By framing sensory design as an organizational performance priority rather than a niche accommodation, they can build broader support for meaningful environmental changes.

In sum, building social, sensory, cognitive, and emotional inclusion across the organization serves to support employee performance, retention, and well-being. It also has an important role in ensuring that neurodivergent people are not locked out of leadership opportunities—which completes and strengthens the cycle of inclusion. Table 14.1 summarizes the holistic belonging framework and its leadership implications, along with holistic inclusion in leadership opportunities, which is discussed in more detail in the following section.

Table 14.1 Holistic Belonging Leadership Framework

Component	Description	Key Leadership Actions
Social Inclusion	Recognition and support for diverse social processing and interaction needs	• Create multiple engagement pathways, including structured and asynchronous options • Make social events truly optional without career penalties • Provide transparent guidance for social interactions • Redefine social effectiveness based on outcomes, not style • Establish clear, direct communication norms • Design structured conflict-resolution processes • Build team understanding of social processing differences
Cognitive Inclusion	Valuing diverse processing and thinking approaches, and problem-solving methods	• Adapt communication for different processing needs (text, audio, etc.) • Implement strengths-based task assignment • Create work environments with work style autonomy and flexibility in scheduling and workspace • Design decision processes that incorporate diverse thinking styles • Provide specific, concrete feedback through preferred channels
Emotional Inclusion	Respecting and normalizing diverse emotional processing, intensity, and expression as natural variations	• Acknowledge emotional processing differences without pathologizing • Model appropriate emotional authenticity • Create environments with privacy for emotional regulation • Normalize communicating emotions explicitly to reduce interpretation demands • Distinguish between emotional expression and experience • Reduce emotional labor disparities from constant masking • Provide processing time in conflict resolution
Physical & Sensory Inclusion	Creating environments that support diverse sensory needs and physical experiences	• Implement flexible lighting, acoustic, and workspace options • Support movement needs and self-regulation strategies • Offer remote/hybrid work as accessibility accommodation • Redesign meetings with sensory considerations • Explicitly welcome individual adaptation tools (noise-canceling headphones, etc.) • Address stigma around sensory adaptations • Advocate for fundamental workspace design changes
Holistic Leadership Inclusion	Ensuring inclusive leadership pathways	• Recognize leadership potential across social, cognitive, emotional, and sensory differences and communication styles, and a broader set of talents • Develop leadership pathways beyond traditional models • Focus on leadership team diversity and complementarity, shared leadership

Developing Neurodivergent Leadership: Beyond the Mythical "Ideal Leader"

Traditional approaches to leadership development have systemically excluded neurodivergent talent from executive positions, creating leadership homogeneity that limits organizational perspective and innovation capacity (Praslova, 2021, 2023, 2024). This exclusion largely stems from narrow definitions of leadership potential that reflect neuronormative biases rather than actual performance requirements (Roberson et al., 2021; Praslova, 2024; Doyle, 2025). Moreover, neurodiversity in leadership remains largely undiscussed in organizational literature, creating the mistaken impression that neurodivergent leadership is rare or exceptional (Praslova, 2021). In reality, neurodivergent leaders exist throughout organizations, often developing innovative approaches to leadership that leverage their unique cognitive, social, and emotional processing styles. These leaders frequently implement adaptations that not only accommodate their neurodivergence but actively transform it into distinctive leadership strengths (Praslova, 2024).

Many successful neurodivergent leaders remain unidentified because they have developed conscious and unconscious coping and masking strategies and appear to be neurotypical. This masking often comes at a significant personal cost, requiring substantial cognitive resources that could otherwise support strategic thinking, innovation, or genuine relationship building. Organizations miss opportunities for authentic leadership development when they fail to create environments where neurodivergent leaders can lead authentically rather than exhausting themselves through constant neurotypical performance (Doyle, 2025; Longmire et al., 2025; Praslova, 2024; Raymaker et al., 2020).

Dismantling Leadership Mythology

Several persistent myths serve to systematically exclude neurodivergent professionals from leadership development opportunities (Praslova, 2024). The "*Ideal Leader*" myth assumes that effective leadership requires a specific constellation of traits and behaviors that align closely with neurotypical social and cognitive patterns. The "*Leadership Pipeline*" myth further constrains neurodivergent advancement by presuming a single, linear development path appropriate for all potential leaders. Finally, the "*Culture Fit*" myth creates perhaps the most significant barrier to neurodivergent leadership development, serving as a proxy for neuronormative social and communication expectations.

The reality of effective leadership contradicts these persistent myths. There are no ideal leaders with perfect, balanced competency across all leadership domains that will shine under all circumstances. Instead, every leader demonstrates a unique profile of exceptional strengths alongside areas of lesser capability. Effective leadership teams leverage these diverse "spiky profiles" to create complementary leadership teams that address complex organizational challenges more effectively than homogeneous groups (Praslova, 2024).

Neurodivergent leaders often demonstrate particularly pronounced spiky profiles, with exceptional capabilities in specific domains alongside areas requiring support or accommodation. Rather than viewing these variable profiles as deficiencies or grounds to exclusion from leadership, neuroinclusive organizations recognize them as potential assets that can bring unique perspectives and capabilities to leadership teams. This approach shifts evaluation from seeking well-rounded *individuals* to building well-rounded *teams* composed of complementary, specialized talents (Praslova, 2024).

Multiple Pathways to Leadership Excellence

Neuroinclusive organizations implementing holistic belonging develop multiple leadership pathways that accommodate diverse strengths and work styles. These varied approaches replace the traditional single pipeline with multiple routes to leadership and organizational impact. Each pathway offers distinct development opportunities aligned with specific aspects of leadership excellence rather than presuming that all leaders must develop identical skill sets.

People-focused leadership pathways can serve professionals whose primary strengths involve interpersonal engagement and talent development. Other, complementary leadership pathways involve minimal people management, but allow for the development of other valuable strengths. For example, *systems leadership pathways* provide advancement opportunities for professionals who excel at analytical thinking and process optimization. *Strategic leadership pathways* capitalize on capacity for long-term thinking and opportunity identification. *Expert leadership* pathways build on the strengths of exceptional specialized knowledge and a continued thirst for learning. For neurodivergent experts with intense interests in specific domains or distinctive creative approaches, these pathways provide advancement opportunities that leverage these talents. Some organizations may also develop *thought leadership*, *global leadership*, or other pathways that help align individual strengths with industry and organizational needs (Praslova, 2024).

Role design flexibility represents a critical component of inclusive leadership development. Rather than creating rigid position descriptions with fixed responsibility allocations, organizations implement modular role design that allows customization based on individual strengths. This approach might create complementary *leadership partnerships* where responsibilities align with natural capabilities—for example, pairing a strategically oriented leader with a people-focused colleague to create complete leadership coverage without requiring either individual to operate primarily in their area of challenge. Instead, individuals are supported in thriving in their areas of strengths, allowing them to maximize their positive organizational impact (Praslova, 2024).

Beyond day-to-day organizational benefits, neurodivergent leadership development offers transformative potential for addressing complex twenty-first-century challenges. As organizations confront ever-accelerating technological change, political instability, environmental concerns,social complexity and ethical dilemmas homogeneous leadership approaches increasingly demonstrate their limitations (Praslova, 2023). Neurodivergent leadership brings different perspectives, innovative approaches, and unconventional thinking that may prove essential for navigating these multidimensional challenges.

Genuine neuroinclusion across the talent cycle is a systemic change. It requires revising fundamental organizational systems including hiring practices, performance evaluation processes, workplace environments, and policy frameworks. This systematic approach addresses root causes of exclusion rather than implementing superficial accommodations that maintain fundamentally neuronormative systems. Moreover, designing work for neuroinclusion, with flexibility and respect for psychological differences, makes it better for everyone.

Consider the true story of canaries in coal mines. Canary birds are much more sensitive to airborne toxins than humans because birds metabolize the air more intensely—both when inhaling and when exhaling (Eschner, 2016).

Because of this intense air metabolism, prior to the transition to modern carbon monoxide detectors in the 1980s, canaries were used to detect toxic air in mines. In the presence of toxic gases, birds became visibly unwell before miners were significantly affected. This allowed miners to evacuate safely and to revive canaries using special air-tight cages with attached mini-oxygen tanks (Eschner, 2016).

Neurodivergent people are canaries in the coal mine of modern work, particularly impacted by the rigid work organization, sensory unwelcoming environments, injustice, bullying, and other organizational ills (Praslova, 2024). Autistic people, in particular, are compared to canaries because of the tendency to process the world more intensely (Markram et al., 2007; Meng et al., 2021; Praslova, 2024). In addition, heightened sensitivity to injustice has been noted among ADHD populations (Bondü & Esser, 2015; Schäfer & Kraneburg, 2012). The analogy of neurodivergent people as canaries in coal mines and neuroinclusion as better air for all illustrates the core idea of the Canary Code: implementing neuroinclusion and intersectional inclusion principles can improve work for everyone. As detailed in Praslova (2024), integrating the six principles of the Canary Code—participation, focus on outcomes, flexibility, organizational justice, transparency, and the use of valid tools in decision-making across the employment cycle—can help build not just neuroinclusive, but generally more human-centric organizational systems. Neurodiversity in leadership is an essential aspect of such systems.

Conclusion

The future of leadership lies beyond the one-size-fits-none approaches that have limited both individual fulfillment and organizational effectiveness. Organizations implementing holistic belonging can lead positive transformation by developing leadership systems that genuinely value human neuropsychological diversity. They recognize that the most effective leadership for complex challenges comes not from enforcing procrustean models of "ideal" performance but from cultivating the full spectrum of human strengths in their authentic forms.

The future of leadership is not about demanding uniformity. It is about nurturing an ecosystem where diverse human talents are not just accommodated, but developed in flexible environments that honor the dignity and authenticity of every human being.

References

Austin, R. D., & Pisano, G. P. (2017). Neurodiversity as a competitive advantage. *Harvard Business Review, 95*(3), 96–103. https://hbr.org/2017/05/neurodiversity-as-a-competitive-advantage

Bailenson, J. N. (2021). Nonverbal overload: A theoretical argument for the causes of Zoom fatigue. *Technology, Mind, and Behavior, 2*(1). https://doi.org/10.1037/tmb0000030

Bondü, R., & Esser, G. (2015). Justice and rejection sensitivity in children and adolescents with ADHD symptoms. *European Child & Adolescent Psychiatry, 24*(2), 185–198. https://doi.org/10.1007/s00787-014-0560-9

Bury, S. M., Flower, R. L., Zulla, R., Nicholas, D. B., & Hedley, D. (2020). Workplace social challenges experienced by employees on the autism spectrum: An international exploratory study examining employee and supervisor perspectives. *Journal of Autism and Developmental Disorders, 51*, 1614–1627. https://doi.org/10.1007/s10803-020-04662-6

Chamorro-Premuzic, T. (2019). *Why do so many incompetent men become leaders? (and how to fix it)*. Harvard Business Review Press.

Crosbie, P. (2016). Autistics: Less biased. Researchers? *The Autism Advantage*. https://autism-advantage.com/autistics-less-biased.-researchers.html

Davies, J., Heasman, B., Livesey, A., Walker, A., Pellicano, E., & Remington, A. (2023). Access to employment: A comparison of autistic, neurodivergent and neurotypical adults' experiences of hiring processes in the United Kingdom. *Autism*. https://doi.org/10.1177/13623613221145377

Deng, C., Gulseren, D., Isola, C., Grocutt, K., & Turner, N. (2022). Transformational leadership effectiveness: An evidence-based primer. *Human Resource Development International, 26*(5), 627–641. https://doi.org/10.1080/13678868.2022.2135938

Denham Smith, D. (2023, October 17). 5 tactics to combat a culture of false urgency at work. *Harvard Business Review*. https://hbr.org/2023/10/5-tactics-to-combat-a-culture-of-false-urgency-at-work

Doyle, N. (2025). *Learning from neurodivergent leaders: How to start, survive and thrive in leadership*. Jessica Kingsley Publishers.

Duke, K. (2006). Faking happiness at work can make you ill. *BMJ, 332*(7544), 747. https://doi.org/10.1136/bmj.332.7544.747-b

Elahi, H., Son, H. M., Calub, C. A., Nasiri, N., Shapiro, D., Isbister, K., Borden, J., Hastings, P. D., Liu, X., & Schweitzer, J. B. (2025). Impact of fidget devices on anxiety and physiological responses in adults with ADHD. *Research in Developmental Disabilities, 158*, 104944. https://doi.org/10.1016/j.ridd.2025.104944

Eschner, K. (2016, December 30). The story of the real canary in the coal mine. *Smithsonian Magazine*. https://www.smithsonianmag.com/smart-news/story-real-canary-coal-mine-180961570

Finnigan, K. A. (2024). Sensory responsive environments: A qualitative study on perceived relationships between outdoor built environments and sensory sensitivities. *Land, 13*(5), 636. https://doi.org/10.3390/land13050636

Frei, F. X., & Morriss, A. (2023). *Move fast and fix things: The trusted leader's guide to solving hard problems*. Harvard Business Review Press.

Grandin, T. (2023, May 23). When great minds don't think alike. *Harvard Business Review*. https://hbr.org/2023/05/when-great-minds-dont-think-alike

Gutmann, M. (2023). *The unseen leader: How history can help us rethink leadership*. Springer.

Longmire, N. H., Vogus, T. J., & Colella, A. (2025). Relational incongruence in neurodiverse workgroups: Practices for cultivating autistic employee authenticity and belonging. *Human Resource Management, 64*(1), 59–76. https://doi.org/10.1002/hrm.22248

Lorenz, T., Frischling C., Cuadros R., & Heinitz, K. (2016). Autism and overcoming job barriers: Comparing job-related barriers and possible solutions in and outside of autism-specific employment. *PLoS ONE, 11*(1), e0147040. https://doi.org/10.1371/journal.pone.0147040

Markram, H., Rinaldi, T., & Markram, K. (2007). The intense world syndrome: An alternative hypothesis for autism. *Frontiers in Neuroscience, 1*(1), 77–96. https://doi.org/10.3389/neuro.01.1.1.006.2007

Meng, C., Huo, C., Ge, H., Li, Z., Hu, Y., & Meng, J. (2021). Processing of expressions by individuals with autistic traits: Empathy deficit or sensory hyper-reactivity? *PLOS ONE, 16*(7), e0254207. https://doi.org/10.1371/journal.pone.0254207

Milton, D. (2012). *So what exactly is autism?* Autism Education Trust.

Parr, A. D., & Hunter, S. T. (2014). Enhancing work outcomes of employees with autism spectrum disorder through leadership: Leadership for employees with autism spectrum disorder. *Autism: The International Journal of Research and Practice, 18*(5), 545–554. https://doi.org/10.1177/1362361313483020

Parr, A. D., Hunter, S. T., & Ligon, G. S. (2013). Questioning universal applicability of transformational leadership: Examining employees with autism. *The Leadership Quarterly, 24*(4), 608–622. https://doi.org/10.1016/j.leaqua.2013.04.003

Patton, E. (2019). Autism, attributions and accommodations: Overcoming barriers and integrating a neurodiverse workforce. *Personnel Review, 48*(4), 915–934. https://doi.org/10.1108/PR-04-2018-0116

Praslova, L. (2021, December 15). Neurodivergent people make great leaders, not just employees. *Fast Company*. https://www.fastcompany.com/90706149/neurodivergent-people-make-great-leaders-not-just-employees

Praslova, L. (2023, January 10). Today's most critical workplace challenges are about systems. *Harvard Business Review*. https://hbr.org/2023/01/todays-most-critical-workplace-challenges-are-about-systems

Praslova, L. (2024). *The Canary Code: A guide to neurodiversity, dignity, and intersectional belonging at work*. Berrett-Koehler.

Praslova, L., (2025). The Future of Leadership: Neurodiversity in Leadership Teams. *Leader to Leader, 116*, 39–45 DOI:10.1002/ltl.20873

Praslova, L., Bernard, L., Fox, S., & Legatt, A. (2023). Don't tell me what to do: Neurodiversity inclusion beyond the occupational typecasting. *Industrial and Organizational Psychology, 16*(1), 66–69. https://doi.org/10.1017/iop.2022.105

Raymaker, D. M., Teo, A. R., Steckler, N. A., Lentz, B., Scharer, M., Delos Santos, A., Kapp, S. K., Hunter, M., Joyce, A., & Nicolaidis, C. (2020). "Having all of your internal resources exhausted beyond measure and being left with no clean-up crew": Defining autistic burnout. *Autism in Adulthood, 2*(2), 132–143. https://doi.org/10.1089/aut.2019.0079

Roberson, Q., Quigley, N. R., Vickers, K., & Bruck, I. (2021). Reconceptualizing leadership from a neurodiverse perspective. *Group & Organization Management, 46*(2), 399–423. https://doi.org/10.1177/1059601120987293

Ruan, Y., Reis, H. T., Zareba, W., Trzebinski, J., Fitzsimons, G. M., & Kashdan, T. B. (2020). Does suppressing negative emotion impair subsequent emotions? Two experience sampling studies. *Motivation and Emotion, 44*, 427–435. https://doi.org/10.1007/s11031-019-09774-w

Schäfer, T., & Kraneburg, T. (2012). The kind nature behind the unsocial semblance: ADHD and justice sensitivity—a pilot study. *Journal of Attention Disorders, 19*(8), 715–727. https://doi.org/10.1177/1087054712466914

Shapiro, J. (2023). Burning bright or burning out: A qualitative investigation of leader vitality. *Frontiers in Psychology, 14*, 1244089. https://doi.org/10.3389/fpsyg.2023.1244089

Walker, N. (2021). *Neuroqueer heresies: Notes on the neurodiversity paradigm, autistic empowerment, and postnormal possibilities*. Autonomous Press.

Whelpley, C. E., & May, C. P. (2022). Seeing is disliking: Evidence of bias against individuals with autism spectrum disorder in traditional job interviews. *Journal of Autism and Developmental Disorders, 53*, 1363–1374. https://doi.org/10.1007/s10803-022-05432-2

SECTION VI
CARING AND EMPATHY

15

The New Frontier of Psychological Safety

Balancing Speaking Up and Accountability in the Workplace

Elisabetta Comini

Leading in a New World

The COVID-19 pandemic has profoundly reshaped workplaces, altering how individuals work, collaborate, and engage with organizational culture. While the pandemic's impact was unprecedented in its scale, global reach, and pace, most of the changes that we witnessed were influenced by underlying shifts already underway. Generational shifts, technological advancements, and evolving societal expectations had been shaping the work environment and transforming how people approached their day-to-day working lives.

For decades, work was seen as an identity, with people picking a career path and then devoting themselves to a career at a single company or a few. The job was the center of peoples' lives. Over the past eight to ten years, perceptions and attitudes toward work have profoundly changed: work has become one aspect of a broader life ecosystem with an increased focus on well-being, a shift that accelerated in the early 2020s.

Attitudes toward leadership have also changed. There is an increased complexity and vulnerability (Brown, 2012) to leadership today. The courage of a leader to be transparent about not having all answers has become more and more acceptable, and the allure of the hero leader "who knows it all" has diminished. As complexity increases, good leaders are expected to maintain responsibility for making decisions, but at the same time to become "orchestrators" and leverage all the available resources. The biggest resource is their team, which means soliciting their ideas and identifying solutions together.

Elisabetta Comini, *The New Frontier of Psychological Safety*. In: *The Changing Leadership Landscape*.
Edited by: Sheri L. Feinzig and Mariangela Battista, Oxford University Press. © Oxford University Press (2026).
DOI: 10.1093/9780197820070.003.0015

Over the last two decades expectations over organizational conduct have also changed. Social movements have attempted to infuse beliefs about the ideal role of business in society and have contributed to influencing public perceptions about the nature and responsibilities of corporations (Georgallis, 2017). In fact, social movement organizations have started to directly engage with firms in their attempts to bring about societal change. Social initiatives typically address a variety of issues, including but not limited to diversity, community development, promotion of education, labor standards, and environmental protection. As a result, social movements have contributed to holding companies increasingly accountable for creating value for a wider range of stakeholders—encompassing shareholders, employees, citizens, local communities, the environment, and future generations. In addition, as technology has made the world more connected and as social media have made an increasing impact on corporate reputations, organizations have come under increasing scrutiny.

These social movements have also manifested inside corporations. Employee resource groups have become increasingly vocal in their demands that their organizations cater to the diversified range of needs and expectations of the diverse workforce in terms of age, gender, sexual orientation, cultures, and abilities. The COVID-19 pandemic has accelerated these existing trends and forced organizations to adapt quickly.

How Organizations Reacted during and after the Pandemic

During the pandemic, the boundaries between personal and professional lives became increasingly blurred. This made it even more evident than before that an individual's well-being is shaped by both their personal experiences and their work environment. As a result, the need for a holistic approach to employee well-being emerged—one that considers the full spectrum of an individual's life and the interconnected impact it has on their performance and overall satisfaction.

While most employees were affected by the pandemic, managers especially were confronted with a particularly daunting task: they had to foster trust, connection, engagement, and high performance in new hybrid settings while at the same time ensuring their employees' well-being. To equip managers for these challenges, training programs were designed and implemented to enhance managerial capabilities in empathy, emotional intelligence, and conversations focused on employee well-being.

Those efforts continued after the pandemic. While the COVID-19 pandemic had underscored the importance of employee well-being, prompting organizations to prioritize supportive work environments, it soon became evident that the effects of COVID-19 were long-term and that the pandemic had exacerbated some issues, like mental health (Roulet & Bhatti, 2023).

Post-pandemic, there has been a focus on "caring" for employees: in our consulting practice we have seen many corporations, across all sectors, expand their well-being programs to address a broader range of employee needs. These initiatives have included mindfulness courses, stress management workshops, nutrition, financial wellness, and mental health programs, on-site or remote psychological support. Comprehensive training and well-being guides, often designed with input from healthcare professionals, were also developed for managers and human resources (HR) professionals to increase their awareness about these issues and their capability to address them. Remote work has become a permanent feature for many organizations, with hybrid models allowing employees to balance personal and professional responsibilities.

What Has Been Achieved

Despite these investments, we are seeing many organizations struggling to achieve their desired outcomes. The data show that stress levels remain high in organizations, and employee engagement has not improved significantly. Recent reports (MeQ, 2025, Introduction, p. 5) mention psychosocial risks—"the complex interplay between workplace conditions, organizational factors, and employee well-being"—as a key challenge in today's business environment.

Looking at the data on well-being, concerning patterns emerge across multiple dimensions of workplace health and satisfaction (see Figure 15.1).

Burnout and stress seem to be pervasive among employees. Half of the respondents reported that negative emotions outweighed positive ones during their workday. When it comes to Gen Z, the situation is even more concerning. According to the report, "As of October 2024, younger workers were 64% more likely to struggle with morning motivation (37.2% vs. 22.6%) and 53% more likely to report job-related anxiety (44.8% vs. 29.3%)" than their older colleagues. (MeQ 2025, Gen Z is a well-being outlier, p. 19). The data refer to the US market but workers in Europe face similar struggles.

Well-being measures show concerning trends

Looking at the broader picture of employee wellness trends over the past two years, we see concerning patterns across multiple dimensions of workplace health and satisfaction.

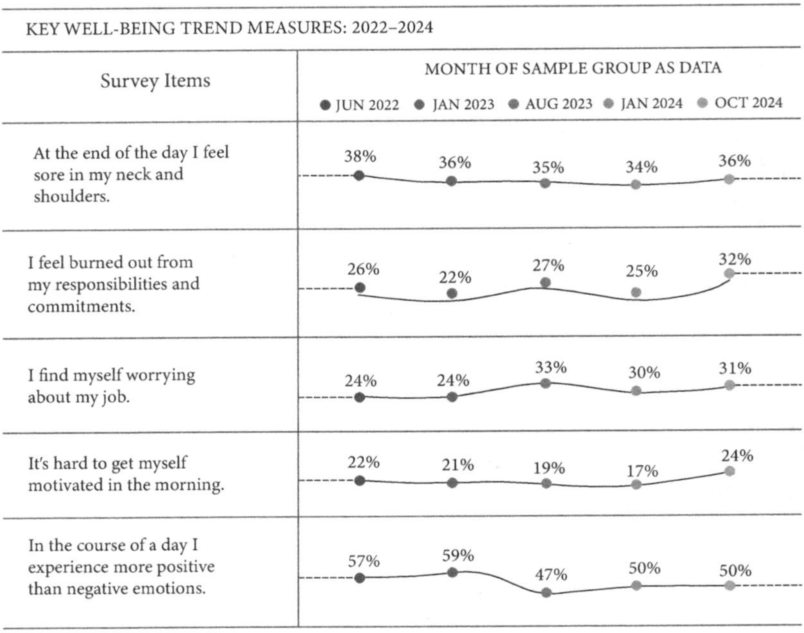

Figure 15.1 Well-Being Measures Show Concerning Trends

Source: MeQ, State of the Workforce Report (2025).

According to Gallup's latest report (2024), Europe has the lowest regional percentage of engaged employees with only about 13% of respondents saying they were engaged at work, while 72% were "not engaged," putting in the minimum effort required, and 16% were "actively disengaged," undercutting their employers' goals. When it comes to the percentage of workers who reported experiencing negative emotions "frequently" in the previous day, stress stands at 37%, anger at 15%, sadness at 17%, and loneliness at 14% (compared to 49%, 17%, 21%, and 18% in the United States). And the percentages are higher for workers younger than 35.

In Italy, according to the latest report on corporate welfare (Censis-Eudaimon, 2025), 32% of employees experience feelings of exhaustion, detachment, or otherwise negative emotions toward their work—symptoms that are consistent with burnout. This psychological condition affects 48% of young workers (aged 18–34), 28% of adults (aged 35–49), and 23% of employees over 50 (see Figure 15.2).

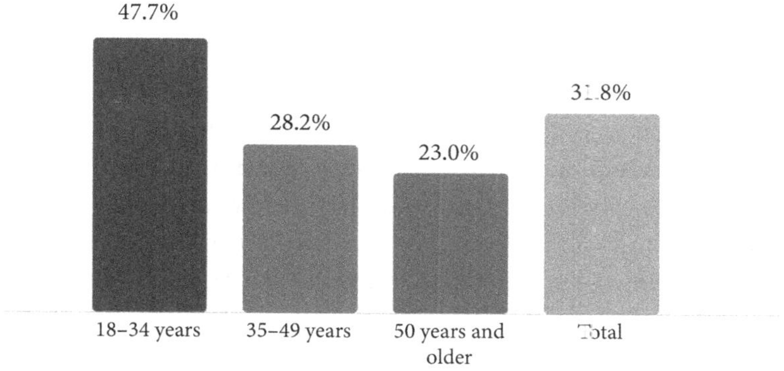

Figure 15.2 Employees Who Reported Feeling Burnout, Detachment, or Other Negative Emotions toward Their Job, by Age Group
Source: Censis-Eudaimon (2025).

Another interesting piece of data that emerges from the MeQ (2025) *State of the Workforce Report* regards work locations. Among remote and hybrid workers, the well-being advantage has slimmed, with on-site employees reporting only slightly higher levels of physical discomfort and burnout. While data may differ in other geographies, that data prompt a reflection about hybrid work being the solution to well-being issues.

The same report shows that in 2024 employees' perceived levels of managerial support for well-being declined. This warrants attention, as managerial support has been consistently associated with lower psychosocial risks for employees.

Back to Normal, with Issues Yet to be Solved

What we make of the latest data and our daily consulting practice in organizations is that while COVID-19 put well-being at the forefront of everyone's attention, in particular managers', that focus has somehow lost momentum because of other priorities related to the "back to normal." In addition, existing corporate well-being initiatives, like mindfulness, stress management courses, and psychological support, while well-intentioned and beneficial in terms of overall well-being education, have tended to focus very much on "fixing" the individual. We have seen less attention given to initiatives that address organizational issues and how work is managed.

As Croft, Parks, and Whillans argue (2024), the approach focused on the individual is not likely to "fix" well-being issues. They mention an Oxford University study of 46,336 workers in 233 organizations that compared employees who did and did not engage in a range of individual-level well-being interventions, including resilience training, mindfulness, and well-being apps. The study concludes that participants were no better off after engaging in these interventions. Furthermore, as those initiatives fall short of delivering the expected results, the risk emerges that this approach is perceived by employees as "carewashing." As Gube et al. (2024, p. 2) explain, carewashing manifests as a "[m]isalignment between what leaders portray as cultures of care (often referencing the organization's stated values) and employees' actual daily experiences at work" and can potentially lead to greater disengagement.

If employees feel that well-being is indeed related to how work is being done, initiatives aimed at only fixing the individual risk backfiring, creating a lack of trust in both leaders and the company and a disillusion regarding the willingness and possibility of actually redressing the situation. In the age of increased scrutiny of organizational conduct, initiatives that sound like a "check-the-box" exercise or designed to only gain media attention will likely not go unnoticed.

What Managers Can Do

Based on our experience as a global consulting firm and the evidence that emerges from the most recent data and research in the field (MeQ Report, Gube et al., and Croft, Parks, and Whillans), we argue that well-being strategies should be integrated with changes to management practices.

We are aware that the topic is complex: Croft, Parks, and Whillans (in their chapter "Moving Toward a Holistic Approach") for example argue that "to truly combat rising need and mitigate the costs of poor well-being (...) systemic change is essential." In this section we focus on an approach to workplace well-being that might offer a greater and more enduring impact while remaining practical for managers to implement.

In our daily consulting practice in organizations, when it comes to designing training programs and initiatives to improve well-being, we suggest working to enhance the quality of conversations between managers and employees. Many authors, starting from the foundational work of Douglas Stone et al. (1999) have written about how to make conversations more candid and authentic in the workplace as well as how to address "difficult" topics. Two aspects must be considered: "what" (which topics should be addressed) and "how" (ways to handle them).

Regarding "what," we argue that there is a case for making emotions part of conversations in the workplace. In fact, emotions have always played a part in people's behavior, including at work. However, before the pandemic, emotions were rarely discussed in professional settings. Demonstrating emotions was often perceived as a form of vulnerability equated with weakness, rather than an act of courage.

The pandemic underscored the importance of conversations about well-being, with "How are you?" evolving into a meaningful and necessary question that deserves attention and eventually further investigation, and as a sign of "caring" by managers. Equally important, the pandemic exposed the many weaknesses of forceful, dominant leaders and highlighted the superiority of those who have the courage to reveal their vulnerabilities.

To address the emotional long-haul of the pandemic, some organizations have gone so far as to foster cultures where it is acceptable to discuss emotional challenges, encapsulated by the phrase "It's okay not to be okay." Based on our consulting experience, we argue that we are still in the early stages of this process. We believe that openness about emotional challenges such as burnout, low motivation, or feelings of stagnation or "languishing," as Adam Grant (2021) puts it (i.e., the "what"), coupled with right strategy to address them (the "how"), can contribute to well-being in organizations.

The New Frontier of Psychological Safety

So, the first question is: How do we speak up about emotions? The answer is that, first of all, we need to have psychological safety in place. Edmondson (2019, in paragraph "What It Takes to Thrive in a Complex, Uncertain World,) popularized the concept of "psychological safety." In her words, "psychological safety is broadly defined as a climate in which people are comfortable expressing and being themselves ... When people have psychological safety at work, they feel comfortable sharing concerns and mistakes without fear of embarrassment or retribution."

	↓ Low Standards	↑ High Standards
↑ High Psychological Safety	Comfort Zone	Learning and High-Performance Zone
↓ Low Psychological Safety	Apathy Zone	Anxiety Zone

Figure 15.3 How Psychological Safety Relates to Performance Standards
Source: Edmondson (2019).

Despite this broad definition of "expressing and being themselves," much of Edmondson's focus is in fact about people sharing ideas, questions, and concerns, to the point that she concludes that "[w]hen people don't speak up, the organization's ability to innovate and grow is threatened (Chapter 1. Takeaways)." In other words, she frames psychological safety as one factor which impacts performance in workplaces and the capability of a team to perform (with the other factor being "performance standards," see Figure 15.3).

We believe that psychological safety is a very powerful construct and would propose broadening its scope to align with the needs of the evolving workplace and the quest for well-being in the workplace, as discussed in the section "Back to Normal, with Issues Yet to be Solved." Similar to the original concept of psychological safety, we believe that the conversations about one's feelings and emotions require an environment that fosters openness and trust. It is crucial to address this topic across all levels, from corporate communication to team discussions.

As with the original concept of psychological safety, the team dimension here is crucial: while speaking up is something that people experience at the individual level, "The sense of safety and willingness to speak up is not an individual trait ... it's an emergent property of the group" (Edmondson A. C. as quoted in Gallo, A. 2023 in the chapter "What Is Psychological Safety?")

Let's see how this idea might apply to a workplace situation. A manager might say during a team meeting, "Stress and burnout are challenges many of us face in the workplace ... we all know this can happen. It can come from a mixture of both professional and personal life demands. I have experienced these issues myself during my career and realized how important it is to talk about them and address them constructively to help us achieve our goals. Please know that I am available and open to having these conversations, if you feel like sharing ... it can be in face-to-face conversations as well as in our team meetings."

When managers share their own personal challenges and encourage others to do the same, they set the tone and normalize these conversations as legitimate. In some cases, it may be the manager who initiates the dialogue by reaching out to a team member they are concerned about. For example, they might say, "Over the past few weeks, you seem a bit down. I could be wrong, but I wanted to check in with you."

Creating the climate of psychological safety where employees feel like speaking up about their feelings and emotions (the "what") is one management practice that may contribute to well-being in the workplace. But there is an important caveat here: speaking up is not enough. Without a second dimension, accountability (the "how"), there is a risk of speaking up turning the workplace into a "free-for-all" where people feel that anything can be said, eventually leading into conversations that are both ineffective and counterproductive for the person speaking and for the organization. We argue that without accountability, speaking up would also put undue pressure on managers, who might feel they are being asked to turn into psychologists, a perception that lately many managers have been voicing in our leadership trainings.

We argue that this should not be the case: managers must care for their team members, but in such a way that resonates with their role and the organizational boundary. We mention "boundaries" because for any management practice to resonate, it must be contextualized to the realities of organizations, which have their own rules that individuals must abide by.

Being aware of the constraints that organizations impose on individuals is important to put "well-being" in the right perspective and avoid delusions about what can be achieved at the organizational level. At the same time, we believe that within those boundaries, there is still a lot that can be done to improve well-being in the workplace when speaking up is paired with accountability.

Accountability and Speaking Up in Action: Jeff and Helen's Case

Let's consider an example: Jeff and his manager, Helen. Jeff decides to approach Helen because he is experiencing a sense of languishing, stress, and depression. Jeff feels psychologically safe and opens up to Helen, sharing these feelings. Helen listens attentively and seeks to understand why Jeff feels this way. At this point, the conversation reaches a critical juncture: whether and how Helen, as a manager, leverages accountability in the conversation.

By accountability, we mean empowering individuals to take ownership of their choices rather than "holding" individuals accountable in the traditional sense, which often implies enforcing consequences or dictating actions (Moran & Lennington, 2022). As Moran and Lennington (2022) explain, there is a difference between that view of accountability and the traditional view: "Too often, accountability is synonymous with consequencesin particular negative consequences ... accountability is typically affiliated with bad behaviour, poor performance, and negative consequences." Usually those negative consequences are applied by some authority to a performer: someone with authority blames or punishes another person who lacks authority. "The authority is active, the person being punished is passive. Accountability ... is profoundly asymmetrical." (chapter 1 "Accountability as Ownership").

We intentionally frame accountability as empowerment, as it focuses on enabling the person to take responsibility for their own decisions and actions. So how does it play out in Helen's case? Let's consider Helen's options:

- *Option 1*: Helen fails to activate the accountability dimension. Helen listens to Jeff in such a way that Jeff returns to his work feeling reassured that he was heard and his emotions were acknowledged. However, as the deeper root causes of his dissatisfaction were not addressed, Jeff risks remaining stuck in the same feelings, potentially slipping into a victim mindset. At the same time, while listening to Jeff, Helen might feel as though she is taking on the role of a psychologist, a responsibility that falls outside her expertise and role. She might feel uneasy herself.
- *Option 2*: Helen does activate the accountability dimension. Helen decides to adopt the role of a coach, a vital skill for today's managers, and guides Jeff to reflect on his challenges, uncover root causes, and take ownership of the solutions. This approach not only empowers Jeff

to address his concerns constructively but also allows Helen to remain firmly within her professional boundaries as a manager.

Helen might ask questions that encourage Jeff to explore the root causes of his concerns and then empower him to take actionable steps. The aim is not simply to gather more information but to prompt Jeff to identify choices, make decisions, and take ownership of his situation. To be clear, we are not suggesting that managers become fully-fledged coaches; rather, they should adopt a coaching mindset and leverage some key techniques of the role.

When it comes to mindset, the focus is on believing the person has the capability to find their own solution, which requires attentive listening and practicing silence, resisting the urge to immediately offer solutions and instead allowing the individual to identify their strategies. As for techniques, the emphasis should be on using "powerful questions" that promote reflection and self-directed problem-solving.

Powerful questions help unravel the situation and emotions, enabling the individual to better understand and articulate what they are truly feeling. In many cases, when managers engage in these conversations, both parties come to realize that the person's initial perception of their experience may evolve or differ significantly by the end of the discussion.

In our consulting experience we have repeatedly seen that many people struggle to accurately label their emotions. Often, they default to a limited set of familiar emotions such as fear, anger, sadness, joy, or happiness, while neglecting the broader spectrum, which includes feelings like anxiety, embarrassment, guilt, amusement, compassion, gratitude, etc. Developing the ability to recognize and name these nuances is crucial for fostering deeper understanding and meaningful conversations.

Identifying and articulating how we feel is a skill that can and should be further developed, as it is a critical life skill. While we may not always fully understand what has caused a particular emotion, simply acknowledging and recognizing the feeling is equally important for our overall well-being (Brown, 2022). In our experience, providing some form of emotional education that helps individuals understand their emotions, label them accurately, and discuss them openly in the workplace can be highly beneficial. Such initiatives not only enhance personal awareness but also foster healthier communication and stronger workplace relationships.

In fact, emotions should be viewed as data that provide valuable insights about us and our circumstances, making them worth examining

(David, 2025). Sometimes, the solutions to emotional challenges may lie outside the workplace, while at other times they may not. However, if managers fail to address these emotions initially, the issues are unlikely to resolve on their own and may, in fact, worsen over time.

So let's see how this might play out in Jeff and Helen's case. In her conversation with Jeff, Helen might ask him to provide specific examples of situations where he experiences languishing and stress, helping him identify recurring patterns and potential causes. From there, Helen could pose questions such as, "What is important for you to achieve in this situation?" and questions aimed at helping Jeff identify his own solution: "If you choose this solution, what are you leaving behind? Alternatively, if you are saying 'yes' to this, what are you saying 'no' to?" These questions encourage Jeff to reflect deeply on his priorities and the trade-offs involved in his decisions, eventually helping him take ownership of his decision.

However, accountability is a two-way street: while we have explored how Helen can help Jeff take ownership of his choices, Helen must also hold herself accountable.

For her, accountability means taking all actions aimed at creating an environment where Jeff's resolutions can be implemented and pursued. To this end she may also solicit Jeff's input: "How can I help you achieve your objectives?" Such collaboration ensures that both parties share responsibility for driving meaningful progress.

Framing accountability as ownership enables both Jeff and Helen to be intentional in determining the best course of action. This approach benefits not only the individual but also the organization as a whole. Simply allowing Jeff to express his feelings and listening to him, while important, would not be sufficient to create meaningful change.

Besides, complaints voiced by one individual are often shared by others in the organization. Addressing these issues through accountability as ownership can lead to changes in work practices and patterns that benefit everyone, avoiding negative emotions that would impact both the person's well-being and the morale of the team.

When accountability is effectively practiced, Jeff will feel empowered to take ownership of his decisions, recognizing himself as an active agent in shaping his outcomes, while Helen, thanks to the conversation with Jeff, might reevaluate work practices that contribute to stress, such as workload management—an area that is well within her responsibilities as a manager.

By doing this, Helen will not only address Jeff's individual concerns but also implement measures that could benefit the broader team. The positive impact will extend beyond Jeff, creating a beneficial ripple effect across the organization.

The Accountability and Speaking Up Model: The Profiles

In the previous section we have argued that shifting the focus from "fixing" the individual to helping the person improve the broader context or setting that they operate in allows managers to regain their agency in designing work practices collaboratively with their teams, ensuring objectives are achieved in a sustainable manner. In fact, by supporting Jeff's speaking up and accountability Helen helps him achieve the role of a "catalyst" for change which benefits Jeff, the team, and the organization. The "catalyst" profile is the one that matches high support for speaking up with high expectations of accountability. When the two dimensions are considered, the four profiles emerge, as shown in our Coreconsulting model in Figure 15.4

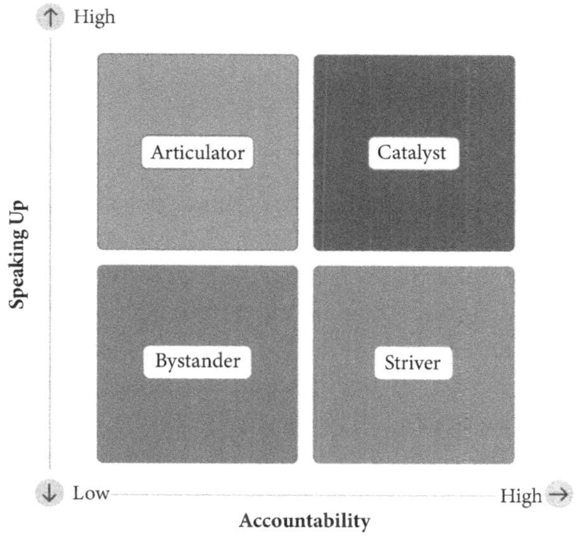

Figure 15.4 The Speaking-Up–Accountability Model
Source: Coreconsulting (2024).

- *Bystander*: Someone who neither speaks up about their personal challenges nor takes initiative to address them. This profile represents a passive stance, often leading to stagnation and disconnection within the organization.
- *Striver*: An individual who takes responsibility for addressing their problems but does so quietly, without sharing their struggles or seeking support. This approach limits the potential positive impact on team or organizational dynamics. Over time it can lead to exhaustion.
- *Articulator*: A person who is open about their challenges or difficulties but lacks the accountability to take action on them. They do not take ownership of their own situation, often blaming others or the overall context.
- *Catalyst*: Someone who openly communicates their difficulties and actively works (often collaboratively) to find solutions. This individual not only improves their own situation but also generates benefits for their team and the broader organization.

Much has been said and written about how to foster speaking up in organizations (Edmondson, 2019). We therefore would like to provide here some pieces of advice about how managers can help their team members develop the other dimension of the model, namely accountability as "ownership."

Here are a few recommendations:

- Practicing the mindset and key techniques of a coach, which includes making time for crucial conversations with the team members, holding the person and the team "capable" rather than accountable—i.e., confronting them with their abilities to make productive choices about their own situation, rather than the negative consequences of not pursuing a way dictated by the manager. This entails relinquishing some control to them as well.
- Changing the language of their conversations by helping the individual to move from a blaming attitude about others or themselves to one that helps them assess how they contributed to a certain situation in the past and how they can choose a different set of actions in the future.
- Helping the person realize that the benefits of being the victim and the good feelings often associated with it, including self-sympathy and ego protection, are short-lived.

- Identifying together with the person and the team a method to monitor the outcomes of the choices that they made to help them own their actions and results.

We believe that today's scenarios call for accountability more than ever: business complexity has increased the need for individual proactivity and self-efficacy. As employees are increasingly expected to take initiative, the ability to balance speaking up and accountability becomes a critical skill for both managers and employees. Besides, as managers need to manage their own increased workload and emotional demand, there is the need for empowering employees to support each other.

A culture of speaking up and accountability can help relinquish the burden of well-being from managers alone, making it a shared responsibility within the team. This is even more important, as speaking up requires psychological safety, and psychological safety is very much the outcome of conversations and interactions that happen at the team level.

Summary

In this chapter we have focused on the relationship between managers and employees and framed well-being as a shared responsibility. We started by stating that managers have the responsibility of building up a climate of psychological safety where their team members feel like speaking up, sharing the personal challenges that affect their well-being alongside their ideas and opinions. Then we argued that by adopting a coaching attitude managers can help employees balance speaking up with accountability. In particular, they can empower individuals by helping them realize that they do have a choice about how they frame and address their personal challenges. By fostering accountability as "ownership" and "capability to act" managers can enable employees to regain agency over their own well-being in a way that is within the boundaries of their role and the organization's rules. Ultimately, managers should be accountable for supporting and accommodating employees' resolutions.

Well-being is a daunting endeavor that requires the commitment of all people and roles in the organization: actions to improve well-being can reside on different levels and include a vast array of initiatives. We have argued that there is an opportunity for organizations today to revise their well-being policies and direct the focus from the individual back to the "individual in the organization." By engaging in the conversations that we have described in this chapter, managers can contribute to building a culture of speaking up and accountability that benefits both the organization and the people in a way that is both practical and sustainable.

References

Brown, B. (2012). *Daring greatly: How the courage to be vulnerable transforms the way we live, love, parent and lead.* Gotham Books.

Brown, B. (2022). *Atlas of the heart: Mapping meaningful connection and the language of human experience.* Penguin Random House Audio Publishing Group.

Censis-Eudaimon. (2025, February 21). *VIII Rapporto Lavoro, aziende e benessere dei lavoratori: Un'epoca nuova, sintesi dei principali risultati.* https://www.censis.it/sites/default/files/downloads/SINTESI%20DEI%20PRINCIPALI%20RISULTATI%20_1550.pdf

Croft J., Parks A., & Whillans A. (2024, October 18). Why workplace well-being programs don't achieve better outcomes. *Harvard Business Review.* https://hbr.org/2024/10/why-workplace-well-being-programs-dont-achieve-better-outcomes?autocomplete=true

David, S. (2022, July 20). *Recognizing your emotions as data, not directives.* https://www.susandavid.com/newsletter/recognizing-your-emotions-as-data-not-directives

Edmondson, A. C. (2019). *The fearless organisation: Creating psychological safety in the workplace for learning, innovation, and growth.* Wiley and Sons.

Gallo, A. (2023, February 15), What is psychological safety. *Harvard Business Review.*

Gallup. (2024). *State of the Global Workplace: 2024 Report.* https://www.gallup.com/workplace/349484/state-of-the-global-workplace.aspx

Georgallis, P. (2017). The link between social movements and corporate social initiatives: Toward a multi-level theory. *Journal of Business Ethics, 142*(4), 735–751. https://www.jstor.org/stable/45022134

Grant, A. (2021, April 19). There's a name for the blah you're feeling: It's called languishing. *The New York Times.*, https://www.nytimes.com/2021/04/19/well/mind/covid-mental-health-languishing.html

Gube, M., Mathieu, C., & Hennelly, D. S. (2024, June 10). How carewashing alienates employees. *Harvard Business Review.*, https://hbr.org/2024/06/how-carewashing-alienates-employees?autocomplete=true

MeQ. (2025). *State of the Workforce Report.* https://go.mequilibrium.com/meQ-winter-2025-state-of-workforce-report_content_submit.html

Moran, P. B., & Lennington, M. (2022). *Uncommon accountability: A radical new approach to greater success and fulfilment.* John Wiley & Sons.

Roulet, T., & Bhatti, K. (2023, April 13). Well-being intelligence: A skill set for the new world of work. *Massachusetts Institute of Technology Sloan Management Review*, https://sloanreview.mit.edu/article/well-being-intelligence-a-skill-set-for-the-new-world-of-work/

Stone, D., Patton, B. M., Heen, S. (1999). *Difficult Conversations: How to discuss what matters most.* Penguin Books.

16

The Generous Check-In

Meisha-ann Martin

Introduction

You probably saw the title of this chapter and thought, "I know check-ins are important but what on earth is a *generous* check-in? What does that even mean?" Traditionally, check-ins are considered as a time for the manager to check in on the tasks assigned to the direct report, a status update of sorts on all things important to the organization.

A check-in is generous when the leader checks in on the person and not just the work the person is doing. A check-in is generous when it creates an environment where the employee receives coaching, feedback, and praise instead of just criticism. A generous check-in includes two-way dialogue, creating an opportunity for an employee to give feedback instead of only receiving it. A generous check-in creates a safe space for employees to be vulnerable, admitting when they are having a difficult time and need extra support. A check-in is generous when it maintains or improves employee well-being instead of creating negative emotional states like anxiety, anger, stress, or burnout.

One of the primary outcomes of a generous check-in is psychological safety. In her book *The Fearless Organization* (2019), Amy Edmondson defines psychological safety as "a climate in which people are comfortable expressing and being themselves" (p. xvi) and talks about a psychologically safe workplace as one where people are not hindered by interpersonal fear but are so comfortable with candor that they fully participate by sharing themselves and their ideas freely. According to Gallup (2015), 70% of an employee's engagement can be attributed to their manager. The check-in meeting is the opportunity for a manager to be a good steward of employee engagement, creating a safe space for employees to give the best of themselves to their organization.

Meisha-ann Martin, *The Generous Check-In*. In: *The Changing Leadership Landscape*. Edited by: Sheri L. Feinzig and Mariangela Battista, Oxford University Press. © Oxford University Press (2026).
DOI: 10.1093/9780197820070.003.0016

In his book *Glad We Met*, Rogelberg (2024) shares seven different outcomes of a good check-in meeting: team member success, manager success, building relationships, diversity and inclusion, promoting employee growth and development, life satisfaction, and employee engagement. These are all positive outcomes, but for all seven outcomes to be accomplished, the check-in meeting needs to be broader than just a status update. In this chapter, we will talk about how to conduct a check-in in a way that accomplishes all these things. We will talk about how to do these check-ins well in a way that serves both the business and the employee.

The Arguments for a Frequent, Generous Check-In

First and foremost, the research is clear that it is important to have check-in meetings and that it is important to have those meetings regularly. Employees who meet with their managers weekly are nearly twice as likely to say their manager keeps them motivated and engaged compared to employees who meet with their managers less frequently or not at all (Workhuman, 2021). Internal studies conducted at Microsoft and Cisco yielded similar findings. Employees who had more frequent and effectively run check-in meetings with their managers were more engaged than their colleagues who did not have such meetings (Flinchum et al., 2023). In fact, Gallup found that on average only 15% of employees were engaged when they did not meet with their manager regularly (Gallup, 2015). Workhuman research finds that employees who meet with their managers weekly are more than twice as likely to say that they see a path to grow in the organization, feel a sense of meaning and purpose at work, feel a sense of belonging at work, and, last but not least, trust their manager (Workhuman, 2021). Plus, people who feel appreciated by their manager report feeling more connected to their colleagues and their company culture (Workhuman, 2022).

As mentioned before, Gallup research shows that 70% of the variance in team engagement is determined solely by the manager (Gallup, 2015). Check-in meetings provide employees with an opportunity to develop a meaningful relationship with their manager, understand how their work contributes to broader objectives, and be appreciated for the work they do; all these outcomes form the foundation for how the employee experiences the rest of the organization.

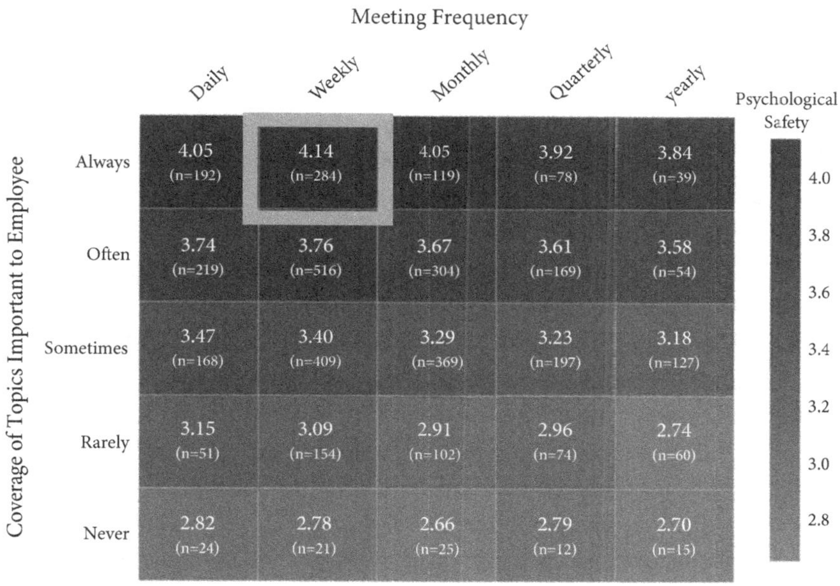

Figure 16.1 Relationship Between Check-In Frequency, Coverage of Topics Important to Employee, and Psychological Safety

There may be a misconception that employees do not want to meet with managers weekly. Rogelberg (2024) found the opposite. In his research with employees based in France, Germany, the United Kingdom, and the United States, he found that employees want three to four check-in meetings a month with their manager. And the best predictor of a desire to reduce the number of check-in meetings was not workload but how well the manager conducted those meetings. Employees want to be supported but they have no desire to have their time wasted. As shown in Figure 16.1, research shows much lower psychological safety for employees who say they never discuss items of importance in their check-ins, even when those check-ins happen frequently (Vicaria & Lauritsen, 2023).

Still, across the board, psychological safety is highest for employees when they meet with their managers at least once per week. This is true regardless of age, tenure, role, and career stage (Vicaria & Lauritsen, 2023). In fact, the group most likely to have weekly check-in meetings are senior leaders (Workhuman, 2024). Not surprisingly, they also tend to rate their managers the highest, compared to middle managers and individual contributors

(Workhuman, 2024). These findings suggest that veterans of the workplace know exactly how important it is to check in weekly.

All of this tells us that good managers are important, good managers have regular check-in meetings with their direct reports, and those check-ins are high-quality and not considered a waste of time by the direct report. So how are organizations overall doing in this respect?

Leaders are failing and it is getting worse. According to Workhuman (2023) research, only 49% of employees met with their manager weekly in 2023. In Workhuman's 2024 study, that number dropped even further to a dismal 21%. And even when leaders check in as frequently as they should (at least once per week), they are not doing it very well. Only 18% of individual contributors consider their check-ins as time well spent. This seems to be a blind spot for leaders. Ninety percent of managers and supervisors think they know how to conduct a productive, supportive, and meaningful check-in with their direct reports (Workhuman, 2024). Given this disconnect, it is not surprising that people are not rating their managers very highly. Fewer than half of individual contributors rate their manager 8 or higher on a 10-point scale. One in four employees rate their manager 5 or lower (Workhuman, 2024).

How to Conduct a Generous Check-In

The first thing for leaders to do, as Nike says, is just do it. Leaders need to make check-in meetings a priority and do it weekly for the best results. The research is compelling that frequency matters and makes a difference. Even for managers who may have no idea how to conduct a good check-in, just doing it over and over may allow them to figure it out, especially if they continuously ask for feedback along the way. Employees who say they meet weekly with their managers are three times more likely to consider that time well spent than employees who meet with their manager less frequently (Workhuman, 2024).

Second, how leaders show up to a check-in meeting absolutely matters. When managers conduct check-ins just to tick the box, it can backfire and can be considered a waste of time by the employee. Workhuman research (2024) shows that even for managers who check in weekly, there is a contingent of employees who say managers are not consistent with discussing items of importance to them (35%) and who do not consider the check-in meeting as time well spent (32%).

One of the most important objectives of a check-in is to provide a safe space for employees to build a relationship with their leader and ask for support if they need it. There is a significant difference in psychological safety when employees say their manager always shows up to the weekly check-in meeting prepared for the conversation vs. if they never show up prepared for the conversation (4.18 vs. 2.94 on a scale of 1–5; see Workhuman, 2024).

Similarly, Rogelberg (2024) finds that even though check-in meetings only have an agenda about 50% of the time, check-in meetings with an agenda were rated as a more valuable use of time. And employees rated the meeting highest when the agenda was co-created jointly by the manager and the direct report.

It should also never be forgotten that a check-in meeting is an opportunity for the leader to signal to their direct report that they matter. Showing up rushed does the opposite. It signals to employees that this is happening as a check-the-box task rather than as time that has been intentionally set aside for the employee's benefit. Employees report feeling significantly more psychologically safe when managers never show up rushed for the weekly check-in than if they show up rushed most of the time or all of the time. As shown in Figure 16.2, psychological safety for employees who meet weekly with a rushed manager is actually a little lower than it is for employees who only meet with their leader once a year but where that leader is fully present in that one meeting.

Another way to signal to employees that they matter is to start the check-in by asking the employee how they are doing. Starting a check-in meeting this way before diving into tasks and action items sends a message that the manager cares about the person beyond what they do for the organization. As with every single element of conducting a great check-in, it is important that this question be more than perfunctory or a check-the-box activity.

Vicaria and Lauritsen (2023) recommend that instead of leaders just asking employees how they are doing, they ask, "How are you doing on a scale of 1 to 10?" and then ask a follow-up question based on the response. An answer of 8, 9, or 10 suggests that there is something that should be celebrated and the leader can ask a question like, "What's going well with you right now?" If the employee gives an answer about their personal life, that is an opportunity for a moment of human connection. If the employee gives an answer about work, it gives the manager insight about what the employee finds engaging and an opportunity to provide more of the same. An answer of 4, 5, 6, or 7 allows for curiosity, and the manager can follow up with a question about what it would take to move the person closer to an 8 or higher. An answer

Figure 16.2 Relationship between Manager Preparedness and Psychological Safety

of 1, 2, or 3 lets the manager know that compassion and support are needed. The manager can inquire about what is happening and how they can help, letting the employee know that it is okay if they choose not to disclose the issue and reinforcing their willingness to support regardless. But a choice not to disclose suggests that perhaps there is an opportunity to improve the relationship so that the employee feels safe to disclose in the future.

This generous check-in, when done well, in time creates the space for employees to answer honestly about how they are doing. And the weekly frequency means that the manager is quickly aware of anything the employee is struggling with, providing them with the opportunity to remove those barriers and retain the employee. In a 2023 Workhuman study (2023), only 29% of employees who talked about intending to look for a new job in the next 12 months reported having weekly check-in meetings with their leader.

Last, check-ins should be used as an opportunity to give employees timely performance feedback. Forty-six percent of employees report receiving less feedback from their manager than they would like (Gallup & Workhuman, 2024). But, Workhuman's 2021 research (2021) shows that employees rate their managers highest when, in addition to checking in weekly, they were giving and receiving feedback at least monthly. Gallup (2023) finds that 80% of employees who said they had received meaningful feedback in the previous week also reported being fully engaged, and this relationship held true for employees who were fully on-site, fully remote, or a hybrid of the two.

Another important element of a weekly check-in that includes feedback is that it can take the anxiety and dread out of upcoming performance reviews. When feedback is being given on a continuous basis, rather than all saved up for an annual meeting, it can make an annual performance review a far more constructive meeting, especially if check-ins have been documented in a check-in tool. In that case, those notes can easily be reviewed, recalled, and pulled into the performance review, which will improve the quality of the review since the manager will be less dependent on their memory. This strategy turns the performance review from a conversation where the manager is focused on the latest things they can remember to a broader, more informed discussion of what has happened over the entire time period since the last review.

In his foreword to Steven Rogelberg's book on check-in meetings (2024), Marshall Goldsmith recalls a client engagement in which he was working on getting leaders to conduct feedback meetings. He said that getting leaders to conduct these sessions "felt like pulling teeth" (p. xiii) because people dreaded a meeting that seemed to be focused only on criticism. To help with this, he required each leader to have consistent check-in meetings that included status updates as well as the opportunity to give and receive feedback. According to Goldsmith, the clients reported feeling more connected to their direct reports and increased team engagement. The check-in meetings became the pillar of their leadership, transformed their culture, and improved productivity.

Feedback from direct reports to leaders is also important. This requires a relationship with the leader that allows for open, honest two-way communication instead of just passively receiving feedback. When employees are checking in weekly and only receiving feedback, not giving it, they rate their manager lower (Workhuman, 2021).

The world of work has changed rapidly since the global COVID-19 pandemic. There was a rise in remote, then hybrid working followed by return-to-office mandates. By extension and necessity, that means more check-in meetings happen virtually. The same rules of being present and checking in on the person in addition to the work the person is doing apply to a virtual meeting. Interestingly, Workhuman (2024) finds that fully on-site workers have the lowest meeting frequency of any working arrangement, with 46% of those workers only meeting once a quarter or less. It is important to intentionally set aside time for a check-in meeting even for people you naturally see frequently in the course of work. And, as times and technology are changing, perhaps it is time to consider different and more creative approaches to a check-in meeting.

One option is a walking meeting. This can be considered for either remote or in-person meetings. In a remote scenario, each person is walking and on the phone for the check-in. To take notes, you can easily record the call using your phone's voice memo feature. There is even technology like smart glasses or a smart watch that allow you to take the phone call without holding your actual phone, and you may even be able to record the meeting. Of course, leaders should obtain their direct report's permission before recording the phone call. With smart glasses, you initiate a video call and have the other person see what you are seeing. This could be a great bonding and humanizing experience for a leader and a direct report and may be particularly helpful for those who have never met each other and/or two people who live very far away from each other, perhaps even in different countries. It is a clever, innovative, and unusual way to get to know someone by seeing their surroundings. In an in-person scenario, the leader and the direct report can walk together while having their meeting. This can be a great alternative to meeting in the leader's office, the direct report's office or in a meeting room. It can set a more casual, personable tone for the discussion.

Almost 50% of employees find a walk or an outside location like a coffee shop an acceptable location for a meeting (Rogelberg, 2024). Obviously, that means there is a large contingent that does not consider those locations favorable. But it is worth asking and offering, especially since this is another opportunity for a direct report to have a say in the check-in experience.

The Organization's Role

The organization's role in the check-in experience is to set expectations, provide training and tools, measure adherence, and conduct analyses that show the impact of this practice. Managers should not be left on their own to figure out how to do a productive and supportive check-in meeting. An organization should support manager check-ins by first setting the expectations for check-ins and also by providing training and tools. Based on all the research, it is completely reasonable to set the expectation that managers check in with employees weekly or at the very least once every two weeks. Organizations can also give leaders some guidance around how to conduct these check-in meetings. Training can and should be provided and be based on research like the research reviewed in this chapter.

A check-in technology tool can also be very helpful. Fundamentally, it is a powerful signal to leaders that this is an important thing for them to get right. Additionally, a good tool can provide in-the-moment guidance to managers and improve the quality of the check-in meeting. And, from a practical perspective, it allows for a manager and a direct report to collaborate on the agenda and meeting items before, during, and after the check-in. This seems like a simple thing, but it can be considered an element of empowering leadership, which is broadly defined as "behaviors that share power with subordinates" (Vecchio et al., 2010, p. 531). This sharing of power has been found to increase employee energy and excitement (Kim & Beehr, 2022), engagement and employee well-being (Park et al., 2017), and innovation (Kim & Beehr, 2022).

Workhuman research (2024) shows that employees are least likely to say their check-in meeting was time well spent when they lacked a check-in tool, and most likely to agree that the check-in was time well spent when they had a check-in tool that they were using. But it is not enough to just have a tool; there needs to be a change management effort to get people to actively utilize the tool provided. Employees who had a tool but were not using it were only slightly more likely to consider their check-in meetings as time well spent.

Automated nudges are another good option for a tool that supports leaders. They have become increasingly popular of late as a human resources (HR) tool. A nudge is a reminder to complete an action, often delivered by email or text notification, and is used to create good habits. Although it is easy to schedule a weekly check-in, there is a potential to use nudges to guide and improve the content of check-in meetings. For example, the research says that employees should get feedback at least monthly. This is a great opportunity for a nudge. Everyone knows how important it is to have regular developmental conversations, but often time passes and the developmental conversations do not happen as frequently as they should. A nudge can help. It is important to celebrate employee's life events. "Date of birth" is a field in every HR management system. A nudge to acknowledge and celebrate a birthday means a manager would never forget a birthday again. The possibilities are endless.

Once expectations are set, and once training and tools are provided, the next step an organization should take is to apply discipline to measuring the frequency and effectiveness of check-ins. For frequency, many organizations are using survey data to estimate the extent to which check-ins are happening. But even for organizations who have a survey item related to this, the survey item usually asks employees if they are meeting with their managers regularly but is not precise about what "regularly" actually means. There is an opportunity to make this type of question much clearer, asking directly if managers are meeting with their direct reports once a week. Not only does this provide better information but it is another opportunity to send the message that once per week is the expectation. There is also an opportunity to use the research on check-ins and feedback to craft other survey questions that will give a better idea of how well leaders are serving employees in this area. For example, the research suggests that employees need feedback at least once per month. If an organization asked a question to see if this is happening and also asked employees if they are receiving enough feedback, this would give an idea of how often people are getting feedback and if there are certain segments of the population that desire feedback even more than once per month.

For organizations employing a check-in tool, this provides another opportunity for measurement, insight, and evaluation. A tool allows an organization to measure the frequency of check-ins, and it also allows for an opportunity to analyze the content of those check-in meetings, perhaps connecting content themes to engagement and other outcomes of interest. This allows us to answer questions like, "Which agenda topics are most related to engagement, psychological safety, and well-being?" These learnings can be shared with the organization and used to improve the quality of check-ins across the board.

In addition to this generous check-in, there are other, complementary strategies that can contribute to the psychological safety that helps employees acknowledge when they need compassion or support. Psychological safety tends to be highest when managers are taking the time to check in with employees weekly, taking time to recognize their employees, and also celebrating things about the employee that have nothing to do with the work they do for the organization like birthdays, running a marathon, or buying a house (Workhuman, 2023). Sixty-six percent of workers want more celebration of personal milestones at work (Workhuman, 2022). When organizations celebrate individuals and their humanity, that has the potential to carry over into check-in meetings, creating a space for honest, candid, and vulnerable conversations.

Conclusion

In conclusion, the research is clear that frequent check-ins are important and that ideally they should happen on a weekly basis. Organizations should set this expectation and provide the tools and support for doing check-ins well in a way that serves the business and the employee. For their part, leaders can commit to effective check-ins: checking in on the person in addition to checking in on the work the person is doing, being fully present in each and every meeting, and working with their direct reports to make sure that each person considers the time well spent. These commitments on the part of the leader and on the part of the organization will improve the quality of the relationships between leaders and their direct reports, increase psychological safety, engagement, and retention, and improve employee experience overall.

References

Edmondson, A. C. (2019). *The fearless organization: Creating psychological safety in the workplace for learning, innovation, and growth.* John Wiley & Sons.

Flinchum, J. R., Kreamer, L. M., Rogelberg, S. G., & Gooty, J. (2023). One-on-one meetings between managers and direct reports: A new opportunity for meeting science. *Organizational Psychology Review, 13*(4), 478–505. https://doi.org/10.1177/20413866221097570

Gallup. (2015). *State of the American manager: Analytics and advice for leaders.* https://www.gallup.com/services/182138/state-american-manager.aspx

Gallup. (2023). *A Great Manager's Most Important Habit.* https://www.gallup.com/workplace/505370/great-manager-important-habit.aspx

Gallup & Workhuman. (2024). *Elevating cultures of recognition through feedback.* https://www.workhuman.com/resources/reports-guides/elevating-cultures-of-feedback-through-recognition-gallup-report/

Kim, M., & Beehr, T. A. (2022). Empowering leadership improves employees' positive psychological states to result in more favorable behaviors. *The International Journal of Human Resource Management, 34* (10), 2002–2038. https://doi.org/10.1080/09585192.2022.2054281

Park, J. G., Kim, J. S., Yoon, S. W., & Joo, B. K. (2017). The effects of empowering leadership on psychological well-being and job engagement. *Leadership & Organization Development Journal, 38*(3), 350–367. https://doi.org/10.1108/LODJ-08-2015-0182

Rogelberg, S. G. (2024). *Glad we met: The art and science of 1:1 meetings.* Oxford University Press.

Vecchio, R. P., Justin, J. E., & Pearce, C. L. (2010). Empowering leadership: An examination of mediating mechanisms within a hierarchical structure. *Leadership Quarterly, 21*, 530–542.

Vicaria, I., & Lauritsen, J. (2023). *Unlocking the power of check-ins: The data behind effective feedback* [Conference presentation]. Workhuman Live 2023 Conference, San Diego, CA.

Workhuman. (2021). *The great resignation.* https://www.workhuman.com/blog/introducing-the-new-workhuman-survey-report-the-great-resignation

Workhuman. (2022). *Two years into COVID: The state of human connection at work.* https://www.workhuman.com/resources/reports-guides/two-years-into-covid-the-state-of-human-connection-at-work

Workhuman. (2023). *The evolution of work.* https://www.workhuman.com/resources/reports-guides/the-evolution-of-work-report/

Workhuman. (2024). *The lost art of the 1:1 check-in.* https://www.workhuman.com/resources/reports-guides/the-lost-art-of-the-check-in/

17

Vulnerability and Agility

How Top Leaders Build Learning Muscle

Cassandra Frangos

Introduction

The context in which leaders operate is becoming fundamentally more complex, and traditional approaches to leadership no longer work. The playbook has changed, and what made Chief Executive Officers (CEOs) and other senior leaders successful in the past is no longer sufficient. Gone are the days of the heroic individual leading from the front. Instead, in most corporations, decision-making has become decentralized, leaders have to operate with less "control," and they need to empower and enable their people to respond to rapidly changing conditions.

Increasingly, success is not possible without learning from mistakes along the way. The leaders who thrive amid complexity and uncertainty embrace vulnerability and a learning mindset. They are inquisitive, agile, and flexible—inviting new information, learning from it, and adjusting.

Our research into what predicts CEO success illuminates the importance of these traits. We studied 75 CEO successions, involving 235 candidates, that took place at large-cap companies in the United States and Europe from 2009 to 2019. We examined the correlation between CEO skills and company performance, measuring shareholder return, revenue growth, and operating margins. In addition, we interviewed a subset of leaders about their development experiences and the styles they used to deliver results; we assessed executives' ability to work through networks to enhance organizational performance by instilling and leveraging people skills.

This research revealed that successful CEO candidates scored higher than unsuccessful ones in three key areas:

Cassandra Frangos, *Vulnerability and Agility*. In: *The Changing Leadership Landscape*.
Edited by: Sheri L. Feinzig and Mariangela Battista, Oxford University Press. © Oxford University Press (2026).
DOI: 10.1093/9780197820070.003.0017

- *Delivering results*: They were able to meet or beat goals and personally improve performance.
- *Collaborating and influencing*: They regularly worked with and through others who were not under their direct control.
- *Self-evaluation and adjustment*: They had the capacity to adjust their point of view and behavior based on new information.

Once candidates became CEOs, their past success delivering results did not have any effect on their performance. The ability to collaborate and influence was associated with higher total shareholder return, while strength in self-evaluation and adjustment was associated with higher revenue growth and greater increases in operating margins.

While there is growing appreciation for the need to draw on this broader range of leadership behaviors, many senior leaders struggle to learn and consistently apply these skills. In this chapter, we explore the interconnection between learning agility, vulnerability, and effective leadership; we discuss how, when done well together, they help build connection and followership.

Letting Go of Being "in Charge"

For senior leaders, especially CEOs, there is a fallacy that being "in charge" means you have all the answers. But when you move into a top leadership role, you do not magically know it all—and you are not supposed to. It is not humanly possible to know all the things all the time, especially in today's rapidly evolving environment.

Assumptions that you should be a master of all the technical processes you are in charge of, have control over your entire management team, and possess the discipline to bring closure to your toughest challenges each week are simply unrealistic. This type of fixed mindset can set you up for failure and frustration—and block your growth and development. Often, when leaders move into the C-suite, they struggle with letting go of things they have relied on in the past, including the idea that they need to have all the answers.

Consider the example of a technology industry engineering leader who left his large (50,000 employees) company to take the role of CEO in a much smaller firm. After the initial honeymoon period, profits flattened, and this leader slipped back into his old methods of managing engineering teams. He joined a key product-development team, energized by the problem-solving of old, and got into the habit of working around the clock. He began complaining to us, "My team isn't stepping up to do the work!"

The problem was not so much that employees resisted a virtuoso engineer's advice, but rather that his performance as CEO was in question as he shifted too much energy away from company leadership and operated in the weeds of engineering problems. This leader's team became frustrated that the CEO was not driving the big-picture strategy, vision, and mission-critical goals. Instead of falling back into old areas of expertise, the CEO needed to assess whether he had the right team and then trust the technical people to deliver.

Perhaps you see a bit of this CEO's behavior in yourself?

It is tempting to let muscle memory lead the way and exert expertise in areas that are comfortable. But time and again, we have seen the most successful leaders push themselves in two areas: they uphold and model a learning mindset and do the work to "unlearn" things from the past that got them where they are. As the saying goes, "What got you here won't get you there."

Let's consider the scenario faced by a corporate board of a global beverage company with a multibillion-dollar valuation considering two CEO candidates. One was a qualified candidate who made it through multiple rounds of screening. On paper, the candidate checked all the boxes: he held an Ivy League MBA, had decades of leadership experience, had spent his career in the snack food industry, and sat on the board of a Fortune 500 organization. His references were strong.

But on the day of his interview with the board of directors, a personality trait came to light: "He just didn't seem very curious," the chair of the board later told us. "We were surprised he didn't ask any questions about our business, processes, or plans. He was just *closed off*."

By contrast, a less "paper-match" candidate met with the same members of the board for final interviews. His background was not as closely aligned; though he had held C-suite roles, he was less experienced than the first candidate, came from general retail, and did not sit on any boards.

He got the job.

Why? This candidate expressed a learning mindset, was genuinely curious about the company's business and background, and was able to clearly explain how his experience in other aspects of retail could be beneficial to the beverage maker. He proved that he was not a "know-it-all" but rather a lifelong learner who would seek multiple viewpoints and avoid stagnation. He asked questions—and listened to the answers; he engaged each person in the room during the interview.

We learn more from people who challenge our thought process than those who affirm our conclusions. Organizational psychologist Adam Grant's (2021, p. 180) research has shown that people who exhibit a willingness to be challenged and continue learning are stronger leaders than those who remain static with existing beliefs:

> Weak leaders silence their critics and shoot the messenger. Strong leaders welcome voice and thank the messenger. Great leaders build systems to amplify voice and elevate the messenger.

Most of us need structure to sustain our motivation amid burnout, boredom, or doubt. Scaffolding, often provided by coaches and mentors, helps us build the resistance to overcome obstacles that threaten to overwhelm us and limit our growth. Grant's research (2021, p. 81) also points to the importance of nurturing to help individuals along their learning journey:

> Many new skills don't come with a manual, and steeper hills often require a lift. That lift comes in the form of scaffolding: a temporary support structure that enables us to scale heights we couldn't reach on our own. It helps us build the resilience to overcome the obstacles that threaten to overwhelm us and limit our growth.

Building Your Learning Muscle

How can leaders overcome the obstacles to growth? *Deliberate play* is one approach to building scaffolding and adding variety and fun as part of expanding one's skills. What does deliberate play look like? Anything that engages your willingness to have a little fun. For NBA star Steph Curry, deliberate play looks like little games that support his development. In one game, Twenty-One, Curry gets one minute to score 21 points and has to sprint to mid-court after each shot.

For executives, deliberate play could be small challenges to learn and implement new skills every day. These challenges could involve experimenting with different leadership styles, seeking out opportunities to engage in cross-functional projects, or even dedicating time each day to read and reflect on industry trends and best practices. By incorporating deliberate play into professional development, executives can maintain a sense of curiosity and adaptability, ultimately fostering continuous growth and innovation within their roles.

One of the most successful CEOs we have worked with—and placed three times—delivers solid results regardless of the organization he leads. What sets him apart is his leadership approach. Much like the candidate who asked questions of everyone in the room at the beverage company board interview, this leader is genuinely inquisitive with all employees of his company—regardless of level, title, or tenure. He is just as likely to ask a junior project manager for their opinion about a project as a senior vice president.

In this manner, he is quite unique—he resists criticizing and leads with learning by asking questions like, "Why do we do *this* that way?"; "What do you think we should do, and why?"; and "Who else should weigh in on this decision?" While he is confident in his ability to lead and make decisions, he recognizes that he cannot know everything and values learning from others.

When it comes to reaching the top box on the organization chart, many are treated as if they are experts, as if they have learned it all and know the path forward. But your success is not "set it and forget it." You may be an expert for a moment in time, but no expert stays that way without continuous effort. In fact, psychologist and author Angela Duckworth (2016, p. 122) suggests that one aspect of maintaining expertise is regularly seeking feedback:

> As soon as possible, experts hungrily seek feedback on how they did. Necessarily, much of that feedback is negative. This means that experts are more interested in what they did wrong—so they can fix it—than what they did right. The active processing of this feedback is as essential as its immediacy.

We have observed that CEOs who are most effective are those who can emotionally connect with their organization through their personalities and are increasingly open to staying current with trends. They stay current and seek to adapt even through the potential discomfort of learning new things. Leadership is in the end often more about understanding when to maneuver and doing it very quickly while learning than about sheer speed in a straight line without paying attention to the signals along the way.

What *Is* Lifelong Learning?

Lifelong learning, *learning mindset*, and *growth mindset* are all buzzwords that cross work and personal circles. You have heard them hundreds of times; you may have even advocated for them yourself.

But what are people trying to express when they say, "It's important to be a lifelong learner," or "At our company, we lead with a growth mindset"? Are they insisting that it is only possible to succeed if you read five books a month and take graduate level classes in your free time?

We don't think so.

When people tout these traits, they are talking about adaptability. They are saying that agility and an ability to listen and learn from others and evolve your perspective trumps old ways of leading—when you "knew something" and stood by it. Leaders who are willing to do everything they can to grow and learn so they can be the best version of themselves are highly valuable, because this trait often helps them deliver on the mission of the organization. This is especially true in our fast-changing, highly competitive environment, where stakeholder demands evolve quickly and market conditions change on a dime.

People with learning agility can look at themselves from the outside and clearly see a situation as it unfolds. Rather than seeing adversity or conflict as a threat, these individuals see it as an opportunity to learn and do better the next time. CEOs with learning agility are prized in the modern business environment because they understand every experience is a teacher; every failure, an opportunity to perfect the product, solution, or process the next time. As Thomas Edison said, "I have not failed. I've just found 10,000 ways that won't work."

One CEO we know stepped into the top role during a period when the business was in crisis. No one else wanted the job, so by default, she was best suited to try to save the flagging company—which was running out of capital, its business model in question, and with a split board in terms of "what to do next." She knew it was a risk—and did it anyway. Most leaders would be wary of a situation that seemed a guaranteed failure, but this leader stepped up. Instead of worrying about what would come next in her career path, she focused on doing everything in her power to help the business succeed.

Unfortunately, the business was too far gone to be saved, and several reductions in force, failed acquisitions, and board restructuring did not solve the underlying problem: the business needed resuscitation much earlier in its demise.

However, this leader learned more about the role of a CEO in two years than many learn in a career and used that learning to her advantage in her next role. Her ability to synthesize and process those lessons helped her step into her next role with confidence that she could handle anything thrown at her, and with the knowledge of how to build the right team to succeed. It is easy to impress when times are good, but resiliency through adversity builds a wealth of knowledge that almost always helps in the future.

Vulnerability and Leadership

What does vulnerability mean to you?

Stop reading for a moment and think about your answer to this question. Perhaps write it down. Don't worry about getting it "right"—this is *your* version of vulnerability.

Did that exercise make you uncomfortable? We are willing to bet, if you took the moment to do it, you experienced some signs of discomfort while doing so.

Why?

While the notion of vulnerability is a hot topic and stands out as a mandatory leadership trait, it can feel overly psychological, self-indulgent, and emotional. Today's leaders are told they need to be vulnerable. But they also need to be strong. And self-confident. And driven.

Achieving this balance of soft and strong can feel impossible. So many leaders instinctively lean on their "strong traits" and avoid vulnerability or, perhaps worse, practice moments of false vulnerability that people see through as veiled attempts at authenticity. But we would argue that leaders who want to build connection and followership must also get comfortable with showing their softer sides—their vulnerability.

Acclaimed research professor Brené Brown (2012, p. 169) highlighted this finding in her interview with Gay Gaddis, owner and founder of T3 (The Think Tank), who said: "There is no vision without vulnerability."

In other words, people will not follow your vision if they do not feel connected to you. Followership is heavily dependent on connection. And connection requires trust. This is even more pertinent as millennials and younger generations become the majority workforce. Studies continue to show that these employee cohorts are most drawn to purpose, work/life balance, and being heard—among other more "self"-focused requirements. Today's leader must earn connection—automatic followership is rapidly waning.

Seventy percent of people say that their sense of purpose is defined by their work. And while 85% of executives report they can live their purpose at work, only 15% of frontline managers and employees report the same, according to a study published by McKinsey & Company (Dhingra et al., 2021). This divide can make the followership gap even larger, due to a perception that leaders get what they want while employees feel left behind or unheard.

A leader with whom we work understands this interdependence inherently. When he took over the CEO role in an arguably successful, profitable, multibillion-dollar organization, it would have been easy to let status quo roll. But, as a longtime employee himself, he was well-acquainted with past leadership's history of making empty promises. Early in his tenure, he called an employee town hall meeting to introduce himself and share his platform. In front of the organization, he proclaimed that the company had made promises to employees over the years that had never been fulfilled, and one of his key tenets of leadership was to fulfill them. His other main pillar was getting the business in order in the following five years, so that when the time came for his succession, the next CEO would be set up for success. He led from a place of vulnerability, especially by planning for succession so early in his tenure. Additionally, he made it clear that the business needed its employees to succeed, and by fulfilling broken promises he was earning the right to ask employees to help the company deliver its broken promises to customers.

This action of admitting the company had fallen short in its responsibilities to employees helped build trust with a base that largely assumed he would be just another stuffed suit in the corner office. By establishing and maintaining trust, this leader was able to get more done across all aspects of the business to fulfill his second mission—optimizing and readying it for succession—because people were on board with him. Of course, a critical piece of maintaining his followership was fulfilling promises made—otherwise, he would have lost people's trust faster than he gained it.

This leader achieved a balance of true self-confidence and vulnerability. He believed strongly in listening to employees and following through with changes—but the risk was in making such a big claim in an organization that lacked trust in upper management. His willingness to take risks and grow—two traits of vulnerable leaders—paid off by fostering trust among employees, and led to significant positive changes in the organization's culture and performance.

One Is the Loneliest Number

The CEO role is one of the most personal roles you'll ever hold, where the lines between your "life" and your "job" are intertwined to an almost inseparable degree. Only those who climb the ranks into the role know another truth: it's lonely at the top.

There are a lot of reasons for the loneliness factor, including a lack of peers (zero, to be exact!), difficulty sharing and unpacking work woes with friends and family, and the "pedestal" treatment from employees. *Harvard Business Review* found that half of CEOs express loneliness, and 61% believe that loneliness hinders job performance (Saporito, 2012). Loneliness affects first-time CEOs even more; nearly 70% of first-time CEOs experiencing loneliness report that the feelings negatively affect their performance.

We have seen it time and again. Executives tell their executive coach that they are the only person able to hold space for them to have meaningful conversations about both work and their personal lives.

And it makes sense. The CEO is the highest authority of a company, and keeping them "happy" is often a primary goal of employees, who have myriad reasons why they do not want to be on the receiving end of an upset, frustrated, or disappointed CEO. So, they are more likely to put a rosy glow on all news delivered to the chief executive (or avoid them altogether) for fear of being put in the hot seat.

But this positive-washing aspect of employee communication—which extends all the way up the organization chart chain to senior leadership—can hinder CEO performance. CEOs often do not have many meaningful or engaging conversations about topics that matter, and therefore can become alienated inside their own organizations. In many ways, a CEO is a type of celebrity and must find a way to productively deal with being observed living their lives, having assumptions made for them, and only receiving superficial and sanitized feedback from their teams.

As CEO, when you walk in the door, your title enters first. People all around are focused on you. Are you smiling? Do you look mad? What are you eating? With whom are you meeting? And the list of questions and observations goes on and on. Part of the role is being on stage all the time—even when you are not. One retiring CEO shared the number-one piece of advice from his mentor with the incoming CEO: "People will pay attention to every word you say, so be careful about everything you say." Can you imagine the strain that approach to communication with everyone around you could take?

When a CEO of a publicly held company went to dinner alone in his medium-sized town, he wanted to be just another customer. His wife was traveling, so he figured he would dine alone at the bar and catch up on some sports TV to unwind after a long day. Not long after, a member of his senior leadership team casually said to him, "I heard you were at this restaurant two nights ago sitting at the bar by yourself." And that's the reality of being a CEO—even if you don't think people are watching you, they are.

Another leader told us that if she says, "I wonder if...," her teams immediately start doing whatever it was she wondered, without stopping to realize she processes out loud and often just wants to brainstorm.

When you are in the constant spotlight, how do you lead with vulnerability, combat isolationism, and maintain a learner's mindset?

We have found that—like most things that come with this role—discipline is critical. While we cannot offer a one-size-fits-all prescription, we have observed that the best CEOs hold space for safe communication, whether the conversation is positive or less-than positive. They actively listen without jumping into judgment or blame, and instead invite dialogue around lessons learned, which creates an environment for CEOs to hear about things that are not working and focus on problem-solving. This type of CEO continually earns trust, demonstrates their human side, and actively engages employees by garnering and listening to feedback. If an authentic conversation is a rare exception, it can be scary when it happens.

When our client took on the CEO role at a major retail organization dominated by men, she knew she would have to combat gender bias, along with all the other aspects of an already challenging role. It was her first chief executive job, and she had a lot on the line. In addition to wanting to prove the board right in its selection, she did not want to disappoint her family, the company's employees, or herself.

From the start, she worked to create an open environment where others could share their perspective, and she acknowledged what she knew and did not know. When she did not know an answer, she made sure that people heard her say, "I don't know. Let me find out and get back to you"—and then she *actually* got back to them. As a former debate team member, she was already comfortable with examining two sides of an issue and used that skill to help gain trust among employees.

This CEO was a natural-born leader and excelled in the role. But privately, she was uncomfortable living under a magnifying glass. As her trusted adviser, we worked together to navigate the experience of suddenly becoming a minor celebrity, board dynamics, team dynamics, and personal growth and fulfillment.

Adapting to the magnifying glass aspect of being CEO required learning that is not unique to this particular leader; almost every CEO needs help navigating some aspect of their role. If you do not have an adviser helping you navigate, we strongly recommend finding one with CEO-specific experience and meeting with them regularly. A great adviser should have an aligned interest in your success with a point of view that adds value to your unique situation and be able to help you understand your own learning blockers and biases. A great adviser also needs to understand the context and bring enough intensity and duration of interaction to help. Otherwise, it's like setting up a monthly workout with a bodybuilding coach to train for a marathon in six months ... six meetings later, we doubt it would be a fun race. Your personal and professional situation is also part of the context when you are a CEO, so find someone you trust.

Learning to "Unlearn"

When former Cisco CEO John Chambers was nine years old, he was diagnosed with dyslexia. In the mid-1950s, there was less understanding of dyslexia, few learning tools to help overcome it, and a stigma that followed anyone who possessed it. Of course, we now know that this condition that affects reading, writing, and speech is very common, with more than three million cases diagnosed each year in the United States alone. Today, we consider dyslexia a neurodivergence—a different way of thinking. Not better, not worse. Just different. But Chambers came from an era when differences were not discussed or acknowledged. He had learned to keep his way of learning quiet—to not discuss or divulge that he might need accommodations to help him process information in the way that his brain best worked.

And then, decades into his career, he accidentally unlearned the perceived need to hide his dyslexia. He began talking about it and eventually became somewhat of a spokesperson, thanks to a vulnerable moment at a Take Your Children to Work Day event at Cisco.

After Chambers's speech to the attendees of the annual event, one of the kids tried to ask him a question but fumbled her words and ended up in tears. When Chambers walked off the stage to talk to her personally, she told him she had dyslexia.

What happened next changed everything for Chambers: he told her that he too had dyslexia, forgetting that his wireless mic was on, and everyone could hear what he was saying. In that moment, he was a person connecting with another person over a shared experience. However, it was the first time he publicly acknowledged his neurodivergence—and he had to unlearn his own personal beliefs about hiding it—quickly. Here is what Forbes says of that pivotal day (Gallo, 2018, para. 7):

> When Chambers returned home that evening, he had several dozen voice messages and emails from employees who wanted to thank him for sharing his story. They told Chambers that he had inspired and connected with them in a way he never had before. John Chambers had learned "the power of admitting my vulnerabilities and sharing my own story."

In the process of learning the power of sharing his story, John Chambers unlearned a lifetime of hiding. And while his story is quite dramatic and on a grand scale, yours need not be. As chief executive, you are required to unlearn and relearn daily (Grant, 2021, inside cover).

> Intelligence is traditionally viewed as the ability to think and learn. Yet in a turbulent world, there's another set of cognitive skills that might matter more: the ability to rethink and unlearn.

Humans are wired to seek comfort—another way of saying "safety." In fact, it is so important to our well-being that in his gold-standard hierarchy, Maslow labeled safety as the second most important essential human need, right after food, water, and shelter (Maslow, 1943, p. 370).

The irony is that comfort is perhaps the biggest potential impediment to our long-term growth. Comfort is the reason we are often hesitant to unlearn. Comfort keeps us from stretching boundaries, trying concepts that may not work, and embracing change. Comfort tries its hardest to keep us from letting go of the known. But to succeed in any senior leadership role, it is important to learn how to become comfortable being *uncomfortable.*

If you are comfortable for too long—if you have stopped learning *and* unlearning—you are likely not growing or benefiting the business, and it is time to move on.

Much like the girl in John Chambers's story, most of us generally need someone else to hold the mirror up for us to change. Every strong leader gets stronger with the right steps for unlearning and relearning, and often you need other people to help you on your journey. This is where it gets tricky for CEOs, and where vulnerability becomes crucial.

Consider the following ideas to assess where you need to unlearn and rethink on a regular basis:

- *Confide in an accountability partner*: Likely your mentor or adviser, this needs to be someone who will be honest with you about what they observe. Where do they see you slipping into old habits? Where are you failing to embrace new ways? Ask your partner to listen to the subtext of what you are saying, as you may not understand your failings yourself.
- *Get candid feedback*: Be sure that you, and other top executives, receive regular feedback from those at different levels of the organization to understand what you are doing well and what needs to evolve or change. This understanding will help guide you in unlearning and rethinking the right things.
- *Give people permission to give you feedback*: Data show that the higher you go in an organization, the less people feel free to be transparent and honest in their feedback. It is up to you to model giving kind and respectful feedback and asking the same of others—even though they are your subordinates. You will be amazed by what you find out when people feel safe to tell you the truth.

Shedding outdated habits, embracing discomfort, and fostering a culture of openness are some of the most effective ways to build trust and followership. Leaders who can unlearn and relearn effectively are ahead of the curve and can better serve their organizations—and their careers.

Overcoming the Fear of Failure

Most people do not like to talk about failure. In fact, until the last decade or so, Harvard Business School rarely included "failure" studies in its revered 100-year-old case study library. But researcher and author Carol Dweck

(2006, p. 49) posits that thinking about, talking about, and learning from failure is precisely what makes great leaders successful:

> In the fixed mindset, everything is about the outcome. If you fail—or if you're not the best—it's all been wasted. The growth mindset allows people to value what they're doing *regardless of the outcome*. They're tackling problems, charting new courses, working on important issues. Maybe they haven't found the cure for cancer, but the search was deeply meaningful.

So many of the products and services we know and rely on today were born out of failures. Post-it Notes were created after a 3M scientist failed to create a super-strong adhesive and ended up with a very weak, repositionable one. Viagra was developed to treat hypertension and angina—and had an unexpected, but popular, side effect. WD-40 (Water Displacement 40th Formula) was a scientist's 40th attempt at creating a product to prevent corrosion in nuclear missiles, and now it can be found in households around the globe. YouTube was originally a video dating site that failed to gain traction, Groupon began as a consumer activist site, and PayPal originally developed security software for handheld devices.

All these examples share a commonality: a willingness to embrace and learn from missteps and pivot, creating wild success in the face of initial failure. Of course, success cannot always be ripped from the jaws of defeat, and failure is just a learning moment for whatever comes next.

What we know to be true is that progress without learning is not possible, and no individual is omniscient. The best laid plans, the most researched endeavors, the "can't-lose" opportunities are all illusions. The fact is that in a life made and sustained by humans, something can always go wrong. It is what you do with the knowledge gained by the missteps, the wrong turns—the "failures"—that matters.

References

Brown, B. (2012). *Daring greatly: How the courage to be vulnerable transforms the way we live, love, trust, parent, and lead.* Avery.

Dhingra, N., Samo, A., Bill Schaninger, B., & Schrimper, M. (2021, April 21). *Help your employees find purpose—or watch them leave.* McKinsey & Company.

Duckworth, A. (2016). *Grit: The power of passion and perseverance.* Collins.

Dweck, C. (2006). *Mindset: The new psychology of success.* Random House.

Gallo, C. (2018, December 13). How Cisco's former CEO turned a secret "disability" into his greatest strength. *Forbes*. https://www.forbes.com/sites/carminegallo/2018/12/13/how-ciscos-former-ceo-turned-a-secret-disability-into-his-greatest-strength/
Grant, A. (2021). *Think again: The power of knowing what you don't know*. Viking Books.
Grant, A. (2023). *Hidden potential: The science of achieving greater things*. Viking.
Maslow, A. H. (1943). A theory of human motivation. *Psychological Review*, *50*(4), 370–396
Saporito, T. (2012, February 12). It's time to acknowledge CEO loneliness. *Harvard Business Review*. https://hbr.org/2012/02/its-time-to-acknowledge-ceo-lo

SECTION VII

DEVELOPING LEADERS FOR THE NEW WORLD OF WORK

18

Leading with Trust

Building Leadership Effectiveness across the Arcs of Time

Ruchin Kansal, Karen Boroff, and Anthony W. Caputo

Introduction

Is there really a unifying set of leadership qualities or outcomes that transcend time? Is the leadership literature comprehensive, or can it be enhanced?

To answer the first question, we reviewed the existing theoretical and empirical literature on leadership effectiveness over the past century. Our analysis leads us to believe that there is no unifying set of leadership qualities or behaviors that transcend time. The more relevant question is: What makes a leader effective at a single point in time or during the critical moments it matters most?

To answer this last question, we introduced the key results of our Future of Leadership Survey (Kansal et al., 2024) on the insight and foresight of leadership and leadership expectations through the eyes of new entrants to the workforce worldwide. This is a longitudinal study that began in 2021. We compared the results to the established body of literature, highlighting where our findings align with the current literature and where they diverge. The survey results, combined with practical insights from the field, suggest that it is leadership effectiveness, rather than individual leadership traits or qualities, that truly matters when measured across an extended arc of time. In the work context, we posit that the antecedent to leadership effectiveness is a leader's ability to instill trust, which becomes the foundational lever that shapes and amplifies a leader's impact over time. As a result, we hypothesize that instilling trust, measured over an extended arc of time, needs to be more salient in the leadership discourse.

Ruchin Kansal, Karen Boroff, and Anthony W. Caputo, *Leading with Trust*. In: *The Changing Leadership Landscape*. Edited by: Sheri L. Feinzig and Mariangela Battista, Oxford University Press.
DOI: 10.1093/9780197820070.003.0018

Further, given that trust is built over time, we also believe that current leadership literature can be advanced by examining leadership effectiveness over certain, defined arcs of time. In this spirit, we offer a new model of leadership effectiveness for future research. We will also offer practical guidance for leaders to enhance their trust with the workforce when working within their organizations.

The Evolution of Leadership Effectiveness

Are leaders born or made? Humanity has long been fascinated with understanding leadership—what it is, where it emerges, and how effective leaders rise. Scientists and practitioners alike have spent lifetimes studying it. And yet, a simple Google search today on leadership or leadership effectiveness still yields billions of results. It is evident that the science of leadership has yet to settle on a clear consensus. While traditional research has long sought to define the characteristics that make someone a leader, the emphasis has now shifted toward understanding what makes a leader truly effective. In the post-pandemic world (since 2020), where technology plays an increasingly integral role in shaping organizational contexts, identifying who holds leadership status is not sufficient in determining leadership effectiveness. Instead, we must rigorously distinguish between the concept of leadership and the demonstration of leadership effectiveness. This distinguishing requires revisiting established leadership frameworks, incorporating credible evidence, and clarifying the difference between "good" and "bad" leadership—where the latter fails to timely apply or adequately adapt insights from the evolving body of leadership research to today's world.

There are five major components to the framework of leadership that need to be considered. These are "The Leader" (e.g., the person, personality traits, characteristics, and demographics), "The Followers" (e.g., the "led" and associated characteristics of this group), "The Situation" (e.g., the internal and external context in time), "The Influence Process" (e.g., the dynamic between the leader and the followers during a specific point in time), and an "Outcome" (e.g., the result of a course of action that would have otherwise not taken place without the intervention of the leader and his/her followers) (House & Aditya, 1997; Northouse, 2019). It can be said that leadership effectiveness then coalesces from these five components as they interact with each other. Recognizing this complexity and the evolving nature of leadership, we will first summarize the last century of leadership theory, leading to modern times, discuss timely and relevant research, and weigh the implications for today's world—keeping in mind the question, "Is there really a unifying set of leadership qualities or outcomes that transcend time?"

Historically, trait theories (Stogdill, 1948; Judge et al., 2002) or focusing on "The Leader" her/himself dominated early leadership studies. Dating back to the early 1920s, these theories are rooted in the belief that certain innate qualities make someone a leader. Of the most prevalent traits at the time, a leader's dominance (Cowley, 1931; Judge et al., 2002; DeRue et al., 2011), intelligence (Bird, 1940; Lord et al., 1986; Judge et al., 2004), charisma (Weber, 1922/1947; Conger & Kanungo, 1998; Antonakis & House, 2013), and physical presence (Cowley, 1931; Judge & Cable, 2004; Re et al., 2013) rose to the top of people's perception of leadership potential. This research also gave rise to an interest in personality frameworks, such as the Big 5 Theory of Personality (Tupes & Christal, 1961; Norman, 1963), which highlighted that traits like extraversion (being sociable, outgoing, energetic, etc.) and conscientiousness (being hard-working, organized, responsible, etc.) are the biggest predictors of leadership potential (Judge et al., 2002). However, the limitations of the approach soon became evident. The sample of many of these studies included mostly white men and excluded diverse populations such as women. As Thomas Carlyle (1841) famously put it in the nineteenth century, "The history of the world is but the biography of great men." As time progressed and the tides of change such as the Industrial Revolution, global conflicts, and social reforms revealed, traits alone could not fully account for effective leadership, as situational dynamics and a leader's ability to adapt to evolving contexts often dictate which qualities are most relevant at any given time.

In response to these gaps, the mid-twentieth century saw the emergence of behavioral theories (Stogdill & Coons, 1957; Likert, 1961), which suggested that effective leadership was not about who you are but what you do. Research like the Ohio State Leadership Studies (Stogdill & Coons, 1957; Hemphill & Coons, 1957) focused on two key behavioral processes of leaders: initiation of structure and consideration for followers. This perspective shifted the lens from the static idea of visible genetic and personality-based traits to observable actions that leaders could intentionally adopt and refine (Blake & Mouton, 1964). However, even this approach had its constraints as it overlooked the variability in followers' responses and the situation, which are primarily shaped by their individual biases and preferences (Fiedler, 1967). As Kurt Lewin (1936) famously stated, the right behavior is a function of the person in a specific environment.

Moving chronologically, after World War II and as we approach the 1960s and '70s, we are introduced to situational theories, asserting that leadership effectiveness depends on the alignment between a leader's style and the demands of the situation (Fiedler, 1967; Hersey & Blanchard, 1969; Vroom & Yetton, 1973). Contingency theories advocated for flexibility (Fiedler, 1967), recognizing that a leader's approach must adapt to the unique challenges at hand. It is at this time that we are also introduced to Power and Influence approaches to leadership (French & Raven, 1959; Pfeffer, 1981), which emphasize that a leader is not only defined by their position in a social system but rather by what they control (Pfeffer & Salancik, 1978), how they make people feel (House & Mitchell, 1974), and who they know. French and Raven (1959) introduced a framework that outlined how all leaders have power, the ability to influence a person or situation, irrespective of formal position in a designated hierarchy. This framework was a notable exception in the literature at the time because it connected the four parts—The Leader, The Followers, The Situation, and The Influence Process as the driver—to the fifth component, Outcomes. Leadership effectiveness hinges on how a leader properly leverages all the resources, relationships, and perceptions at the present time to shape outcomes.

At this point, our question is still, "Is there really a unifying set of leadership qualities or outcomes that transcend time?" Up until the mid- to late-twentieth century, research focused on leaders or outcomes of leader activities at a point in time. Further, the subjects of a given study on leadership were mainly white males in the 1920s (trait-based theories) or soldiers/officers in the 1940s (behavior-based theories); one can easily suggest that the research is not generalizable, given the truncated populations and contexts under study. Beyond that, as research has demonstrated, contingency or situational theories demand that one understands the environment or context in which the leader operates.

From the 1980s to today, literature on leadership has ballooned. Transformational and transactional leadership theories (Burns, 1978; Bass, 1985; Bass & Riggio, 2006, Hunt, 1999) have gained prominence, focusing on a leader's role in inspiring and motivating their followers, as well as the reciprocal relationship between leaders and followers, as seen in the Leader–Member Exchange (LMX) theory (Graen & Uhl-Bien, 1995). We are also seeing the reemergence of trait-based theories in the form of values

(Avolio & Gardner, 2005; Brown & Trevino, 2006) and character-based leadership styles (Hannah & Avolio, 2011; Zaccaro et al., 2004).

Consensus across all these theories is clear: a leader is neither solely born nor exclusively made. It is a dynamic interplay of personality, behaviors, and situational demands over a specific arc of time. This leads us to posit that our question—"What unifying set of leadership qualities or outcomes makes a leader effective?"—should be reframed as, "What unifying set of leadership qualities or outcomes makes a leader effective at a *specific point in time?*" We believe that it is more important to ask what leaders need to be mindful of *today* if they want to respond effectively to current demands, rather than simply relying on models or personas of the past. We must then ask what those gaps in understanding are, and whether the current leadership literature can be enhanced.

Trust Matters Most

Our research (Kansal et al., 2024) has been both unique and important, as it has gathered insights on perceptions of leadership from the next generation of leaders, adding to the discourse on advancing the science and practice of leadership. Centering on 18–30-year-olds living and working in North America, South America, Europe, Asia, and Africa, this research project has attempted to overcome the biases that may rest in earlier research and add to our understanding of what makes a leader effective. In aggregate, over the last four years that we have offered the survey, we now have more than 11,000 data points. The research has widened the pool of respondents to include men and women, and their race/ ethnicity and national origin. Our respondent pool was purposely fashioned to include only those newly emerging into their professional lives to understand better their formative positions on leadership and current workplace issues. The positions included the degree to which the physical appearance of leaders matters, the values and competencies they wish to see in those who lead them, and their assessment of the challenges of today's leaders (Kansal et al., 2024). In addition, this cohort, whose entry into their professional lives was marked by the COVID-19 pandemic, lived through a context and point in time not paralleled by a generation since, perhaps, the entry of the United States into World War II.

We completed the fourth iteration of the study, administered in the first quarter of 2024. This study again surveyed respondents between the ages of 18 and 30 on a leader's traits, values, competencies, challenges, leadership development preferences, and impact of remote work and artificial intelligence (AI). In total, 4,200 people participated in this iteration and agreed or disagreed on a 5-point scale to each of the questions presented. To measure physical traits of a leader, eight items were utilized. To measure value and character traits of a leader, 13 items were utilized, one of which was "instills trust." To measure competencies of a leader, 15 items were utilized. The analysis has revealed some important insights into the broad discussion of leadership effectiveness. First, these young professionals have discarded prior research's "leaders are born" plank. To seek to validate prior research on physical traits, we asked respondents to reflect on the physical traits of a leader. The respondents indicated that they place diminished value on genetically leaning physical traits, such as height ($M = 2.78$, $SD = 1.08$), depth of voice ($M = 2.79$, $SD = 1.05$), left-handedness ($M = 2.47$, $SD = 1.03$) or attractiveness ($M = 3.13$, $SD = 1.05$). These older traits, once seen as important, have faded. Even so, emerging professionals know that their leaders represent their organizations. Hence, they desire to see leaders who are groomed appropriately ($M = 3.58$, $SD = 1.03$), who dress the part ($M = 3.90$, $SD = 0.94$), and who are healthy ($M = 3.72$, $SD = 0.97$). All who aspire to leadership roles can undoubtedly develop and enhance these latter traits, showing evidence that this generation believes today's leaders can be "made" (see Table 18.1). Our findings revealed some geographical differences among respondents, but these differences did not upend the basic finding—that the perception

Table 18.1 Survey Responses to Physical Traits of a Leader Measure

	Range	Mean	Std. Deviation
A leader's attire is appropriate.	1–5	3.90	0.944
A leader is healthy.	1–5	3.72	0.968
A leader's hair is well-groomed.	1–5	3.58	1.030
A leader is physically fit.	1–5	3.31	1.042
A leader is attractive.	1–5	3.13	1.048
A leader has a deeper voice than their peers.	1–5	2.79	1.051
A leader is above average in height than their peers.	1–5	2.78	1.079
A leader is left-handed.	1–5	2.47	1.033

Note: Respondent n = 1102.

of physical traits as important factors in measuring leaders or leadership effectiveness has dropped in importance over time.

The second significant finding has emerged from the responses to this question accumulated from our research. Over the last four years, our respondents have expressed their opinions on the challenges that leaders face. For the research cycle concluded in May 2024, our respondents reported shifts in what they believed to be the most prevalent challenges leaders face today. While the actual challenges are less important, we highlight that *challenges change with time*, and we pointedly underscore that today's leaders may need a specific competency to deal with challenge X. However, that same competency may not be enough to overcome challenge Y, which emerges two or three years hence. In turn, without a specific measurement scale or index on nimbleness, our findings nonetheless cause us to posit that young professionals know "things change" and, in turn, want their leaders to be able to act and pivot focus quickly. Whether that pivot rests in changing the talent needed for the organization, changing products or services, responding to political or legal challenges, or developing new technologies is still an open question. Nevertheless, our data suggest that the mental agility to recognize the challenge and the organizational acumen to respond to it is a desired skillset in leaders today since the organization and the environment in which it operates changes more rapidly.

Our third important finding rested on competencies. We asked the survey respondents to state which competencies or values they would most want to see in a mid-level leader who may be competing for a position in their organization. Clearly, the respondents respond as "follower," which means "the leader for whom they wish to work." Here are the most compelling attributes or competencies of a leader according to our respondents (see also Table 18.2):

1. Effectively deals with crises ($M = 4.27$, $SD = 0.94$)
2. Ensures that employees' work is valued ($M = 4.26$, $SD = 0.94$)
3. Creates adaptive organizations ($M = 4.19$, $SD = 0.94$)
4. Manages work–life balance ($M = 4.19$, $SD = 0.94$)

There is some convergence of these compelling competencies among CEOs who were asked what keeps them up at night (The Conference Board, 2021). These high-level executives were most concerned about uncertainty

Table 18.2 Survey Responses on Competencies of a Leader Measure

	Range	Mean	Std. Deviation
Deal with crisis and failure	1–5	4.27	0.942
Create an environment where employees' work is valued	1–5	4.26	0.936
Create an adaptive organization	1–5	4.19	0.887
Manage work–life balance	1–5	4.19	0.947
Create an empathetic and inclusive culture	1–5	4.18	0.943
Create jobs that provide job security	1–5	4.18	0.937
Manage legal, privacy, and security risks	1–5	4.16	0.938
Create ethical and socially responsible organizations	1–5	4.16	0.953
Attract, recruit, and retain top performers	1–5	4.15	0.888
Keep organizations financially viable	1–5	4.14	0.922
Create jobs that pay well	1–5	4.13	0.946
Manage conflicting stakeholder perspectives, staying true to the organization's mission	1–5	4.05	0.950
Develop a robust pipeline of diverse leadership talent	1–5	4.03	0.934
Manage geopolitical risks	1–5	3.84	0.962
Prepare the organization for an AI future	1–5	3.66	1.120

Note: Respondent n = 1052.

in the global economy, ensuring the acquisition of talent to meet the organization's goals, digital transformation management, and regulatory pressure. The two populations were surveyed at different times and at very different stages in their careers, signaling that change management is essential, as is managing talent in the organization.

In probing how these four competencies for change were related, we found that these four were the most significant building blocks of respondents' belief of trust in their leaders. Through a series of regression and correlational analyses (see Table 18.3), we found that the one common thread across all these competencies is a leader's *ability to instill trust.* We also found that a leader's *ability to create a culture of trust* emerged as the most impactful determinant of leadership effectiveness in today's world (see Table 18.4). In addition, we found that for this population, trust is most

Table 18.3 Stepwise Regression Analysis on Predictors of Trust

Model	Survey Item	R	R2 Change	P
1	Create an environment where employees' work is valued	.465	0.216	<.001
2	Deal with crisis and failure	.518	0.053	<.001
3	Manage work–life balance	.544	0.027	<.001
4	Found and implemented creative solutions to problems	.563	0.022	<.001
5	Manage legal, privacy, and security risks	.575	0.014	<.001
DV	Instills trust			

Table 18.4 Survey Responses to Values of a Leader Measure

	Range	Mean	Std. Deviation
Instills trust	1–5	4.42	0.866
Admits mistakes	1–5	4.41	0.848
Recognizes the dignity of employees	1–5	4.36	0.880
Is a continuous learner	1–5	4.35	0.853
Is ethical	1–5	4.32	0.904
Is authentic	1–5	4.30	0.887
Encourages open dialogue	1–5	4.27	0.878
Persists despite failure	1–5	4.25	0.897
Is empathetic	1–5	4.24	0.919
Seeks diverse perspectives	1–5	4.24	0.913
Makes hard choices in the face of resistance	1–5	4.23	0.886
Pursues excellence	1–5	4.22	0.881
Is driven by a higher purpose	1–5	4.05	0.994

Note: Respondent n = 1086.

related to leadership satisfaction, a higher level of job commitment, and a lower sense or belief that they are contemplating leaving their jobs (Kansal et al., 2024). These findings are supported by prior research showing that trust in leadership is strongly associated with key organizational outcomes such as job satisfaction, commitment, and reduced turnover intentions (Dirks & Ferrin, 2002). This creates a compelling link between leadership, handling challenges, and trust. Given (1) that there are uncertainties and, more significantly, disruptions in the context in which leaders operate; and (2) that all stakeholders, including followers, seek that their leaders can bring about the changes warranted by uncertainties, trust in the leader becomes the glue that we hypothesize will make the leader most effective. We hypothesize that instilling trust needs to be elevated in the leadership discourse as the first enhancement to leadership literature.

Trust, Time, and the Paradox of Leadership

Prior research on trust (Colquitt et al., 2007) lays out the three important ingredients of trust:

1. Does the leader have the ability to do the job? This ability necessarily includes the technical, conceptual, and human resources components.
2. Does the leader act with integrity?
3. Does the leader act with benevolence—that is, make decisions for the betterment of the organization? And is the leader not self-serving?

These three elements form the foundation of trust between leaders and followers. However, it is crucial to view them through the lens of time. Followers observe leaders' behaviors over time, collecting data points bolstering or undermining their trust in these leaders. In effect, it is the passage of time that affirms whether the leader is fulfilling the three elements of trust, thereby growing the follower's capacity to conclude that this is the leader they will follow. This parallels Warren Buffett's famous investment philosophy, "Our favorite holding period is forever", underscoring the idea that trust, like value, compounds with time (Berkshire Hathaway Inc., 1988). Recalling that our research population already knows that "things change," they appear willing to follow a leader they can trust to lead them through changing environments. The willingness to follow emerges not from any single snapshot in time but from the accumulation of evidence that the leader will adapt their ability, and act with integrity and benevolence over time.

It is this notion of time that fuels a paradox of leadership. Leaders are hired or promoted based on past performance, assuming their former success will predict future success. However, this logic is flawed because it presumes that the original conditions and followers, those who once validated the leader's effectiveness, remain fixed in the new (future) setting. Instead, new followers who have not yet developed trust, coupled with altered contextual factors, create a blank slate and opportunity. Current research does not reveal how long it takes for trust to emerge in these new circumstances or whether a leader's traits and values will fully transfer. Nor does it clarify which events most strongly signal ability, integrity, and benevolence. Together, these gaps point to the need for a new model of leadership effectiveness, which is the second enhancement we propose to the leadership literature.

Building Trust: Leadership Effectiveness as an Arc of Time

Literature to date has focused on leadership effectiveness as performance over a snapshot in time. We suggest that it is a short-term perspective as it does not fully account for trust as the key determinant of leadership effectiveness. We believe that studying leadership over different arcs of time can close gaps in understanding what makes a leader effective. A better evaluation of leadership effectiveness can only happen over an arc of time. We propose the "3 Ps": Potential, Performance, and Permanence (see Figure 18.1) as the long-term building blocks of trust and, in turn, leadership effectiveness. This model further aligns with Silzer and Church's (2009) emphasis on identifying and assessing high-potential talent as a foundation for long-term leadership success.

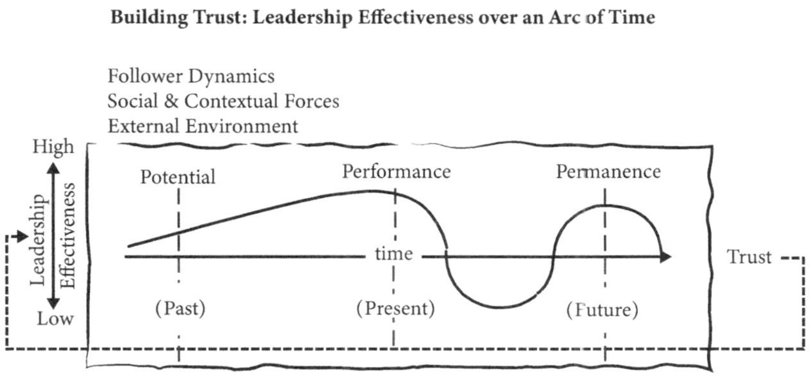

Figure 18.1 Three Ps Leadership Effectiveness Framework

Potential: Leaders are hired into roles based on their potential (ability as evidenced by past performance) to influence the context they are hired into. Just like potential energy is a function of an object's position, properties, and external forces acting upon it, a leader's potential is determined by their position, their expertise, and the environment that they are currently operating in, past experiences, or an accumulation of competencies fit for a role. Building credible potential takes time (Campion et al., 2011; Silzer & Church, 2009).

Performance: Potential provides the platform to perform. Performance takes time. However, tenures can be short-lived if leaders cannot garner their followers' trust quickly (Dirks & Ferrin, 2002). That is the paradox of leadership that we discussed earlier.

Permanence: They say history is written by those who won. We say that history is interpreted by the ones who read it. Moreover, that reveals the third pillar of our leadership effectiveness model: permanence. In retrospect, every leader is judged over an arc of time (Hunt, 1999). The time may extend into centuries for some (Jesus Christ, Marcus Aurelius, Alexander the Great) or decades for others (presidents, CEOs, philosophers). The question then is: Should leaders perform to garner trust in the short term and hope that permanence will be the outcome, or should they do so with an eye toward permanence that may lead to actions that conflict with the demands of the future?

This conceptual model illustrates trust and leadership effectiveness evolving over an arc of time. The horizontal axis represents the progression from the leader's past to the present and future. Trust serves as the primary outcome of the model, resulting from the leader's impact though each stage (arcs of time). Further, trust has to be rebuilt anew for each phase of a leader's new role. The vertical "High-Low" scale suggests that effectiveness, trust, or other key attributes may fluctuate in intensity across different points in the leader's journey. The dotted line looping back to the start symbolizes that leadership effectiveness is part of a continuous, iterative process. As a leader's actions and outcomes move through each arc of time, the lessons learned, the trust established or eroded, and the shifts in context are never lost. Instead, they cycle back, informing how future leaders are evaluated, how trust is granted or withheld, and which attributes are considered essential at the outset of a new arc. This feedback loop highlights that each generation of leadership builds upon the positive and negative legacy of those who came before, both within the same leaders and across different leaders. Above, the broader social and contextual forces, including follower dynamics and the external environment, shape and respond to the leader's actions across the arcs of time. The model emphasizes that trust-building must be sustained across changing contexts and time horizons by viewing leadership effectiveness through these multiple interacting layers—a complex endeavor. Since this is a conceptual model based on empirical research, we wanted to introduce it here as a model that still needs to be measured, validated, refined, and studied in future research.

Conclusion

We opened this chapter with two questions: whether a unifying set of leadership qualities transcend time, and whether current leadership literature can be enhanced. Our review and analysis of the science of leadership leads us to two key conclusions. First, rather than a single, universally accepted set of qualities that transcend time, what truly matters is a leader's effectiveness at a given point in time. Second, what has been underappreciated in literature is the critical role of trust, built and reinforced over different arcs of time, that defines their effectiveness and outcomes. By examining leadership effectiveness through a longitudinal lens, we highlight that leaders must earn and re-earn trust in every situation they find themselves in as contexts and followers change. This perspective advances the current thinking on leadership beyond static traits and behaviors, emphasizing that effectiveness emerges from a dynamic interplay among the leader, followers, and the unfolding environment. As a result, trust becomes the enabling lever of leadership effectiveness. Future research should focus on the independent variables of trust and time, with outcomes focused on leadership effectiveness and related variables.

In the meantime, there are countless ways for a leader to build (and re-build) trust on a day-to-day basis. The Employee Lifecycle framework (Bernthal et al., 2001) is a conceptual framework used to describe the series of stages an employee experiences during their tenure with an organization—from attraction and recruitment, through onboarding, development, retention, and ultimately separation or exit. This lifecycle view is a good framework for leaders to consider when thinking about building trust in their organization since many researchers and practitioners agree on the general notion that employees pass through each of these identifiable phases regardless of where they are working. The question to ask is: How can leaders demonstrate ability, integrity, and benevolence at each of these life stages of an employee?

As a leader, there are three things you can do today to advance trust employees have in you:

- Strive for transparency and process fairness in your behavior and organizational policies, whether hiring, developing, retaining, or separating employees.
- Be a continuous learner. This signals your constant efforts to enhance your ability at work and improves confidence in your ability in all aspects of work, including the ability to deal with crisis and failure, and building new business opportunities.
- Reflect upon the last five communications you sent out to your teams. Were they more about you and your needs, or balanced with those of employees? If not balanced, pause, and reflect if you need to change the tone of your communications with a view to build trust.

References

Antonakis, J., & House, R. J. (2013). The full-range leadership theory: The way forward. In J. Antonakis, D. V. Day, & B. Schyns (Eds.), *The nature of leadership* (2nd ed., pp. 3–20). SAGE Publications.

Avolio, B. J., & Gardner, W. L. (2005). Authentic leadership development: Getting to the root of positive forms of leadership. *The Leadership Quarterly*, *16*(3), 315–338. https://doi.org/10.1016/j.leaqua.2005.03.001

Berkshire Hathaway Inc. (1988). *1988 letter to shareholders*. https://www.berkshirehathaway.com/letters/1988.html https://www.berkshirehathaway.com

Bass, B. M. (1985). *Leadership and performance beyond expectations*. Free Press.

Bass, B. M., & Riggio, R. E. (2006). *Transformational leadership* (2nd ed.). Lawrence Erlbaum Associates.

Bernthal, P. R., Wellins, R. S., & Smith, A. B. (2001). Towards a sharper focus: HR measures for the workforce or the workplace? *Human Resource Planning*, *24*(4), 36–48.

Bird, C. (1940). *Social psychology*. Appleton-Century.

Blake, R. R., & Mouton, J. S. (1964). *The managerial grid: Key orientations for achieving production through people*. Gulf Publishing.

Boroff, K., Lorenzet, S., & Kansal, R. (2024). The future of leadership survey: 2024. *In the Lead*.https://www.shu.edu/leadership/news/the-future-of-leadership-survey-2024.html

Brown, M. E., & Treviño, L. K. (2006). Ethical leadership: A review and future directions. *The Leadership Quarterly*, *17*(6), 595–616. https://doi.org/10.1016/j.leaqua.2006.10.004

Burns, J. M. (1978). *Leadership*. Harper & Row.

Carlyle, T. (1841). *On heroes, hero-worship, and the heroic in history*. James Fraser.
Colquitt, J. A., Scott, B. A., & LePine, J. A. (2007). Trust, trustworthiness, and trust propensity: A meta-analytic test of their unique relationships with risk taking and job performance. *Journal of Applied Psychology, 92*(4), 909–927. https://doi.org/10.1037/0021-9010.92.4.909
Conger, J. A., & Kanungo, R. N. (1998). *Charismatic leadership in organizations*. SAGE Publications.
The Conference Board. (2021). *C-Suite Challenge™ 2021: Leading in a post-pandemic recovery*. https://www.conference-board.org/publications/c-suite-challenge-leading-post-covid-recovery
Cowley, W. H. (1931). The traits of face-to-face leaders. *Journal of Abnormal and Social Psychology, 26*(3), 304–313.
DeRue, D. S., Nahrgang, J. D., Wellman, N., & Humphrey, S. E. (2011). Trait and behavioral theories of leadership: An integration and meta-analytic test of their relative validity. *Personnel Psychology, 64*(1), 7–52.
Dirks, K. T., & Ferrin, D. L. (2002). Trust in leadership: Meta-analytic findings and implications for research and practice. *Journal of Applied Psychology, 87*(4), 611–628. https://doi.org/10.1037/0021-9010.87.4.611
Fiedler, F. E. (1967). *A theory of leadership effectiveness*. McGraw-Hill.
French, J. R. P., & Raven, B. (1959). The bases of social power. In D. Cartwright (Ed.), *Studies in social power* (pp. 150–167). University of Michigan, Institute for Social Research.
Graen, G. B., & Uhl-Bien, M. (1995). Relationship-based approach to leadership: Development of leader–member exchange (LMX) theory of leadership over 25 years: Applying a multi-level multi-domain perspective. *The Leadership Quarterly, 6*(2), 219–247. https://doi.org/10.1016/1048-9843(95)90036-5
Hannah, S. T., & Avolio, B. J. (2011). The locus of leader character. *The Leadership Quarterly, 22*(5), 979–983. https://doi.org/10.1016/j.leaqua.2011.07.012
Hersey, P., & Blanchard, K. H. (1969). Life cycle theory of leadership. *Training & Development Journal, 23*(5), 26–34.
House, R. J., & Aditya, R. N. (1997). The social scientific study of leadership: Quo vadis? *Journal of Management, 23*(3), 409–473. https://doi.org/10.1177/014920639702300306
House, R. J., & Mitchell, T. R. (1974). Path-goal theory of leadership. *Journal of Contemporary Business, 3*, 81–97.
Hunt, J. G. (1999). Transformational/charismatic leadership's transformation of the field: An historical essay. *The Leadership Quarterly, 10*(2), 129–144. https://doi.org/10.1016/S1048-9843(99)00006-4
Judge, T. A., Bono, J. E., Ilies, R., & Gerhardt, M. W. (2002). Personality and leadership: A qualitative and quantitative review. *Journal of Applied Psychology, 87*(4), 765–780. https://doi.org/10.1037/0021-9010.87.4.765
Judge, T. A., & Cable, D. M. (2004). The effect of physical height on workplace success and income: Preliminary test of a theoretical model. *Journal of Applied Psychology, 89*(3), 428–441.
Judge, T. A., Colbert, A. E., & Ilies, R. (2004). Intelligence and leadership: A quantitative review and test of theoretical propositions. *Journal of Applied Psychology, 89*(3), 542–552.
Kansal, R., Boroff, K., Caputo, A., & Johnson, B. (2024). The future of leadership survey (2021–2024). *Seton Hall University*. https://www.shu.edu/leadership/news/the-future-of-leadership-survey-2024.html
Lewin, K. (1936). *Principles of topological psychology*. McGraw-Hill.
Likert, R. (1961). *New patterns of management*. McGraw-Hill.
Lord, R. G., De Vader, C. L., & Alliger, G. M. (1986). A meta-analysis of the relation between personality traits and leadership perceptions. *Journal of Applied Psychology, 71*(3), 402–410.
Norman, W. T. (1963). Toward an adequate taxonomy of personality attributes: Replicated factor structure in peer nomination personality ratings. *Journal of Abnormal and Social Psychology, 66*(6), 574–583.

Northouse, P. G. (2019). *Leadership: Theory and practice* (8th ed.). SAGE Publications.
Pfeffer, J. (1981). *Power in organizations*. Pitman.
Pfeffer, J., & Salancik, G. R. (1978). *The external control of organizations: A resource dependence perspective*. Harper & Row.
Re, D. E., DeBruine, L. M., Jones, B. C., & Perrett, D. I. (2013). Facial cues to perceived height influence leadership choices in simulated voting. *The Leadership Quarterly, 24*(2), 159–168.
Silzer, R., & Church, A. H. (2009). Identifying and assessing high-potential talent: Current organizational practices. *Consulting Psychology Journal: Practice and Research, 61*(4), 284–293. https://doi.org/10.1037/a0017159
Stogdill, R. M. (1948). Personal factors associated with leadership: A survey of the literature. *Journal of Psychology, 25*(1), 35–71. https://doi.org/10.1080/00223980.1948.9917362
Stogdill, R. M., & Coons, A. E. (Eds.). (1957). *Leader behavior: Its description and measurement*. Bureau of Business Research, The Ohio State University.
Tupes, E. C., & Christal, R. E. (1992). Recurrent personality factors based on trait ratings. *Journal of Personality, 60*(2), 225–251. https://doi.org/10.1111/j.1467-6494.1992.tb00973.x
Vroom, V. H., & Yetton, P. W. (1973). *Leadership and decision-making*. University of Pittsburgh Press.
Weber, M. (1922/1947). *The theory of social and economic organization* (A. M. Henderson & T. Parsons, Trans.). Free Press.
Zaccaro, S. J., Kemp, C., & Bader, P. (2004). Leader traits and attributes. In J. Antonakis, A. T. Cianciolo, & R. J. Sternberg (Eds.), *The nature of leadership* (pp. 101–124). SAGE Publications.

19

Leading through Change

Navigating Acquisitions and Integrations

Jane Wu and Patricia Pedigo

Introduction

Many companies continue to use mergers and acquisitions (M&A) to gain strategic advantage and grow. In their 2024 outlook article, PricewaterhouseCoopers noted that 60% of surveyed Chief Executive Officers (CEOs) planned to acquire a company that year. Unfortunately, according to several surveys, between 50% and 75% of all post-merger integrations fail to meet their original objectives due to factors directly related to leadership action or inaction (Christensen et al., 2011).

M&A pose unique challenges for leadership as they manage the complexities of bringing multiple organizations into one. An *acquisition* refers to the process by which one company purchases most or all of another company's shares or assets with the goal of gaining control of the other company (Bruner, 2004; Koller et al., 2010). Acquisitions can be friendly or hostile and are often aimed at achieving strategic objectives such as expanding market share, acquiring new technologies, or entering new markets. In contrast, a *merger* is a strategic decision in which two or more companies come together to form a new entity, typically with the goal of improving efficiency, expanding market reach, or enhancing competitive advantage. Unlike an acquisition, where one company buys another, a merger usually implies a more equal partnership between the merging companies (Gaughan, 2017). With a merger, a new entity is formed, typically involving the exchange of stock and the dissolution of the previous companies (DePamphilis, 2010). This chapter will focus exclusively on the role leaders play within the context of acquisitions, and provide food for thought in terms of potential actions and considerations.

Jane Wu and Patricia Pedigo, *Leading through Change*. In: *The Changing Leadership Landscape*
Edited by: Sheri L. Feinzig and Mariangela Battista, Oxford University Press. © Oxford University Press (2026).
DOI: 10.1093/9780197820070.003.0019

Acquisitions occur for a variety of purposes that enable the organization to grow, whether that be in revenue, market share, or skills. These strategic reasons may include:

- diversification or growth by entering a new market
- purchasing cutting-edge technology or products
- bringing new talent into the organization
- removing a competitor from the market

Acquisitions include a series of complex and often time-pressured events which involve individuals across every function of each organization (see Figure 19.1 for an example). There are a variety of factors that influence the amount of time spent within each phase, such as size of the acquired and acquiring organization, marketplace regulations, legal requirements, etc. Each of the phases provides numerous opportunities for misalignment, fear of the unknown, confusion, lack of clarity, etc. to pervade through the organizations.

Phase 1: Negotiations ("Courtship")

At this phase, the acquiring company learns why the target company is "for sale." Here are a few possible reasons:

- Company-funding entities (venture capital or private equity) want to cash out their holdings (this is common after approximately five years of funding), or the founders want to cash out their positions.
- The cost of "going public" via an Initial Public Offering (IPO) is too high.
- The company has reached a perceived limit of what it can strategically and/or financially achieve on its own.

Leaders of the acquiring company begin initial conversations with the target leaders and can assess motivations. The target company can evaluate for organizational fit with the acquiring company. Terms and conditions are agreed upon and movement to the next step is planned; or, if the companies are too far apart on the price, interest, strategy, etc., they may agree to end discussions. In many cases there are other interested parties seeking to purchase the target company as well as other potential targets for

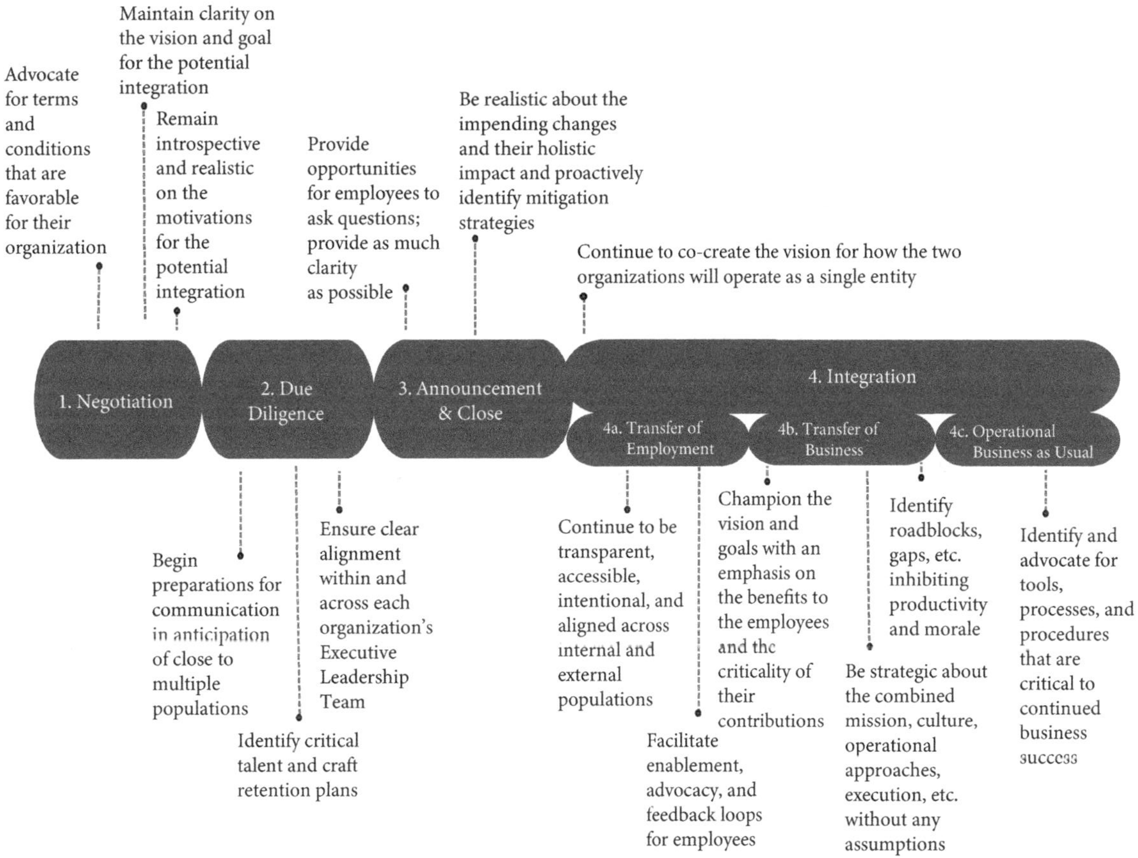

Figure 19.1 An Example of a Typical Sequence of Phases of an Acquisition and Subsequent Integration

the acquiring company. The acquiring company may also fine-tune their strategy for the acquisition.

Phase 2: Due Diligence ("Getting to Know You")

At this phase, acquiring leaders perform a deep dive into the details of the target organization and how it operates at each of the functional levels—e.g., marketing, sales, product development, human resources (HR), finance, legal, etc.

The leaders of both sides are interested in "selling" their company to the other. It is up to the due diligence functional teams to dig beneath the "covers" to identify issues of risk that the acquiring company would be taking on if the deal were to proceed. The identified organizational risks (such as legal issues, financial irregularities, etc.) and estimates of mitigation costs or actions are included in the terms of the final offer.

This phase also allows the leaders of both sides to build rapport and begin developing the relationships needed for success. Despite the more virtual work environment in many companies, it is recommended that, and far more effective when, due diligence is in-person. This allows for, and enables, informal time for leader conversations and a group dinner or cocktails. This human interaction helps further strengthen the relationships that will be necessary to carry through the integration.

In addition, formal leader assessments by the acquiring company are recommended to identify the leaders' personal motivations, expectations, and strengths and weaknesses. Identification of key senior leaders and compensation expectations will also be discussed with the target CEO at this phase.

All findings from due diligence are input to the final offer and terms and conditions from the acquiring company to the target. Any additional negotiations and other regulatory approvals will happen at this phase.

It is important that all required target leaders (business, operational, and technical) have formally agreed to join the acquiring organization as these leaders will be key to securing a successful integration. Often, the deal will not be signed without formal agreement from critical leaders to join the acquiring organization. On the acquiring organization side, key functions such as communications, HR, organizational change, operations, and event planning are engaged to plan the announcement. Once formal agreements are signed, the deal will move to the next phase.

Phase 3: Announcement and Close ("Getting Married")

At this phase, the union is announced to employees, contractors, clients, vendors and suppliers, and the press. Dedicated communications, HR, and organization change staff from both organizations will be required through typically the first six months of the integration. This sets the tone for the amount of information that will be available to employees throughout the upcoming integration period.

Leaders from both sides meet with key acquired clients to help them understand the impact of this union on their business and reassure them of ongoing support. Key vendor conversations will also occur to ensure continued support and partnership. Acquiring company leaders will also meet with their relevant clients to discuss any impacts to their ongoing relationship and support.

Acquired leaders will meet with their employees to discuss the announcement and answer any questions as best they can. Enabling acquired leaders with information and frequently asked questions (FAQs) is critical for them to address employee concerns and "What's in it for me?" questions. The risks of attrition among key employees can also be mitigated through open and frequent communications.

When announcement and close happen on the same day, employees will be welcomed into the acquiring company with a celebration and new badges, etc. Basic overview education about the acquiring organization will occur. Acquired leader participation in these events along with acquiring leaders introducing them to the acquiring organization opens the door for collaboration across the organizations.

For some acquisitions, close (when the organizations finally become one) can happen months after the announcement. This delay (often impacted by country-based regulatory approval processes) can cause confusion and uncertainty in acquired employees. Leaders from both sides must be prepared to effectively manage this phase to retain talent during this time of significant change and ambiguity.

Phase 4: Integration ("Living Together")

Critical milestones for this phase include *Transfer of Employment (ToE)*, where acquired employees become official employees of the acquiring company. They receive new email addresses in alignment with the acquiring company and are assimilated into the acquiring company's payroll, benefits, and other HR programs. At *Transfer of Business* (ToB), business functions and operations, such as sales, marketing, customer support, product development, etc. become branded and managed by the acquiring company. ToB often also marks the point at which the acquired organization ceases to exist as a legal entity. The exact dates and format of these changes can be impacted by conditions such as country-level laws and practices, or business strategy.

Early in this phase, acquiring employees and leaders participate in education and sharing sessions to learn about the acquired business and how it operates. The goal of such sessions is to help the acquiring employees understand the organizational interrelationships, technologies, and other linking elements of the acquired company and avoid any potential unintended disruption to them during the integration.

The integration phase includes acquired leaders and employees beginning to learn about and assimilate into the new company. Due to the multiple factors that impact integrations from a people, operational, etc. perspective, it is critical to be intentional, deliberate, and holistic with these meetings as they will enable a successful assimilation.

Critical activities during this phase include (but are not limited to) merging products and services; rebranding and/or developing new logo materials; migrating clients to new terms and conditions and contracts; aligning employees with new job roles and new compensation structures, enrolling in benefits, and enacting organizational changes.

A "hostile" acquisition (a.k.a. a *takeover*) is rarer and riskier as there is little time to fully investigate the target company and how it operates. In this case, the acquiring company attempts to take control of the target company against the wishes of their leadership team by going directly to the company's shareholders and board of directors. If the takeover is successful, the target leaders often resign, leaving the acquiring leaders to quickly learn about and assimilate the products, employees, customers, etc. The focus of this chapter will be the more common "friendly" acquisition environment and the role acquired leaders play to ensure integration success.

Role of the Leader in an Acquisition

Leaders of both sides of the acquisition process play vital roles in guiding the structure, timelines, and myriad details surrounding the operational aspects of an acquisition. Also entangled in the various technical steps are the leaders' personal aspirations and expectations. While acquired leaders have a vested interest in presenting their company in the best light possible to representatives from the acquiring organization, they also have a responsibility to ensure their teams disclose all relevant information during the due diligence process, including risks and issues in areas such as tax, technology, operational, financial, legal, and HR.

Leaders, however, also inevitably have themselves in mind as acquisitions involve massive changes that will impact their professional, personal, and financial lives. There are countless examples of how things can go awry for leaders in an acquisition. Here is what can happen at the time of close and into the integration period:

- Acquired leaders may receive "life-changing" money when the company is sold, which changes their motivation, interest, and commitment to the newly integrated/merged organization.
- They may lose personal perks, especially as related to business travel and other "luxury" expenses such as the company plane.
- They may feel powerless to address their own and employee questions and concerns because of lack of knowledge of the acquiring company's processes, organizational structure, and informal networks.
- They may become distracted by acquiring business leaders and the business growth plans. As a result, they may not be available for employee questions and concerns.
- They may experience real and/or perceived lack of freedom as they cope with the processes and procedures of the acquiring company.
- They may leave the new organization and cause others to question their own interest and motivation to stay.
- They may feel a lack of alignment with other leaders (both acquired and acquiring) on the vision, strategy, and governance for the new organization.

Facilitating a smooth transition with an expressed unified vision while also maintaining a thriving business are key activities that leaders engage in to drive acquisition success. A steady, transparent, and intentional leadership presence—physical and virtual—is critical to easing the inevitably disruptive process of integrating two companies together.

"Death by a thousand papercuts" is a term that is used all too often when organizations are adjusting to one another. Whether it be small changes such as the availability of beverages and snacks to broader changes such as employee benefits, or contract terms and renewals, leaders have a key role in defining the future combined organization's culture, processes, structure, operations and vision while addressing the changes needed to live it. Their enthusiasm or skepticism about the future has a tremendous impact on the acquired employees and is contagious.

Much of the existing research has focused on the acquiring leadership (Junni & Sarala, 2014) with little attention paid to the important role of the acquired leadership, and the partnership that must be established with the acquiring organization. This chapter will cover the key role of both acquired and acquiring leaders and how they can be enabled to help lead the integration effort to successful outcomes, while providing context and insights to acquiring leaders.

Who Are the Leaders?

Who a leader is in a workplace may be initially clear as described via an organization chart. However, as with many things related to acquisitions, assumptions can open the door to ambiguity, confusion, and misalignment. Within the context of acquisitions, leaders include the executive leadership teams of both the acquired and acquiring organizations. This typically includes the C-suite of the acquired and acquiring organizations as well as the acquiring general managers and senior vice presidents. Additionally, business-function leaders also play an essential role in sharing and integrating functional knowledge. These leaders understand the intricacies of their functional areas and where more attention may be needed compared to other areas. These are the detail areas that contribute to the degree of success realized by the acquisition. The due diligence phase is also a point in time to uncover non-executive managers and non-managers who may play key leadership roles and who should be included in the planning.

One leadership role that is unique to the world of acquisitions (for those transactions that are large enough to justify such a role) is that of an integration executive (IE). This is someone from the acquiring business unit who has "line of sight" across the various functional areas and acts as the "go-to" person for all executives over the course of the integration lifecycle. This person serves as a champion for the acquired company and becomes embedded in their organization to provide invaluable understanding of the acquired

Cameron has been selected as the IE for Organization A's acquisition of Organization X. He was selected due to his previous experiences with Organization A and knowledge of M&A as well as his empathetic disposition. Cameron is a mid-level executive, which is commensurate with the level of leaders he will be working with and influencing. He will be able to effectively advocate for organization X and have the sponsorship and backing of his fellow executives within Organization A. Having had 8+ years of tenure at Organization A Cameron has broad knowledge of Organization A's operations and overall business, which he can leverage to put the high-level puzzle pieces together across the two organizations' various functional areas. This is considered a growth and development opportunity for him with significant senior executive exposure.

His ability to see the broader vision and truly understand the value of the integrated organizations allows Cameron to effectively guide all parties through the necessary tasks. Cameron was selected and put in play from the very beginning to ensure there would be no knowledge gaps and rapport could be established early on with the executives of Organization X.

Cameron is responsible for ensuring alignment across all functional areas within the organization. He has an experienced team of functional experts working for him and he has accountability for the quality and execution of all integration-related tasks from headcount planning to go-to-market strategies and beyond.

Figure 19.2 An Example of an Integration Executive Profile

company and establishes rapport with the acquired teams. An example of the experiences and responsibilities of an IE is described in Figure 19.2.

Role of Acquired and Acquiring Leaders

In addition to business knowledge and experience, leaders play a critical role in culture, communication, and governance. All these areas are fundamentally intertwined throughout each phase of the acquisition process. Acquired and acquiring leaders need to be cognizant of how essential their role is within each of these areas in order to facilitate both the operational and person-related integration activities. The manner and intentionality with which leaders assume each of these roles is important in reducing push-back and resistance, anticipating challenges and roadblocks, providing clear structure and guidance, and mitigating risks, among other things.

While each organization has unique circumstances and cultures which will require leaders to adapt and adjust their approaches to best fit the acquisition scenario for the specific organizations in play, but the role of the leader remains constant. Leaders (both acquired and acquiring) who are adept at understanding the needs of the organization will be able to adjust their energies to meet those needs in a way that best facilitates success.

Role of Leaders in Shaping the Organization Culture

Many organizations cite their culture as part of the winning equation or their organization's "secret sauce," and oftentimes organizational founders take intentional steps to curate and maintain their organization's culture. With such intentionality and uniqueness to many organizational cultures and reputations, it should not be a surprise that true cultural alignment across organizations is rare (especially when there is an organizational-size discrepancy between the two organizations) and that a lack of culture fit is often cited as a key reason an acquisition fails. Cultural differences can significantly impede the success of an acquisition. Mismatched values, resistance to change, communication breakdowns, loss of key talent, ineffective leadership, and inadequate cultural due diligence (or ignoring the cultural aspects of a deal and focusing solely on the financial ones) all contribute to the challenges faced during the integration process. Leaders and organizations must prioritize cultural alignment to enhance the likelihood of successful acquisitions.

How, whether, and to what extent an acquired organization can maintain bits and pieces of their culture while integrating into the acquiring organization is often of paramount concern and also contributes to their combined success. For example, having an open discussion about what each company values and believes can often highlight areas of communality that can be leveraged in how these values are manifest in behaviors and are rewarded. Aspects of both companies' cultures should be evaluated and understood to facilitate synthetization and optimization, where possible. Leaders must be willing to look at themselves and their organizations with a critical eye and be honest about their organizations' way of working, communication, and decision-making styles, as well as about unspoken rules of engagement.

Time and energy need to be expended on identifying the critical and emblematic elements of each organization's culture to understand what differences may exist and where communality can be leveraged. Risk areas need to be identified and mitigated early to ensure employees do not have preconceived notions or misconceptions, and/or come face to face with a situation where they feel so disconnected that it becomes a reason to leave the company. Having a clear understanding of, and being able to tangibly communicate, the culture beyond catchphrases and lists of values enables employees to more easily embrace the new culture and can better direct change management and employee experience activities. Such discussions can result from initial due diligence, or more often because of surveys and focus groups with acquired employees post-acquisition. Using this information, acquired leaders can more effectively advocate for the critical parts of their organization's culture and provide an opportunity for the acquired employees to share their perspectives on critical components of their organization's culture. Drawing upon this information allows the employees to see and feel their organizational culture being reflected in the acquired organization's culture.

For example, office locations of the acquired companies will often be closed, and employees will be expected to move to the acquiring company's offices. Concerns may exist on how to maintain a company's culture when their defined space has been eliminated, commute times increased, office amenities and office setups altered, etc. Or, in cases where the acquired company has an entirely remote working environment, employees may worry about the personal changes they will need to make if required to work in an office. In other cases, where rapid growth is pursued, significant hiring can dilute the acquired company culture and cause unanticipated consequences.

Acquired leaders can be actively engaged in creating energy around the upcoming changes and rally their organization toward something employees can be a part of, or they can acquiesce to the acquiring organization's culture and increase the risk of their employees exiting the organization. However, it is not just the acquiring organization's executives that play a guiding role in an organization's culture. Management sitting right below the executive suite (often referred to as the "operational leadership team") have a tremendous impact on employees' lived experience. These leaders often set, and influence, the tone of their teams. Executive leaders must recognize this level of management's role in "selling" the new organization to their employees. If the leaders themselves are not confident and bought into the culture and future of the organization, it will trickle down to their teams and negatively influence morale and job performance. In essence, they must champion the culture and lead the changes needed to realize the new/modified culture.

When an organization with a tight-knit culture starts seeing it erode, the resignations that occur tend to snowball, leaving the acquiring organization with an attrition problem that may threaten the business case and overall success. It is recommended that information and insights be gathered anonymously from employees via surveys and focus groups, as well as round tables and one-on-one meetings. Timely, visible action by acquired and acquiring leaders on the concerns raised is paramount to securing employee trust and commitment, and identifying and managing any issues that impact the business case. Dedicated project management by the IE and/or HR can ensure progress is being made on the issue areas. Sometimes acquired organizations may institute dedicated employee experience and change management teams for this purpose.

An acquisition can impact an organization long after the deal has closed and the integration completed, as the cultural changes may take years to be manifest. For example, the recent problems with Boeing aircraft quality were reported to have roots in their acquisition of McDonald-Douglas in 1997 (Tang, 2024). In this case, company leadership began prioritizing a financial return culture (McDonald-Douglas) over that of product engineering and quality (Boeing). Where the product has a long production time, it may take decades for the lack of culture alignment to manifest as significant quality or other customer-impacting issues. Leaders must recognize that they play an indispensable and continual role in defining and sustaining a shared culture that strongly contributes to the achievement of the deal's goals and long-term success.

Role of Leaders in Communications

Leaders play a vital role in communication within organizations by setting the vision, fostering open dialogue, practicing active listening, providing feedback, adapting their communication styles, managing crises, and building a communication-centric culture. Their ability to effectively communicate influences employee engagement, organizational alignment, and overall performance. In an acquisition, leaders should err on the side of overcommunicating in the face of a new and ambiguous situation. The sentiments of empathy, care, and concern must start from the top of the organization, with acquired CEOs assuming five different roles (Gadiesh et al., 2002):

- *Visionary*: Articulating the organization's future.
- *Cheerleader*: Addressing employee and customer concerns while building excitement for what is to come.

- *Closer*: Bringing the acquisition to fruition by closing the deal.
- *Captain*: Overseeing integration activities.
- *Crusader*: Setting forth the rules of engagement in terms of ways of working.

Acquired leaders sometimes fail to consider the key role they must play in reducing fear, uncertainty, and doubt, while also maintaining, rebuilding, or establishing trust that their employees should experience during the integration process. In essence, sometimes acquired leaders stop leading. In the absence of clear and transparent communication, individuals tend to fill in the gaps with their own worst-case scenarios. Initially, acquired employees will often be confused and surprised by an announcement, or have their suspicions and fears confirmed. Misconceptions and/or stereotypes about the acquiring company's brand and business model may lead to immediate concerns. Acquired employees will wonder how the deal will impact them personally. Concerns will often include who they will be working with, their compensation, day-to-day activities, etc. Naturally, employees from both sides of the acquisition will have numerous questions and concerns ranging from why the acquisition is occurring and how the acquired organization will fit into the acquiring organization, through to tactical and personal concerns such as compensation and benefits plans, ways of working, etc. Leaders must recognize that the impact of acquisitions is not relegated only to the operational aspects of the organizations but also has substantial person-level impacts leading individuals to go through the various stages of grief (Kubler-Ross, 1969). It is at this level that acquired and acquiring leaders play a critical role in keeping employees engaged and committed.

Crafting communication plans must begin during the due diligence phase as rumors regarding the acquisition will fill the informal communication channels long before formal communication messages are executed. Rumors and misinformation find fertile ground in the ambiguity surrounding an acquisition. If not addressed with open and honest communications, they can fester into suspicion and distrust.

Acquired employees often look to their senior leaders and managers for information rather than the leaders of the acquiring company. However, too often, acquired leaders have limited information, feel reluctant to share anything if they are not certain about the accuracy and relevance of the information, or do not feel "authorized" to share it. The integration team must arm and enable acquired leaders with accurate and transparent information to help them lead their organization through the impending changes. The lack of information or perceived lack of information from the acquired leadership team can alter how acquired employees view their leaders in terms of how much power or influence their leaders will have in the new organization. Should employees see their leaders lose confidence, or perceive them to be relegated to passengers that are just along for the ride, they will become even more anxious and uncertain about the future ahead.

An open management forum is also recommended to ensure all leaders have access to the same information and the opportunity to ask questions and discuss needs. This forum can be hosted weekly by the IE early in the integration and slowly reduced in frequency as the integration progresses. Additionally, acquired leaders must feel comfortable in reaching out to secure answers to their employees' questions while also anticipating concerns and intentionally addressing them. The integration team, led by the IE, should also have an overall communications plan and timeline that is coordinated and managed by communications staff, which reassures employees on when information will be shared.

Leaders must avoid any temptation to state or imply that nothing will change following an acquisition, as employees will feel deceived after being told by acquiring leaders that "nothing changes," which is impossible. Breaking employee trust and psychological contracts at the early stages of such a monumental event can have catastrophic consequences leading to resentment as well as perceptions of "us vs. them" and "winners vs. losers" throughout the integration period. Open and ongoing communications can help leaders navigate through these change dynamics.

If inaccurate or misleading information has been circulated, it behooves leaders to be intentional and transparent with their organization in identifying the miscommunication and providing clarity to the employees. Oftentimes the cliché "there are so many moving parts" is quite true during an integration, and having a holistic handle on every downstream implication is nearly impossible. Being open and honest about the complexities, decisions, and considerations being taken will help bring employees into the fold and provide a sense of shared understanding.

Leaders must actively articulate clear and tight alignment between the future vision of the combined organization and the acquired organization's original goals and vision, as well as the timing of the integration and associated milestones that will be met. This alignment is critical to avoid the "us vs. them" mentality across the leadership teams of the different organizations, which inevitably would trickle down to the rest of the employee populations. Each stakeholder population should have a clear understanding of the value proposition for them. For example, employees should understand their future learning and career development opportunities, and acquiring managers need to understand the talent and skills available to them.

In addition, it is critical for leaders to be intentional about communicating a drumbeat of successes and wins right after the close and then on a regular basis, to assist in the perception of information being meaningfully shared with the broader organization and provide an opportunity to celebrate. Furthermore, it is crucial to emphasize why the acquired employees are critical to the path for future success. Oftentimes the employee mission in the acquired company is clear and they have been cohesively working toward the same goal. Clarity around what that unified vision, strategy, and mission will be as part of the acquired organization will be essential for employees to embrace their new reality. Leaders should generate excitement for the journey ahead and the opportunities that it will afford everyone, or in some cases, how any downsizing will be managed as part of the plan.

While words and communications are critically important for acquired employees to feel connected and informed, leaders must not discount the impact their presence and actions have on their employees. Multiple communication methods and tools should be utilized extensively. For example, hosting "Ask Me Anything" sessions and town halls, crafting and disseminating integration newsletters, creating an acquisition-specific internal communication forum (e.g., Slack or Teams channel), deploying an acquisition-specific chat bot, creating a web page that serves as a hub for FAQs and other pertinent information are often among the ongoing communications toolsets. If the organizational culture has been one of transparency, open-door policies, etc., ensure that leaders remain readily accessible. Continuing with the modes of communications that have served the employee population well in the past helps ease the transition.

In addition, remaining visible and having continuity in leadership (Birkinshaw et al., 2000) as well as leaders' levels of initiative (Teerikangas et al., 2011) contribute to more positive post-acquisition outcomes. Too often, acquired leaders spend significant time away from the office meeting with various acquiring company groups and customers. While important for operational reasons, acquired employees may feel abandoned if this absence is not managed appropriately. A list of some common pitfalls and associated recommendations can be found in Table 19.1.

Table 19.1 Sample Leader Pitfalls and Associated Recommendations

Pitfall	Recommendation
Implementing arbitrary timelines for various integration activities	Be and keep others informed about the time and resources required for the execution of each major integration activity. Attend integration briefings.
Assuming the acquiring organization has a known playbook for all integration activities	While the overarching set of integration activities are set, depending on the business case for the acquired organization, exceptions may be beneficial for all parties involved. Remain flexible.
Assuming all processes and procedures within the acquiring organization are nonnegotiable	Collect data on any overly onerous processes and procedures and the impact they have in order to recommend changes. Advocate for your teams.
Not fully recognizing the resources needed to complete integration activities	Recognize that revenue and productivity will be temporarily negatively impacted during the integration phase as specific, often critical, employees will split their time between integration activities and their standard roles and responsibilities. Be mindful of burnout. Request additional resources as needed.
Assuming communications and messaging are being received and landing as intended	Keep all parties apprised of changes, updates, vision, and future activities with intentional focus on the "why" in addition to the "what" and "when." Communicate as much as possible (and needed) via multiple types of channels. Do not assume that sending a communication means it is received and/or understood.
Focusing only on the operational necessities of an integration	Make sure to stay apprised of employee sentiments. An acquisition is a life-changing event for employees as they are joining a new organization via a move based on a decision that they did not have a say in. Provide avenues for employees to share thoughts and feedback. Act on feedback.

Organizational structure changes require strong partnerships and communication not just within but across organizations to ensure the appropriate messages and rationales are shared, especially if downsizing or reorganizations are planned. Again, open and honest communications on any downsizing plan needs to address employee concerns and questions. Often, employees in general and administrative functions (legal, HR, finance, etc.) are given transition payments to secure support during a defined transition period. Once the transition or integration is complete, some may be given offers of jobs in other organizations or assistance in finding a new role in the new organization. The IE plays an important role in assisting the reassignment of impacted employees.

Ideally, thoughtful conversations covering individual employee skills, criticality to business continuity, attrition risk, and growth potential will take place prior to any workforce management decisions being executed. The profiles of employees who have been identified for resource management should be made available to the broader acquiring company to see if they can be slotted into open requisitions. Skip-level interviews and stay interviews can provide insights into individual person-level challenges, misalignments, and other issues employees have that may have otherwise been overlooked. Additionally, celebrating the contributions of the "transitional" employees prior to their exit demonstrates good will and acknowledgment of their work.

Providing an open path for communication and feedback from the broader employee population back to the leadership team, along with a concerted effort to address any problem areas, maintains leader engagement with employees during the integration. Here are some questions that are consistently of great interest to acquired employees:

- What does it mean to be an employee in the new organization?
- How will my day-to-day activities differ?
- How does my reporting structure change?
- How will my career path and growth be impacted?
- How will my work team change?

A sample of commonly asked employee questions is shown in Figure 19.3.

Communication is a two-way street. In addition to leader messages out to the organization, they must also actively pursue and address input from the acquiring and acquired employees. Similarly to what was described in the section "Role of Leaders: Culture," this can be done via periodic surveys and focus groups that protect anonymity to enable open and honest feedback. One of the most critical pieces of the puzzle is that leaders must be willing to acknowledge and act on incoming feedback in a timely manner. For a leader to demonstrate commitment to understanding issues, engaging employees in problem-solving, and openly sharing actions is essential to facilitating acquisition success. Acquiring company employees may also have similar questions and concerns about how the new company impacts them.

In addition to securing employee engagement, acquired leaders are often the key contact with their customers during the acquisition process. Like

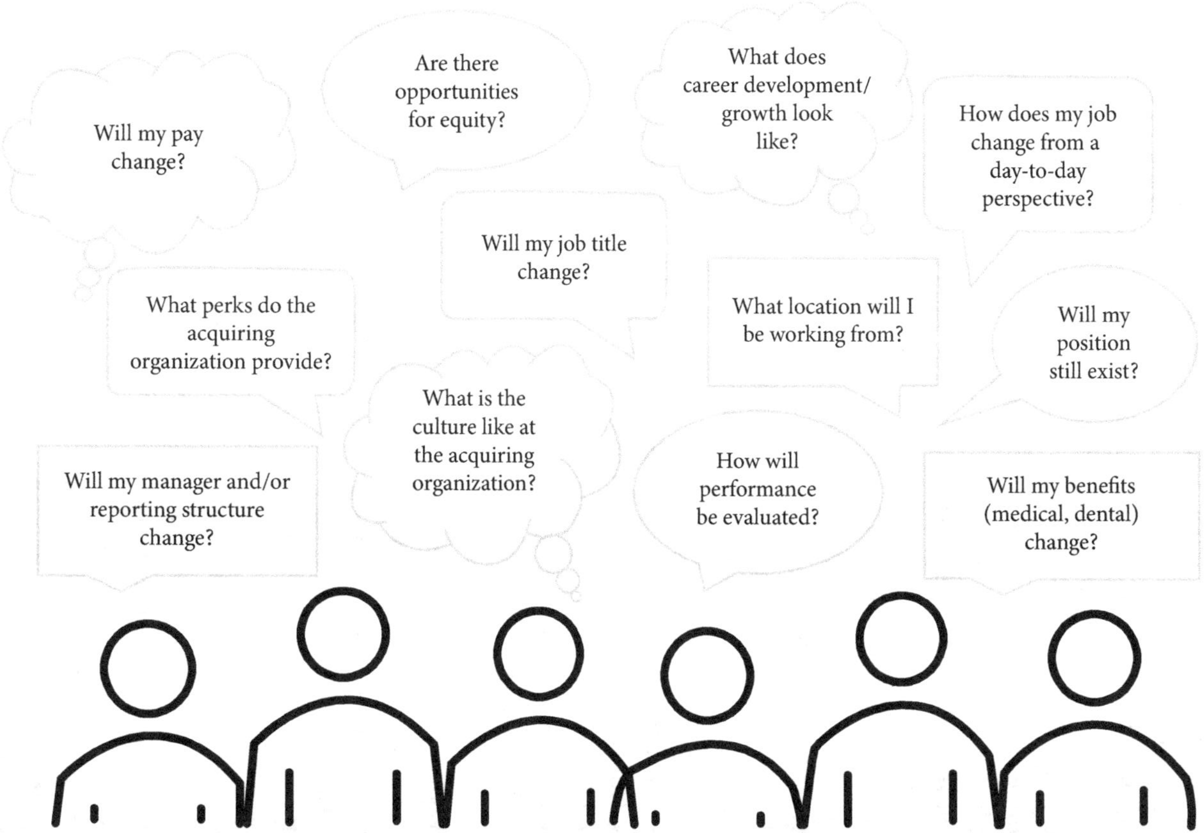

Figure 19.3 Examples of Questions Employees Have after an Acquisition Is Announced

employees, customers will want to know what the changes mean to them and their business. The customer may have a past relationship with the acquiring company that will influence their perceptions of the acquisition. When a small company is acquired by a larger one, clients may worry about getting "lost" in the larger company, concerned that there may be changes to the pricing of services or assets, or that previous agility will now be replaced with bureaucracy, etc. Active engagement with customers on the value proposition of the combined organization to their business success will be critical to prevent churn. Acquired leaders need to clearly communicate the vision, impending changes, and any relevant information to client-facing employees, who are often the face of the acquired organization to their clients. Without a unified understanding and approach, different client teams may hear different "stories," which will ultimately cause unwarranted frustration and concern. Managing these messages while also being available to address employee concerns is a balance leaders need to make during the integration process.

Furthermore, multinational acquisitions pose added communications challenges for leaders as county and local language, laws, customs, cultures, and practices often dictate what, how, and when communications can occur. For example, an acquisition with a European component will often have a significant delay in transitioning employees into the acquiring organization when compared to their North American or Asian colleagues, due to negotiations with works councils and other legal requirements. Leaders need to be aware of the communication differences and be mindful to ensure the European employees do not feel neglected or get mixed messages through the informal communications channels. The impact of international time zones on communications cannot be underestimated as sentiments of inequity can quickly build. While inconvenient, leaders must be willing to accommodate different time zones to ensure their messages are received and understood (Battista et al., 2010).

Role of Leaders in Governance

Organizational governance involves processes and structures for decision-making, accountability, controls, and behaviors designed to accomplish an organization's objectives (Bahrman, 2011). It refers to how the organization manages itself through policies and processes that serve as guardrails and frameworks for power sharing and decision-making behavior by the organization to protect the interests of stakeholders—be it customers, employees, investors, or society at large—and efficiently and effectively achieve the organization's goals. It encompasses establishing management processes and organizational culture, and promoting shared values.

The top executives are responsible for defining and managing their organization's governance processes. These processes have likely been instituted and evolved based heavily on the influence and insights of these leaders. When organizational governance is done well, roles, responsibilities, and accountabilities are effectively defined and employees are aware of who or what group of individuals have accountability and authority for specific areas (Bahrman, 2011).

Establishing a governance system early in the acquisition process will reduce issues with role clarity (the clear definition of responsibilities, expectations, and authority associated with a particular position within an organization) and plays a crucial role in reducing conflict among employees and teams. Establishing clear governance among leaders and teams early in the integration process significantly reduces conflict in organizations by minimizing ambiguity, enhancing collaboration, improving accountability, aiding conflict resolution, and increasing job satisfaction (Bakker et al., 2008; Hackman & Oldham, 1976; Kahn et al., 1964; Rizzo et al., 1970; Tjosvold, 2008). By ensuring that employees understand their (and others') roles and responsibilities, organizations can create a more harmonious and productive work environment. It will also provide the foundation for ongoing collaboration during the integration process and enable ongoing positive relationships among the leadership teams.

Collaborating on, and establishing, an effective governance system from day one will avoid significant confusion over decision ownership and daily management (Merger Integration, n.d., para. 1):

> Good governance is about setting up the team structure and protocols, so the right people get involved at the right times, take the right steps in the right sequence, provide the right information, and achieve the right goals, as opposed to having the teams scattering in all directions absent any coordination.

Prior research also highlights the importance of role clarity to enable effective performance and avoid conflict (Tjosvold, 2008). Additionally, defining task accountability (e.g., via a framework such as Responsible/

Accountable/Consulted/Informed, often referred to as "RACI") can help further define and document key activities.

Governance systems for an integration often include the following elements:

- Defining how decisions are made, who makes them, and whether there is an appellate process
- Addressing scope of authority, "powers reserved," and delegations
- Documenting how problems are escalated and conflicts resolved
- Establishing a framework for joint review processes
- Enabling and facilitating communications

The establishment of a governance system is, however, only one part of the process. Organizational governance can only be effective when it has been clearly communicated and broadly accepted, with an ongoing mechanism to assess effectiveness. There can be no misconceptions or assumptions. Everyone involved needs to be speaking the same language and be on the same page.

As described in the section "Role of Leaders: Communications," one of the key roles of leaders, is enhanced and enabled through the governance system where employee questions can be raised and consistent answers developed. One best practice for acquisitions is for the acquisition IE to host a full-day, in-person meeting at the beginning of the integration process to discuss the governance system and the associated support mechanisms. Securing the appropriate attendees is critical and should include both leaders from the acquired and acquiring businesses. This meeting is also a good opportunity to begin building the trusting relationships needed for integration success.

A sample leadership alignment session agenda, which can be split into two days, is shown in Figure 19.4.

A regular cadence of follow-up meetings after leader-alignment session(s) ensures that issues are raised and addressed quickly, and that timely decisions are made, communicated, and executed upon. While this is an important element of any smooth-running business, it is especially critical in the early stages of an integration to avoid siloed thinking and facilitate a holistic integration strategy. As the integration progresses, these meetings are often folded into existing business-as-usual governance processes.

One important leadership decision made early in the acquisition process is the degree of company integration that is desired or needed to secure the expected business outcomes. In some cases, it may be preferable to

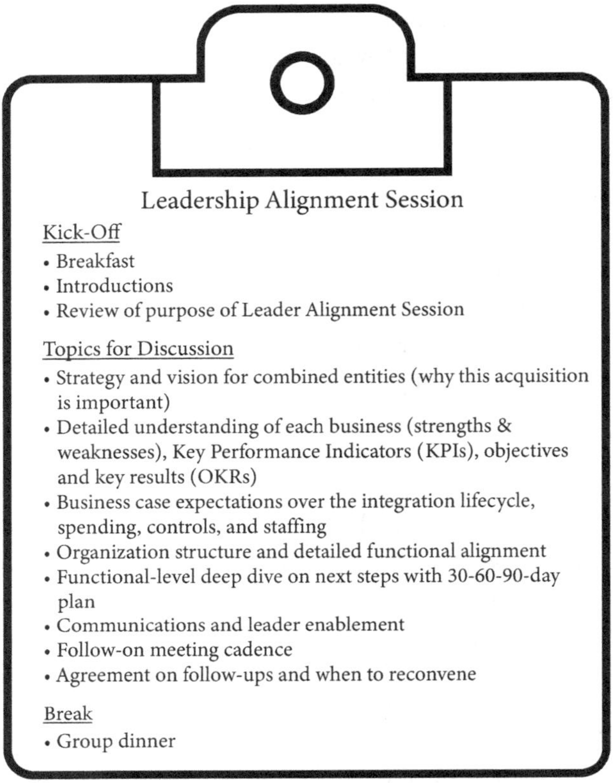

Figure 19.4 A Sample Leadership Alignment Session Agenda

keep the organizations separate. In other cases, varying levels of integration may be most appropriate. Regardless of the decision, leaders will need to communicate the decision and reasoning to give employees reassurances about their future.

Leaders as People and the Relationships They Hold

While managing productivity, changes in processes, systems and policies, and all the other areas of execution related to an acquisition, leaders must also reflect on what their own futures will look like in the new organization. In the case where a smaller, innovative startup is acquired by a larger, legacy organization, there most likely will be an inherent incongruence between what it means to be a founder of the startup and what it means to be an employee in a large organization.

Founders typically will have a strong entrepreneurial mindset that may or may not be in alignment with their new role within the larger organization. Leaders will need time to assess their own interests and motivations for remaining with the acquiring organization. For example, these leaders may want to ponder the following questions:

- Why are we selling the organization?
- Do we have a clear vision of what the organization looks like moving forward?
- What does the future look like for me personally?
- How will the organization survive if I leave?

Many acquired leaders have invested years of their "blood, sweat, and tears" into the establishment and success of their company. Not only will their job titles change, but their organization will often cease to exist—not just in terms of the name and brand of the organization no longer being a legally recognized entity, but often also because their employees will be disbanded and absorbed into existing teams within the acquiring organization.

Having had the freedom and responsibility of full control of their organizations, leaders' job titles often hold a special place in their hearts. In many cultures, individuals have been trained, and in some ways indoctrinated, to respect and be deferential to people based on the job title they hold. For many, their job titles become deeply entangled with their identity and therefore feed into their self-perceptions of worth and esteem, which then impacts their motivation. In a larger, more bureaucratic organization, one's job title also impacts whether you receive a "call back" or attention from others in the new organization. Losing the impact and influence that a title carries may be a factor in the decision to remain in the organization or to leave. In many cases, and especially where a smaller company is brought into a larger one, the acquired leaders at the Senior Executive or C-suite level may become lower-level executives, or even non-executives, in the acquiring organization. Even when compensation may be comparable, the perceived value and impact the job title carries is very different. This can cause regrettable attrition if not managed effectively.

An acquisition has a tremendous impact on the leaders of both the acquired and acquiring company in terms of the amount of direct influence each individual leader will have. For example, you are the CEO of your successful startup. You are the leader of your company, and, while you have been a key driver of the acquisition process, the day the transaction of sale closes, everything changes (possibly despite expectations, and potential assurances from the acquirer, that "nothing will change"). On Monday you were making key investment and business direction decisions, the deal closed on Tuesday, and by Wednesday those decisions and plans are being reviewed by another company's leadership team, and that team is now the ultimate decision maker. The changes to a leader's power, influence, and personal impact after the acquisition closes cannot be overemphasized.

Furthermore, "serial entrepreneurs" and leaders hired by any funding agency (e.g., venture capital or private equity) are more likely to leave once the deal closes. Founders may be more likely to remain with the organization if they feel committed to the vision for the new organization and/or if they are bound by contracts with financial incentives tied to staying. Oftentimes retention packages (with payouts structured over multiple years) are awarded to key leaders in an attempt to maintain a level of stability during the integration.

Acquiring leaders need to have a clear understanding of the leadership skills and talents they need to sustain and grow the new integrated organization. Rapid enablement including education on the acquiring organization, ability to partner with acquiring leaders to define the go-forward mission and strategy, maintaining their level of influence and scope, access to mentors/coaches, and financial incentives can assist in building a compelling value proposition for remaining with the organization. Often, when acquired leaders feel they have impact, are valued, and are being heard, they are more likely to remain with the new company. This includes providing additional support to build their resilience and enabling them to adapt to, and champion, the changes the organization will experience during the integration. Providing a meaningful role with associated title (as well as compensation, benefits, and perquisites) can also secure the leaders' commitment to the new organization and open doors to the acquiring company.

Unfortunately, in many cases, acquisition scenarios will result in a reduction in headcount. For an acquisition, the general and administrative (G&A) function of the acquired organization, including the C-suite leaders of the G&A function, is often the hardest hit. Being able to effectively lead their teams through the anxious times while attempting to secure their own futures is a scenario that requires finesse and fortitude. These leaders' own insecurities about their personal futures and goals need to be set aside when they attempt to quell the anxiety and ambiguity of the future for the broader employee population. Oftentimes these leaders have built their business functions from scratch and have personally hired many of their team members. The leaders will need to serve as an advocate for their organization, their teams, and themselves to provide a smooth transition for all. As noted earlier, transition bonus pay (typically a retention payment for key individuals to retain them for a specific amount of time) for functions impacted by downsizing will help smooth the transition over a set timeline. Typically, these individuals are within the finance, accounting, HR, legal, IT, and facility operations functions, wherein these individuals have specific insights and experience to facilitate integration activities (e.g., transferring employee data, closing financial books, paying out incentives on discontinued systems, etc.).

Developing Acquired Leaders

One of the key challenges faced by incoming acquired leaders is understanding the basics of their new organizational home as well as building their skills as leaders in the organization. There is often tremendous variability in acquired leader skills. Many leaders have significant acquisition experience and have worked at larger, sophisticated companies in the past, when they were included in ongoing leadership development activities. In other cases, such as with leaders of small startups, leaders may not have been exposed to dedicated leadership training. This variability requires initial leadership assessments to tailor development offerings beyond the basics of the new organization. Once assessed, focused classes and experiences can be offered to build the leadership strength needed for success. Securing mentors or "buddies" in the acquiring organization can provide real-time insights into the organization. In some cases, executive coaching may be valuable to assist with the transition. For an acquisition, enabling resilience and adaptability can provide support to the change sponsorship and champion roles the leaders must fulfill.

While there may be pressure to immediately grow revenue and focus on customers to meet the acquisition's business case, it is critical that training

Table 19.2 Sample List of Knowledge Areas for Acquired Leaders

What Acquired Leaders Need to Know
The basics of the acquiring organization (e.g., organization structure, functions/business units, senior executives, culture, etc.)
The basics of people leadership (supported by a needs assessment to tailor offerings to the acquired leaders)
How to gain alignment and support across multiple parties
How to get connected with mentors, buddies, and other key relationships
The new organizational structure and how it will operate (governance)
How to be a change leader and effect change within a new environment
The importance of, and how to increase, personal resiliency and adaptability
How to get plugged into existing career and talent management processes (e.g., succession planning, career paths, etc.)
How to operate within a new organization; the informal ways of work
The concerns, questions, and needs of your employees and how to facilitate their engagement
How to identify and mitigate potential risks

and skill building be timely, as establishing the foundation is easier than trying to correct it at a later point. Providing such training six months after the acquisition closes, while still valuable, is often too late. A nimble leadership development delivery mechanism and team to rapidly address the needs of the acquired leaders is required as it is the "fast start" to their success. Table 19.2 includes a sample list of knowledge areas beneficial for acquired leaders.

Key Takeaways

Acquisitions represent a unique challenge to each affected organization's leadership with significant and far-reaching consequences. From organizational direction and strategy to personal implications for role and influence, enabling the acquired leadership team during the integration phase will help secure long-term success and business case achievement. Here are the key roles leaders play in an acquisition:

- Defining and aligning the differing organization's cultures and actively advocating for the organization's culture and ways of operating
- Crafting communications to sustain employee morale and secure needed input during the integration
- Securing and acting on employee issues and concerns in a timely and visible manner
- Building a governance system to provide role clarity, avoid conflict, and ensure that timely decisions are made
- Managing the additional complications of multinational integration and ensuring appropriate and culturally sensitive communications are distributed across countries and time zones
- Creating a shared vision of the future that all employees can be excited about and aligned with
- Understanding and managing employees' personal desires and motivations

Effective leadership makes the difference between success and failure, achieving the business case or falling short, as well as the ease with which necessary integration activities are conducted. By understanding and embracing the multifaceted roles and responsibilities leaders must undertake, they can better guide their organizations through the integration process, minimize disruptions, and foster a unified, high-performing entity. We hope that the insights and recommendations provided in this chapter will enable leaders to make informed decisions that will ultimately contribute to the success of their organization regardless of the type or industry of the acquisition.

References

Bahrman, D. (2011). Evaluating and improving organizational governance. *The Institute of Internal Auditors Research Foundation.* https://www.theiia.org/en/content/guidance/recommended/supplemental/practice-guides/assessing-organizational-governance-in-the-private-sector/

Bakker, A. B., Schaufeli, W. B., Leiter, M. P., & Taris, T. W. (2008). Work engagement: An emerging concept in occupational health psychology. *Work & Stress, 22*(3), 187–200.

Battista, M., Pedigo, P. R., & Derosiers, E. (2010). Navigating the complexities of a global organization. In Kyle Lundby & Jeffrey Jolton (Ed.), *Going global: Practical applications and recommendations for HR and OD professionals in the global workplace* (pp. 1–21). Jossey-Bass.

Birkinshaw, J., Bresman, H., & Hakanson, L. (2000). Managing the post-acquisition integration process: How the human integration and task integration processes interact to foster value creation. *Journal of Management Studies, 37*(30), 395–425.
Bruner, R. F. (2004). *Applied mergers and acquisitions.* John Wiley & Sons.
Christensen, C. M., Alton, R., Rising, C., & Waldeck, A. (2011). The big idea: The M&A playbook. *Harvard Business Review, 89*(3). https://hbr.org/2011/03/the-big-idea-the-new-ma-playbook
DePamphilis, D. M. (2010). *Mergers, acquisitions, and other restructuring activities.* Academic Press.
Gadiesh, O., Buchanan, R., Daniell, M., & Ormiston, C. (2002). A CEO's guide to the new challenges of M&A leadership. *Strategy & Leadership, 30,* 13–18.
Gaughan, P. A. (2017). *Mergers, acquisitions, and corporate restructurings* (7th ed). John Wiley & Sons.
Hackman, J. R., & Oldham, G. R. (1976). Motivation through the design of work: Test of a theory. *Organizational Behavior and Human Performance, 16*(2), 250–279.
Junni, P., & Sarala, R. M. (2014). The role of leadership in mergers and acquisitions: A review of recent empirical studies. *Advances in Mergers and Acquisitions, 13,* 181–200.
Kahn, R. L., Wolfe, D. M., Quinn, R. P., Snoek, J. D., & Rosenthal, R. A. (1964). *Organizational stress: Studies in role conflict and ambiguity.* John Wiley & Sons.
Koller, T., Goedhart, M., & Wessels, D. (2010). *Valuation: measuring and managing the value of companies.* John Wiley & Sons.
Kubler-Ross, E. (1969). *On death and dying.* The Macmillan Company.
Merger Integration. (n.d.). *Step 2: Establishing M&A integration governance.* https://www.mergerintegration.com/integration-strategy-and-governance
Rizzo, J. R., House, R. J., & Lirtzman, S. I. (1970). Role conflict and ambiguity in complex organizations. *Administrative Science Quarterly, 15*(2), 150–163.
Tang, C. (2024, February 8). The merger that brought Boeing low. *Newsweek Opinion.* https://www.newsweek.com/merger-that-brought-boeing-low-opinion-1867937
Teerikangas, S., Very, P., & Pisano, V. (2011). Integration managers' value-capturing roles and acquisition performance. *Human Resource Management, 50*(5), 651–683.
Tjosvold, D. (2008). Conflict avoidance and effectiveness in work teams. *International Journal of Conflict Management, 19*(2), 151–169.

20

Innovations in Developing the Intrapreneurial Mindset

Archie Jones Jr., Xolani Nghona, and Angela Jackson

Introduction

The rapid acceleration of technological change, combined with volatile global market conditions, has fundamentally reshaped assumptions about what effective leadership entails. Traditional, hierarchical leadership models—once considered reliable for maintaining efficiency and stability—are increasingly giving way to more adaptive, entrepreneurial frameworks (Christensen, 1997; Heifetz et al., 2009). Within this evolving landscape, intrapreneurship—the cultivation of entrepreneurial thinking and behavior inside established organizations by employees—has emerged as a pivotal force driving sustainable growth and competitive advantage (Pinchot, 1985; Morris et al., 2011; Jackson 2025). Leaders who succeed in this new environment are not merely reactive; instead, they proactively foster innovation from within, anticipate customer needs, and guide their organizations to pivot ahead of market disruptions (Dyer et al., 2011; Ibarra, 2015).

In this context, developing an intrapreneurial mindset is no longer a luxury reserved for a visionary few; it has become essential for leaders at all levels of an organization who aspire to keep their organizations relevant and resilient (Dess et al., 2003; Jackson, 2025). It is imperative for companies striving not only to succeed but to also thrive in the future to cultivate an intrapreneurial culture—one that encourages intelligent risk-taking, embraces lessons from experimentation, and supports creative problem-solving. These qualities enable organizations to uncover new opportunities amid uncertainty (Kuratko, 2017).

Such organizations and their leaders establish psychological safety—an environment in which individuals feel safe to express their ideas, take

Archie Jones Jr., Xolani Nghona, and Angela Jackson, *Innovations in Developing the Intrapreneurial Mindset*. In: *The Changing Leadership Landscape*. Edited by: Sheri L. Feinzig and Mariangela Battista, Oxford University Press. © Oxford University Press (2026). DOI: 10.1093/9780197820070.003.0020 risks, ask questions, and admit mistakes without fear of punishment or humiliation—and cultivate a culture that views failure not as a setback but as a learning opportunity, thereby empowering employees to iterate ideas rapidly (Schein, 2010; Edmondson, 2019). Moreover, they harness open communication channels and social networks to connect individuals across silos, facilitating the flow of knowledge and fostering the kind of collaborative climate that gives rise to breakthrough innovations (Baker, 2000; Pentland, 2014).

This chapter leverages the Leadership Capital Framework (LCF) to demonstrate how five core elements—Capability, Culture, Communication, Connection, and Confidence—can be deliberately cultivated to foster intrapreneurial leadership (Jones, 2024). As research suggests, building the right capabilities (technical, interpersonal, strategic) enhances an organization's adaptability and responsiveness (Goleman, 2000). Shaping a supportive culture encourages experimentation and continuous learning, while clear and transparent communication ensures that information moves fluidly throughout the firm (Snowdon & Boone, 2007). Fostering strong connections within and beyond organizational boundaries taps into social capital and strengthens the idea-sharing networks essential for sustaining innovation (Baker, 2000). Finally, instilling confidence in employees fosters the courage to test new approaches, learn from failures, and refine their strategies—an ongoing cycle vital to intrapreneurial success (Duhigg, 2016).

This chapter will provide real-world examples drawn from recognized organizations to illustrate how these principles translate into practice. By examining how companies have incorporated the LCF elements, leaders can glean insights into how to architect organizations that are more agile, resilient, and poised for continuous renewal. Ultimately, the goal is to equip leaders with the mindset, tools, and evidence-based strategies to thrive in an era where change is not an occasional disruption but a constant driver of opportunity.

Understanding Intrapreneurship: The New Leadership Paradigm

Sweeping technological advancements, ongoing disruptions to global supply chains, and ever-evolving customer preferences have dramatically transformed the environment in which organizations operate. We once lived in a world where a firm's success hinged largely on its capacity to refine established business models and execute well-defined processes at scale (Christensen, 1997). That era, however, is fading quickly. Companies now face an environment marked by volatility, uncertainty, complexity, and ambiguity (VUCA), concepts first popularized by leadership studies in the US Army War College and subsequently discussed in strategic management literature (Bennett & Lemoine, 2014). In such conditions, the notion of "stability" has become elusive, and sustainable competitive advantage cannot be taken for granted.

To remain relevant, firms must identify new growth opportunities, adapt swiftly, and challenge entrenched assumptions about what customers want and how best to serve them (Heifetz et al., 2009; Dyer et al., 2011). It is against this backdrop that intrapreneurship emerges as a compelling new leadership paradigm. Traditional notions of leadership often evoke images of hierarchical chains of command and the careful stewardship of existing resources (Schein, 2010). In contrast, intrapreneurship reframes leadership as the capacity to cultivate entrepreneurial behaviors inside established organizations (Pinchot, 1985; Kuratko, 2017). It does this by allowing employees to look beyond their job descriptions and core business terrain and encouraging them to explore unmet customer needs, which enables an organization to develop new business models to offer innovative value propositions.

This is not entrepreneurship in the classic, external sense, where founders start a new venture from scratch. Instead, intrapreneurs operate within existing firms—often large, complex, and historically successful enterprises—leveraging established brand equity, supply chains, marketing channels, and customer relationships (Morris et al., 2011). Yet intrapreneurs face their own hurdles: overcoming organizational inertia, navigating internal politics, and persuading colleagues to embrace novel concepts. It takes a distinctive skill set to drive innovation in environments originally designed for execution rather than exploration (Christensen, 1997; Edmondson, 2019).

To fully understand intrapreneurship, consider the attributes of intrapreneurs. They seek and seize new opportunities, even when these opportunities challenge the firm's legacy logic (Dyer et al., 2011). Intrapreneurs are comfortable with uncertainty and, like external entrepreneurs, exhibit a tolerance for failure, recognizing that not every idea will succeed. Learning from missteps is part of the innovation process. Crucially, they do this work from within, leveraging institutional knowledge and resources while navigating established hierarchies and metrics of success.

Intrapreneurs lead, but their leadership does not always depend on title or formal authority. Rather, they lead through influence, persuasion, and the audacity of their ideas. They challenge the status quo and encourage organizations to reexamine core assumptions. Consider how many once-dominant firms were overtaken by disruptive innovations they failed to recognize or respond to in time (Christensen, 1997). Kodak hesitated as digital photography gained ground, Blockbuster was slow to counter Netflix's DVD-by-mail model, which paved the way for streaming's eventual dominance, and Borders found itself outmaneuvered by Amazon's online capabilities. In each case, entrenched assumptions and rigid processes got in the way of responding effectively to shifts in customer needs. An intrapreneurial mindset within these organizations might have prompted earlier, bolder experimentation, and thus a more agile response to emerging threats.

Research on disruptive innovation (Christensen, 1997; Dyer et al., 2011) suggests that established firms often stumble not due to ignorance or complacency, but because they excel at serving their core customers and executing a proven formula. This very success can hinder their ability to notice and capitalize on new opportunities. By cultivating intrapreneurship, organizations introduce a form of productive discontent—a mechanism for asking uncomfortable questions, exploring new technologies or business models, and anticipating changes in customer jobs to be done. Intrapreneurs help organizations look beyond their current success and consider how markets and technologies might evolve.

The growing importance of intrapreneurship is increasingly recognized. A global recruitment firm, Michael Page (2020), identified intrapreneurship as the most desirable skill of the year in 2020, reflecting a broader shift in what businesses consider essential leadership competencies. No longer is it enough to preserve the status quo. The modern leader must not only welcome intrapreneurial thinking but actively foster it within teams. Leaders who do so enable individuals and groups to experiment, learn rapidly, iterate ideas, and propose new offerings in response to shifting conditions (Ibarra, 2015; Kuratko, 2017).

Intrapreneurial leaders do more than encourage creativity; they build the environment that allows innovation to flourish. This involves fostering a culture in which failure is not stigmatized but recognized as part of the exploration process (Edmondson, 2019). They may design structures such as internal incubators or "innovation labs" where employees can test ideas quickly and at low cost. Some organizations have allocated "20% time" for employees to pursue passion projects, as was famously done by Google, fostering a pipeline of intrapreneurial concepts. Others stage hackathons and ideation challenges to surface employee-driven initiatives. By instituting these cultural and structural supports, leaders create conditions in which intrapreneurship becomes a natural, ongoing practice rather than a sporadic exception.

Crucially, unlike the traditional approach to innovation, where organizational innovation is exclusively expected from research and development (R&D) units, intrapreneurial capacity can emerge from anywhere within the firm. It might be found in middle management, customer-facing teams, or specialized R&D units (Morris et al., 2011). The key is that the organization learns how to identify and nurture such talent. By encouraging employees at all levels to interact with customers, observe emerging needs, and bring forward new ideas, companies ensure a steady stream of intrapreneurial opportunities. Social capital and robust communication networks within the organization are vital here (Baker, 2000; Pentland, 2014), as they enable the rapid circulation of insights and feedback that feed the iterative innovation cycle.

Another distinguishing factor of intrapreneurship is its risk-and-reward profile. Entrepreneurs who launch startups often do so because of their high tolerance for ambiguity and the potential for significant personal gains if they succeed. Intrapreneurs, conversely, operate in an environment where risk is mitigated by the firm's established infrastructure and resources. While personal financial rewards might be more modest, intrapreneurs can derive intrinsic satisfaction from seeing their ideas shape the company's future, influence strategic direction, and deliver greater value to customers (Dyer et al., 2011).

From a strategic perspective, cultivating intrapreneurship is about building organizational agility and optionality. When markets shift due to disruptive technologies or sudden changes in customer preferences, organizations equipped with intrapreneurial capabilities can pivot more smoothly. They have a reservoir of partially tested concepts, internal talent accustomed to experimentation, and leaders who understand the need for balanced exploration and exploitation (March, 1991). This optionality acts as a buffer against obsolescence and stagnation, helping the firm navigate complexity and remain relevant over time.

However, intrapreneurship is not without its challenges. Tensions can arise between short-term targets and long-term innovation efforts. Managers may resist radical new ideas if they fear cannibalizing existing products or distracting them from core operations. Performance metrics designed for stable environments can punish the kind of experimentation that intrapreneurship requires. Overcoming these barriers demands leadership at the top that clearly communicates the strategic importance of intrapreneurship and aligns incentives to reward risk-taking, learning, and adaptation (Goleman, 2000; Edmondson, 2019).

Intrapreneurs themselves must also develop certain skills. They must master the art of storytelling—articulating the value of their ideas in ways that resonate with key stakeholders. They need to build coalitions, garner support from peers, and manage upward to gain executive sponsorship for their projects (Ibarra, 2015). Soft skills—also known as interpersonal skills—such as communication, adaptability, and problem-solving, become just as important as creativity in ensuring that bold ideas can move through the internal pipeline from concept to market test. Effective intrapreneurs understand how to navigate the company's structures, policies, and norms, turning potential obstacles into opportunities for refinement and engagement.

As the business environment continues to evolve, the pressure on organizations to cultivate intrapreneurial mindsets will only intensify. Disruptive technologies—artificial intelligence (AI), quantum computing, biotechnology, and others—promise to upend established industries and create entirely new ones. Consumer expectations, fueled by digital experiences and personalized services, will continue to rise. Against this backdrop, relying solely on old forms of leadership and management invites obsolescence. Intrapreneurship stands as a proactive response to these forces, granting firms the ability to sense and respond to shifts more rapidly and effectively. As a result, while Pinchot and Soltanifar (2021) noted that digitalization and digital transformation have opened new intrapreneurial possibilities, World Bank (2016) is of the view that digital intrapreneurs must possess the skills to identify new digital-technology-enabled business opportunities and bring them to fruition, either as a new concept altogether or as an existing, but transformed, business system.

In sum, intrapreneurship represents a fundamental rethinking of what it means to lead inside an organization. Rather than focusing exclusively on operational excellence and incremental improvements, leaders must become catalysts for internal innovation. They must create a climate in which employees are encouraged to think entrepreneurially, to experiment, and to develop new growth paths from within. By aligning culture, structure, and incentives to support these behaviors, leaders help their organizations become more adaptive, more resilient, and ultimately more capable of competing in a world of relentless change.

This new leadership paradigm is not a passing trend; it is a strategic imperative. As global markets morph and customer demands evolve, the organizations that successfully internalize intrapreneurship are those most likely to thrive. Intrapreneurs ensure that a company's relevance extends into the future, not just by meeting today's challenges, but by anticipating tomorrow's opportunities.

The Leadership Capital Framework: A Blueprint for Developing Intrapreneurial Leaders

The LCF provides a structured approach for developing the key traits and capabilities required for intrapreneurial leadership. This framework, illustrated in Figure 20.1, emphasizes five core components—Capability, Culture, Communication, Connection, and Confidence—that are essential for fostering a leadership style and environment that encourages creativity, risk-taking, and innovation (Jones, 2024).

Capability: Recognizing and Leveraging Individual Superpowers

The first C in the LCF is *Capability*. Every leader possesses unique strengths, or what we refer to as "superpowers." These capabilities are not always tied to job titles or formal roles but are often the innate or developed talents that

Figure 20.1 Leadership Capital Framework Elements

allow individuals to excel in specific areas. For some, their capability might be a talent for inspiring others, while for others, it could be the ability to analyze large amounts of data and distill them into actionable insights. Leaders who are aware of their capabilities and those of their team members are better positioned to drive intrapreneurial efforts. They can identify which individuals are best suited for specific opportunities and encourage employees to develop their strengths in ways that align with organizational goals. Intrapreneurial capability often involves a deep sense of curiosity, creativity, and a willingness to challenge existing norms.

The founding of OUTsurance is a compelling example of how harnessing and combining capabilities can lead to innovative business ventures. In the late 1990s, a group of forward-thinking employees at the South African insurance company Mutual & Federal recognized the need for a more customer-focused approach in the insurance industry (Jacobs, 2016). Encouraged by a culture that valued creativity and innovation, these intrapreneurs proposed a new model that emphasized direct interaction with clients and transparent pricing.

This vision culminated in the launch of OUTsurance in 1998, driven by the idea of rewarding customers for their loyalty and good behavior. By allowing employees to act as entrepreneurs and leverage their individual superpowers within the company, OUTsurance was able to rapidly develop and implement unique offerings that set it apart from traditional insurers (Jacobs, 2016). Recognized as an insurance pioneer for their OUTbonus—a cash-back program given to customers who are claim-free after three consecutive years (OUTsurance, 2025), OUTsurance was awarded News24's 2025 Short-Term Insurer of the Year Award for the third consecutive year (News24, 2025). This spirit of intrapreneurship not only led to the creation of a successful brand but also transformed the landscape of the insurance market in South Africa, demonstrating the power of fostering innovation within established organizations.

Culture: Building an Environment That Supports Intrapreneurial Behavior

The second C is *Culture*. A culture that promotes intrapreneurial behavior is one that values innovation, embraces risk-taking, and supports employees who challenge the status quo. In such a culture, failure is not stigmatized but is instead viewed as an essential part of the innovation process. Leaders who cultivate this type of environment enable and encourage employees to experiment, take calculated risks, and bring new ideas to the table.

In organizations with strong intrapreneurial cultures, employees feel empowered to step outside their formal roles to solve problems and pursue innovative solutions. This requires a shift from traditional, hierarchical leadership styles to more flexible, collaborative models. An excellent example of a company culture leading to intrapreneurial innovation is Pixar's development of its short films. Pixar fosters a culture of creativity, allowing employees to experiment with new ideas and storytelling techniques through short films (Catmull, 2008). The company encourages risk-taking and learning from failure, giving employees the confidence to pursue innovative projects without fear. Pixar emphasizes collaboration and open feedback, helping employees refine their ideas and develop high-quality content. Short films serve as a testing ground for new animation techniques and storytelling methods, which can later be applied to feature films. While no Pixar short films directly became feature films in the sense of being extended or re-released as a longer version, several shorts have inspired or influenced feature films. For example, the short film *Tin Toy* (1988) won an Academy Award and was a key project that helped Pixar secure a deal with Disney to create the feature film *Toy Story* (1995). This culture of creativity and support has led to groundbreaking advancements in animation and storytelling, solidifying Pixar's reputation for innovation.

Communication: Transparent and Empowering Dialogue

The third C is *Communication*. Transparent and open communication is essential for fostering intrapreneurial behavior. Leaders need to create environments where employees feel comfortable sharing their ideas and feedback, and where communication flows freely across departments and hierarchical levels. Intrapreneurs often rely on collaborative teams to bring their ideas to life, so effective communication is critical. Leaders must ensure that there are clear channels for employees to share their innovative ideas and that those ideas are taken seriously by decision makers within the organization. Moreover, leaders should articulate a clear vision that aligns intrapreneurial efforts with the broader strategic goals of the organization. A great example of intrapreneurship fostered by strong corporate communication is 3M's Post-it notes. 3M encourages employees to share ideas openly. Spencer Silver, a 3M scientist, originally developed a low-tack adhesive but did not have a clear application for it (3M, 2002, 2015; Krishnamurthy, 2011). Through open communication channels, this idea was shared across the company. Art Fry, another 3M employee, learned about Silver's adhesive through internal networks and identified its potential use as a bookmark that wouldn't slip out of his hymnal. 3M's leadership communicated their support for experimenting with innovative ideas. This allowed Fry to develop and refine the product with company resources. By highlighting successful intrapreneurial projects, 3M promotes a culture of innovation, encouraging employees to pursue and communicate their own ideas. This open communication and support system led to the creation of the Post-it Note, one of 3M's most successful products.

Connection: Building Networks That Drive Innovation

The fourth C is *Connection*. Innovation does not happen in a vacuum; it often occurs at the intersections of different disciplines, experiences, and perspectives. Leaders who prioritize connection foster cross-functional collaboration and encourage employees to build networks both within and outside the organization. Leaders must create opportunities for employees to work on cross-functional teams, share knowledge, and collaborate with external partners. These connections enable employees to tap into a wider range of ideas and resources, which can lead to groundbreaking innovations. An excellent example of intrapreneurship through connection is the development of Amazon Web Services (AWS) (Butler, 2015; Miller, 2016). AWS began as an internal project when Amazon engineers, led by Andy Jassy, identified the need for scalable IT infrastructure. They communicated this internally, recognizing that other companies might face similar challenges. The team's intrapreneurial spirit led to the idea of offering Amazon's infrastructure as a service. Strong communication of this vision within Amazon secured the necessary support and resources. As AWS developed, Amazon formed partnerships with companies like Netflix and Airbnb. These partnerships were game-changing, as they allowed AWS to demonstrate its capabilities while providing scalable solutions to its partners. AWS's success helped Amazon become a leader in cloud computing, transforming the industry and setting a standard for IT infrastructure services. Through intrapreneurship and strategic networking inside and outside of Amazon, AWS not only became a significant revenue stream for Amazon but also reshaped the landscape of corporate partnerships in the tech industry.

Confidence: Empowering Employees to Act with Courage

The final C is *Confidence.* Intrapreneurs need the confidence to take risks, challenge the status quo, and advocate for their ideas. This requires a level of psychological safety within the organization, where employees feel empowered to act without fear of punishment or failure. Leaders play a critical role in building this confidence by celebrating small wins, providing constructive feedback, and demonstrating their belief in their employees' abilities. Confidence is often built incrementally, through a series of small wins, continual experimentation, and learning experiences. W. L. Gore's history of innovation and intrapreneurship demonstrates how confidence inspires calculated risk-taking and market leadership. An example is how W. L. Gore & Associates inspired confidence in their employee, Bob Gore, leading to the invention of Gore-Tex. W. L. Gore & Associates encouraged a flexible and innovative workplace, allowing employees to explore new ideas without fear of failure (Shipper et al., 1999). Bob Gore, along with his father Wilbert "Bill" Gore, explored the properties of polytetrafluoroethylene (PTFE), a polymer also known as Teflon, and its potential applications. The company's nonhierarchical structure empowered Gore to pursue his curiosity and build his confidence in experimenting with the materials. Leadership recognized the potential of Gore's discovery and provided the resources needed to develop it into Gore-Tex fabric. By fostering a supportive and empowering environment, W. L. Gore & Associates inspired the confidence that led to the creation of a groundbreaking product.

Organizations can leverage the LCF to foster innovation in their organizations and develop intrapreneurial leaders that will create competitive advantage.

Developing Intrapreneurial Leaders through Educational and Corporate Programs

This section will explore how higher education institutions and corporate leadership programs can play a pivotal role in cultivating an intrapreneurial mindset in both future and current leaders. Intrapreneurial capabilities should be nurtured early, both in educational institutions and within organizations (Wetten et al., 2020; Deprez et al., 2021). To assist in the development process of transforming students and employees to become intrapreneurial leaders, this section will provide real-life examples from universities and corporate leadership programs.

Fundamentally, employees become intrapreneurs when they think beyond the norm (i.e., job description) and introduce innovations in one of two ways: by improving work procedures or by creating new offerings (such as services, products, divisions, or corporate startups) that address unmet customer needs (Pinchot & Pellman, 1999; Pinchot & Soltanifar, 2021). In whatever form or shape the innovation begins, we now know that its success depends on problem–solution fit. This is captured by the Steve Jobs quote, "You've got to start with the customer experience and work backward to the technology. You can't start with the technology then try to figure out where to sell it" (Landoni, 2022).

Over the years, intrapreneurs existed under the shadow of superstar entrepreneurs or under the radar of the corporate brands. For instance, people think of Steve Jobs, not Tony Fadell, when they hold an iPod; they think of Sony, not Ken Kutaraji, when they use a PlayStation; and they think of First National Bank, not Philani Potwana, when they deposit cash without a bankcard at an ATM. This state of affairs is evolving. As the Michael Page study shows (2020), intrapreneurs are now increasingly in demand, mostly because of the VUCA world. As intrapreneurship is increasingly gaining momentum as a highly desired skill set, it is important for companies and universities alike to understand that intrapreneurs first and foremost are leaders (Jackson 2025). Therefore, as in the case of the leadership skill set, employees at any organizational level can be trained and mentored to become successful intrapreneurial leaders.

The Role of Higher Education in Developing Intrapreneurs

While entrepreneurship education is now common in business schools, intrapreneurship education remains relatively underdeveloped (Kikas, 2022). Most entrepreneurship programs focus on starting new ventures, but few offer training on how to be an entrepreneur within an existing organization—a key skill for most graduates who will go on to work in established companies (Kikas, 2022).

A common misconception is that entrepreneurship—and by extension, intrapreneurship—stems from a set of innate traits tied to a specific kind of person. This perspective implies it is something that cannot be taught. However, if we treat "entrepreneurship" (and "intrapreneurship") as processes—systematic ways of approaching problems—then they become teachable.

By focusing on how to identify opportunities, experiment at low cost, pivot when needed, and persevere through challenges, educators can break intrapreneurship down into skills, frameworks, and methods that many can learn and practice. Aspiring intrapreneurs can be equipped to do the following:

1. Ideate thoughtfully and proactively, generating innovative ideas that address real problems
2. Experiment efficiently, quickly testing hypotheses to validate and refine ideas with minimal resources
3. Communicate effectively via storytelling and persuasion to inspire buy-in from stakeholders
4. Mobilize resources internally, building networks and social capital within the organization, enabling access to the people, time, and financial support needed to bring ideas to life

Educational programs should therefore provide these toolkits and frameworks—often taught in entrepreneurship courses—to increase the likelihood of success within both startups and established organizations. Furthermore, universities can partner with "intrapreneurship-minded" companies to create internships and project-based experiences, allowing students to put their classroom training into practice and develop a deeper, hands-on understanding of the intrapreneurial process.

Corporate Programs: Coaching Intrapreneurial Leaders

Once inside organizations, employees and leaders alike need support to develop their intrapreneurial potential. Corporate leadership programs should be reimagined to foster intrapreneurial thinking among employees at every level—rather than just top earners. By integrating entrepreneurial values into the company culture and performance reviews, organizations can encourage everyone to innovate, collaborate, and drive growth (Jackson, 2025). These initiatives can help employees build the skills and mindset needed to become successful intrapreneurs. These programs should focus on building confidence, problem–solution fit validations, how to conduct cheap and quick product–market fit experimentations, and design thinking (Molotsi & Zias, 2018). One wonderful example of a corporate intrapreneurial leadership program is the Innovators Program from First National Bank (FNB). FNB was recognized as the Most Innovative Bank in the World from among more than 150 entries from over 30 countries by the Financial Global Banking Innovation Awards (Bronkhorst, 2012).

FNB's Innovators Program showcases and celebrates innovations by employees, acting as a platform to help drive and celebrate relevant innovation across their organization (First National Bank, 2022). Apart from giving employees the opportunity and training to be innovators, there are four key features of the Innovators Program that other organizations can utilize to transform employees into intrapreneurial leaders. One is creating a real bottom-up approach to innovation that can create concrete changes to the corporate strategy. Former FNB CEO Michael Jordaan says, "Effectively, every employee can be an innovator and can change the way we conduct business. This is an inversion of the historical top-down application of corporate strategies" (quoted in Bremmen, 2012 p. 9). Second, organizations should view employees as leaders who can drive growth. In the case of FNB, for instance, "The Innovators programme allows our employees to lead the evolution of our business from a digital era to platform era" (FNB Media Release, 2019, p. 3). Third, companies should allow close collaboration between employees and customers. Last, the program has a strong recognition and reward system for employees' innovations: "Nearly R80 million in prize money has been awarded to employees over the years" (FNB Media Release, 2019, p. 2). In summary, this demonstrates that an intentional intrapreneurship program can both transform employees into intrapreneurial leaders and help companies to achieve competitive advantage by leading the market as a "Strongest Banking Brand in the World" (FANews, 2023, p. 1).

Conclusion

In an increasingly volatile and complex world, the intrapreneurial mindset is no longer just a bonus; it is essential for organizational survival and growth. By leveraging the LCF, organizations can foster a culture that encourages innovation, risk-taking, and adaptability. The leaders of tomorrow must be equipped with the mindset and skills to think like entrepreneurs within their organizations, driving innovation from the inside out.

In this chapter, we have explored the key elements of the LCF and provided practical examples of how organizations can nurture intrapreneurial leaders. Whether through higher education programs, corporate leadership development initiatives, or a combination of both, the future of leadership lies in the ability to inspire, empower, and enable employees to take ownership of their ideas and their roles. Leaders who master this form of leadership will not only survive but thrive in the new world of work.

References

3M. (2002). *A century of innovation: The 3M story*. 3M Company.

3M. (2015). *3M megatrends and the future of innovation*. http://www.artba.org/wp-content/uploads/2015/12/Lindekugel-TransOvation-Nov-17.pdf

African FinTech Awards. (2016). *FNB is the most innovative bank in Africa* [Press release]. https://www.firstnationalbank.com.gh/downloads/Ghana/FinTech_Awards_2016.pdf

Baker, W. (2000). *Achieving success through social capital: Tapping the hidden resources in your personal and business networks*. Jossey-Bass.

Bennett, N., & Lemoine, G. J. (2014). *What a difference a word makes: Understanding threats to performance in a VUCA world. Business Horizons*, *57*(3), 311–317. https://doi.org/10.1016/j.bushor.2014.01.001

Bremmen, N. (2012, October 10). FNB named world's most innovative bank. *Memeburn*. https://memeburn.com/2012/10/fnb-named-worlds-most-innovative-bank

Bronkhorst, Q. (2012, October 10). FNB named most innovative bank in the world. *BusinessTech*. https://businesstech.co.za/news/banking/23968/fnb-named-most-innovative-bank-in-the-world

Butler, B. (2015, March 2). The myth about how Amazon's web service started just won't die. *Network World*. https://www.networkworld.com/article/936248/the-myth-about-how-amazon-s-web-service-started-just-won-t-die.html

Catmull, E. (2008, September). How Pixar fosters collective creativity. *Harvard Business Review*, *86*(9), 64–72.

Christensen, C. M. (1997). *The innovator's dilemma: When new technologies cause great firms to fail*. Harvard Business Review Press.

Deprez, J., Peeters, E. R., & Gorgievski, M. J. (2021). Developing intrapreneurial self-efficacy through internships: Investigating agency and structure factors. *International Journal of Entrepreneurial Behavior and Research*, *27*(5), 1166–1188. https://doi.org/10.1108/ijebr-09-2020-0642

Dess, G. G., Ireland, R. D., and Hitt, M. A. (2003). Strategic Entrepreneurship: Creating Competitive Advantage Through Streams of Innovation. *Academy of Management Executive* *17* (1): 73–87. https://doi.org/10.5465/ame.2003.9474818

Duhigg, C. (2016). *Smarter Faster Better: The Secrets of Being Productive in Life and Business*. Random House.

Dyer, J., Gregersen, H., & Christensen, C. M. (2011). *The innovator's DNA: Mastering the five skills of disruptive innovators*. Harvard Business Review Press.

Edmondson, A. C. (2019). *The fearless organization: Creating psychological safety in the workplace for learning, innovation, and growth*. Wiley.

FNB. "Trailblazing Platform Innovations Awarded Top Honors." Press release, December 2, 2019. https://www.fnb.co.za/downloads/pressOffice/2019/FNBInnovatorsPressRelease.pdf.

Goleman, D. (2000, March–April). Leadership that gets results. *Harvard Business Review, 78*(2), 78–90.

Heifetz, R., Grashow, A., & Linsky, M. (2009). *The practice of adaptive leadership: Tools and tactics for changing your organization and the world.* Harvard Business Press.

Ibarra, H. (2015). *Act like a leader, think like a leader.* Harvard Business Review Press.

Jackson, A. (2025). *The win-win workplace: How thriving employees drive bottom-line results.* Berrett Koehler Publishers.

Jacobs, J. (2016, July 28). OUTsurance: Playing the long game. *News24 Business.* https://www.news24.com/fin24/outsurance-playing-the-long-game-20160728

Jones, A. (2024). *The treasure you seek: A guide to developing and leveraging your leadership capital.* Forbes Books.

Kikas, M. (2022). *Managerial perspectives on fostering intrapreneurship in organizations through education and training* (Doctoral dissertation, Estonian Business School). https://doi.org/10.13140/RG.2.2.28614.96325

Krishnamurthy, P. (2011, April 4). How Post-it never stuck: Case study on intrepreneurship. *SSRN Electronic Journal.* https://doi.org/10.2139/ssrn.1857795

Kuratko, D. F. (2017). *Entrepreneurship: Theory, process, and practice.* Cengage Learning.

Landoni, P. (2022) *Steve Jobs—Start with the customer experience* [Video]. YouTube. https://www.youtube.com/watch?v=QGIUa2sSYFI&t=40s

March, J. G. (1991). Exploration and exploitation in organizational learning. *Organization Science, 2*(1), 71–87.

Michael Page. (2020). *Top skills of 2020.* https://www.michaelpage.co.uk/sites/michaelpage.co.uk/files/mp_skills_ebook_for_2020.pdf

Miller, R. (2016). How AWS came to be. *TechCrunch.* https://techcrunch.com/2016/07/02/andy-jassys-brief-history-of-the-genesis-of-aws

Molotsi, H., & Zias, J. (2018). *The intrapreneur's journey: Empowering employees to drive growth.* Jeff Zias.

Morris, M. H., Kuratko, D. F., & Covin, J. G. (2011). *Corporate entrepreneurship & innovation.* Cengage Learning.

News24. (2025, March 13). *News24 business awards 2025.* https://specialprojects.news24.com/the-news24-business-awards-2025

OUTsurance. (2025, March 18). *The legendary OUTbonus from OUTsurance.* https://www.outsurance.co.za/car-insurance/outbonus

Pentland, A. (2014). *Social physics: How social networks can make us smarter.* Penguin Press.

Pinchot, G. (1985). *Intrapreneuring: Why you don't have to leave the corporation to become an entrepreneur.* Harper & Row.

Pinchot, G., & Pellman, R. (1999). *Intrapreneuring in action: A handbook for business innovation.* Berrett-Koehler Publishers.

Pinchot, G., & Soltanifar, M. (2021). Digital intrapreneurship: The corporate solution to a rapid digitalization. In M. Soltanifar, M. Hughes, & L. Gocke (Eds.), *Digital entrepreneurship: Future of business and finance* (pp. 233–262). Springer.

Schein, E. H. (2010). *Organizational culture and leadership.* Jossey-Bass.

Shipper, F. M., Manz, C. C., Nobles, B., & Manz, K. P. (1999). W. L. Gore & Associates, Inc.: A Case Study. In A. A. Thompson & A. J. Strickland (Eds.), *Strategic management: Concepts and cases* (11th ed., pp. C–491–C–513). Irwin.

Snowden, D. J., and Boone, M. E. (2007). A Leader's Framework for Decision Making. *Harvard Business Review, 85* (11): 68–76.

Van Wetten, S. J., Gerards, R., & de Grip, A. (2020, April). Are graduates' intrapreneurial skills optimally used for innovation? *Technovation, 96–97*(3). https://doi.org/10.1016/j.technovation.2020.102131

World Bank. (2016). *World Development Report 2016: Digital Dividends.* World Bank. https://doi.org/10.1596/978-1-4648-0671-1

21

Coaching beyond Performance

Building Trust, Presence, and Meaning

Barbara Toffolo

Introduction: Leading in Complexity Requires a New Kind of Presence

The landscape of leadership is shifting. Today's managers are expected to deliver results in a world marked by increasing complexity, rapid change, and competing stakeholder demands. Yet it is not only what leaders do that defines their effectiveness—it is how they show up. This chapter explores a critical but often overlooked dimension of leadership: relational presence and attunement. As organizational life grows more paradoxical—requiring leaders to act and reflect, to push forward and pause—traditional managerial habits centered on problem-solving and control are no longer enough. Leaders must now embrace the tension between "doing" and "being," and learn to meet their teams with greater emotional clarity, presence, and humanity.

Through real coaching cases and grounded research, we investigate how managers can develop the capacity to attune to themselves and others—creating the conditions for trust, mutual understanding, and shared accountability. Coaching is presented not just as a tool for performance development, but as a relational learning space where leaders cultivate new ways of engaging with complexity. This chapter offers practical insights and reflections for those seeking to lead not just with expertise, but with presence. It invites readers to consider how the quality of their relational engagement—not just their strategy—may be the most powerful leadership resource they bring to the table.

Barbara Toffolo, *Coaching beyond Performance*. In: *The Changing Leadership Landscape*.
Edited by:Sheri L. Feinzig and Mariangela Battista, Oxford University Press. © Oxford University Press (2026).
DOI: 10.1093/9780197820070.003.0021

The New Context of Coaching: Helping Managers Lead in a Paradoxical World

Expectations placed on leaders have always been high. In recent years, however, they have intensified due to the growing need for organizations to keep pace with unprecedented and disruptive shifts in the business context, rapid technological advancement, profound changes in workplace dynamics, particularly following the COVID-19 pandemic, as well as rising societal demands.

Expectations come from a wide array of stakeholders—including employees, shareholders, customers, communities, and the broader society—and frequently pull in different directions: to deliver short-term results while remaining committed to long-term impact, to drive innovation while ensuring stability, to adopt new technologies while fostering a human-centered culture, or to embrace diverse individual needs while preserving collective cohesion. In a nutshell, the level of complexity leaders must navigate has markedly increased.

These persistent tensions between competing elements that are interdependent and mutually reinforcing are what Smith and Lewis call "paradoxes" (Smith & Lewis, 2011). They are embedded in the fabric of organizational life and have become even more pronounced in today's volatile, uncertain, complex, and ambiguous (VUCA) environments. Unlike dilemmas, which call for choosing between alternatives, paradoxes cannot be resolved by favoring one side or seeking compromise; instead, they must be embraced and navigated simultaneously over time, creating opportunities through a "both/and" approach. Smith and Lewis (2011) identify four core categories of paradox that leaders must navigate:

1. Performing paradoxes, such as pursuing financial performance while upholding social responsibility
2. Learning paradoxes, like balancing operational efficiency with continuous innovation
3. Organizing paradoxes, including the need to centralize for control while decentralizing for agility
4. Belonging paradoxes, which involve reconciling individual identity with a shared sense of community

The belonging paradox—the tension between honoring individual uniqueness and cultivating group cohesion—has gained renewed prominence in the wake of the COVID-19 pandemic. During and after the crisis, employees have increasingly sought recognition not only as professionals but as whole human beings navigating complex emotional, social, and personal realities. This shift has placed new demands on leaders, who are expected to attend to individual needs with sensitivity and presence while still sustaining a shared sense of purpose and unity across their teams.

The tension described by Smith and Lewis (2011) as the belonging paradox is echoed by Tim Elmore (2021), who frames this dynamic as one of the central challenges for contemporary leaders, stating that "great leadership is deeply personal and inherently collective." This paradox, he argues, requires leaders to engage empathetically and meaningfully with individuals, offering presence and support, while also maintaining a coherent collective direction that binds the team together.

These paradoxes become visible in our coaching conversations with leaders. Managers often describe feeling pulled between distinct sets of expectations; what emerges is a sense of being overwhelmed, of facing tensions that appear irreconcilable, yet demand to be managed simultaneously.

Data from 2023 Gartner research confirms this feeling of "being overwhelmed." (Gartner, 2023, HR survey). Managers today are accountable for 51% more responsibilities than they can effectively manage and they are starting to buckle under the pressure: 54% are suffering from work-induced stress and fatigue and 44% are struggling to provide personalized support to their direct reports. Ultimately, one in five managers said they would prefer not being people managers given a choice. While managers are increasingly overwhelmed, employees are simultaneously raising their expectations: the same Gartner study reports that 77% of employees place increasing importance on the role of their manager in providing support.

The Manager's Challenge of Being Deeply Personal

Getting personalized support is what employees expect of their managers, but the challenge of being deeply personal is often more complex than it seems. A coaching session we held with Nicholas, a senior manager, illustrates this. Nicholas reported to his coach a one-on-one call with Mary, a member of his team. During that call, Nicholas started what looked like a "normal" habitual conversation by asking how Mary was doing. She opened up, explaining that she felt overwhelmed by the workload. She shared that her team was composed largely of junior colleagues who lacked the experience needed to carry out the work effectively. She wanted to support them but doing so took time, and that time was being diverted from the more strategic responsibilities on which her performance was evaluated.

Mary was aware that her priorities should lie with those strategic tasks, yet she felt that without her involvement, the project risked falling short, with potential consequences for the client. Nicholas listened attentively and, with sincere concern, began offering solutions. He suggested reallocating resources by bringing in more experienced support, renegotiating timelines with the client, conducting a detailed workload analysis, and identifying tasks that could be completed by drawing on resources developed as part of previous activities, in order to save time and reduce effort.

While his suggestions were thoughtful and well-intentioned, a quiet disconnect began to surface: Mary grew increasingly silent. It seemed as though his words were not landing. Despite her polite thanks at the end of the conversation, her expression and tone betrayed a sense of unease. During the talk with his coach, Nicholas recalled that he had left the conversation with a vague but persistent sense of dissatisfaction, unable to name exactly what had not worked, but aware that something important had not landed. He felt as though he had failed as a manager: despite all his efforts and genuine concern for Mary's well-being, despite his sincere desire to support her, he sensed that she had left the call even more burdened than when they had started it.

While recalling the interaction with Mary during the coaching session, Nicholas came into contact with a part of himself that he was not used to confronting: his vulnerability as a leader. A seasoned manager, accustomed to finding answers and offering direction, he was now facing a situation where something had clearly fallen short, yet he could not fully grasp what that was. During the conversation, the coach offered space to Nicholas to deep-dive into his feelings: she encouraged him to face his discomfort, to acknowledge the frustration of not knowing how to help and at the same time the genuine care he felt for his team member. This eventually led him to approach the issue with curiosity and a willingness to better understand both himself and the other person.

A few days later Nicholas made the courageous move to follow up with Mary. That move opened the door to a deeper insight. Mary explained that in that moment she had not been looking for solutions. What she truly needed was to feel heard, to know that her manager was present with her, and genuinely attuned to the difficulty of what she was going through. It was not advice she was looking for, but connection and presence.

The situation led Nicholas to an important reframing: being present, refraining from action as he had always understood and practiced it, was in that specific moment precisely what his team member needed. And that presence was in itself a way of acting and exercising leadership.

The tension Nicholas experienced is one we frequently encounter in coaching sessions. It is not only a cognitive tension, a challenge to the leader's assumptions and problem-solving reflexes, but also an emotional discomfort that unsettles even the most experienced leaders. These signals are symptoms of another paradox that defines contemporary leadership: the tension between "doing" versus "being." Leaders are trained to act, to respond, to solve. Yet the current context increasingly demands that they know when to pause, when to simply accompany, and sense when presence is more impactful than action. What Nicholas had failed to appreciate during his conversation with Mary was that Mary was implicitly asking Nicholas to "do less and be more."

Smith and Lewis (2022), in their ABCD framework for navigating paradox (see Figure 21.1), provide a lens through which to interpret Nicholas's case. In the diagram, "people" and "context" are cross-cutting elements that influence and shape all four core dimensions: Assumptions, Boundaries, Comfort, and Dynamics. They are not separate circles, but overarching categories that permeate the entire paradox system.

People: This refers to the agents who experience and manage paradoxes: leaders, teams, managers, coaches, and collaborators. They bring their own experiences, emotions, values, and mindsets. They are the ones who shape assumptions, define boundaries, experience discomfort, and activate dynamics. Their individual capacity to recognize and integrate tensions is crucial. Paradoxes are not managed in the abstract—they are navigated through people, in their concrete roles and lived realities.

Context: This represents the broader environment—social, cultural, institutional, and organizational—in which people operate and where paradoxes emerge. It determines which paradoxes become salient (e.g., during times of crisis, growth, or transformation). It shapes the norms, values, and expectations that govern how paradoxes are addressed. It can either enable or constrain creative responses (e.g., rigid environments may limit adaptive

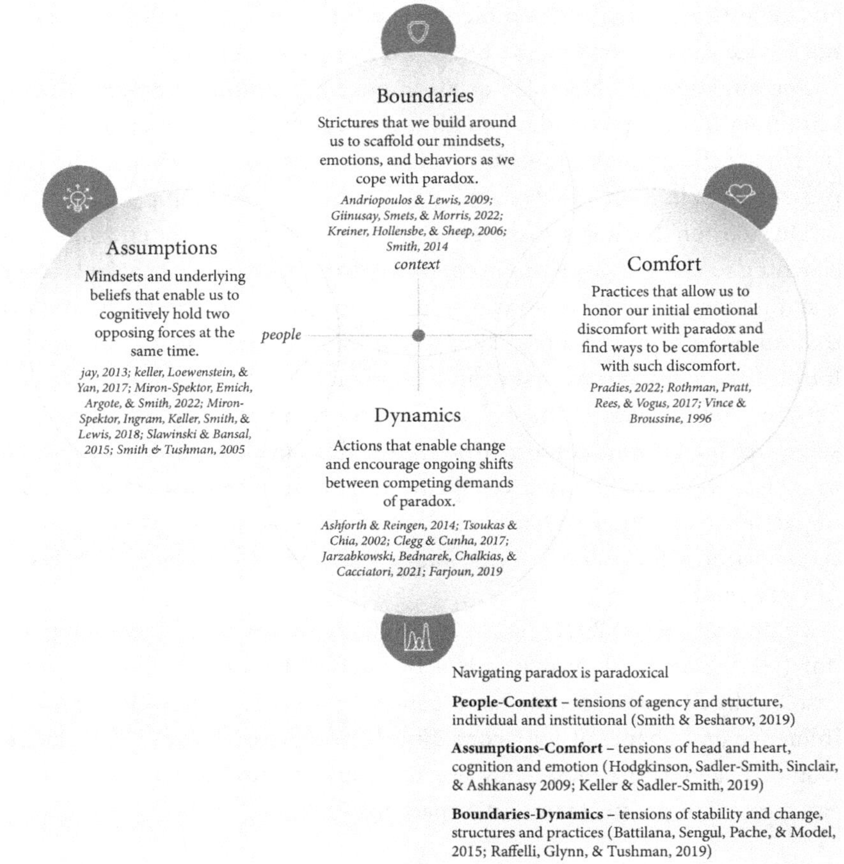

Figure 21.1 Smith and Lewis ABCD Framework for Navigating Paradox
Source: Adapted from Smith & Lewis (2022). Copyright 2022 by Harvard Business Publishing. Used with permission.

> dynamics). In short, context is the frame that influences and moderates how paradoxes are managed.
>
> The People–Context Relationship: The model suggests that navigating paradox is a situated process, happening at the intersection of the subjective capacities of individuals (emotional, cognitive, behavioral), and the objective conditions of the context (structures, rules, culture).
>
> Smith & Lewis (2022, pp. 145–149)

The reframing that Nicholas experienced in his coaching session and the interaction with Mary closely mirrors the process described by Smith and Lewis (2022) in their ABCD framework for navigating paradox (see Figure 21.1). In particular, his experience reflects the first two elements of the strategy: A for Assumptions and C for Comfort.

Reframing "Assumptions" means challenging one's underlying beliefs about what knowledge, control, and effective leadership look like. For Nicholas, this meant questioning the assumption that being a "good manager" necessarily involves offering solutions and directing others. Reframing "Comfort" refers to the leader's capacity to honor their initial emotional discomfort with paradox and find ways to be comfortable with such discomfort, resisting the urge to resolve tension too quickly. Like mindsets, emotions can both support and hinder our ability to navigate paradox. With the help of his coach, Nicholas acknowledged both his frustration and his sincere care for his team member; this eventually resulted with him approaching Mary with a curious attitude rather than a defensive one.

This reframing enabled Nicholas to access what Smith and Lewis (2011) describe as the "engagement zone," a space where the leader neither avoids the paradox nor seeks to prematurely resolve it, but instead engages with it fully, allowing the tension to generate new insight and possibility. Figure 21.2, The Paradox Mindset Inventory, illustrates how individuals deal with paradoxes based on two dimensions:

Figure 21.2 Paradox Mindset Inventory: Zones of Navigating Paradoxes

Source: Adapted from Smith & Lewis (2022). Copyright 2022 by Harvard Business Publishing. Used with permission.

- Experiencing Tensions (Vertical Axis):
  - *High*: Strong awareness and experience of conflicting demands
  - *Low*: Minimal awareness or avoidance of tensions
- Mindset (Horizontal Axis):
  - *Either–Or (Dichotomous)*: Chooses between opposing options
  - *Both–And (Paradoxical)*: Integrates opposing forces

The interaction of these dimensions gives rise to four distinct zones

1. Avoiding Zone (Low tension, Either–Or mindset):
   - Ignores or denies tensions
   - Low engagement with complexity
2. Anticipating Zone (Low tension, Both–And mindset):
   - Open to paradox but not yet actively experiencing tensions
3. Resolving Zone (High tension, Either–Or mindset):
   - Feels the tension but responds rigidly, choosing one side over the other
4. Engagement Zone (High tension, Both–And mindset):
   - Embraces paradox and complexity
   - Most adaptive and effective in dynamic environments

The *Engagement Zone* represents the ideal state—where people actively navigate tensions with a mindset that seeks integration, not division.

The Basis of "Feeling Felt": Attunement

During the coaching session with Nicholas, another aspect was investigated: the disconnection between Nicholas and Mary and what caused it. What had been missing in Nicholas's conversation with Mary was neither knowledge, expertise, strategy, nor goodwill. What was missing was attunement.

As Thomas Hübl describes (2020), attunement is more than a relational competence: it is a neurophysiological capacity that allows us to connect deeply and meaningfully with others. It is "the capacity of our nervous systems to actually feel another person, group, or system—not just think about them—and in turn, receive information that we can feel, emotionally and somatically. This interplay forms the basic building blocks of relating: 'I feel you, feeling me'" (p. 48).

According to Daniel Siegel (2010), clinical professor of psychiatry at the University of California, Los Angeles, and a leading voice in interpersonal neurobiology, it is attunement that gives rise to the deeply human experience of "feeling felt."

The neurobiological foundation of this capacity has been explored extensively by neuroscientist Vittorio Gallese (2005), whose research on mirror neurons provides a compelling explanation for how attunement operates at the level of the brain. Mirror neurons are a class of brain cells that fire both when we perform an action and when we observe someone else performing that same action. This mechanism enables a process Gallese refers to as "embodied simulation," through which we internally replicate the emotional and motor states of others.

Rather than simply interpreting others' behavior through cognitive inference, we literally simulate their experiences in our own neural systems. It is through this shared embodied activation that attunement becomes possible. Gallese (2005) terms "intentional attunement" the mutual neural and affective alignment enabled by the embodied simulation system that allows us to grasp others' intentions and internal states This mirroring underlies our ability to empathize, allowing us to experience the other's state as if it were our own, without losing the awareness that it is not. (Gallese, 2005).

As such, empathy builds upon attunement. While attunement allows us to resonate with another's inner world, empathy involves an additional capacity. In Siegel's words, it is "moving from the resonance and feeling-with to the more complex perceptual capacity to see from another point of view: we sense the other's intentions and imagine what an event means in his or her mind" (Siegel, 2010, p. 31).

While empathy has received considerable attention in the management science, attunement has often remained in the background. Yet attunement is what enables leaders to truly sense and connect with others on an emotional level. This capacity is becoming increasingly important, as more and more people in organizations are struggling and expressing a clear need for support.

According to Gallup's workforce indicators on employees' well-being from February 2025, 40% of global workers report feeling a lot of stress, 38% report feeling a lot of worry, 23% report feeling a lot of sadness and 21% report feeling a lot of anger. In Italy, according to the latest report on corporate welfare (Censis-Eudaimon, 2024), 32% of employees experienced feelings of exhaustion, detachment, or otherwise negative emotions toward their work, symptoms that are consistent with burnout. This psychological condition affects 48% of young workers (aged 18–34), 28% of adults (aged 35–49), and 23% of employees over 50. Leaders who cultivate attunement are better equipped to offer the kind of presence and connection that today's workplace requires.

Attunement "in Action"

As we have seen in the previous section, we are biologically wired for connecting with other humans, but in Hübl's words, "We have rarely cultivated or celebrated it with the depth it deserves" (Hübl, 2020, p. 56). One reason for this neglect lies in how traditional leadership development has been conceived. Managerial training has long prioritized other capabilities offering little room for cultivating emotional presence or embodied awareness. However, today's complexity demands a fundamental shift in how leadership is practiced.

Coaching offers a powerful example of what happens when these underutilized capacities are engaged. In coaching conversations, leaders are engaged in a relational space with their coach that includes presence, attunement, empathy. The quality of presence modeled by the coach becomes a learning experience in itself for the managers, and something that managers struggle to experience in training or other development opportunities. Over time, the coachee has the opportunity to internalize the mode of engagement of the coach and bring it back into their teams. Through this form of modeling, coaching becomes not just a tool for individual development, but a catalyst for relational transformation in organizations.

Another coaching conversation that one of our coaches had with a manager illustrates this point. Helena, a manager at a large organization, walked into her coaching session visibly tense. She was concerned about Holger, a member of her team: "He misses deadlines, shows no initiative, and seems completely disconnected from what's happening in the company and the team. I've tried everything: more structure, clearer expectations, even tough conversations. Nothing works. I honestly do not know what else to do." As Helena spoke, the coach was observing her posture: leaning forward, hands tightly clasped, jaw tense. Her voice was composed, but clipped and sharp.

After a pause, the coach gently asked, "As you talk about all this, what are you noticing in your body right now?" Helena paused, then said, "I hadn't thought about it ... but now that you ask, my shoulders feel like stone. And my stomach is tight."

The coach continued, "Let's stay with that for a moment ... What might that heaviness in your shoulders be trying to tell you?" Helena closed her eyes briefly: "It's saying ... if you don't hold everything together, no one else will." Her voice cracked slightly as she spoke.

"And that tightness in your stomach: what might be living underneath it?"

After a long silence, Helena replied, "Fear. Fear of failing, of not being taken seriously. And maybe ... disappointment. I thought he would be different. Or maybe I thought I would be."

They continued to explore—not Holger's behavior, but Helena's inner experience. The language she had been using ("He doesn't care," "He's a lost cause"), the brisk tone, the rigidity in her body. The coach mirrored some of these elements back with gentle curiosity, creating space for Helena to notice, rather than analyze or judge. Slowly, something began to shift.

They did not end the session with a plan. No action points. No next steps. But something in Helena's presence had changed. Her breathing was slower, her tone softer. She left the room with no new tools, just a new intention: to get back to Holger, not to fix the situation, but to truly listen.

At their next session, the coach asked, "How did it go?" Helena paused, then smiled with a mix of surprise and humility: "I'm not even sure what I did. Honestly ... not much. I didn't push. I didn't suggest anything. But something shifted. He started to talk. To share things I had not heard before. I do not think we have solved everything, but something opened up. Eventually he thanked me and said that he had felt heard."

Helena's experience is not unique. In many coaching sessions, we observe a similar pattern: coachees often leave without being able to clearly articulate what they have learned, yet with a deep awareness that something has shifted both within themselves and in their relationship with others. These sessions reveal a crucial insight for today's leaders: presence and the capacity to establish attunement are no longer peripheral skills but essential dimensions of leadership.

As a result, coachees do not emerge from the coaching process equipped with a set of techniques to apply. Instead, they leave with a new way of being, a more grounded, attuned presence in their relationships. This shift marks a departure from doing to being, from control to connection.

Attunement, however, is not an end in itself. In a manager–collaborator relationship, it serves as a necessary condition for co-creation, for helping one another navigate difficulties and jointly develop solutions. It is a prerequisite for effectively addressing today's complex challenges. This need is even more pressing in the current context, where managers often do not hold all the answers, and where organizational structures and the surrounding complexity increasingly demand shared accountability across all members of the organization.

As Hübl (2023) notes, attunement enables managers to connect with their team members through all their senses and to "create functional, transparent communication and feedback loops. (para. 4)" It allows them to draw on the full range of resources available to both parties—including intellectual, sensory, spiritual, and emotional capacities—thus unlocking the "bountiful reserves of creativity, ingenuity, innovation, and radical disruption we need to tackle complexity" (Hübl, 2023, para. 6).

How to Build Attunement

How can leaders learn to cultivate presence, attunement, and empathy, the core relational capacities of coaching? As we have argued, these qualities are often considered exclusive to the coaching relationship, yet they are increasingly essential in broader leadership practice. In today's complex work environments, we propose that leadership development should intentionally incorporate elements that help leaders access and strengthen these capacities even outside formal coaching contexts.

We suggest that leadership development programs should address cognitive, emotional, and relational dimensions through an integrated approach—treating them not as separate levers to be pulled, but as interdependent layers of the same process. This may involve framing leadership topics using an integrated "I–We–It" model.

Leadership training often still places a strong emphasis on the "It" dimension—how to assign objectives, how to delegate, how to provide feedback. The focus tends to remain on technical aspects and tools, rather than on the "I"—the identities of the individuals involved, how they relate to themselves, to the topic, and to the context in which they operate—or the "We," the quality of the relational space they are able to generate when addressing those topics.

This pattern is often mirrored in workplace conversations: when facing problems, managers and collaborators tend to concentrate on the "It," as it is the most visible, tangible part, the tip of the iceberg. Yet the "It" is usually only one element of the equation. It is deeply influenced by the self-awareness, beliefs, and personal perspectives that individuals bring to the interaction (the "I"), and by the quality of their relationship (the "We"). When the "I"s are attuned to one another, the "We" becomes a generative space, one in which solutions can be co-created in a way that allows everyone to feel seen, heard, and acknowledged.

Revisiting Nicholas's and Helena's cases can help illustrate why addressing the "I" dimension is essential. In her work with Nicholas, the coach noticed the underlying tension that he was experiencing. Rather than focusing solely on the "It," the topic Nicholas initially brought into the conversation, the coach first guided him to explore the "I" dimension. She supported Nicholas in adopting a paradoxical mindset, acknowledging that being a leader today means accepting the frustration and vulnerability that come with not always being able to "do" or offer solutions in every situation. The coach helped him reframe leadership as encompassing both doing and being.

The coach also supported Nicholas in cultivating internal attunement, helping him connect with the physical sensations, emotions, and thoughts associated with this paradoxical mindset. This led to a second transformation: not only did Nicholas's mindset and internal narrative evolve, but so did his physical presence, his tone, voice, and even the quality of his silences.

Nicholas became more curious about his internal states, taking time to "check in" with himself before engaging with Mary. By doing so, he brought a "different self" into the conversation, both cognitively and emotionally. He approached her with a paradoxical mindset, genuine curiosity, and a sincere willingness to better understand both himself and the other person. Helena was encouraged to do the same. Her coach guided her to explore her emotions through reflective questions: What am I feeling? Where do I feel it in my body? What is this telling me about myself?

In both cases, the coaches supported their clients in working on the "I" dimension, integrating cognitive awareness with emotional insight. This enabled a transformation in the relationship between Nicholas and Mary as well as Helena and Holger (the "We"). In the second call, Mary felt that Nicholas's frustration had faded and left room for true curiosity and attunement. This had an effect on Mary too: Mary ceased to feel the burden of being a cause of frustration for Nicholas, of not performing, of not living up to her manager's expectations, which enabled her to have a candid and honest conversation with her boss. In that second call, Nicholas also stopped another leadership habit: trying to reduce his team members' discomfort with uncertainty by making decisions that minimize complexity and emphasize stability. In the second call, Nicholas refrained from this habit and gave space to true listening and the creation of a new space where co-design with the counterpart could take place. Equally, Helena's attunement helped Holger to come forward, to open up and feel heard.

In both Nicholas's and Helena's cases, attunement enabled them to approach their interactions with a mindset of exploration rather than evaluation. This openness allowed them to uncover new layers within the conversation, the context, and the other person, ultimately creating space for jointly identifying solutions with their team members. When addressing leadership topics, training should therefore engage all three dimensions: I, We, and It.

Another recommendation for enhancing leadership development is to help managers embody a relational presence. Training should support leaders in becoming aware of how they sit, breathe, speak, and listen. This was precisely what Nicholas and Helena experienced in their coaching sessions and what many managers report in their own coaching journeys, where the coach's presence is often "felt" more deeply than their words.

Leadership training could, for example, help managers observe and appreciate the coach's behaviors and its components, and integrate these into their own conversations with team members. Training might focus on what contributes to a sense of safety during dialogue: the coach's voice and tone, the way emotions are acknowledged with empathy and respect, and the relational cues that foster trust and connection.

Managers can learn to replicate their coach's ability to read facial expressions, tone of voice, posture, and pacing—cues that often reveal what words do not—to deepen relational insight and responsiveness. They can also learn to validate emotional experience and acknowledge emotions with empathy and respect. Phrases like "that sounds difficult" or "I can understand why that's upsetting" communicate presence and respect more than solutions often do.

Figure 21.3, Relational Presence Practice Table, summarizes five key dimensions of relational leadership—each linked to specific key behaviors and reflection or practice ideas that support development. The dimensions are:

Dimension	Key Behaviors	Reflection / Practice Ideas
1 Self-Awareness	• Recognize emotions, judgments, and automatic reactions • Practice emotional regulation • Stay centered under stress	• Keep a reflection journal after key interactions • Note emotional "triggers" and patterns
2 Deep Listening	• Suspend judgment during conversations • Tune into tone, body language, pauses - Ask open, non-directive questions	• Practice "listening to understand" in meetings • Notice when you interrupt or rush to reply
3 Intentionality & Coherence	• Clarify your relational intent before engaging • Align actions, tone, and message with that intent • Use silence intentionally	• Ask: "What is my purpose in this conversation?" • Revisit alignment after interactions
4 Somatic Presence	• Pay attention to breath and posture • Use grounding practices before key moments • Stay embodied during conflict	• Take 30 seconds to ground before meetings • Check physical sensations during tough talks
5 Relational & Systemic Intelligence	• Observe relational patterns and group dynamics • Ask deeper follow-up questions • Consider the broader system/context	• Map team dynamics or invisible roles • Use dialogic facilitation in group conversations

Figure 21.3 Relational Presence Practice Table

Source: Adapted from Core.School internal materials (2024). Used with permission.

1. *Self-Awareness*: Recognizing emotional triggers and maintaining emotional regulation under stress
2. *Deep Listening*: Suspending judgment, attuning to nonverbal cues, and asking open, non-directive questions
3. *Intentionality & Coherence*: Clarifying one's relational intent and aligning behavior accordingly
4. *Somatic Presence*: Staying physically grounded and aware of bodily sensations, especially in moments of tension
5. *Relational & Systemic Intelligence*: Understanding group dynamics and engaging with the broader organizational context

Each dimension includes practical exercises and reflective prompts aimed at building embodied, emotionally intelligent leadership in complex relational settings.

Summary

Traditional "manager-as-coach" approaches have often focused on techniques: asking the right questions, adopting a developmental stance, and encouraging people to find their own solutions. While these tools remain valuable, they are no longer sufficient in today's increasingly complex and emotionally demanding organizational environments. As more people express a clear need for support, what is required of managers is not only what they do, but how they show up.

What makes the difference is the manager's ability to be fully present, to attune and create a relational space that mirrors the quality of a coaching relationship. Coaching, in this sense, becomes not only a support system but a learning opportunity: a space where managers can mirror and internalize the presence and attunement they receive. Attunement is what allows people to "feel felt." It enables trust. It creates the conditions for co-design, mutual understanding, and shared responsibility. It also enables managers to navigate the paradox of "doing" and "being." When attuned, a manager can sense whether a team member needs direction and structure—or, on the contrary, whether the moment calls for presence, stillness, and an open, empathetic space. The ability to discern and respond appropriately is contextual, and it emerges not from applying a model, but from being genuinely connected to the other person.

Leadership development curricula should integrate the relational dimensions that characterize effective coaching. This would allow more managers—not just those who experience coaching firsthand—to embody these essential capacities and bring them into their everyday practice.

References

Andriopoulos, C., & Lewis, M. W. (2009). Exploitation–exploration tensions and organizational ambidexterity: Managing paradoxes of innovation. *Organization Science*, *20*(4), 696–717. https://doi.org/10.1287/orsc.1080.0406

Censis & Eudaimon. (2024). *7° rapporto Censis-Eudaimon sul welfare aziendale.* Censis-Eudaimon.

Coreconsulting. (2021–2024). *Coaching cases with managers (unpublished internal material).* Coreconsulting.

Elmore, T. (2021). *Leading Gen Z: The New Rules for Managing and Motivating Today's Workforce.* Atlanta, GA: Grow Leaders.

Gallese, V. (2005). Embodied simulation: From neurons to phenomenal experience. *Trends in Cognitive Sciences*, *9*(1), 23–29. https://doi.org/10.1016/j.tics.2004.12.008

Gallese, V., & Sinigaglia, C. (2011). *The shared mind: The cognitive neuroscience of intersubjectivity.* Harvard University Press.

Gartner, Inc. (2023). *Gartner HR survey reveals less than half of employees are achieving optimal performance.* Gartner. Retrieved from https://www.gartner.com/en/newsroom/press-releases/05-23-2023-gartner-hr-survey-reveals-less-than-half-of-employees-are-achieving-optimal-performance

Hübl, T. (2023). *Attunement: A leadership capacity for navigating complexity.* Sounds True. https://www.soundstrue.com/blogs/authors/thomas-hubl-attunement-leadership

Kreiner, G. E., Hollensbe, E. C., & Sheep, M. L. (2006). Where is the "me" among the "we"? Identity work and the search for optimal balance. *Academy of Management Journal*, *49*(5), 1031–1057. https://doi.org/10.5465/amj.2006.22798186

Pradies, C., Tunarosa, A., & Lewis, M. W. (2022). From vicious to virtuous paradox dynamics: The social-symbolic work of supporting actors. *Organization Studies*, *43*(2), 271–293. https://doi.org/10.1177/0170840621997448

Siegel, D. J. (2010). *Mindsight: The New Science of Personal Transformation.* New York, NY: Bantam Books.

Smith, W. K. (2014). Dynamic decision making: A model of senior leaders managing strategic paradoxes. *Academy of Management Journal*, *57*(6), 1592–1623. https://doi.org/10.5465/amj.2011.0932

Smith, W. K., & Lewis, M. W. (2011). Toward a theory of paradox: A dynamic equilibrium model of organizing. *Academy of Management Review*, *36*(2), 381–403. https://doi.org/10.5465/amr.2009.0223

Smith, W. K., & Lewis, M. W. (2022). *Both/and thinking: Embracing creative tensions to solve your toughest problems.* Harvard Business Review Press.

22

The Direction and Future of Executive Education

Building the Plane while Flying

Edward Barrows Jr., Randall P. White, and Sandra L. Shullman

Past to Present: The Mix of Academic and Practical Contributions

Since its inception, executive education has continually evolved to meet the dynamic requirements of its constituents: commercial leadership, academic research and teaching, talent at all levels, political leadership, and shareholders. Starting within the halls of Harvard Business School in the first decade of the twentieth century, and other universities that followed, there quickly emerged a "great divide" between the mission of degreed education, undergraduate and master's level, and the first Master of Business Administration degrees (MBAs) on the one hand and, on the other, the real-world dynamic demands of business that called for more rapid preparation of executives, which brought about the non-degreed Advanced Management Program (AMP) in 1945. That year was notable as the conclusion of World War II—Harvard's AMP was a direct result of the school's participation in the US war effort in which more business leaders were needed quickly to run nationalized business missions (Amdam, 2016).

The split between classical education and the more technical preparation for a newly defined profession is academically defined by two logics. One of these logics, which has been a focus of historical research, has led to the rise and development of a series of degree programs, from bachelor's and master's programs to Executive MBA (EMBA) and PhD programs. The other logic, which from the 1960s began to be labeled "executive education" in the United States, led to a new sector of shorter, non-degree courses

Edward Barrows Jr., Randall P. White, and Sandra L. Shullman, *The Direction and Future of Executive Education*. In: *The Changing Leadership Landscape*. Edited by: Sheri L. Feinzig and Mariangela Battista, Oxford University Press. © Oxford University Press (2026). DOI: 10.1093/9780197820070.003.0022 and programs within the framework of the business school as an institution (Amdam, 2016). The former sector enrolls students based on their grades or enrollment exams, the latter basically on their hierarchical position within an organization.

From the start, an opposing cycle emerged between the two logics, manifested in the business schools' experimentation and development of curricula and who taught the curricula—traditional business professors or adjunct business leaders from the leading corporations of the day (Amdam, 2016). This opposition, observable in how business learning happened early on and continues to the present, has produced a great deal of innovation, knowledge, and understanding. It is still shaping how executives and leaders are developed. This ongoing tension between the two logics has three significant characteristics:

1. The historically documented symbiotic relationship between the academy and the corporate sphere has opened doors behind the scenes of the world's leading businesses to generate groundbreaking academic research and case studies (Amdam, 2016). This academic and business relationship enabled faculty to establish contacts with top leaders of leading corporations of the time—such as Corning, Mellon Bank, Chase, Merrill Lynch, Westinghouse, and General Electric. Through those contacts, the doors of those various organizations were opened for research by faculty engaged in teaching executives.
2. A continually evolving variety of paths for students of business leadership emerged, from the original 13-week AMP at Harvard to today's stackable certificate programs, just-in-time contract courses, and commercially offered credentials of many stripes (Amdam, 2016).
3. Hybrid faculty cross-pollinated business and the academy, as instructors shifted from professorial positions to business engagements, and their own consultancy startups, along with adjunct instructors who have come from business to universities.

Given this history, our overarching inquiry pertained to how the two logics and underlying tensions affect executive education and, more broadly, leadership development today. For that we turned to representatives from all three factions highlighted at the outset: academia, industry, and consultants.

Triangulating Executive Education Today: Our Approach

Each of the authors brings business consulting and academic experience—somewhere over 100 years combined—drawn from academic teaching at schools including Brown University, IE University, Cornell University, Duke University, HEC Paris, and Ohio State University, along with leadership development, notably at The Center for Creative Leadership. Our scope has been global, on all continents.

Reaching out to a dozen current executive education experts was deemed to be the most up-to-date way of checking our own experiences with other experts. We sought a qualified consensus on the executive education trajectory at the time of writing. Specific questions probed current trends in content and delivery modes, as well as where the bulk of the spending takes place and what novel practices are emerging. We agreed to keep all interviews anonymous. What follows is our distillation of respondent perspectives with a focus on providing both a snapshot in time of challenges leaders face today and how these challenges impact the business of executive education.

Major Trends Impacting Leaders Today

To gain an appreciation for the ways in which executive development is changing, we first asked respondents to give their assessment of the major, high-level trends affecting leaders across industries and geographies today. We identified six that currently impact leaders and their organizations:

1. *Environmental Dynamism*: The era of punctuated equilibrium—long-term stability periodically jolted for a short time by shocks—is long gone. Volatility and change are now constant. Leaders can expect the future to be an environment characterized by accelerated, unpredictable, at times chaotic change with very little stability.
2. *Technology Advancement*: Developments in technology have been and will continue to be the most disruptive trend that leaders and their organizations face. Big data, analytics, and machine learning have made their way into mainstream business decision-making. Further, well over 90% of organizations are engaged in some type of digital transformation, and artificial intelligence (AI) adoption is a

priority. Emerging leaders will be expected to capture the value of these current investments and will need to determine how to leverage this technology to make better, faster, and more impactful decisions.

3. *Geopolitical Instability*: The global political situation is taking on a much more significant role. At present, there are major conflicts underway in Europe and the Middle East. Political tensions are rising both in the United States and abroad. To keep pace, leaders will have to be more than citizens of the world, they will need to be skilled diplomats, adept at navigating the challenges of doing business in regions where tensions are high and addressing new alliances that were heretofore previously unseen.
4. *Demographics Shifts*: Workforce composition has changed. Five generations of workers populate the workplace, each bringing with them a different set of values, behavioral norms, and expectations. While senior leaders continue to push for workers to spend most of their time in the office, remote and hybrid structures are strongly favored by employees and will require a balancing act by leaders who are charged with managing multigenerational, international, and widely distributed workers.
5. *Talent Management Complexities*: Developing talent is becoming more difficult as a function related to changes in the working environment. At the long-tenured end of the talent pipeline, seasoned workers with decades of experience are marching into retirement. Leaders will need to be able to make strides in attracting talent, but they will also need to develop strategies for retaining employees with the kinds of training, motivation, and incentives that will keep them in place in organizations.
6. *Sustainability Reemergence*: A trend impacting leaders is sustainability; after being sidelined by the pandemic, organizations are gaining new awareness of the importance of sustainable business practices. Leaders across a wide range of businesses are being called upon to step up and make major strides in advancing sustainability. According to our sources, this may be more prevalent in the European Union than in the United States.

Combined, these trends require leaders to change the way they lead. The demand for results will continue to increase, but leaders will need to deliver results with approaches that incorporate increased levels of empathy. Leaders will have to balance greater performance demands with the ability to lead with greater humanity, recognizing the value of every individual and their unique contribution to the culture and the mission. All of this must happen while adopting new ways of working with AI.

Effects on Executive Education

Our discussion on trends provided the context for understanding from respondents the ways in which executive education is evolving to meet leaders' current needs. From academia to corporations and consulting firms, providers see the following responses:

- *Continued Growth*: The investment in leader development alone is likely over $60 billion (Yemiscigil, 2023).
- *Ongoing Disruption*: As predicted by Harvard Business School's Clayton Christensen, disruption has taken hold in business education as evidenced by non-traditional institutions like Quantic School of Business (Christensen, 2011).
- *Mass Customization*: We see the advent of contract or closed courses and much more tailoring of courses, where organizations work together with a university faculty to design a class just for people at a single organization that delivers an experience versus a degree.
- *Program Compression*: Programs offer shortened classroom time that is focused on real problems that hail from students' work environments.
- *Degree Proliferation*: We see the explosion of programs—MBA, Executive MBA, and non-degreed—across universities and non-university alike with an intensifying focus on the annual rankings by periodicals like *The Financial Times*.
- *Widespread Specialization*: A plethora of specialist master's degree programs are being created where the motto is, "If you can think it up, we can design it."
- *Increasing Globalization*: While geographical regionalization demonstrates that certain topics are more relevant in some regions than in others, there is still a demand for truly global educational experiences that broaden leaders' perspectives, such as TRIUM Global Executive MBA, the IE Brown Executive MBA, and other multi-university partnerships.

On the ground, these dynamics appear to be affecting leader education in several important ways. Here is what we learned from our conversations:

1. *Less Emphasis on Traditional AMPs*: Today, there are fewer of these programs, as AMPs evolve to meet market demand. Students and their underwriters are saying they want the programs to hit the high points on relationship skills and emotional intelligence, as well as tacit knowledge and agility issues, across situations and diverse people. We are seeing more relevance given to the things that the organization is facing. So, broad-based general programs are probably not as prolific, or as honored, as they once were.
2. *A Come-Back of Corporate Universities*: We heard of trends toward bringing executive education more in-house with the concept of corporate universities, branded by the corporation—The <insert company name> University—often with a director of executive education on the organizational chart, full-time. This is not new, but a return with an updated revival from the 1990s and the first decade of the twenty-first century. A key difference, from our interviews, is that the trend is not going to be as broad but instead will present more targeted programming for executives.
3. *The Enduring Importance of EMBAs*: EMBAs have filled the need for some of the more traditional AMPs, and organizations are a ready market for contract programs that are very targeted to a particular level in an organization. This is specifically for leader development, where management wants them immersed in topics, typically along the lines of leadership strategy, finance, and customer-centricity.
4. *Expansion of Online Options*: Over the three-to-five-year horizon we expect a proliferation of online options for people who are not in EMBA/MBA programs. In the cases of people in leader development who might want to do it themselves, or companies that have limited resources, we are going to see a lot of access to online materials—a fundamental shift. A lot of the general programs that exist now will go online and in-house.
5. *Bringing Education In-House*: The courseware may be generated by academics or private companies that may buy a subscription series or usages. In some cases, individuals will be able to access this and cut out all the costs of the residential programs. It remains to be seen if these are effective or not, but we heard indications that this is coming.

Executive education will have to become better, faster, and cheaper. From the Key Performance Indicator (KPI) perspective of "butts in seats," executive education is having to use different tactics. Organizations are no longer going to send candidates off for days and weeks at a time. As one executive said about long educational experiences, "If it takes longer than a few days, my business has already changed!" They are going to use technology with a focus on development that will be delivered in addition to your day job.

Key Dimensions of Executive Education Today

The bulk of our interviews spent time gaining an in-depth understanding of the state of the practice across four key dimensions of executive education: employees, content, modalities, and methods. We first present our main insights from within each area followed by illustrative points from the interviews.

Employees: Who's Getting Developed?

Much of the focus for leader development is still targeted at *high-potential programs*, as those leaders currently form (or are expected to form) the cadre that comprises senior management. These top-talent programs are the source for all successors to future roles in the company, so they garner the lion's share of the attention. With these programs, leaders are often grouped into cohorts that not only learn together but also network to create linkages across the enterprise and, furthermore, cascade what they have learned to their various teams using a "leaders-developing-leaders" approach.

An area that has gained greater attention recently is *development of teams*. In many organizations, the skills needed among learning populations are shared across teams; learning is more systemic; thus, teams are the starting point for collective leader development. Starting with top teams and cascading downward, development consists of a few days of targeted instruction and/or coaching around a business or team-specific challenge, all within the team's unique context.

Along with high potential and team development, there is still *organization-wide individual development*. What's changed with the democratization of learning for the individual is that single learners have more platforms to engage with and course options to pick from than ever before. Topics like innovation, data security, digital transformation, and sustainability are taught along with functional and technical skills.

Finally, *team development is going in-house.* The main takeaway here is that at the team level, development is being done, but it is primarily in-house within organizations, more as a consulting process, rather than engaging in an executive education process.

Interview Insights on "Who's Getting Developed?"

Several interviewees mentioned their corporations will either hire contract personnel or employ their own technical people, who will do nothing but develop these problem-solving simulations for their teams to go through. They are creating jobs within the organization to do that. A couple of places where they have already done this were cited. A clear consensus from our conversations is that the emphasis is on cohorts and their individuals working with outside institutions or commercial Training and Development (T&D) providers, while team development has been mostly brought in-house.

Content: What Are They Learning?

Most leaders readily admit that the pace of change is accelerating. To keep pace, leaders are being called upon to routinely engage in various levels of *organizational renewal.* At the most fundamental level, evolving technology in areas such as advanced connectivity, applied and generative AI, cloud computing, and digital trust/cybersecurity is changing the very nature of how leaders design and execute their work.

Effectively incorporating these advancements into the fabric of process inside the organization requires improved skills in the areas of *collaboration and change leadership.* Business transformation reaches farther and touches more parts of the corporate body than ever before; to succeed, leaders need to adopt an enterprise perspective that enlists the support of highly diverse and, in some cases, divergent constituents.

Because of technological advancements and the accelerated pace of change coupled with increased environmental complexity, business models are adapting rapidly, spurring a need for an improved understanding of *strategy at all levels* (functional, business, corporate, and global). To maintain competitiveness in the worldwide arena, leaders must have sharpened abilities in both critical and creative thinking—both elements of effective strategy development and implementation.

In conjunction with macro level change, leaders and the firms they guide are operating with a greater *global orientation.* Social media use has grown explosively due to the development of the internet and smartphones. Events that took days to report and communicate now happen in real time. Events that unfold halfway around the world have both a profound and instantaneous impact. This presents a massive challenge and opportunity for leaders striving to stay relevant in a highly globalized and dynamic environment.

Additionally, leaders and their organizations are working across cultures more frequently, demanding greater cultural awareness and sensitivity. A global mindset has never been a more vital element of leader education.

As important as sustainability is globally, it is also essential individually only in this vein: *resilience.* To absorb the demands of a highly diverse workforce, new technologies, intensifying competition, and shifting global context, leaders need to develop their mettle. As importantly, they need to ensure they enable their teams to build their endurance capability. Leaders must learn how to recharge and refocus if they are to remain sturdy in the face of mounting intellectual and physical demands.

Emotionally, leaders must enhance their *self-awareness and empathy.* The workforce of today houses up to five generations of employees, many of whom now work remotely while seeking a greater balance of work and life. To understand, appreciate, and advocate for diverse employees with divergent needs, leaders must enhance their awareness and sensitivity of the wide range of colleagues that work around them—whether that be in an adjacent office or another nation.

Regardless of gender or generation, a growing number of employees seek greater *meaning and purpose* in their work. People want to know that their work matters—not only to them personally, but to their organizations and the broader settings in which they work.

Talent management will continue to be an ever-present challenge and opportunity for leaders. Hiring, onboarding, developing, and advancing employees throughout the various phases of their careers will be central to leader effectiveness.

While the talent management function within organizations will continue to play a central role, leaders will be called upon to provide the *coaching* needed to grow employee capabilities to their fullest.

Interview Insights on "What Are They Learning?"

Respondents note that uncertainty is a fact of life, but it is no longer traumatic. VUCA (volatility, uncertainty, complexity, and ambiguity) and related acronyms like BANI (brittle, anxious, nonlinear, and incomprehensible), RUPT (rapid, unpredictable, paradoxical, and tangled), and TUNA (turbulence, uncertainty, novelty, and ambiguity)—in general—ireflect the various shorthand created to make sense of persistent volatility Still, it is not so much about the demonization of change that characterized discussions in the recent past. Today, especially with Generation Z, change is often experienced as, "This is the way it is, and this is the way it's going to remain." Continual change is not aberrant, but normal and natural.

They also find that learning is always accelerating because there is no choice. The speed of learning continues to simply be the speed of everything—the speed of change, the speed of technology. Today's executive education requires and will continue to require a different pace of learning, adjusting, and adapting.

Interviewees find that development is less event-driven and more organic—executive education is no longer as event-focused as it was in prior decades. Classes are not being asked to sit back for a talking-head lecture on what was once a required curriculum for everyone, regardless of their organization or their role. Now, learning is becoming much more organic and relevant to the organizations served, with the perspective being, "This is what we're faced with."

Old models are being replaced with faster, more relatable ones. There is simply no time for a plodding linear curriculum. Just like the speed of everything else, this speaks to the way education is going to be delivered in more bite-size points, very quickly. Attention spans are shorter. Thus, we are seeing ways to make it fun, relevant, and quickly digestible. Also, teaching is done according to the ways that people learn, by using the information immediately, or what might be better termed "just-in-time learning."

Respondents also note more immersive teaching. What's been described to us now might be characterized as more immersion experiences. One source spoke about this in their organization, where, for example, they are bringing people together and saying, "You want to do strategy?" Then, they do an immersion—such as a real-world project together—but they explore it with a game or simulation where they actually learn the important pieces and experiment with those pieces in a discovery-learning model. They may not have a formal instructor, they might have a convener, and they teach each other through this immersion.

Finally, more relational content is the norm. We heard a lot about how learning is happening faster and with greater concentration to adapt in the moment, just in time. But with the content itself, such as leadership, it is more focused on people and interpersonal engagement—very relational, real-world, and practical. This also addresses diversity and inclusion across a combination of many generations in the workspace and bridging those different generations.

Location: Where Are They Engaging?

Prior to the pandemic, the preponderance of leadership education was delivered in person for all program types. But the duration, intensity, and almost exclusive nature of online program delivery during the pandemic across all program formats proved to leaders, colleges and universities, and public and private organizations alike that education can be delivered with good effect virtually, both from the learning and cost-saving standpoint.

Leader development programs must consider the needs of the audience. Where educational experiences involve senior leaders or incorporate a strong desire to aid in the development of organizational culture or connect leaders across institutional boundary lines, in-person programs remain the standard. Because of the significant challenges some entities face, in-person programs are not only the preferred option, but their frequency also *surpasses* pre-pandemic rates. Many purely in-person programs have begun incorporating online components to both accelerate learning and reduce overall costs. Still, for upper managers and senior leaders, live, face-to-face development programming is among the highest priority.

That said, *hybrid learning* is taking on a more significant role. Larger organizations, with larger populations to train, are increasingly turning to hybrid and online learning to both accelerate rollout and save money—and to bridge the gap between the classroom and application. Hybrid programs continue to grow, and the findings are clear that hybrid is here to stay.

To augment programs for upper-middle and senior leaders while providing education to the entire employee base, organizations often provide suites of custom-built or curated online, *asynchronous learning platforms.*

This type of learning is often associated with short courses focused on technical skills or early-career manager development. In some instances, online learning platforms are used to track the deployment and completion of mandated training. However, much of the online learning is self-selected and self-paced at the discretion of the individual learner.

Interview Insights on "Where Are They Engaging?"

The interviewees said that hyrbrid is here to stay, but it still needs work. We heard some initial resistance to hybrid learning—paradoxical to how online learning, either real-time or self-directed, has been embraced with success. It appears likely that hybrid can become broadly accepted, but the mode of mixing online with face-to-face has yet to be figured out to make sure all participants have the same learning experiences. The pandemic forced the hand of executive education to go remote. Our interview subjects mirror what we have read and learned in the media: people are adaptable to online learning. Remote learning is here to stay for the near future because we have become more effective in using it.

Executive education has successfully moved online. We heard that the lecture concept is far less popular, and even the in-person concept is way down, except for at the very top of the organization. So, while we see the trend to go online, executive education programs must now evolve their platforms for being online so that they are more interesting and so they incorporate experiences that challenge what is being taught in the moment. Online does not mean just Zoom conferences. What we heard is that it really means much more interaction. Today's attention spans are being addressed with quick bursts of learning, which works best when the learning is just-in-time so the material can be immediately used in the organization.

The pandemic ushered in helpful changes, but we still have work to do. Our conversations around the topic of modes of learning make it apparent that we need to address how to make hybrid as appealing as pure face-to-face or remote. Hybrid settings have an intuitive appeal, but the challenges of reaching two classrooms congruently need to be ironed out. A very robust technological solution that presents a seamless virtual and face-to-face reality, simultaneously, is needed. There clearly is a trend to move more learning online to take advantage of better technology while reducing cost of delivery. Regardless of modality, the post-pandemic environment made it clear that we must get our technology up to speed.

Approach: How Do They Learn?

More than ever before, leaders want *socially grounded, experientially oriented* learning. In short, leaders want to learn together in cohorts through techniques that are application-oriented. Leaders today enter the classroom with considerable experience—senior leaders in particular. They want to take advantage of their knowledge via shared applications—and not exclusively for textbook-type exercises and sterile business cases.

Leaders want experiences to be *customized to their contexts* and reflect the realities of the challenges and opportunities they face. Moreover, today's learners want the ability to experiment with new tools, techniques, and approaches that sharpen their skills and broaden their capabilities. Certainly, there are out-of-the-box learning experiences—such as improvisation and business simulations—that foster new skills, but more often leaders are pushing for customization to their context. Mid-to-upper-level managers want to be sure the investment of their time yields payback in the form of work on actual business challenges.

Closely related to experience-oriented programs is *action learning.* Leaders—and upper echelons of management especially—want learners to take the skills they acquire in the classroom and apply them to real-time business challenges—challenges that yield tangible benefits for the organization.

Academic rigor remains essential, but learners—experienced learners in particular—want *relevance* from academics and practitioners alike (i.e., people who face the same challenges as their students). The model blends learning, consulting, and design thinking—which Tim Brown defines as, "A methodology that imbues the full spectrum of innovation activities with a human-centered design ethos" (Brown, 2008)—all into one curated project-focused experience.

The output from these evaluations is often used as part of an *executive or a peer-coaching program* that enables leaders to not only consider but also work on developing key skills through the duration of the leader development program and beyond.

Unsurprisingly, technology is playing an increasingly central role in leader education. *Business simulations*—both standard and custom—continue with widespread use, but growth is happening around learning driven by mobile applications (apps) and AI. Education providers, and organizations themselves, are developing custom applications, often gamified and bite-sized—that enable frequent engagement similar to standard social media platforms today.

Despite the experiential and highly customized focus, *self-paced learning*, which is largely standardized and widely distributed, will continue to be a feature in contemporary leader development for most mandated, technical, and early-career topics.

Interview Insights on "How Do They Learn?"

The experts we spoke with indicated that Executive Education is, right now, at a tipping point—The combination of all the aforementioned factors will affect learners at every level—individuals, teams, and cohorts. But the impact will vary in terms of mix and proportion over the next five years. We're undergoing a revolution, and Executive Education is at the forefront of that because businesses are pushing it.

Many interviewees talked about improvisation, evolution, and responding to demand. Our interviews suggest that some of them want an approach that is a bit like, "Let's try a lot of different modalities all at once." This preference is partially born out of necessity, partially out of the urge to try something different, and partially out of customer demand.

The biggest point that we gleaned is that the classroom is not going to be the traditional classroom much longer. There will be a new definition of the classroom. It may be a meeting place of some kind, but it will not have a traditional talking head in the front. It may look very different; likely, it will be some co-created space where individuals can come together and explore technical information, models, and approaches to a topic in a safe way, taking guidance from some expert source—human or AI—to learn by direct application how to approach and solve problems essential for the organization's growth and survival.

Conclusion

In addition to the rapid pace of change in education in general, the content focus of executive education and the primary methods and modalities for the design and delivery of executive education are all in considerable flux. Different worldviews are emerging for what is needed to prepare leaders for leadership in major organizational endeavors. The task for the leader-in-progress is no longer about finding the right business school; it is about contemplating a whole series of experiences, modalities, and opportunities for learning that are all changing at the same time. In the analogy of "building the plane while flying it," we are also changing the building materials, passenger list, and, perhaps, the destination. We are even changing the design of the airplane while in motion.

The changing emphasis from historic expertise to just-in-time learning, expected when people now go into leadership roles, can be seen in current organizational and political life in the United States, where there is often advocacy for the replacement of highly experienced leaders with less-experienced applicants, with appointees expected to learn while on the job. This emerges from both ideological change and the necessity of modifying mindset to meet rapidly changing pressures to acquire and retain talent. Such rapid change also creates rapidly evolving ethical challenges for leaders. It is currently unclear both how and where executive education will address significant ethical issues.

The looming questions are: Who will set the future direction of executive education in general? What role can or should business schools play? Will higher education guide executive education, or will the impetus and models for executive education shift more emphatically to outside vendors or corporations themselves?

References

Amdam, R. P. (2016). Executive education and the managerial revolution: The birth of executive education at Harvard Business School. *Business History Review*, 90(1), 671–690. https://doi.org/10.1017/S0007680517000010

Brown, T. (2008). Design thinking. *Harvard Business Review*. https://hbr.org/2008/06/design-thinking

Christensen, C., & Eyring, H. (2011). The innovative university: Changing the DNA of higher education from the inside out. *Jossey-Bass*. https://a.co/d/53UU4qU

Yemiscigil, A., Born, D., & Ling, H. (2023). What makes leadership development programs succeed? *Harvard Business Review*. https://hbr.org/2023/02/what-makes-leadership-development-programs-succeed

SECTION VIII

BRINGING LEADERSHIP PRACTICES TO LIFE: CASE STUDIES

23

Leading Peace Globally

The United Nations' Role in Shaping Leadership for Today and Tomorrow

Anton I. Botha, Mathian Osicki, and Chelsi Campbell

From a Cubicle to the Frontline: Mary's Story

Mary sits in a bunker-like office, scrutinizing a map of Eastern Ukraine. Her desk is cluttered with reports and communication devices. Her task is critical yet perilous: today, she coordinates routes and security escorts for her World Health Organization colleagues to deliver urgent humanitarian aid to children in a hospital ravaged by recent bombings, in a city still under siege.

Her responsibilities include leading the efforts to orchestrate military support, briefing all parties involved, and meticulously planning contingencies. Her goal is singular: ensure the safe delivery of aid with minimal risk to her team and the beneficiaries. Having served as a security risk analyst and now as a chief of section for two years, Mary occasionally finds the gravity of her duties overwhelming, yet she remains steadfast, driven by the tangible impact of her work.

Reflecting on her journey, Mary finds it surreal. Just four years prior, she was ensconced in a gray cubicle, analyzing risks for a major global insurance company. The leap from corporate risk analytics to frontline humanitarian missions was sparked by a simple LinkedIn post—a call for individuals with her expertise to join the United Nations (UN). Despite her having no field experience and being a woman in a traditionally male-dominated arena of field security, the UN saw Mary's leadership potential. Her successful transition underscores a significant evolution within the UN: a shift toward inclusivity and a recognition of the diverse talents essential to meeting contemporary challenges.

Anton I. Botha, Mathian Osicki, and Chelsi Campbell, *Leading Peace Globally*. In: *The Changing Leadership Landscape*. Edited by: Sheri L. Feinzig and Mariangela Battista, Oxford University Press.
 DOI: 10.1093/9780197820070.003.0023

A decade or so ago, the thought of Mary, with her background, taking on such a pivotal role in the field would have been nearly unthinkable. Her story not only highlights her personal growth and bravery but also reflects the broader transformation within the UN—how this organization has adapted to integrate and empower individuals beyond traditional paradigms, fostering a workforce that is as diverse as the challenges it faces and the populations it serves (Office of Human Resources, 2020).

However, this is not the whole story—not Mary's and the UN's. Faced with a rapidly changing world where the challenges of the past no longer resemble the challenges of the future, the UN had to adapt its approach to developing its future leaders (e.g., United Nations General Assembly, 2017). Mary is being developed through an entirely new values and behaviors framework where humanity and humility now take center stage, complemented by cutting-edge skills such as understanding behavioral sciences, data analytics, and digital innovation (United Nations Chief Executive Board for Coordination, 2017). This development is part of the broader "UN 2.0" strategy, which aims to revamp the UN system with the Quintet of Change—innovation, data, digital, foresight, and behavioral science—toward a forward-thinking culture that not only meets contemporary and future global challenges, but also creates opportunities for leadership that emphasizes adaptability and inclusiveness (United Nations, 2023a).

Why Look to the UN?

Since its inception in 1945, the UN has stood as a beacon of global cooperation and leadership (Mingst et al., 2022). Born from the ashes of the world's most devastating conflicts, this organization was designed not as a path to utopia but as a means to avert global catastrophe—its founding mission was to save succeeding generations from the scourge of war (United Nations, 1945). Today, the UN represents a dynamic forum for 193 member countries, wielding a diverse global workforce that spans its Secretariat and numerous funds (e.g., UN Population Fund), agencies (e.g., International Labour Organization), and programs (e.g., UN Development Program) with a diverse set of mandates (United Nations, n.d.a).

The landscape of global threats has evolved dramatically since the mid-twentieth century. While the specter of nuclear conflict still looms, the UN also confronts challenges that are vast in scale and complexity, such as climate change, pandemics, artificial intelligence (AI), and bioengineering (Economic Commission for Africa, 2018; United Nations, 2024a; United Nations, 2021a; United Nations, 2023b). These modern challenges test the limits of the institution's original mandate and its adaptability (Dempsey, 2023; Stauffer, 2023; Tharoor, 2020). Despite significant successes in mitigating global warfare and improving health and poverty outcomes, regional conflicts and the rising tide of new global risks have exposed gaps in the UN's capacity to effectively manage such crises (Kalantar, 2019; Owuamanam & Nwagbo, 2024).

Acknowledging these pressures, the UN is not static; it is an institution in transformation, recognizing that foundational reforms—especially in leadership—are crucial to its continued relevance and effectiveness (Dag Hammarskjöld Foundation, 2020). This chapter explores the UN's reformative efforts to reshape its internal leadership to better navigate the complexities of today and prepare for tomorrow's challenges. Indeed, there are few global institutions whose leadership standards carry as much influence.

In assessing why the UN remains a pivotal institution for understanding and influencing global leadership, we delve into its internal environment—how it is redefining leadership within its own ranks—and its external influence, shaping leadership principles and practices on the world stage (e.g., Hendra, 2024; United Nations, 2017). The UN's unique position as a long-standing and universally recognized symbol of global leadership gives it a pivotal role in directing the global response to emergent threats and in fostering leaders that are capable, inclusive, visionary, and, most importantly, humble (Jacquand, 2024).

The UN's approaches to fostering diverse, innovative leadership not only set a benchmark for public institutions worldwide, but also inspire myriad private sectors, non-governmental organizations (NGOs), and even grassroots movements such as international corporations adopting the UN's sustainability goals through the UN Global Compact and NGOs modeling their governance on UN frameworks (e.g., Berrone & Ricart Costa, 2024; Reimann, 2006; United Nations, 2021a; United Nations Global Compact, 2019; Van Tulder et al., 2021). This pervasive influence underscores the critical importance of the UN's leadership evolution—not just for the organization itself, but for the broader global community it serves.

As we delve deeper into the UN's proactive measures to develop effective leaders, both internally and externally, for today and the challenges of tomorrow, it is crucial to understand the specific programs and initiatives in place.

Table 23.1 Strategies for Cultivating Leadership: The UN's Approach for Today and Tomorrow

	Today	Tomorrow
Internal	• DEI Talent Pipelines • UN Leaders Program	• UN 2.0 & Quintet of Change • New Values and Behaviors
External	• UN Youth Envoy • Leadership Capacity-Building Programs in the Field	• Young Leaders for the SDGs • UN75 Consultations

The UN's leadership development strategies are structured not only to adapt to the emerging global landscape but also to set a standard for excellence in leadership across various sectors (United Nations, 2017). Table 23.1 categorizes these efforts into "Today" and "Tomorrow," illustrating a clear trajectory from current initiatives to plans for the future. This bifurcation helps clarify how the UN invests in immediate capabilities while also planning for the progressive development of leadership that aligns with the Sustainable Development Goals (SDGs)[1] and beyond. Through these diversified programs, the UN is actively shaping a new generation of leaders equipped with the skills and values necessary to navigate and mitigate the world's complex issues today and in the future.

UN Internal "Today" Programs: DEI Talent Pipelines

The UN's Diversity, Equity, and Inclusion (DEI) talent pipeline initiative was initially developed to address gender and geographic imbalances within peacekeeping roles, but has now broadened in scope and is also employed in the selection and development of the UN's top representatives in each country—the Resident Coordinators (United Nations, 2023c; United Nations Sustainable Development Group & Inter-Agency Standing Committee, n.d.; United Nations Sustainable Development Group, n.d.). This reflects the organization's commitment to creating a workforce that mirrors its diverse global constituency. Given the constraints against direct affirmative action policies due to the provisions set out in the UN charter, which enshrines a meritocracy (United Nations, 1945, Article 101), the UN has had to innovate to foster greater gender and geographic transformation effectively.[2]

The process of building a talent pipeline begins with an outreach campaign for women and individuals from underrepresented regions possessing specific skills, qualifications, and experience. They are then either encouraged to apply or can be nominated for inclusion. No specific UN experience is required (e.g., United Nations, 2017; United Nations Women, 2022). While traditional channels like social media are often used, it is informal channels that have proved most useful. Individuals already working for the UN who come from underrepresented states are asked to nominate individuals they feel would make suitable candidates provided they meet the criteria (e.g., Pehrman et al., 2019; see also *Report of the Secretary-General's Task Force on Addressing Racism and Promoting Dignity for All* in the United Nations Secretariat, 2021). This strategy opens the doors to a talent pool that would have otherwise likely never considered a career in the UN. Shortlisted candidates undergo a rigorous assessment process to verify their qualifications for targeted management positions. Successful candidates then participate in developmental activities designed to enhance their prospects of securing these roles. Participants receive specialized training on crafting personal history profiles (akin to resumes), writing effective cover letters, preparing for job-specific tests, and navigating the organization's somewhat esoteric competency-based interview process (Department of Management, Strategy, and Compliance & Department of Operational Support, 2022). Specific job openings are then circulated among eligible talent pipeline members, who are encouraged to apply (United Nations Careers, n.d.b). This encouragement and comprehensive preparation aims to maximize both application rates and success rates.

Furthermore, other activities, such as lectures by seasoned UN staff, provide female talent pipeline participants insights into the roles' context and challenges. These experiences are traditionally more readily accessible by their male counterparts in field operations (United Nations, n.d.c; United Nations, n.d.d). This is akin to providing members of the talent pipeline a realistic job preview by preparing them for the realities on the ground, which is often not adequately covered in vacancy announcements.

Since its inception in the mid-2010s, this initiative has significantly increased the representation of women from underrepresented countries in peacekeeping roles. Data show that participants are twice as likely to be selected for positions if they successfully participated in the pipeline (United Nations, 2023c). The percentage of women in management roles within peacekeeping missions has risen from a low of 20–30% to 35–40% across different nations since the program's inception (United Nations, 2023d). Additionally, and perhaps more critically, it has reduced turnover rates thanks to realistic job previews, coaching, and mentoring, as well as equipping participants with both the mental and practical tools required for the demanding conditions of UN peacekeeping missions (L. Otti personal communication, July 10, 2024). In particular, the support provided through mentoring within the pipeline has been vital, offering guidance on the potential impacts of such career choices on participants' families and strategies to mitigate these effects (United Nations, 2023d).

While the initiative requires substantial resources—including staff time and funding for applicant reviews, selection processes, and training coordination—the investment, made available through special funding for a handful of UN member countries, has proven to be a worthwhile endeavor for the UN (United Nations, 2023d). The success of these talent pipelines is evident, prompting considerations for their expansion to address other demographic challenges within the UN global workforce, and allowing the organization to source more qualified people from under- and unrepresented regions (e.g., Office of Human Resources, 2020).

Talent pipelines provide one example of how the UN delicately balances the need to reflect the diverse people of the world it serves while adhering to member states' reservations about the use of tools such as affirmative action, which is seen in some corners as against the spirit of the UN Charter and a form of reverse discrimination.

UN Internal "Today" Programs: UN Leaders Program

The UN Leaders Program is a tailored initiative designed to enhance the strategic, ethical, and adaptive leadership capabilities of top management within the UN. Developed by the UN System Staff College, this program is a response to the evolving learning, training, and knowledge management needs of UN staff and their partners across the globe (United Nations System Staff College, n.d.a). As an inter-agency learning institution, the UN System Staff College acts as a strategic partner in fostering leadership that is adept at navigating the complexities of global challenges (United Nations System Staff College, n.d.b).

At the heart of the program is the goal to inspire UN leaders to provide visionary guidance and practical solutions to the world's most pressing issues. Embracing a growth mindset, the program requires participants to approach problems not as "experts," but as curious investigators who see failure as an opportunity to learn and continuously improve while also immersing participants in an environment that values innovation, transformation, resilience, and collaboration. Through a blend of interactive online learning experiences and practical applications, leaders are encouraged to reflect on their own leadership practices and explore novel approaches (UNSCC, 2023).

Previously, the UN Leaders Program was hosted in person at a variety of host sites, including New York, Geneva, Turin, Bangkok, and Nairobi. In a post–COVID-19 world, the program was reimagined to meet the needs of modern leaders, including transitioning to an "interactive online solution" (United Nations Systems Staff College, n.d.c; UN Leaders Programme Online, n.d.d). The nomination process involves either open enrollment or internal nomination, with some UN organizations following their own internal processes to identify suitable candidates for the program (HR Portal, n.d.).

The program begins with an exploration of core leadership concepts and progresses through various phases of personal and professional development. Leaders engage in thematic webinars that discuss successful leadership strategies and their application to UN and international contexts (United Nations System Staff College, n.d.d). These sessions are designed not only to impart knowledge but also to facilitate a deeper connection with peers from across the international and UN system, enhancing the collaborative experience.

An integral component of the program is executive coaching, where leaders receive personalized guidance to contextualize their learning experiences to their specific roles within the UN (United Nations System Staff College, n.d.d). This coaching is crucial in helping leaders align their personal development with the UN's overarching goals, ensuring that they are prepared not only to meet current organizational demands but also to anticipate future challenges.

Overall, the UN Leaders Program serves as a critical platform for senior UN staff to refine their leadership skills, ensuring they are well equipped to foster an organizational culture that is innovative, inclusive, and forward-thinking. The outcomes of this program are evident in the enhanced capacity of leaders to effect meaningful change, driving the UN toward achieving its mission more effectively in an increasingly complex global landscape (United Nations System Staff College, 2018).

UN External "Today" Programs: The UN Youth Envoy

The UN recognizes the critical role of young people, defined as individuals between the ages of 15 and 24, in shaping the future. This age group primarily comprises Generation Z and makes up around 1.3 billion individuals globally—the largest generation in history (Department of Economic and Social Affairs, Population Division, 2024; Wood, 2018). Their unique perspectives and energies are essential for driving sustainable development and peace worldwide. At the forefront of this effort is the UN Office of the Secretary-General's Envoy on Youth, which plays a vital role in amplifying the voices of these young leaders and integrating their contributions across the spectrum of the UN's work (Office of the Secretary-General's Envoy on Youth, n.d.a).

Among the most impactful initiatives of the UN Youth Envoy program are the Young Leaders for the SDGs and the UN Youth Delegate Program. The Young Leaders program selects 17 exceptional individuals aged 15 to 24 every two years, each representing one of the 17 SDGs, to engage in global advocacy, capacity-building, and networking over a two-year term (see the "UN External "Tomorrow" Programs: Young Leaders for the SDGs" section for a comprehensive overview of this program; see also Office of the Secretary-General's Envoy on Youth, n.d.b).

The UN Youth Delegate Program is another program engaging youth. It allows youth delegates from various countries to participate for several weeks in UN General Assembly sessions, where they engage in debates, draft resolutions, and contribute to policy discussions (Department of Economic and Social Affairs, n.d.). These programs combine courses, workshops, face-to-face meetings, and simulations to empower young people, enhance their leadership skills, and integrate their voices into UN processes, thereby advancing sustainable development and peace worldwide (Department of Economic and Social Affairs, 2020).

More than just an advocate, the UN Youth Envoy also serves as a crucial bridge between the UN and young people around the globe, facilitating a meaningful two-way dialogue. Through various programs and partnerships, such as the UN Youth Delegate Program, the Envoy enables an exchange of ideas and perspectives that enrich both sides (Office of the Secretary-General's Envoy on Youth, n.d.c). Young people are given a platform to voice their concerns and aspirations and to interact with the global community, bringing fresh insights that are vital for the UN to stay relevant and effective in its mission.

Ultimately, the work of the UN Youth Envoy is about investing in the future. By empowering young people and fostering their active participation, the Envoy not only strengthens the fabric of the UN but also ensures that the UN is better prepared to face the complex challenges of today and tomorrow (e.g., Altiok & Grizelj, 2019). This forward-thinking approach promises to foster a more inclusive and dynamic UN, ready to be led by the next generation of global leaders.

UN External "Today" Programs: Empretec Entrepreneurs and Technology Leader Training

The Empretec Entrepreneurs and Technology Leader Training, established by the UN Conference on Trade and Development (UNCTAD), is a global initiative aimed at fostering sustainable and competitive small- and medium-sized enterprises (SMEs) (UN Trade & Development, n.d.). Launched in Argentina in 1988, Empretec has expanded to over 40 countries, where it tailors its training to meet local needs while maintaining a core focus on entrepreneurial leadership and capacity-building (Denis et al., 2000; United Nations Conference on Trade and Development, 2023).

A key component of the program is the Entrepreneurship Training Workshop (ETW), which is based on the research of Harvard University's Professor David McClelland (United Nations Conference on Trade and Development, n.d.). The ETW typically spans six days and involves around 60 hours of intensive, hands-on learning. The training emphasizes the development of 10 essential entrepreneurial competencies, including opportunity-seeking, risk-taking, systematic planning, and persistence. Through a combination of experiential learning methods, simulations, and peer discussions, participants are challenged to refine their leadership and decision-making skills (Empretec, n.d.).

For example, in Brazil, the Empretec program annually engages thousands of entrepreneurs, selected through a competitive application process that assesses their business potential and commitment (International Trade Centre, 2013). Participants come from diverse sectors, including technology, agriculture, and manufacturing, with an emphasis on supporting underrepresented groups such as women and youth. The training sessions in Brazil are delivered by certified facilitators and are designed to simulate real-world business scenarios, enabling participants to apply new skills directly to their enterprises (Coelho et al., 2018; International Trade Centre, 2013; Martins et al., 2021).

In Ethiopia, the program similarly supports women entrepreneurs, tailoring its content to address specific challenges they face in the market. The selection process is inclusive, actively recruiting women-led businesses, and the training includes modules on overcoming gender-based barriers to entrepreneurship (Entrepreneurship Development Institute Ethiopia, n.d.; United Nations Development Programme Ethiopia, 2019). This local customization ensures that the core Empretec principles are applied in ways that maximize impact within the country's unique economic and cultural context.

The program is not just limited to a single training session. In many countries, such as Nigeria, participants receive ongoing mentoring and coaching to help implement their business strategies effectively. This long-term engagement includes networking events where entrepreneurs can connect with investors and industry leaders, as well as support for accessing financing (e.g., BusinessDay NG, 2017; UN Trade & Development, 2024). In Nigeria, the program is integrated into national economic development strategies, with a focus on sectors such as technology and agriculture, leading to significant contributions to economic growth and job creation (e.g., Nwanguma, 2022; United Nations Conference on Trade and Development, 2015).

The adaptable nature of Empretec allows it to be successfully replicated across diverse markets. It fosters entrepreneurship in a way that aligns with local economic realities while maintaining a strong foundation in entrepreneurial skill development. Through its combination of interactive training, local adaptation, and ongoing support, the program contributes meaningfully to the UN's broader goals of sustainable development and poverty reduction, making it a powerful tool for economic resilience worldwide (Coelho et al., 2018).

UN Internal "Tomorrow" Programs: UN 2.0 & Quintet of Change

As the UN reaches the midpoint of the 2030 Agenda, many of the SDG indicators suggest that we may fall short if a change in approach is not made (United Nations, 2023e; Yuan et al., 2023). A transformative overhaul is essential—not of the goals themselves, but of how the UN pursues them. The transformation needed focuses on the UN system's internal culture, operational methods, and collaborative approaches. By pinpointing these areas for change, the UN aims to achieve an even greater return on investment through accelerated progress toward the SDGs (United Nations, 2021b). This imperative is encapsulated in Secretary-General António Guterres's vision of UN 2.0, representing a modernized and rejuvenated UN equipped with a forward-thinking culture and advanced skills for the twenty-first century (United Nations, 2023e). This vision is crucial to turbocharge the UN's support for people and the planet.

Central to this vision is the Quintet of Change, which zeros in on five key areas: data, innovation, digital transformation, strategic foresight, and behavioral science (United Nations, 2023f). These areas emerged as top priorities because they address the fundamental competencies needed to effectively realign the UN's efforts with the SDGs. By enhancing capabilities in these domains, the UN seeks to become more agile, responsive, and impactful in tackling global challenges (UN 2.0, n.d.).

Concrete examples of this transformation are already underway. For instance, the Secretary-General's Data Strategy is a pivotal initiative aimed at harnessing the power of data across the UN system (United Nations, 2020). Launched to strengthen the organization's ability to collect, analyze, and utilize data effectively, the strategy transforms raw data into actionable insights. This enables smarter decision-making and more impactful results, directly contributing to the achievement of the SDGs.

Each element of the Quintet plays a vital role in this transformation and applies to everyone at all levels across the organization (UN 2.0, n.d.):

- *Data*: Enhancing capabilities to gather, process, and utilize data from diverse sources to drive smarter decisions and achieve impactful outcomes.
- *Digital Transformation*: Embracing technological advancements and integrating them into work processes to enhance efficiency, foster collaboration, and amplify results.
- *Innovation*: Cultivating environments that encourage creativity, risk-taking, and continuous learning, viewing challenges as opportunities for groundbreaking solutions.
- *Strategic Foresight*: Equipping the organization with the ability to anticipate emerging trends, discern shifts, and respond proactively, embodying a commitment to long-term strategic planning.

- *Behavioral Science*: Applying insights from human behavior to design evidence-based strategies and interventions that promote positive change.

Another practical example is the evolution of the UN's selection and development systems, with the Quintet of Change forming the backbone of these initiatives (United Nations, 2023c). Specifically, the UN is leveraging AI and data analytics to enhance recruitment processes (e.g., Alnamrouti et al., 2022). AI tools are used to screen applications more efficiently, identifying candidates with skills in innovation and strategic foresight while reducing unconscious bias to promote diversity and inclusion. For instance, AI algorithms analyze large volumes of applicant data to match candidates whose competencies align with the Quintet's focus areas, such as digital proficiency and innovative thinking. This is done with the necessary safeguards in place to continually check for adverse impacts and undue bias, ensuring a balanced and fair approach to AI utilization (e.g., Avagyan, 2022; Brookland, 2019).

On the development front, the UN is incorporating behavioral science into leadership training programs to foster a culture of agility, creativity, and adaptability. By applying insights into human behavior, these programs help leaders develop skills in strategic foresight and innovation (Ghazaryan, 2022). Practical applications include workshops that simulate complex decision-making scenarios, coaching sessions that promote a growth mindset, and interventions designed to nudge employees toward collaborative and innovative behaviors (e.g., Foster, 2017; Ghazaryan, 2022; Office of Counter-Terrorism, n.d.). Additionally, digital platforms are utilized to deliver interactive learning experiences (e.g., ECLAC Training and UNICEF's Agora), allowing staff to engage with new technologies and data-driven tools directly.

By accelerating efforts already in motion within these areas, the UN aims to reshape itself into a forward-thinking international organization suited for the twenty-first century. This strategic focus is anticipated to have the greatest impact on propelling progress toward meeting the SDGs (UN 2.0, n.d.). The implementation of the Quintet of Change positions the UN not just to lead by example but to actively shape global leadership for today and tomorrow (United Nations, 2023f). This progressive approach ensures that the UN remains at the forefront of global governance, ready to meet future challenges with innovative solutions and a deeply human-centric perspective.

UN Internal "Tomorrow" Programs: New Values and Behaviors

The UN has always been at the forefront of global leadership and organizational culture, but with the introduction of the new "UN Values and Behaviors Framework," it is taking a progressive step toward defining the future of its ethos in alignment with the evolving global landscape (Economic Commission for Africa, 2022). This framework, which emerged from an extensive co-creation process involving nearly 4,500 staff members, builds on the 1999 "Competencies for the Future" and revitalizes them to better reflect the goals of the organization for the 2030s and beyond (Office of Human Resources, n.d.).

The new UN Values and Behaviors Framework marks a significant shift from the UN's previous Values and Competency Framework, which centered on competencies like Professionalism, Respect for Diversity, and Commitment to Continuous Learning. While the old framework focused on individual skills and attributes necessary for effective performance, the new framework comprises nine elements—four values and five behaviors—that collectively establish a more holistic blueprint for daily interactions and long-term strategic goals within the organization (Office of Human Resources, n.d.).

The values of Inclusion, Integrity, Humility, and Humanity now take center stage, reflecting a deeper commitment to embracing diversity, ethical conduct, modest leadership, and compassion in service. Accompanying these values are behaviors such as Connect and Collaborate, Analyze and Plan, Deliver Results with Positive Impact, Learn and Develop, and Adapt and Innovate (Human Resources, n.d.). These behaviors serve as actionable guidelines for how UN staff engage with each other, execute their duties, and interact with the global community.

This new approach is more forward-looking because it not only emphasizes ethical and interpersonal values but also prioritizes adaptability and innovation in response to a rapidly changing world (United Nations Office of Human Resources, n.d.). By incorporating behaviors like "Adapt and Innovate," the framework encourages staff to be flexible and creative—essential qualities for addressing complex global challenges. The inclusion of "Learn and Develop" fosters a culture of continuous improvement, ensuring that the organization remains dynamic and responsive to new developments. Moreover, "Connect and Collaborate" underscores the importance of teamwork and partnership, which are crucial for multifaceted problem-solving (United Nations, 2024b).

In contrast to the previous framework's focus on static competencies, the new values and behaviors align closely with the Quintet of Change, which includes data, innovation, digital transformation, strategic foresight, and behavioral science (United Nations, 2023f, see *Our Common Agenda: Policy Brief 11 UN 2.0 Forward-Thinking Culture and Cutting-Edge Skills for Better United Nations System Impact*). This alignment ensures that the UN's workforce is not only skilled but also agile and prepared to leverage modern tools and methodologies. By evolving its foundational principles, the UN is better positioned to meet current and future challenges, making the new framework a strategic asset in achieving the SDGs.

Particularly notable is the emphasis on humanity and humility. These values underscore a commitment to upholding human rights and dignity, embodying compassion not only toward each other but also toward those served by the UN (United Nations, 2023d). This human-centered approach fosters an organizational culture that is both aspirational and grounded in the current realities of the global landscape. Humility, viewed not as a weakness but as a strength, promotes a culture of mutual respect and recognition that no single individual holds all the answers (Gerber, 2024; Office of Human Resources, n.d.). This perspective is crucial for collaborative problem-solving and effective leadership.

The introduction of these values and behaviors into the UN's organizational fabric is expected to influence various human resources processes, including workforce planning, recruitment, learning, and performance management. By embedding these principles into everyday practices, the UN aims to not only enhance its internal culture but also to strengthen its role as a global leader (United Nations, 2022). The framework ensures that the UN remains adaptive and innovative, prepared to meet the complex challenges of today and to shape a sustainable and just world for tomorrow (Ghazaryan, 2022).

This progressive framework provides further evidence of the UN's role modeling more progressive and inclusive approaches to leadership for tomorrow. By focusing on values such as humanity and humility, the UN is setting a global standard for leadership that prioritizes ethical conduct, inclusiveness, and a deep-seated respect for human dignity. This approach not only enhances the effectiveness of the UN's global initiatives but also ensures that it continues to lead by example in the evolving international arena (Gerber, 2024).

UN External "Tomorrow" Programs: Young Leaders for the Sustainable Development Goals

The Young Leaders for the SDGs program is a flagship initiative of the UN, managed by the Office of the Secretary-General's Envoy on Youth. It is specifically designed to identify, recognize, and elevate exceptional young changemakers who are making significant strides toward achieving the SDGs in their communities and beyond (Office of the Secretary-General's Envoy on Youth, n.d.d).

Practically speaking, the program acknowledges the vital contributions of these young leaders by selecting 17 outstanding individuals every two years, each representing one of the 17 SDGs. Participants are found and nominated through an open global application process. Young people between the ages of 18 and 30 are invited to apply by submitting detailed information about their work, impact, and alignment with specific SDGs. The selection process is highly competitive, attracting thousands of applications worldwide (Office of the Secretary General's Envoy on Youth, n.d.d; Office of the Secretary-General's Envoy on Youth, n.d.e).

The selection involves multiple stages, beginning with an initial screening where applications are reviewed for eligibility and completeness. Shortlisted candidates are then evaluated by expert panels based on criteria such as leadership qualities, innovative approaches, proven impact, and the ability to inspire others. The Office of the UN Youth Envoy makes the final decision, ensuring a diverse cohort representing different regions, backgrounds, and SDG focus areas (United Nations Office of the Secretary-General's Envoy on Youth, 2016).

The program duration is two years, during which the Young Leaders serve as advocates and ambassadors for the SDGs. They are provided with critical support, mentorship, and opportunities to connect with a global network of like-minded individuals committed to sustainable development. Mentorship from experienced UN officials and experts helps them refine their strategies, enhance their projects, and increase their effectiveness (Office of the Secretary-General's Envoy on Youth, 2022).

Throughout the program, Young Leaders gain access to global platforms. They participate in high-level UN events, such as the UN General Assembly and the High-Level Political Forum (e.g., Sustainable Development Goals, 2016). This exposure allows them to advocate for their causes on a global stage, share insights, and learn from other cultures and approaches. The program fosters a supportive ecosystem where Young Leaders can connect with each other, leading to cross-border collaborations and innovative solutions to global challenges. Their projects and ideas received increased attention through UN channels, media coverage, and speaking engagements, helping attract additional resources and support to expand their impact (e.g., Sustainable Development Goals, 2019; Sustainable Development Goals, 2023).

For example, in the 2022 cohort, the Young Leaders included individuals like Heela Yoon, a peace advocate from Afghanistan, and Ronelle King, a gender justice advocate from Bermuda. They worked on issues ranging from environmental sustainability to gender equality, robotics, entrepreneurship, and education (United Nations Office of the Secretary-General's Envoy on Youth, n.d.f). By spotlighting these young innovators, the program ensures that their contributions are not only recognized but also amplified.

The practical approach of selecting a limited number of participants allows for tailored support and meaningful engagement. The two-year term provides ample time for the Young Leaders to develop their initiatives and build lasting relationships within the UN system (United Nations Office of the Secretary-General's Envoy on Youth, n.d.d). Organizations looking to replicate this program can consider defining clear objectives focused on recognizing and supporting young leaders who align with specific goals or values, and implementing an open and competitive selection process with transparent criteria ensuring diversity and representation. Providing structured support through mentorship, resources, and platforms enhances participants' impact, while facilitating networking opportunities connects them with peers, experts, and potential collaborators. Enhancing visibility through media and events increases awareness of their work, attracting further support and engagement.

In essence, the Young Leaders for the SDGs program encapsulates the UN's commitment to integrating the energy, creativity, and unique perspectives of youth in driving global change. By providing practical support and global recognition, the UN not only bolsters the current generation of young leaders but also ensures sustained momentum toward achieving the SDGs, paving the way for a sustainable future that benefits all (United Nations Office of the Secretary-General's Envoy on Youth, n.d.d).

UN External "Tomorrow" Programs: UN75 Consultations

In 2020, marking its seventy-fifth anniversary, the UN embarked on the UN75 consultations, pioneering global consultation process aimed at integrating the ideas and perspectives of young people into the future trajectory of the organization. This inclusive approach underscored the UN's commitment to engaging with a generation that will inherit the outcomes of today's policies and global initiatives (Office of the Under-Secretary-General and Special Adviser on Preparations for the Commemoration of the UN's 75th Anniversary, 2020). The insights gathered through this process were instrumental in shaping the report *Our Common Agenda*, a comprehensive document that articulates a vision for a world that is more peaceful, just, and sustainable (United Nations, 2021b).

The UN75 consultations reached out across continents, drawing in diverse voices from various backgrounds to ensure a rich tapestry of viewpoints was represented (Office of the Under-Secretary-General and Special Adviser on Preparations for the Commemoration of the UN's 75th Anniversary, 2020a). Young participants were encouraged to share their thoughts, fears, and hopes about the future, providing the UN with a unique and valuable perspective that is often missing from high-level diplomatic discussions. This engagement not only brought fresh ideas to the table but also fostered a sense of ownership and participation among the youth, making them feel more connected to the UN and its global mission (United Nations, 2021b).

The outcome of these consultations, encapsulated in *Our Common Agenda*, outlines a forward-looking blueprint for international cooperation and governance. The report emphasizes the need for collective action to address global challenges such as climate change, inequality, and conflict, and highlights the critical role of youth as agents of change within this framework (United Nations, 2021b).

The UN75 consultations exemplify how the UN is adapting to the demands of a rapidly changing world by placing youth at the heart of its agenda. By listening to and incorporating the views of younger generations, the UN is ensuring that its plans for the future are robust, relevant, and inclusive. This initiative not only enriches the organization's understanding and approach but also empowers young people to actively shape a world that aligns with their aspirations for peace, justice, and sustainability.

Conclusion

As the UN family of organizations navigates a world that has changed dramatically since its inception in 1945, it continues to serve as a pivotal body of institutions providing stability in an increasingly uncertain global landscape. Despite facing numerous challenges and undergoing significant transformations, the UN has remained the cornerstone of international cooperation and development (Griffin, 2019; Mingst et al., 2022).

The UN's progressive initiatives, such as the Quintet of Change, the UN Values and Behaviors Framework, and leadership development programs, underscore its role as a trailblazer in setting trends and approaches for reshaping global leadership. These efforts demonstrate a commitment not only to adapt to a changing world but also to actively shape the leadership that will navigate the complexities of today and the uncertainties of tomorrow.

In a world where change is the only constant, the UN's ability to integrate a broad spectrum of perspectives—garnered through its truly global representation—ensures that its strategies and solutions are not only culturally sensitive but also shaped by extensive and inclusive consultations (e.g., Dag Hammarskjöld Foundation, 2024). This inclusivity enhances the credibility and applicability of the UN's approaches, making it a trusted leader in international governance.

As the global community continues to grapple with unprecedented challenges, the UN stands out as one of the few multilateral institutions equipped to guide us toward a more stable, just, and sustainable world. The leadership models and strategies developed and implemented by the UN are not merely responses to global trends but are proactive measures that set the standard for governance and cooperation worldwide. Thus, for better or worse, the world continues to look to the UN for guidance on navigating the future, relying on its extensive reach and deep-rooted principles to lead the way.

Notes

1. The SDGs are a set of 17 global objectives, adopted in 2015, that aim to address major global challenges and promote prosperity, peace, and environmental sustainability. These goals unite all 193 UN member states in a shared mission to end poverty, protect the planet, and ensure well-being for all by 2030. Examples include "Goal 1: No Poverty," "Goal 5: Gender Equality," and "Goal 13: Climate Action."
2. While the UN employs objective selection criteria and validated selection methods, these have traditionally resulted in differential outcomes. A simple criteria like "years of work experience in a particular field," which is rigidly set for each level in the UN system, immediately creates a gender disparity in the applicant pool. This is because, across the globe, women have historically had less access to professional opportunities and, therefore, have fewer years of experience, on average, in most fields. Other selection methods, such as competency-based interviews, had a similar impact. These backward-looking assessments, which require candidates to provide concrete examples of actions they took in specific situations, placed female candidates at a distinct disadvantage in many instances. This is because women, who on average have less work experience due to historical inequalities, had fewer, and often less compelling, examples to draw on. The same outcomes applied to many applicants from the Global South who come from socioeconomic backgrounds where, on average, there were less educational and work experience opportunities available.

References

Alnamrouti, A., Rjoub, H., & Ozgit, H. (2022). Do strategic human resources and artificial intelligence help to make organisations more sustainable? Evidence from non-governmental organisations. *Sustainability, 14*(12), 7327. https://doi.org/10.3390/su14127327

Altiok, A., & Grizelj, I. (2019). We are here: An integrated approach to youth inclusive peace processes. *United Nations.* https://www.un.org/youthenvoy/wpcontent/uploads/2019/07/Global-Policy-Paper-Youth-Participation-in-Peace-Processes.pdf

Avagyan, A. (2022, November 20). Refining artificial intelligence for recruitment of UN Volunteers. *UN Volunteers.* https://www.unv.org/Success-stories/refining-artificial-intelligence-recruitment-un-volunteers

Berrone, P., & Ricart Costa, J. E. (2024, July 30). This is how companies can make the UN's SDGs their own. *World Economic Forum.* https://www.weforum.org/stories/2024/07/companies-can-make-the-uns-sdgs-their-own-heres-how

Brookland, J. (2019). Revolutionizing recruitment: A test for AI in the United Nations. In Parater, L. & Park, H. (Eds.), *The United in UNCHR Innovation Service in 2018–2019: Explorations and discoveries in innovation at UNCHR* (pp. 96–110). https://www.unhcr.org/innovation/wp-content/uploads/2019/06/Innovation18-19-WebV.pdf

Business Day NG. (2017). *Fidelity Bank, Empretec empower 300 youths with entrepreneurial skills.* https://archive.businessday.ng/enterpreneur/article/fidelity-bank-empretec-empower-300-youths-entrepreneurial-skills

Coelho, F. J. M., Marques, C., Loureiro, A., & Ratten, V. (2018). Evaluation of the impact of an entrepreneurship training program in Recife, Brazil. *Journal of Entrepreneurship in Emerging Economies, 10*(3), 472–488. https://doi.org/10.1108/jeee-10-2017-0077

Dag Hammarskjöld Foundation. (2020). *The art of leadership in the United Nations: Framing what is blue.* https://www.daghammarskjold.se/wp-content/uploads/2020/03/un_leadership_2020.pdf

Dag Hammarskjöld Foundation. (2024). *The art of leadership in the United Nations: Our duty to find new forms*. https://academic.oup.com/edited-volume/27974/chapter-abstract/211645540?redirectedFrom=fulltext

Dempsey, J. (2023, September 21). Judy asks: Is the United Nations still fit for purpose? *Carnegie Endowment*. https://carnegieendowment.org/europe/strategic-europe/2023/09/judy-asks-is-the-united-nations-still-fit-for-purpose?lang=en

Denis, J.E., Bullon, A.L., & Sherif, K. (2000). *Evaluation of UNCTAD Empretec program* (TD/B/WP/129). United Nations.

Department of Economic and Social Affairs. (n.d.). UN Youth Delegate Program. *United Nations*. https://social.desa.un.org/issues/youth/un-youth-delegate-programme

Department of Economic and Social Affairs. (2020). The United Nations guide to the Youth Delegate Program. *United Nations*. https://social.desa.un.org/sites/default/files/migrated/21/2020/05/Youth-Delegates-Guide_May-20200-WEB-1.pdf

Department of Economic and Social Affairs, Population Division. (2024). World population prospects 2024. *United Nations*. https://www.un.org/development/desa/pd/sites/www.un.org.development.desa.pd/files/undesa_pd_2024_wpp_2024_advance_unedited_0.pdf

Department of Management, Strategy, and Compliance & Department of Operational Support. (2022). Applicant guide. *United Nations Secretariat*. https://careers.un.org/media/contactus/contactus/QuickGuide/Applicant_guide_262023163740.pdf

Economic Commission for Africa. (2018). Building biomedical engineering innovation capacity for improved health outcomes in Africa. *United Nations*. https://archive.uneca.org/sites/default/files/PublicationFiles/pb_building_biomedical_engineering.pdf

Economic Commission for Africa. (2022, September 30). ECA's acting chief discusses UN values and behaviours framework with staff. *United Nations*. https://www.uneca.org/stories/eca%E2%80%99s-acting-chief-discusses-un-values-and-behaviors-framework-with-staff#:~:text=Mr%20Pedro%20underscored%20the%20four,%3B%20and%20Adapt%20and%20Innovate.%E2%80%9D

Empretec. (n.d.). *Empretec training workshop*. https://www.empretec.in/workshops.php#:~:text=A%20typical%20ETW%20is%20about,the%20success%20of%20an%20entrepreneur

Entrepreneurship Development Institute Ethiopia. (n.d.). *Business development service (BDS)*. https://edi-ethiopia.org/bds.html

Foster, L. (2017). *Applying behavioural insights to organisations: Theoretical underpinnings* (OECD Regional Development Papers, No. 92). OECD Publishing. https://doi.org/10.1787/48a7e6de-en

Gerber, B. (2024, June 1). When norm-based leadership turns into ethical decision-making at the United Nations. *UNToday*. https://untoday.org/when-norm-based-leadership-turns-into-ethical-decision-making-at-the-united-nations

Ghazaryan, A. (2022). Leadership from where you sit: Behavioural challenge. In T. Weiss & S. Daws (Eds.), *The art of leadership in the United Nations* (2nd ed., pp. 131–153). https://www.daghammarskjold.se/wp-content/uploads/2022/06/leadership-report-2022-web.pdf

Griffin, M. (2019). The UN's role in the changing global landscape. In Weiss, T. & Daws, S. (Eds.), *The Oxford handbook on the United Nations* (pp. 823–842). https://academic.oup.com/edited-volume/27974/chapter-abstract/211645540?redirectedFrom=fulltext

Hendra, J. (2024). Pivoting for more dynamic impact: Enhancing UN development policy leadership during times of policy crisis. *Dag Hammarskjöld Foundation*. https://www.daghammarskjold.se/wp-content/uploads/2024/08/arts-of-leadership-digital-96ppi-2024.pdf

HR Portal. (n.d.). Leadership and management development (LMD). *United Nations*. https://hr.un.org/page/leadership-and-management-development

International Trade Centre. (2013, April 15). *Empretec: Inspiring entrepreneurship*. https://www.intracen.org/news-and-events/news/empretec-inspiring-entrepreneurship

Jacquand, M. (2024). Leadership and identity. *Dag Hammarskjöld Foundation*. https://www.daghammarskjold.se/wp-content/uploads/2020/03/un_leadership_2020.pdf

Kalantar, N. (2019, July 18). The limitations and capabilities of the United Nations in modern conflict. *E-International Relations*. https://www.e-ir.info/2019/07/10/the-limitations-and-capabilities-of-the-united-nations-in-modern-conflict

Martins, M. F., Cfp, M. H. P., & Garcia, M. R. (2021). The impact of Empretec entrepreneurship training workshop on Brazilian businesses. *SSRN Electronic Journal*. https://doi.org/10.2139/ssrn.3937662

Mingst, K.A., Karns, M.P., & Lyon, A.J. (2022). *The United Nations in the 21st century* (6th ed.). Routledge. https://doi.org/10.4324/9781003038269

Nwanguma, B. (2022). Youth entrepreneurial ecosystem: The case of Nigeria. In *Youth entrepreneurial ecosystem for sustainable development in Sub-Saharan Affrica* (pp. 98–113). https://aap.isp.msu.edu/files/1316/4916/9659/AAP_Youth_Report_FINAL_DIGITAL_04.05.2022.pdf

Office of Counter-Terrorism. (n.d.). Behavioural Insights Academy. *United Nations*. https://www.un.org/counterterrorism/behavioral-insights-academy

Office of Human Resources. (n.d.) Values and behaviors. *United Nations*. https://unu.edu/sites/default/files/2023-01/Values-and-Behaviours-Framework_Final.pdfValuesandBehaviours

Office of Human Resources. (2020). Geographical diversity strategy. *United Nations*. hr.un.org/files/OHR%20Geographical%20Diversity%20Strategy_EN_0.pdf

Office of the Secretary-General's Envoy on Youth. (n.d.a). United Nations Office of the Secretary-General's Envoy on Youth. *United Nations*. https://www.un.org/youthenvoy

Office of the Secretary-General's Envoy on Youth. (n.d.b). About Young Leaders for the SDGs. *United Nations*. https://www.un.org/youthenvoy

Office of the Secretary-General's Envoy on Youth. (n.d.c). Workplan. *United Nations*. https://www.un.org/youthenvoy/workplan

Office of the Secretary-General's Envoy on Youth. (n.d.d). Become a Young Leader for the SDGs. *United Nations*. https://www.un.org/youthenvoy/becomeyoungleader

Office of the Secretary-General's Envoy on Youth. (n.d.e). FAQ. *United Nations*. https://www.un.org/youthenvoyFAQ

Office of the Secretary-General's Envoy on Youth. (n.d.f). Meet the 2022 cohort of Young Leaders for the SDGs. *United Nations*. https://www.un.org/youthenvoy/2022class

Office of the Secretary-General's Envoy on Youth. (2016, September 19). United Nations announces Young Leaders for the Sustainable Development Goals. *United Nations*. https://www.un.org/youthenvoy/young-leaders-sdgs

Office of the Secretary-General's Envoy on Youth. (2022). Year in Review. *United Nations*. https://www.un.org/youthenvoy/wp-content/uploads/2023/01/OSGEY-Year-in-Review-2022-1.pdf

Office of the Under-Secretary-General and Special Adviser on Preparations for the Commemoration of the UN's 75th Anniversary. (2020). Updated on the work of the UN75 Office resolves to combine our efforts: Preliminary assessment of the UN75 survey and dialogues. *United Nations*. https://www.un.org/sites/un2.un.org/files/un75_update_report_april_2020_final.pdf

Office of the Under-Secretary General & Special Adviser on Preparations for the Commemoration of the UN's 75th Anniversary. (2021). Shaping our future together: Listening to the people's priorities for the future and their ideas for action. *United Nations*. https://data.undp.org/sites/g/files/zskgke476/files/2023-11/UN75_final_report_ShapingOurFutureTogether2.pdf

Owuamanam, C. M., & Nwagbo, S. N. C. (2024). The United Nations' approach towards global peace and security: Understanding the challenging issues. *Social Science Research*, *10*(1), 89–105.

Pehrman, K., Emerson, L., Anderson, M., Arnò, I., Turunen, S., & Ronda, S. (2019). Supplementary guidance on the enabling environment guidelines for the United Nations System. *UN Women*. https://www.unwomen.org/sites/default/files/Headquarters/Attachments/Sections/Library/Publications/2019/Gender-parity-Enabling-environment-guidelines-Supplementary-guidance-en.pdf

Reimann, K. D. (2006). A view from the top: International politics, norms and the worldwide growth of NGOs. *International Studies Quarterly*, *50*(1), 45–68. https://doi.org/10.1111/j.1468-2478.2006.00392.x

Secretary-General's Task Force on Addressing Racism and Promoting Dignity for All in the United Nations Secretariat. (2021). *Strategic action plan: Report of the Secretary-General's Task Force on Addressing Racism and Promoting Dignity for All in the United Nations Secretariat*. https://hr.un.org/sites/hr.un.org/files/sap_final_report_0.pdf

Stauffer, M., Seifert, K., Aristizábal, A., Chaudhry, H. T., Kohler, K., Hussein, S. N., Salinas Leyva, C., Gebert, A., Arbeid, J., Estier, M., Matinyi, S., Hausenloy, J., Kaur, J., Rath, S., & Wu, Y.-H. (2023). Existential risk and rapid technological change. *Simon Institute for Longterm Governance & United Nations Office for Disaster Risk Reduction*. https://www.undrr.org/media/86500/download?startDownload=20241104

Sustainable Development Goals. (2016, September 20). SDG advocates highlight the formal opening of the General Assembly and engage in SDG Media Zone dialogues. *United Nations*. https://www.un.org/sustainabledevelopment/blog/2016/09/sdg-advocates-highlight-the-formal-opening-of-the-general-assembly-and-engage-in-sdg-media-zone-dialogues

Sustainable Development Goals. (2019, April 10). Youth advocates demand immediate action to address urgent challenges. *United Nations*. https://www.un.org/sustainabledevelopment/blog/2019/04/youth-advocates-demand-immediate-action-to-address-urgent-challenges

Sustainable Development Goals. (2023, April 25). World youth leaders gather at UN for ECOSOC Youth Forum to accelerate COVID-19 recovery and SDG Implementation. *United Nations*. https://www.un.org/sustainabledevelopment/blog/2023/04/press-release-accelerating-the-covid-19-recovery-and-full-implementation-of-the-2030-agenda-with-and-for-youth

Tharoor, S. (2020, October 5). *The UN's existential crisis*. Project Syndicate. https://www.project-syndicate.org/commentary/united-nations-anniversary-covid19-existential-crisis-by-shashi-tharoor-2020-10

UN 2.0. (n.d.). *UN 2.0 Quintet of Change*. https://un-two-zero.network

United Nations. (n.d.a). *Our work*. https://www.un.org/en/our-work

United Nations. (n.d.b). *Careers*. https://inspira.un.org/psc/REGISTER/EMPLOYEE/HRMS/c/UN_SKILL_REG.UN_SKILL_REG.GBL&languagecd=ENG

United Nations. (n.d.c). *United for gender parity: FAQ*. https://www.un.org/gender/faq

United Nations. (n.d.d). *United for gender parity: Key facts*. https://www.un.org/gender/about-us

United Nations. (n.d.e). *Chapter I: Purposes and Principles (Articles 1–2)*. https://www.un.org/en/about-us/un-charter/chapter-1

United Nations. (1945). *Charter of the United Nations*. https://www.un.org/en/about-us/un-charter

United Nations. (2017a). *System-wide strategy on gender parity*. https://www.un.org/gender/sites/www.un.org.gender/files/gender_parity_strategy_october_2017.pdf

United Nations. (2017b, Annex I). *United Nations system leadership framework* (CEB/2017/1, Annex I). https://documents.un.org/doc/undoc/gen/n17/178/23/pdf/n1717823.pdf

United Nations. (2020). *Data strategy of the Secretary-General for action by everyone, everywhere*. https://www.un.org/en/content/datastrategy/images/pdf/UN_SG_Data-Strategy.pdf

United Nations. (2021a). *Review of the management of the implementing partners in United Nations systems organizations* (JIU/REP/2021/4). https://www.unjiu.org/sites/www.unjiu.org/files/jiu_rep_2021_4_english.pdf

United Nations. (2021b). *United Nations comprehensive response to COVID-19*. https://www.un.org/sites/un2.un.org/files/2021/12/un-comprehensive-response-covid-19-2021.pdf

United Nations. (2022). *Leadership dialogue 2022—Living the UN Values: What this means in practice for each of us*. https://www.un.org/en/ethics/assets/pdfs/Leadership%20Dialogue%202022_Leaders%20Guide.pdf

United Nations. (2023a). *Our common agenda* [Policy brief]. https://www.un.org/two-zero/sites/default/files/2023-09/UN-2.0_Policy-Brief_EN.pdf

United Nations. (2023b). *Alarmed by risk of nuclear escalation among major powers, speakers in General Assembly warn growing distrust, divisions are driving multilateral system towards dysfunction* [Press release] (GA/12538 2023). https://press.un.org/en/2023/ga12538.doc.htm

United Nations. (2023c). *Diversity, equity, and inclusion: Compilation of practices* (CEB/2023/HCLM/29, Annex 3). https://unsceb.org/sites/default/files/2024-01/DEI%20Compilation%20of%20Practices.pdf

United Nations. (2023d). *Navigating challenges and driving change: Women, peace, and security highlights of the UN* Peacekeeping in 2023. https://peacekeeping.un.org/sites/default/files/dpo_wps_report_2023-may24-digital.pdf

United Nations. (2023e) *The Sustainable Development Goals Report: Special Edition. https://*unstats.un.org/sdgs/report/2023/The-Sustainable-Development-Goals-Report-2023.pdf

United Nations. (2023f). *Determined: Report of the Secretary-General on the work of the organization*. https://www.un.org/sites/un2.un.org/files/sg_annual_report_2023_en_0.pdf

United Nations. (2024a, May 9). *Speaker focus on potential of artificial intelligence to address climate change, as Science, Technology, and Innovation Multi-Stakeholder Forum opens* [Press release] (ECOSOC/7162). United Nations Economic and Social Council.

United Nations. (2024c). *United Nations values and behaviors framework* (ST/SGB/2024/4). https://documents.un.org/doc/undoc/gen/n24/268/00/pdf/n2426800.pdf

United Nations Chief Executive Board for Coordination. (2017). *UN system leadership framework*. https://www.unssc.org/sites/default/files/un_system_leadership_framework.pdf

United Nations Conference on Trade and Development. (n.d.). *Empretec Programme: The entrepreneur's guide*. https://unctad.org/system/files/official-document/diaeed20093_en.pdf

United Nations Conference on Trade and Development. (2015). *Policy guide on youth entrepreneurship*. https://unctad.org/es/node/27135

United Nations Conference on Trade and Development. (2023). UNCTAD Empretec—Inspiring entrepreneurship. In *SDG Pulse 2022* (pp. 185–188). United Nations. https://doi.org/10.18356/9789210018418

United Nations Development Programme Ethiopia. (2019, May 16). *Entrepreneurship trainers certified by UNCTAD*. https://www.undp.org/ethiopia/news/entrepreneurship-trainers-certified-unctad

United Nations General Assembly. (2017). *Shifting the management paradigm in the United Nations: Ensuring a better future for all* (A/72/492). https://documents.un.org/doc/undoc/gen/n17/297/60/pdf/n1729760.pdf

United Nations Global Compact. (2019). *Making global goals local business: Responsible business in the era of the Sustainable Development Goals*. https://unglobalcompact.org/library/4321

United Nations Sustainable Development Group. (n.d.). *The Resident Coordinator/Humanitarian Coordinator (RC/HC) talent pipeline*. https://unsdg.un.org/2030-agenda/leadership/resident-coordinator-humanitarian-coordinator-rchc-talent-pipeline

United Nations Sustainable Development Group & Inter-Agency Standing Committee. (n.d.). *RC/HC talent pipeline numbers: Key data.* https://data.uninfo.org/Home/_LBRCTalent

United Nations System Staff College. (n.d.a). *UN Leaders Program.* https://www.unssc.org/un-leaders-programme

United Nations System Staff College. (n.d.b). *United Nations Systems Staff College.* https://www.unssc.org

United Nations System Staff College. (n.d.c). *Celebrating a 20-year learning and training journey.* https://www.unssc.org/celebrating-20-year-learning-and-training-journey

United Nations System Staff College. (n.d.d). *UN Leaders Programme online* [PowerPoint slides]. https://www.unssc.org/sites/default/files/inline-files/UNLP24_OnlineOverview.pdf

United Nations Systems Staff College. (2018, June 13). UN Leaders Programme celebrates 10-year anniversary. https://www.unssc.org/news-and-insights/news/un-leaders-programme-celebrates-10-year-anniversaryUNSCC. (2023, December 21). *UN Leaders Programme 2023* [Video]. Vimeo. https://vimeo.com/896927550?share=copy

UN Trade and Development. (n.d.). *Empretec—Entrepreneurship global network.* https://unctad.org/topic/enterprise-development/Empretec

UN Trade and Development. (2024, June 27). Micro-, small, and medium-sized enterprise day: Empretec global network event. *United Nations Conference on Trade and Development.* https://unctad.org/meeting/micro-small-and-medium-sized-enterprises-day-empretec-global-network-event

UN Women. (2022). *How can we reach gender parity at the UN by 2028?* https://www.unwomen.org/sites/default/files/2022-12/How-can-we-reach-gender-parity-at-the-United-Nations-by-2028-en.pdf

Van Tulder, R., Rodrigues, S. B., Mirza, H., & Sexsmith, K. (2021). The UN's Sustainable Development Goals: Can multinational enterprises lead the Decade of Action? *Journal of International Business Policy, 4*(1), 1–21. https://doi.org/10.1057/s42214-020-00095-1

Wood, J. (2018, August 23). Generation Z will outnumber millennials this year. *World Economic Forum.* https://www.weforum.org/stories/2018/08/generation-z-will-outnumber-millennials-by-2019/#:~:text=Writer%2C%20Forum%20Agenda,the%20intergenerational%20cut%2Doff%20point.

Yuan, H., Wang, X., Gao, L., Wang, T., Liu, B., Fang, D., & Gao, Y. (2023). Progress towards the Sustainable Development Goals has been slowed by indirect effects of the COVID-19 pandemic. *Communications Earth & Environment, 4*(1). https://doi.org/10.1038/s43247-023-00846-x

24

Creating Empathetic Managers at Walmart

Lorraine Stomski

Introduction

In March 2024, *The New York Times* wrote an article detailing how the world's largest retailer, Walmart, is teaching store managers how to be compassionate leaders (Holman, 2024). In a business that focuses heavily on operational excellence, it was a surprise to highlight the importance of soft skills. However, emerging from a global pandemic, social unrest, and the rise of generative artificial intelligence (AI), it seems timely that organizations will now shift more of their focus to the human side of leadership. Walmart's tagline— "People-led. Tech-powered."—also emphasized the people focus. With an estimated 250 million customers that pass through Walmart's doors each week, the opportunity to demonstrate compassion to our customers and fellow associates was of the utmost importance to our then CEO, Doug McMillon. In this chapter, I will provide an overview of why empathy and compassion are key to not just leadership success, but for the success of the business.

Walmart's roots date back to 1962 when Sam Walton had an idea to find goods at the lowest price possible and pass those savings on to their customers. The business began in 1962 in Rogers, Arkansas, with the goal to reach customers in underserved communities—primarily in rural areas. Sam, a pilot, flew all over the country, visiting stores and listening to his associates (i.e., employees) to hear their feedback. His curiosity was never satisfied; his ambition to win never tempered. He was a tough but fair leader and he would always say, "there is only one boss: the customer" (Walton & Huey, 1992, p. 13).

Lorraine Stomski, *Creating Empathetic Managers at Walmart*. In: *The Changing Leadership Landscape*.
Edited by: Sheri L. Feinzig and Mariangela Battista, Oxford University Press. © Oxford University Press (2026).
DOI: 10.1093/9780197820070.003.0024

Walmart is a founder-led company, and with its rural origins, it broke the model of retail in many ways; the tagline "every day low cost/every day low price" (EDLC/EDLP) is the centerpiece of Walmart's business model today. Its humble founder spent the bulk of his time with associates, *listening*, a key aspect of the culture. He strongly believed that the frontline associates were the most important asset of the company given their proximity to the customer. This sentiment holds true today at Walmart. But in 1962 there was one store, and today there are over 10,000 globally with 2.1 million associates. This creates a unique situation. How does one not just *select* associates who are empathetic and customer centric, but how do you continue to *train and develop* those skills when you have an employee population of 2.1 million, of which 1.6 million are in the United States? And, given that 90% of people in the United States live within 10 miles of a Walmart store, the need for our associates to serve our shoppers in a consistent and compassionate way can feel daunting.

In this chapter, I will share a unique approach to teaching empathy and compassion to Walmart's store managers. I will start by discussing the literature on listening and empathy, and whether it can be taught, followed by the role of culture and values in organizations to anchor desired behaviors expected by employees. We will then move into the actual design of the intervention ("Manager Academy") and metrics of success. Finally, we will discuss how to maintain the momentum of such programs.

Empathy

Empathy is the ability to understand and share another's emotions, needs, and thoughts. It involves "putting oneself in another's shoes" to experience their perspective or feelings (Ioannidou & Konstantikaki, 2008, p. 118). Empathy is critical as it helps us connect to each other—to understand when people are in pain, happy, struggling, etc. It is the core to our humanity. The question that many have asked—"Can you develop empathy?"—has been studied for many years. The short answer seems to be "yes," but like any human emotional capacity, it is probably a bit more complicated than taking a training course.

Let's start with brain science. Cook et al. (2014) discovered that it is mirror neurons that are responsible for humans' ability to develop connections with others and also to interpret why people act the way they do. Further, it is postulated that the part of the brain that is engaged when we feel emotions is the same area activated in the interpretation of others' emotions (Heyes & Catmur, 2021). Ferrari and Coudé (2018) cite three things we must be capable of doing in order for us to connect with others,: we must be capable of: (1) understanding what others are doing within our social group, (2) empathizing with how they feel, and (3) grasping their intentions. They go on to say that it is the mirror neurons that enable us to translate facial expressions and human interactions, enabling us "to perceive and understand others' feelings without words" (Trieu et al., 2019, p. 25). Given the underlying shared brain functions, we can engage and experience others' emotions. In addition, the role of oxytocin is critical in that it can regulate or enhance these empathic processes (Trieu, 2019). While the science of the brain and how it drives empathy will continue to be studied, another consideration is: What is the role of personality? Is empathy teachable, or are you just born with it?

Personality Theory and Empathy

What does personality theory tell us about empathy? Park and Lee (2020) looked at the relationship between the Five Factor Model of Personality (FFM) (Costa & McCrae, 1992) and empathy. The five factors—openness, extraversion, conscientiousness, agreeableness, and neuroticism—were examined across 63 studies. In their meta-analysis, Costa and McCrae (1992) found a strong relationship between agreeableness and empathy. The other four factors showed inconsistent or moderate relationships to empathy. Individuals with high agreeableness approach situations with a "people centric" view and communicate with others easily. The authors also found that openness was closely related to the "perspective taking" dimension of empathy. Further, Park and Lee (2020) found the following additional attributes to be closely related to empathy: compassionate, good-natured, eager to cooperate and avoid trouble.

Teaching Empathy

The general consensus in the literature is that empathy can in fact be taught. There are several studies that address how it can be taught in many different contexts, such as education and healthcare (Foster et al., 2017; Hojat et al., 2001; Zhou, 2022). Much of the approaches cited center around role-playing, reflection, mindfulness, emotional intelligence training, and mentorship, among other techniques. Some of the research suggests the use of technology such as virtual reality (VR) to help facilitate the learning. In this scenario, the goal is to achieve empathy by putting the individual in an immersive scenario that replicates representative situations encountered on the job—for example, an angry customer whom an associate would need to interact with. Here, VR can closely replicate the experience, using prompts like, "What would you do next?" It can immediately provide feedback on whether the response is appropriate or what a better approach would be. This can be a powerful way to mirror real life, putting the core principle of empathy in play, creating scenarios that put people in the shoes of others. It replicates the emotional sentiment and teaches people the best response. Given what we understand about personality theory and empathy, if we know that not everyone is going to be high in agreeableness or have attributes of perspective taking, this may be a great way to help teach and reinforce empathy and compassion. In Walmart Academy, this technology is used with our store associates to help them address some of the toughest customer scenarios.

Building Listening Skills

As discussed in the prior section, empathy is putting yourself in another person's shoes. In order to do that, it can be argued that it involves deep listening. One of the premier researchers in the field of listening is Avi Kluger. Kluger has focused his work on the core premise that developing listening skills in leaders can increase both performance and engagement in organizations (Kluger & DeNisi, 1996; Kluger & Nir, 2010). In his research, he has identified various listening styles such as analytical, empathetic, and comprehensive listening. *Analytical listening* is defined as being focused on the details of the message. People who engage in this kind of listening are seeking the evidence, logic, and facts behind the message. *Comprehensive listening* is seeking to understand and retain the information that is being communicated. Finally, *empathetic listening*, which I am postulating as being a requirement for an empathetic leader, is about trying to understand others' perspectives. Its goal is to emotionally connect with the communicator in attempting to understand the individual's feelings. I will focus on the building of this kind of listening skill to help create empathic leaders and managers. The genesis of empathetic listening can be traced back to Carl Rogers, considered to be one of the founding fathers of humanistic psychology (Rogers, 1951). Here is how Rogers (1975, p. 6) described the role that empathetic listening plays in learning and change:

> Over the years ... the research evidence keeps piling up and it points strongly to the conclusion that a high degree of empathy in a relationship is possibly the most potent factor. Certainly, one of the most potent factors in bringing about change and learning.

He goes on further to discuss the seven unique aspects of empathetic listening (Rogers, 1975, p. 4):

1. *Entering the Other's World*: Rogers describes empathic listening as "entering the private, perceptual world of the other, and becoming thoroughly at home in it."
2. *Moment-to-Moment Sensitivity*: Being sensitive to the changing feelings and meanings of the speaker, including their fears, anger, tenderness, or confusion.
3. *Temporary Suspension of Judgments*: Empathic listening requires temporarily laying aside one's own views, values, and prejudices to fully understand the other person's perspective.
4. *Not Trying to Uncover Unconscious Feelings*: Rogers cautioned against trying to uncover feelings of which the person is totally unaware, as this could be too threatening.
5. *The Power of Understanding*: Rogers believed that accurate empathic understanding can be a powerful force for personal growth and change.
6. *Self-Awareness*: Rogers also emphasized the importance of self-awareness for the listener, as they must be secure enough in themselves to avoid getting lost in the other person's world.
7. *Not Just a Technique*: Empathic listening is not just a technique but a way of being, a way of relating to others with genuine care and understanding.

In sum, the literature is fairly clear: we can teach both empathy and listening, even if individuals are not naturally possessing the personality attributes associated with these capacities. If we are to believe that we can teach empathy, and it requires deep and empathetic listening, how do we construct learning at scale to help leaders? The next section discusses how, by leveraging Walmart's unique culture, we have built manager training at scale to help our leaders become even more compassionate and empathetic.

Building Compassionate Leaders at Walmart Academy

One of the critical beliefs that Sam Walton had was about building a culture that placed the associates at the center. He believed that if we took care of our associates, they would take care of their customers. Mr. Sam, as he is affectionately referred to, famously said, "Our people make the difference. That's the way we built the company." That mindset led the company to create a set of four timeless values that were meant to guide the behaviors in their everyday work. The four values are (1) Respect for the individual, (2) Act with integrity, (3) Serve our customers and members, and (4) Strive for excellence. The tenet is, if our associates acted in accordance with the four values, we would create a workforce that would treat our customers and each other with respect and care while holding each other accountable.

Yet, this naturally became more challenging as the company grew to 2.1 million associates (as of 2025). How does one deploy our Walmart culture and values across 19 countries? In the early days of the COVID-19 pandemic, one of the jobs that the communities could count on to keep them fed and in supply of goods was the frontline retail worker. While many people ended up working from the comfort of their own homes during the pandemic, the frontline workforce showed up every day for their customers and remained steadfast, serving them and keeping them connected to the community. Additionally, when social unrest happened following the George Floyd murder in 2020, tensions were high in the United States and acts of incivility were reported across the country. This created an even stronger need for managers to show empathy.

While Walmart Academy has always included training on dealing with tough customers, it felt timely to refresh. Going back to the literature on empathy and listening, it was critical to identify ways in which we could create a safe experience for our associates to learn how to address some of these newer kinds of tough customer scenarios. As discussed in the section "Teaching Empathy," we did this through VR. This approach is especially useful in situations we describe as RIDE—rare, impossible, dangerous, and expensive to replicate.

Creating the Global Walmart Academy

In 2021, our Chief People Officer Donna Morris made the decision to centralize learning to modernize the approach, align it to the future of work, and scale it globally. The core problem we were trying to solve is: How do we reinforce and continue to teach the culture and values that Walmart has held true for decades? How does Walmart do this at scale three decades after Sam Walton's death? Back in the 1990s, Sam and Helen Walton created what was called the "Walton Institute." The primary goal of the Institute was to upskill managers across a wide variety of capabilities to keep them up to date from a business perspective. The other goal was to reinforce the Walmart culture and values. This was a successful initiative for many years, until it eventually ran its course.

Fast forward to the pandemic days, when several questions emerged from our most senior leaders: How can we ensure all our managers are tightly connected to our purpose, culture, and values? Especially when they are all over the world? How could we "reimagine" the Walton Institute, and provide all store managers the same understanding of our culture and values but in a new way? And how do we do this at scale and at a rapid pace? With close to 5,000 stores and clubs across the United States alone, this was a formidable task.

Enter Walmart Academy. Prior to the centralization of learning, the Walmart Academies were approximately 200 physical learning centers, typically attached to a supercenter, that taught a variety of courses, mostly business processes or "one-best-way" programs. It served primarily to provide the training and education to Walmart store associates on how to do their jobs. There are thousands of processes and procedures to running stores, and Walmart Academy teams focused their energy on ensuring that training was delivered in a consistent way—it was called "one best way." That training was helpful and needed at the time; however, a decision was made to create a global Walmart Academy that serves the entire enterprise: The United States, Sam's Club (our club membership business), and International, along with our corporate headquarters populations. We rebranded from a focus on the 200+ physical entities to one global Walmart Academy, serving our associates wherever and however they need learning. Now, an associate could access training and learning through several ways: the physical Academy, at Home Office, in one of our countries of business, on their handheld devices, or online. Our goal was to meet our associates where they want to access learning.

This enabled us to shift our focus from mostly process and procedure (e.g., how to cut meat) to training on culture, leadership, and values. Given the expressed needs of the business, they asked that all store managers complete this training to ensure consistency. This meant a learning strategy that would engage 5,000+ store and club managers, over an accelerated timeline—a not-so-easy feat. As we looked back at the former Walton Institute, there were many lessons learned—the power of the manager community, learning from each other, and strengthening the emotional connection to the Walmart culture whether the manager is in Bentonville, Arkansas, or Milpitas, California. We wanted to ensure that in building the program, we were respecting the past but focused on equipping our current workforce with the tools needed to lead in our increasingly complex environment while using our culture and values as the guidepost. Further, the store and club manager roles are critical to the business. They are the "Chief Executive Officers" (CEOs) of the stores they run, they are the leaders in the communities we serve, and they are accountable for all the hiring and operations of the stores. We quickly made the decision to celebrate the manager focus and called this new learning initiative "Manager Academy," built and designed for our store/club managers.

At the core, the Manager Academy vision is anchored to our culture and four timeless values. These values are well-understood in the Walmart culture. They are taught during onboarding, displayed in our stores, clubs, and facilities, and used as a rubric for decision-making among our 2.1 million associates. That said, given how many new associates are hired each week and the movement of talent across the organization, we needed to ensure that the teaching of culture is "always on," through role-modeling behavior and through our new Manager Academy training.

Keeping our timeless values front and center of the training, Manager Academy was designed as an immersive experience. Managers come to Walmart Headquarters in Bentonville, Arkansas, for five days. Approximately 25–30 managers attend per week from across the country. Prior to them coming, each complete a 360-degree survey focused on Walmart's Leadership Expectations (our competency model). During the five-day in-person experience, we cover four core leadership areas, as shown in Figure 24.1.

Note the heavy focus on values, the customer, leadership, resilience, and listening. The model used reflects adult learning models of experiential learning theory (Kolb, 1984). As illustrated by Figure 24.1, managers come together across a wide variety of learning experiences.

WEEK AT A GLANCE

DAY 1	**Live Our Values - Part 1** Our Mission Aligning Our Values Walton Culture
DAY 2	**Live Our Values - Part 2** Home Office Tour Walmart and the Community Community Service Event
DAY 3	**Focus On The Associate** Tour | Distribution Center Leading with a Focus on Well-being Resilience Coaching and Active Listening
DAY 4	**Deliver for the Customer** Know Your Customer Tour | Store of the Future Tour | Sam's Club Building Loyalty
DAY 5	**Embrace Change** Digital Ways of Thinking Ambassador for Change Lead Like Sam

Figure 24.1 Overview of Manager Academy

Importantly, in addition to our Walmart Academy master facilitators, we have retired Walmart leaders teach during the week. We have had former operators and Chief Merchants lead sessions. To keep the culture at the forefront, they share stories of working with Sam Walton, bringing in artifacts of the time he was alive, such as letters written by him, and share the learnings they received under his leadership. It is one of the most powerful moments during the week. In addition to classroom activities, managers tour stores, do case studies, role-play, and share the problems they are solving. The goal is to create a community of peers that can serve as a resource moving forward.

The highlight for many is the Home Office tour, not because of the physical aspect of seeing the office, but because they get to interact with so many senior leaders, mostly in a spontaneous way. On any given day, the US CEO or Chief Operating Officer (COO) could be there, and our CEO Doug McMillon is often there and speaks to the visiting managers. It provides an opportunity for listening, sharing stories, and expressing gratitude for the work our store and club managers do for our customers and associates. Sometimes, managers will get to speak with other long-term associates at the Home Office; notably, level is insignificant as all associates are expected to be culture carriers. All these experiences, both formal and informal, create a connection to the culture and mission of Walmart, which is to "help people save money so they can live better." It also highlights how, through every interaction and experience, it provides a way in which to teach and reinforce the desired attributes of Walmart leaders—humility, servant leadership, empathy, and active listening.

Conclusion

We held our first Manager Academy in 2021; as of 2025, we have had almost 5,000 store and club managers go through the program. Following each in-person session in Bentonville, the lessons are brought back to the store and shared with the associates. Additionally, all managers go through another 360-degree survey six months following their participation, and we are seeing statistically significant elevated leadership ratings post-participation. While our net promoter score (NPS) for the program is impressive at 96, the more telling measure is going back to the listening literature: Does the program actually increase engagement of associates and enhance their performance? Our results demonstrate a statistically significant engagement score improvement of 3% for associates of managers who have completed Manager Academy versus those who have not. Store performance on critical key performance indicators (KPIs) are stronger for those stores and clubs who have had managers go through Manager Academy than those who have not, a testament to the intervention and likely the strengthened emotional connection created to the organization.

The success of Manager Academy has led us to expand it to other audiences—including supply chain general managers and the recently created Market Manager Academy—a higher-level program aimed at those who manage regions. In addition, we have built a program focused on those who are new to leading, called License to Lead. This new program has resulted in a 7% increase in customer satisfaction for those who have attended the program. Further, we have seen a 9% increase in retention of hourly workers for those leaders who manage that population. At our scale, single digit percentages translate into thousands of associates and meaningful business impact. While we are still early in our journey, we will continue to strengthen the immersion, continuing to reinforce our culture and values and create empathetic and compassionate managers, all while driving strong business results.

References

Cook, R., Bird, G., Catmur, C., Press, C., & Heyes, C. (2014). Mirror neurons: From origin to function. *The Behavioral and Brain Sciences, 37*(2), 177–192.

Costa, P. T., Jr., & McCrae, R. R. (1992). Four ways five factors are basic. *Personality and individual differences, 13*(6), 653–665.

Ferrari, P. F., & Coudé, G. (2018). Mirror neurons, embodied emotions, and empathy. In K. Z. Meyza & E. Knapska (Eds.), *Neuronal correlates of empathy: From rodent to human* (pp. 67–77). Elsevier Academic Press. https://doi.org/10.1016/B978-0-12-805397-3.00006-1

Foster, A., Trieu, M., Azutillo, E., Halan, S., & Lok, B. (2017). Teaching empathy in healthcare: From mirror neurons to education technology. *Journal of Technology in Behavioral Science, 2*, 94–105.

Heyes, C., & Catmur, C. (2021). What happened to mirror neurons? *Perspectives on Psychological Science, 17*(1), 153–168. https://doi.org/10.1177/1745691621990638

Hojat, M., Mangione, S., Gonnella, J. S., Nasca, T., Veloski, J. J., & Kane, G. (2001). Empathy in medical education and patient care. *Academic Medicine, 76*(7), 669.

Holman, J. (2024, March 12). Walmart wants to teach store managers compassion. *The New York Times*. https://www.nytimes.com/2024/03/12/business/walmart-manager-training.html.

Ioannidou, F., & Konstantikaki, V. (2008). Empathy and emotional intelligence: What is it really about? *International Journal of caring sciences, 1*(3), 118.

Kluger, A. N., & DeNisi, A. (1996). The effects of feedback interventions on performance: A historical review, a meta-analysis, and a preliminary feedback intervention theory. *Psychological bulletin, 119*(2), 254.

Kluger, A. N., & Nir, D. (2010). The feedforward interview. *Human Resource Management Review, 20*(3), 235–246.

Kolb, D. A. (1984). *Experiential learning: Experience as the source of learning and development.* Prentice-Hall.

Park, H. J., & Lee, J. H. (2020). Looking into the personality traits to enhance empathy ability: A review of literature. In C. Stephanidis & M. Antona (Eds.), *HCI International 2020-Posters: 22nd International Conference, HCII 2020, Copenhagen, Denmark, July 19–24, 2020, Proceedings, Part I 22* (pp. 173–180). Springer International Publishing.

Rogers, C. R. (1951). *Client-centered therapy: Its current practice, implications, and theory.* Houghton Mifflin.

Rogers, C. R. (1975). Empathic: An unappreciated way of being. *The counseling psychologist, 5*(2), 2–10.

Trieu, M., Foster, A. E., Yaseen, Z. S., Beaubian, C., & Calati, R. (2019). Neurobiology of empathy. In Foster, A.E. and Yaseen, Z.S. (Eds.), *Teaching empathy in healthcare: Building a new core competency* (pp. 17–39). Springer Nature.

Walton, S., & Huey, J. (1992). *Made in America.* Bantam Books.

Zhou, Z. (2022). Empathy in education: A critical review. *International Journal for the Scholarship of Teaching and Learning, 16*(3), 2.

25

Developing Leaders at Scale

Gaurav Mukherjee, Lynn G. Collins, and Sandra B. Hartog

Introduction

In an era marked by a digital labor revolution, economic volatility, and evolving workplace dynamics, the importance of developing our employees cannot be overstated. Organizations today are navigating an increasingly complex environment where the ability to adapt, innovate, and lead with agility is not a luxury—it is a necessity. Developing our talent sits at the core of this strategic imperative, providing the foundation for sustained high performance.

As highlighted in recent industry insights, investing in employee development is not merely a response to external factors but a proactive strategy to ensure organizational continuity, scalability, and success. Employees are not just strategic contributors; they are partners in innovation and value creation. Investing in their careers and their growth equips them to meet challenges with confidence, while also fostering engagement and sustained performance.

The stakes are high. Without strategic talent development, organizations risk falling behind in the war for talent, losing out on opportunities for innovation, and failing to adapt to a world where humans and non-human AI-enabled agents work in tandem to deliver unprecedented business results. Embedding a forward-looking, people-centric approach to learning and leadership, organizations can secure not only their future but also the enduring success of their workforce.

At Salesforce—a pioneer in data, artificial intelligence (AI), and customer relationship management—investing in building a strong leadership pipeline and manager capability has been an important driver of business.

Gaurav Mukherjee, Lynn G. Collins, and Sandra B. Hartog, *Developing Leaders at Scale*.
In: *The Changing Leadership Landscape*. Edited by: Sheri L. Feinzig and Mariangela Battista,
Oxford University Press. © Oxford University Press (2026). DOI: 10.1093/9780197820070.003.0025

Its success reaffirms the continued need to invest in employees and leaders to drive sustainable high performance.

The Business Imperative for Developing Talent

For organizations like Salesforce, investing in developing talent addresses immediate and long-term business needs, ensuring a pipeline of capable leaders who can drive growth and innovation. From the company's perspective, well-developed leaders enhance organizational agility, employee engagement, and productivity—all critical to maintaining a competitive edge. At Salesforce, this investment is driven by the business need to enable fast, aligned decision-making across a matrixed, high-growth environment. In Salesforce's case, internal surveys have consistently revealed that employees identified their direct manager as their most valued source of information and support. Frontline leaders therefore play a significant role in shaping company culture, developing teams, and driving operational excellence. Investing in developing leadership capability is an investment in the company's overall success, particularly in an era where humans and agents work in tandem to drive value for the business.

For employees, structured developmental programs provide opportunities for growth and self-actualization. These interventions not only prepare employees for leadership roles but also build their confidence and capabilities in their current positions. As participants grow, they feel more engaged and committed to their roles, contributing to a positive work environment and better team dynamics.

For shareholders, the return on investment in talent is tangible and measurable. High-performing leaders drive improved financial performance, enhance customer satisfaction, and reduce turnover costs. Studies consistently show that companies prioritizing employee development experience stronger performance, reflecting the link between engaged workforces and shareholder value. Salesforce's leadership programs—Accelerate for aspiring leaders and Elevate for in-role frontline managers—are directly aligned to key business priorities: building trust, accelerating accountability, and scaling high-performing teams globally. Salesforce's leadership programs serve as a prime example of this dynamic, with measurable outcomes such as increased retention, productivity, and quality of work directly tied to the company's strategic goals.

Building Personalized Leadership Development Experiences at Scale

Traditional leadership development programs often cater to a group of identified senior executives, with minimal support for aspiring and frontline managers. In the case of Salesforce, however, building frontline managerial capability through investing in aspiring managers, as well as developing in-role frontline managers, is essential for driving alignment, accountability, and sustained high performance. This approach was designed to ensure that the business can meet its growth goals while maintaining a consistent leadership culture across functions and geographies, prioritizing development opportunities where they are needed most.

In service of this approach, Salesforce crafted not one, but two industry-leading programs to cater to the development needs of its frontline leader population. These programs rank among the most extensive industry initiatives of their kind. Over 15,000 people have participated in them to date, and more than 2,000 leaders are on track to complete these programs in 2025.

These distinct yet interconnected programs were specifically developed to expose leaders to what it means to lead at Salesforce, deepen the knowledge and skills of both aspiring and in-role frontline leaders, and ultimately strengthen the organization's ability to deepen trust and cultivate leaders who have the desire and ability to lead high-performing teams. Doing so addresses both Salesforce's immediate and long-term business needs by fostering an environment where every leader is equipped to contribute significantly to the organization's success.

The two programs developed are:

- *Accelerate*, which focuses on equipping aspiring frontline leaders with the skills and knowledge they need to adopt a leadership mindset and excel in a future leadership role.
- *Elevate*, which develops results-driven frontline people managers with critical mindsets, behaviors, and skills, and strengthens accountability in Salesforce's ability to deepen trust within high-performing teams.

Accelerate and Elevate are each designed to address distinct aspects of frontline leadership skills. The two programs offer complementary experiences that provide a comprehensive learning pathway for frontline leaders.

While Accelerate is not a prerequisite to participate in Elevate, both programs are offered to leaders depending on what stage they are at in their leadership journey. Accelerate is designed for aspiring people leaders—individual contributors or program/practice leads who are preparing to step into a formal people manager role—while Elevate is for those already managing others. Elevate builds on skills learned in Accelerate, so leaders can take both programs in succession.

Accelerate serves as the foundational stage in developing Salesforce's frontline leadership pipeline, focusing on developing leaders' self-awareness and understanding of core people leadership skills and competencies. This program aims to prepare leaders by helping them understand their role expectations and the skills needed to meet those expectations effectively. The program also aims to provide opportunities for participants to take what they have learned and immediately apply that knowledge within their current role, creating a space where they can practice and continue to build that leadership muscle without being in a direct leadership role.

Elevate further builds skills and practice on the basis set by Accelerate, with a specific focus on accountability, which is a critical element within Salesforce's high-performance teaming. This program aims to translate the self-awareness, emotional intelligence, and key leadership skills developed in Accelerate into actionable leadership behaviors, such as strategic alignment, active listening, and trust-building. By focusing on these areas, Elevate seeks to enhance leaders' ability to drive team performance and contribute to organizational success. The progression from Accelerate to Elevate is strategic. By connecting Accelerate's focus on self-awareness and resilience with Elevate's emphasis on accountability, Salesforce creates a clear path for developing effective frontline leaders aligned with the organization's goals.

Accelerate Goals and Their Connection to Organizational Objectives

The Accelerate program's core goal is that by the end of the seven-month journey, participants will understand the expectations of a frontline people leader's role and the skills required to perform in the role effectively. Over the years, it has also become a very aspirational program from a career development and capability development standpoint among individual contributors. The program's learning objectives include:

- Develop a deeper self-awareness of purpose and values, and how these contribute to effective leadership
- Establish and nurture meaningful connections while expanding the participants' professional networks across the company
- Implement strategies that build resilience to navigate through common leadership pitfalls
- Adopt a beginner's mindset to grow and learn from others with different backgrounds, perspectives, and experiences
- Promote a culture of feedback through balancing constructive and positive input, while fostering an environment of psychological safety
- Effectively use strategic alignment tools such as V2MOM (which outlines Vision, Values, Methods, Obstacles, and Measures to align goals and drive focus), Einstein (Salesforce's AI technology), and customized agents
- Demonstrate impactful communication skills using storytelling and emotional intelligence

Elevate Goals and Their Connection to Organizational Objectives

Elevate also has a core goal tied to Salesforce's organizational objectives. The core program goal is that by the end of the journey, participants will understand and practice key behaviors necessary to ensure accountability within the business, their teams, and their role as a leader. This means that upon graduation, participants will be able to:

- Apply a framework to lead effectively in an era where humans and agents work together to drive business results
- Practice active listening and asking powerful questions that garner better insights they can apply toward conversations
- Learn strategies and actions that deepen trust with their teams
- Build a stronger community among fellow frontline people leaders

Design and Delivery: Both programs—designed with accessibility, blended learning, and a modular approach in mind—were developed and delivered in partnership with an external consulting firm (BTS) and leverage multiple learning modalities and a structured yet flexible curriculum to enhance participant engagement and retention. Alignment to Salesforce values and the V2MOM for greater relevance and application are key considerations for program design.

Blended Learning: The programs utilize a blend of learning methods to cater to different learning styles and to maximize knowledge retention. This includes multiple engagement touchpoints, consisting of peer-driven pod coaching sessions (small-group sessions focused on shared learning, feedback, and support) and virtual simulation workshops (interactive sessions where participants practice leadership in realistic business scenarios). This mix of formats ensures that learning is not only interactive, but also allows for the application of concepts in varied, realistic scenarios. The different points of engagement are designed to facilitate deeper understanding, encourage sharing of insights, and foster a collaborative learning environment. By incorporating both peer-driven and facilitated learning experiences, participants are offered a tapestry of perspectives and techniques, which enhances their learning journey.

Accessibility: Salesforce designed both Accelerate and Elevate to be virtual-first, accessible to leaders across the globe, and reflective of different learning styles and modalities. The design ensures that both programs are scalable and grounded in Salesforce's values of equality. Both programs incorporate virtual best practices such as optimizing activity duration, streamlining questions and reflection exercises, and fostering continuous peer discussions over traditional classroom teaching methods. The virtual format not only maintains high levels of engagement, but receives consistent, positive feedback from participants regarding their engagement with and the effectiveness of all journey sessions.

Practical Learning: The programs' design encourages participants to actively engage in peer discussions, experiments, and reflections within each module. This engagement is not only about absorbing knowledge, but also about applying it practically, allowing participants to directly observe the impact of their learning. Moreover, the focus on building Individual Development Plans (IDP) within the context of the modules enables participants to tailor their learning journey to their specific development needs, making the experience highly personalized and relevant.

Small-Group Coaching Sessions (Pods): Pods leverage the power of human networks and the digital workplace to accelerate context-rich learning, systems-centric transformation, and a timely flow of information. These pods are targeted, 90–120 minute personal coaching sessions where seven participants, supported by an experienced facilitator explore the practical and emotional side of leadership together and work through content and activities. In Accelerate, participants engage with the same group members in six pod sessions. Through staying with the same people for all pods, they form strong relationships; participants use their group as a safe space to share with one another. In Elevate, there are two pod sessions, and the groups are varied for each one. This is to enable participants to deepen their networks across the organization and share knowledge across business units. To prepare prior to each pod session, participants receive targeted pre-work that consists of reading and reflection.

Focus on Accountability: From a program design point of view, both programs are intentionally structured to help Salesforce leaders emphasize and practice accountability. This goal is directly reflected in the program's components, aiming to develop team dynamics, increase job satisfaction, and improve team efficiency. Key elements like the V2MOM framework, regular meetings, and quarterly check-ins are built into the programs' design to set clear goals and ensure everyone is accountable for their actions. These aspects are chosen specifically to make discussions on performance more straightforward, encourage setting specific targets, and achieve better outcomes for the company. Essentially, embedding accountability within these programs is crucial for meeting Salesforce's objectives.

Team-Based Simulations: The simulation elements for both Accelerate and Elevate are built around realistic business scenarios that demand strategic decision-making, putting participants in the shoes of leaders who must navigate the complexities and competitive pressures of the business world. The inputs for their simulations have been sourced after having extensive conversations with business leaders, previous alumni, and other functional stakeholders.

Participants are arranged into teams in a simulated market environment. This setup fosters a competitive spirit as teams vie for improvement across multiple leadership-focused metrics. Both simulations include continuous feedback on team performance, allowing participants to see the immediate effects of their decisions. This feedback loop is instrumental in creating a competitive learning environment where teams strive to improve their standing through iterative learning and strategic adjustment.

Accelerate Design

Multiple Modalities for Increased Retention and Sharing: The journey includes nine varied engagement touchpoints: six peer-driven pod coaching sessions and three virtual simulation workshops. These occur across three modules, accompanied by ample opportunities for practice and reflection.

Modular Design: The entire seven-month journey is designed into three distinct modules that align competency and skill development with Salesforce's People Performance Process, which is powered by their V2MOM. The modular design enables participants to focus on a few critical competencies at a time—with in-depth peer discussion, experiments, and reflections—and to build what they learn into their IDP.

All-Encompassing Online Portal: Participants are granted access to a comprehensive digital learning platform that offers a holistic view of their journey, housing all necessary content for activities such as pre-work and application, facilitating easy access to engagement sessions, and generating a personalized PDF document that encapsulates their contributions and the utilized content.

Gamification: To motivate leaders and increase engagement, track progress, and add an element of fun, the entire journey incorporates gamification. Participants earn points for learning, collaborating, practicing, and taking action, both individually and in teams, creating a sense of competition. However, all competitive program aspects are balanced with content that encourages participants to acquire new skills directly applicable to their roles. Although participants require a minimum number of points from each module to graduate at the end of the journey, they prioritize learning and application over competition.

Accelerate Modalities

Pre- and Post-Program Assessment: At the beginning and end of the Accelerate journey, participants complete a 30-minute, high-fidelity moments-based assessment, designed to simulate common challenges a frontline leader is likely to face on the job. After completing this tryout, participants receive a report detailing the decisions they made against predetermined behaviors and competencies of a frontline leader. This tryout helps them identify their development objectives for the Accelerate journey. For example, a participant might be asked to respond to a well-liked team member who is consistently missing deadlines and putting a project at risk—forcing the leader to balance accountability, empathy, and delivery under pressure.

Virtual Workshops/Competitive Simulation (Also Available as Self-Paced): Participants attend three two-hour-long virtual workshops across the modules. Each module features one workshop, with approximately 100 participants from other pods on the Accelerate journey. In their pod groups, participants progress through a simulation featuring job-related scenarios built around the most critical moments that distinguish great leadership from good leadership. These moments were identified through internal research, feedback from Salesforce leaders, and analysis of common leadership breakdowns. The pod groups compete against each other as their decisions are evaluated in relation to the following predefined metrics:

- *Team Execution*: Measures the ability of the team to complete assigned tasks, manage workload, and execute on deliverables in a timely manner. A high team execution score means the leader has provided their team with the tools and support needed to get the job done.
- *Team Alignment*: Measures how in-sync team members are with each other, the leader, and the project at hand. Strong people leaders ensure each team member knows their role, as well as the skillsets they each bring together to contribute to the project. Scoring well on team alignment shows that the team has the ability to work well together and is aligned working toward a single vision.
- *Team Trust*: Measures the level of trust and respect the team has for their leader. Team members expect their people leaders to understand their jobs and offer support and guidance. A high team trust score means that the leader has successfully created a comfortable work environment and built strong relationships, while maintaining a level of authority.

Stretch Assignments: In each module, participants have the chance to directly apply the content and concepts they learn through experiments called "stretch assignments." Each stretch assignment has three levels of activity based on time commitment. Participants can choose one, two, or all three to complete. These assignments require participants to complete an action or activity and offer reflection/feedback on it, both verbally in the next session and in writing.

Alumni Portal: After the program, if they graduate, participants gain access to a new portal which contains numerous resources that assist with their leadership development and progress. These resources include a Manager Conversation Guide to discuss progress and next steps, an Accelerate Graduation Certificate, and suggested activities for knowledge development.

Elevate Design

Multiple Modalities for Increased Retention and Sharing: The Elevate journey includes three touchpoints—two peer-driven pod coaching sessions and one virtual simulation workshop occurring across three modules, accompanied by ample opportunities for practice, reflection, networking, and community building.

Modular Design: The entire three-month journey is designed to strengthen accountability in Salesforce's ability to deepen trust among high-performing teams. Participants focus on deepening skill development aligned with Salesforce's People Performance Process, which is powered by their V2MOM.

The modular design enables each participant to dig deeper into their role as frontline people leader. First, they connect self-awareness to the impact their behaviors have on their teams. Then, in a simulated environment, participants apply tools to respond to critical moments that frontline people leaders experience. Finally, they learn how to lead high-performing teams, deepen trust, and accelerate results through developing relationships. The journey centers on the frontline people leader looking inward and assessing their behaviors and performance. Then, through peer coaching interactions, simulated experiences, experiments, and reflections, participants build their IDP using what they learn.

Elevate Modalities

Virtual Workshop/Competitive Simulation: Participants attend one six-hour-long virtual workshop, spread over two half-days with approximately 100 participants from other pods that are also on the Elevate journey. In their new simulation teams, participants progress through a simulation featuring job-related scenarios, built around critical moments that distinguish great leadership from good leadership. The simulation teams compete against one another, as their decisions are evaluated in relation to choices made in the simulation. For example, participants may be asked to lead through a scenario where their team is falling behind on deliverables and showing signs of misalignment. They must decide how to respond—whether to hold a team reset, deliver individual feedback, or escalate concerns—while maintaining trust and clarity. Their choices directly impact simulation scores in areas like team execution, team alignment, and team trust, with results visible in real time.

Practice and Learn Assignments: In each module, participants have the chance to directly apply the content and concepts they learn through experiments called "Practice and Learn Assignments." After each assignment is completed, participants share their experience with their pod groups and discuss ways to integrate what they have learned into the simulation and on the job. In addition, peer coaching pods are encouraged to set up monthly recurring meetings to check in on action plans, share progress, and get support from peers.

Program Adoption

Many of Salesforce's strategies in use increase the adoption rate of the programs. Here are some of the key features that make them a success.

Senior Leadership Endorsement: The Accelerate and Elevate program has seen substantial adoption rates, underpinned by explicit endorsement and support from senior leadership including the Chief People Officer (CPO). Their active support not only elevates the program's visibility across the organization, but also underscores its alignment with Salesforce's values and cultural priorities. This top-down endorsement is pivotal in encouraging broad participation and anchoring leadership development as a critical organizational focus.

Serialized Content: By chunking content and establishing a consistent delivery schedule, learners focus on one concept at a time and progress through the structured learning schedule. Completion milestones and opportunities for continuation further incentivize learners to stay engaged and pursue ongoing learning opportunities.

Gamification: A points system in Accelerate ensures participants stay engaged with the program. In Elevate, a simulation-based workshop promotes an immersive virtual experience that promotes social interaction among learners and enhances their motivation to engage. Both programs maintain a balance between healthy competition and collaboration. By fostering a cooperative learning environment where learners can share knowledge, collaborate on projects, and celebrate each other's successes, the programs promote an effective learning experience that prioritizes understanding and skill development over mere achievement or ranking.

Pod Accountability: In Accelerate, pod groups remain the same over the course of the program. This creates a safe, structured place for participants to learn, share, and develop together—and provides a platform for them to reinforce their commitments, actions, and mutual accountability. In Elevate, pod group members could in some cases differ to encourage network building and knowledge sharing. In both cases, participants consistently provide feedback that the pods allow them to leverage the power of human networks in a digital workplace to accelerate context-rich learning and timely flow of information.

Regional Networks: Program participants come from different functional backgrounds and are grouped with other members in their region to ensure that sessions take place at a suitable time within their working hours. Furthermore, participants are paired with a coach in their region to ensure their ways of working and regional cultures are reflected in the interactions with their coach and other group members.

Scaled Communications: With multiple touchpoints, point thresholds, deadlines, new operating systems, and new ways of working, participant communications are vital in supporting leaders and their line managers throughout the journey. A virtual communication plan takes the place of in-person updates. Salesforce's communication plans for both programs outline the stakeholders that need to be reached, the information that is critical for them to know, and methods of communication. Through the plan, participants and their line managers are informed about the program: what activities are taking place, what activities are upcoming, and what actions need to be completed before a certain date.

Measurable Benefits

To prioritize and identify what's important, the first thing Salesforce did was listen to their employees. As per internal surveys, most Salesforce employees consistently selected their direct manager as their most valued source of information and support, further reaffirming the importance of direct management and making it clear that investing in leadership development across these programs is a critical part of improving the business ecosystem.

Salesforce further engaged with frontline leaders and other stakeholders to gather insights into their specific learning needs and challenges. This was achieved through surveys, focus groups, and interviews with the goal of understanding their expectations, pain points, and desired outcomes from the learning programs. Using this feedback, the organization worked with the consulting firm BTS to tailor the content and delivery methods to address learner needs effectively.

Throughout the implementation of both programs, continuous monitoring and tracking of engagement metrics and feedback are analyzed to assess the program's effectiveness in achieving their targeted objectives.

Accelerate Benefits

Effectiveness of Learning

Throughout the program, participants learn new skills and develop new mindsets that relate to the critical elements of leadership at Salesforce. Working together in small groups, whether in small-group sessions or in breakout groups from larger workshop settings, is impactful when used to support real-time, system-wide culture change. This is reflected in participants' self-reported results:

- Ninety-seven percent of participants strongly agree or agree that they are motivated to work on specific shifts on their journey to becoming a better leader following Pod Session One: "Knowing What I Stand For" (based on 1,205 responses).
- Ninety-three percent of participants strongly agree or agree that they are more aware of their emotional states following Pod Session Two: "Choose Your Attitude" (based on 1,102 responses).

- Ninety-one percent of participants strongly agree or agree that they felt capable of improving their response(s) to stress following Pod Session Two (based on 1,086 responses).

Effect on Confidence and Competence

At the end of each module, participants reflect on their progress and what they have learned in the Accelerate journey by taking a self-assessment on their skills and capabilities. Between Module One and Module Three, reports showed increased confidence in key areas like giving and receiving feedback, connecting their work to the corporate V2MOM, etc. This demonstrates that participants not only gained a deeper understanding of the subject matter covered in the program, but as they progressed through modules, they accumulated more knowledge and skills. Furthermore, it shows that as participants engaged in self-reflection and introspection, they were able to identify personal growth and development.

Achievement in Business Outcomes

On average, 96% of participants report that they either mostly or completely achieved their Leadership Shift by the end of the program. A Leadership Shift is a personalized mindset or behavior change that each participant identifies at the start of the journey—such as becoming more intentional with feedback, improving delegation, or leading with greater empathy. They also selected the business outcomes that coincided with them making their shift and achieving their desired results. These data reflect outcomes from 10 cohorts of Accelerate since its launch in 2022.

The top business outcomes reported are as follows:

- Increased employee engagement (98% participants note some or significant change in this area)
- Increased efficiency (96% participants note some or significant change in this area)
- Increased quality of leadership (96% participants note some or significant change in this area)

Scale of Sessions

These metrics reflect the overall scale and delivery volume of the Accelerate program since its launch. They represent the total number of facilitated learning hours delivered across all cohorts.

- In total, 42 two-hour-long virtual workshop sessions were run, which equals 84 hours of workshop learning.
- In total, 1,441 pod coaching sessions were run, which equals 2,882 hours of pod coaching.

To date, 15,000+ aspiring frontline leaders have completed Accelerate, making it one of the largest leadership development programs in the industry.

Engagement of Learners

Here are a few data points indicating the strong engagement of program participants

- Average attendance rating across sessions is 92% and remains consistent throughout each program launch.
- Applications are not slowing down—cohorts consistently draw more than 2,000 participants. The twelfth cohort launched in March 2025 with over 1,800 participants, indicating excitement across the company for the Accelerate program.
- Average session effectiveness rating is at 92%.
- On average, 92% of participants enrolled in the program obtain sufficient points to graduate from each module.
- Participants spend an average of 11 minutes and 30 seconds navigating portal activities on each visit, indicating strong engagement with self-paced, bite-sized learning activities.

On-the-Job Application

In total, 57,263 Stretch Assignments (on-the-job-actions) were completed, allowing participants to translate their new skills and capabilities

Table 25.1 Summary of Accelerate Program Outcomes

Metric	Result
Participants graduated in 2024	Over 3,000
Average graduation rate (across 11 cohorts)	90%
Graduates who found the program relevant and impactful	95% (2024 cohort)
Participants who better understood expectations of people leaders post-program	95%(2024 cohort)
Participants who felt more productive due to tools/resources from Accelerate	94%
Maximum percentage of detractors across all evaluation Parameters[1]	~2%

[1]Defined as participants who rated the program 1 or 2 on a 5-point scale.

into behaviors. These assignments are designed to be part of a leader's natural workflow, bringing genuine behavioral change and accountability back on the job.

End-of-Program Results

Salesforce's end-of-program survey indicates that the Accelerate program is highly effective and well-received by participants, particularly for its relevance, impact, and the practical tools and resources it offers. The operational aspects of the program, including the portal and support systems, are particularly impactful, demonstrating that the program has struck an effective balance between participant learning and experience. Salesforce continues to evaluate participant feedback and refine the program accordingly. As shown in Table 25.1, participant satisfaction and program impact remain consistently high across cohorts.

Elevate Indicative Impact Measures

Supporting Frontline Manager Capability at Scale

Here are a few data points indicating the impact that the Elevate program has had since inception:

- Over 2,000 managers representing the length and breadth of Salesforce have taken part in Elevate over the past two cycles (at the time of writing).
- A majority of participants were senior managers and directors.
- The program included participants from over 25 countries.
- 50+ business units across Salesforce have been represented through the program.
- The program has been run in both English and Japanese.
- By investing in over 2,000 managers, the program has seen a significant multiplier effect, in terms of managers taking their learnings to their teams.

Scale of Sessions

Here are a couple of data points to indicate the scale at which the Elevate program is delivered:

- Over 40 virtual workshops were run, totaling ~300+ hours of workshop learning reaching over 2,000 participants since inception.
- Over 750 Peer Learning Pods facilitating exchange of best practices, creating opportunities to practice skills and building new networks.

Engagement of Learners

Here are a couple of data points referencing the qualitative feedback received from program participants:

- Ninety percent of those who registered attended sessions or workshops.
- Ninety-four percent of participants believed they had built new networks for connection and exchanging of ideas through Elevate.
- Ninety-two percent of participants found their small-group peer learning sessions impactful.
- Ninety-five percent found their aggregate Elevate experience meaningful as frontline leaders.
- Ninety-three percent of participants believed that Elevate had provided them with impactful tools and resources to be more effective on the job.

- The maximum percentage of detractors across evaluation parameters, like Accelerate, was again in the 2% range.

Elevate has seen these results in just two cohorts, in comparison to the 10 cohorts for Accelerate. In 2024, the Salesforce and BTS teams have taken the feedback from the first cohort to enhance the format of the experience; shifting from one day to two half-days, improving the insights and resources for participants to apply throughout the simulation workshop and on the job, and enhancing the user interface leveraging BTS's Momenta portal. The program team also piloted the first in-person Elevate program, which received an aggregate Net Promoter Score of a staggering 98.

Blueprint for the Future

Frontline leaders play a critical role in Salesforce's success. Employees rely on their leaders to support their growth and development, work–life balance, and overall success in their roles. Investing in programs that support the growth and development of current and aspiring leaders is a top-of-mind priority for Salesforce.

Salesforce's journey does not end here. With plans to integrate AI-powered personalization and expand in-person workshops, the company is poised to further elevate its leadership development initiatives. Aligning program content to strategic business objectives and the V2MOM ensures continued relevance and impact. By embedding these programs into its organizational fabric, Salesforce demonstrates a profound commitment to empowering its people. Accelerate and Elevate are not merely training programs; they are investments in the future of the company, its employees, and its customers.

Salesforce continues to emphasize continuous advocacy for both learning programs. The team maintains visibility and momentum through ongoing efforts to highlight the value and impact of these programs. They strive to regularly showcase participant achievements, success stories, and program milestones to leadership. They also celebrate program accomplishments through various channels such as Slack and internal meetings.

By consistently reinforcing the programs' significance and demonstrating their positive outcomes, Salesforce is generating internal excitement for the programs and investing in their long-term successes. By the end of 2024, these two programs had provided leadership development to nearly

17,000+ employees—almost a quarter of the Salesforce employee population. With the continued investment in and development of these programs, their impact and influence will only continue to grow.

Why Investing in Talent Matters

The story of Salesforce's leadership programs serves as a powerful reminder of why companies must prioritize developing their talent. Investing in employees is a key driver for innovation, resilience, and growth, particularly in an era of digital labor. When leaders at every level are equipped to succeed, the multiplier effects are felt across the organization—increased engagement, greater collaboration, and a culture of trust and sustained high performance.

26

Driving a People-First Culture to Support the Nation's Cybersecurity Mission

Elizabeth Kolmstetter

Prologue

It is an honor to share with you a three-year journey (2022–2024) to create a people-first culture of excellence at the Cybersecurity and Infrastructure Security Agency (CISA). In my more than thirty-year career across nine federal agencies, I have never worked for a more inspired senior leader, and committed senior leadership team, dedicated to creating a *real* people-first culture. Director Jen Easterly—Chief Executive Officer (CEO) equivalent—was unanimously confirmed by the Senate on July 12, 2021, to lead CISA during President Biden's administration (2021–2025). Standing up a new agency while coming out of the COVID-19 pandemic, and in the wake of serious cyber incidents of data breaches (i.e., Microsoft, Marriott, Twitter, Solar Winds), malware, and ransomware attacks (i.e., Colonial Pipeline, Apple, Accenture) among others, has been an enormous feat. Even with all this, Director Easterly *always* prioritized people and culture, and personally led the effort to define and role-model our culture. She hired me to be the first Chief People Officer (CPO) at CISA to take on what I consider the most critical work to drive a thriving and successful organization. This chapter describes our efforts during 2022–2024 and does not address any changes that might take place as a result of the second Trump administration (as a political appointee, Director Easterly is required to resign as of January 20, 2025). The views expressed in this chapter are those of the author and do not necessarily represent the views of CISA, the Department of Homeland Security (DHS), or the United States government.

Elizabeth Kolmstetter, *Driving a People-First Culture to Support the Nation's Cybersecurity Mission*.
In: *The Changing Leadership Landscape*. Edited by: Sheri L. Feinzig and Mariangela Battista,
Oxford University Press. © Oxford University Press (2026). DOI: 10.1093/9780197820070.003.0026

Background

CISA is one of the newest federal agencies of the United States (established in 2018 as an agency within the DHS). It serves as the nation's risk advisor, working with partners to defend against today's threats and to collaborate on building more secure and resilient infrastructure for the future (Cybersecurity and Infrastructure Security Agency, n.d.-a). Americans rely on our lights turning on, our water being clean, our public transit moving as expected, our banking transactions occurring, and our communication and information technology services connecting without wondering what makes these possible or whether they will be safe and reliable. The threats our nation faces—whether digital or physical, man-made, technological, or natural—are more complex, and the threat actors more diverse and distributed, than at any point in our history. CISA is at the heart of mobilizing collective defense as we lead efforts to understand and manage the risks posed by cyberattacks and attacks on our critical infrastructure. As a partnership agency, rather than a regulatory one, we partner with all sectors and organizations to understand and mitigate the risk environment and increase resilience, using all available resources. In summary, CISA partners with industry and all levels of government to manage risk affecting our national infrastructure, coordinate response to threats and incidents, promote and build critical infrastructure security and resilience, secure federal networks, improve emergency communications, provide training to cybersecurity and infrastructure security experts, and provide public awareness (see Figure 26.1).

Cyber threats are among the greatest risks our nation faces, and the cyber skills and talent gap remains the biggest challenge in resisting and combating cyberattacks (Cyberseek, 2024; World Economic Forum, 2024). With

We Are Team CISA

Our Team: We are the nation's Cyber and Infrastructure Security Agency: One Team, One Fight, One CISA.

Our Mission: We lead the national effort to understand, manage, and reduce, risk to our cyber and physical infrastructure.

Our Vision: Secure and resilient infrastructure for the American people.

Figure 26.1 CISA Vision and Mission

over 750,000 unfilled cybersecurity jobs in the United States (Cybersecurity Ventures, 2023), CISA must be able to compete for high-impact talent and then motivate, develop, and retain them. Competition is fierce and that talent can make a lot more money in the private sector, not have to wait six to 12 months to get through the federal hiring process, nor go through the difficult security clearance process. We learned that our people come to CISA because they are *attracted* to our mission and want to make a meaningful difference through their work. We *engage and retain* them by providing a healthy culture where they can grow their skills, work with amazing teammates and leaders, and bring their best to the mission every day.

We recognize the direct link between CISA's ability to deliver on our mission and its reliance on a healthy culture. That is why we have made driving a people-first culture a mission imperative—and it is proving successful. CISA has grown its workforce by hiring more than 2,200 since July 2021, bringing the total to about 3,400 in December 2024. We understand and support healthy attrition (e.g., mobility, promotion, career opportunities). Still, we are also keenly aware of our need to retain our talent and manage turnover (as of this writing, at about 8–10%). The key to retention has been improving employee engagement, and CISA reached an all-time high of 76% positive engagement in 2024 (with a 72% survey response rate), with many engagement-related areas achieving over 85% positive ratings from our employees.

Defining CISA's Culture

CISA's culture journey started with our Core Values: Collaboration, Innovation, Service, and Accountability (see Table 26.1). These represent the fundamental tenets of our organization that guide our actions.

However, to make our values real and part of the "felt experience," we took them a step further and co-created 12 CISA Core Culture Principles (CISA, n.d.-b) with our workforce (see Table 26.2). These core principles articulate *the ideal behaviors* we aspire to experience every day by every person across our agency, behaviors that make us individually and collectively successful. While they are represented on a poster around our offices, in an *Our CISA Culture* booklet (CISA, n.d.-b), and on my personal Microsoft Teams background, at CISA, we have *intentionally* anchored many of our operational and talent programs to teach, assess, and reinforce these as our underlying

Table 26.1 CISA Core Values

Collaboration	Strong and vibrant partnerships are critical to everything we do; we will approach every engagement as an opportunity to build trust with our teammates, our partners, and our customers.
Innovation	We face threats at machine speed and adversaries unbound by bureaucracy; we must move with creativity and agility at the speed of ideas to stay ahead of threats and to our nation and our way of life, and be grounded in the strength of our resilience.
Service	We are defined by our dedication to selflessly serving the American people; more than a mission, our commitment is a calling to protect and defend the infrastructure Americans rely on every hour of the day.
Accountability	We will only succeed if every one of us takes active ownership of our mission, our words, and actions. We will model the behavior we want to see in others; we will hold ourselves and our teammates responsible for our actions; we will empower our workforce through trust, transparency, and radical honesty.

Table 26.2 CISA Core Principles Description and Sample Practices

Core Principle	Description	Sample Practices
1. People First	We put the human first. We actively create an environment where people can be their best selves, bring their top talent to their work every day, and feel ownership and connection with our mission.	• Dedicated Chief People Office • Gather employee input
2. Do the Right Thing. Always.	A responsibility rooted in integrity, honor, moral courage, and trust. Always choose the harder right over the easier wrong. Always take accountability for our actions and our words.	• Create psychologically safe environment • Senior leaders share their stories
3. Lead with Empathy	Always treat others with respect and kindness. We cultivate the talents of everyone around us by caring for and getting to know one another.	• CISA Cares well-being services • Self-awareness assessments
4. Seek & Provide Honest Feedback	We learn what we are doing well and where we need to improve. Treat feedback as a gift. Actively provide quality feedback to others to help them succeed.	• 360-degree feedback program

continued

Table 26.2 *continued*

Core Principle	Description	Sample Practices
5. Communicate Transparently & Effectively	Share and seek information continuously with respect, honesty, and integrity. We use communications to break down silos, hold constructive discourse, and connect with audiences.	• Dedicated resources to workforce communications • “Theme years” to create cohesion
6. Foster Belonging, Diversity, Inclusion, & Equality	Champion an environment where all teammates feel not just safe and welcome but truly cherished for who they are and for their diverse perspectives.	• Neurodiverse Federal Workforce Initiative • Culture Council
7. Imagine, Anticipate, & Innovate to Win	Imagination is the magic that fuels our ability to solve our most complex problems, that drives our spirit of innovation, that generates the big ideas.	• CISAlutions platform to crowdsource solutions • Employees as “Ambassadors”
8. Make It Count	It is truly important to love what you do, to like who you do it with, to feel you are valued, and to know that you are making an impact. We embrace our mission while maintaining balance in our lives.	• Flexible work arrangements • CISAThanks!
9. Build & Cultivate Your Network	Having, using, and sharing a strong and broad network is necessary in today’s work environment. Developing strong partnerships is key to our collective success.	• “Give 12/Take 12” Leadership Program • One day a month with no scheduled activities
10. Play Chess	Ability to be agile and adaptive in this increasingly complex and uncertain world. We must be strategic, take initiative, and keep the long game in mind.	• Organizational health measurement process
11. Stand in the Arena	Do the hard work. Take risks. We own our actions, even if we “fail,” and view them as learning opportunities, a chance to grow and improve.	• Critically analyze program performance • Launch “first-evers”
12. Commit to a Lifetime of Learning	We approach learning with a growth mindset—continuously examining what we have done well and areas where we can improve with open minds.	• Reverse shadowing • Individual Development Plans • Leadership development for all

core behaviors (e.g., trust, moral courage, teamwork, empathy, imagination, inclusion, agility, ownership, lifelong learning, and resilience). Four values and 12 principles are a lot—but our leadership and workforce did not want to simplify or cut back on them; instead, we embrace the idea that we can all aspire to exhibit and experience these values and principles every day.

Intention and Purpose

To create and sustain a healthy, strong organizational culture, it must be worked on with intention and purpose. Actions speak louder than words. Leaders do not simply say "people are our most valued asset" and then hope things will happen that make employees feel that way. Following through with visible, meaningful actions that support our people-first culture and excellence goals is key. At CISA, we realize that culture starts at the top, but everyone has a role and responsibility in working on it. Much of an organization's culture stems from its leaders. Senior leadership behaviors that reflect and reinforce the values and principles are necessary but not sufficient. Managers and frontline supervisors must also emulate and evaluate the behaviors that contribute to the desired culture. And to truly achieve a strong, healthy organizational culture, *every* employee should understand their role and responsibilities.

To drive this enterprise approach to culture with intention and purpose, we took three major actions: (1) embedded culture as a formal strategic objective, (2) adopted a human-centric approach to the work experience, and (3) created the first-ever CPO position and office to drive this agency-wide effort.

First, to ensure that culture becomes an actual strategic priority and not a competing "nice to do" effort, it was written in as a direct objective in the CISA Strategic Plan 2023–2025 (Cybersecurity and Infrastructure Security Agency [CISA], 2022). Specifically, Objective 4.4 is "Advance CISA's Culture of Excellence" (CISA, 2022, p. 33) (see Figure 26.2 for description). In this way, it became part of the formal strategy, planning, resourcing, reporting, and measurement process (e.g., quarterly reporting on metrics). This also helped ensure that *all* leaders and employees across CISA recognized and understood the critical role culture plays in our mission success.

In addition, workforce and culture were explicitly linked in the strategic plan. Objective 4.3 is "Cultivate and Grow CISA's High-Performing

Objective 4.4 The strength of CISA's culture is critical to our mission and foundational to our success as One CISA. We will continue building our culture through promulgation of our core values and core principles. Our culture will be incorporated in our day-to-day tasks, mission-enabling functions, service to our partners and stakeholders, and in our everyday behaviors. We will prioritize an environment of psychological safety where people can be their authentic selves; where they feel cared for, supported, empowered, and always treated with dignity and respect; where they feel a sense of ownership for mission; and where accountability and responsibility are welcome. We will prioritize wellness and resilience across our agency by systematically mitigating burnout and providing access to mental health resources. Advancing an organizational culture of fairness and justice requires that leaders at CISA promote transparency and equity around rewards, decision outcomes, communications, and employee treatment. To drive organizational performance, CISA will cultivate an environment where feedback, learning, growth, and innovative perspectives are welcomed and cherished. Capitalizing on our culture of excellence, CISA will be a recognized leader in the cyber community and a premier destination to work within the federal government.

Figure 26.2 CISA Strategic Plan: Advance CISA's Culture of Excellence

Workforce," which includes the commitment, "We will build upon our success in cultivating and growing a workforce and culture that attract and retain our Nation's most talented cyber and infrastructure defenders." (CISA, 2022, p. 32).

Second, we intentionally began creating a human-centric workplace at CISA to ensure our people thrive in the "new normal" of work that is characterized by an "always on and always ready" urgent and dynamic mission. This means we must take employees' perspectives and needs to heart. We know our people want to make a difference and bring their best selves and talents to work. They want to grow, be heard, and share their ideas and perspectives. They also need flexible work arrangements, autonomy, and supportive leaders. If our agency processes and procedures are not working for our people, they are getting in the way of mission accomplishment. For example, if we are not assessing the right qualities and selecting the right leaders, our people will not feel supported in bringing their best talent to the mission every day. Or, if our people are burned out or lack the new skills needed for their work, our mission is negatively affected. Our people make our mission possible, therefore we must listen to our people, understand their experience, and strive to continuously improve it.

Third, the new CPO role is intended to be laser-focused on people and culture. The Office of the Chief People Officer (OCPO) is not the same as the Office of the Chief Human Capital Officer (OCHCO). The OCHCO is primarily focused on human resources (HR) operations, including hiring, compensation, benefits, performance management, and compliance with the vast federal HR requirements and regulations. The pioneering CPO role serves as a strategic lead and partner to everyone across CISA. It is responsible for bringing strategic vision and capability to create an effective organizational culture and data-informed people strategy for mission success. The OCPO's mission and unique capability are to "build and sustain CISA's employee capacity and work environment to effectively execute CISA's growing complex mission to secure the Nation's cyber and physical infrastructure" (Kolmstetter, 2024, p. 2). The vision and desired outcome driven by OCPO is "agile, resilient, knowledgeable, engaged, and skilled employees committed to fulfilling CISA's mission" (Kolmstetter, 2024, p. 2).

I was hired in 2022 as the CPO, and during my first year at CISA, I completed a Strategic Functional Analysis to define and create this new office. The new office is officially responsible for six functions: (1) strategic advisor to CISA senior leadership for employee engagement, workforce capability, and work environment; (2) culture, engagement, and work environment strategies, plans, and initiatives (including organizational development and effectiveness, and associated metrics and workforce analytics); (3) leadership and career development; (4) training and education; (5) internal workforce communication; and (6) OCPO business management and operations. As an organizational psychologist, I was well-positioned to build a team to conduct research and analyze data to gain insights into how best to embed a positive culture into CISA's "DNA" and sustain it. From these data-informed insights, we developed and implemented actions, programs, and initiatives. Many of these began as "pilots" or "prototypes" and were then scaled across the agency once we were on a track for success. We took a multi-pronged approach because we knew there was no "one size fits all," and that our strategy must be agile, tackling short-, mid-, and long-term needs.

The rest of this chapter will discuss how we operationalized our culture and provide practical and relevant examples organized by each of our 12 Core Culture Principles (see Table 26.2). These are not mutually exclusive concepts or practices but provide a useful organizing framework to share our approach and impact. All of these required leadership at various levels to come to fruition, and those are described throughout. Measures and early indicators of our progress are presented at the end of the chapter (see the section "Measuring Our Progress: Early Returns").

(1) "People First" (What It Means)

Like any high-performing organization, we recognized that our people are the most important asset to CISA. We must continue to attract, motivate, and retain world-class talent to succeed in our mission. Director Easterly consistently emphasized in all of her addresses how important our people are to her and to our mission. But words are not enough, even from the head of the organization. We defined our people-first culture of excellence in three ways, and operationalized how these tenets show up in our behaviors and actions.

First, we began creating an environment of *psychological safety* where people can be their authentic selves; where everyone feels cared about, supported, empowered, and always treated with dignity and respect. This also meant that our people would feel a true sense of ownership and connection to our mission, and welcome accountability and responsibility for their actions.

Second, we required *selflessness*—as public servants and in upholding our oath of office. This often meant putting the interests of others, such as our partners, customers, and team, before our own. Seeking what is best for others, rather than ourselves, means realizing that the only way to create our own success is to "flip the telescope around": broaden our focus and drive results for everyone through collaboration, empowerment, and teamwork. If we focused only on maximizing our individual interests, others would realize we could not be counted on. As we say at CISA, "The goal is not about becoming a star, it's about building a constellation of a great team with great leaders."

Third, the focus on people first was even more critical for those who have the privilege of supervisory responsibilities; we strove always to remember that while our title may make us a manager, our people make us a leader. Leaders put their people first by obsessing about their growth, development, and well-being, and by empowering them—striving to bring out the best of their talent every day to ensure their success and that of their team. As Director Jen Easterly put it during a Town Hall address to the workforce:

> How we put our people first is by creating a work environment where you wake up in the morning excited by what you do, you admire and respect your teammates, you are empowered by your leadership, and you feel like you are making a difference every single day. (Easterly, 2022)

(1) "People First" (Practices)

Dedicated Chief People Officer Role

Dedicating a CPO role and office to serve as a strategic lead and partner to everyone across CISA, intentionally driving a people-first culture of excellence, was a visible, tangible action that made it real to the workforce. The OCPO was designed to foster trust and collaboration—to partner with leaders and all employees to improve the employee experience and build workforce capability. OCPO focused on motivating, developing, and retaining our high-impact talent—through organizational effectiveness, internal communications, and workforce development (the Chief Learning Office is part of OCPO).

In this way, CISA made OCPO accountable for this key workforce strategy—to invest in our employee experience and skill development as necessary to build and maintain capability in our workforce. This included developing strong leaders who reflected our core values and principles as well as skilling our workforce to meet career goals and mission needs. Dedicating an office with experts (e.g., organizational psychology, training and learning, communications, data science and analytics) and resources meant that OCPO was not competing with but *complementing* other workforce management efforts—and that investment in the employee experience and workforce capability building would be done as agency priorities.

In addition, organizationally, the CPO worked in the front office of CISA reporting to the Director, met weekly with the Director, hosted workforce Town Halls, and literally sat in the Director's suite. This not only visibly demonstrated the importance of the role and responsibilities but also kept the CPO strategic and "at the table" to implement a human-centric experience across everything from communications and policy changes to restructuring and new mandates. Even if the "what" of a new requirement was mandated, the "how" of communicating it and leading our employees through the change is what contributed to a healthy culture.

Gathering Employee Input

Operationalizing our human-centric approach required multiple methods for gathering our employees' perspectives, needs, and experiences.

Designing metrics and collecting *quantitative* and *qualitative* data helped us understand what was working well, what was not, and whether we were realizing the desired outcomes. The OCPO was responsible for conducting agency-wide workforce surveys, including the annual engagement survey and various pulse surveys, as well as program evaluations (e.g., training and development programs, Town Hall programs).

Gathering qualitative input can take many forms. As CPO, I hosted at least two "sensing sessions" per month on different topics where any employee could openly discuss and share experiences, perspectives, ideas, and concerns. Our Director and Deputy Director hosted listening sessions, coffee chats, and office hours to reinforce their accessibility to the workforce and their desire to hear from all levels of the organization. Our agency ombudsman (who reports to the CPO) summarized the types of issues raised to him and also conducted the agency exit interviews with departing employees.

In 2024, OCPO engaged over 900 employees through dynamic activities such as focus groups, sensing sessions, pulse surveys, and action teams, enabling us to improve inclusion across our organization-wide culture change movement. For the first time, we developed and implemented a fully inclusive engagement action plan that involved every division and office at CISA. As CISA addressed workforce needs and solutions, we shared them with our employees through "in our employees' words" short videos, Town Halls, *CISA Vision* articles, and our engagement intranet hub.

(2) "Do the Right Thing. Always." (What It Means)

CISA's mission is to lead the national effort to understand, manage, and reduce risk to the cyber and physical infrastructure Americans rely on every hour of every day. This mission is monumental. In some cases, what we do or fail to do may mean the difference between life and death. We play both a reactive and a proactive role in this responsibility. To us, this is a sacred responsibility—rooted in integrity, honor, moral courage, trust, and always doing the right thing; always choosing the harder right over the easier wrong—and knowing the difference; always taking accountability for our actions and our words.

Our character is defined by what we do and how we act—especially when no one is watching or knows it is us. Every interaction within and outside of CISA, from a simple email to a national strategy, reflects who we are and must be in the best interest of our team, our partners, and the American people. We expect our people to treat every day and every interaction as an opportunity to build trust among our teammates and our partners, to exercise sound judgment, and to make and inform the best decisions with honesty and transparency. Trust is the foundation of relationships, but it can be easily destroyed by a lie or by failing to take responsibility for our words or actions. At CISA, we set our moral compass to true North—meaning that our words are our bonds, our reputation is one of unfailing integrity, and our team's success and our nation's success depend on it.

(2) "Do the Right Thing. Always." (Practices)

Psychological Safety

We recognized that we had to create a culture that allowed our people to act with honesty and integrity. Many implicit and explicit reward systems in organizations reinforce behaviors that get people noticed and are favored by leaders, such as agreeableness, the similar-to-me effect, ego stroking, compliance, and positive reinforcement (e.g., groupthink). Speaking "truth to power," expressing opinions or raising data that counter the majority's thinking, and/or bringing forth expert perspectives that differ from those of the leaders are the hardest actions employees have to take. Employees simply are not going to risk being "labeled" as a troublemaker, endanger a promotion, jeopardize their performance rating, or otherwise be considered in the "out-group" if the environment our leaders create does not welcome anything other than "yes behaviors." At the same time, employees have to learn and use professional, appropriate, and effective techniques to gain the trust and credibility to raise new or different ideas or issues. We chose to instill a culture of psychological safety across CISA to ensure our people could speak up with work-relevant content, share ideas, and address concerns without fear of rejection, humiliation, or punishment.

Psychological safety is a concept researched by Amy Edmonson, who defines it as the belief that one will not be punished, humiliated, ignored, or blamed for speaking up with ideas, questions, concerns or mistakes, and that the team is safe for interpersonal risk-taking (Edmonson, 2019). Since 2023, we have included awareness and thoughtful discussion of psychological safety in our New Employee Orientation (NEO) held every two weeks.

As of early 2024, all leaders receive refresher training on psychological safety through our leadership courses. In September 2024, we hosted Amy Edmondson as a guest speaker at our Town Hall. Director Easterly engaged her in a "fireside chat" format to share and explore how we were operationalizing psychological safety and risk-taking across CISA. Edmondson helped us unpack "failure" and embrace mistake-making as vital to learning, resilience, and growth.

Leading by Example

Senior leaders "walking the talk" may be the most powerful demonstration of a culture's value to the workforce. Integrity is a pillar of every federal agency because of the core need to gain and maintain public trust. Chris Krebs served as CISA's first Director, appointed by President Trump and confirmed by the Senate in 2019. He was famously fired by President Trump via Twitter after declaring the 2020 presidential election the safest and most secure in United States history.

Current CISA Director Easterly invited former Director Krebs to return to CISA as a Town Hall guest speaker in 2022. Krebs began with a heartfelt message to the workforce, calling them the best team in government and saying he always trusted career civil servants to do their jobs (Krebs, 2022). He believed CISA's fundamental role was to "increase transparency, operate with a clear set of guidelines, build trust and partnerships, and reduce harm." As a leader, he said he was "constantly engaging with people and building relationships to create trust" (Krebs, 2022).

When Krebs was asked about his decision to declare the 2020 election secure, he said first that it had to be a data-informed community decision—he gathered data from the CISA centers, from states facing floods of disinformation, and from election security partners. Second, as CISA Director, he said his role was to serve as the national spokesperson on election security, so he was responsible for delivering that message to the American people. Third, he told us,

> "Do the right thing because your character is yours. Every single one of you is incredibly employable ... never sacrifice your values because you are scared of losing your job ... the American people depend on us every day to be a trusted partner and do the right thing" (Krebs, 2022).

(3) "Lead with Empathy" (What It Means)

Treat others with respect and kindness. At CISA, we believe everyone can be a leader, and lead from wherever they serve. By cultivating the talents of everyone we work with, we demonstrate genuine interest in our teammates' lives, career goals, strengths, and developmental areas. We seek to make emotional intelligence and authenticity our superpowers. By leading with the platinum rule, "treat others as they would like to be treated," we strive to truly get to know ourselves and one another. Each of us must be self-aware. We practice active listening and stay mindful of how our words and actions might affect others. We strive to always assume noble intent and give our colleagues the benefit of the doubt before jumping to conclusions or letting our unconscious biases come into play. Relentless positivity is a force multiplier and can be contagious.

We aspire to have every teammate be someone everyone wants to work with or for—to be the person others seek out for advice or inspiration; someone who embodies confidence grounded in experience and knowledge, and who is also open to new and alternative ideas. Conflict is inevitable, but we will handle it with grace and appropriate humor. We talk with each other, not at or over each other. Given the stress of our work and the unrelenting urgency of our mission, we must be calm and unflappable in the face of stress or crisis, remembering that others are always watching us to see the example we set, no matter our title, role, or position.

(3) "Lead with Empathy" (Practices)

CISA Cares

A people-first culture can only exist when our people believe their health and well-being really matter. Our data showed that high stress and burnout were taking a negative toll on our workforce. The CISA Cares program is committed to supporting a healthier workforce by providing CISA employees, including supervisors, and their family members, with free, confidential access to Employee Assistance Programs (EAP), LifeCare resources, and Well-Being and Resiliency training to help them manage life challenges and remain healthy, engaged, and productive on their wellness journey. LifeCare includes articles, webinars, expert access, and other resources to help manage work and personal life responsibilities, such as child care, elder care, financial and legal needs, education and career changes, health, and wellness.

Other parts of this program include providing the Headspace App free of charge to our employees. Employees rave about using this app to improve their sleep, do stretches and movements to relieve ergonomic issues from sitting at a computer all day, and practice mindfulness to reduce burnout and improve their energy levels. We also provide the robust FedStrive online wellness website, which allows employees to create an account, complete an annual Wellness Profile, access a library of healthy recipes and health articles, participate in virtual wellness programs (such as wellness challenges and daily health-related goals), and use fitness, food, and hydration trackers. Our goal with CISA Cares is to provide our employees with the support, tools, and resources they need to manage their health and wellness *before* health issues negatively affect their well-being and work performance. We train our supervisors and managers to be informed about these services and to support their employees' use of them.

Assess and Learn

We implemented a variety of assessments that help our people gain valuable insights into themselves. For example, we use the CliftonStrengths assessment (Gallup, n.d.), which includes 34 themes such as empathy, and we have certified coaches to help our leaders and teams understand and use the results. Because this assessment uses a strengths-based, positive psychology approach, our people feel empowered and good about the insights they gain. We have used this assessment with leaders and their teams during office retreats and in our leadership development courses. Through it, we teach actionable strategies to play to our strengths and to seek assistance from those around us to improve.

(4) "Seek and Provide Honest Feedback" (What It Means)

We treat feedback as a gift. We actively seek it out, ask for honest feedback that will help us, and strive to improve every day. People are not perfect and we do not expect anyone to be flawless. We say "thank you" and view feedback as advice from someone who wants to help us be even better—rather than becoming defensive or making excuses—even when our brain wants to jump into that mode. We take ownership and accountability for our actions rather than treating constructive or critical feedback as failure—and we ask, "What can I learn from this?" even if we do not agree. We practice giving feedback authentically, thoughtfully, and constructively.

None of us can advance in our careers without candid, honest developmental feedback that makes us more effective. Achieving success requires self-awareness and the humility to know yourself and where you are working on self-improvement, regardless of position, tenure, or seniority. In fact, the more a person advances in their career, the more responsibility they have to listen to feedback from others to grow as a leader. They must also provide quality feedback to others, enabling those people to grow and succeed. To be a great leader, you need to be a great coach—willing to roll up your sleeves and get in the arena with your teammates. Great coaches make other people successful.

We must work collectively to create a safe space for providing constructive, critical feedback and for telling each other what we did well and where we can do better. Not giving someone helpful feedback robs them of the opportunity to improve. Practicing giving and receiving feedback, or advice, often makes it "the norm" and more comfortable for everyone. We can make each other better every single day, and we owe it to each other to do so.

(4) "Seek and Provide Honest Feedback" (Practices)

To reinforce, measure, and further develop our leaders in line with our culture principles, we designed a 360-degree feedback questionnaire that included actual behaviors aligned with the 12 Core Culture Principles, as well as other leadership competencies. Feedback was gathered from direct reports, peers, managers, and participants (self). With over 98% participation from all supervisors, managers, and executives, we received meaningful feedback on how others experienced these behaviors. The program also required that at least one goal on each individual's annual development plan be based on this feedback.

We learned from the data that employees overwhelmingly report that supervisors (1) treat them with dignity and respect; (2) foster a culture where their views, opinions, and suggestions are welcomed, even when they differ from others (psychological safety); and (3) actively work to make telework/remote work successful for them. In addition, employees reported enjoying working for their supervisors. In terms of our 12 Core Culture Principles, respondents across all 360-degree feedback perspectives (i.e., self, direct reports, peers, managers) consistently identified "People First" and "Do the Right Thing" as the strongest culture principles experienced across CISA, followed by "Lead with Empathy" and "Foster Belonging, Diversity, Inclusion, and Equality."

(5) "Communicate Transparently and Effectively" (What It Means)

CISA is headquartered in Arlington, VA, operates ten regional offices nationwide, and has numerous remote teams and employees. This necessitates constant communication to ensure we are on the same page and working as a cohesive unit.

Communication is more than transmitting information. It requires active listening. We use active listening to seek understanding by listening more than speaking. While creating a psychologically safe space for disagreement, we expect constructive discourse and respectful communication. We seek never to condemn, gossip, or complain—but rather to be thoughtful, positive, and authentic.

Communication is also about how the message gets out and about recognizing that every message drives and reflects our culture. Effective workforce communications are essential because they form a vital bridge between management and employees, conveying the organization's objectives and strategies while considering the workforce's perspectives and concerns.

Presentation matters. Attention to detail matters. We seek to connect with our audience and communicate in terms and concepts that resonate. We recognize that people often do not remember what you said, but they do remember how you made them feel.

(5) "Communicate Transparently and Effectively" (Practices)

Emphasis on Internal Communications

Another unique aspect of the OCPO is that we are responsible for internal communications across CISA (this includes the CISA Intranet, *CISA Vision* digital newsletter, CISA calendar of events, Director/Deputy Director/CPO messages to the workforce, and Town Halls). In so many ways, communications contribute to employee engagement. Our people want to be "in the know" about what is happening and what might impact them. We also know that our people feel a deep sense of commitment to our mission. Therefore, drawing connections for them between what is going on and our mission operations is critical to our agency's performance.

As humans, we pay attention to how things are said. The OCPO deeply understands the importance of effectively conveying leadership intent while considering employees' viewpoints and situational factors that might affect the impact of the communications. All messages to the workforce from the Director and senior leaders are either written by or cleared through the OCPO (we had over 90 in 2024). These messages deeply resonated with employees, fostering a strong sense of unity, purpose, and motivation—from heartfelt condolence notices for the passing of a CISA team member to agency-wide imperatives, from announcing leadership changes to recognition of our federal holidays.

Two-Way Communications

At the end of most of our Town Hall events, we hosted a "Question and Answer" session with the guest speaker, panel members, senior leaders, the CPO, and/or the Director. In this way, we heard from our employees on substantive topics and answered their questions. In addition, we hosted virtual "Ask Me Anything" sessions during which the workforce asked questions on a number of topics (e.g., Return to Onsite Work/Hybrid Work, new Drug Testing Program) and received answers from experts across the agency. We found these sessions very well received because they offered employees transparency and access to senior leaders and experts, quickly corrected misinformation and rumors, clarified confusion, and built trust. These sessions also provided senior leaders with insight into a broad spectrum of employee perceptions, questions, and concerns.

Employee Portals

Employees are the ones who can tell us what is working well and what is hindering them. We hosted several "portals" on our internal CISA Intranet where employees submitted suggestions or asked questions about various initiatives. For example, during our "Thriving in Hybrid: Return to Office" implementation, employees posted questions on our "Hybrid Hub," which were compiled into "Frequently Asked Questions and Answers" for all to view. We also had a portal where employees could leave comments and make suggestions about our Town Hall speaker series and watch recordings of previous sessions.

Theme Years

Culture and engagement, even with clear definitions of our core values and principles, are broad and complex constructs to address. As part of a unique culture initiative, CISA adopted a "focus theme" each year to directly engage, educate, and support our workforce, aligning our culture priorities with our mission. Our themes were Year of Mental Health and Well-Being (2022), Year of Leadership and Learning (2023), and One CISA: Year of Unity and Resilience (2024). These themes helped rally our workforce, foster team cohesion, and focus on a "North Star" culture priority for each year. Many of our leadership and culture activities and programs each year were tied directly to these themes.

(6) "Foster Belonging, Diversity, Inclusion, and Equality" (What It Means)

CISA champions an environment where individual and cultural differences are a defining strength; where all teammates feel not only safe and welcome, but truly celebrated and cherished for who we are. We seek to understand, recognize, and appreciate our diverse perspectives, backgrounds, and unique challenges. It is vital to embrace open dialogue about how to foster equality for all with a focus on taking action to achieve that ideal. We all strive to be the change we want to see in the world.

In the words of Martin Luther King, "Injustice anywhere is a threat to justice everywhere." We strive to recognize that unless you have personally lived the experience of being a minority, whether by race, ethnicity, neurodiversity, gender identity, sexual orientation, or ability, it may be hard to imagine the everyday challenges of being excluded, misunderstood, or overlooked simply for being oneself. We foster empathy to create awareness and understanding.

We must acknowledge that we all carry unconscious and conscious biases from our upbringing and experiences that affect our ability to promote diversity and equality. When we recognize and counter those biases, we help foster a culture of inclusion. We recognize that we arrived where we are today with the help of many others—to pay it forward is to spread that support and encouragement. We strive to invest extra time mentoring and coaching those with backgrounds different from our own. We expect our teams to reflect the full diversity of society that we serve. In this way, we celebrate our differences and seek diverse opinions, input, and perspectives to promote a CISA culture of belonging, which will lead to superior outcomes for ourselves and our partners.

(6) "Foster Belonging, Diversity, Inclusion, and Equality" (Practices)

Neurodiverse Federal Workforce Initiative

CISA actively addressed neurodivergence in an inclusive way. Autism, attention-deficit/hyperactive disorder, and dyslexia are among the conditions commonly associated with neurodivergence. In 2024, CISA was the second federal agency to launch the Neurodiverse Federal Workforce (NFW) Initiative. The initiative aimed to address critical cyber and IT talent shortages by drawing on underutilized populations of talented neurodivergent adults with skill sets (e.g., pattern recognition, rule detection, systems thinking, attention to detail) that are well suited to CISA's mission.

CISA partnered with MITRE, a nonprofit federally funded research and development center, and with Melwood, a nonprofit that supports the employment of neurodivergent people and people with disabilities, to implement this program. The team developed an orientation session on neurodiversity in the workplace and strategies to support neurodivergent workers for supervisors and managers. CISA hosted five NFW participants who received career coaching throughout the program. These participants performed excellent work and completed tasks ahead of schedule. CISA hired several into full-time positions. In this way, CISA is helping to eradicate stigma and demonstrating that neurodivergent talent adds significant value to our mission and can help the broader federal government address the talent supply shortage.

CISA Culture Council

The CPO chaired the chartered CISA Culture Council, which the Director sponsored. Every office was represented on the council. The CHCO and the Chief of Diversity, Equity, Inclusion, and Accessibility (DEIA) served as senior advisors. A key feature of this multidisciplinary council was its embedding of inclusion, equity, and accessibility across our culture and engagement efforts.

In 2023–2024, the council made significant contributions to the priority areas of Future of Work and CISA's Transition to Hybrid, Employee Engagement Action Planning, Workforce Recognition, and the new CISAlutions innovation portal (described in the section "Imagine, Anticipate, and Innovate to Win (Practices)"). These programs supported CISA's DEIA Strategy, and we did not need a separate DEIA group to review the proposals or perform the work, as that was already embedded in the Culture Council's role.

(7) "Imagine, Anticipate, and Innovate to Win" (What It Means)

Imagination is the magic that fuels our ability to solve our most complex problems, drives our spirit of innovation, and generates big, bold ideas. Our ability to imagine the best and the worst of what is possible will make the difference in ensuring the nation is prepared to respond to the full range of complex threats to our infrastructure, including cyberattacks, weather events, acts of terrorism, and pandemics.

We remember the famous saying from hockey legend Wayne Gretzky: "A good hockey player plays where the puck is. A great hockey player plays where the puck is going to be." Being able to skate "ahead of the puck" is particularly critical to CISA's work, where understanding and analysis of the operational environment will enable us to proactively anticipate disruptions to our critical infrastructure and effectively reduce risk. We encourage our people to hone their imagination to see where the puck is headed, helping prepare for the most probable as well as the most disruptive scenarios.

We develop and exercise against a range of scenarios to ensure preparedness and response and to build resilience. We focus on opportunities to improve our response and share the insights gained from these improvements. Given the high stakes of our mission, every "game" could be a playoff. Having the imagination to determine where the puck is going and skating ahead of it is how we will consistently deliver security and resilience for the nation.

(7) "Imagine, Anticipate, and Innovate to Win" (Practices)

CISAlutions

The OCPO implemented a modern-era, reimagined "suggestion box" platform that leveraged crowdsourcing capabilities to allow all federal CISA employees to submit ideas, comment on and vote on them, and send kudos to idea submitters. This program encouraged innovation, provided transparency into ideas under development, and fostered dialogue to improve mission effectiveness, quality of work life, and agency "pain points."

Crowdsourcing can be one of the fastest and most engaging ways to address enterprise problems related to workplace issues. We found that unleashing employees to help solve problems and be part of solutions that improve the workplace improved organizational processes and employee engagement. In its first year, CISAlutions received over 100 solution suggestions; about a third underwent full adjudication (some were found not to be legal, affordable, or practical), and about a quarter of them have been implemented. Examples from this program include improving the Voluntary Leave Transfer program (e.g., the ability to donate earned leave to other employees with qualifying medical needs), creating a "Report Phishing Button" in the email system to make it much easier to report suspicious emails, installing filtered water in the kitchen sinks (which eliminated the cost of water coolers), making it easier for employees to find and use the Student Loan Repayment program, and streamlining official name change procedures (e.g., changing to a married name).

Employee Ambassadors for One CISA "Secure by Design" Campaign

One of CISA's significant national efforts is "Secure by Design" (SbD), issued in April 2023 in support of the White House's National Cybersecurity Strategy (CISA, 2023). Our workforce is among the most effective "marketers" of this movement. The goal of SbD is to shift the cybersecurity burden from technology customers to technology manufacturers. During the design phase of a product's development lifecycle, companies should implement SbD principles to significantly reduce the number of exploitable flaws before introducing the product to the market for widespread use or consumption. Out-of-the-box products should be secure, with features such as multi-factor authentication (MFA), logging, and single sign-on (SSO) available at no extra cost. Hundreds of companies have signed the voluntary pledge to participate in the program.

Our Cybersecurity Division launched the SbD Ambassadors program for the entire CISA workforce and hosts training and a monthly expert speaker series. Each month a featured speaker from industry shares how they operationalize and advance this initiative. An effective way to create a "whole of agency approach," SbD Ambassadors spread the word and gain additional voluntary industry pledges through their professional networks and affiliations, speaking and conference engagements, volunteer activities, and even personal lives (e.g., as "tech consumers").

(8) "Make It Count" (What It Means)

This principle is the intersection of four simple precepts from life-purpose frameworks (e.g., Burnett & Evans, 2016; Collins, 2001):

- Do what you love.
- Do what you are good at.
- Do what the world needs.
- Do what you can be rewarded for.

While most of us want to work to live, not live to work—the truth is that we spend most of our adult lives working. So, it is essential to love what you do, to like who you do it with, to feel you are valued, and to know that you are making an impact—whether this involves excelling at your job, helping a teammate, or volunteering your time or resources to give back to your community.

We believe that every member of team CISA contributes to this culture of impact—where we embrace our mission and take ownership of our actions and behaviors to effect positive change; take the initiative to recognize problems and work to solve them; strive every day to make a difference rather than complain that something is not our job or beyond our control; and take the time to show gratitude for work well done and to say "thank you."

Making it count also means ensuring we maintain balance in our lives—that we spend time with friends and family, rest, recharge, and reorient ourselves—intellectually, physically, and emotionally. Taking a vacation is as important as working. Without it, we burn out, depriving us of our best career successes and our team of our top contributions. Maintaining balance in our lives is key to achieving that ideal combination of mutually reinforcing career and personal success.

(8) "Make It Count" (Practices)

Flexible Work Arrangements

A people-first culture requires supporting people in their inextricably intertwined work and personal lives. If we expect our people to work when our mission needs it (and we do!), we must provide flexibility in how and where they perform that work. Our people tell us they want and need flexibility and the ability to have focused, deep-thinking time. CISA embraced work flexibility through flexible schedules, telework/hybrid (approximately 72% of employees in 2024), fully remote work (approximately 25% of employees in 2024), and mobile IT devices/access—and this flexibility has created significant value. We have been able to recruit and hire some of the nation's top experts and a highly diverse workforce with unique skills and experience by offering hybrid and fully remote work arrangements. Our people tell us they are more productive, more engaged, and more likely to stay at CISA when they can determine when they are most productive, when they are empowered to organize their day (in-office vs. telework days), and when they are trusted by their supervisors to co-design their schedule. Telework/hybrid employees must work onsite between one and three days a week, depending on their specific job and Division requirements. According to our 2024 annual engagement survey, 91% of employees felt supported in their work–life balance needs.

As we sought to mature into a healthy hybrid posture (from fall 2023 to spring 2024), employee feedback indicated that supervisors were establishing different work norms and not applying them consistently across their teams. This was leading to confusion, a breakdown in team cohesion, and concerns about fairness.

The Culture Council took on this challenge and led an enterprise-wide effort to define "One CISA Flexible Work Environment Principles" establishing CISA-wide norms and expectations to ensure that the hybrid way we work would be engaging and successful *for all employees*. These principles aimed to provide agency-wide consistency where it mattered most while also allowing managers to determine what would work best for their specific work functions. These 11 principles included such things as requiring appropriate "cameras on" during virtual meetings; requiring "out-of-office" messages when away; requiring meeting organizers to provide the meeting purpose and agenda before meetings; requiring leaders to hold regularly scheduled one-on-one time with each employee regardless of remote or telework status; ensuring that all workers receive equitable consideration for special projects, assignments, development opportunities, and training, regardless of remote or telework status; requiring leaders to make every effort to conduct performance counseling sessions in person; and requiring leaders to regularly seek feedback and discuss how flexible work arrangements are or are not working with the team, and then adjust as needed.

CISA Thanks!

Showing appreciation is one of the easiest things we can do for our people. Our team members have been recognized every day through our *CISA Thanks!* portal where any employee can recognize another for being helpful and/or for standing out in one of our core values or principles. In just a few "clicks," employees select a core principle and add a statement of thanks to their colleague. Employees who receive a *Thanks!* receive an email with a link to the *CISA Thanks!* portal where they can read their message. Employees love receiving these and often quote them in their self-evaluations during performance review time.

(9) "Build and Cultivate Your Network" (What It Means)

CISA will achieve nothing by itself. Collaboration is at the core of how we work. We view every engagement as an opportunity to build trust and strengthen partnerships. Time is precious; it is one thing none of us ever gets back. We value our people's time and the time we put into our partnerships. If we come unprepared, we might not get another chance, and it is on us not to waste anyone's precious time. Developing strong partnerships is inextricably linked to our collective success. These partnerships span the federal government, industry, academia, and our state, local, tribal, and territorial colleagues. They also span our teams. We seek to break down organizational silos to be the agency the nation deserves—One CISA. We encourage and expect all employees to build and share their networks (inside and outside of CISA).

(9) "Build and Cultivate Your Network" (Practices)

Give 12/Take 12 Leadership Program

CISA participates in the DHS's "12/12 Leadership Program." This program requires leaders to complete at least 12 hours of development each year and to provide 12 hours of development to others. By and large our leaders are giving their time in ways that expand networks and partnerships—through mentoring others, speaking at leadership courses and professional meetings, attending annual conferences, and participating in recruiting and educational activities for cybersecurity, IT, STEM, and other professionals for CISA, DHS, and the federal government.

ADONSA

Building networks takes time, and our workforce tells us they never have enough of it. CISA implemented "ADONSA" (A Day of No Scheduled Activities) on the last Friday of every month. ADONSA provides a day for uninterrupted writing and analysis, catching up on emails, connecting with colleagues, or building personal networks, and much more. It is not a day of no work. Instead, our people tell us that these designated "No Regular Meetings Days" are helping enhance resilience across our workforce, giving everyone the space to focus, recharge, make new connections, and bring their best ideas forward.

(10) "Play Chess" (What It Means)

We embrace the "new normal" by accepting that two fundamental realities are change and complexity. Our ability, as individuals, teams, and organizations, to be agile and adaptive in this increasingly complex world is critical to the success of CISA's dynamic mission. We think of it as "we get to play chess" rather than "be pawns in someone else's game." We must be strategic in how we think and what we do, every single day. We act boldly with intention and purpose, and we take initiative in all things. We always keep the long game top of mind, even when we are inevitably pulled into the urgent and tactical. We step back and think big-picture, envisioning the whole chessboard, and seek to play several steps ahead—thinking critically about the consequences. We work smart to make the best use of our time. Activity does not necessarily mean productivity—anyone can work long hours but long hours do not necessarily equate to quality work.

Being strategic means having a clear understanding of priorities and next steps. Leadership requires providing clarity on what is important, especially when competing priorities arise. We expect leaders to ensure their teams understand priorities and can allocate time and resources effectively, recognizing that if everything is a priority, then *nothing* is. In today's world of work, we seek to share the "chessboard" with all our employees—to provide transparency and clarity on what we are doing, why we are doing it, and how we are doing it.

Each of us is responsible for understanding what is important to achieve on any given day, having a plan to accomplish those activities, and applying the necessary creative and critical thinking skills to ensure we always deliver a high-quality product or service. Solutions to complex problems are found at the intersection of multiple disciplines. Our people need time to find those intersections and make those connections. We must be agile thinkers, constantly adapt, and play the long game.

(10) "Play Chess" (Practices)

To be agile and adaptive, you need data and goals. With almost "too much data" these days, it is essential to invest time in defining which metrics to capture, what goals we are aiming for, and what priorities we can take on. CISA has become excellent at reporting on mission outputs and outcomes, but wanted to improve how we assess and manage the health of our six divisions.

A cross-divisional team created a quarterly review process, the Division Management Review (DMR), which included a template and a method to pull together quarterly data across standard categories (e.g., financial, human capital, acquisitions, performance, operations, compliance, policies, etc.). The team's biggest hurdle was collecting the data, an arduous manual process across disparate systems, tools, and repositories, all of which depended on specific timing related to the financial briefings to Congress each quarter. Another challenge was reaching consensus on the data, which proved to be tedious and time-consuming.

In less than one year, collaborating across offices, the team successfully established a reporting process that made the work meaningful to all involved and illuminated each division's ability to deliver on its mission. The head of each division presented their DMR each quarter allowing them to share an overview of their division's health, challenges, roadblocks, and opportunities. Team members from across CISA attended these briefings so they could support one another as needs arose.

The DMR process has been institutionalized within CISA and has evolved from highly manual processes to a more automated approach via dashboards, improving efficiency in data collection and reporting for quarterly meetings. As a result of these DMRs, CISA has streamlined contract management and awards, gained a better understanding of our funding as it relates to operations and contract support, and can assess hiring metrics and address bottlenecks and challenges. The agency has implemented many changes to its processes (financial, procurement, human capital, etc.) as a result of these quarterly reviews, thereby strengthening our overall management operations.

(11) "Stand in the Arena" (What It Means)

Any worthy cause is worth doing well and it takes effort—in all things personal and professional. At CISA, we embrace and take ownership of our mission. We know it, understand it, and pursue it relentlessly. In his famous "Citizenship in a Republic" speech, Teddy Roosevelt said:

> It is not the critic who counts... The credit belongs to the man who is actually in the arena, whose face is marred by dust and sweat and blood; who strives valiantly; ... who spends himself in a worthy cause; who at the best knows in the end the triumph of high achievement, and who at the worst, if he fails, at least he fails while daring greatly. (Roosevelt, 1910, para. 9)

These words ring true to us. Our mission requires that we sometimes take risks, make tough calls, try something new and unproven, take a leap of faith, or even do something scary or uncomfortable. It also means sometimes failing—which is okay. This does not mean we should take uncalculated risks, make poor decisions, or repeatedly make the same mistakes. It means we should not fear the prospect of failure, allowing that fear to paralyze us.

What sets us apart is how we respond to inevitable mistakes. We take ownership and accountability as appropriate, viewing them as learning experiences and opportunities to improve and grow. Because so much of what we do at CISA is unprecedented and unproven, we accept that risks, mistakes, and even failure will be part of our work. In this way, we must know how to respond, recover, and learn—together as a team.

(11) "Stand in the Arena" (Practices)

After-Action Hot Wash

We conduct immediate post-event discussions and debriefings to analyze performance and outcomes, capture fresh insights and key takeaways, and reinforce lessons learned and improvements. This is not just an evaluation but also an opportunity to ask ourselves what went well, what did not go as expected, what was surprising, and what can be improved. Program evaluation is often conducted against the goals and objectives by examining output and outcome measures. We purposefully build in a critical review of the unexpected, which can be both negative and positive.

As one example, we conducted an after-action review of our new supervisor leadership development course. According to the data, it was a resounding success—meeting the training evaluation criteria and receiving very high participant satisfaction scores. By asking instructors, facilitators, and participants critical questions about what could be improved, we learned about additional key changes that would enrich the learning and enhance application back on the job: participants wanted to continue as a cohort with peer coaching (implemented), found great value in CISA leader-instructors and CISA-centered examples (we will increase their use in future offerings), and faced various challenges with the action project requirement (we will significantly revise this activity).

Launching and Recognizing First-Evers

Standing in the arena at a new agency requires courage, fearlessness, and persistence—because much of what we do will be "first-evers" in government. That is hard—and it is exciting. In 2024, we appointed our first Chief Artificial Intelligence (AI) Officer to build CISA's AI capabilities, integrate AI into the agency's core missions of cybersecurity and critical infrastructure protection, and set a national standard for AI.

A significant achievement was the team's role in fulfilling Executive Order 14110 on AI security, which involved delivering a comprehensive AI vulnerability detection report to the White House. The project required overcoming significant technical, policy, and coordination challenges while ensuring that CISA's AI approach was aligned with both national security objectives and emerging AI risks.

The agency-wide working group (which included OCPO) laid the groundwork for AI governance, not only within CISA but also across DHS and the broader federal government. The team also developed key AI security standards and practices that have shaped how the federal government approaches AI integration and risk management. The AI vulnerability detection report delivered to the White House directly influenced national policy on AI security and risk management. All of these deliverables required extensive collaboration, wide-ranging debate, and courageous leadership.

This work set standards for the ethical and secure use of AI in critical infrastructure protection, ensuring that AI technologies are deployed in ways that prioritize security and public trust. The OCPO was proud to nominate this pioneering effort for recognition and, in 2024, the Chief AI and a small core team was awarded the Gold Award, CISA's highest annual honor.

(12) "Commit to a Lifetime of Learning" (What It Means)

Be curious. Ask questions. At CISA, we encourage each other to learn one new thing every day. We recognize that learning is central to our team's mission and a foundational skill for our success. If someone, especially a leader, reaches a point where they think they know all they need to—they by definition will not succeed. We challenge ourselves and each other to seek out new learning opportunities or revisit old ones. We approach learning with a growth mindset—continuously examining what we have done well and where we can improve with an open mind. Through continuous learning, we become better at our jobs, build stronger rapport with our teammates, and help everyone achieve our own and our team's goals.

Learning comes in many forms. CISA offers many formal training and education opportunities and also provides a wide array of self-paced development programs. In addition, we are firm believers in experiential learning—learning by doing—and we incorporate it into our work and career development.

(12) "Commit to a Lifetime of Learning" (Practices)

Reverse Shadowing

Not only do we have a shadowing program for all employee job levels that we run in the fall and spring, but we also launched a reverse shadowing program. In reverse shadowing, managers and senior leaders shadow a more junior member of the workforce, often in a different division or function. This has three main benefits: (1) creating new network connections that would not occur organically, (2) demonstrating that our managers and leaders are lifelong learners, and (3) showing that teaching is not only top-down and that we can all learn from any level of employee. Even the Director participated in reverse shadowing and declared broadly how much she learned from shadowing a frontline early-careerist. She encouraged all senior leaders to participate to ensure they experienced "a day in the life on the front line."

Individual Development Plans

With the Director's support, we mandated Individual Development Plans (IDPs) for all employees to foster professional growth at all levels. In 2024, we implemented the new "IDP Vault," a groundbreaking tool that streamlined the creation of IDPs for individual employees and served as an essential accountability tool for the agency. CISA's new IDP is no longer the traditional "training and education" form but rather a comprehensive career growth plan that helps employees build skills for their current jobs *and* future career goals. The IDP now incorporates experiential learning through rotational assignments, serving on working groups or councils, receiving mentoring or coaching, shadowing, and more. This program achieved an unprecedented 96% participation rate, strengthening our focus on workforce development and career growth.

Democratize Leadership Development

The OCPO designed ways to "democratize leadership development," ensuring employees would actively benefit from leadership development opportunities without having to wait until they were formally in a supervisory role or at a senior grade level. This approach aligns with the strategic plan which states "To foster employee retention, we must ensure equal access to professional development and educational opportunities for employees and leaders at all levels" (CISA, 2022, p. 32). To strengthen "leaders at all levels" we vastly improved and broadened access to leadership development across CISA.

In December 2023, we used an online learning platform (Percipio) to make leadership resources available to all CISA employees. These resources included over 2,000 books, 80 audiobooks, 30 learning channels, 300 courses, and 700 videos covering leading-edge leadership development competencies, practices, and tips. In less than a year, nearly a quarter of CISA employees used this cost-effective, self-service program, which was also available via a mobile app.

We also reviewed feedback on a new leadership development program which had been initially designed for current supervisors (GS14–15 levels). Our review found that the course content would benefit emerging leaders (GS11–13 levels), that there was interest from that population for the course objectives, and that we had unfilled "seats" in each class. Starting in 2024, we opened the course to GS11 and above. Throughout that year, we had fully enrolled classes and high participant satisfaction.

One CISA Town Halls

Starting in 2022, CISA reserved Thursdays at 1:00 p.m. ET as our common hour during which we hosted a virtual Town Hall for the entire agency.

Between 2022 and 2024, we hosted over 100 Town Halls featuring Director addresses to the workforce, internal senior leader and expert presentations and "fireside chats," panels on operational or new mission programs, employee panels on our culture and engagement efforts, and external guest speakers who brought a wide range of timely and relevant "learnings" to our workforce. External speakers included interpersonal influence expert Zoe Chance, FEMA Administrator Deanne Criswell, organizational psychologist Adam Grant, Future of Work strategist Seth Mattison, author Jennifer Pahlka, NASA James Webb Telescope Director Greg Robinson, business leader Simon Sinek, presidential speechwriter Terry Szuplat, and DHS Deputy Secretary John Tien. Each year these events drew over 50,000 attendees, with an average of about 1,400 virtual participants. Employees overwhelmingly enjoyed the diverse topics and speakers (ratings averaged 4.7 on a five-point scale), the opportunity to "step away" from their daily work and come together across the agency, and exposure to ideas from internal and external experts.

Role of Leaders

Organizational culture is inextricably linked to leadership. It starts at the top and flows down through all levels of management. Not only have CISA's first two Directors role-modeled our core values, but they have also ensured that a people-first culture is embedded in the agency's strategy, priorities, and goals for accomplishing its mission. All CISA executives (about 60) are expected to create the conditions for their supervisors and managers to coach, embody, and foster our core values and principles across their teams. With this top-down support and expectation, our approximately 660 supervisors and managers are supported and rewarded for strengthening our people-first culture. Finally, all employees are expected to embody and act in accordance with our values and principles.

All levels of management play a role in upholding culture, but our line supervisors are the "accountability coaches" closest to employees' day-to-day behaviors. Celebrating our people's successes is one of the easiest and most enjoyable parts of being a supervisor. Holding employees accountable when they exhibit counter-cultural behaviors is hard and often unpleasant—but it is required of people-first leaders. It is necessary to fortify culture principles by addressing non-achievers or "bad actors" through mentoring/coaching, feedback, performance counseling, reassignment (when it is a fit issue), discipline, demotion, and/or removal. Our supervisors have told us they feel more supported and skilled in 2024 than a few years ago when it comes to taking consequential action to address counterproductive, counter-cultural employee behaviors (and the data support this).

Specific dynamics make it particularly essential to proactively support our line leaders in their critical roles helping them personally and collectively sustain our people-first culture within their teams. Those dynamics include:

1. Being a federal government agency with a national security mission entails a highly hierarchical structure and a necessary "chain of command," as well as an intense focus on accountability for delivering results to the American people, Congress, the president, and the administration.
2. CISA has a highly technical and analytical workforce, and our supervisory cadre is composed of experts in their fields with deep technical expertise.
3. The demands on supervisors are more complex than ever, including leading success in a hybrid, flexible work environment, caring for and addressing employees' unique needs in work–life blending, managing increased work demands amid shrinking budgets, staying abreast of new approaches and impacts related to data analytics, AI and technology, and navigating the uncertainty and changes expected with new political leadership.

Table 26.3 provides examples of actions we have taken in performance, development, awards, and communications to reinforce the essential role of the supervisor/manager and instill accountability for the culture.

Measuring Our Progress: Early Returns

Culture is a long game. Leadership support is necessary but not sufficient to truly achieve culture excellence. Purposeful, dedicated, and expert work is also required to measure progress and identify what is working well and where improvements are needed. So how will we know that we are focusing on the right things and that this work is making a difference? The answer is measurement through multiple methods over the years.

Table 26.3 Actions Taken to Instill Accountability for Culture

Type	Action	Description
Performance	Executive Element for Employee Engagement	"Fosters an employee centered, high performing organization ... a culture that engages employees and provides an environment that fosters high morale, makes employees feel heard and valued, and enhances the organization's ability to improve individual and unit performance" (U.S. Department of Homeland Security, 2024a, p. 4).
Performance	Executive Element for Culture Improvement	"Supports the agency wide culture improvement efforts with executive leadership skills and deliberate, organizational actions. Provides clear communication of workforce culture, objectives, programs, and improvements" (U.S. Department of Homeland Security, 2024b, p. 4).
Performance	Supervisor Elements	Mandatory performance elements cover communications, leading with respect and empathy, giving feedback, continuous learning, developing others, teamwork, collaboration, networks and partnerships, psychological safety, customer service, and fairness.
Performance	FEVS Results Dashboard and Action Plans	One hundred percent of leaders provided with highly useful FEVS data to share; all offices implemented action plans.
Development	Mentoring, Coaching, Shadowing	Leaders expected to participate in and support their employees' participation in mentoring, coaching, and shadowing programs.
Development	Leadership Development	Implemented five new leadership courses aligned to core principles.
Development	Leadership Development Dashboard	Online dashboard for supervisors to log and track progress fulfilling their development requirements.
Development	Psychological Safety Training	Training for all supervisors (started in 2022); added to New Employee Orientation (started in 2023); added to leadership development refresher courses (in 2024); hosted expert speakers (e.g., Amy Edmonson, Simon Sinek).

Type	Action	Description
Development	360-Degree Feedback	Designed CISA-specific 360-degree instrument; Town Hall with 360-degree feedback expert Dave Bracken; offered numerous resources and required development plan.
Development	Executive Retreat	Director and CPO hosted a two-day offsite retreat for all senior executives to work on building One CISA.
Recognition	Agency Awards	Annual Honorary Director Awards (non-monetary) with 15 categories reinforcing agency values and core principles.
Communications	Quarterly Supervisor Forums	Supervisors/managers required to attend information exchange forums hosted by the Deputy Director and facilitated by the CPO.
Communications	Town Hall Events	Town Hall events on operation and agency updates, Director addresses, and external speakers. At least one event each month was focused on one of the culture principles.
Communications	Leadership Messages to the Workforce	Averaging 90 per year, from Director, Deputy Director, Chief of Staff, and CPO.

Participation Rates

Our people do not have time for things that do not matter or do not help them. But our people cannot benefit from our programs unless they participate. One of the easiest measures is to see whether people are attending the programs. We track participation rates for our events, programs, surveys, and sensing sessions. For example, we set a goal of 900 participants per Town Hall on average. In 2023, we hosted 32 Town Halls, averaging about 1,200 participants per event. In 2024, we hosted 35 Town Halls, averaging over 1,340 participants per Town Hall. In 2024, our goal was to increase CISA Intranet visits to 80,000, and we exceeded that, reaching over 120,000. We ran two pilot shadowing sessions in 2023 for 100 participants; in 2024, we opened two sessions and had over 300 participants. In 2023, only 17% of CISA supervisors had completed their required training; in 2024, we increased that to over 83%.

We used these data to better understand why employees do or do not attend. For example, we learned that employees were unaware of specific programs, so we improved our communications and advertising by sending group calendar invites, sending Director or CPO messages, posting an event calendar on our CISA Intranet home page (and highlighting events for the week ahead), and streamlining our digital *CISA Vision* newsletter. We have also selectively used the Director's willingness to make specific talent programs "mandatory" to gain attention and participation for new programs deemed most essential to driving our people and culture efforts (this is important for initial participation, but having them experience value from the program is what keeps them participating).

Satisfaction Rates

Most of our programs ask participants to complete a short voluntary evaluation survey but response rates vary widely. Some examples of satisfaction rates follow. Our evaluation survey at the end of each Town Hall event achieved high satisfaction scores (4.5/5 in 2023 and 4.7/5 in 2024); however, the response rates were very low (typically less than 20%). The 20 executives who participated in our on-site "Upside of Uncertainty" Workshop reported 95% satisfaction, with 84% requesting a follow-up session on the same topic (100% survey participation). Ninety percent of participants in my CPO sensing sessions said they would recommend the sessions to their colleagues, and about 80% provided specific input on each session topic. Across our suite of leadership development courses, we averaged satisfaction rates of 75% positive or higher (2023–2024).

Gathering general satisfaction rates can be informative; however, receiving suggestions for improvement and feedback on specific aspects of these programs that we were striving to improve is proving even more actionable. We plan to add additional longitudinal evaluation metrics to understand how our employees apply their learning over time.

Engagement Survey Results

CISA participates in the mandatory Federal Employee Viewpoint Survey (FEVS) administered and managed by the Office of Personnel Management (OPM). FEVS has been implemented at CISA since 2019. In 2024, CISA achieved the highest response rate (72%) across all of DHS (45%) (for the second year in a row); the government-wide response rate was 41%.

We believe this is the result of our three-part effective communications campaign that explains why the workforce should participate: (1) showing how FEVS results led to real change (e.g., a video highlighting employees talking about initiatives in their units that were born from FEVS results); (2) linking participation to mission success (e.g., when we improve CISA on the things measured on FEVS, we achieve our agency goals); and (3) linking participation to other strategic initiatives (e.g., in our 2024 theme of Unity and Resilience we focused on uniting people via the "Our Voices Are Stronger Together" campaign to take the FEVS). Notably, in 2022, less than 50% of respondents believed the FEVS results would be used to improve the agency, but by 2024, over 62% did (a more than 25% increase).

In 2024, CISA achieved its *highest ever* positive ratings across all five FEVS indices— employee engagement, global satisfaction, diversity and inclusion, employee experience, and performance confidence—a true testament to the transformative power of our people-centered approach (see Table 26.4). Since creating the Chief People Office in 2022, we have dedicated year-round efforts to real organizational development, including a new Organizational Development and Effectiveness office with four Industrial/Organizational Psychologists and a data scientist, a new Chief Learning Officer, and a dedicated Leadership and Talent Development office. We implemented more robust employee listening programs (e.g., sensing sessions, pulse surveys). We built stronger partnerships across the agency (e.g., CISA Culture Council [including the Offices of the CHCO and DEIA], FEVS Action Planning Working Group) to ensure we were collectively using results to drive meaningful improvements. We have seen increases in all five FEVS indices: a 10% increase in global satisfaction; a 5% increase in employee engagement and diversity, equity, and inclusion; a 3% increase in employee experience; and a 2% increase in performance confidence. CISA also improved on all three employee engagement subindices and the three items measured annually to determine the best places to work in the federal government (see Table 26.4; Partnership for Public Service, 2024a). While I would not suggest direct causation, as many factors contribute to these results, there is evidence that our concerted programs and new human-centric efforts are making a positive impact.

CISA is countering the general decline in employee engagement in the United States. Across the nation, engagement has been declining and reached

Table 26.4 Percent Positive (% Pos) on Federal Employee Viewpoint Survey Indices and "Best Places to Work" Index

FEVS Index/Items	2022 % Pos	2023 % Pos	2024 % Pos	% Increase Since 2022
Employee Engagement	73	75	76	5
Global Satisfaction	66	71	72	10
Diversity, Equity, and Inclusion	75	77	79	5
Employee Experience (new in 2023)	N/A	76	78	3
Performance Confidence	86	87	88	2
Employee Engagement Subindices				
Perceptions of Senior Leaders	63	67	69	8
Supervisor Effectiveness	83	84	85	3
Intrinsic Work Experience	71	73	74	4
Best Places to Work Index	65	70	72	10
Three Best Places to Work Items from FEVS				
I recommend my organization as a good place to work	65	71	74	14
How satisfied are you with your job	68	71	72	6
How satisfied are you with your organization	63	67	70	9

Note: OPM considers anything over 65% positive a strength.

its lowest level in a decade in 2024, with only 31% of employees engaged (Gallup, 2024). Gallup's research found that engagement peaked in 2020 at 36% engaged but has generally decreased since then. Even NASA, named the "Best Place to Work" in the federal government (large agencies) for 12 years in a row, is seeing declines in some key employee engagement items and indices. After a steady increase in "Best Places" engagement levels from 2011 to 2020 (high of 87% positive), NASA engagement, while still very high, has declined by 6% since then (to 82% positive in 2024) (NASA, 2024; Partnership for Public Service, 2024b).

As described in this chapter, CISA has intentionally focused on key areas that drive employee engagement, achieving a 76% positive engagement index score in 2024. According to Gallup's longitudinal research (Harter, 2024), "best practice organizations" achieve 70% or higher on engagement (72% in 2022, 70% in 2023, and 70% in 2024 across the United States). This research on "best practice organizations" shows that employee engagement improves when organizations take the following actions: implement the right strategies, focus on communication, invest in manager development, and prioritize accountability. Indeed, CISA has seen meaningful increases in scores for unity, resilience, learning, leadership, inclusion, and well-being after implementing year-long campaigns and special programs (e.g., 360-degree feedback) focused on strengthening these areas.

When we take care of our people, they take care of the mission. Based on our analyses, our core strengths indicate that a people-focused approach is associated with the attitudes and behaviors CISA needs to deliver on our mission. For example, our strongest areas were respecting our employees and their views, as well as supporting well-being and development. In turn, we saw very high service orientation, team cooperation, adaptation to changing priorities, accountability for quality work and results, and support for agency performance. Our challenge areas (none of which fell below 50% positive) were improving business and decision processes, and some areas of talent management, such as workloads and recognition of performance.

We plan to evolve our metrics program to more directly measure perceptions and experiences of our culture principles in practice. For now, we have linked some OPM FEVS items to provide indicators across our 12 Core Principles (see Table 26.5 for examples).

Table 26.5 Percent Positive (% Pos) on Sample Survey Items Linked to 12 Culture Principles

Culture Principle	FEVS Item Example	2022 % Pos	2023 % Pos	2024 % Pos
People First	I can be successful in my organization being myself	73	77	79
	Comfort in expressing different opinion	75	78	80
	Employees in work unit consider customer needs top priority	86	86	88
	Employees protected from health & safety hazards	79	86	86
	FEVS will be used to make the agency better	50	59	63
Do the Right Thing	I have trust & confidence in supervisor	79	80	81
	My organization's senior leaders maintain high levels of honesty & integrity	64	67	69
	Can disclose suspected violation of law, rule, or regulation without fear	73	74	77

continued

Table 26.5 *continued*

Culture Principle	FEVS Item Example	2022 % Pos	2023 % Pos	2024 % Pos
Lead with Empathy	Supervisors listens to employees	84	86	86
	Supervisor treats me with respect	87	89	90
	Employees in work unit care about me as a person	80	81	84
Honest Feedback	Organization shares FEVS results	NA	89	91
	Supervisor provides constructive feedback	74	78	79
	Supervisor provides performance feedback throughout the year	78	82	83
Communicate Effectively	Managers promote communications across groups	71	75	77
	Managers communicate goals of organization	67	73	74
Foster Belonging, DEI	People's differences are respected	78	80	84
	Supervisor demonstrates commitment to diversity	81	82	83
	My team makes me feel I belong	81	82	85
Innovate to Win	Management encourages innovation	65	68	71
	Feel encouraged to come up with new & better ways	70	72	74
	Work unit commits resources to develop new ideas	56	64	65
Make It Count	Supervisor supports need to balance work & life issues	88	89	91
	Important that my work contributes to common good	92	94	95
	I know how my work relates to agency goals	79	82	83
	I identify with the mission	81	82	85
	My work gives me sense of accomplishment	72	75	76
Cultivate Your Network	Employees in my work unit share job knowledge	81	82	83
	People I work with cooperate to get the job done	84	87	87
Play Chess	Employees in work unit adapt to changing priorities	84	85	85
	Employees in work unit approach change as opportunity	63	66	70

Culture Principle	FEVS Item Example	2022 % Pos	2023 % Pos	2024 % Pos
Stand in the Arena	Supervisor holds me accountable for results	90	91	92
	I am held accountable for quality work	89	88	90
	Management makes effective change to address challenges facing our organization	54	58	62
Lifetime of Learning	I am given opportunity to improve my skills	71	75	77
	Supervisor supports employee development	83	85	87

Measurement Next Steps

Admittedly, we are in the early stages of building a robust workforce analytics capability. We plan to mature our analytics by expanding the use of quantitative and qualitative measures. We are reviewing more detailed hiring and retention data to better understand where further interventions are needed to improve our talent acquisition and retention goals (e.g., application rates, offers accepted, new hires onboarded, new hire survey feedback, promotion rates, and voluntary and involuntary turnover rates).

We also use focus groups, sensing sessions, exit interviews, open-ended questions, and one-on-one interviews to focus on specific experiences, feedback, and sentiment trends. We plan to continue developing qualitative analytic techniques to further understand the impact of our people-first culture efforts.

Conclusion

There is nothing more critical for today's leaders than driving a healthy organizational culture that engages the workforce. Culture starts at the top and requires a concerted effort across the management ranks. Programs, initiatives, and accountability must also involve all employees at all levels for a healthy culture to really take hold. We know we will have a new Director and other leaders at CISA in the next administration and beyond, so it is incumbent on all of us to embody and sustain the culture we have begun.

In conclusion, driving a healthy, strong organizational culture and high employee engagement is essential to CISA's mission success. We cannot do the hard work required for mission success without high-impact talent that is motivated, skilled, and supported. We know organizational culture will always be a "work in progress" because the new normal of work includes constant reorganizations, frequent leadership changes, continuous improvements to procedures, adoption of new technology and AI, shifts in where and when work is performed, changing expectations and needs across the workforce, and changes in priorities and budgets.

We have learned that what *attracts* people to work at CISA is our critical mission and knowing their work contributes to a purpose greater than themselves. Our people tell us they *stay and thrive* when they work for excellent leaders, have support for flexible work arrangements, and can develop their skills for today and tomorrow. Through our employee surveys and listening efforts, our people have told us that when they feel supported, they will go above and beyond for our mission.

Culture improvement is a journey, and we still have *much* work to do. This journey must begin by ensuring the workforce knows that leadership cares about them and is actively working to build and sustain a healthy culture. We have defined our culture in terms of the mindsets and behaviors we all aspire to have and experience, and we have implemented actions and programs to build and sustain them. We have incorporated our culture and workforce goals into our CISA Strategic Plan, established accountability in our talent management programs, and instituted a dedicated OCPO to drive, measure, and deliver on these goals. We are on our way.

The innovative strategies I have shared in this chapter have not only elevated CISA's culture—they have also ensured that an engaged, capable workforce is at the heart of our agency's success in cybersecurity. Our people-first culture of excellence has proven that when employees are empowered, informed, and truly valued, remarkable things happen—for our people, mission, and nation.

References

Burnett, B. & Evans, D. (2016). *Designing your life: How to build a well-lived, joyful life.* Knopf.

Collins, J. (2001). *Good to great: Why some companies make the leap... and others don't.* HarperBusiness.

Cybersecurity and Infrastructure Security Agency. (n.d.-a). *About CISA.* U.S. Department of Homeland Security. Retrieved December 30, 2025, from https://www.cisa.gov/about

Cybersecurity and Infrastructure Security Agency. (n.d.-b). *Our CISA culture* [Internal pamphlet]. U.S. Department of Homeland Security.

Cybersecurity and Infrastructure Security Agency. (2022, September 1). *Cybersecruity and Infrastructure Security strategic plan 2023–2025.* U.S. Department of Homeland Security. https://database.cyberpolicyportal.org/api/files/1677058627155xlpdb16e3m.pdf

Cybersecurity and Infrastructure Security Agency. (2023, April). *Secure by Design (SbD).* U.S. Department of Homeland Security. https://www.cisa.gov/securebydesign

Cybersecurity Ventures. (2023). *2023 official cybersecurity jobs report* [Report]. https://www.esentire.com/resources/library/2023-official-cybersecurity-jobs-report

CyberSeek. (2024). *CyberSeek* (National Institute of Standards and Technology [NIST] National Initiative for Cybersecurity Education [NICE]). https //www.cyberseek.org

Edmonson, A. (2019). *The fearless organization: Creating psychological safety in the workplace for learning, innovation, and growth.* John Wiley & Sons.

Easterly, J. (2022, April 13). *People first: Live event CISA Town Hall* [Speaker Series internal presentation]. Cybersecurity and Infrastructure Security Agency, U.S. Department of Homeland Security.

Gallup. (n.d.). *CliftonStrengths.* Retrieved December, 30, 2025, from https://www.gallup.com/cliftonstrengths/en/252137/home.aspx

Gallup. (2024). *Employee engagement index.* https://www.gallup.com/394373/indicator-employee-engagement.aspx

Harter, J. (2024, September 4). World's largest ongoing study of the employee experience. *Gallup.* https://www.gallup.com/workplace/649487/world-largest-ongoing-study-employee-experience.aspx

Kolmstetter, E. (2024, July 23). *Office of the Chief People Officer organizational structure* [Memorandum for the Director, internal document]. Cybersecurity and Infrastructure Security Agency, U.S. Department of Homeland Security.

Krebs, C. (2022, May 5). *Do the right thing, always: Live event CISA Town Hall—Fireside chat with former CISA Director Chris Krebs* [Speaker Series internal presentation]. Cybersecurity and Infrastructure Security Agency, U.S. Department of Homeland Security.

National Aeronautics and Space Administration. (2024, October). *2024 NASA annual employee survey results.* https://www.nasa.gov/wp-content/uploads/2024/10/2024-annual-employee-survey-aes-results.pdf?emrc=671a24c795b88

Partnership for Public Service. (2024a). *Best places to work in the federal government(2024): Government-wide findings overall.* https://bestplacestowork.org/analysis/government-wide-findings-overall

Partnership for Public Service. (2024b). *Best places to work in the federal government (2024): National Aeronautics and Space Administration.* https://bestplacestowork.org/rankings/detail/?c=NN00

Roosevelt, T. (1910, April 23). Address at the Sorbonne in Paris, France: "Citizenship in a Republic" [Speech transcript]. The American Presidency Project. https://www.presidency.ucsb.edu/documents/address-the-sorbonne-paris-france-citizenship-republic

U.S. Department of Homeland Security. (2024a). *Senior Executive Service performance management: Executive element* (Performance periods 2022–2024) [Internal document]. Critical Element 2: Leading People—Employee Engagement.

U.S. Department of Homeland Security. (2024b). *Senior Executive Service performance management: Executive element* (Performance periods 2022–2024) [Internal document]. Critical Element 2: Leading People—Culture Improvement.

World Economic Forum. (2024, January). *Global cybersecurity outlook 2024.* https://www3.weforum.org/docs/WEF_Global_Cybersecurity_Outlook_2024.pdf

SECTION IX

SUMMARY AND CONCLUDING THOUGHTS

27
The State of Leadership
Reflections on Where We Are and Where We Are Headed

Sheri L. Feinzig and Mariangela Battista

Introduction and Context

As described in the introduction to this volume (Chapter 1) and reiterated throughout its chapters, this book was conceived and written during increasingly volatile and unpredictable times that can be characterized as "polycrises." Such circumstances permeate every aspect of society including our workplaces, and require leaders to adapt and evolve. We strongly believe, based on the preponderance of evidence, that the leadership described in these chapters is the leadership we need now, more than ever. As these chapters have made clear, diversity brings strength to organizations and should be strived for and celebrated. Every individual deserves to feel included and respected at work and in society, and concerted effort is needed to "level the playing field" to even begin to achieve an equitable meritocracy. Similarly, leadership styles grounded in empathy, with sincere concern (accompanied by enabling actions) for all workers' well-being, will yield positive outcomes for employer and employee alike. Leaders need to lead with humanity and humility. Optimizing outcomes means creating and sustaining safe—not toxic—work cultures.

If we wish to have a planet that will support the organizations that leaders are responsible for and that we all wish to inhabit, we must not let our guard down on sustainability. We must be vigilant in deepening our understanding of evolving technologies such as artificial intelligence (AI) and automation, and the implications such technologies have on our organizations and society at large. It is our sincere hope, as you read these pages, that evidence-based outcomes triumph, that truth prevails, and that the leadership insights

Sheri L. Feinzig and Mariangela Battista, *The State of Leadership*. In: *The Changing Leadership Landscape*.
Edited by: Sheri L. Feinzig and Mariangela Battista, Oxford University Press.
DOI: 10.1093/9780197820070.003.0027

shared in these chapters will inspire and instruct leaders of today and tomorrow how to operate most effectively in a rapidly evolving and ever-changing world of work.

Volume Summary

Through the chapters in this volume, we have strived to present a balanced perspective of varying viewpoints and experiences in navigating through challenging times. We aimed to provide trusted research- and experience-based insights and guidance for leaders operating across a range of settings, as well as for those tasked with developing leaders, and for anyone interested in more deeply understanding what effective leadership looks like and how it is experienced by those being led. Across these chapters, we have seen varying takes on what constitutes leadership, what skills and capabilities are required for leading through today's—and tomorrow's—global challenges, the ever-evolving knowledge and ability to navigate a changing technology landscape, and the role of humanity demanded of leaders amid a pervasive and persistent march toward automation and algorithmically driven optimization. We intentionally sought a diverse range of voices in this volume, representing a spectrum of viewpoints and lived experiences. Reflected in the chapters are perspectives from academics, consultants, and practitioners; European, African, and North American citizens; and authors of various ethnicities, religions, skin colors, genders, and thinking styles. We hope that by bringing you a range of perspectives, this volume will help you feel well-informed and enabled with knowledge of the rich complexity that is leadership.

The Rapidly Evolving World of Technology

We began our in-depth discussion with the changing technology landscape, as technology has been permeating every aspect of society, and capable leadership is needed now more than ever to understand the implications and take the appropriate actions to both reap the benefits and minimize the risks. With the advent of generative AI, the 2020s have been characterized by a great deal of enthusiasm around the potential of algorithmic technologies to drive the next wave of business transformation with visions of increased efficiencies, improved profit margins, and growth. Leaders have been expected to embrace these technologies and integrate them into business operations, and many have done just that. Risks with algorithmic technologies—data exposure and breaches, privacy violations, poor decision-making resulting in individual, group, and societal harm—have been observed and well-documented for over a decade, with standard admonishments to "keep a human in the loop" and "verify the output" tacked onto AI discussions like so many obligatory warnings on many consumer packaged goods products—always there, barely noticed, rarely acted upon.

So, what is the role of leadership in this *fear-of-missing-out* but *proceed-with-caution* environment? Pointedly, leaders bear the responsibility of upskilling and educating themselves about the use and implications of AI adoption and algorithmic automation, while simultaneously doing so for the people in the organizations they lead. Boyce (Chapter 2) emphasized this point, using the employee lifecycle as a framing device. Boyce highlighted specific leadership tasks and skills required of leaders as each lifecycle stage is potentially transformed by AI, as well as leadership responsibilities that span the employee lifecycle—namely, decision-making and change management. Throughout this AI-focused discussion, Boyce notably highlighted the need for more—not less—humanity from leaders in a technology-immersed world. This human-centric, empathetic emphasis is echoed strongly throughout the chapters in Section II (and throughout the other sections in this volume).

Similar to Boyce, Tavis and Derler (Chapter 3) point out that algorithmic technologies have already been embedded extensively in workplaces. The presence of these technologies is changing the nature of management and leadership—which, Tavis and Derler argued, is a false distinction that is being further blurred by contemporary technologies. They described specific use cases for AI in organizations—autonomous AI agents, digital twins for scenario planning, and AI coaching—that manager-leaders will need to understand and work with.

Niederhoffer and colleagues (Chapter 4) also discussed the manager's role in the rapid and seemingly inevitable incorporation of AI into the workplace. With an implied underlying assumption that embracing AI in the workplace will yield positive outcomes in the way of efficiency and innovation, these authors argued that a key to such adoption lies in employees' mindsets and leaders' ability to foster the desired mindsets among their workforce members. Specifically, they distinguish between the Pilot mindset characterized by readily embracing AI at work and reaping the resulting benefits, and the Passenger mindset that is more cautious, skeptical, and feeling threatened by AI. Interestingly, Niederhoffer and colleagues identified very few Passengers in their research sample relative to Pilots, which itself was substantially smaller than the percentage of participants categorized as "undecided." Again, assuming that widespread AI adoption is desired, this suggests that managers have a substantial opportunity to influence "undecideds" to become Pilots. As with other chapters in this section, Niederhoffer and colleagues also strongly emphasized the importance of "deeply human" skills required of managers to motivate their teams and effectively lead through this changing technology landscape.

Woodward (Chapter 5) focused the AI conversation on the technology's influence on executive coaching, with an in-depth discussion of the numerous variations of AI coaching capabilities in supporting, delivering, and enhancing coaching engagements. The chapter described a taxonomy of current and emerging capabilities and the role they play in developing leaders, including streamlining administrative tasks, scaling support, and personalizing feedback to both coaches and the leaders they coach.

The authors of all these chapters included a note of caution about the risks of algorithmic technologies, including the propensity for producing questionable and inaccurate output, data privacy concerns, and potential loss of human connection. Boinodiris (Chapter 6), while recognizing the potential benefits these technologies can offer, shared a stark warning of the substantial risks that are often overlooked or underestimated in the zeal to adopt AI and reap the anticipated positive outcomes. In addition to explicating the wide array of risks and the widespread reality of disappointing returns on investment in these technologies, Boinodiris provided practical guidance on what leaders need to know and do when bringing these technologies to their organizations and actually realizing benefits. A key action proposed by this author is investing in a new leadership role—the AI governance leader—to provide ongoing risk identification and mitigation and to increase the likelihood of benefit realization while protecting the business, the workforce, customers, and society from harm.

Data and Analytics through a Leadership Lens

Section III took a step back to the basics of data and analysis, on which this technology landscape is built. Foundational to algorithmic technologies are the underlying data that power them, and this is the focus of Fink and Reiswig's chapter (Chapter 7): understanding data fundamentals, identifying key patterns in data, and recognizing the implications of analytical output as required core competencies for effective leadership today. Fink and Reiswig highlighted the knowledge, skills, and actions required of leaders for managing and utilizing data to properly extract reliable insights and apply those insights to positive effect. Practical, experience-based guidance and illustrative examples were provided on accessing, handling, and analyzing both quantitative and qualitative data, highlighting the special sensitivities associated with people data.

Nalbantian (Chapter 8) emphasized the importance of understanding the context and culture surrounding data and analysis, highlighting the game-changing nature of incorporating "the hand a leader is dealt" when evaluating their performance and drawing conclusions about leadership effectiveness. Nalbantian's real-world examples provide compelling illustrations of how to put these insights—and guidance such as that described by Fink and Reiswig—into action. Both chapters argued that leaders of today and tomorrow must get comfortable with proper use and application of data and analytics. Both also emphasized the invaluable role that qualitative data play in providing contextual as well as future-oriented information essential to complementing and interpreting quantitative data analysis. Analyzing and modeling based on historical data will yield predictions consistent with what worked in the past; understanding what will work in the future requires a different approach.

Global Challenges

In Section IV we turned our attention to the big picture of global challenges, with a focus on the existential urgency of environmental sustainability and, more broadly, the art of leading through various types of crises. It is in the interest of everyone—individuals, organizations, and societies—to sustain a habitable environment. Absent this, there will be fewer and fewer people to purchase the products and services proffered by organizations. Pure self-interest and short-term profit optimization are not winning strategies. And it is critical to recognize that the current technology landscape is not a separate and distinct topic from sustainability but rather deeply intertwined with it: the unrelenting demand for energy to train, optimize, and use algorithmic models is directly at odds with organizations' stated goals of radically reducing their carbon footprints.

Birrell Ivory and Mackay (Chapter 9) compellingly argued that sustainability is a necessity for a thriving business. Particularly powerful is their framing of why businesses exist: to support a thriving society (first and foremost), by producing goods and services (needed by society), and in doing so make a profit (a necessary outcome in a market economy). Similar to the primacy of mindset in Niederhoffer and colleagues' discussion of AI adoption, Birrell Ivory and Mackay emphasized the importance of leadership mindset in incorporating sustainability into the strategic mission of an organization, coupled with explicit acknowledgment of the risks of failing to consider sustainability and the opportunities afforded by proactively embracing it. The essential role of top leadership in bringing this mindset to the entire organization was highlighted. Their "Of/On Sustainability Framework" offered practical guidance for leaders to navigate this existential challenge.

While the effects of the climate crisis are not always felt on a daily basis and are often deprioritized as a result, other crises facing leaders are impossible to ignore or defer. Cyberattacks, supply chain disruptions, data breaches, and pandemics (to name a few examples) require immediate action. Further, crises are characterized by an environment where decisiveness is paramount yet the information on which to base decisions is typically inaccurate and incomplete. Grubb and Anderson (Chapter 10) provided guidance on how to lead effectively through such scenarios, explicating steps to take before, during, and after such incidents.

Grubb and Anderson make it clear that effectively leading through a crisis requires a plan of action long before the crisis emerges. Further, crisis management does not end with the resolution of the crisis; it continues with after-action reviews for refining and honing preparations for the next (inevitable) crisis. Also noteworthy (as echoed throughout this volume) is the essential focus on the human aspects of leadership for successfully navigating crises: simply executing a series of technical actions will fall far short of what's needed during a crisis. Rather, leaders need to also create a psychologically safe environment where employees are comfortable bringing problems forward, and where they can build the resilience to withstand uncomfortable day-to-day challenges as well as more substantial crisis-level shocks. This requires empathy, compassion, and transparent communication to build and nurture a culture of trust.

Leadership and Diversity

Section V shared perspectives on a long-standing topic that tragically, at the time of this writing, has become highly politicized and weaponized: diversity. While the term "diversity, equity, and inclusion" (and specifically the acronym "DEI") has fallen out of favor and is under attack at the time of writing, the reality undergirding these concepts cannot be denied: all people—both those historically favored and those historically disadvantaged—are worthy of the same respect, dignity, and opportunities. Failure to enable all individuals, regardless of personal circumstances and physical and cognitive attributes, to fully contribute and succeed amounts to a catastrophic waste of talent and potential. It is truly heartrending to contemplate all that could have been but was not, due to unfounded perceptions, biases, and fears that have systematically held people back over millennia.

Cox and Wilson (Chapter 11) provided important context for understanding the long-standing and ongoing systemic barriers faced by minoritized groups in organizations, the slow progress made in addressing and overcoming these barriers, and the current backlash against such efforts. With this as a backdrop, they offered practical guidance for leaders to shift the conversation and address organizational challenges impacting the entire workforce, minority and majority members alike. They made the strong case that leadership entails leading the *entirety* of the workforce, which requires viewing every worker as a dignified human being, all equally worthy of respect.

This section of the volume has also sought to remind readers of the value of recognizing human diversity in all its dimensions, the benefits diversity brings to organizations, and what it means to lead the *entirety* of the workforce: White, Black, Brown, Jewish, Muslim, Christian, Hindi, Buddhist, neurodivergent and neurotypical, abled and disabled, all genders, all ethnicities—everyone. Valerio and Ronske (Chapter 12) focused specifically on the lost opportunities associated with the unique barriers faced by women (and particularly women of color) who are pursuing leadership roles, and Praslova (Chapter 14) highlighted the experiences of neurodivergent individuals whose opportunities to bring their valuable talents to the workplace have historically been vastly limited. Both of these chapters made the compelling case that diversity, equity, and inclusion must be present in the leadership ranks as well as among those being led. And Smith and Stuart (Chapter 13) provided practical guidance that leaders can utilize as a decidedly low-tech, highly human, and evidence-based approach for creating more inclusive and equitable workplaces across all the various dimensions of diversity: allyship. This simple yet effective technique is available to every leader in every organization, requires no capital investments, and yields long-term, lasting benefits that reverberate throughout the organization.

Caring and Empathy

Leading the entirety of the workforce in a genuine manner means demonstrating empathy and care to all, which Martin (Chapter 16) described as taking the time to understand employees through meaningful conversations, creating a safe environment where they can speak up and share their concerns, and seeing team members as more than simply the work that they do. Martin described a deceptively simple yet impactful method for doing this: generous check-ins. When planned and implemented with consistency and purpose, this approach paves the way for employees to safely express their feelings and concerns, to develop and grow professionally, and to choose to stay and contribute to the organization's success. As with allyship, this low-tech, highly human approach is available to all leaders in all organizational contexts.

Comini (Chapter 15) concurs with and expands on the power of employee conversations. Based on years of experience coaching leaders, Comini has found that showing genuine concern for all members of the workforce involves not only listening and creating space for raising issues but also sharing accountability for solutions, and empowering employees to identify actions and take ownership of their decisions and behaviors. Leaders and workers alike have a role to play in creating the space to be heard, responsibly raising issues and expressing concerns, agreeing on appropriate actions, and embracing accountability for positive action and problem resolution.

Frangos (Chapter 17) highlighted that, while the challenges may be vastly different, even the most senior leaders in an organization, up to and including the chief executive officer (CEO), experience vulnerability and need to be recognized for their humanity. Top leaders are often shielded by their staff from receiving information that is accurate and candid yet challenging to hear, which impedes their ability to lead effectively. Top leaders also need to unlearn ways of working that have served them well in the past, relearn new ways of working for new situations, and learn how to build and sustain trust with the people they are leading, each and every time they take on a new job or expanded scope of responsibility.

Taken together, chapters of Section V and Section VI cautioned us against the futility of expecting individuals and groups to address and remediate, on their own, the challenges they experience in the workplace. Interventions aimed at "fixing" the individual by offering "solutions" such as well-being apps and mindfulness training do not appear to yield positive results, likely because they fail to address such root-cause issues as suboptimal working conditions, deep-seated biases, poorly designed work, and work overload based on outsized expectations to "do more with less." Conversely, addressing such factors as ill-configured work environments, inefficient processes, and inflexible work arrangements prove beneficial for all employees, not just those who are disproportionately negatively impacted by such hindrances. Similarly, investing resources and time in proven approaches such as allyship and generous check-ins stand to benefit the entirety of the workforce.

Developing Leaders for the New World of Work

Section VII considered the myriad factors and dynamics described in the previous sections, addressing the challenge of how to develop and enable leaders—current *and* future—to effectively lead in this new world of work. Addressing this challenge depends on how one views and defines the construct of leadership. Is it a set of immutable traits, a set of acquired skills and learned behaviors, or some combination of those? Kansal, Boroff, and Caputo (Chapter 18) made the case that much of the required knowledge base and skillset of effective leadership is in fact learnable, with the focus being on leadership effectiveness, evaluated within the context and timeframe in which it takes place. Past performance is merely an indicator of the *potential* for current effectiveness, and no guarantee that effectiveness will carry forward into future circumstances. Ongoing learning is required, as are the abilities to continually adapt and to establish (and reestablish) trust through changing contexts. Frangos in Chapter 17 similarly argued for the need to continually learn, adapt, and establish trust with the workforce. Nalbantian's Chapter 8 agreed with the importance of context in evaluating and developing leaders. Relying on old models that served an organization well in the past is not an effective approach for building the leadership required in the new world of work. Real-world examples of organizations taking context into account, and adjusting their leadership development approaches accordingly, powerfully demonstrated the rewards (e.g., strategic goal attainment and positive shareholder return) to be reaped by doing so.

One important context to consider is the unique challenge of leading effectively through organizational mergers and acquisitions (M&A). M&A activities are often the largest—and riskiest—investments for companies seeking to increase competitive advantage, protect their market position, and grow their businesses. Wu and Pedigo (Chapter 19) illustrated how leaders of both the acquiring and acquired companies have pivotal, proactive roles to play in merging disparate organizations into a single cohesive entity and realizing the envisioned return on investment. Specific guidance and practical examples were provided for leaders tasked with this challenge. This type of focus on leaders in the M&A process, while often overshadowed by financial and tactical actions needed to "get the deal done," is essential to achieving the business case and represents entirely learnable skills and behaviors for leaders in these pivotal roles.

Jones, Nghona, and Jackson (Chapter 20) examined the oft-overlooked opportunity to bring an entrepreneurial focus internally within organizations, adapting traditional entrepreneurial skills and approaches to develop and enable an "intrapreneurial" mindset for sustainable innovation. Intrapreneurship is the cultivation of entrepreneurial thinking and behavior *inside* established organizations by employees, and has emerged as a strong potential source of innovation for driving growth and competitive advantage. The success of this approach hinges on leaders' establishing and reinforcing a culture where it is safe for employees to take calculated risks and to learn from, rather than be punished for, setbacks. Leading in this manner is another example of a learnable approach to leadership that can be successfully incorporated into leadership development curricula.

Similarly teachable is the idea of shifting leaders' mindsets in how they interact with their team members. Returning to the fundamental notion of humanity, oftentimes we as human beings simply want to be heard. While leaders are typically adept at problem solving and "doing," sometimes people turn to their leaders as sounding boards first and foremost. Toffolo (Chapter 21) argued that leaders need to be comfortable with simply "being" and listening when the moment demands it, and to defer the "doing" until the individual is ready. Toffolo made the case for explicitly incorporating this mindset shift into leadership development programs, providing examples of how to enable managers and leaders to be more in tune with their people by applying "attunement" techniques that recognize people's humanity while helping them navigate their challenges. And Comini in Chapter 15 proposed incorporating content into leadership development programs to address well-being challenges facing many organizations today, by enabling managers to create an environment where employees are comfortable both speaking up and taking accountability for decisions and actions.

As discussed, several chapters have made the case that the evolving technology landscape, and the basics of data and analytics, must be explicitly incorporated into leadership training. Tavis and Derler (Chapter 3) in particular argued that traditional leadership development programs are ripe for a substantial overhaul, given the anticipated transformative impact of technologies such as generative AI on the roles of managers and leaders.

Reflecting again on earlier sections, recall that recognizing individuals' humanity and affording each individual the respect they deserve is a fundamental, underlying concept in Cox and Wilson's Chapter 11, which argued that *all* employees (and by extension, all human beings) deserve to be seen, heard, and valued. This idea reverberates through to the highest levels of leadership and how we should think about leadership development, as we saw in Wu and Pedigo's Chapter 19. These authors emphasized that acquired leaders must feel that they have impact, are valued, and are being heard, and discussed how important this is in retaining critical leaders in the combined integrated company. Frangos (Chapter 17) emphasized the importance of top leaders (CEOs and C-suite executives) demonstrating their human side by actively engaging with employees at all levels and listening to their feedback. Birrell Ivory and Mackay (Chapter 9) reminded us of the essential roles that top leaders play in establishing a sustainability mindset, accompanied with organization-wide education on how sustainability is an integral component of the organization's core strategy.

Looking through the lens of how leadership development is delivered, Barrows, White, and Shullman (Chapter 22) briefly reflected on the history of executive development programs and the roles that academic, consulting, and in-house approaches have played. The expectation is that all will continue to play a role, collaboratively, while responding to the new world of work in which executives need to operate. Insights from a range of executive development experts highlighted key trends impacting leaders today, many of which have been addressed in this volume and will need to be meaningfully and explicitly incorporated into executive development curricula—including disruptive technology, geopolitics, demographic changes (notably, the multigenerational workforce), shifting work environments, and sustainable business practices. And as with many of the chapters in this volume, Barrows and colleagues highlighted the necessity of incorporating a humanity-focused aspect of leadership into executive education programs.

Bringing Leadership Practices to Life: Case Studies

Organizations are operating in an extraordinarily complex environment, requiring a complex, multi-pronged approach to developing and sustaining the leadership needed to succeed through tumultuous times. Section VIII brought the insights and lessons from the prior sections to life through illustrative case studies that have served organizations well and proven effective in leading through the continually changing world of work. These case studies represent a range of sectors and organization types, from the truly global (the United Nations [UN]), to US-headquartered large and influential global corporations (Walmart, Salesforce), to the US public sector (Cybersecurity and Infrastructure Security Agency). Each of these has provided a unique demonstration of successfully navigating the enormous challenges facing leaders today. Through these examples, we have seen powerful illustrations of the effectiveness of embracing the core leadership themes discussed throughout all sections of this volume, including the focus on humanity and empathy, adaptability and continual learning, possessing working knowledge of technology, data and analytics, and embracing diversity and inclusivity.

Botha, Osicki and Campbell (Chapter 23) shared how the UN, formed in 1945, has continually adapted its approach to leadership throughout the course of its history. The UN's current focus powerfully illustrates the effectiveness of embracing these core leadership themes. These areas are embraced not because they reflect the latest trends, but because they have proven effective in addressing very real challenges, such as needing to look beyond traditional candidate sources to build sufficient pipelines for filling essential roles. The UN's story is particularly informative for its dual focus on fulfilling its own leadership needs while simultaneously recognizing its role in developing leaders external to the UN, serving as a model and inspiration of effective leadership throughout the world.

Shifting to the private sector, two large US-headquartered global corporations were highlighted, with details shared of their respective imperatives and approaches to comprehensively developing their early-career and future leaders. As described by Stomski in Chapter 24, with more than 2.1 million employees, Walmart faces a formidable challenge in consistently developing leaders aligned with the company's core values and culture, and in creating and sustaining a sense of community that translates into positive experiences for employees and customers alike. The company tackled this challenge by creating a new Manager Academy in 2022, with an emphasis on empathy as a key construct for reinforcing corporate culture and driving business performance. Stomski shared how the program, rooted in behavioral science, has been designed and scaled to reach their large target audience. Results to date indicate a positive return on Walmart's leadership development investment.

Salesforce, another US-headquartered global firm, has similarly made a large-scale investment in developing their leaders. In Chapter 25, Mukherjee, Collins and Hartog describe Salesforce's focus on sustaining a culture of accountability and trust, and on equipping leaders to operate effectively in a world where humans will work collaboratively with AI agents. This focus on the role of AI in the world of work is consistent with guidance from Tavis and Derler (Chapter 3) and Niederhoffer and colleagues (Chapter 4), who foresee the inevitable integration of AI at work, and the need for leaders to cultivate mindsets within the workforce for successful adoption. The Salesforce effort focuses on two key constituencies: current front-line managers and aspiring people managers. Similar to Walmart, results to date indicate a positive return on Salesforce's leader development programs.

One of the trends highlighted in Barrows and colleagues' Chapter 22 is the need for experiential, cohort-based learning, as well as "action learning" where real business challenges are incorporated in the educational experience and yield tangible value for the organization. We saw these concepts robustly illustrated in both the Salesforce and Walmart case studies, with their focus on solving actual business challenges and the emphasis on bringing cohorts of leaders (or aspiring leaders) together to help them build their personal networks and support each other throughout the learning process and beyond.

We closed this section with a return to the public sector and an inspiring roadmap for creating a people-first culture in the Cybersecurity and Infrastructure Security Agency (CISA) of the US federal government. Kolmstetter's Chapter 26 described the three-year journey from 2022 to 2024, when the agency was in its formative years, to create a culture based on core values and principles as driving forces of decisions, behaviors, and actions expected throughout the agency. These values and principles were deemed essential for the agency to achieve its formidable mission of keeping the nation safe from cyberthreats. The people-first culture of excellence needed to emanate from the highest levels of leadership and flow throughout the entire agency; this was achieved by aligning programs and initiatives with the core principles and with accountability—at all levels of the organization—for consistency with the desired culture. Again, we saw how core themes such as diversity, inclusion, empathy, and continuous learning can be intentionally designed and incorporated into the daily operations of an organization to extraordinary positive effect, and the essential role of leaders in creating and sustaining this type of environment.

Further Reflections and a Look to the Future

Considering the volume as a whole, we close this chapter by highlighting some big-picture themes and considerations as we head into the future: what it means to be a leader, additional technology considerations, and the essential role of humanity.

What Is Leadership Anyway?

This may seem a strange question to ponder in the final chapter of a book on leadership, but we pose it nonetheless, recognizing the evolving nature of the construct. As Boyce stated in Chapter 2, "definitions of leadership continue to be numerous and varied" (p. 25). While not all chapters offer an explicit definition, those that do define (or allude to a definition of) leadership bring a range of perspectives that collectively reflect the complexity that is leadership today.

Several chapters emphasized the people aspect of leadership, specifically, putting people first to bring out their best (Kolmstetter in Chapter 26), and creating an inclusive environment where all employees feel seen, valued, and supported (Smith and Stuart in Chapter 13; Cox and Wilson in Chapter 11). Others defined leadership as the combination of interpersonal skills and empathy with intelligence (Boyce in Chapter 2) and with achieving results

(Barrows and colleagues in Chapter 22). The ability to inspire and influence others is at the core of Woodward's definition in Chapter 5, and this is similarly highlighted by Jones and colleagues (Chapter 20) in the context of creating an enabling environment where intrapreneurship can thrive. Kansal and colleagues (Chapter 18) focus on the ability to establish trust, in each new leadership experience, as a fundamental aspect of being a leader. Some see strategic vision as core to the definition of leadership, when combined with operational excellence (Tavis and Derler in Chapter 3) and with understanding, clarity, and agility (Birrell Ivory and Mackay in Chapter 9). For Frangos (Chapter 17), leadership is ultimately about continuous learning and the ability to evolve one's perspective.

As we have seen, the authors' varying perspectives share much in common while also bringing specific, complementary ideas to defining the construct of leadership. What's absent is the notion that leadership is based on immutable traits that individuals are born with—i.e., you either have what it takes or you don't. While the aspiration and motivation to serve in a leadership role must come from within the individual, the skills and competencies required of leaders today are largely learnable, bringing home Frangos's (Chapter 17) point that recognizing the need to continuously learn, and having the ability to do so, really are essential ingredients for leadership success.

Navigating Rapid Technological Change

We started this volume with the role of technology in the rapidly changing world of work, and the topic has reverberated throughout. We have seen examples of what is possible, and we have learned of how the practice of leadership must evolve in response to this technological transformation. We also saw words of caution regarding the very real errors and harms that can be caused by these technologies. Concrete, practical guidance has been provided to leaders on how to navigate the perils and pitfalls while deriving benefits from targeted, purpose-built, properly trained models. But it will be no small task to balance the proper levels of caution with the unrelenting push (and pull) of immediate and widespread adoption. To help with this balancing act, we offer additional thoughts on leadership responsibilities and considerations with respect to algorithmic technologies, with the hope of tilting the balance to slowing down and proceeding with caution.

We worry about the effects of rapid, widespread adoption of such a poorly understood technology as complex algorithmic models, and in particular generative AI (e.g., Metz & Weise, 2025). When the very people developing these technologies are surprised and baffled by the resulting output, it speaks volumes to the lack of understanding about how the models operate and their implications. Standard parenthetical asides to "keep humans in the loop," "check the output," and "beware of hallucinations" do not seem to result in the investments in labor and infrastructure needed to actually do these things, and examples continue to come to light (e.g., Hill, 2025) where users of AI-enabled tools (students, professors, attorneys, journalists, etc.) who failed to take these precautions expose how things can go awry.

We believe that it is in leaders' best interests to apply the same rigor and approach to AI as they would with any other substantive investment: fully accounting for the potential benefits and costs, considering the complete spectrum of relevant perspectives, and distinguishing realistic expectations from hype. Some research-based perspectives to consider include *The AI Con* (Bender & Hanna, 2025), *Empire of AI* (Hao, 2025), and the Distributed AI Institute (DAIR), which focuses on targeted use cases with demonstrated benefits to organizations and society (e.g., Baker and Wee, 2024).

To assist with thinking more deeply about the implications of rapidly embracing these technologies, we pose some questions for leaders to consider for their organizations, for their fellow leaders, and for themselves:

- Why are we far more accepting and forgiving when AI makes mistakes than when our human employees do?
- Why are we more willing to invest in training and fine-tuning algorithms than in helping human employees learn and improve?
- Why are we choosing to disregard the ravaging toll that large language models take on the environment (e.g., Penn, 2025) when we are already struggling with a global climate crisis?
- Should we be investing our limited resources in technology with unsubstantiated benefits and known shortcomings, diverting those resources from other investments with proven returns?

We advocate for proceeding with caution, fully educating ourselves and our organizations on all aspects of these technologies, wisely choosing appropriate use cases, and verifying the processes, data, and approaches used to build the models we plan to adopt. We believe these steps will greatly increase the likelihood of bringing benefits that outstrip the totality of the costs.

The Human Element

At the risk of sounding repetitive, we close out this volume with a return to the topic of humanity and the essential role leaders must play in retaining and nurturing this very essence of leadership—that of humans guiding and supporting fellow humans in fulfilling their organization's reason for being. Across the range of topics covered in the sections and chapters, the need for humanity in our leaders—for showing up as human and for recognizing the humanity in every individual—has reverberated throughout. We have seen that humanity and humility are fundamental to understanding and motivating the workforce, to driving efficiency and effectiveness by helping every member of the organization fulfill their potential, and for enabling every leader to be the best they can be. We have seen that humanity and empathy are core aspects of effective leadership development programs. We have seen how centering humanity keeps an organization's priorities properly grounded and enables long-term success. This focus effectively guides organizations through day-to-day operations and builds the resilience needed to navigate through a crisis. And we have seen that a people-centered approach helps organizations maximize both near- and long-term value derived from investments in technologies, M&A, and other strategic actions. With this focus and emphasis on humanity, we are confident that the leaders of today and tomorrow will be well-equipped to successfully navigate the myriad known and unknown challenges that lie ahead.

References

Baker, D. & Wee, P. (2024, August). Towards truly community centered research. The Distributed AI Research Institute. https://zines.dair-institute.org/research-philosophy-zine.

Bender, E. M., & Hanna, A. (2025). *The AI con: How to fight Big Tech's hype and create the future we want.* Harper Collins Publishers.

Hao, K. (2025). *Empire of AI: Dreams and nightmares in Sam Altman's OpenAI.* Penguin Press.

Hill, K. (2025, May 14). The professors are using ChatGPT, and some students aren't happy about it. *The New York Times.* https://www.nytimes.com/2025/05/14/technology/chatgpt-college-professors.html?unlocked_article_code=1&trk=feed_main-feed-card_feed-article-content.

Metz, C., & Weise, K. (2025, May 5). A.I. is getting more powerful, but its hallucinations are getting worse. *The New York Times*. https://www.nytimes.com/2025/05/05/technology/ai-hallucinations-chatgpt-google.html

Penn, I. (2025, May 16). Data centers' hunger for energy could raise all electric bills. *The New York Times*. https://www.nytimes.com/2025/05/16/business/energy-environment/data-centers-utilities-electricity-bills.html

Index

For the benefit of digital users, indexed terms that span two pages (e.g., 52–53) may, on occasion, appear on only one of those pages.

Tables and figures are indicated by *t* and *f* following the page number